THE LAKOTA GHOST DANCE OF 1890

The Lakota Ghost Dance of 1890

RANI-HENRIK ANDERSSON

University of Nebraska Press   Lincoln & London

Library of Congress
Cataloging-in-Publication Data

Andersson, Rani-Henrik.
The Lakota ghost dance of 1890 / Rani-Henrik Andersson.
p. cm.
Includes bibliographical references and index.
ISBN 978-0-8032-1073-8 (cloth: alk. paper)
1. Ghost dance—South Dakota.
2. Teton Indians—Rites and ceremonies.
3. Teton Indians—Government relations. I. Title.
E99.T34A63 2008
299.7'9809034—dc22
2008015838

Set in Dante.

The man had died and yet he had not died,
And he had talked with God, and all the dead
Were coming with the whirlwind at their head,
And there would be new earth and heaven!

JOHN G. NEIHARDT,
"The Song of the Messiah," in *A Cycle of the West*

CONTENTS

ILLUSTRATIONS

TABLE

PREFACE

There were at least one hundred and fifty tepees forming almost a complete circle within which the Indians had gathered to the number of six hundred[,] a part to engage in the exercises and a part to look on. At a given spot a young tree was planted on which was placed the American flag, around it gathered the priests who sat down on the ground and remained silent for some time. Around this tree about equally distant therefrom men, women, to the number of near four hundred formed a circle and assumed at first a sitting position. The men were arrayed in their war paint, consisting of red, black and yellow, feathers in their hair, leggings on their lower limbs, blankets wrapped round their bodies and moccasins on their feet. The women were clad in dresses of variegated colors, some were beaded in the most artistic style and their faces painted profusely.

The Indians forming the outer circle sat down on their feet and remained quiet for some time, when they broke out in a sort of plaintive cry, which is pretty well calculated to affect the ear of the sympathetic. Then some one passes around with a vessel in his hand containing some kind of roots . . . after this is partaken of, at a given command the Indians rise to their feet [and] join hands thus forming a complete circle. Having occupied this position for a moment they begin to chant their opening hymn . . . and commence a slow measured movement from right to left, increasing the pace as they go[,] and it is not long until all[,] old and young[,] are singing and becoming excited. This is kept up for a half hour when many being overcome with the exercises and excitement connected therewith, fall where they were standing in the ranks or leap wildly from the circle into the open space, fall flat on their faces upon the ground, strike the ground furiously with their hands as though they were endeavoring to dig a hole therein, leap up wildly again, rush from one side of the circle to the other throwing out their arms and finally fall exhausted and apparently lifeless. When a certain number had thus exhausted themselves the dancing stopped and all sat down again. As the exhausted ones revived they gathered into a group in the center of the space and the proclaimers received an account of their experiences while in this state and then proclaimed it to the Indians. . . . A young woman said when she fell an eagle hovered over her and picked her up[,] carrying her to a house, the door being open the eagle went in first and she followed, and saw Christ who shook hand[s] with her three times and said He was glad to see her as she had been there before. Another [said] that the dead would all soon come back and meet them and that buffalo and other game would be plentiful.

In the late 1880s a revitalization movement known as the ghost dance swept across the North American plains and galvanized tens of thousands of Indians from more than thirty tribes. The epigraph is a description of the ghost dance ceremony among the Lakota Indians, the western branch of the Sioux people, as reported by U.S. Special Indian Agent Elisha B. Reynolds in September 1890. He was perhaps the first white observer ever to witness and describe the ceremony as it was performed by the Lakotas.[1]

The ghost dance was a religious movement that took many forms as it passed from one tribe to another, yet its core message of return to the old ways and a future of peace and happiness remained the same. The ghost dance was the physical expression of a religious movement that advocated peace. The most important instructions of the prophet of the religion, a Paiute Indian called Wovoka, were these, later published in "The Messiah Letters" (see appendix 3): "You must not . . . do harm to anyone. You must not fight. Do right always." According to Wovoka, the white people were going to disappear in a great earthquake, and only those Indians who believed in his message would survive. Then they would live forever in a world of happiness where there would be no hunger or disease. To make this happen, the Indians need only dance a certain sacred dance. Thus no hostilities were required to bring about the new Indian paradise.[2]

In the late 1880s most Indians in the United States lived on reservations, where they were fed and clothed as wards of the government. They had little hope for the future. They had been forced to surrender their lands and abandon their traditional ways of living. Even their religious ceremonies were forbidden. The ghost dance offered them hope and returned religious ceremonies to a central place in their daily lives. Throughout the western United States Indians started to dance and pray as Wovoka taught. Unfortunately, among the Lakotas the dance produced tragic consequences. The U.S. military, under orders to put a stop to what many whites thought was a war dance, opened fire on a group of Lakotas in December 1890, resulting in what would become known as the Wounded Knee massacre.[3]

For my doctoral thesis, "*Wanáǧi Wachípi kį*: The Ghost Dance among the Lakota Indians in 1890—A Multidimensional Interpretation," I studied the ghost dance among the Lakotas and its significance in their culture. As I studied the events leading to the Wounded Knee tragedy, I discovered that many mixed feelings about the ghost dance prevailed and that different interest groups perceived the events in different ways.

The Lakota ghost dance has been the subject of wide scholarly and public interest from the late nineteenth century throughout the twentieth century. The first publications about the dance that used historical documents as source material were published as early as 1891. James P. Boyd's *Recent Indian Wars: Under the Lead of Sitting Bull and Other Chiefs; With Full Account of the Messiah Craze and Ghost Dances* and Willis Fletcher Johnson's *The Red Record of the Sioux: Life of Sitting Bull and History of the Indian War of 1890–1891* were among the very first to set the tone in studying the Lakota ghost dance. Articles in various journals and magazines soon followed.

The first and foremost study of the ghost dance is *The Ghost-Dance Religion and the Sioux Outbreak of 1890* by the early anthropologist James Mooney. His book resulted from several years of investigating the ghost dance among various Indian tribes. Mooney's work is still essential and invaluable, but also somewhat problematic and includes some statements that time has proved to be erroneous. For example, Mooney was not able to get any information from the Lakotas. The Lakotas simply refused to talk to him: "The dance was our religion . . . we will not talk any more about it," was their reply to his requests. For this reason his study, although the first attempt to understand the ghost dance as a religious movement, lacks information from the Lakotas themselves. Even the Lakota ghost dance songs he published he obtained from a local schoolteacher, Emma C. Sickels, who in turn got them in written form from George Sword, a literate Lakota who was captain of the Indian police at Pine Ridge Agency. Mooney constructed his story of the Lakota ghost dance and the "outbreak," as he calls it, from primary government documents and newspapers, but not with the help of Lakota participants, as he was able to do among several other tribes.[4]

From the very beginning the Lakota ghost dance was studied mainly from the perspectives of white Americans, and the Lakotas' views were only briefly incorporated into this main narrative. Those earliest accounts created a tradition of treating the Lakota ghost dance as a military, political, or religious-political movement. This approach is characterized by phrases such as the "Sioux outbreak," the "Messiah Craze," and the "ghost dance war," which are so often used even in the titles of those works. This tradition continued into the late twentieth century, when alternative interpretations began to emerge. While some of these accounts do incorporate the Lakotas' point of view as a legitimate part of the story, most fail to put the ghost dance in a wider cultural and social context. Often these accounts are written to convey a particular perspective or narrow focus on some specific aspects of the Lakota ghost dance. All too often the story of the Lakota ghost dance, even in some of the most recent accounts, is based on the published literature or on one-sided interpretations of primary documents. However, critical analysis of primary sources is essential, since they do not simply reveal "facts" but must be interpreted in the context of the late nineteenth century.

Mooney's work, however, has been the cornerstone on which scholars throughout the twentieth century have based their interpretations of the Lakota ghost dance. It has become a tradition to treat Mooney's study almost as a primary source on the Lakota ghost dance; his interpretations have survived in the works of several historians and anthropologists. Some of these include Robert H. Lowie's *Indians of the Plains* (1954), George E. Hyde's *A Sioux Chronicle* (1956), Robert M. Utley's *The Last Days of the Sioux Nation* (1963), and Rex Alan Smith's *Moon of the Popping Trees* (1975).

Thus a standard tradition of writing the history of the Lakota ghost dance emerged. Only more recently have different interpretations been proposed. One of these was written by the anthropologist Raymond J. DeMallie. In his brief but insightful article, "The Lakota Ghost Dance: An Ethnohistorical Account" (1982), DeMallie looks at the Lakota ghost dance from the point of view of the Lakota people. Another recent attempt, by the historian William S. E. Coleman, seeks to move beyond the traditional mainstream interpretation of the Lakota ghost dance. In *Voices of Wounded Knee* (2000), Coleman presents several documents relating to the Lakota ghost dance and the Wounded Knee massacre. In *The Plains Sioux and U.S. Colonialism from Lewis and Clark to Wounded Knee* (2004), the historian Jeffrey Ostler places the Lakota ghost dance in the context of U.S. expansionist politics. In her recently published book, *Hostiles? The Lakota Ghost Dance and Buffalo Bill's Wild West* (2006), Sam A. Maddra analyzes the Lakota ghost dance using several documents that present the ghost dancers' point of view. In a new introduction to a reprint of his *Last Days of the Sioux Nation* (2004), Robert Utley expresses a changed opinion about his earlier assessment of the ghost dance among the Lakotas. He addresses some of the problematic issues and acknowledges the need for more nuanced interpretation of the Indian side of the story. All these recent works are interesting and valuable, but there is still need for additional reevaluation.[5]

In the present work I consider the Lakota ghost dance from a larger perspective. I have drawn on the growing number of studies that stress multicultural approaches, that is, include a multidimensional interpretation.[6] One example of this approach that I have found valuable is Patricia N. Limerick's *Legacy of Conquest: The Unbroken Past of the American West* (1987), in which she considers the American West as a meeting ground of several groups who compete over economic, cultural, and political control of the area.[7] Recent theoretical work by Robert F. Berkhofer Jr. that emphasizes the importance of identifying conflicting "voices," including gender, ethnicity, race, and class, suggest new approaches to writing history.[8]

Berkhofer suggests that by presenting different voices of events, historians can develop a more comprehensive picture of the past. When conflicting voices are accepted as legitimate "sub-stories" of the same (hi)story, and when the "various viewpoints of evidentiary sources, others' stories, other scholars' texts, and the historian's own text are incorporated into one interpretive system," a multidimensional interpretation of the past can ultimately be achieved. Berkhofer refers to this synthesis as "the Great Story." The more comprehensive the selection of voices and viewpoints is, the fuller the final historical analysis, "the Great Story," is. However, the historian's task, Berkhofer argues, is not only "to reclaim voices, but also to contextualize them, to reconstruct the discursive world, which the subjects inhabited and were shaped by."[9]

In this study Berkhofer's ideas serve as the basis for constructing "a Great Story" of the Lakota ghost dance. Each of the chapters presents a story of the Lakota ghost dance viewed from a certain perspective, thereby presenting the voice of that particular group of historical actors. In the conclusion, "Toward 'a Great Story,'" the historian's interpretation is achieved by combining the different voices into a single interpretive account of the Lakota ghost dance.

In my study, the voices of six different groups of actors are presented: the Lakotas, the Indian agents, the U.S. Army, the missionaries, the press, and the U.S. Congress. My basic questions are these: Did misunderstandings exist about the ghost dance, and, if so, how were they compounded, leading eventually to the tragic end at Wounded Knee? My study seeks to demonstrate that the multidimensional method I have chosen can provide a more realistic and historically sound reconstruction of the Lakota ghost dance than any other now available. I attempt to go beyond a mere collection of conflicting viewpoints and seek to explore and analyze the political, cultural, and economic linkages among them in order to gain a fuller understanding of what the ghost dance represented.

This study is arranged so that the voice of each of the six groups of actors is analyzed in a separate chapter. Because the Lakotas were living at several different agencies and events took place simultaneously at each one, strict chronology is necessary to avoid confusion. News of the ghost dance spread from west to east, so I have arranged the chapters in a similar—natural—order; the Lakota voice is dealt with first, followed by the voices of the agents, the army, the missionaries, the press, and, finally, the Congress.

Limerick argues that events that took place in the West have usually been portrayed from the perspective of the East. In this sense the East is the center, representing white civilization, while the West represents the uncivilized frontier that merely reacts to decisions and actions originating in the East. In this study the actual center of events is indeed in the West, but my approach allows us to look at several centers that reacted to one another and created a complex structure of conflicting but equally important viewpoints. These viewpoints, as the anthropologist Raymond J. DeMallie has noted, "may contradict one another not because one is right and one is wrong, but because they are composed for different purposes and are based on different cultural premises."[10]

The method used in this study proves especially valuable in understanding the relationships among these various groups, how they acted and reacted to events during the ghost dance period, and how they affected one another by setting events in motion that had multiple culmination points, including the arrival of the military on the Lakota reservations, Sitting Bull's death, and the Wounded Knee massacre. By studying these different voices it is possible not only to identify these culmination points, but also to understand how and why they came about.

This study demonstrates how the different groups developed their respective views about the Lakota ghost dance. For example, how the Lakota agents' views of the ghost dance developed and changed during the period from April 1890 to January 1891 has not previously been examined in detail. The facts surrounding Agent Daniel F. Royer's and Agent James McLaughlin's actions are well documented, but their—and especially the other Lakota agents'—actual views of the ghost dance have not been thoroughly studied. More important, how their views affected those of the army, the press, and Congress, and vice versa, has not been previously explored. It is, in fact, this interaction and these linkages among the different groups that ultimately constitute "a Great Story" of the Lakota ghost dance. Therefore, this study presents the ghost dance as a whole, as a phenomenon in which many interests collided and many misunderstandings prevailed on both collective and individual levels. The method used shows the linkages and interactions among several groups of people, and has also been used whenever possible to explore the critical points, relationships, and interactions within those groups. Revealing the connections among these voices is, in fact, one of the major contributions of this method.

The voices presented here represent different viewpoints on the Lakota ghost dance, but none of them alone provides a satisfactory interpretation of what the Lakota ghost dance was about. Together, these voices help us to understand not only the events, but also the ideologies behind the actions of each group. This study allows us to look at the collective viewpoints of these groups and also to consider the viewpoints of some important individuals within the groups. Thus, the method chosen for this study demonstrates how an approach that takes multiple perspectives into consideration can further our understanding of the past. This methodology provides us with a fuller understanding of the Lakota ghost dance than has been achieved before. It is, however, not yet the fullest account possible; for example, the voices of various groups of Indian and white women would provide further insight. Moreover, the six voices presented here could be further broken down. For example, in addition to the army officers' voices, the viewpoints of the soldiers themselves could be investigated. The Lakota voice could be further studied by looking in detail at the various reservations, bands, and interest groups. The perspective of the mixed bloods could constitute an additional voice. The lack of source material left by any of these groups, however, greatly restricts what is possible in this respect.

Each of the chapters in this study presents different kinds of challenges. To understand the Lakota voice, I have put the Lakota ghost dance in a larger cultural perspective. As DeMallie notes: "To attempt an understanding of the Sioux [Lakota] past it is essential to come to an understanding of Sioux [Lakota] culture, which provides the context."[11] For this reason, the history and culture of the Lakota people is briefly reviewed in the beginning of this study and further discussed whenever necessary. To achieve an understanding of the Lakota ghost dance from the Lakota perspective, I have found that the traditional historical approach is not sufficient to answer all the questions raised in this study. To gain a fuller understanding I have incorporated methodology derived from ethnohistory and anthropology that enables me to deal with problems that arise from studying a culture so different from Western culture. I have, for example, used oral history as source material, and I have portrayed the Lakota ghost dance in terms that derive from Lakota culture and that were familiar to the Lakotas. In this, knowledge of Lakota language has been invaluable.[12]

The chapters on the army, the missionaries, the agents, and Congress presented fewer methodological challenges, but it was enough of a challenge simply to decipher the handwritten historical documents. These chapters required extensive reading on various topics: Congress, the Bureau of Indian Affairs, the Indian agents, missionary work among the Lakotas, and U.S. Indian policy in general. Becoming familiar with the U.S. military and its relations with Indians throughout the nineteenth century was essential for the writing of the voice of the army. The voice of the press presented yet another challenge: how to deal with material that was not only voluminous, but also contradictory and inconsistent. To study the voice of the press, I selected the *New York Times* and the *Washington Post* to represent the eastern newspapers for the simple reason that they were widely read and very likely influenced eastern decision makers. The *Chicago Tribune* was important since the army headquarters for the 1890–91 campaign was located in that city. Furthermore, the *Chicago Tribune* was geographically located between the Lakota reservations and Washington. The *Omaha Daily Bee* represents the local western newspapers. Its importance lies in the fact that it was the most widely quoted newspaper during the ghost dance "trouble." The *Yankton Press and Dakotan* from Yankton, South Dakota, was chosen to give additional depth to the local newspapers' reporting. *Harper's Weekly* magazine here represents national magazines and was chosen mainly because of its long tradition of writing about Indian-related issues.

To aid in a fuller understanding of the ghost dance, a brief survey of revitalization movements as well as some main features of official U.S. Indian policy are presented. The Lakota ghost dance has to be understood in these broader contexts, although the emphasis of this work is on the events of the year 1890.

In this study, some Lakota names and words are used to give authenticity to the Lakota voice. Generally, English names are used, but when a name appears for the first time the Lakota name is provided in parentheses, for example, Red Cloud (Maȟpíya Lúta). In writing Lakota words I have chosen the orthography introduced by Allan R. Taylor and David S. Rood, which is, as the anthropologist and linguist Douglas R. Parks put it, by far the best orthography for the Lakota language currently available.[13] A brief phonological key is provided in appendix 2.

ACKNOWLEDGMENTS

This book is the result of years of hard work and dedication, but it is also the result of a lifelong interest in Native American cultures. The fact that I am a Finn, living far away from the Indians and far away from the primary sources, has made this project challenging. To some people it has even seemed rather strange. Why did I not heed the advice of those who urged me to choose a more familiar and easy topic? Once you are interested in something, however, you have to pursue that ambition; otherwise, inaction might lead to a lifelong questioning of *what if?* Now I do not have to ask myself that question; I have traveled this journey and the result is this book.

Still, there has been great understanding toward my work here in Finland. It would have been impossible to complete this study without this support. When I look back, I can see that I always met exactly the right people at the right moment. Because I am a historian, I feel that it is only natural that these people should be mentioned here in the order in which they appeared in my life.

My academic life began at the History Department of the University of Tampere in 1988. During my first years as a student I pushed aside my interest in Native Americans; there was simply too much other work to do. When I finally had to decide on a topic for my master's thesis, I naturally thought of Indians. But I was afraid of taking the first step. I knew that there would be no return from that path; it would be a life-altering decision. At a critical moment my good friend Riitta Savola said: "If you don't do it, you will regret it all your life." I would like to thank her for those encouraging words.

In 1992, I visited my former middle school teacher Dr. Rainer Smedman, who laughed at me when learning about my interest in Indians. His amusement was not malicious; on the contrary, he was working on his PhD dissertation, focusing on the history of the Lakota people. From that moment he has helped and guided me; he has been a good friend, and he has read and commented on many versions of my manuscript. Without his help this work would not have been possible. I owe him my deepest gratitude. During the early period Professors Seikko Eskola, Olli Vehviläinen, and Marjatta Hietala supported my doctoral work and helped me to receive funding for several years. When I was starting my dissertation, I met again with Professor Markku Henriksson, who had introduced me to the field of American studies years earlier. He encouraged me to continue my work and has helped and supported me ever since. In 1998 he grabbed me by the arm and threw me into an office; there I met, for the first time, with Professor Robert E. Bieder. I spent several hours with Professor Bieder talking about my project and listening to him sing Iroquois songs. Afterward I was convinced that I did not make a good impression because I was thrown in front of him totally unprepared. Now I have to thank Markku Henriksson for his wise action; despite my fears, Professor Bieder took me under his wing and has been a constant supporter and a friend ever since. He has tirelessly read, commented on, and corrected my text. His help has been of utmost value, and he deserves my warmest thanks.

Professor Bieder also introduced me to Professor Raymond J. DeMallie, who has taught me more about the Lakota people than anyone else. His advice has been worth more than I can put into words. He also guided me to archives and manuscripts that might have eluded me and generously gave me access to his personal collections. At the American Indian Studies Research Institute (at Indiana University) I was allowed to study the Lakota language under Professor Douglas R. Parks. The fact that he put up with me, and with my pronunciation of the Lakota *z*, says a lot about his attitude toward me. I am glad to express my gratitude to these two men, and I am delighted that we were able to establish a good professional relationship but also a friendship that I hope will last for years to come. I also want to express my thanks to the people at the American Indian Studies Research Institute, who helped me feel at home. Especially Deb Speer, who efficiently took care even of my daily problems, deserves my special thanks. I am also indebted to Francis Flavin, who was always there for me when I had problems adjusting to the American way of life. Damon D. Bergen, Sebastian Braun, Mark Van DeLogt, and Dennis Christafferson made my life in America a pleasant experience.

I owe my gratitude also to the nice people at various libraries and archives in the United States. Especially worth mentioning are the people at the Government Documents room and the Microfilm Reading room at the Indiana University Main Library. Mark Thiel at the Marquette University Archives also helped me to locate important documents. It would have been impossible to carry out this project without proper funding. I express my thanks to the Fulbright Foundation for awarding me the ASLA-Fulbright Graduate Grant, which enabled me to start my dissertation project in 1999. The Academy of Finland deserves my gratitude for awarding me several research grants. The University of Tampere also supported my work with several grants, the Nordenskiöld Foundation assisted me with a travel grant, and Ella and Georg Ehrnrooth's Foundation helped with another research grant, and I am grateful for their assistance.

I have also received support from Professors Auvo Kostiainen and Markku Hyrkkänen, who both showed understanding toward my work. Sari Pasto at the University of Tampere has helped me with various practical problems, and I am glad to express my thanks to her. Countless discussions with Riku Hämäläinen have been both fun and helpful. I am also grateful to the University of Helsinki, Renvall Institute, where I have felt welcome after returning from the United States. I am indebted to my American friends who read and corrected the final version of the manuscript. Raymond J. DeMallie showed exceptional patience with me and my countless problems. It was an enormous challenge to write several hundred pages in English. I thought that I was quite a fluent writer, but I discovered that nothing that I know about Finnish grammar applies to English. Still, all the mistakes that can be found in the book are mine, and I would like to think that some Finnish expressions here and there give a special character to the book—a character that makes this work ultimately mine.

Finally, I want to thank Siiri and Martti Tikka, who have always welcomed me to their home and who have helped me in so many ways. Martti, Ville Smedman, and Toni Lassila have helped with countless computer problems. My sister, Aretta, and her friend Susanna allowed me to establish a base in their home. My sister always found the best, not the cheapest, but the most flexible airplane connections. I know it was not always an easy task. My parents, Auli and Mauno, have always been there for me and believed that I would be able to carry out this project. They deserve very special thanks. Then there is Marianne, who has put up with me for the past years; she even followed me across the Atlantic Ocean and spent two years with me in the United States. Although she never said that she would like to see this project finished as soon as possible, I am certain that she finds it a welcome change in our lives. Even if this project has been fun and exciting, I believe that when this book is finally published, she will find it as rewarding as I do.

The Lakota Ghost Dance of 1890

Introduction

Isolation and Assimilation

Early contact between Europeans and Native Americans made it clear that these different peoples could not coexist without conflict. As early as 1763, by a royal proclamation of King George III of England, a boundary line was drawn along the Appalachian Mountains, leaving the area to the west for the Indians. Separation became U.S. national policy during the early nineteenth century.[1] In this way conflicts with Indians could be avoided, and as Indians gradually became civilized they would need less land. The whites could then inhabit the surplus land. The policy of separation culminated in the reservation policy, which still exists.[2]

To understand the ghost dance and its impact not only on the Indian people of the United States, but also on the white population, it is essential to understand the ideologies behind the relations between whites and Indians.

The reservation policy can be roughly separated into two phases. The first phase was adopted as official Indian policy in the 1820s, although similar ideas had been presented even earlier. The aim of this policy was to create an Indian territory in the western United States. In the second phase, which started officially in the 1850s, Indians were removed tribe by tribe to individual reservations that were established for them.[3] Indian removal was considered necessary to prevent the total extinction of the Indians, but also to free more land for white settlers. Indians could not remain a hindrance to the expanding nation as it fulfilled its destiny of exploring and conquering new lands. This idea of western expansion became known in the United States as Manifest Destiny.[4]

At the beginning of the nineteenth century the U.S. population was divided into citizens and noncitizens. Indians, as well as African Americans and later also Asians, were excluded from citizenship, whereas European immigrants were taken in as full members of society. After the Civil War the situation changed as slavery was abolished and as the number of immigrants increased. The nonwhite minorities were given second-class membership in the nation—a membership that allowed them to serve the white upper class but at the same time "feel at home."[5] Indian policy after the Civil War, initiated by President Ulysses S. Grant, was known as the Peace Policy. Its basic idea was to locate the Indians on tribal reservations where they could be civilized and gradually absorbed into the social and economic system of the United States. This task was given to the Indian Office, which at first was situated within the War Department. In 1849, however, when the Interior Department was created, the Indian Office was taken out of the War Department and relocated into the new department and renamed the Bureau of Indian Affairs. Under the Peace Policy the Interior Department handed actual control of the reservations to different church groups.[6]

Despite the Peace Policy, many famous Indian wars were fought during the 1860s and 1870s. By the 1880s Indian resistance was basically over, and the tribes were confined to reservations. Confinement brought with it the need for change in official Indian policy. The Peace Policy was considered a failure, and the struggle over the control of Indian affairs continued between the Interior and War Departments and among the different religious denominations, which were "fighting over souls."[7]

By the 1880s dissatisfaction with Indian policy was growing in the U.S. Congress. The Peace Policy was considered to be partly responsible for the disturbances that had occurred on several reservations.[8] Both the Democrats and the Republicans were tired of the fact that money invested in Indian affairs had no lasting effects. A well-known Peace Policy supporter, Henry L. Dawes, the Republican senator from Massachusetts, even claimed that 2.7 million dollars had been appropriated to solve what he called "the big Indian question." According to Senator Dawes, "We have made no advance toward it; we have not even touched it; but we have aggravated it."[9]

The basic question was whether or not the reservation system should be continued. The reservations helped Indians to maintain their tribal autonomy and protected them from white encroachment. Indian education was another problem—not whether Indians should be educated, but who would educate them.[10]

Behind these basic issues was the question of whether the Indians should be considered an exceptional minority, to be protected and civilized separately, as had been the case during the Peace Policy. Already by the end of the 1860s powerful groups had formed to find solutions for these difficult problems. The so-called Friends of the Indians were religious and humanitarian leaders who thought that their duty was to help the Indians to become civilized. Their aim was to benefit the Indians, but because their work was based on their own values and not on those of the Indians, the results were—despite their sincere efforts—devastating for the Indians. However, Friends of the Indians was a powerful group, and the government could not ignore their suggestions for the reorganization of official Indian policy.[11]

Before the 1880s the argument for Indian "exceptionalism" was based on the issue of land, that is, the question of whether the Indians owned their lands in common as tribes or as individual persons. After the 1880s almost all Indian land was confined to reservations, so such reasoning was no longer relevant. Because there were so few Indians left on the continent, and because rather than inhabit the land they "roamed on it as the game they hunted," policy makers believed they were justified in confiscating the remainder of their land. Demands to dismantle the whole reservation system arose during the 1880s. The reservations were seen as "islands surrounded by civilization," where barbarism could continue to exist. Many whites also thought that the reservations denied Indians the benefits open to others.[12]

Fundamental to Indian policy was the idea of the superiority of the white race, although it was generally believed that Indians had the potential to develop from savagery to civilization. Some of the most notable American ethnologists, such as Lewis Henry Morgan and Henry Rowe Schoolcraft, believed that converting to Christianity would gradually civilize the Indians.

Others, such as Samuel G. Morton, believed that the Indians could not progress at all and would eventually die out as a race. Those ideologies provided a scientific basis for the Indians' inferior position as well as for the taking of their lands.[13] The fact that white society offered Indians the road to civilization justified their treatment. Becoming civilized and ultimately achieving U.S. citizenship was believed to be sufficient compensation for the Indians' loss of their land and culture.[14]

The question of Indian exceptionalism was discussed in Congress for several years, especially in the 1880s. At times the Indians were believed to have a kind of treaty right for exceptional treatment, and at other times they were considered to be in a position no different from that of other landowners. At the same time it was thought peculiar that Indian illiteracy remained high despite the large amount of money that was spent on Indian education. Senator Dawes demanded that the United States spend as much money on Indian education as it had spent in vain trying to kill off the Indians. Many Indians, in fact, understood how important education was for their future; reading especially was considered a valuable skill.[15]

Despite the debate, the idea of exceptionalism stayed strong: many reservations were divided or reduced, but they remained. One solution to the Indian question was sought in the General Allotment Act of 1887 (also known as the Dawes Act), which provided the mechanism for dividing the ownership of reservation lands among individual Indians.[16] This was a satisfactory solution for many whites for whom an independent Indian engaged in farming had long been the goal. Farming was thought to be the highest form of civilization and a God-given duty. Moreover, those supporters of exceptionalism saw the General Allotment Act as the last chance to protect Indians from land-hungry settlers, who were growing in number and power. The allotment of Indian lands would at least allow individual Indians to keep some of the land they previously had owned communally. The General Allotment Act signaled a change in Indian policy from isolation to assimilation.[17]

The General Allotment Act meant in practice that the Indians who took up allotments could no longer maintain tribal ownership of the reservations and the tribes would no longer be considered independent nations. The land was to be divided among individuals and the surplus lands were to be sold to white settlers.[18] The act meant also that Indians had to learn to work like white men. As Senator Dawes put it, "The Indian will be an Indian as long as he lives unless he is taught to work." And working he could learn only through education. Thus Indian education and the allotment of the Indian lands were inseparable goals.[19] However, it remained the duty of the government to protect the individual Indian in his efforts toward civilization and eventual citizenship.[20]

Even if the General Allotment Act was an answer to many problems, and it seemed to satisfy all the white interest groups that were involved, it also produced many more problems, especially in the 1890s, as surplus Indian land was diminishing. Indian education continued to cause problems as well.[21]

Whereas Indian policy in the 1860s and 1870s had separated whites from Indians, in the 1880s, especially toward the end of the decade, the policy tried to protect the Indians from the whites; now reservations became areas of refuge. Reservations were a way to protect a conquered race; on reservations the Indian could become the "beginning of a man."[22] During the 1880s, especially among the so-called Friends of the Indians, the goal was no longer to destroy Indians, but to raise them up to civilization. As Senator Dawes expressed it, white men had a duty to "take him [the Indian] by the hand and set him upon his feet, and teach him to stand alone first, then to walk, then to dig, then to plant, then to hoe, then to gather and then to *keep*."[23] Whether these efforts benefited the Indians is a totally different question.

Thithųwą: Dwellers on the Plains

Until the beginning of eighteenth century, the Lakotas were living between the Minnesota and Missouri Rivers on the prairies of today's Minnesota and the Dakotas. By the mid-eighteenth century pressure from Ojibwas and eastern Santee Dakotas forced the Lakotas to move westward. As they acquired horses they crossed the Missouri River in small groups and pushed west, reaching the Black Hills sometime during the second half of the century. The Great Plains, with their tremendous herds of bison, drew the Lakotas west. The plains offered everything that was needed, not only in daily life but also in the expanding trade with the white man.[24]

The Lakotas were a part of the people known as the Sioux or Dakotas.[25]

The Sioux were divided into seven groups, also known as the seven council fires (*ochéthi šakówį*), the mythological origin of the Dakota people.[26] Despite having different dialects, the seven groups spoke the same language and were fully capable of understanding each other. The easternmost groups living in Minnesota were called the Santees. Together with the Yanktons and Yanktonais, the Santees formed the branches of the nation that called themselves Dakhóta. Although scholars frequently refer to the Yanktons and Yanktonais as "Nakotas," the term Nakhóta is the self-designation of Assiniboine Indians, who were close relatives of the Sioux.[27] The Lakotas (Lakhóta) formed the western branch of the seven council fires. They are also known by the name Teton, a name deriving from the Lakota word *thíthųwą* ("dwellers on the plains"). The Lakotas, the subjects of this study, are further divided into seven tribes: Oglalas (Oglála), Hunkpapas (Húkpaphaya), Minneconjous (Mnikhówožu), Brulés (Sichágu), Two Kettles (O'óhenupa), Sans Arcs (Itázipcho), and Blackfeet (Sihásapa).[28]

The Lakotas arrived on the plains in small, independent groups. They were able to drive away some of the other tribes already living there, partly due to the diseases that took their toll on the Plains Indian population, and partly due to the numerical strength of the Lakota people. The Lakotas adapted quickly to life on the plains, and by the late eighteenth century had become a dominant Plains Indian tribe. On their way farther west, the Lakotas pushed aside the Kiowa, Arikara, and Crow tribes. Alongside the Cheyennes and Arapahos, the Lakotas became the masters of the North-Central Plains. By 1825, they occupied an area stretching from the Missouri River to the Black Hills.[29]

Hunting buffalo provided the Lakotas with their primary means of living. The acquisition of horses allowed them to hunt more efficiently, which immediately resulted in a higher living standard and a rise in population. Diseases caused havoc among the Lakotas also, but because they lived in small groups constantly on the move, they were less vulnerable to epidemics than were the tribes living in larger, permanent villages. While other plains tribes were struggling, the Lakotas were prospering. Their population growth was rapid: in 1804 whites estimated that there were approximately 8,000 Sioux, perhaps 3,000 Lakotas among them, but in 1850 the numbers were 24,000 Sioux and 13,000 to 14,000 Lakotas. In the early nineteenth century the whites were not yet their enemies but important trade partners who provided the Lakotas with guns, ammunition, and utensils that helped support their daily life.[30]

Warfare was an essential part of Lakota life—not constant, full-scale war, but periodic skirmishing. Their main enemies were the Pawnee, Shoshone, Crow, and Arikara Indians. The goal was not to destroy the enemy but to show individual courage or to steal horses. Counting coup, that is, touching the enemy, was considered the highest form of bravery, one of the most highly respected virtues in a Lakota man.[31]

Indian wars were fought mainly during the summer; war was put aside for the winter. Summer in general was a time of great activity. It was the time for communal buffalo hunts and for the most important religious ceremonies, such as the sun dance (*wiwáyąg wachípi*). For this ceremony the Lakotas gathered into a great summer camp. Afterward, the people dispersed for the coming winter into small individual groups called *thiyóšpaye*.[32]

The basic unit of society was the *thiyóšpaye*, the extended family or lodge group. Every *thiyóšpaye* had its own headman or chief (*itháchą*). The *itháchą* was a man who possessed the virtues that made him respected among the people. He was a person to be trusted and followed, although his authority was limited; every man could basically decide for himself, for example, where to live, when to hunt, and how to behave toward whites. The next higher level in Lakota society was the band, which consisted of several *thiyóšpaye*. The bands then formed the various *oyáte*, best translated in English as "tribes." Thus a Lakota could, for example, belong to the band of Itéšica (Bad Face) of the Oglala tribe, as did the famous Red Cloud (Maȟpíya Lúta). Traditionally and ideally the Lakotas constructed their society following their sacred number, seven, reflected in the seven council fires. Still, the structure was very flexible, and the number seven seldom was actually the exact number of the bands.[33]

The Lakotas, however, consisted of the seven tribes mentioned above: Hunkpapas, Oglalas, Brulés, Blackfeet, Two Kettles, Sans Arcs, and Minneconjous.[34] During larger gatherings each of these tribes had its own position in the camp circle, which was of extreme importance to the Lakotas.

Everything inside was Lakota (*ólakhota*, alliance); outside was the hostile world. Indians not belonging to the Lakota people were potential enemies (*thóka*); they shared with the Lakotas the designation "common men" (*ikcéwichaša*) and were "related as enemies" (*thókakičhiyapi*). Sometimes, however, a peace was made with other Indians, who then became a part of the Lakota alliance (*lakhólkičhiyapi*). This was the case, for example, with the Cheyennes and Arapahos. The whites were not considered enemies; they were called *wašícu*, a term referring to guardian spirits, particularly those related to war. The whites acquired this name because of their mysterious powers, especially those associated with their powerful guns.[35]

The camp circle, *hóčhoka*, symbolized this unity of the Lakota people. Within the circle the sacred hoop (*čhagléška wakhá*) was unbroken. In the middle of the circle was a large lodge (*thíyothipi*) where important meetings were held. The Hunkpapas camped at the edges of the circle, close to the opening (*húkpa*), which always faced east. From there, each tribe put up its tipis in the accustomed position. Even within tribal camp circles, the bands camped in a certain order, so that the most important band or family was closest to the back of the circle, opposite the opening. Here too the flexibility of the society can be seen, as the rise in status of a band or family allowed it to move to a more respected place in the camp circle. Thus, as the structure of society was constantly changing, there were changes in the daily lives of the Lakotas. Although there were different rules for large camp circles in which different tribes were present, the basic form of the circle was present in the camp of the smallest *thiyóšpaye*.[36]

The camp circle also affected the power structure in the society. At different times and in different situations the power structure shifted from the chief of the *thiyóšpaye* to the warrior societies (*akíchita*) or to a war leader, *blotáhuka*, during times of war. In larger camp circles, power was held by the chiefs' council (*načá omníciye*), which consisted of elderly men who were no longer active hunters and warriors. The chiefs' council selected men to perform different duties in the camp and during hunting and war. The council appointed men called "deciders" (*wakíchuza*), whose task was to mediate between the chiefs and the people and to direct the camp's movements. Other important leaders selected by the council were the "shirt wearers" (*wicháša yatápika*), prominent younger men known for their bravery and success in war . All these different leaders were known as the *wichášha ithácha*, "leader men." So, among the Lakotas, there was never a single chief who could make decisions on behalf of all the people. Power was distributed; individuals belonged to certain groups and associations depending on their kin relationship and on their own actions.[37]

The whites never really understood this system, in which the leading warriors were more visible than the actual chiefs, who acted in the background. In fact, not even the chiefs were able to act on behalf of the people unless all the chiefs and the chiefs' council approved their decisions. This caused many misunderstandings in the negotiations between the whites and the Lakotas. There were times when the whites announced that they had an agreement with all Lakotas when, in fact, they had an agreement only with a representative of a village or a band. The whites mistook such famous men as Red Cloud and Crazy Horse (Thašúke Witkó) as head chiefs who could decide for the whole tribe, whereas they were leading warriors, not chiefs at all. Partly because the whites deemed Red Cloud the primary chief, he achieved such a powerful position that even the Oglalas themselves started to consider him their head chief.[38]

Until the 1840s, the Lakotas had relatively little contact with whites. By then, however, immigrants traveling to California and Oregon started to arrive in Lakota country. Most immigrants traveled along the Oregon Trail, which followed the Platte River. The Oglalas and Brulés living in the Platte River valley gradually became dependent on the white man's trade goods. Alcohol had been introduced to the Lakotas around the 1820s, but when contacts with immigrants became more frequent the availability of alcohol increased. This brought problems to the Lakotas, and drunken brawls became common. Under the influence of alcohol, small disputes were resolved with violence more often than before. For example, in 1841 a dispute between two Oglala chiefs resulted in the death of one of them, and eventually in a division within the Oglala tribe.[39]

As the number of immigrants traveling west increased, the U.S. government considered it necessary to protect the travelers. In 1845 soldiers entered the Platte River valley for the first time. Four years later a military base was established on Lakota lands. This base, Fort Laramie, was the scene of the first major negotiations between the U.S. government and the Plains Indian tribes in 1851. The government sought to establish safe passage for the immigrants; to this end, the primary goal of the U.S. negotiators was to end hostilities among the warring Indian tribes. Even though the Indians seldom attacked travelers, Indians fighting each other caused instability in the region, making traveling unsafe. Another goal was to define boundaries for the various Indian tribes. These were not actual reservations but areas where each tribe was supposed to be able to live and hunt without interference from other tribes. Almost 10,000 Indians attended the negotiations at Horse Creek, near Fort Laramie.[40]

The Indians agreed to let the government build forts on their lands, promised to let the immigrants travel freely, and promised to end all hostilities among themselves. The boundaries for each tribe were explained. But intertribal peace on the plains did not last long. Peace with the whites, however, did last for a short while. This was partly due to the annual appropriations the government gave to the Indians in compensation for peace.[41]

In 1854 that peace ended. The cause of the hostilities was a cow. A Minneconjou shot a cow belonging to Mormon immigrants, and even though the Indians offered to pay compensation for the cow, Lt. John L. Grattan set out to arrest the Indian responsible. In the ensuing battle Lieutenant Grattan and all thirty of his men were killed. The Lakotas did not understand that they were now at war with the United States; they saw no reason to sustain hostilities after inflicting what they considered a major blow to the U.S. Army. The U.S. government, however, was of a different opinion: in September 1855 the army destroyed a Brulé village in retaliation. In 1856 the Lakotas again made peace with the United States, giving away the Platte River valley.[42]

After this, the Lakotas called together a council, which may have been attended by as many as 7,500 Lakotas. They unanimously decided to oppose the white man's further encroachment on their lands. Instead of taking action, however, the Lakotas dispersed into their traditional winter camps. They compensated themselves for the lost Platte River valley by taking the Powder River country from the Crow Indians and expanded their territory farther west to the Big Horn Mountains. The Treaty of 1851 thus caused the Lakotas to expand their influence at the cost of other Indian tribes. Before the 1851 treaty, U.S. and Lakota interests were not necessarily in conflict, but now these two expanding peoples were competing over the same land base.[43]

During the early part of the 1860s, the Lakotas tried to avoid hostilities with the whites. War arrived on the Northern Plains from the East, where the Santee Sioux were thrown into a war against the U.S. Army in 1862. The army defeated the Indians, and some of the Santees sought refuge among their relatives living on the plains. The army followed the refugees, drawing the Lakotas into the war.[44] Most of the Lakotas did not want to fight against the U.S. Army, but at the same time they were prepared to defend their country against white encroachment. Some of the people were convinced that the best way to survive was to stay at peace with the whites. Thus, already by the 1860s, the Lakotas were divided in their basic approach toward the white man. The whites used this division to differentiate between the so-called friendly and hostile Lakotas. Those who preferred to "walk the white man's road," that is, those who maintained a friendly attitude toward the whites, were called "progressives." Those who preferred to defend their lands and their way of life were called "nonprogressives." In times of war these respective groups were referred to as "friendlies" and "hostiles."[45]

During the summer of 1864 the Oglalas and Brulés were at war with the whites, and even gained some victories, but in the fall they stopped fighting, as they always did in traditional warfare. Spotted Tail (Šįté Gleška), the most powerful leader among the Brulés, was in favor of peace, but Col. John M. Chivington's brutal attack against a Cheyenne village in November 1864 doomed his efforts. The massacre of Indian women and children caused the Cheyennes, Arapahos, and Lakotas to unite against the common threat.[46] The war continued throughout the winter of 1864 and summer of 1865. Red Cloud's status was rising among the warring Indians; Spotted Tail still sought peace, however, and to prove his intention not to fight he finally led some Oglalas and Brulés close to Fort Laramie.[47]

The fighting in the summer of 1865 was remarkable for the havoc the Indians caused, almost humiliating the U.S. Army. The summer was very successful for the Indians, but by fall they again dispersed to hunt buffalo in preparation for the winter. They could not wage war indefinitely; they had to take care of their families.[48]

In 1866 the government again called the Lakotas to Fort Laramie for negotiations. Spotted Tail arrived early with his followers, but Red Cloud, now a leader of the warring faction, stayed in the Black Hills and the Powder River country, as did Sitting Bull (Thatȟáka Íyotake), who led the other major Lakota group living in the area. Red Cloud's presence at the negotiations was considered essential, and when he finally arrived the government officials were jubilant. A permanent peace was now thought possible.[49]

The whites obviously thought that Red Cloud, although most likely only a war leader (*blotáhųka*), had the power to decide tribal matters on his own.[50] During the negotiations the government tried to convince the Lakotas of the benefits of peace. More important, they wanted to get the Indians' permission to open roads through Lakota lands and to build forts alongside the roads to protect travelers. During the negotiations, however, the Indians learned that there was already a military detachment on the way to build forts along the already existing Bozeman Trail, which ran through the Lakota country to the gold fields in Montana.[51]

This news enraged most of the Lakotas, who, led by Red Cloud, marched away from the conference. The final result of the negotiations of 1866 was that only a few of the most progressive headmen signed the treaty. The most notable of these was Spotted Tail, who was the first Indian to sign. When the treaty was finally concluded, the government representative officially declared that a satisfactory result had been achieved and that the Indians had participated in great numbers. He did not mention Red Cloud's leaving the conference or that the majority of Lakotas did not sign at all. Whether or not the negotiators' intention was to deceive the government is not known; at least, their report was not completely truthful. Thus the government in Washington thought that the problems with the Lakotas were solved when, in fact, the United States was at war with Red Cloud's Lakotas.[52]

The war, known as Red Cloud's war, lasted for two years, during which the Indians fought very successfully. Their military tactics resulted in some of the most famous Indian victories, and the U.S. government was eventually forced to give in to the Lakotas and their allies. The forts along the

Bozeman Trail were abandoned, and Red Cloud could declare a victory over the army.[53] But the victory was not due solely to the Indians' ability to wage war; the government's new Indian policy also played a role. The new Peace Policy sought to put an end to the hostilities. Furthermore, the war against the Lakotas turned out to be extremely expensive. It was cheaper to feed the Indians than to fight them.[54]

The war officially ended in 1868, when a new treaty was signed that established a reservation for the Lakotas, which included the sacred Black Hills and a large area north of the Platte River. White men were not allowed to enter this Great Sioux Reservation without permission. In addition, the Indians were allowed to continue to hunt to the north and west in an area designated as unceded Indian territory.[55]

According to the treaty, any future land cession would require the signatures of 75 percent of all adult male Lakotas. This, Article 12, was to serve as a guarantee for the Lakotas that they would have control over their lands in the future. The Indians promised to maintain peace, and as a reward for this the government agreed to give them annual provisions. The provisions, however, were to be distributed far away from the Lakota homelands at new Indian agencies on the Missouri River. The goal was to force the Lakotas to move eastward and to live permanently within the borders of the Great Sioux Reservation. This particular article of the treaty was apparently not properly explained to the Lakotas before 1870, when Spotted Tail and Red Cloud visited Washington.[56]

The 1868 treaty resulted in a division within the Lakota people. Red Cloud and Spotted Tail, with their respective followers, decided to live within the Great Sioux Reservation, but thousands of Lakotas who did not want to have anything to do with the treaty remained off the reservation, living in the unceded territory. The whites soon referred to these Lakotas as the "wild" Indians. Several Indian agencies were established within the reservation. Red Cloud and Spotted Tail were given agencies that carried their names. In addition to these, the Standing Rock, Cheyenne River, and Lower Brulé Agencies were later established. The old Upper Missouri Agency, on the east side of the Missouri, became the new Crow Creek Agency.[57]

At first, life on the reservation was not particularly restricted. The Lakotas were still able to go on hunting trips, visit their relatives on and off the reservation, and live far away from the Indian agencies. Some of the Lakotas returned to the agencies only on the days when rations were issued.[58] Despite this flexible arrangement, life on the reservation was constantly balanced between war and peace. The regular visits by the "wild" Lakotas also kept tensions alive. Furthermore, the government moved the Lakotas from one place to another, hoping that they would eventually settle down and take up farming. The Lakotas strongly opposed this idea. The Friends of the Indians, who were now directing the government's Indian policy, were convinced that in only a few years the Lakotas would be self-supporting farmers. The reality was that by 1873 no farms, or even gardens, were established by full-blood Lakotas at either the Red Cloud or the Spotted Tail Agency.[59]

The government spent large sums of money to support the Lakotas, and there were many whites who wanted to take their share of this money. Inexperienced and often dishonest Indian agents cheated the Indians as well as the government. At times the Lakotas were able to run things as they pleased; weak agents were no match for strong leaders like Spotted Tail and Red Cloud. By 1874 military forts were established near the Spotted Tail and Red Cloud Agencies. The policy of civilizing the Indians by means of Christianity seemed not to be working for the Lakotas; order was to be maintained by force if need be.[60]

In 1874 gold was discovered in the Black Hills and white fortune seekers rushed to the Lakota lands. The U.S. Army was ordered to stop and arrest the white men entering the Black Hills, but the few men who were arrested were quickly released, and consequently many returned to the gold fields. The threat of war was imminent already in 1875, when the government invited the Lakotas to listen to a new proposal. To avoid war, the government proposed to buy the Black Hills, reasoning that, since the Indians were not able to feed themselves but were supported by the government, the land the Indians did not use belonged to the government. The government offered the Lakotas six million dollars for the land, far less than its true value. The Lakotas refused to sell. The government did not want to use force to stop the white gold miners, so their rush to the Black Hills continued.[61]

Because the Lakotas refused to sell the Black Hills, all Lakotas, including those who lived outside the reservation, were ordered to move to within the reservation boundaries by January 1, 1876. Those who failed to do so would be considered hostiles. This was an ultimatum and practically a declaration of war. Most Lakotas had no chance of reaching the agencies by the date they were given; traveling in the middle of the winter was difficult and slow. Furthermore, some of the Indians learned about the ultimatum only after the deadline had passed. The date given by the government actually meant little to the Lakotas anyway; unlike the whites, they were not used to strict time schedules. They could wait until the following spring.[62]

Because the Lakotas failed to meet the deadline, the army marched into Lakota country during the winter and spring of 1876. From the beginning of the war it was clear that the government had underestimated the Lakota forces. Crazy Horse, Gall (Phiží), and Sitting Bull, among others, were leading a fighting force of united Lakotas, Cheyennes, and Arapahos. During the summer of 1876 many of the most famous battles between the Lakotas and the U.S. Army were fought, in which the Indians were able to defeat the army. The culmination of the fighting took place on the Little Big Horn River on June 25, when the Indians completely destroyed the troops of the 7th Cavalry led by Lt. Col. George Armstrong Custer. After the battle, however, the Indians again dispersed; some even returned to the agencies, expecting to get provisions and the same kind of treatment as before.[63]

Following Custer's death more troops were sent to force the Lakotas onto the reservation. Small groups gradually came to the agencies, but the army was not capable of destroying all the hostile Lakotas. Sitting Bull and Crazy Horse, for example, decided to continue the war. The government could not pressure those Indians who were living outside the reservation the same way it could pressure those on the reservation, for example, with food rationing; as a result, the peaceful Indians living on the reservation were made to suffer. By the fall of 1876 they no longer received the provisions that the government had promised them. They were threatened with starvation, and unless they gave up the Black Hills, the government threatened to remove them by force.[64]

With the war still going on, it was highly unlikely that 75 percent of adult male Lakotas would surrender the Black Hills, as the 1868 treaty required. It is of interest to note that, starting in 1871, the U.S. government ceased to make treaties with Indians as sovereign nations. Instead, the government signed agreements with Indian tribes, which became law only when passed as acts of Congress.[65] Under tremendous pressure, even Red Cloud and Spotted Tail, who had not joined the fighting Indians, signed a new agreement by which the Lakotas gave away the Black Hills and their rights to the unceded Indian territory that had been reserved for their use by the 1868 treaty.[66]

The army under Gen. George Crook and Col. Nelson A. Miles followed the Indians led by Crazy Horse and Sitting Bull all through the winter of 1877. In the spring even Crazy Horse surrendered, and Sitting Bull led his people to Canada. After Crazy Horse's surrender, life at the Indian agencies was restless. Almost 10,000 Lakotas were starting a difficult journey of adaptation to reservation life. Crazy Horse's presence, and rumors of his plans to escape and resume hostilities, kept tensions alive. Only after he was killed at Fort Robinson, Nebraska, in September 1877 did the tensions subside.[67]

At this time, the Lakotas were forced to move east to the Missouri River, where a new agency was established. The government refused to distribute provisions elsewhere. Because there were no longer any buffalo in the vicinity of the Lakota agencies and the army prohibited the Lakotas from following the buffalo off the reservation, the Lakotas had no other option but to move east. The next summer, however, Red Cloud and Spotted Tail were allowed to take their people to locations of their own choosing. After many problems, Red Cloud settled the Oglalas on Pine Ridge, and Spotted Tail with his Brulés chose a location along the Rosebud River for their new agency.[68]

The whites considered Spotted Tail and Red Cloud the most powerful Lakota leaders on the reservation in the late 1870s. Because of this, their influence among the Lakotas grew in proportions never seen before. After Spotted Tail's death in 1881, the government considered Red Cloud alone head chief of the Lakotas, even though there were other chiefs who were more entitled to such a position. The government's policy, in fact, was to try to undermine the power of the chiefs. The idea was to dissolve the traditional structure of Indian societies by emphasizing individualism. The government thought that by breaking up the band structure of the Lakotas, they could transform the Indians into individual farmers. The chiefs were seen as obstacles to individual initiative and civilization. Indians were considered to be under their chiefs' tyrannical rule. In daily life ordinary Lakotas still turned to their chiefs; they could not function individually as the whites hoped. The chiefs, like Red Cloud and Spotted Tail, who visited Washington several times, understood the white men better than other Indians, so their influence grew even as the government tried to minimize it. In fact, whenever there was major trouble on the reservation, government agents had to turn to the chiefs. The chiefs were leading the Lakotas' struggle for survival on the reservations.[69]

In 1881 Sitting Bull returned from Canada and surrendered. These last "wild" Lakotas eventually settled around Standing Rock Agency. After Sitting Bull's return all the Lakotas were settled on the Great Sioux Reservation. The Lakotas' era as independent hunters on the plains was over. Their culture had changed dramatically in a very short time. They had resisted white encroachment as well and as long as they could, but now they faced a new kind of challenge: life on the reservation.[70]

U.S. Indian Policy in the 1880s and the Lakotas

The goal of the U.S. government was to make all Indians—including the Lakotas—self-supporting through farming. For most of the Lakotas the concept of work as the whites knew it was totally unfamiliar. For them, hunting was the only natural means of living. In the 1880s the Lakotas also believed that the government owed them support in compensation for lost lands.[71] Moreover, the lands and the climate prevented the Lakotas from adopting farming. The Indian agent at Pine Ridge Reservation, Valentine T. McGillicuddy, described the situation, saying that if 7,000 white settlers were located on the same land and given all that they needed for one year, they would starve to death if they had to live on the products of their own farms.[72]

The government emphasized farming, built schools, and created the Indian police system in a deliberate effort to break down the traditional structure of Lakota society. In 1878 a law was passed creating an Indian police force on all Indian reservations. Among the Lakotas, the creation of the police force was difficult, since they saw the police as rivals to traditional men's societies.[73] Gradually the Lakotas' attitudes toward the police changed as they realized that, if they did not allow the police to keep order on the reservation, that duty would be left to the U.S. Army. In the end the police system was not so strange to the Lakotas. In traditional society the "camp police" (*akíčhita*) kept order; the Indian police system basically replicated this structure and gradually replaced it to some extent. Eventually the Indian police forces became very loyal to the white agents.[74]

Schools were also dividing the Lakota people. The people whom the whites called progressives were willing to send their children to school. They saw the schools as a chance to learn the ways of the white man, which would eventually benefit all the Lakota people. The nonprogressives resisted education in all possible ways. For them, school was a hateful place where the boys' hair was cut off and they were forced to wear white man's clothes.[75]

Reservation life for the Lakotas in the 1880s was a constant struggle over power. This struggle was fought both between the agents and the chiefs and among the chiefs themselves. The most bitter struggle was between Red Cloud and Agent McGillicuddy. This struggle for control of Pine Ridge Reservation lasted for seven years and can be said to have ended in Red Cloud's favor when the agent was removed from duty in 1886.[76]

According to some scholars, one sign of the success of the government's policy to undermine the power of the chiefs was the explosive increase in the number of chiefs, even though many of those who wanted to be referred to as chief lacked the achievements that were traditionally needed for that position. For example, in 1878 the Lakotas had twelve chiefs, but at the beginning of the 1880s there were sixty-three men who called themselves chief. The number of sub-bands also rose dramatically. The historians George E. Hyde and Robert M. Utley claim that this lessened the power of the traditional hereditary chiefs, but it also made possible the tremendous rise in authority of Red Cloud and Spotted Tail.[77]

There is some indication that the structure of Lakota society was not as badly broken in the late 1880s as scholars have suggested. The fact that the number of chiefs and sub-bands increased does not necessarily indicate the breakdown of traditional society. It may reflect the traditionally very flexible structure of Lakota society. As noted earlier, Lakota society could adapt

to the needs of the time; in reservation life, the traditional band structure
was gradually replaced by a district structure, according to where each band
lived. Despite this, basic elements of traditional Lakota society remained;
people moved to these districts in traditional *thiyóšpayes*, where the strong
bonds of kinship remained as a unifying force. For example, the Lakotas
acted in the councils held with the so-called Sioux commissions in the late
1880s as they had traditionally acted in councils. This suggests that the structure of society had suffered a blow, but that blow was not as dramatic as is
generally believed.[78]

In 1882 the government planned to reduce the size of the Great Sioux
Reservation. Threatening and cheating, the government representatives tried
to make the Lakotas cede almost half of the area of their reservation. The
Lakotas, however, were once more able to unite, and with the help of some
eastern white friends, were able to keep their lands. Despite all the restrictions there was still plenty of room on the Great Sioux Reservation to escape the white man's influence. As long as this was possible, there was no
way of making the Lakotas into farmers. But the government did not give
up. By reducing the size of the reservation, the government sought to force
the Lakotas to be bound to the land. Since the Lakotas did not cultivate their
land, they would still have unused land even if they gave away half of it. The
government's plan culminated in 1887 when the General Allotment Act was
passed. This act decided the fate of Lakota lands.[79]

In 1876 the Great Sioux Reservation had been divided into six separate
Indian agencies, but this division was only for administrative purposes. In
1887 these agencies served as the basis for the planned reduction of the Great
Sioux Reservation. The government sent delegations to negotiate with the
Lakotas over the reduction of their lands. The first attempt, in 1888, was a
failure. The Lakotas confronted the commissioners, refusing almost unanimously to surrender their lands. The next year another commission was sent.
This time, one of the members was a famous Indian fighter, Gen. George
Crook, who knew the ways of the Indians. This commission acted differently
from the previous one: by trying to persuade individual Indians behind the
scenes, the commission sought to break the strong opposition of the previous year. Indeed, this strategy proved to be successful. By means of threats

and promises, the commission was able to obtain enough names to legally carry out the reduction of the Great Sioux Reservation. The agreement was then ratified in the Sioux Act of 1889. During the negotiations the Lakotas' strong unified opposition gradually broke down. This would prove a major blow to the Lakota people. The split within the Lakotas deepened dramatically, and seeds of the troubles of 1890 were planted as those who opposed the reduction started to draw away from those who signed the act.[80]

Thus, after tremendous pressure from the government, in 1889 the Lakotas were finally forced to give away land that the whites considered surplus. The Great Sioux Reservation was divided into smaller reservations based on the former administrative areas. The Hunkpapas, Minneconjous, Sans Arcs, Two Kettles, and Blackfeet settled on two adjoining reservations, Standing Rock and Cheyenne River. Pine Ridge Reservation became the home of the Oglalas, the Brulés settled on Rosebud Reservation, and the Lower Brulés were established at Lower Brulé Reservation, across the Missouri River from Crow Creek Reservation.[81]

After 1881, the Lakotas living on the Great Sioux Reservation—and later on the smaller reservations—were in different phases in their assimilation to white culture. The Loafers were so called because they had been living with the whites since the 1850s. Some of the Lakotas settled on the reservation in the 1860s, some in the 1870s, and the last group as late as the 1880s. Thus a very rough division was recognized: those who had lived for a longer time on the reservation formed the group that the whites called progressives, while the newcomers were considered nonprogressives. This, however, is too simplistic a picture, because there were many nonprogressives among those who had lived on the reservation since the 1860s, and there were also progressives among those who had moved onto the reservation in the 1880s. Furthermore, it is almost impossible to say definitely who was really progressive and who was not.

This artificial division existed throughout the 1880s and, although a white invention, started to affect the daily lives of the Lakotas. Despite the efforts and partial success of white officials to break down the unity of the Lakotas as a people, it was clear by the end of the 1880s that an Indian could not live outside the tribal community without his chief or headman. Individualism, as the whites understood and wanted it, had not yet taken root in Lakota society. Despite all the efforts to break down the tribal structure and the power of the chiefs, even Agent James McLaughlin at Standing Rock Reservation said that it was much easier to deal with the Indians through their chiefs than to try to deal with them as individuals.[82]

An understanding of the division into progressives and nonprogressives is somewhat easier if we look at the most notable chiefs. This division occurred on all Lakota reservations, where the people followed the example of their chiefs, as they had always done. More important, the whites considered the people who followed a progressive chief to be progressives, and the same with nonprogressives. Thus the whites automatically considered an Indian living, for example, in Sitting Bull's village to be a nonprogressive, like Sitting Bull himself. Sitting Bull, although also a medicine man, was the leading nonprogressive chief on Standing Rock, while Gall and John Grass (Phežĺ) were the leading progressive chiefs. On Pine Ridge, Red Cloud and Big Road (Čhaŋkú Tháŋka) were leaders of the nonprogressives, while, for example, Young Man Afraid of His Horse (Tȟášuŋke Khókiphapi), Little Wound (Thaópi Cík'ala), and American Horse (Wašíču Tȟašuŋke) led the progressives. Hump (Caŋkáhu) and Big Foot (Sí Tháŋka) were the leading nonprogressives on Cheyenne River Reservation. On Rosebud, Two Strike (Núpa Apȟápi) and Crow Dog (Khaŋǧí Šuŋka) were the leading nonprogressives. After Spotted Tail's death in 1881, the leadership among the progressives on Rosebud was unclear. Those men were, of course, only the most notable leaders at the time, but this allows us to some extent to track the division within the Lakota people.[83]

In 1883 traditional Lakota religious ceremonies were forbidden by the Office of Indian Affairs. The last sun dances of the nineteenth century were held on Pine Ridge in 1882 and on Rosebud a year later. This was a very great blow to Lakota society, since religion and religious ceremonies had always been a part of their daily life. When these ceremonies were forbidden, the culture lost an essential foundation. The Lakotas tried to continue their traditional practices secretly, but the time for large public religious ceremonies, such as the sun dance, was over. In this impossible situation many Lakotas turned to Christianity, preached by missionaries for decades but previously ignored or rejected by many Lakotas. The reality, however, was that for many, the Christian God was only one godlike being among others. So, by the end of the 1880s, the Lakotas were also divided into different religious groups; there were Christians, those who tried to find a balance between Christianity and traditional beliefs, and those who tried to perpetuate the old system of belief.[84]

On the reservations the life of the Lakotas changed rapidly. Nonetheless, by the end of the 1880s they had not yet assimilated as much as the whites had expected. The nonprogressives kept tensions constantly alive, among the Lakotas as well as between the Indians and their white agents. In the late 1880s the Lakotas faced a serious famine. There was no more game left to hunt, the crops failed year after year, and the government added to the Lakotas' distress by reducing the annual appropriation and delaying the delivery of food and supplies. In 1890 the government justified the cut in rations partly by blaming lack of funds and partly by pointing to the decrease in the Lakota population. If the 1890 census was accurate, the decrease was probably the result of famine and disease, but that was not taken into account when the decision to reduce the rations was made. The cut was included in the Sioux Act of 1889, which reduced not only the Great Sioux Reservation to almost half of its size, but also the annual beef allowance. The cut in rations was part of a government policy that sought to use the gradual reduction of rations, and subsequent hunger, to make the Lakotas realize that labor was the only way to survive and achieve self-sufficiency. As late as December 1890 Senator Henry L. Dawes noted that hunger was the only way to make an Indian work.[85]

The famine brought with it devastating epidemics; measles, the grippe (influenza), and whooping cough spread among the desperate Lakotas. Furthermore, the planned reduction of the Great Sioux Reservation caused great anxiety. The Sioux Commission of 1889 made many promises to the Lakotas in order to acquire enough signatures to reach the 75 percent requirement, but the government carried out the partitioning of the Great Sioux Reservation without fulfilling practically any of the Commission's promises. When the division of the Great Sioux Reservation was accomplished in 1890, many Lakotas saw it as the final evidence of the white man's untrustworthiness.[86]

In 1888–89, when life for the Lakotas seemed hopeless, a rumor reached them: somewhere in the west a messiah was preaching a better future for the Indians. Thousands of Indians were reportedly listening to him, and the Lakotas decided to learn more about the wonderful things he was promising.

Revitalization Movements: Hope for Suppressed People

The ghost dance that spread among the many North American Indian tribes in the late 1880s was not a peculiarity of the history of the American Indians. Similar phenomena have occurred all over the world when indigenous peoples have come face-to-face with European expansion and colonialism. The roots of the North American ghost dance can be found in this collision between Native American and Euro-American cultures and in the devastation this contact gradually brought to Indian cultures.[87]

Europeans and, in the case of North America, Euro-Americans tried to replace all aspects of native cultures with the achievements of their own culture. Among the native peoples this caused strong resistance, resulting in cultural conflict and warfare. This conflict eventually led to cultural assimilation, as the weaker culture had to yield to the demands of the stronger.[88]

When Europeans and Euro-Americans succeeded in suppressing the political, military, economic, and religious resistance of the natives, they sometimes encountered another, often unexpected form of resistance. When the structure of a certain society had been crushed, or when that society no longer had the power to continue traditional forms of resistance, new possibilities arose through a religious prophet. These prophetic leaders combined aspects deriving from the new, dominant culture with their own traditional cultures.[89]

These "religious-prophetic" mass movements have occurred all over the world. Among American Indians similar movements occurred among the Pueblos in the late seventeenth century and among the Iroquois and the Shawnees in the early nineteenth century. All of these movements were typically born as a result of tremendous cultural change and in the midst of cultural crisis.[90]

Such movements mainly aimed at getting rid of the dominant culture and restoring traditional ways of living. Through religion and religious ceremonies and with the help of a religious prophet, the object was to bring about a new world without the conquerors. Typically, the destruction of the world was prophesied; it would then be replaced by a new paradise promised by the prophet or messiah. These movements are also called eschatological or messianic movements. A messianic doctrine is usually a doctrine of peace; the believers need only pray, perform certain ceremonies, and wait. The fact that, in the Native Americans' case, the whites are excluded from the new world does not necessarily reflect hatred toward whites. Very often it simply symbolizes the fulfillment of the expected return of the old ways of life. The birth of these movements is often preceded by a deep feeling of spiritual, physical, and social deprivation, as well as social disintegration. The attraction of a messianic movement is that it includes all those things that previously brought pleasure to life. When those things are lost, the result is the prevalent destitute state of society.[91]

Because the object of these movements is to create a more satisfactory culture by reviving the old way of life, they are also called revitalization movements. As defined by the anthropologist Anthony Wallace, a revitalization movement can be at the same time nativistic, messianic, millenarian, and revivalist. Thus the term "revitalization movement" can be used as a general designation for these various religious movements.[92]

The ghost dance of 1890, the object of this study, was in a way a typical revitalization movement; it was born in the midst of cultural change, it included aspects that allow us to designate it by all the names mentioned above; it was nativistic, eschatological, religious-political, and messianic; its object was to create a new kind of world; and it was born at a time when the military resistance of North American Indians had been crushed—a time when most Indian cultures were in deep crisis and the Indians were forced to live on reservations set aside for them by the U.S. government.

 The prophet of the ghost dance of 1890, Wovoka, was a Paiute Indian born about 1858 in Mason Valley, Nevada. Not much is known about his early life, but his father, Tavivo, was a well-known shaman and medicine man. Through him Wovoka learned the secrets of the spirit world and religion. As a young man Wovoka was famous for his ability to hear voices and see visions.[93] During his younger years, the Paiutes were forced to give up their old ways of living as well as their lands. Like many Paiutes, Wovoka went to work on a farm owned by a white man, David Wilson, where he became known by the name Jack Wilson. There he also learned about Christianity.[94]

In 1887 Wovoka taught his people a new dance, which was basically his transformation of the traditional Paiute circle dance. The dance did not cause great excitement among the Paiutes, although they danced for a while as Wovoka instructed.[95] His real religious revelation came on January 1, 1889, when he was sick and lying in his cabin. On that day there was an eclipse of the sun, and as the sun "died" Wovoka also "died." He traveled to heaven, where, he reported, he saw God and people who had died a long time ago. These people were happy and young forever. God gave Wovoka a new dance and new instructions for life, which he was supposed to teach to his people. He also received power to control the weather. When Wovoka came back from heaven, he began to preach as he had been instructed. After this incident, his influence as a shaman and mediator between God and human beings was guaranteed among the Paiute Indians. His influence grew when he made some correct predictions about the weather; he also performed many miracles.[96]

Wovoka's message appealed to Indians. The news of his message, and the hope of his predictions about a new world that was about to appear in the near future, spread across Indian reservations throughout the West. During the years 1888–90 several Indian tribes sent representatives to Mason Valley to hear his message.[97]

The roots of Wovoka's doctrine can be found in several earlier revitalization movements among North American Indians.[98] In most of these movements Christianity played an important role. The idea of loving your neighbor as yourself was adopted into the new doctrine, although it was generally thought to apply only to Indians. Typical of these movements was also the idea of resurrection after death and the arrival of a paradise on earth. The followers made it clear that Indian customs were respected; only things and ideas that were not harmful to Indians were taken from white culture. For example, the use of alcohol was rejected. These movements were usually

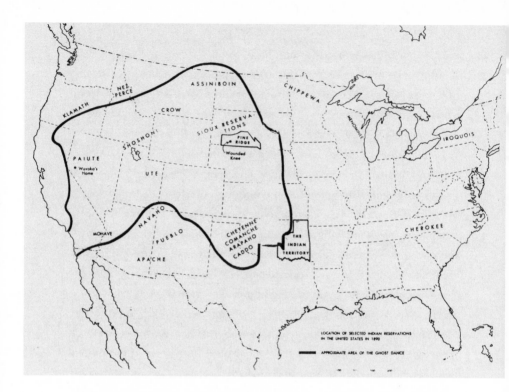

FIGURE 1. The area covered by the ghost dance. From James Mooney, *The Ghost Dance Religion and the Sioux Outbreak of 1890*, 14th Annual Report of the Bureau of Ethnology to the Secretary of the Smithsonian Institution 1892–1893, Washington DC 1893, (Lincoln: University of Nebraska Press, 1991).

peaceful in their basic nature, but violence was often present in one way or another.[99]

The movement that most affected Wovoka originated in 1869 in western Nevada; it was led by a Northern Paiute shaman named Wodziwob. He taught new prayers, songs, and a certain dance for his people, the Northern Paiutes. The aim was to bring back to life all the dead Indians and to restore the old ways of life. This movement, known as the ghost dance of 1870, spread widely among the Indians in the Great Basin area. As Wodziwob's promises were not fulfilled, however, the religion died out in a relatively short time.[100] Wovoka was well acquainted with Wodziwob's religion, since his own father was one of Wodziwob's followers.[101]

The 1870 ghost dance appealed not only to Indians, but also to the Mormons, who saw it as an answer to the expectations of their own religion. They too expected a messiah to arrive in the near future. How much Mormons actually affected or participated in the 1870 ghost dance, and later in the 1890 ghost dance, remains unclear.[102]

The second movement that is generally believed to have affected Wovoka was the Dreamer movement, founded in the Northwest by the prophet Smohalla in the 1870s.[103] The Shaker movement that was founded in 1881 by John Slocum (known also as Squasachtun) and Mary Slocum was the third movement that is believed to have affected Wovoka.[104]

Wovoka's doctrine is similar to all these movements and includes aspects of each as well as aspects from Christian, and specifically Mormon, beliefs. His doctrine was probably most strongly affected by Christianity and Wodziwob's teachings.

The basic idea of the ghost dance was that there would be a time when all the Indians, the living and the dead, would live happily forever in a world where no death, sickness, or misery would exist. There was no room for white people in the new world; only the Indians were to survive the great transformation, whether an earthquake or some other kind of natural phenomenon, that would bring about the new world. This was supposed to happen through supernatural power, without the help of humans and without their interference. Humans were expected only to dance, pray, and believe. Wovoka left the day of the great transformation open, but generally it was expected to take place in the spring, when nature was recovering from winter. Wovoka himself spoke of several different years, but his followers generally believed that the spring of 1891 was the time of the expected transformation.[105]

Even though Wovoka's doctrine left the white race destroyed in the trembling of the earth, the doctrine was not directed against the whites. According to Wovoka, there was no need to fight the whites; there would simply be a natural transformation into the new world, where no whites would exist. Wovoka's religion was a religion of peace. He told his people to do right always; he prohibited telling lies as well as harming other people. Above all, he forbade fighting.[106]

Wovoka gave precise instructions concerning how the Indians should act in order to survive the great earthquake unharmed. He ordered them to dance for four consecutive nights, and on the fifth night dancing should continue until morning. After the dance, everyone had to take a bath in a river. The dances were to be held every sixth week, and during the dancing great festivities were to be arranged. Wovoka introduced two sacred things that should be worn when dancing. One was a feather, which would transform into a wing that would lift the wearer up in the air when the earth was trembling. The other was red paint, which was supposed to ward off illness until the new world appeared. There was nothing else the Indians were expected to do but to live according to these instructions and wait.[107]

Wovoka's religion was very simple and clear, but as it spread from one tribe to another it changed. Each tribe understood his message in its own way and explained it according to its own cultural traditions. The lack of a common language among the different tribes led to transformations and misrepresentations of the original message. Thus the earthquake was replaced by flooding among some tribes, and others wanted to give even the whites a place in the new world. Wovoka, however, forbade anyone from telling the white people anything about what was going to happen. The ghost dance was meant to benefit only the Indians.[108]

Whereas the 1870 ghost dance spread mainly toward the west, Wovoka's religion attracted followers from all directions. By the fall of 1890 it covered an area reaching from Canada to Texas and from California to the Missouri River. More than thirty tribes and tens of thousands of Indians were following the teachings of the Paiute medicine man.[109] Ironically, the inventions of the whites were helping to spread Wovoka's religion. Educated Indians spread the news by letter and telegram, and the railroads helped Indians to travel long distances to meet Wovoka. Furthermore, the Indians were able to read newspapers; thus the English language, as well as the traditional Indian sign language, became primary means of communication between different tribes.[110]

Many tribes sent delegations to Mason Valley to meet with Wovoka. When those delegations returned home, they told their people of the wonderful things they had seen and heard. Wovoka performed many miracles and convinced the Indians of his powers.[111] As noted above, the doctrine changed as it traveled through the country, and so did the name of the dance. Some tribes called it "the dance in a circle" or "the dance with clasped hands." On the Great Plains the Lakotas called it wanáǧi wachípi kị, best translated as "the spirit dance," the word *wanáǧi* referring to the spirits of the dead. Frightened whites, however, gave it the name it became known by all over the world: the ghost dance.[112]

Wovoka's religion was a mixture of traditional Indian beliefs and customs added to teachings from Christianity. Dancing and feasting had always been vital parts of religious ceremonies among the Indians; seeing visions and believing in their message was also natural for them. Those aspects that were taken directly from Christianity were probably less familiar, but it has to be taken into account that by the late 1880s thousands of Indians were members of Christian churches. How much the Mormons affected the ghost dance is not clear, but perhaps Wovoka got the idea of a returning messiah from them, since the Mormons were awaiting their own revelation in 1890. Thus many of the ideas that Wovoka gave to the Indians were not strange to them at all, but old familiar concepts put in a slightly new package. Whites looked upon the ghost dancers with suspicion throughout the western United States, but only among the Lakotas did the ghost dance have tragic consequences.

ONE

Wanáǧi Wachípi kį

The first news of the ghost dance (wanáǧi wachípi kį) reached the western-most Lakota reservation, Pine Ridge, by early 1889, perhaps in late 1888. The news was mainly received through letters written in English by Shoshone and Arapaho Indians. William T. Selwyn, a full-blood Yankton Sioux who worked as a postmaster on Pine Ridge Reservation, translated these letters for the Oglalas.[1] According to these first letters the Son of God had come upon earth somewhere to the west of the lands of the Shoshones and the Arapahos.[2]

Because of these letters and other rumors, the Lakotas wanted to learn more, and eventually decided to send a delegation to meet with the messiah. Sending this official delegation was a matter of great importance to the Lakotas; before selecting the men who would represent the Lakota people, a council that included both the progressive and the nonprogressive chiefs was held on Pine Ridge. The meeting was conducted in the traditional way, and every chief was allowed to present his views. After much discussion and even some arguing, the council decided to send the delegation to the West to determine the reliability of the rumors. The chiefs' council appointed Good Thunder (Wakįyą Wašté) the leader of the delegation.[3]

There has been extensive debate among scholars regarding the events lead-ing up to the Lakotas' decision to send a delegation to the West. Scholars have usually followed the anthropologist James Mooney's interpretation, which suggests that the Lakotas sent two different delegations; the first trav-eled only to the Arapahos and Shoshones, the second went all the way to Nevada to meet with the messiah. The dates and members of these Lakota delegations have been, and still are, somewhat unclear. This is partly due to the conflicting accounts by Indian informants, and perhaps due to misinterpretations and errors in translations. Short Bull (Thatháka Ptécela), one of the key members of the so-called second delegation, for example, provides us with conflicting accounts. In one account he maintains that the delegation left in June 1889, and in another he says that they left in the fall of 1889; his accounts also report two different lists of names. Other Indian informants also give varying lists of names. My research leads me to believe that there was only one official delegation, which left between June and September 1889 and returned in early 1890. There is no clear evidence that there really was a previous official delegation, but, of course, contacts between these tribes were frequent. Therefore, a visit by some Lakotas to the Arapahos and Shoshones earlier in 1889, maybe even 1888, is possible, even probable. This might be one of the reasons that so many different names have been mentioned in this context. Clearly, however, based on the information gained from these visits, an official delegation was sent out. This delegation traveled all the way to Nevada and most likely returned to Pine Ridge in early 1890. Once back, the delegates were fully convinced that the story of the messiah was true.[4]

Accompanying Good Thunder on this official delegation were other Oglalas from Pine Ridge: Short Bull, from Rosebud Reservation, represented the Brulés; Kicking Bear (Mathó Wanáhtaka), from Cheyenne River Reservation, represented the Minneconjous; a few Cheyenne and Arapaho Indians also joined the delegation en route. Both Short Bull and Kicking Bear were veterans of the war of 1876. They were among the last of Sitting Bull's followers to surrender, and they were openly nonprogressive. They were against the reforms forced upon the Lakotas by the white men. Short Bull was known as a warrior as well as a medicine man. These two men became the leaders of the ghost dance religion among the Lakotas.[5]

The trip to Nevada, where the messiah lived, was in itself a journey to the unknown for the Lakota delegates. They had almost no knowledge of the lands and peoples west of the Shoshones. That a part of the trip was made by train added to the strangeness of the journey.[6] Short Bull provides us with the following account of the journey:

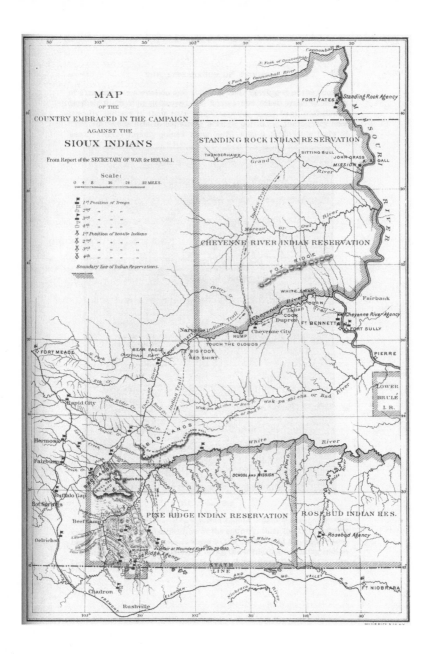

FIGURE 2. The Lakota reservations, 1890. From *The Annual Report of the Secretary of War, 52nd Congress, 1st Session, House Executive Document*, Vol. 2, No. 1, Part 2, Vol. 1, Serial 2921, (Washington DC: Government Printing Office, 1892).

In the year 1889, in June, we went from Pine Ridge; four of us were from Rosebud, and from Pine Ridge there were three, so we were seven. And after eleven nights we reached Arapaho Agency, Wyoming, and there we rested seven days. And then from there we went to the Bannock (Wabanaka) Agency and after nineteen nights we reached there and the people came together and held an Omaha dance, and we took part in it. There a man who was said to be holy participated, a Bannock (Banake); he spoke to us as follows: "Three days from here is the place of God (Wakhą́ Tňą́ka) so four tribes will go see him. So, my friends, you will join them", he said. . . . Then when it was morning that man came and said, "My friends, now they will go together so you should join them. Hurry!" Then we saddled our horses. . . . We went with them for six nights and we arrived there at the Paiute (Rabbit-skin Blanket Wearers) Agency and stayed two days. And from there we went with four Paiutes and after three days we camped; we arrived at the foot of the Rocky Mountains (White Mountains).[7]

Once in Nevada, the delegates met Wovoka and other Indians from many different tribes. When the delegation returned to Pine Ridge they told George Sword, captain of the Pine Ridge Indian police, about their meeting with Wovoka, the Messiah. Sword then wrote the story of the delegates' journey in the Lakota language. The English version of the story was initially published in 1891 in *The Folk-Lorist* magazine by Emma C. Sickels and later reprinted in James Mooney's work.[8]

According to Sword, the delegates told him that smoke came from heaven to the place where the Messiah was to appear. When the smoke disappeared, there was a man about forty years old, who was the Son of God. The delegates said that they had seen the signs of crucifixion on the man's body. This was considered a true sign and evidence that they were indeed dealing with the one who was called the Son of God by the Christians. He had come to earth again. Because the whites had once abandoned and crucified him, he had now come to help the Indians and to punish the whites for their wickedness and wrongdoing toward the Indians. According to the delegates, Wovoka promised also to destroy those Indians who would not believe his message or who would take the side of the whites. Wovoka announced that he was able to destroy the whites simply by stretching out his arm. He also urged all Indians to take up farming as well as to send their children to school.[9]

The delegates described many miracles they had seen on their journey. They were able to meet their relatives who had been dead for a long time. On their way home they killed a buffalo, and after they ate only those parts that the Messiah had advised, the buffalo came to life again. Wovoka had also promised to shorten their way home; this came true, because after making camp in the evenings in one place, in the mornings they woke up in a different place, much closer to home. In addition, Wovoka taught them a new dance and wanted them to call him Até, "Father."[10]

This is the standard interpretation of the Lakota delegation's journey. A slightly different version of the events, with additional information, was told by Short Bull himself:[11]

> Then [after arriving at the Paiute Agency] one of the Paiutes spoke to us as follows: "We will stay here for two days, waiting for two tribes to arrive here, then they will reach us here at midday," he said. Then we stayed right there. And then on the second day some Cheyennes and Shoshones, those two, arrived; there were three Cheyennes and five Shoshones, and so eight arrived. Well, then we went and they stopped at midday, and when they finished eating they said this: "We will sit on this hill and then he will arrive," they said. And then we went to a hill, the biggest and highest one in the Rocky Mountains. I was the last one to join them and then we stopped beneath it . . . we dismounted and we tied our horses to little pine trees. . . . We put on red earth paint. And then, one behind the other, we climbed the hill. We climbed to the top. And in the middle there was a huge flat rock and around it was a grove of pine trees, and everything was visible in all directions. And then they sat in a circle. And one of the Paiutes sat down in the middle where we were sitting and shouted something.
>
> After a while a white man came and stood in the middle of them, but not one of us looked steadily at him. He stood with his head bowed and all at once, surprisingly, he made a speech in the Lakota language. He said as follows: "My pitiful children," meaning these [the

35

gathered Indians], "because you come to me suffering, you will hear those things that are right and you will act accordingly," he said. "By means of a dance you will see again those of your relatives who died long ago; but only if you do it properly will you truly see your people. And because Father told me these things, remember me! Behold me, my sons, I myself was killed long ago by the white men, and therefore now there are many holes in me," he said, "but because you Indian people are suffering I am paying you this visit so in the future you and your relatives who have died will see one another. From this time on, by dancing and [doing] those things that I will say, you will live well. My beloved sons, do not murder one another! Whoever commits murder does evil. And love one another! And take pity on one another! If you act in this manner, I will give you more concerning the ceremony. And those people should take sweat baths. While you are dancing you must not eat any at all of the white man's food! And fast! And you must not wear any metal. And while you dance you must dance with your eyes closed. If you think about one of your relatives who died long ago you will see him. Well, it is not possible for you Indians and the whites to become the same as long as your generations continue. Therefore my father made you of a different nature and also gave you a country. And he will see any bad things that you do, so from this time on whatever you do, I will watch over and keep [you]. The Indians are far below because my father made you last. Now I will help you and you will live well. In the future these things will be fulfilled.

Behold! There is a village. These are your relatives of past generations so you will go there," he said, and turning around he looked to the west, so we looked there. Then there was a village of people and many were walking about and the village was smoky. And some were coming this way on horseback. And on this side there was a hill so they were coming up on the other side. Then he said as follows: "You will be with them, but then you will not truly be with them; then you will see your relatives, so then you will see them in the normal way," he said, "and from now on, do not forget this visit! And whatever the whites with whom you will live want, do it accordingly! This will not

36

be for long. Well, I give you these things, so remember them well! ... Well, my sons, do not overdo these things! And do them properly! Everyone close their eyes!" he said. So I sat there with my head bowed and I sat with my eyes closed. And then I looked. Then he was gone, so, "Look there!" I said. Then one of them looked up furtively, pointing behind, so I looked that way. Then he was standing high up. And the land and that village of people, too, were slowly disappearing. So those who I had joined were crying.

So then we went back and we arrived at the Paiute Agency. And we stayed there four days and from there again we went back and arrived at the Bannock Agency and we stayed there six days. And from there we went to Pine Ridge, South Dakota; we arrived there and at White Clay we told our story.[12]

The Lakota delegates traveled far from home and undoubtedly experienced many strange things, yet it is very difficult for us to comprehend these remarkable stories, told by men highly respected among their own people. Either the delegates agreed to tell such stories, or they simply believed them. The following text, in fact, shows how Short Bull and his companions felt after the meeting with the Messiah: "And then I [Short Bull] asked them, 'Did you understand clearly what he said?' 'Yes,' they said. Then I asked the Cheyenne named Porcupine, 'My friend, did you understand what Father said?' Then, 'Yes,' he said. Then I asked a Shoshone and he, too, said they understood him. So I told them how we understood him and when I finished they all said it was right. So again I spoke as follows: 'When you return and arrive home, will you dance?' Then, 'Yes,' they said."[13] Short Bull was clearly highly impressed by what he saw and heard, but also needed reassurance from his companions. After this, it seems, they were true believers in the Messiah's powers. It is very hard to imagine that they would have consciously fabricated these stories, as some historians have claimed. One explanation is presented by James Mooney, who claimed that perhaps these men were "under some strange psychological influence as yet unexplained."[14]

When considered from the Lakota point of view, however, the stories the delegates told are not so unusual. For example, the idea of the return of the buffalo makes sense when the Lakota concept of the buffalo is taken into account. To the Lakotas, human beings and buffalos were linked to each other; they had both originated from the earth and would eventually go back there. From beneath the earth they could then be restored to the earth, perhaps by a messiah. One of the delegates gave a simple reason for believing: he said that he was an ordinary man, but he had to believe, because he had seen, though he could not explain.[15]

Once back home the Lakota delegates started to spread a message that was somewhat different from the doctrine preached by Wovoka. According to the Lakota delegates, Wovoka announced that he himself was the Son of God, who had been crucified by the whites. Mooney states that Wovoka never claimed to be the Son of God or Jesus; he was only a mediator. However, in the so-called Messiah letters, Wovoka said, "Jesus is now upon the earth." Porcupine, a Cheyenne Indian who was with the Lakota delegation, told about the Son of God and the signs of crucifixion; as Short Bull put it, they had made "holes" in his body.[16] That the Lakota delegates and other Indians were confused about Christian teachings can probably be explained by the fact that—in the end—they were not that familiar with Christianity, and they interpreted Christian beliefs in the context of their own belief systems. Furthermore, there is little evidence that the Lakota delegates were particularly interested in the Christian aspects of the Messiah's doctrine. In fact, the Lakotas had been largely negative toward Christianity and the white man's civilization. Very soon the Lakotas started to consider the "Father" one aspect of their own Great Spirit (Wakhą́ Tháka) rather than the Christian God.[17] Nonetheless, the Lakota delegates did retain some Christian elements in their teachings, as will be seen throughout this study.[18]

The Lakota delegates made several small changes in Wovoka's "doctrine."[19] According to George Sword's version, Wovoka was able to destroy the whites with a wave of his hand. In addition, the delegates said that because the whites were bad and had treated the Indians badly, they had to be punished. It was for this reason that Wovoka came to help the Indians. This, however, was not the original message. Wovoka did explicitly demand that the Indians live in peace with the whites until the dawn of the new world. No one was to be harmed, but the white race would perish in the forthcoming transformation to a new world. So it seems that, as interpreted by Sword, the doctrine preached by the Lakotas took a more negative tone toward the whites than the doctrine preached by other Indian tribes. This has become the standard interpretation of how the doctrine developed among the Lakotas. Short Bull's account, however, clearly shows that the Lakota delegates' ideas did not differ significantly from the original message. It is also important to realize that Short Bull's account of the meeting with the Messiah is full of symbolism, completely understandable and reasonable from the Indians' point of view. Most important, he does not mention destroying the white men, as suggested in the account given by Sword. On the contrary, he repeats the Messiah's peaceful teachings, saying, "Whatever the whites with whom you will live want, do it accordingly," albeit he notes that the Indians and whites could "not be the same." This, however, does not contradict the accounts of the ghost dance told by other Indian informants, nor does it render the Lakota ghost dance more hostile toward the whites than the ghost dance among other Indian tribes. Short Bull, in fact, later claimed that the dance was for whites and Indians alike.[20]

The Lakota delegates understood Wovoka's doctrine in their own way, in terms of their own attitudes, expectations, and beliefs. It has to be taken into account that delegates like Kicking Bear and Short Bull were nonprogressive traditionalists. They refused to live as the whites demanded, and they expected the destruction of the white man and the return of the old way of life. Thus the doctrine probably transformed in their minds to meet their own expectations. There is no evidence, however, that the delegates deliberately made changes in the doctrine at this point. Such changes have to be understood in relation to the delegates' personal values and expectations, and also in relation to the events that led to the destitute situation in which the Lakotas were living. The delegates returned home to tell about things they had seen and heard, but also to tell about things they had wanted and hoped to see and hear.

There is also no doubt that the lack of a common language led to distortions in the ghost dance doctrine. The only common languages these Indians from many different tribes had were the sign language and—ironically—English. Translating and interpreting through several Indian languages must inevitably have resulted in changes to Wovoka's doctrine.[21] Considering these facts, it would be far too strong an argument to claim that the Lakota delegates "perverted Wovoka's doctrine into a militant crusade against the white man," as suggested by the historian Robert Utley. Also far too simple an explanation is presented by the historian Robert W. Larson, who has suggested that, "being a more militaristic people, the Lakota Sioux also gave the ghost dance a certain twist never endorsed by the pacifistic Wovoka." This, however, has remained a mainstream interpretation of the Lakota ghost dance doctrine.[22] In fact, the Lakota delegates did not talk about war against the whites; they said that the whites would be punished, but it would be the Messiah who would punish them.

Furthermore, there was never any single doctrinal form of religion in the traditional Lakota belief system. As the anthropologist Raymond J. DeMallie has noted, "Each individual man formulated a system of belief by and for himself. There was no standardized theology, no dogmatic body of belief. Basic and fundamental concepts were universally shared, but specific knowledge of the spirits was not shared beyond a small number of holy men. Through individual experience every man had the opportunity to contribute to and resynthesize the general body of knowledge that constituted Lakota belief."[23] Thus the traditional Lakota system of belief was constantly changing and adapting to new circumstances. The Lakota ghost dance followed perfectly this pattern for the evolution of belief. There was no single universal doctrinal teaching in the Lakota ghost dance, and it was constantly changing through personal experiences. This can already be seen in the message the delegates brought home with them, but it is even more obvious in later phases, when individual trances and visions started to have their effect on the Lakota ghost dance ceremony.[24]

Drawing enthusiastic crowds of Lakotas, the first meetings and ceremonies to consider the ghost dance were held on Pine Ridge and Rosebud Reservations in April 1890, not long after the return of the delegation. The first meeting was held at White Clay Creek, a half-mile north of Pine Ridge Agency, and was led by Kicking Bear. On Rosebud Reservation, Agent J. George Wright arrested Short Bull after learning that his preaching was taking the Lakotas away from their farms. Under pressure from the agent, Short Bull promised to stop the ceremonies. On Pine Ridge Reservation, Agent Hugh D. Gallagher also arrested the apostles of the new religion and ordered them to stop preaching. They promised to do so. Thus it seemed that the agents were able to prevent the organization of large public meetings and dance ceremonies, but on both reservations the Lakotas continued their ceremonies in secrecy.[25]

Kicking Bear returned to the Cheyenne River Reservation, where he was able to preach without intervention. He invited all Lakotas to take part in a great dance there, but since the agents had prevented the Lakotas from attending the ceremonies on other reservations, the dance was never held and enthusiasm faded also on Cheyenne River. At this point Kicking Bear left the reservation and traveled to visit the Arapaho Indians, who were already dancing frequently.[26] On the other Lakota reservations the ghost dance had not yet taken hold of the people. In fact, it was never really adopted by the people of Crow Creek and Lower Brulé Reservations. So far, no one had introduced the dance on Standing Rock Reservation, since they had not sent a representative to join the delegation to the West.[27]

None of the agents on the Lakota reservations considered the ghost dance a serious threat in the spring and summer of 1890. They were too busy with farming programs and other daily routines. The situation was reported to be perfectly peaceful.[28]

The reports and actions of the agents in June do show that at that time the ghost dance had not become a major movement on the Lakota reservations. However, Mooney states that already on June 20, there was a large and dramatic ceremony in the village of No Water (Mní Waníce) at White Clay Creek. Mooney bases his account on an eyewitness description that he says is dated June 1890. Nonetheless, this description starts with the words "We drove to this spot about 10.30 am on a delightful October day." The text continues with a description of a large and "fanatic" ceremony, which became typical later in the fall. If such a major ceremony had been organized already in June, it is unlikely that the agent would not have been familiar with it and therefore mentioned it in his letters. The agent's letters, however, do not report any such gatherings. This seems to be a mistake on Mooney's part. He most likely took this eyewitness account from a report

FIGURE 3. Lakota leaders at Pine Ridge. Chief Kicking Bear (left) wears a breech-cloth, tunic, and vest; his blanket is on the ground. Chief Young Man Afraid of His Horse, an intermediary (center), wears a combination of traditional and white-style clothing. Standing Bear holds a ceremonial pipe and wears a suit with a watch chain and a Christian pin. Denver Public Library, Western History Collection, North Western Photo Co., call number x-31367.

by Daniel Dorchester, the superintendent of Indian schools, but misread the date. The camp of No Water was a major religious center for the ghost dance, but became so only later in the summer. Utley concurs that there were no large gatherings of ghost dancers on any of the Lakota reservations as early as June 1890.[29]

The ghost dance religion might have died out altogether if July had not brought with it yet another drought and crop failure. The crops failed even

worse than in previous years, and the drought was followed by severe famine. Even white settlers were abandoning their farms. Unlike them, the
Lakotas were unable to move away. During this time of greatest hardship,
Congress again reduced the annual appropriations for the Lakota reservations. This left the Lakotas in a devastating condition. They asked for help.
Several chiefs wrote letters to the commissioner of Indian affairs in which
they tried to explain the destitute situation they were facing and the effect
the cut in rations would have on their people. They feared another winter of
starvation might lead to trouble. They could not understand why the government had done this to them. They simply wanted to live in peace and
receive what was promised to them in treaties and in the negotiations with
General Crook the previous year.[30]

As the summer of 1890 advanced, the Lakotas became more desperate.
Obviously no relief could be expected from the whites, and more and more
people gathered around their traditional leaders, looking to them for help
and guidance. On Pine Ridge, Red Cloud was still a prominent figure among
the nonprogressive traditionalists, even though he had joined the Roman
Catholic Church. Big Road and Little Wound were among the leaders whose
influence was growing. The so-called progressive leaders American Horse
and Young Man Afraid of His Horse found themselves in a difficult situation. This was especially true of American Horse, who, having signed the
Agreement of 1889, was considered by many to be responsible for the pitiful situation in which the Lakotas now found themselves.[31]

In fact, American Horse himself complained to the commissioner of
Indian affairs that the Lakota people had never faced such hard times as they
had since signing the Agreement of 1889. American Horse had signed that
agreement because he thought that some good would result from it, but it
had brought only misery and divisiveness to the Lakotas. Now the split between the progressives and the nonprogressives was intensifying, American
Horse observed. Those who had not signed the agreement joined the ghost
dance to separate themselves from those who had signed.[32]

By the end of July dissatisfaction among the Lakotas was deepening and
defiance toward whites was more openly shown. Just at this time Kicking
Bear returned from his visit to the Arapahos. His return coincided with a

time when the Lakotas were desperate to believe anything that offered them hope. He told the Lakotas that the Arapahos were already dancing, and as he told them about the miracles he had seen and experienced among the Arapahos, as well as about the bright future those Indians had ahead of them, he found many interested listeners among his people. Short Bull "forgot" the promise he had made to his agent and started to preach again.[33]

The helplessness and hopefulness felt by the ghost dancers in general is well illustrated by this famous Arapaho ghost dance song:

> Father, have pity on me,
> Father, have pity on me,
> I am crying for thirst,
> I am crying for thirst;
> All is gone—I have nothing to eat,
> All is gone—I have nothing to eat.[34]

Soon after Kicking Bear's return the Lakotas started to organize ceremonies in several places under the leadership of the ghost dance apostles. Despite being a Roman Catholic and later claiming that he had never even seen a dance himself, Red Cloud gave his blessing to the dances. He commented that the religion would die by itself if it were not true.[35] Little Wound, who was also Christian—an Episcopalian—and considered very progressive, urged the people to organize a dance quickly, so that the Messiah would not leave them behind when the time came. He did not know whether the dance would help, but he saw nothing wrong in it.[36]

In early August 1890 approximately 300 Oglalas were dancing in Little Wound's camp. Other dance camps were established in various places around Pine Ridge Reservation under the leadership of Little Wound, Big Road, Good Thunder, and Jack Red Cloud, the son of the famous chief. Large dance camps emerged on Pine Ridge in four places. The biggest was No Water's camp at White Clay Creek, where as many as 600 people were reported to be dancing. Big Road was the leader of the 250 Lakotas who took up ghost dancing at Wounded Knee Creek. At Porcupine Creek 150 Lakotas started to dance, and at Medicine Root Creek more than 500 people were dancing under the leadership of Little Wound. In August, almost 1,200 Oglalas of

the more than 5,500 Lakotas living on Pine Ridge Reservation were participating regularly in the ghost dances; their numbers grew during the fall,
reaching perhaps 1,500 by November.[37] Many moved out of their log cabins and away from the agency to be able to live in the dance camps in traditional tipis. After the problems of midsummer, Oglalas were rapidly turning to the new religion.[38]

The ghost dance enthusiasm on Pine Ridge grew as August wore on. Agent
Gallagher became worried about the situation, and on August 22 he tried to
stop a dance, taking with him thirty members of the Indian police force. But
the Indians knew about his arrival in advance and were ready to defend their
new ceremony, with arms if necessary. In the end, the presence of Young
Man Afraid of His Horse prevented further trouble. For the first time the
ghost dancers had defied the authority of the agent and were ready to fight
the Indian policemen, even though they were also Lakotas.[39]

The news of the ghost dancers' success spread across the Lakota reservations, but it also spread among the white settlers. By late fall even officials
in Washington grew restless as the rumors of Indians arming themselves
reached the capital.[40] The focus of the ghost dances on Pine Ridge in August
was the camp of No Water at White Clay Creek, where more and more
people were falling into trances and "dying." After returning from the land
of the spirits, they told wonderful stories about their journey. Hope started
to replace the despair that had prevailed during the summer.[41]

On Rosebud, where Short Bull was preaching the new religion, the news
of the ghost dancers' success on Pine Ridge was greeted with enthusiasm.
The Brulés began to abandon their homes and take their children out of
school, heading for the dance camps.[42] Later in August a rumor spread across
Rosebud Reservation that the army had arrived at the reservation and captured some Lakota women and children. The news caused anger and dis-
may, and both the progressives and the nonprogressives started to go for
their arms. The Indians rushed to meet the soldiers and free the captured
women and children. The rumor, however, turned out to be false. The panic and the confusion following the spread of this rumor demonstrate the
delicate situation that defined life on the Lakota reservations at that point.
According to Luther Standing Bear (Mathó Nážį), an Indian put the rumor
forward, but the reason for this remained unclear.[43]

During the fall of 1890 the new Republican administration replaced the agents appointed by the previous Democratic administration; only James McLaughlin at Standing Rock remained. The new agent at Pine Ridge was Daniel F. Royer, who did not have much experience with Indians; in fact, he seemed to be afraid of them. At least the Indians felt that he was afraid, since very soon the amused Lakotas at Pine Ridge gave him the name Young Man Afraid of His Indians.[44]

The new agent at Rosebud, Elisha B. Reynolds, was unconcerned about the ghost dance, a fact of which Short Bull and his followers took advantage. The Rosebud ghost dancers were camped approximately five miles west of the agency at Little White River. The camp was quite large and was continually growing larger. The ghost dances were reportedly going on daily, but the dancers were not particularly enthusiastic. Luther Standing Bear reports that the camp moved away when a rumor circulated that soldiers were coming.[45]

On Cheyenne River, Kicking Bear gathered almost all the nonprogressives away from the agency to a safe place where the new agent, Perain P. Palmer, could not bother them. Altogether about 700 Minneconjous joined Kicking Bear's believers under the leadership of Hump and Big Foot at Cherry Creek. Although Hump had previously served in the Indian police force, he now joined the ghost dancers. Big Foot had been hoping to get more schools on the reservation, but as nothing happened despite many promises, he became disillusioned and looked to the ghost dance for help.[46] Cheyenne River soon became the center for the Lakota ghost dance. People from other Lakota reservations came to watch, to participate, and to learn the ceremonies and the doctrine of the ghost dance as Kicking Bear taught it.[47]

By the end of September 1890 ghost dancing started to interfere with daily reservation routines. The ghost dancers no longer obeyed their agents or the Indian police, who could not perform the duties they were given. Under normal circumstances the policemen had been faithful to the agents, but now they had to choose over and over again between the white agents and their own people.[48]

The ghost dance, together with the disasters of the summer of 1890, led many Lakotas to turn once again to their chiefs and medicine men. Even those who did not take up the new religion sought guidance from their chiefs instead of siding with the agents. When the Lakotas moved to the ghost dance camps, they re-created the traditional camp circles. These camps embodied the sacred hoop of the Lakota people, and the feeling of unity grew stronger. The ghost dance camp was a reflection of the old way of life.[49] Thus the government policy that sought to break the unity of the Lakota people and the power of the chiefs faced a serious setback during the fall of 1890.[50]

Historians such as Utley and Larson claim that only the so-called non-progressives and those older Lakotas who had experienced most of the conflicts between the old and the new values were interested in the new religion. They say the progressives and the young who had already partly adapted to reservation life considered the promises of the ghost dance unbelievable.[51] However, there is no evidence to support this claim. The ghost dance, as I will show, was extremely appealing to the Lakotas regardless of their feelings about the whites. The ghost dance's religious nature appealed to the Lakotas across the artificial progressive–nonprogressive line. DeMallie noted, "Even Lakota nonbelievers accepted the religious motivation of the ghost dance."[52]

By the end of the summer of 1890, even greater numbers of those considered progressive turned to the ghost dance. Commissioner of Indian Affairs Thomas J. Morgan noted in his annual report that the progressive Indians were almost "universally loyal" and did not turn to the ghost dance unless forced to do so.[53] But this claim is proven false by Little Wound's actions alone as well as by the actions of many other progressives who followed his example in joining the ghost dancers. Their attraction to the ghost dance was partly due to the failure of crops and the resulting famine. When the annual appropriations were cut further, the ghost dance seemed to be the only way of surviving. The exact number of progressives who actually joined the ghost dancers at this point is very difficult to determine. The fact that during the fall of 1890 schools and churches were left empty and farms were abandoned reflects the actions of the progressives. Still, it has to be emphasized that those people can not be directly counted as ghost dancers, since many simply left things unattended when order on the reservations collapsed. Many joined the ghost dance only as spectators, and in general there was extensive movement to and from the ghost dance camps.[54]

After considering all these aspects, we have to conclude that the ghost dance was not simply a protest by the old, nonprogressive Lakotas trying to advance their own political and military goals, as suggested by so many scholars. Its religious nature appealed to the Lakotas, who were left in religious confusion after their own sacred ceremonies were forbidden. Without the catastrophes of the summer of 1890 the ghost dance might even have died out altogether, but during the fall the ghost dance became the religion of a growing number of Lakotas. It was developing, it was changing, and it was adding new features and new meanings.

The Traditional Lakota Belief System and the Ghost Dance

For the Lakotas, religion was an inseparable part of everyday life. There was no idea of atheism or life without religion. Like other Plains Indians, the Lakotas believed in a sacred cosmic system that manifested itself everywhere in the surroundings of human beings. They differentiated between the ordinary, everyday world and the supernatural, mysterious world. The Lakota sacred cosmic world was embodied in religious beliefs, mythology, and ceremonies. Through these, the original, sacred world was re-created in religious symbols.[55]

The basis for Lakota religion lay in the belief in a general spirit force that was everywhere in the visible as well as in the invisible world. This force was known as Wakhą́ Thą́ka, which is usually translated as the Great Spirit or the Great Mystery. Wakhą́ Thą́ka was not really a god in the Euro-American sense, but a divine or a godlike being. It embodied all those things that could not be understood or explained. It was above all, all-governing, paramount among all supernatural powers and beings. However, it was a spiritual being without any physical form; it was always present and it incorporated the visible and the invisible, the material and the immaterial; it was the highest spirit. Perhaps the best way to characterize Wakhą́ Thą́ka is as divine or godlike.[56]

Wakhą́ Thą́ka was not one single godlike being, but had sixteen different forms, which were divided hierarchically in four categories, each of which included four aspects of Wakhą́ Thą́ka. Thus Wakhą́ Thą́ka was composed of the multiples of the Lakota sacred number four (*tóbtob kį*).[57] The highest category of Wakhą́ Thą́ka was the sun (*wí*), energy (*šką́*), earth (*makhá*), and rock (*įyą*), and these were given very great value in religious life. For this study the most significant is the fourth category, the *wakhą́lapi*, which includes those godlike beings that are usually called spirits.[58]

The spirits were extremely important beings. They helped people, took care of them, and warned them of dangers. People gave them gifts in order to appease them and to ask them to be helpful and beneficial. Without proper attention, spirits could also be dangerous. The Lakotas believed that all things that move or do something have a spirit. In a way, spirits were like shadows from another world. The human spirit, however, was different from other spirits, because after an individual's death it went to a special spirit world. From there the spirit of the dead could return to the world of the living to meet people and even to take part in their daily lives. However, this spirit, called *naǧí,* was only one of the four spirits that were part of the human being. In addition to *naǧí*, there was *niyá* (life breath), *naǧíla* (the little ghost,) and *šicų́* (the spirit of personal power). Evil spirits too wandered the earth, causing trouble and pain for people, and they were greatly feared. Their actions, however, could be restricted with proper ceremonies. Spirits were therefore not strange beings for the Lakotas, but a part of their normal, everyday world. Meeting the spirits and visiting the spirit world were totally normal events.[59] The Lakotas actually used the word *wanáǧi yatapi*, "where the spirits are," to designate the spirit world. The way to the spirit world was the Milky Way, called *wanáǧi tháchąku*, or "spirits' path."[60]

Spirits and all other things that could not be understood were called *wakhą́*. *Wakhą́* can be conceptualized as a kind of power best described by the words "sacred," "holy," and "mysterious." Human connection to *wakhą́* things was established through holy men. They were able to perform "wakanlike" things and were therefore called *wicháša wakhą́*, holy men, or, as they are usually called in the English literature, medicine men. These medicine men were the leaders of religious ceremonies, and they held the secrets of Lakota religion and ceremonies in their possession. Thus they can be considered the "priests" of the Lakotas.[61]

The holy men were divided into groups according to their purpose and the manner in which they gained their power. The most powerful were the men who had received their power in a vision from a bear or a buffalo. The holy men were divided into four main groups and further into subgroups. Some were healers or doctors (*phežúta wichášа*) who cured people with medicines; although the English literature usually uses the term "medicine men" to designate all holy men, this term should perhaps be restricted to refer only to this one group, the *phežúta wichášа*.[62] Above these men in the hierarchy of medicine men were the true holy men, who could heal and knew the use of medicines but who also cured through their own power. They were men whose visions had been particularly powerful.[63] These medicine men acted as leaders of religious ceremonies as well as mediators between the spirit world and the human world. Their actions were always shadowed by great secrecy, and they were often the most respected members of their society. For example, Sitting Bull, who is often referred to as a medicine man, was not only a healer but also a holy man. Since medicine men were the leaders of ceremonies, it was only natural that many of the leaders of the ghost dance—Short Bull, Black Elk (Heȟáka Sápa), and Sitting Bull—were holy or medicine men.[64]

The Lakotas practiced many religious ceremonies. Through them things that could not be understood were transformed into the sacred (*wakhą́*).[65] The unifying symbol for all these ceremonies was the sacred pipe, or more correctly, the Buffalo Calf Pipe (Ptéȟįčala hú chąnúpa). The pipe symbolized the whole Lakota universe. Smoking the pipe was a part of all religious ceremonies, and the smoke had a special, purifying effect. The smoking, or rather the offering of the pipe, was always performed with certain rituals. Smoking the sacred pipe and even touching it was allowed only in the presence of a medicine man and under his instructions. Although every man could own a pipe of his own, all pipes were considered sacred and related to the Buffalo Calf Pipe.[66] Smoking the pipe was so sacred that, for example, a person suspected of a crime who wanted to prove his innocence could do so by smoking the pipe. A guilty person would not have dared to take the pipe.[67]

One of the oldest sacred rituals included as a part of all major Lakota ceremonies was the sweat lodge ceremony (*inípi*). The sweat lodge ceremony was always performed under strict rules and it often preceded other rituals.

The purpose of the *inípi* was to purify a person both physically and mentally and to strengthen the human spirit, the *ní*.[68] Especially sacred too was the ceremony of ghost keeping (or keeping of the soul). The purpose of this *wanáǧi yuhápi* was to keep the spirit of a dead person close to home for a while. Sometimes a lodge was erected for the spirit of the departed, where it could live until finally released to the spirit world in a special ceremony.[69]

Visions were at the heart of Lakota religion. They helped a person to find a direction for his or her life. Many religious ceremonies were also born in visions. The vision quest, *hąblécheyapi*, was a very important ceremony for every male (and sometimes also female) Lakota, although some never received a vision. The idea was to find a connection to the spirits and acquire power from them or to get their protection for life. In a vision one might be given a medicine bundle and a song for oneself, and also knowledge of one's guardian spirit, *šicú*. The visions were then interpreted by the medicine men, who gave instructions on how to live according to the vision. As suggested earlier, people with powerful visions could become medicine men themselves.[70]

The annual sun dance (*wiwáyąǧ wachípi*) was the only Lakota calendrical ritual. It was connected with the annual communal buffalo hunt. For the ceremony the Lakotas gathered into great summer camps, where several religious ceremonies and rituals were held over consecutive days. The high point was reached in a dance held around the sacred tree. In the sun dance, the dancer was attached to the sacred tree with a rawhide thong, which was looped around a stick inserted through pairs of slits in the chest or back. The goal was to dance and pull against the thong until the skin tore and the dancer was released. No food or drink was allowed during the dance; the pain and suffering helped the dancer reach another world. Self-mortification convinced the spirits of the dancer's sincerity and pitifulness. The suffering and offering of one's own body was the most valuable sacrifice. The rite itself was a ceremony of renewal and regeneration, during which everything was reborn; it reflected the mythical and supernatural events that took place in early times, when the world was first created. The ritual sought to establish and maintain unity between the earth, the sun, and the spirits, to ensure that the buffalo would never disappear and that the people would prosper.[71]

In addition to these four, the other sacred ceremonies were the girls' puberty ceremony (*išnála awíchalowąpi*), the throwing of the ball (*thápa wąkáyapi*), and the making of relatives (*hųká*). The *hųká* ceremony was especially important because it was a means for establishing kinship. In Lakota society, blood relationship was not the only determinant of kinship, and *hųká* was one way of making relatives of people who were not related by blood or marriage.[72]

Thus there were altogether seven most sacred ceremonies. The numbers seven and four were sacred for the Lakotas. In Lakota beliefs almost everything was conceptualized in terms of fours and sevens or their multiples. There were four cardinal directions, four seasons, and four stages of human life; the Sioux nation was formed of seven council fires, and *Wakhą́ Thą́ka* had sixteen different aspects (4x4=16). These numbers were frequently present in religious ceremonies, which often lasted four consecutive days; there were seven songs in the sun dance and they were always sung four times.[73]

Also sacred was the circle, which united human beings with nature. In nature, many things operated in circles. The sun and the moon were round and moved across the sky along the path of a circle. The heavens were also a circle, and the seasons came in circles. Thus the form of the circle was taken as a part of everyday life, from the camp circle to sacred dances.[74]

To understand the Lakota ghost dance, it is essential to have knowledge not only of the history of the Lakota people, but also of their cultural heritage. For that reason a very general picture of Lakota religion and traditions is presented in this chapter.

Lakota religious life continued on the reservation until 1883, when the government forbade the practice of traditional religious ceremonies, including the sun dance. Christianity's ceremonies were the only acceptable form of public religious ceremony. Indeed, Christian churches had already found supporters among the Lakotas, since the Indians' own understanding of religion did not rule out the possibility of accepting the Christian God as well. This new God did not replace Wakhą́ Thą́ka, but joined the other sacred beings as a part of the totality of Wakhą́ Thą́ka. Some Lakotas tried to go on with their lives relying on their old traditions, while others turned to Christianity. However, many of those Christian Lakotas saw Christianity as an extension of their old religion. In a way, they lived between two different religious worlds, and therefore it is extremely difficult to say exactly how many of the Lakotas were Christians at the time of the ghost dance.[75]

An interesting comment comes from the anthropologist Marla Powers, who claims that only those who were listed as Christians were able to receive their annual appropriations. If this really was the case, the number of the so-called nominal Christians was probably higher than is generally stated. Clifton Olmstead, a religious scholar who believes that as late as 1914 more than 40 percent of American Indians were nominally Christians, substantiates this view. In the case of the Lakotas, for example, the official report for 1878 says that one-fifth of the Lakotas (4,751) were Christians, while the report of Agent Gallagher in 1889 claims that there were 2,213 Christian Lakotas on Pine Ridge alone. The question of numbers is a difficult one to answer, but need not be investigated further in this study. I raise the issue only to demonstrate how complex the situation was at the time of the ghost dance.[76]

When the ghost dance arrived on the Lakota reservations in 1890, the people there had already lived for many years between the forbidden worldview of their own beliefs and the worldview delivered by Christian missionaries and schoolteachers. For Christian Lakotas, and those Lakotas who were trying to find a balance between two different religions, the ghost dance offered a means of combining the old and new worldviews. Fast Thunder (Wakíyą Lúzahą), a Christian ghost dancer, provides a clear example of such a combination. He described his ghost dance vision:

> Two holy eagles transported me to the happy hunting grounds. They showed me the Great Messiah there, and as I looked upon his fair countenance, I wept, for there were nail-prints in his hands and feet, where the cruel white men had fastened him to a large cross. There was a small wound in his side also, but as he kept his side covered with a beautiful blanket of feathers this wound could only be seen when he shifted his blanket. He insisted that we continue the dance and promised me that no whites should enter his city nor partake of the good things he had prepared for the Indians. The earth, he said, was now worn out and it should be repeopled. He had a beard and long hair and was the most handsome man that I ever looked upon.[77]

For those who longed for the traditional life, the ghost dance brought back dancing and the possibility of actually practicing religion. Although seven years had passed since the U.S. government had forbidden Lakota religious ceremonies, there were still many Lakotas who looked back nostalgically to the old ways. Many features of the teachings of the ghost dance were very familiar to them. The idea of spirits returning to earth was not strange; on the contrary, spirits had always been an integral part of life, and so were the visions, which were so important in the ghost dance. Equally familiar was the promise that the buffalo would return. Those who missed their old ways and religion found the ghost dance easy to accept. For example, Black Elk provides us with a description of his development into a ghost dancer after seeing a ghost dance ceremony that included so many features that were familiar to him. He believed that his duty was to try to restore the unity of the Lakota people with the help of the ghost dance.[78] As with Christianity, the ghost dance itself did not threaten the power of Wakhá Tháka, but became incorporated into Lakota religion. Thus to understand the Lakota ghost dance it is essential to study it with this background, not as an isolated phenomenon. As DeMallie says, the ghost dance was not a break in the Lakota way of life; it was a continuation. Today it is still part of ongoing Lakota tradition and history.[79]

The Ceremony of the Lakota Ghost Dance

The ceremony of the Lakota ghost dance was not performed according to a single formula. In fact, there were many variations, for example, in the use of songs and in the number of leaders of the ceremony. Nonetheless, the general characteristics remained the same from one ceremony to another, which allows us to create a picture of a representative ghost dance ceremony.

The preparation for the ghost dance began with a purification ceremony. The dance was often preceded by a fast, and the dance ground was blessed by the medicine men. Sometimes the medicine men also blessed the dancers by first touching the blessed ground and then touching the head of the dancer.[80] The most important purification ceremony was the sweat lodge ceremony, which was performed in the same manner as it had been in the past. The sweat lodge was built so that the entrance faced east, the sacred

54

path to the fireplace where the stones were heated, and inside the lodge the
ritual was performed as usual. Some variations occurred, however, when
the sweat lodge was attached to the ghost dance. There were several sweat
lodges erected for both men and women to allow as many as possible to
be purified. They were also larger than normal, and in the ghost dance the
sweat lodge sometimes had two doors, an entrance and an exit. Individuals
who came into the lodge through the entrance were considered to be heavy
with dirt; after the ceremony they left from the other door, cleansed, and
were then given clean clothing. In this way the sweat lodge served the purpose of cultural purification. As the anthropologist Raymond A. Bucko says,
it was a symbolic universe purged of foreign elements and a return to the
origins of the power of the past.[81] Although many other Indian nations used
the sweat lodge, it appears that only the Lakotas, and perhaps the Shoshones
and Cheyennes, associated it with the ghost dance.[82]

   All traditional Lakota ceremonies started with the smoking of the sacred
pipe, but in the ghost dance, smoking the pipe was associated only with the
preparatory sweat lodge ceremony. In the actual ghost dance the pipe was
also present, but in a different way. During the ceremony, a young woman
stood in the center of the dance circle holding the pipe up, pointing to the
west, the direction of the Messiah. In this case the woman symbolized the
sacred Buffalo Calf Woman, who, according to legend, had first brought
the pipe to the Lakotas.[83]

   After purification in the sweat lodge the Lakotas prepared for the dance
itself. The faces of the dancers were painted with sacred symbols, including circles, stars, and crescents. This preparation could take all morning, so
the dance often did not start until afternoon, when the dancers gathered
around the sacred tree. The sacred tree, *chą wakhą*, was an essential part of
the sun dance and symbolized the unity and the center of the Lakota people.
Before the actual dance began, a vessel filled with beef was passed to each
of the participants, the meat symbolizing the vanished buffalo. Alongside
the woman who held the pipe stood another woman, who shot four arrows
to the four cardinal directions, symbolizing the Lakota, Arapaho, Crow, and
Cheyenne Indians. The arrows were picked up and hung together with a
gaming hoop on the sacred tree.[84] The gaming hoop itself symbolized the

four directions and the reproduction of buffalo and human beings. The hoop and pole game was a traditional ceremony of renewal, and was thus naturally incorporated into the ghost dance.[85]

In the center of the circle were the leaders of the dance and the lead singer, who started the ceremony with an opening song. The following is one of the commonly used opening songs:

Até héye é ya yo	The father says so—E'yayo!
Até héye é ya yo	The father says so—E'yayo
Até héye lo	The father says so,
Até héye lo	The father says so.
Nithŋkášila waníglakį	
kta é ya yo	You shall see your grandfather
Nithŋkášila waníglakį	
kta é ya yo	You shall see your grandfather
Até héye lo	The father says so,
Até héye lo	The father says so.
Nitákuye wanieglakį	
kta é ya yo	You shall see your kindred—E'yayo!
Nitákuye wanieglakį	
kta é ya yo	You shall see your kindred—E'yayo!
Até héye lo	The father says so,
Até héye lo	The father says so.[86]

During the song the dancers stretched their hands toward the west, which was the direction of the land where the Messiah lived and also the direction in which the Buffalo Calf Woman had departed. When the song ended the dancers cried together, then took each other by the hand, joined in the singing of the next song, and started to move slowly in a circle from left to right. Dancing in a circle was not unfamiliar to the Lakotas, but dancing in a circle holding each other by the hand was a cultural innovation produced by the ghost dance. Dancing in this manner had great symbolic meaning for the Lakotas. In the dance circle, the sacred hoop, the unity of the Lakota people, was re-created.[87]

Gradually the leader increased the pace, crying and praying toward each cardinal direction, especially toward the west. When the leader became excited, the dancers started to share his excitement and the dance grew more intense.[88] As the people danced, they also cried out the names of their dead relatives and expressed their grief loudly. The dancers threw dirt on their hair to signify their grief and tried to work themselves into a state in which they might see visions.[89]

As the singing and dancing continued, the excitement grew, and increasing numbers of people left the circle, making tremendous leaps into the air. Finally, those who left the circle fell to the ground with trembling limbs and lay motionless, seemingly dead. According to one witness, there could be as many as one hundred unconscious ghost dancers lying on the ground simultaneously.[90]

In an article on January 17, 1891, the *Illustrated American* claimed that the ghost dancers were sacrificing human flesh and blood to their sacred tree, which was covered with blood. Other newspapers also reported that the Lakotas were sacrificing human flesh in the ceremony, or were even resorting to cannibalism. However, Black Elk says that the sacred tree was often painted red, which was the sacred color of the ghost dance as well as the sacred color of the sun. Mooney notes that the offerings for the sacred tree were small gifts for the spirits; these gifts included tobacco or small ceremonial objects, such as stuffed animal skins. Such offerings had previously been made in the sun dance.[91]

The ghost dance ceremony ended when enough people had fallen into a trance. Then everybody sat down in a circle, and the medicine men who led the dance began to interpret the dancers' visions. After a while, the ceremony began again. There could be as many as three ceremonies a day; in between, people feasted and played traditional games.[92] The ceremony always ended at the command of the medicine men, with a final song. The circle dispersed, the dancers shook their blankets to remove any bad influence from them, and finally they purified themselves by bathing in water.[93]

By the late fall of 1890 the Lakota ghost dance ceremonies had grown more intense. According to the original instructions given by Wovoka, the dances were to be organized at six-week intervals, four days in a row, and on the fifth day the dance was supposed to last all night long. The Lakotas, however, danced much more frequently, and the dances might continue for several days and nights.[94]

The Lakotas made many changes to the original, rather simple ceremony. They attached to the ghost dance their own traditional ceremonies, such as the sweat lodge and dancing around a sacred tree under the protection of the sacred pipe. Also, traditional games were revived during the ceremony. By attaching their own traditions to the ghost dance the Lakotas made the ceremony more familiar and meaningful. In the ghost dance, Lakota traditions became alive again. The visions and songs of the Lakota ghost dance reflect these traditions.

In traditional Lakota religious ceremonies, such as the sun dance, drums and rattlers were used, but the ghost dance was always performed without musical instruments. On the other hand, there were many songs, and trance experiences were often turned into songs. Because there were very many such experiences, it seems obvious that there must have been a great number of songs also. James Mooney published almost two hundred ghost dance songs, but only twenty-seven of them are Lakota. Those Lakota songs were originally collected by Emma C. Sickels, a schoolteacher on Pine Ridge, and later included by Mooney in his ghost dance monograph. The anthropologist William K. Powers gathered fifty-five Lakota ghost dance songs from various sources, including those used by Mooney and Sickels. In his brief book *Voices from the Spirit World: Lakota Ghost Dance Songs* he provides a short analysis of each song. A similar collection was published by Wilhelm Wildhage as *Geistertanz-Lieder der Lakota: Eine Quellensamlung* (Lakota ghost dance songs: A collection of sources). He, however, does not attempt to analyze the songs.[95] Those songs that have been preserved provide a good picture of the expectations and hopes the Lakotas had for the ghost dance.

Several of the songs refer to ancestors and to meeting dead relatives, which, of course, were among the basic ideas of the new religion. Other very popular themes included the return of the buffalo, as well as organizing and leaving on hunting trips. Many songs referred to the Messiah or Father and to the eternal life he promised.[96] The following two songs are examples of these:

Wanáyą máni ye,	Now he is walking,
Wanáyą máni ye,	Now he is walking.
Thatáka wą máni ye,	There is a buffalo bull walking,
Thatáka wą máni ye,	There is a buffalo bull walking,
Até héye lo,	Says the father,
Até héye lo,	Says the father.
Até hé ú we,	There is the father coming,
Até hé ú we,	There is the father coming.
Até eyáya hé ú welo,	The father says this as he comes,
Até eyáya hé ú welo,	The father says this as he comes,
Yanípi kta ú welo,	"You shall live," he says as he comes,
Yanípi kta ú welo.	"You shall live," he says as he comes.[97]

The songs did not speak about violence or the destruction of the white race. In general the songs were sad, but they reflected the hope the Lakotas had in the new religion. For example, the next song was born of a young woman's vision, in which she saw her dead mother:

Iná hé kúwo;	Mother, come home;
Iná hé kúwo,	Mother come home.
Misúkala chéyaya	My little brother
omániye,	goes about always crying,
Misúkala chéyaya	My little brother
omániye,	goes about always crying,
Iná hé kúwo,	Mother come home;
Iná hé kúwo.	Mother come home.[98]

Often the songs told about the spirits and the spirit world. Messages from that world were brought over to this world by such sacred birds as the eagle (*wąblí*) and the crow, or raven (*khąǧí*). Traditionally among many Plains tribes these birds—especially the crow—acted as a mediator between humans and spirits.[99] Many of the songs that refer to crows, or belonging to the "crow nation," in fact symbolize union with the spirits and the spirit world.[100]

The following song well illustrates the whole message of the ghost dance, promising the return of both the buffalo and the spirits of the dead, just as the Father had prophesied. In the song, the knowledge of these events is brought to the Lakotas by the eagle and the crow:

Makhá sitómniyą ukíye,	The whole world is coming,
Oyáte ukíye, Oyáte ukíye	A nation is coming, a nation is coming
Wąblí oyáte wą,	The eagle has brought
hošíhi yelo,	the message to the tribe,
Até héye lo,	The father says so,
Até héye lo.	The father says so.
Makhá ówąchaya ukíye,	Over the whole earth they are coming.
Pté kį ukíye,	The buffalo are coming,
Pté kį ukíye,	The buffalo are coming,
Khąǧí oyáte wą,	The crow has brought
hošíhi yelo,	the message to the tribe,
Até héye lo,	The father says so
Até héye lo.	The father says so.[101]

The songs of the Lakota ghost dance provide no support for the belief that the Lakotas were organizing the ghost dances to make war against the whites, as suggested by many contemporary white observers and later scholars alike. If the Lakota ghost dance doctrine had been hostile toward the whites, it seems likely that this sentiment would have been expressed in at least some of the songs. Furthermore, these songs differ from Lakota war songs in all respects; the words and the rhythm are completely different. Although only a fraction of the Lakota ghost dance songs are preserved, it is obvious that they have nothing to do with the destruction of the white race. Instead, they are like the ghost dance songs of other Indian peoples, such as the Arapahos, the Cheyennes, the Kiowas, and the Paiutes.[102] What is revealed in the songs is that the Lakotas were extremely unhappy and longed for the traditional way of life and for the time before the white man interfered with their lives.

Trances and visions were the source of many of these songs, and falling into a trance and seeing visions were major elements in the ghost dance ceremony. Those who received a vision were considered special. They were expected to help other people reach the emotional state in which seeing visions became possible. At the time the ghost dance was beginning to be established among the Lakotas, hypnotism may have been used to help people see visions. The correspondent of the *Illustrated American* describes how a medicine man was able to hypnotize and make the young men and women act as he pleased simply by looking at them. However, by the late fall of 1890 more and more people fell into a trance without the need for hypnotism.[103]

These trances could be very deep and spectacular. Mrs. Z. A. Parker described a person falling into a trance:

> One woman fell a few feet from me. She came toward us, her hair flying over her face, which was purple, looking as if the blood would burst through; her hands and arms moving wildly; every breath a pant and a groan; and she fell on her back, and went down like a log. I stepped up to her as she lay there motionless, but with every muscle twitching and quivering. She seemed perfectly unconscious.[104]

Young Skunk (Maká Cįcála) described his trance experience during a ghost dance ceremony at White Clay Creek:

> Again we danced and after a little while, all of a sudden, as I danced with my eyes closed, a bright light came on me and my heart was beating fast. Although it seemed that I was becoming overcome, I danced without fear. Then I had pain in my liver, shortness of breath and at once I was suffocating and was about to faint and . . . I became unconscious.[105]

Young Skunk then described how, in a vision, his dead sister came to him, and as they were both crying for joy she showed him a large camp of Indians. In this camp he was given food and was told how he could soon join his relatives in this new and wonderful world.[106]

Pretty Eagle (Wąblí Wašté), also a ghost dancer, gave the following description of his experiences:

I danced the dance with my eyes closed and it seemed like [I heard] those sounds of buffalo hoofs galloping and then little by little the sound of bird wings was mixed in and it seemed that the buffalo really bellowed and grunted, and it was like a buzzing noise and the dance songs disappeared and were soon gone. And more [people] were really overcome and quickly I looked, but thus they were dancing and they were only ordinary people and my heart was beating fast and I was shaking. . . . And then they stopped and when they were about to finish there were still some lying fainted. . . . And so it was, and many were overcome and fainted. And some were overcome for a long time. The dance lasted a long time and for a long time they recovered. I sat there and one [man] was overcome for a very long time, so I sat watching him. And then he was babbling something incomprehensibly, so I watched him. Then I would again see this eagle with outstretched wings at his head. And then it was gone and the one lying fainted, it seemed like it came for him, I thought. Then he told about it: "An eagle came for me" he said.[107]

During their trances, ghost dancers such as Young Skunk were able to see their dead relatives, who were living happily in the spirit world. Some saw a whole new world where white men did not exist. In a vision, the medicine man Black Elk met men who took him with them and showed him spectacular things:

Then I went to the center of the circle with these men and there again I saw the tree in full bloom. Against the tree I saw a man standing with outstretched arms. . . . The man with outstretched arms looked at me and I didn't know whether he was white or an Indian. He did not resemble Christ. He looked like an Indian, but I was not sure of it. He had long hair, which was hanging down loose. On the left side of his head was an eagle feather. His body was painted red. . . . I stood there gazing at him and tried to recognize him. I could not make him out. He was a nice-looking man. As I looked at him, his body started to transform. His body changed into all colors and it was very beautiful. All around him there was light. Then he disappeared all at once.

It seemed as though there were wounds in the palms of his hands.
. . . The day was beautiful—the heavens were all yellow and the earth
was green. You could see the greenward [*sic*] of the earth [the plains].
The men that I saw were all beautiful and it seemed there were no old
men in there. They were all young.[108]

Little Wound described his vision:

A great and grand eagle came and carried me over a great hill, where
there was a village such as we used to have before the whites came into
the country. The tepees were all of buffalo hides, and we made use of
the bow and arrow, there being nothing of white man's manufacture
in the beautiful land. Nor were any whites permitted to live there. The
broad and fertile lands stretched in every direction, and were most
pleasing to my eyes. I was taken into the presence of the great Messiah,
and he spoke to me these words: "My child I am glad to see you. Do
you want to see your children and relations who are dead?" I replied:
"Yes, I would like to see my relations who have been dead a long time."
The God then called my friends to come up to where I was. They appeared, riding the finest horses I ever saw, dressed in superb and most
brilliant garments, and seeming very happy. As they approached, I recognized the playmates of my childhood, and I ran forward to embrace
them while the tears of joy ran down my cheeks. We all went together to another village, where there were very large lodges of buffalo
hide, and there held a long talk with the great Wakan Tanka [Wakȟą́
Tȟą́ka, or the Great Spirit]. Then he had some squaws prepare us a
meal of many herbs, meat, and wild fruits and wasna [pounded dried
meat and chokecherries]. After we had eaten, the Great Spirit prayed
for our people upon the earth, and then we all took a smoke out of a
fine pipe ornamented with the most beautiful feathers and porcupine
quills. Then we left the city and looked into a great valley where there
were thousands of buffalo, deer, and elk feeding. After seeing the valley
we returned to the city, the Great Spirit speaking meanwhile. He told
me that the earth was now bad and worn out; that we needed a new
dwelling-place where the rascally whites could not disturb us. He fur-

ther instructed me to return to my people, the Sioux, and say to them that if they would be constant in the dance and pay no attention to the whites he would shortly come to their aid. If the high-priests would make for the dancers medicine-shirts and pray over them, no harm could come to the wearer; that the bullets of any whites that desired to stop the Messiah Dance would fall into the ground without doing any one harm, and the person firing such shots would drop dead. He said that he had prepared a hole in the ground filled with hot water and fire for the reception of all white men and non-believers. With these parting words I was commanded to return to earth.[109]

Given the situation among the Lakotas in 1890, it is easy to understand that such experiences made an impact. In the visions, happy people were hunting, dancing, and playing games and did all those things that were done in the past. The traditional way of life seemed to be returning. Because this was happening in the visions, it was clear that this was going to happen in real life as well.[110] There was no reason not to believe the message of the visions. Visions had always been an important part of Lakota life, and medicine men had always been able to interpret them, so why not now? Visions were always believed, and the leaders and medicine men could interpret them to suit their own expectations and hopes. Thus as religious excitement among the Lakotas grew and the tension between whites and Indians increased, the original doctrine and ceremony of the ghost dance was in the process of changing through visions and their interpretations. Perhaps the most dramatic of these developments was the new kind of dance shirts mentioned in Little Wound's vision.

During the fall of 1890 the ghost dances gradually became more intense on both Pine Ridge and Rosebud Reservations. The ghost dancers started to arm themselves. There is some dispute about the presence of guns during the ghost dance ceremony, but according to many contemporaries and some scholars, dancers carried rifles when they danced. This despite the fact that according to the Lakota ghost dance doctrine they were not supposed to wear anything that reminded them of the white man. Bows and arrows, however, were a part of the ceremony from the very beginning.[111]

Short Bull later denied that arms were carried during the dances: "We went unarmed to the dance. How could we have held weapons? For thus we danced, in a circle, hand in hand, each man's fingers linked in those of his neighbor." On November 26, 1890, Big Road too denied that arms were carried in the ceremony.[112] In fact, there is no evidence that the Lakotas carried arms during the ghost dance ceremonies; it seems that no one actually saw them do so. Elaine Goodale Eastman witnessed a ghost dance as late as November 1 but saw no guns in the ceremony.[113] Therefore, it has to be concluded that it was not a common feature among the Lakota ghost dancers to carry arms while dancing, although perhaps they started to keep arms at hand to be ready at any moment to defend themselves should the whites try to interfere with their religious ceremonies.

On October 9, 1890, Kicking Bear arrived at Standing Rock without authorization from the U.S. government to teach the new religion to the people there and to meet with Sitting Bull, who had invited him. Agent James McLaughlin sent a detachment of Indian policemen to escort Kicking Bear off the reservation. The policemen, however, did not dare to carry out their assignment; the ghost dance also affected these men, even though they were used to discipline and the ways of the white man. Kicking Bear's teachings seemed to appeal to the policemen, who were afraid of his power. Finally, on October 15, two policemen dared to escort Kicking Bear off the reservation.[114]

After Kicking Bear left, Sitting Bull's camp became the center of the ghost dance religion on Standing Rock Reservation. It is not clear whether Sitting Bull himself really believed in the doctrine of the ghost dance. Utley suspects that Sitting Bull hated the whites too much to believe in a religion that had so many Christian aspects, but his interpretation seems far-fetched. Several people who knew Sitting Bull suggest that he was not opposed to all Christian teachings and had many friends among the missionaries. It seems that Sitting Bull tried to believe in the ghost dance at first, but when he did not experience a vision, he just gave his blessing to others who wanted to dance. He had nothing against the new religion. He reportedly told the policemen who came to his camp that the most important thing there was their schoolhouse, not the ghost dance, which would eventually stop. Even Agent McLaughlin thought that Sitting Bull did not really believe in the ghost dance.[115]

Many scholars believe that Sitting Bull saw the ghost dance as his final chance to rise up against the white man and to gain more prestige among his people. These arguments are often supported by accounts of Sitting Bull's alleged actions. He is said to have stated that he was ready to fight the white men and to die for the ghost dance. As an assurance of this he supposedly broke the sacred pipe that he had used to seal the peace. If he really did that, there is no doubt what it meant for the Lakotas; it was an extreme act of disrespect and, in this case, an extreme form of provocation.[116] But it seems unlikely that Sitting Bull would have abused a sacred pipe.

Also, Sitting Bull's words have been used against him. He supposedly urged all of his people to continue the dance and predicted that the winter would be warm and mild. He believed that the whites were afraid of the Indians, and, as an example, he used the incident on Pine Ridge in which the agent was forced to retreat in front of the ghost dancers. The Indians were to be as brave as ever, since the Great Spirit was ashamed of cowards. He also maintained that the Indians had every right to dance as they pleased on their own reservation.[117]

Sitting Bull's biographer, the historian Stanley Vestal, offers an interesting interpretation of Sitting Bull's words and actions. According to him, Sitting Bull simply told the people they could dance and the weather would be good for that purpose, nothing more. Indian accounts suggest that Sitting Bull could not forbid ghost dancing; a Lakota leader had no power to coerce his people. Personally, Sitting Bull remained skeptical about the ghost dance. This view is substantiated by several Indian accounts and also by the missionary Mary C. Collins, who knew Sitting Bull well. Kicking Bear tried to convince Sitting Bull by claiming that Wakhą́ Tȟą́ka could easily intervene in the life of the Indians since, according to the Bible, the Christian God had done the same for the white people several times. Indian accounts maintain that Sitting Bull considered it stupid even to try to resist the power of the whites, saying several times that the dance was not a very important undertaking and that it would eventually stop.[118]

Despite this, the ghost dance excitement grew rapidly in Sitting Bull's camp after Kicking Bear's visit. Agent McLaughlin wanted to arrest Sitting Bull and other "troublemakers" but did not get permission to do so. He demanded that Sitting Bull negotiate with him, but Sitting Bull would not come to the agency, where he would have been at the mercy of the agent and perhaps the army. Sitting Bull probably felt that he was safe only among his own people, far away from the agency. Still, he did not object to talking to the agent. At least once he asked John Carignan, the schoolteacher at the Grand River Day School, to speak in his behalf to Agent McLaughlin. Some Indian accounts suggest that Sitting Bull actually did go to the agency to talk to McLaughlin, but the agent was not there. Catherine Weldon, of the Indian Rights Association and a good friend of Sitting Bull, warned him about plans for his arrest. She even pleaded with the officials not to arrest him.[119]

During October dances were organized almost daily on the four Lakota reservations.[120] The dancers now lived at the campsites, making it easy to keep the dances going every day. The fact that work on the reservations was left undone and schools and churches were basically empty was justified by the ghost dancers, who claimed that they had to go to their own church, the dance grounds, every day. They had no time to take care of other daily tasks.[121]

It seems that the sacred shirts mentioned by Little Wound started to become more common in late October, when the ghost dances were becoming more frequent and the number of participants was increasing. At this point, as tensions rose between the ghost dancers and the agents, and also between the ghost dancers and Lakotas who did not participate, the dancers started to prepare to defend themselves. In this situation the sacred shirt rapidly became an essential part of the Lakota ghost dance religion.[122] In defiance of the orders of the agent and the Indian police, the ghost dancers started to kill cattle for food.[123] The ghost dancers showed more openly that they were no longer afraid of the authorities.

Ógle Wakhą́ kį: The Sacred Shirt

During the Lakota ghost dance ceremony men, women, and children started to wear a sacred garment prepared only for this purpose. The Lakotas called it *ógle wakhą́ kį*, "the sacred shirt"; the whites called it "ghost shirt." These shirts were worn during the ceremony as the primary clothing, but at other times they could be worn under everyday clothes.[124] The ghost shirts and dresses were made of cloth and were decorated with symbols of the sun, the

moon, the stars, eagles, crows, and buffalo. The colors had their own significance. Red was common, since it was the sacred color of the ghost dance
and traditionally the color of the sun. The yoke of the shirt was often dyed
blue, the color of the sky. Other colors, such as yellow, were also used. In
addition, the shirts were decorated with feathers; eagle, magpie, and crow
feathers were especially valued.[125] The motifs used in the decorations often
symbolized the Lakota belief in world renewal and re-creation, which were
important features in the traditional sun dance. The theme of world renewal was, of course, central to the ghost dance doctrine.[126]

The eagle and the crow were extremely important symbols: the eagle
and its feathers symbolized the unity of the Lakota people; the crow feathers were reminiscent of the past, when the crow had acted as a pathfinder
for hunting parties.[127] In addition to decorating the shirts, the feathers of
these birds were attached to the hair of the dancers, both men and wom-
en. Traditionally, Lakota women never wore feathers, so this feature was a
cultural innovation of the ghost dance. Each dancer was supposed to wear
either one eagle feather or two crow feathers. The Lakotas believed that
when the final whirlwind and flood came to destroy the earth, these feathers would lift the ghost dancers from the ground to safety. In many visions
the eagle also acted as a pathfinder in the spirit world.[128]

Only objects that derived from Lakota culture were used to decorate the
ghost shirts. For example, metal objects were not used at all, since as they
came from the whites. Many other tribes, however, decorated themselves as
beautifully as possible regardless of the origin of the objects used.[129] In his
description of his vision Little Wound explains that no objects from white
culture were to be used, and this fact has often been interpreted as a definite
sign of the hostility the ghost dancers felt toward the whites. The historian
David Miller gives another, very simple explanation. A former ghost dancer told him that the idea came from Kicking Bear "in the heat of the moment," and then just caught on. The idea had no deeper roots.[130] It is of interest that no firearms were depicted on the ghost shirt, even though bows
and arrows were a common motif in its decorations.[131]

The ghost shirts were not used by all Indian tribes practicing the ghost
dance. The Southern Cheyennes, for example, heard of these shirts for the

first time as late as January 1891, when Mooney was among them recording material for his study.[132] The origin of these shirts has remained somewhat unclear. Wovoka denied any responsibility and said he never gave any instructions to make them.[133] Mooney maintains that the original idea came from the gown used by the Mormons, who were very interested in the Indians and whose influence among the tribes close to the birthplace of the ghost dance had been strong. Mooney believes that the idea of this kind of sacred garment passed from tribe to tribe and finally reached the Lakotas.[134]

Mooney's assumption might be correct, since among the tribes that did use the ghost shirts were the Arapahos and Shoshones, from whom the Lakotas learned about the ghost dance in the first place. Although Mooney assumes that the Lakotas frequently used the ghost shirts as early as June 1890, it is difficult to establish a definite time when they were introduced. Mooney bases his assumption on the eyewitness account quoted in the report of Daniel Dorchester, mentioned earlier, but because Mooney misread the date of the report this automatically renders incorrect his assumption concerning the date the shirts were first used. There are no eyewitness accounts that would place the ghost shirts at such an early date. For example, in his description of a ghost dance in September 1890 Special Agent Elisha B. Reynolds relates that the dancers did not wear any clothing except for leggings and blankets wrapped around their upper body. The ghost shirts probably became more common among the Lakotas after Kicking Bear returned from his visit to the Arapahos late in the summer of 1890. This might suggest that the Lakotas really learned about the ghost shirts from the Arapahos, and through Kicking Bear.[135] On the other hand, the medicine man Black Elk claims that he received instructions in a vision that he was to bring a special kind of shirt to his people. He also claimed that he himself made the first ghost shirt. It is highly likely that Black Elk received his vision of the shirt after talking with Kicking Bear; in fact, he even says that he received the vision in a ceremony led by Kicking Bear and Good Thunder. Pretty Eagle too described how he was given instructions to make these sacred garments:

> I went to sacred dance on the White Clay Creek on the flats there. There was going to be a dance and the people gathered and they formed a circle. Then they danced and I joined in. Then again, I was overcome.

Again, I fainted and was unconscious for a long time. . . . I stood in the middle of the flat. The grass was very green and I climbed up and I was standing with someone. Then he said: "Look at this, make shirts in this way and give them to them," he said. So when I looked there an eagle was flying off spreading his wings and on both sides there were stars. And a sun was attached to the back of the eagle. And it went flying off. And again it reached there and said this: "Make four in this manner: two [for] men and two [for] women." . . . And now it flew to the west and right there, I turned around and I came to. There again, I was sitting in the middle of the dance circle and right there I woke up. And then they questioned me, so I told about it. "This evening I will paint two shirts and two dresses." . . . And then, right there two young men and two young women came and they wanted to wear them. . . . And in the evening those young men and women arrived and came to me. So they put up a tipi in the middle. And inside they spread out sweetgrass. And there I painted the shirts and the dresses: on the upper part of the back I painted an eagle; and then on both shoulders I painted stars; and on the chest I painted the moon. And then in the evening I finished. And early in the morning, there was going to be dance again, so they gathered. . . . And we danced and those who I made shirts for, those then were overcome and moved about and both of them fainted.[136]

Whatever the actual origin of the shirts, they became an essential part of the Lakota ghost dance ceremony. On October 17, 1890, Agent James McLaughlin at Standing Rock reported to Commissioner of Indian Affairs Thomas J. Morgan that Kicking Bear claimed in a speech to Sitting Bull's people that bullets could not harm the Indians; the powder made by the white men would be so weak that the bullets could no longer penetrate the skin of the Indians.[137] According to the historian George E. Hyde, Kicking Bear further claimed that if the Lakotas would wear the sacred shirts the bullets would not harm them, and that the shirts were so powerful the whites could now be destroyed altogether. Whether this speech was the one in which Kicking Bear initially introduced the bulletproof shirt cannot be determined. According to Agent McLaughlin, Kicking Bear spoke about the useless powder without mentioning the shirts at all.[138]

Short Bull also assured the Lakotas at the end of October that the white man's bullets could no longer harm the Indians. He, however, did not actually mention the bulletproof shirts; he said only that sacred shirts would help the ghost dancers if soldiers were to attack them.[139]

Even though the origin of the ghost shirts is uncertain, it is clear that their bulletproof nature is a Lakota idea; no other tribe gave them such a feature. It might be that the Lakota idea of the bulletproof shirts derived originally from Wovoka, who, among other miracles, let someone take a shot at him and was unharmed.[140] Kicking Bear, Short Bull, or one of the other delegates might have seen or heard about this miracle on their journey to meet Wovoka. It is also noteworthy that shirts impervious to arrows and bullets were an old cultural tradition among Plains Indians.[141]

The final assurance of the power of the shirts was received through visions, such as that of Little Wound and Pretty Eagle.[142] Like many other visions, those of the sacred shirts ended up in songs:

Mióȟ'ą kį chic'ú che,	Verily, I have given you my strength,
Até héye lo,	Says the father,
Até héye lo,	Says the father,
Ógle kį níniyą kte,	The shirt will cause you to live,
Até héye lo,	Says the father,
Até héye lo.	Says the father.[143]

Belief in the protective features of the shirts grew rapidly as their power was affirmed in visions and songs. The belief in them was also strengthened by highly regarded leaders and medicine men, including Kicking Bear, Short Bull, Black Elk, and Little Wound, who preached about the shirt's power—and undoubtedly believed in it. Short Bull at least seems to have been fully convinced of the power of the ghost shirts; many years later he told James Walker, the doctor at Pine Ridge, that the "ghost shirt is Wakan [wakhą́, sacred]. It is impervious to missiles."[144] The ghost dancers had absolutely no reason to question the power of the shirts. In addition, all kinds of stories soon began to spread concerning people who had been protected by the shirts. One eyewitness told of a young girl who had attempted to stab herself with a knife, but the knife did not penetrate her shirt.[145]

The use of the ghost shirts reflects the Lakotas' traditional customs and beliefs. In traditional warfare the shields that were decorated with sacred symbols protected them from the enemies' weapons. In fact, the shield's power was in the symbols and paintings rather than in the material that was used. The Lakotas also believed that special paintings on the body of the warrior protected him and could make him bulletproof. The symbols depicted in these paintings were derived from visions. This was the case, for example, with Crazy Horse, who was thought to be bulletproof. The same principle applied to the ghost shirt: the material was not important; the power was in its inherent sacredness and in the sacred symbols.[146]

When the ghost shirts are considered in this context it is no wonder that the dancers believed their medicine men and leaders who told about the power of the shirts. The protective nature of the shirt made it easier for the Lakotas to maintain their belief in the ghost dance. With these shirts there was no need to be afraid of the Indian police or the white men. Even when tensions between the Lakotas and the whites increased, with their new sacred shirts the ghost dancers could defy the whites and even the U.S. Army. Thus, as tensions rose, there seemed to be a social need for these sacred shirts. The bulletproof ghost shirts united the ghost dancers both before and after the arrival of the military. In that sense it can be said that the ghost shirts added to the dancers' defiant attitude. However, suggesting that the ghost dancers had "these dresses for war," as George Sword's words have been translated in Sickels's and Mooney's works, is too strong a supposition. A better translation of Sword's account would be this: "They said that they would wear those [the ghost dance shirts and dresses] when they dance and that they would wear them when they fight." The historian Sam Maddra has also correctly pointed out that Sword was a member of the Indian police and opposed the ghost dance. His comment has to be understood in this context.[147] The vision of Little Wound further explains that the shirts would protect the wearer from "the bullets of any whites that desired to stop the Messiah Dance."[148]

The Lakota ghost dance ceremony differed from the ceremony of other Indian tribes, not by being more militaristic than others, but because it reflected Lakota traditions. Other tribes also made changes in the ghost dance ceremony that reflected their own traditions; this was not a peculiarity of the Lakota ghost dance alone. Neither the ghost dance nor the songs and visions so closely related to it were anything to the Lakotas other than expressions of their religious belief. Still, the growing excitement, the more intense and frequent dancing, and the appearance of the ghost shirts started to worry the whites. Many began to feel that the frequent dancing was a sign that the Indians were preparing for war.[149]

From Pine Ridge to Standing Rock: First Blood and Chaos

On October 27, 1890, Maj. Gen. Nelson A. Miles visited Pine Ridge. He tried to convince the ghost dancers that it would be better to give up the new religion.[150] Little Wound told the general that the Indians were going to stop living like white men and planned to dance as long as they pleased. Little Wound wanted the Lakotas to be Indians again; as a token of this, he invited people to join him in a great dance and feast where plenty of beef would be available. He wanted the general to tell all this to the president. It is remarkable that the Indians dared to use such strong words to a general of the U.S. Army. It demonstrates how firmly they believed in the power of the ghost dance.[151]

Red Cloud seemed to play a balancing role between the two sides. On several occasions he stated that he did not take part in the ghost dance. Yet his son Jack acted as a leader in the ceremonies. It is not too profound a conclusion to see this as a sign of sympathy the old chief felt for the ghost dancers.[152]

On October 31, Short Bull announced to the Lakotas who had gathered to listen to him at Rosebud that because the white men were interfering too much, he would shorten the time of the coming of the new world. He promised that all the beautiful things would happen after one more moon instead of the next spring, as previously expected. Thus Short Bull took upon himself the position that had originally been Wovoka's: he made himself the Messiah and the fulfiller of promises. He urged all believers to join together to dance for a month at Pass Creek, a location between Rosebud and Pine Ridge Reservations. He promised that, if the soldiers came, he would instruct three men wearing the sacred shirts to sing, and that would cause the soldiers to fall off their horses and die. The ghost shirts would protect them from all evil, so there was no need to be afraid. Short Bull's speech reflects his personal combination of Lakota traditions, Wovoka's doctrine, and Christianity.[153]

Short Bull's promise of the earlier coming of paradise led the Brulés and Oglalas to start moving toward the meeting point at Pass Creek. Kicking Bear also arrived, and Sitting Bull was urged to leave Standing Rock and join them.[154]

Short Bull emphasized that the supernatural powers would destroy the whites only if the whites attacked the ghost dancers. They would help only if the Indians had to defend themselves. Utley, however, states that in the minds of many Lakotas who were "animated by religious excitement and driven by hatred of the whites," the differences between defense and attack disappeared. He claims that talk about a holy war against the whites increased.[155] This view is not substantiated by Indian accounts. Short Bull, for example, explains that they did have a great ghost dance at Pass Creek, but the following morning rumors that soldiers were coming frightened the people and they started moving toward Pine Ridge. Another rumor stated that the soldiers were coming specifically for Short Bull. He therefore remained behind the main body, attempting to avoid hostilities between the soldiers and the Indians. When the soldiers failed to show up, he joined the main group, which gradually made its way to the Badlands in order to stay away from the soldiers.[156]

On November 11, the Indian police at Pine Ridge tried to arrest an Indian who was accused of killing some cattle. Two hundred angry ghost dancers led by Jack Red Cloud surrounded the policemen. When American Horse, who opposed the ghost dance, tried to intervene, Jack Red Cloud put a gun to his head and threatened to kill him. In the end, the chief's brave demeanor resolved the situation. The policemen, however, failed to perform their duty.[157] The ghost dancers had once again gained a victory over the Indian police and the agent, but the life of a Lakota chief had been threatened. It's true that the hostility between the Red Cloud faction and the American Horse faction was a very old one, yet this incident demonstrates that the Lakotas at this time were clearly divided into two groups: those who danced the ghost dance and those who did not.[158] The people were almost ready to fight one another. After this incident, life on Pine Ridge became extremely tense.[159]

The fact that the ghost shirts created a sense of security must be regarded as a factor contributing to the growing ghost dance excitement. When, in addition, Short Bull promised that intensive dancing for one more month would hasten the arrival of the new world enthusiasm rose dramatically. Beginning at the end of September the defiant attitude toward the authorities increased among the ghost dancers. The tensions between the ghost dancers and the nondancers were often manifested in clashes with the Indian police; however, the ghost dancers did not threaten the white population on the reservations.

Some individuals, such as Kicking Bear, Short Bull, and perhaps Sitting Bull, intensified this defiant attitude. However, these three men alone cannot be held personally responsible for the increased agitation. The importance of the medicine men and other leaders should not be underestimated. As religious leaders and interpreters of visions, the medicine men could use their influence to guide the ghost dancers in the direction they wanted or in the direction that became necessary after the arrival of the military. The problem in any study of their influence and motives is that only a few records are left for us to examine. Still, Black Elk gives us a rare glimpse into the ideas of a religious leader. He said that his goal in the ghost dance was to try to restore the unity of the Lakota people and to make all Lakotas walk again "the good red road." No idea of using the ghost dance for war, let alone for a "holy war" as suggested by Utley, is present in Black Elk's memoirs. The ghost dance was only a way to help the Lakota people.[160] It has often been said that Sitting Bull, at least, saw the new religion as a last chance to lead a struggle against the whites, but that view is doubtful. There is no reason, however, to doubt the sincere belief Kicking Bear and Short Bull had in the message they were preaching.

As the excitement and the possibility of war increased, some Lakotas perhaps saw their chance to once more excel on the battlefield. In part, that

Table 1: The Number of Lakota Ghost Dancers

Reservation	Tribe	Population	Ghost Dancers (%)	Number of Ghost Dancers
Standing Rock				
	Blackfeet	571		
	Hunkpapa	1,734		
Total		2,305	10	231
Cheyenne River				
	Two Kettle	Not available		
	Sans Arc	Not available		
	Minneconjou	Not available		
	Blackfeet	Not available		
Total		2,823	15	423
Rosebud				
	Brulé	1,961		
	Loafer	1,052		
	Wazahzah	1,184		
	Two Kettle	228		
	Mixed	762		
Total		5,187	30	1,556
Pine Ridge				
	Oglala	4,486		
	Mixed	528		
Total		5,014	40	2,006
Grand Total		15,329	28	4,216

might explain the warlike reputation that the ghost dance acquired. But even those who hoped to gain honor in war were sincere believers in the dance. Despite some changes in the original doctrine, there is no indication that the Lakota ghost dancers were hostile toward the whites when the ceremonies were first started on the Lakota reservations. The Lakota ghost dancers became hostile, or warlike, only when the whites tried to interfere in their religious ceremonies.[161]

At the time of the troops' arrival on November 20, 1890, the situation on Pine Ridge and Rosebud was very volatile, and without the interference of the army it was only a matter of time before a serious confrontation would have erupted between the ghost dancers and the Indian police, or between the ghost dancers and the agents. However, to evaluate the situation properly we have to look at the number of Lakota ghost dancers. The exact number is impossible to determine, but by comparing different sources it is possible to give a rough estimate. Although the numbers in the table are not exact, they are sufficient to estimate the number of ghost dancers compared to the total number of the Lakota population.[162]

Utley used the reports of the agents and some eyewitness accounts when he constructed his estimate of the number of ghost dancers. According to him, in November 1890, approximately 40 percent of the Pine Ridge Indian population were ghost dancers. On Rosebud 30 percent were openly practicing the doctrine, whereas the rate at Cheyenne River was 15 percent and at Standing Rock only 10 percent.[163] Mooney, relying most likely on government documents, claims that as many as 50 percent of "the 26,000 Sioux took active part" in the ghost dances, but there is reason to believe that his estimate is not accurate, since there were not 26,000 Lakotas in the first place. Following Mooney the number of ghost dancers would then be almost 13,000, which is quite high given that the total Lakota population did not number more than some 15,000.[164]

However, Mooney's estimates do demonstrate that Utley's are likely accurate. Mooney claims that on Standing Rock approximately 450 Hunkpapas led by Sitting Bull were participating in the ghost dances. According to the table, 10 percent of the population would make the number of ghost dancers on Standing Rock approximately 231, even less than Mooney's estimate. As mentioned earlier, the Hunkpapas were divided into the progressives, led by Gall and John Grass, and the nonprogressives, led by Sitting Bull. And as Mooney himself notes, only the followers of Sitting Bull took part in the ghost dance.[165] Gall never took up the dance, saying that he could not believe in it until he could truly see something good resulting from it. At the time of the ghost dance Gall was considered a devoted Christian, an Episcopalian. During the ghost dance troubles he summoned his followers to St. Elizabeth's Church, where they prayed, read the Bible, and sang gospel hymns in the evenings. In this way he kept his people safe throughout the trouble.[166] In addition, there were the very progressive Yanktonai Sioux living on Standing Rock Reservation. So it is highly unlikely that there would have been more actual ghost dancers on that reservation than 10 percent of the population.

The danger of war seemed to be more imminent on Pine Ridge and Rosebud, where the numbers of ghost dancers were greatest. Considering the matter from the white point of view, calling in the army was reasonable, especially when the official estimates of the number of ghost dancers were extremely high.[167] However, as shown in the table, only about 28 percent (4,216) of the total Lakota population were ghost dancers, and there was much movement between the ghost dance camps and other camps, which makes it impossible to distinguish clearly who was a ghost dancer and who was not. It is especially difficult to determine the actual numbers of the progressive, Christian Lakotas who became devoted ghost dancers. Many visited the ghost dance camps simply out of curiosity; some were deeply affected and stayed. Others stayed for a while, perhaps attended one or two ceremonies or participated as onlookers, and eventually returned to their homes in the progressive camps. Furthermore, especially after the arrival of the military, many of those who fled to the ghost dance camps were not ghost dancers at all; the camps became places of refuge for the frightened people. Thus even 28 percent may be a high estimate.

The excitement on the Lakota reservations finally led to the arrival of U.S. Army troops at Pine Ridge and Rosebud Reservations on November 20, 1890. Their intervention was prompted by several emotional communications from the new Lakota agents, especially from Agent Daniel F. Royer. For the first time in almost a decade the Lakotas found themselves face-to-face with the U.S. Army.[168]

Although the Lakotas struggled with the agents almost from the beginning of their reservation life, nothing occurred during the 1880s that was serious enough to call for military intervention.[169] The power of the U.S. Army was well known and it was feared. The arrival of the army caused much confusion and panic among the Indians on Pine Ridge and Rosebud. Fearing possible military action, hundreds of the so-called progressives moved close to the agencies to show they were friendly, but hundreds also fled from the soldiers to the ghost dancers' camps. Both Charles Eastman, a doctor at Pine Ridge Agency, and Luther Standing Bear described the "friendly" Indians at Pine Ridge and Rosebud Reservations as extremely frightened, even panic-stricken.[170]

At first the arrival of the troops caused confusion among the ghost dancers. Still, the dances on Pine Ridge continued, at least in the camps of Little Wound, Big Road, and No Water. Little Wound acted as the principal leader. Utley and Miller claim that on November 21 and 22 his warriors rode around the reservation urging people to join the ghost dancers. They announced that they were planning to dance all winter and were ready to defend themselves if the army attacked. They were not going to initiate hostilities, but if necessary they would humiliate the army as they had humiliated the Indian police and the agent.[171] According to one ghost dancer, however, they were riding around the reservation that night singing ghost dance songs because they wanted to be ready to flee if the soldiers charged their village. "The priests called upon the young men at this juncture not to become angry but to continue the dance. . . . We did not carry our guns nor any weapons, but trusted to the Great Spirit to destroy the soldiers," he explained later.[172]

After the arrival of the troops several hundred, perhaps as many as 1,100 Brulés started to move camp toward the western border of Rosebud Reservation. Under the leadership of Two Strike and Crow Dog, they planned to meet with Short Bull and his followers in order to join the Oglalas at Pine Ridge. On the way some 700 Oglalas, who had been living close to the border of the reservation, joined the Brulés, increasing the total to approximately 1,800 people.[173]

The news of the arrival of the troops led also to the unification of the Cheyenne River ghost dancers under two chiefs. Altogether approximately 600 to 700 Minneconjous were dancing in the camps of Big Foot and Hump. At this point both men were true believers in the ghost dance. According to Agent Perain P. Palmer, Big Foot urged all believers to stay together and to gather as many arms and as much ammunition as possible. The whites considered Hump so dangerous that they did not even dare to contact him. Progressive Indians who visited the camp on November 22 informed Agent Palmer that the ghost dancers were prepared to fight at any moment.[174] On Standing Rock Reservation Sitting Bull was leading the dancers, although the Indian police and Agent McLaughlin were watching them closely.[175]

The arrival of the troops did not calm the Indians, as the military and other officials expected.[176] On the contrary, it united the ghost dancers and caused hundreds of frightened Indians to flee their homes and seek protection among the dancers. In fear of being treated as hostiles by the army, others decided to leave their homes in order to seek protection at the agencies. They sought to cooperate with the army; for example, forty Oglalas were immediately recruited as scouts.[177] In this way, the arrival of the U.S. Army led to a deepening split within the Lakotas. The military's presence caused much tension and confusion among the Indians.

The presence of the military on Pine Ridge and Rosebud Reservations made tensions mount between whites and Indians also. Several delegations of chiefs and army scouts who were not engaged in the ghost dancing, but whom the ghost dancers knew, went to their camps to try to negotiate with them. On November 27 their efforts bore fruit when Little Wound and Big Road brought their people close to Pine Ridge Agency, announcing that they had left the ghost dancers. The events leading to their decision remain somewhat unclear, but perhaps the "overwhelming show of force" by the army had affected them, or perhaps Little Wound, who had been a Christian before joining the ghost dancers, had begun to doubt the new religion.[178]

The defection of the two chiefs did not affect the rest of the ghost dancers, now led by Two Strike, Short Bull, and Kicking Bear. This group consisted of several hundred Brulé and Oglala men, women, and children. They had decided to move to the Badlands in the northern part of Pine Ridge Reservation, where they sought protection on a plateau that was easy to defend. On their way to what became known as the Stronghold, called by the Lakotas *onáži* (place of shelter), the ghost dancers destroyed some property and stole cattle owned by Indians and mixed bloods who had left their homes and moved to the agency. The Stronghold was an ideal place: all the routes to it were easy to guard and defend, making it practically invincible, and it offered food and water for the people and animals.[179]

The destruction caused by the ghost dancers worried the nondancers living at the agencies. It seemed that the army was unable to stop them from plundering. Even the property of American Horse was destroyed. According to George E. Hyde, for some Christian and progressive Lakotas these acts were convincing evidence that the ghost dance was stronger than Christianity; consequently they turned their backs on the white man's civilization and joined the ghost dancers.[180]

By joining the ghost dancers and sometimes even turning to violence, a few educated Lakotas sought to show that they were still Lakota, despite having attended white men's schools. An extreme example of this is the case of Plenty Horses (Thašųke Óta), who in January 1891 shot and killed an army officer. When asked later why he did it, he simply said that now he had shown that he was a Lakota.[181] This and a few other cases clearly demonstrate the difficult situation in which many of the progressive Indians found themselves. Miller relates the example of a girl who had been a devoted Christian. She visited the mission church, left her belongings there, and went away to join her ghost-dancing relatives; she would not leave her family despite her Christian beliefs. Another example, told by Luther Standing Bear, is the case of Hollow Horn Bear (Mathó Hé Ȟloǧéca), who, though he intended only to go and see the ceremony, never returned to the progressive camp.[182]

By early December the ghost dancers from Rosebud had gathered at the Stronghold, and dancing was resumed. Ghost dancers from Pine Ridge and Cheyenne River also arrived. This made the total strength of the ghost dance camp approximately 3,000 people. In the Stronghold, the old Lakota camp structure was put into effect. The camp circle was formed in a traditional manner, with the opening to the east. The camp was in wartime mode, and Kicking Bear took the role of the head war leader (*blotáhųka*). The Stronghold camp was probably the biggest Lakota camp since the Little Big Horn.[183] From the Stronghold the ghost dancers carried out raids to capture livestock from the ranches of Indians and mixed bloods inside the reservation, but they never committed any depredations outside the reservation. The Stronghold was to be their sanctuary until the coming of the new world.[184]

During late November and early December the nondancers gathered closer to the agencies, fearing possible military action. At Pine Ridge, the people of Little Wound and Big Road had now moved closer to the agency but were not allowed to join the "real" progressives, since the commanding general did not trust them. Many of the people still spoke in favor of the ghost dance and came to the agency only out of fear of the army, because their chiefs wanted to, or because food was issued there. Several thousand Oglalas living at Pine Ridge were gathered around the agency.[185]

The people gathered at the Stronghold were dancing frequently. They had fortified the area, making the natural fortress even more inaccessible. However, they soon realized that they were surrounded by troops. Almost daily from the beginning of December they received emissaries, mainly Indian scouts and progressive chiefs, sent by Brig. Gen. John R. Brooke, commander of the Department of the Platte, who tried to use the tactics of negotiation rather than open warfare.[186] According to these emissaries, the ghost dancers were very sullen; they even shot at the emissaries, who reported on fanatical speeches given by Kicking Bear and Short Bull. The dances were growing very intense; the people were planning to dance all winter. They believed that they had enough food and water and that the army could not attack them there. After several days of negotiation, the ghost dance leaders announced that they did not want to talk about surrender; they were sure there was only prison waiting for them if they gave up. They wanted to die in freedom and planned to defend their final sanctuary until the end. Furthermore, they expressed their dissatisfaction with the reduction in their rations. They also complained about the new reservation boundaries established by the Act of 1889.[187]

The Lakotas gathered at Pine Ridge Agency wanted to talk to their former agent, Valentine T. McGillicuddy, who had arrived at the reservation as an emissary from the governor of South Dakota. Even Red Cloud, who had opposed McGillicuddy when he was an agent, welcomed him. Red Cloud considered him a man of courage, since he had never called in the army. The Indians told the former agent that they were suspicious of the army and hoped he could have the soldiers sent away. The people in the Stronghold also wanted to talk with McGillicuddy rather than with the emissaries sent by General Brooke. However, McGillicuddy was not able to, or rather Brooke did not allow him to, contribute significantly to matters at Pine Ridge, and he left without accomplishing anything.[188]

One of the emissaries sent by General Brooke was a Jesuit, Father John Jutz. This man, according to Black Elk, was the Black Robe who came out and persuaded some of the chiefs to go to the agency for negotiations. Indeed, on December 7, Father Jutz led a delegation of Lakota ghost dancers to Pine Ridge Agency. Two Strike came riding in a wagon surrounded by fully armed warriors. The ghost dancers had decided to come to the agency in war regalia to make an impression, but they agreed to give up their arms during the negotiations. Many expressed willingness to leave the Stronghold but feared to come closer to the agency, as General Brooke requested. They explained that there was not enough food for the horses and cattle near the agency. During the negotiations the ghost dancers and the Indians already at the agency held a great feast and a dance together, but no real results were achieved. The delegation returned to the ghost dance camp.[189]

Kicking Bear and Short Bull tried to use all their influence to keep the ghost dancers united. To show the power of the ghost shirts, one dancer agreed to be shot at while wearing the sacred shirt. When the man was seriously wounded, some Indians rationalized that the man's own medicine or power had failed him, not the ghost shirt. But a number of other miracles promised by the ghost dance apostles also were not fulfilled, and together they caused friction among the dancers.[190]

This friction among the people in the Stronghold deepened as well because of the emissaries General Brooke continued to send. These delegations were led by the mixed-blood interpreter Louis Shangrau and a few prominent Oglalas. They reported to Brooke that the people had been dancing for more than thirty hours and feelings were very intense; that Short Bull replied angrily to all requests to go to the agency to surrender; that the general feeling among the ghost dancers was that the army was not to be trusted, that they feared the army would kill all the ghost dancers in retaliation for their depredations. Short Bull wanted the people to remember that Crazy Horse had been killed after he surrendered in 1877.[191] The dance continued for three more days. Finally, on December 12, when Two Strike and Crow Dog announced that the time to surrender had arrived, the ghost dancers came close to fighting each other. After some skirmishing, more than half of the Oglalas and some of the Brulés started to move their lodges toward Pine Ridge Agency.[192] The ghost dancers' unity was broken. Only a few hundred of the most committed ghost dancers remained in the Stronghold with Short Bull and Kicking Bear. They continued to raid the nearby farms under Kicking Bear's leadership. Some shots were exchanged with local cowboys, but the skirmishing caused no casualties.[193]

At Standing Rock the situation among Sitting Bull's ghost dancers remained unchanged. Agent McLaughlin still watched them closely. Sitting Bull stayed at his camp on the Grand River, forty miles from the agency. He did not respond to requests by the agent to come to the agency for talks. One Indian policeman tried to persuade Sitting Bull to put an end to the ghost dances and come to the agency; in response, Sitting Bull replied that he wanted to have nothing to do with the Indian police. He wanted the policemen to remember the old times, when the young men had depended on him and he in turn could depend on them. But now, he said, "You have turned with the whites against me. I have nothing to say to you." Sitting Bull did not refuse to talk with the agent, but he would do so only in his own camp, where he felt safe.[194]

During one of these meetings with Agent McLaughlin Sitting Bull suggested that he and the agent make a journey to the West; there they could decide together whether or not the new religion was true. Although Sitting Bull promised that he would stop the dances if the story of the Messiah turned out to be false, the agent never warmed to the idea, and the journey was never made.[195]

Dances were organized in Sitting Bull's camp throughout November. Early in December he was believed to be planning a trip to the Stronghold, since Kicking Bear had invited him there. Sitting Bull requested several times that Agent McLaughlin grant him permission to go to Pine Ridge, but he was refused each time. He wanted to go to see the people who best knew the new religion. He publicly announced that he did not believe the message of the ghost dance, but he still urged the people to dance despite his own beliefs. After publicly denouncing the ghost dance, Sitting Bull lost some of his followers, who moved their camp away from him.[196]

Mary C. Collins, a missionary who visited Sitting Bull a week before he was killed, knew that Sitting Bull did not really believe in the ghost dance. According to her, he said that there was nothing harmful in the dance itself, but they had already gone too far to stop now, even though he knew it would result in trouble. Sitting Bull said that their own religion was best for the Lakotas, but he believed that they should be allowed to worship as they pleased.[197] The Indian policeman Grey Eagle (Wąblí Ȟóta), who was sent by

Agent McLaughlin to watch Sitting Bull, warned him that he would be arrested in the near future. Grey Eagle's sister was one of Sitting Bull's wives, but the two men did not get along. In fact, Grey Eagle was one of the men who informed McLaughlin that Sitting Bull intended to leave the reservation. Catherine Weldon of the Indian Rights Association, who tried to work on Sitting Bull's behalf, increased Sitting Bull's apprehension.[198] About this time, during a morning walk, Sitting Bull received a special message from a messenger very familiar to him: a bird. The bird told him that he was going to be killed by his own people.[199] Sitting Bull's fears were realized on December 15, 1890. Early in the morning the Indian police force sent by Agent McLaughlin entered Sitting Bull's cabin. The force consisted of forty men, who were led by some of Sitting Bull's enemies, including Lt. Bull Head (Thatháka Phá). The policemen tried to take Sitting Bull with them quickly, but finally allowed him to dress before escorting him out of the cabin. At first he followed without resistance and, according to one eyewitness, even said that he would go with the police to the agency to see what they wanted of him. But as some of his followers gathered around his cabin, the women wailing and the men abusing the policemen, he changed his mind. According to one Indian policeman, Sitting Bull's son Crow Foot (Sí Khąǧí) told his father, "[The police] are making a fool of you," after which Sitting Bull refused to go. Mary C. Collins suggested that Grey Eagle's presence at the arrest might have been the final reason Sitting Bull changed his mind.

Lt. Bull Head asked the people to let them through, but then Catch the Bear (Mathó Wawóyuspa), Sitting Bull's old friend and Bull Head's enemy, came from behind the corner of the house with a rifle in his hand. It seems that the first bullet was fired from his gun. That bullet struck Lt. Bull Head, who, as he was falling, shot Sitting Bull. At the same time Sgt. Red Tomahawk (Cháȟpi Lúta) shot Sitting Bull in the head, killing him instantly.[200]

The tensions that had been growing between the ghost dancers and the nondancers finally culminated on December 15; Sitting Bull's death set the Lakotas against each other, precipitating a fight between his followers and the Indian police. The Indian policemen withdrew to Sitting Bull's cabin, where they were finally rescued by a detachment of the U.S. Cavalry that had been left behind as backup. Sitting Bull's followers tried to continue the fight but were soon driven away by the army. One of the policemen later claimed that they were all drunk from whiskey the agent had sent them the previous night. Another commented that their mission had been very strange and frightening, since they were all relatives.[201] In the end, eight ghost dancers and six Indian policemen died. The army had no casualties.[202] Sitting Bull had been killed, and the ghost dancers on Standing Rock were left without a leader.

During the fighting a remarkable event took place. A Hunkpapa warrior rode several times into the middle of the crossfire wearing his ghost shirt. He was not harmed by the policemen's bullets. This was taken to be a sign of the power of the ghost dance.[203]

Although the situation seemed to be calming down on other reservations, fighting broke out between the ghost dancers and the Indian police force, backed by the U.S. Army, on December 15 on Standing Rock Reservation. Most interesting is the fact that the fighting did not start on Pine Ridge or Rosebud, where tensions had been much higher than on Standing Rock. That fighting broke out on Standing Rock may be attributed to many factors, the ghost dance being only one of them, and not even the most important.[204] Other factors included the power struggle between Agent McLaughlin and Sitting Bull, the power struggle between the progressive chiefs and Sitting Bull, and the power struggle between Sitting Bull and the Indian police.

These internal conflicts on Standing Rock Reservation had kept tensions rising throughout the 1880s, and events during the negotiations in 1889 worsened the situation.[205] When Sitting Bull put himself at the head of the ghost dancers, he also gave Agent McLaughlin a good excuse to get rid of him, even if the new religion did not present any imminent threat of hostilities on that reservation. If Sitting Bull had joined Kicking Bear's and Short Bull's ghost dance camp at Pine Ridge, his influence might have added to the ghost dancers' determination and hostility. Whether the arrest should have been organized otherwise is an unanswerable question. Perhaps Sitting Bull would have followed an army detachment more willingly than a detachment of Indian police that included some of his enemies. Some of the policemen belonged to Yanktonai Sioux, whom the Hunkpapas generally considered inferior to themselves, not worthy of capturing a man of Sitting Bull's stature. Maybe

FIGURE 4. *The Capture and Killing of Sitting Bull*. An 1890s engraving by H. R. Locke of Deadwood, South Dakota, depicting Sitting Bull's arrest and death. The picture does not reflect the events as they happened in reality, but is a typical contemporary dramatization. Denver Public Library, Western History Collection, call number x-33620.

he already knew when the policemen entered his cabin that this would be the day the bird had foretold. Whatever the case, Sitting Bull had been killed and the ghost dancers on Standing Rock were left without a leader.

After Sitting Bull's death approximately 150 to 200 frightened Hunkpapas fled to Cheyenne River Reservation, seeking security in Big Foot's camp. Some also found their way to Hump's camp, arriving in a destitute condition. Rumors of the fight spread rapidly across the reservations; neither Indians nor whites knew what really happened in Sitting Bull's camp. Several groups of Indians were traveling around the reservations, some of them

openly hostile and others simply looking for shelter from the cold and safety from the soldiers.[206]

The news of Sitting Bull's death caused much anger in the Stronghold.
Kicking Bear started to prepare the men for war; dancing was no longer
enough. Attacks on ranches continued, and the ghost dancers suffered their
first casualty. The dancers also attacked an army supply wagon, which was
rescued by the 6th Cavalry.[207]

On Cheyenne River, the Minneconjous were also dancing, even though
Hump's faith had been wavering before Sitting Bull's death. Back in 1877
he had surrendered to General Miles and acted as a scout for his army afterward. Hump always considered Miles to be a man of honor, and Capt.
Ezra P. Ewers was his friend during the time he served as an Indian agent
on Cheyenne River Reservation. In December 1890, after negotiating with
Ewers, who was sent by General Miles, Hump decided to give up the ghost
dance. On December 9 he brought his people to Cheyenne River Agency
and enlisted as a scout. One of the most influential ghost dance leaders abandoned the religion without bloodshed.[208]

Now Big Foot was the only ghost dance leader left on Cheyenne River
Reservation. The army surrounded his people, and the chief saw no way
out other than to agree to follow the soldiers back to their village at Cherry
Creek, which they had left in order to live in the ghost dance camps. Young
men, who had expected much from the ghost dance, were unhappy and
asked Big Foot to lead them to Pine Ridge, where they could join the other
ghost dancers. Red Cloud and other prominent leaders at Pine Ridge had
invited Big Foot to come there and help them negotiate for peace. Still, Big
Foot hesitated; he did not want to cause trouble. He only wanted the army
to allow his people to stay in their own village instead of going to the agency as the army officers demanded.[209]

The confusion on Cheyenne River continued to grow as Hump tried to
persuade some of Sitting Bull's Hunkpapa refugees to follow him to Fort
Bennett at Cheyenne River Agency. Finally a few of them joined him, but
the rest decided to follow Big Foot. Thirty-eight young men with their families, who belonged to Hump's own Minneconjou band, turned their backs
on their leader and joined Big Foot.[210]

General Miles sent Lt. Col. Edwin V. Sumner (known as "Three Fingers" to the Lakotas), commanding the 8th Cavalry, to watch over Big Foot and his ghost dancers. On December 15 the soldiers surrounded Big Foot's band. Big Foot assured Colonel Sumner that he wanted only peace. He promised to go to Fort Bennett but warned that the younger men were anxious to join the ghost dancers on Pine Ridge and that it might be difficult to keep them quiet. He also worried that if they did not go voluntarily to the fort, the soldiers would force them to go.[211]

The news of Sitting Bull's death and the arrival of the Hunkpapa refugees on December 19 frightened the Minneconjous. Big Foot still wanted to obey Colonel Sumner's instructions and follow the soldiers to Cherry Creek, their former village site. Big Foot and his people hoped to stay there before going on to the fort the next morning. This was agreed to, but during the march to the village the Indians sighted another army detachment, which caused much alarm. So did the behavior of the soldiers. One of the members of Big Foot's band explained later that they had felt uneasy because the soldiers acted in a strange manner.[212]

Their uneasy feeling was escalated by John Dunn, a white rancher known to the Lakotas as Red Beard, who came to the camp as a messenger from Colonel Sumner. The interpreter Felix Benoit heard Big Foot saying to an assembly of Indians that Dunn told him that the soldiers would shoot them if they refused to go to Fort Bennett. Andrew Good Thunder (Wakįyą Wašté) and Joseph Horn Cloud (Maȟpíya Hethų), both members of Big Foot's band, were present when this discussion took place in Big Foot's cabin. They later related that Dunn urged them to go to Pine Ridge if they wanted to live. According to them, Dunn claimed that a force of 1,000 soldiers was on its way to kill the Indians. What Dunn really told Big Foot has remained unclear, but after his visit Big Foot seemed convinced that they had to get out of harm's way and go to Pine Ridge. According to Andrew Good Thunder, Big Foot said, "It seems that Three Fingers [Colonel Sumner] has been trying for the past few days to make trouble and if his intentions are as you [Dunn] say, I will give him room and get out of his way." Big Foot then asked Benoit whether Dunn's words were true. Benoit replied that they should not follow Dunn's advice; they really needed to go to Fort Bennett instead of going to Pine Ridge. After that, however, the Indians seemed to be very scared and started packing. In his own statement Dunn later claimed that he had told the Indians the soldiers were not there to harm them and that he did not tell them to go to Pine Ridge. Still, after much confusion, Big Foot decided to lead his people to Pine Ridge. On December 21, the flight of the Minneconjous began.[213]

At first the journey of the approximately 350 refugees progressed rapidly. However, when reaching the borders of Pine Ridge Reservation, they had to slow down because Big Foot had developed pneumonia and could not keep up the pace. The weather was extremely cold and the people were starving. On December 24 they made camp in a blizzard and, according to some sources, saw a strange light in the sky, which was generally believed to be Sitting Bull's spirit. At this time Big Foot sent some of his people to try to find the ghost dance camp in the Stronghold, while the rest continued their journey toward Red Cloud's camp. He also sent messengers to Pine Ridge Agency to report that he was coming in peacefully. When these messengers returned he learned that there were soldiers camped at Wounded Knee Creek, but instead of trying to avoid them, he decided to meet them openly. By December 27, however, the Indians had almost stopped, which gave the army a chance to close in on them.[214]

Andrew Good Thunder was among the men who were sent ahead to scout. On their way, they met an Indian from Pine Ridge who told them that there were two factions there. One was peaceable and stayed at the agency, while the other remained at the Stronghold, although they were believed to be ready to come in. The man was taken to Big Foot, who said, "We have come to this reservation to avoid trouble and I will take the main road to the agency to join the peaceable people there." The men still continued to scout and met three Indians who were doing the same for the army. They all sat down and smoked a pipe. Big Foot's men learned that the army was looking for them, since it had been reported that they had been in a fight with Colonel Sumner.[215]

The next day the Indians met a column of soldiers who, to their surprise, came toward them from the south rather than behind them from the north. Although the Indians were waving a white flag, the soldiers closed in and lined up in front of them as though ready for a fight. After discussion among themselves, the Indian men also lined up and sent their women and children behind. Andrew Good Thunder reported later, "We agreed not to fight but get in line and go toward them abreast and if the soldiers began firing we would charge and wipe them out." However, after a short parley with Maj. Samuel Whiteside, Big Foot agreed to surrender as the officer demanded.[216]

According to Beard (also called Iron Hail, Wasú Máza), the officer was happy to learn that Big Foot wanted peace, but the behavior of the regular soldiers was suspicious. They were laughing as they helped Big Foot to the wagon given to him by the officer. The Indians were afraid for their leader. Beard even asked a medicine man to lead a ghost dance and seek help from the Messiah. The column of Indians was then escorted to Wounded Knee Creek, where they camped. While the Indians put up their tents, the army encircled them, causing much fear, confusion, and anger. Rumors that the army was going to disarm them were also worrying; the Lakotas did not want to be without arms at the mercy of the soldiers. However, they planned no resistance. Once again the medicine man was asked to seek help from the Messiah. In the evening a crier went around the camp announcing that there would be a council early in the morning and that they would then be taken to Pine Ridge Agency. During the night, more soldiers were heard to arrive, their movements sounding warlike to the Indians. In the morning the 120 Lakota men and 230 women and children woke up to find their camp surrounded by some 500 soldiers, who had brought Hotchkiss guns with them. During the night they had aimed their cannons directly at the Indian camp.[217]

In the morning food was issued, then the Lakotas were asked to give up their arms. The disarmament started about 8:30 in the morning of December 29. The Lakota men were separated from the women and children, who remained in the camp. The men were sitting in a semicircle in front of Big Foot's tent, peacefully smoking their pipes. When the men refused to give up all of their arms, Big Foot tried to explain to the officers that they had given up most of their arms previously, when they surrendered to Colonel Sumner the first time. The soldiers then started to search the camp, but the weapons they found were old and almost worthless. The soldiers believed the men had hidden weapons under their blankets. The search for weapons was carried out brutally. Some women were especially thoroughly searched. Even sharp objects, such as knives and axes, were confiscated.[218]

While the soldiers continued their search and the army moved around them, the Indians grew more and more restless. According to Beard and Joseph Horn Cloud, the interpreter told the Lakota men to march past the soldiers, who would be holding their guns toward them. The Indians understood that the soldiers would be pointing their guns at them rather than holding the guns in front of them, as the interpreter meant. This was seen as a plan to shoot the unarmed Indians, and once again the medicine man's help was requested. The medicine man, Yellow Bird (Zįtkála Zí), started to sing and threw dust in the air. He was wearing a ghost shirt, praying to the Great Spirit and singing about the power of the shirt. According to the interpreter Phillip Wells, he was only planning to dance around the semicircle and then sit down, but Col. James W. Forsyth, who was now in command, tried to stop him. Yellow Bird did stop for a while, but then continued, again promising that no harm would come to those who wore ghost shirts.[219]

The actions of the medicine man have often been interpreted as encouraging the Indians to fight. Especially the fact that he was throwing dust in the air has been interpreted as a sign for the warriors to open fire on the soldiers. To some degree his actions probably caused restlessness among the Indians, but more than that, he caused restlessness among the soldiers. However, throwing dust in the air was part of the ghost dance ceremony, a sign for the Lakotas to show grief and pity.[220] This was probably what the medicine man was actually doing. As Phillip Wells explained, he clearly was urging the people to believe in the power of the ghost shirts in this time of trouble, but he was not making specific signs to start a battle; rather, he was praying for supernatural help. Furthermore, it has to be taken into account that all the women and children were in the danger zone. Some children were even said to have been harmlessly playing in the camp. It is highly unlikely that the Lakotas planned any resistance when their families would have been in danger. All the Indian and mixed-blood accounts I have studied convince me that no plan of resistance existed.[221]

Suddenly, one Indian was spotted wandering about with a gun in his hand. According to some eyewitnesses, he was a deaf and mute man who did not really understand what was going on. Miller claims that this person told him later, through sign language, that he was Sitting Bull's son, and that he was only planning to put his gun down on the pile of other weapons. No other source mentions his identity in relation to Sitting Bull. Whether he really was his son and whether he really was the man who fired the first shot will remain in doubt forever. Whoever he was, he pulled the trigger when the soldiers grabbed him. Whether this was intentional is unclear. Beard said that the shot was fired during the confusion of the medicine man's performance; he heard a shot fired, but could not tell who fired it.[222] Mooney claims that the first shot was deliberately fired by a fanatical Minneconjou named Black Fox (or Black Coyote, Šųgmánitu Sápa). This is also the opinion of Andrew Good Thunder, who claims that he saw Black Coyote fire the first shot. However, this is not substantiated by other Indian accounts, or even by army sources used for this study. Nonetheless, Mooney's interpretation has survived in many accounts of the Wounded Knee fight. For example, Utley's interpretation of the fight was mainly constructed from Mooney's study and from the official army investigation, which includes accounts given by two Indians. It seems obvious that these two accounts were included in the army investigation because they agree in detail with the statements of the army officers.[223]

The stories of other Indian survivors present a different interpretation. Several Indian and mixed-blood accounts describe an officer (evidently Forsyth) giving orders, which the Indians could not understand, in a very loud voice. His commands were followed by a sound like a "lightning crash" when the first volley was fired. Only Beard, Joseph Horn Cloud, and Andrew Good Thunder describe a single shot that preceded the first big volley. After the first shot, the army responded by opening fire on the Indians. The women and children were caught in the middle of the firing. Big Foot was immediately shot and died instantly. Suddenly all expectations of a peaceful march to Pine Ridge Agency were destroyed.[224]

In a few minutes dozens of Lakotas and a handful of soldiers were lying on the ground, dead or wounded. After the first volley, a hand-to-hand fight began, while the soldiers continued to fire on the Indians' camp. The women and children tried to find refuge in the nearby ravine, but the soldiers kept shooting at the fleeing Indians regardless of their sex or age. A number of Lakota men managed to break through the soldiers' circle and tried to organize some resistance.

During the fight there were many brutal acts, and women and children were shot mercilessly. Some soldiers were yelling revenge for Custer, and John Shangrau, a mixed-blood scout, claimed that an officer told him that now the soldiers had gotten their revenge. When asked what the revenge was for, the officer simply replied, "The Custer massacre." Other accounts by mixed-bloods and white men alike claim that the soldiers were more or less drunk, and their plan was to fire on the Indians if they showed any signs of resistance.[225]

The sounds of gunfire were heard as far away as Pine Ridge Agency, where the Oglalas and Brulés who had just arrived from the Stronghold were camped. Hearing the sounds of the battle they broke camp immediately and fled once again. Approximately 150 Lakota men rode to Wounded Knee and took part in the fighting. Partly because of these men the Lakotas were able to organize some resistance. The fight was over by 3 o'clock in the afternoon; 25 soldiers and between 150 and 250 Lakotas were dead. Several soldiers and an unknown number of Lakotas were also wounded in the affair. The exact number of Lakota casualties is almost impossible to know. A total of 146 Lakota dead were found on the battlefield, and an unknown number likely died later.[226]

The situation among the Indians on Pine Ridge was chaotic. Some opened fire on the agency buildings and employees. The fleeing Lakotas, led by Two Strike, Little Wound, and Big Road, met Short Bull's and Kicking Bear's ghost dancers, who were on their way to the agency. The dancers quickly abandoned the idea of continuing toward the agency and joined the people who were fleeing. The refugees stopped at the abandoned village of No Water at White Clay Creek. They numbered roughly 4,000, 800 to 1,000 of whom were men. This, of course, was quite a considerable fighting force. Among them was also old Red Cloud, who barely had time to lower his American flag to half-mast before the fleeing people took him with them. Some ac-

FIGURE 5. Interior of Holy Cross Episcopal Church at the Pine Ridge Agency, South Dakota. Army corps men and a Lakota man stand around wounded from Wounded Knee on the hay-covered floor of the church, still decorated with Christmas garlands. Denver Public Library, Western History Collection, photographer A. G. Johnson, call number x-31471.

counts claim that Red Cloud left after learning that an officer wanted to shell his house and the Indian camp behind it. Others claim that the fleeing people forced Red Cloud to leave because he was their leader and they needed him.[227]

Those Indians who had already come in to make peace were now angrier and more afraid than ever. There was extreme tension among them. Even many of the progressives on Pine Ridge and Rosebud, who had not wanted to have anything to do with the ghost dance, started to arm themselves; the news of Wounded Knee was too much even for them. According to Luther Standing Bear, many of the progressives who did not join the fleeing people and remained at the agency were preparing to take part in the fighting if necessary.[228]

All through the following night the wounded from Wounded Knee were streaming into the refugees' camp, where the mood was extremely warlike. The ghost dancing resumed, even though the new religion had not helped the people at Wounded Knee. The ghost dance, however, started to fade into the background as the people became more concerned with their very survival. The freezing weather and lack of food heightened the misery for the Lakotas, who had fled in haste and with poor equipment. Big Foot's fate did not encourage them to surrender. The promises made by the soldiers were mistrusted more than ever. Desperate ghost dancers decided that no one was allowed to leave the camp. For many of Kicking Bear's and Short Bull's followers it seemed to be better to die fighting than to surrender. Of the major chiefs only Red Cloud wanted to return to the agency, but the ghost dancers threatened to kill him if he tried. Thus even the influence of Red Cloud vanished in the winds of the ghost dance.[229]

During the next few days the Lakotas had several skirmishes with the troops. Kicking Bear led a force of a few hundred warriors. They managed to gain some small victories, but each time the superior equipment and the overwhelming power of the army forced the Lakotas to withdraw. At one point, at the so-called Drexel Mission fight, the Lakotas almost managed to annihilate Colonel Forsyth and his 7th Cavalry. The Indians, possibly numbering only forty men, kept the troops cornered for several hours. Only the arrival of additional troops saved the soldiers.[230]

During the first days of January 1891, the Indians found themselves surrounded by the army. Even if they had managed to break through the first line of troops, they would almost immediately have faced a second line.[231] The feeling in the Indian camp was becoming divided. More and more people started to talk in favor of surrender. These opinions were encouraged by messages from General Miles, who promised fair treatment to all. Big Foot and his people were a good example of what could happen to those the army considered enemies. On the other hand, they also served as an example of what could happen to those who trusted the army. Thus the feelings among the Indians were very mixed. Despite the fear the Lakotas felt toward the army, the messages sent by Miles from January 1 to 4 affected most of the leaders. Many of the Oglalas had surrendered to General Miles in the 1870s; they respected him as a man whom they could trust. In addition, according to Black Elk, Red Cloud gave a speech in which he urged an end to the fighting since the winter was going to be hard on them. Also, Young Man Afraid of His Horse, who had returned from a trip to Wyoming, arrived at the camp and emphasized the fact that winter was no time for warfare. Eventually, the Oglalas decided to surrender.[232]

The ghost dancers directly under the leadership of Kicking Bear and Short Bull did not want to surrender. The apostles of the dance, supported by the young men, rose against the Oglala chiefs. They appointed traditional *akichita* (camp police), who were ordered to stop anyone from leaving the camp. There were several small skirmishes between the two parties and some Lakotas were killed. On January 3, Big Road with four lesser leaders managed to escape. The results of their talks with General Miles at Pine Ridge Agency were brought back to the camp, and many more wanted to surrender. Several Oglala groups left the camp. On January 7, Red Cloud escaped and was soon followed by seventy-five more Oglalas. Only younger men wanted to continue the struggle. Older men like Red Cloud wanted to give up the fighting as the weather and the lack of food threatened especially the women and children.[233]

Young Man Afraid of His Horse continued to negotiate with the remaining ghost dancers. On January 10, his efforts, together with the cold weather, the lack of food, and the tightening army cordon around the Indians, convinced the ghost dancers to gradually start moving their camp back toward Pine Ridge Agency. Although Kicking Bear and Short Bull, along with some younger men, still objected to coming in, they had no choice but to follow. They could not go anywhere else since the army surrounding them moved at the same pace as they did. Tensions were extremely high all the time. A false move on either side had the potential to precipitate a battle or another panic-stricken flight.[234]

On January 13, a noteworthy event took place in the camp of the ghost dancers. Standing Bear (Mathó Nážį), a progressive leader and the father of Luther Standing Bear, went into the camp and offered a pipe to the ghost dancers. He did not know whether he would be killed or whether the pipe would be accepted. Finally, after much tension, the pipe was accepted. What makes this event significant are its similarities to an event during the war of 1876–77, when George Sword went to Crazy Horse's camp and offered a pipe to his people. The effect that the offering of a pipe had upon the ghost dancers must not be underestimated. Here, as in 1877, a Lakota offered a pipe to other Lakotas. In this act we can see how strong the traditional bonds of Lakota relationship still were. Despite the confusion and the division within the Lakota people, the ghost dancers could not reject the messenger's offer. How much this event affected the decision to surrender cannot be estimated, but it must have had an impact. At the very least it shows that Lakota traditions were still important to both the ghost dancers and the nondancers, to the progressives and the nonprogressives.[235]

The battle at Wounded Knee caused a major exodus of the frightened Lakotas. They escaped and were led by the most influential ghost dance leaders and those chiefs who had only recently abandoned the ghost dance. Even progressives, who had nothing to do with the ghost dance, were ready to fight. Immediately after Wounded Knee it seemed that the Lakotas were forced to be ready for a full-scale war. After a few skirmishes that ended unfavorably for the Lakotas, many considered it impossible to carry on a war against the U.S. Army. Because the ghost dance did not help, the internal division deepened among the Indians in the final camp. The division was so complete that the young men led by Kicking Bear and Short Bull turned against the Oglala chiefs. The influence of Red Cloud as head chief also suffered a blow, and Lakotas even killed one another.

Kicking Bear and Short Bull tried to stay in control until the end, but they were unable to both keep the ghost dancers united and lead a successful war against the army. After Wounded Knee the cause of the ghost dance was hopeless. For many, the belief in it died with Big Foot. In the later stages Kicking Bear and Short Bull were probably very much motivated by the fear of being sent to prison. Whether they still believed in the ghost dance is unknown, but some of their later actions and words reveal that their belief never faded.[236]

The events in the final camp show how far the unity of the ghost dancers had disintegrated. The ghost dance had restored the unity and reinvigorated the traditions of the Lakota people, but these effects proved to be only temporary. Strong leaders who could keep the people united either were dead or their influence had vanished.

On January 15, 1891, the resistance of the ghost dancers ended. A caravan of almost 4,000 Lakotas, 7,000 horses, and 500 wagons marched to Pine Ridge Agency. The formal end of the ghost dance came when Kicking Bear surrendered his weapon to General Miles.[237] Thus ended the year of the ghost dance, which the Lakotas later remembered on their winter counts as Sí Tháka ktépi, the year "Big Foot Was Killed."[238]

TWO

The Indian Agents and the Lakota Ghost Dance

The government-appointed agents for the Lakota reservations were a mixed lot, some of them political appointees with no actual experience of the Indians, others strong and independent men who made good agents but often collided with the Lakota chiefs. From the beginning of the reservation period to the end of the 1880s the agents were constantly at odds with the Indians. Military support was usually close by, but tensions never escalated to open warfare.[1] The agents' daily tasks varied from dealing with civilizing programs, such as education and farming, to issuing rations and trying to find compromises between the progressive and nonprogressive Indians. In addition to all this, the agents were forced to deal with officials in Washington; every little incident, every request for money or other supplies had to be carefully explained and justified. The agents were indeed in a difficult situation; they were expected to carry out the government's programs that were designed to lead the Indians to civilization, but at the same time they were forced to face the realities of reservation life. This dilemma can clearly be seen in their annual reports. Even as the agents were complaining about the daily problems, they tried to convince their superiors that, despite all, the Lakotas were advancing toward civilization.[2]

In addition to these daily issues, land issues caused problems. The Lakotas possessed much more land than they actually needed, at least from the whites' perspective. For this reason the government tried several times to reduce the size of the Great Sioux Reservation (see introduction). To accomplish this, the officials in Washington needed extensive help from the agents. When the reduction was finally carried out in 1889, the government negotiators were long gone, and the agents were left to explain away the commissioners' empty promises. The agents generally agreed that the reduction was justifiable, but the manner in which it was carried out was not satisfactory. The negotiations left the Indians with reduced lands, reduced rations, and reduced faith in the government and its agents. The Lakota agents complained that the negotiations planted the seed for future trouble. The Indians had suffered from lack of food and from disease even before the negotiations began, and the months following the reduction of the reservation only aggravated the situation. But the agents could do nothing to help the Indians.[3]

The situation became so serious during 1889–90 that the agents several times asked Commissioner of Indian Affairs Thomas J. Morgan to help ease the suffering among the Indians. Farming proved impossible once again; the crops were almost a complete failure and the Indians were on the brink of starvation. The cut in beef rations, which was carried out in the wake of the reduction of the Great Sioux Reservation, motivated the agent at Pine Ridge to inform the commissioner, "Our beef allowance for present fiscal year was reduced one million pounds below any previous year, which is working a great hardship among the Indians." The tone of some reports approaches begging: "Considerable distress prevails among the Indians of this agency. . . . I am anxious to learn if it is intended that this deficiency will be made up [so that] I can at once afford some relief." This agent complained rather pathetically, "We have several times been out of flour." In another report he asked, "When will allowance of sugar, bacon, beef, beans and corn be shipped. Please hurry it up."[4]

While the Lakota agents were struggling with these problems they failed to take notice of the rumor of an Indian messiah who was causing excitement among the Lakotas in the fall of 1889. Without the agents' permission the Lakotas sent a delegation to meet with the new messiah. The Lakota agents did not take notice of the ghost dance until late spring 1890, when the commissioner of Indian affairs officially asked for information about the ghost dance excitement among the Lakotas. Secretary of the Interior John W. Noble had received a letter from an alarmed citizen living in Pierre, South Dakota, who believed that the Lakotas were planning an outbreak in the near future. In addition, the newspapers, including the *New York Times*, the *Washington Post*, the *Chicago Tribune*, and the *Omaha Daily Bee*, were already in April reporting a threatened uprising among the Lakotas. Secretary Noble promptly ordered the commissioner of Indian affairs to investigate the matter.[5]

The agent at Pine Ridge Reservation, Hugh D. Gallagher, was the first to respond to the commissioner's request. Gallagher assured him that no danger existed. The Indians on his reservation were all quiet and harbored no plans for an uprising, but he noted that they were somewhat excited by news regarding a "great Medicine Man in the North," who promised to bring about an end to "their primitive condition surrounded by herds of buffalo." The Indians' first meeting on this matter had been held without the agent's permission, and he ordered the Indian police to disperse the meeting, after which three leading men were arrested and given "a good lecture about the silliness of their teachings." What did concern Gallagher was the deplorable condition of the Indians caused by crop failure and the reduction in their beef rations. This, he believed, not the ghost dance, might lead to trouble. Despite this, he did not consider the situation dangerous in any way and thought the excitement would soon die out.[6]

Charles E. McChesney, the agent at Cheyenne River Reservation, replied in a similar manner, denying all rumors of an uprising. From Rosebud Reservation came a somewhat more detailed explanation. Agent J. George Wright also denied all stories suggesting trouble, but reported that there had been excitement and secret communications passing from one reservation to another as early as March 1890. The agent noted that these messages were exchanged between the "disgruntled, dissatisfied, non-progressive Indians, who refused to sign the recent treaty and [who were] at one time recognized as chiefs, representing the older men who cannot accept the new order of things," and who were "jealous of younger men." The agent reported that he was carefully watching the Indians' meetings and had promptly arrested some ringleaders. This had the desired effect, and he expected no further trouble. Very little importance was to be attached to this matter, but Wright suggested that Crow Dog and his followers should be removed from the reservation.[7]

With what seemed to be a growing tendency, Agent James McLaughlin at Standing Rock Reservation replied with a very long letter, the essence of which was that there was absolutely no reason for concern. He had traveled among the Indians for nineteen days and was welcomed everywhere. "Best possible feeling prevailing," wrote the agent, and he emphasized that there were few malcontents on Standing Rock Reservation. These men were discouraging the more progressive element, but in the end the agent believed that only a very few would unite in open resistance. The remedy for any uneasiness, he suggested, was to arrest Sitting Bull and his followers at Standing Rock Reservation, Big Foot at Cheyenne River, Crow Dog at Rosebud, and "many of the same kind" on Pine Ridge Reservation. This would quiet things down and give confidence to the majority of Indians, who were loyal to the government. McLaughlin was confident that his Indian police force would be able to control the reservation. He finished his letter by saying that he had "every confidence in the good intentions of the Sioux as people" and that "they will not be aggressors in any overt act against white settlers, and if *justice* is only done them no uneasiness need be entertained."[8]

The first comments made by the Lakota agents were thus quite calm; for them the rumor of a messiah was no particular threat. They all considered it more or less harmless, or, as Agent Gallagher put it, "silliness." They absolutely denied all rumors that the ghost dance would be the cause of an uprising. There were enough other problems on the reservations without the ghost dance. The agents believed that, if there was going to be an outbreak, it would be caused by hunger and the general feeling of dissatisfaction rather than religious excitement. They were concerned about the non-progressive element causing problems, but that was nothing new and had nothing to do with the ghost dance.

As the summer of 1890 wore on, the Lakota agents were busy with their daily tasks, and the ghost dance seemed to be dying out. In his report in August, however, Gallagher briefly mentioned the ghost dance and noted that there had been some agitation among the Lakotas in the spring. To his surprise, the dance seemed to gain more followers as the summer passed. He wrote, "Strange as it may seem this story [of the messiah] was believed by a large number of Indians and is [to] this day." Still, his and the other agents' reports reveal that during the summer the ghost dance was not a major issue on the Lakota reservations.[9]

In late August, however, the first trouble between the ghost dancers and the agents occurred. Agent Gallagher at Pine Ridge learned that a dance camp of 2,000 Indians was established near White Clay Creek, eighteen miles north of Pine Ridge Agency. He sent a detachment of the reservation Indian police to disperse the dancers, but they were not able to do so. On August 24, Gallagher, accompanied by twenty Indian policemen and Special Agent Elisha B. Reynolds, set out in secrecy to witness the dance. When the company arrived, however, the dance was stopped; to the agent's great surprise, the Indians were expecting them. Instead of 2,000 Indians, as had been reported, Reynolds states that there were approximately 150 lodges and 600 Indians, men, women, and children, in the ghost dance camp. Interestingly, Mooney disregards Reynolds's statement and, relying on the initial estimates given by Gallagher, claims that there were 2,000 ghost dancers in the camp.[10]

Some men, according to Gallagher, were "stripped for fight, with Winchester rifles in hands and cartridge belts around their waists," and were "prepared to do or die in defense of their new faith." The agent exchanged some angry words with the Indians, but the interpreter Phillip Wells realized that the situation was becoming dangerous and advised the agent to use caution. Gallagher then urged the Indians to disperse, since they had no authorization to dance. He assured them that he meant no harm and was there only to

witness the ceremony himself. Surprisingly, the ceremony was resumed, and Reynolds and Gallagher became probably the first white men to witness the ghost dance ceremony among the Lakotas. Agent Gallagher reported four days later: "While nothing serious may result from this *new religion* as it is called by the Indians, I would greatly fear the consequences should there be no restrictions placed upon it." Reynolds fully agreed that measures should be taken to stop the dancing, but noted that it was a religious ceremony that fulfilled the hopes the Indians had cherished for years.[11]

In September the ghost dance spread to Rosebud Reservation, where in the summer Agent J. George Wright had arrested some of the leaders, including Short Bull, who, in fact, had remained quiet for the rest of the summer. In September, however, the agent realized that Short Bull was again preaching. The agent was clear in his view of the ghost dance: it had to be stopped, not because it was going to lead to an outbreak, but because it was "interfering with schools and causing a total neglect of stock"; it caused the Indians to become "completely exhausted physically, morally, and intellectually," making them "reckless and defiant." After a rumor that soldiers had entered the reservation caused a major commotion among the Indians, Wright considered it necessary to act. He ordered all rations to be withheld until the ghost dancing stopped. As a result of this action the excitement subsided and, according to the agent, dancing was confined to only a few of its originators.[12]

But Agent Wright's problems were not over. Special Census Agent A. T. Lea, conducting a census among the Rosebud Indians, filed a report stating that there were more than 2,000 fewer Indians living on Rosebud Reservation than Wright had been drawing rations for. Lea concluded that Wright had sold the excess rations and kept the money for himself. Wright was removed from office, pending charges of corruption. Meanwhile, Special Agent Reynolds arrived from Pine Ridge to take his place. Reynolds was not familiar with the Indians or with the circumstances on Rosebud Reservation, which enabled the ghost dancers to resume their ceremonies.[13]

Rosebud was not the only Lakota reservation where a new man took charge. The term for Agents Hugh D. Gallagher and Charles E. McChesney, both Democrats, was over. These men were relatively able as Indian agents, but the Republican administration wanted to replace them with their own appointees. The commissioner of Indian affairs was, in fact, very critical of Agent Gallagher, complaining that he was not up to the standards of an Indian agent. Still, he emphasized that Gallagher's removal was not his decision; the orders came from the president, and his decision was a part of the so-called spoils system and the new home rule, which allowed the governor of each state to appoint Indian agents for the reservations located in his state.[14] Finally, only James McLaughlin at Standing Rock was allowed to remain in charge of his reservation. The new agent for Pine Ridge was a small-town Dakota politician, Daniel F. Royer, a man totally unfamiliar with Indian affairs and who did not want to become an agent in the first place.[15] Perain P.

Palmer took charge of Cheyenne River Reservation. The change could not have occurred at a more unfortunate time. The new agents did not know how to deal with the growing ghost dance excitement.[16]

Although ghost dancing was in progress on Pine Ridge, Rosebud, and Cheyenne River Reservations in October 1890, the new agent on Cheyenne River was at first unaware that ghost dances were being held on his reservation. The ghost dance leader, Kicking Bear, arrived at Cheyenne River in mid-September, and the camps of Hump and Big Foot on this reservation became centers for the new religion. Their camps were located far away from the agency, which made it difficult for the agent to act. When finally learning about the ghost dances, Agent Palmer repeatedly sent his Indian police to stop them. The police, however, were not able to do anything; instead, many of them resigned their jobs and joined the ghost dancers. On October 11, Palmer informed the commissioner of Indian affairs that Big Foot and his band were growing very agitated over the coming of the messiah. He reported that the Indians, armed with Winchester rifles, were growing hostile.[17] This was the first time Big Foot's alleged hostile intentions received the agent's attention. Two months later Maj. Gen. Nelson A. Miles took up the idea, declaring that Big Foot was the most defiant and hostile of the ghost dance leaders.[18]

A couple of weeks later, however, on October 29, Agent Palmer wrote that Big Foot was at the agency and was very friendly, talking freely about his concerns. He told the agent that the whites too had been waiting for a messiah many times and were always disappointed, and it would be so with the Indians. Hump, on the other hand, appeared quiet and sullen. He complained that he had lost influence by signing the 1889 agreement, and as a result of this resigned his job as a policeman and joined the ghost dancers. The agent wrote that Hump was by far the most dangerous character on Cheyenne River Reservation. He wrote to the commissioner that by removing Hump from the reservation, all problems would be resolved.[19]

By early October the ghost dance was introduced at Standing Rock Reservation. Sitting Bull invited Kicking Bear to his camp on Grand River; he arrived on October 9. Agent McLaughlin was quick to blame Sitting Bull for taking up the doctrine and becoming "the high priest and leading apostle of this latest Indian absurdity." Already on October 1, McLaughlin had suggested to the commissioner of Indian affairs that all demoralizing Indian dances should be stopped. At that time, however, the ghost dance was not a problem at Standing Rock Reservation. Only a few days later McLaughlin learned about Kicking Bear's presence in Sitting Bull's camp. This made the agent furious; he ordered his Indian police to go to Sitting Bull's camp and escort Kicking Bear off the reservation. Once again the policemen failed to perform their duty. They came back in a "dazed condition," McLaughlin reported. A second police detachment finally succeeded in escorting Kicking Bear off the reservation on October 15. This, according to McLaughlin, showed that the Indian police were brave enough to maintain order on the reservation. For McLaughlin, however, the damage was done; ghost dancing had started on Standing Rock Reservation, and the idea of Sitting Bull being a leader of a forbidden ceremony was difficult for him to accept.[20]

In a long letter to the commissioner Agent McLaughlin launched his assault on Sitting Bull and the ghost dance. In it he referred to his letter of June 18, in which he had suggested Sitting Bull's arrest. Now, in October, Sitting Bull was still at large and heading the most nonprogressive element on the reservation. McLaughlin asserted that, if Sitting Bull had been removed, there would have been no sign of the ghost dance on Standing Rock. He blamed Sitting Bull for all the trouble and described him in words that clearly reveal his personal hatred toward him: "worthless," "coward," "liar," "a man of low cunning," and "devoid [of] all noble traits of character." According to the agent, Sitting Bull was a "man of low-cunning, devoid of a single manly principle in his nature, or an honorable trait of character. . . . [He is] a coward and lacks moral courage." Indeed, McLaughlin and Sitting Bull had not gotten along from the beginning. After meeting Sitting Bull for the first time in 1881, McLaughlin described him as "a stocky man with an evil face and shifty eyes." Their relationship remained tense throughout the 1880s. Even long after Sitting Bull's death McLaughlin kept blaming and accusing him. In his letter to, among others, Herbert Welsh of the Indian Rights Association on January 12, 1891, he blamed Sitting Bull for open rebellion and for misleading the Indians. In his memoirs, *My Friend the Indian*, McLaughlin described Sitting Bull very negatively: "Crafty, avaricious, mendacious and ambitious, Sitting Bull possessed all of the faults of an Indian and none of the attributes which have gone far to redeem some of his people from their deeds of guilt." It is remarkable that McLaughlin focused so much attention on Sitting Bull's actions if he really considered him to be a man of low cunning. It is also remarkable that a man who presumably had so little ability could have so much influence among the Lakotas. In the end McLaughlin had to admit that Sitting Bull was "by far the most influential man of his nation for many years."[21]

In October, however, McLaughlin's major problem was Sitting Bull's relationship to the ghost dance. McLaughlin was convinced that Sitting Bull was the "high priest and apostle" of this new religion and was using the ghost dance to promote his own leadership, which, according to the agent, was diminishing among the Indians. "Like a drowning man grasping at a straw [he] is working upon the credulity of the superstitious and ignorant Indians and reaping a rich harvest of popularity," McLaughlin wrote. War, he believed, was on Sitting Bull's mind, convincing evidence for which was the report that Sitting Bull had broken his peace pipe. McLaughlin quickly ordered the ghost dancing to be stopped and called for Sitting Bull to come to the agency for a talk. Sitting Bull refused. The agent sent several detachments of Indian police to Sitting Bull's camp to enforce his orders. Despite this, the dancing continued. McLaughlin again suggested to the commissioner that Sitting Bull be removed from the reservation. After that, an end could be put to the dance, which he deemed "demoralizing, indecent, and disgusting."[22]

Thus by late October the ghost dance had spread to all of the major Lakota reservations. All the agents, old and new, condemned it as immoral and dangerous. They did not, however, consider the ghost dance dangerous in a military sense. They did not believe that it would lead to an uprising. Special Agent Reynolds and Agent Gallagher even called it a religious rite, and Agent McLaughlin considered it dangerous only in the sense that Sitting Bull was leading it on Standing Rock Reservation. For the Lakota agents the ghost dance at this time was dangerous because it excited the Indians and thus interfered with daily reservation routines. Schools, churches, and farms were left unattended and the Lakotas' advancement in civilization came to a halt.

Agent Royer at Pine Ridge summarized the agents' concerns by saying that unless the ghost dancing, which was "the most heathenish practice," was stopped, the Indians would "go backwards until they reach the savage mark of the sixties." That was the agents' real concern in September and October, but their emphasis was about to change.[23]

The Question of Control

Agent Daniel F. Royer assumed charge of Pine Ridge Reservation in October 1890. Quite soon after his arrival he informed his superiors at the Office of Indian Affairs that, because of the present disturbance, he was not able to perform the duties he was sent there to do. He complained that his job was to lead the Indians ahead in civilization, but under the present circumstances there was no way of doing that. "They are tearing down more in a day than the government can build up in a month," he wrote. The agent got some relief for his concerns from General Miles, who visited the reservation on October 28 and negotiated with the Indians as well as with Royer. The agent, however, was not fully convinced by the general's assurances that the excitement was dying out.[24]

On October 30, Royer complained that half or even as many as two-thirds of the reservation Indian population supported the ghost dance and were thus beyond control (for comparison, see the table in chapter 1). The agent complained that the ghost dancers defied the law, threatened the police, took children out of schools, and harbored wanted criminals. He listed Red Cloud, Little Wound, and Big Road as the main leaders, although he reported that Red Cloud's role was to encourage the ghost dancers rather than to lead them. Little Wound, according to the agent, was the most difficult person to deal with. He allegedly urged all the Lakotas to join the ghost dancers and to "be Indians again." He told the agent that they would not stop dancing in any case. Royer tried to use the "friendly" leaders, American Horse and Young Man Afraid of His Horse, against the ghost dance, but to no avail. Even these influential men could not stop the ghost dances. Royer saw only one option: military intervention. This was the first time any of the Lakota agents asked for military protection against the ghost dancers.[25]

At Rosebud, Agent Reynolds took a similar tone in a letter to the commissioner on November 2. Three weeks earlier, he reported, the ghost dance was thought to be abandoned, but it had since then gained new adherents. The ghost dancers were becoming more threatening and defiant. They were openly killing cattle, saying that they were given them by the Great Father (the president), so they could do whatever they pleased with them. The policemen, who were sent to arrest those who killed cattle, were forced to withdraw. The agent feared the policemen would lose their lives in the process. The ghost dancers were thus beyond the control of the police, and Reynolds thought that an outbreak was imminent. He noted that the ghost dancers' actions were partly due to the lack of food; the ghost dance was "religious excitement aggravated by almost starvation," he wrote, and "the Indians say better to die fighting than to die a slow death of starvation." He believed that the Indians were clearly more in favor of war now than before. As evidence of this he mentioned that he had received several reports indicating that the Indians were trading their belongings for ammunition. Furthermore, the ghost dancers were no longer afraid of being killed, since their new religion promised that everyone would be resurrected in the near future. Realizing this state of affairs the agent decided to call for troops.[26]

Meanwhile, at Pine Ridge Royer was growing more and more concerned. On November 8, he reported that there were four major ghost dance camps on his reservation. Six hundred people were dancing in a camp at White Clay Creek, he wrote, not far from the agency. At Wounded Knee Creek 250, at Porcupine Creek 130, and at Medicine Root Creek 300 Indians were regularly participating in the ghost dances. Thus altogether almost 1,300 Indians were engaged in these ceremonies, and the agent believed that they were all very hostile and out of control. Little Wound was again singled out as the leader of the ghost dancers. According to the agent, Little Wound was the most "stubborn, head-strong, self willed, unruly Indian on the reservation." Kicking Bear was the other one who caused major concern for the agent. These two men, he wrote, kept exciting the others, who grew more boisterous every day. The condition of things was such, according to Royer, that it was going to "render this administration a failure."[27] Only a week earlier Royer claimed that 50 percent of the reservation population, approximately 2,500 Indians, were participating in the ghost dance ceremonies; now he was able to count only 1,300. Nonetheless, he believed that the situation was going from bad to worse and he was absolutely powerless to enforce his orders. Troops were needed to stop "this most outrageous practice." "We have no protection and are at the mercy of these crazy dancers," he wrote on November 12.[28]

His request was probably triggered by a minor incident that took place on November 11, when the Indian policemen were ordered to arrest a man accused of killing cattle. Tensions were extremely high, and violence was narrowly avoided (see chapter 1). The policemen, however, were not able to arrest the offender. The agency physician, a full-blood Santee Sioux, Charles A. Eastman, later described how this incident affected the agent. Royer summoned some of the chiefs, policemen, Dr. Eastman, and Special Agent James A. Cooper, who was sent to Pine Ridge to assist Royer, to the agency building and frantically asked for their advice. Despite all their efforts to calm him, Royer was certain that the incident had been planned by the ghost dancers from the beginning. While others tried to convince him that intervention by the army would only worsen the situation, he ignored their warnings and called for troops.[29] In the wake of this scare, Royer asked both the commissioner and the acting commissioner of Indian affairs for permission to come to Washington to explain things in person: "Please grant me authority to come at once," he begged. He promised that during his absence no trouble would occur at Pine Ridge; the Indians would remain quiet. His request was denied.[30]

Three days later, on November 15, Royer sent another frantic telegram to Acting Commissioner of Indians Affairs R. V. Belt. This telegram has become a standard quotation in almost every study of the ghost dance, since it has been seen as the final appeal that prompted military action. "Indians are dancing in the snow and are wild and crazy. I have fully informed you that employees and government property at this agency have no protection and are at the mercy of these dancers. Why delay further by investigation, we need protection and we need it now."[31]

In fact, this appeal was unnecessary. President Benjamin Harrison had already, on November 13, directed the military to assume full responsibility for the ghost-dancing Lakotas.[32]

Agent Royer has often been accused of being the major cause of the decision to send the military to the Lakota reservations. Indeed, his appeals for help were by far the most alarming and frantic, but Agent Palmer on Cheyenne River Reservation and Agent Reynolds on Rosebud Reservation also contributed significantly to the general scare that prompted the military action. In the beginning of November both agents were still sending relatively mild letters to their superiors, but, at about the same time as Royer was growing more scared the tone in the reports by Palmer and Reynolds also changed. Palmer especially exhibited concern. He reported that the Indians were trading cattle for guns and ammunition. He also complained that Indians from other reservations were coming to Cheyenne River, where they together planned an outbreak. He reported that the Indians were being very bold in their replies to the agent's request to stop dancing. When he told them that the government was displeased with them, they replied that they were displeased with the government, and would continue to dance. This, the agent thought, was the ultimate defiance; he even labeled the ghost dancers "hostiles." Reynolds was concerned about the killing of cattle and about the fact that several hundred Indians were heading from Rosebud toward Pine Ridge. Both Reynolds and Palmer listed several of the ghost dance leaders, recommending that they be arrested as soon as possible.[33]

All those repeated pleas for help, together with the alarming newspaper accounts, prompted President Benjamin Harrison to act.[34] Consequently, on November 20, the military arrived at the Pine Ridge and Rosebud Reservations. Before that, however, one peculiar event took place. When Agent Royer was denied permission to visit Washington he decided to leave Pine Ridge without permission. On November 17, he packed his belongings, left his clerk in charge of the reservation, and headed to the town of Rushville, Nebraska. There he stayed until the troops arrived, and then returned to the reservation under military protection. He claimed that he wanted to meet the troops in advance to explain the situation, but his actions seem more like an escape out of fear that his life was threatened. Supported by Special Agent Cooper, who joined him on his trip to Rushville, Royer later denied that he had left his post out of fear. Cooper first stated that Royer never left his post, but later emphasized that it was necessary for him to leave. Brig. Gen. John R. Brooke, in command of the arriving troops, later reported that Royer had gone to Rushville at Brooke's request. Whatever the truth, Royer's rush to Rushville made headlines in the newspapers, and, at least in the public eye, it appeared that he was not in control of either his nerves or his reservation.[35]

Agent Royer's growing fear can be traced to the incident on November 11, but the other agents' rapid change in attitude is not so easily explained. It seems that nothing more alarming or serious took place on either Cheyenne River or Rosebud Reservations than what had been going on for the past few months. Still, by November the two agents had joined Royer's pleas for military help. Perhaps repeated minor incidents exhausted their patience, or perhaps, inexperienced as they were, they simply could not deal with the situation. The latter possibility is supported by the actions of the experienced James McLaughlin at Standing Rock Reservation. He did not call for troops; on the contrary, he wanted to deal with the situation himself.

On Standing Rock Reservation McLaughlin's view of military intervention was the antithesis of those of his colleagues on the other Lakota reservations. From the beginning, he emphasized that the danger lay in Sitting Bull, not in the ghost dance. McLaughlin disapproved of the ghost dance, of course, but for him there was only one problem on the reservation: Sitting Bull. It is noteworthy that, while the other agents were clamoring for troops, McLaughlin's views did not change at any stage in favor of military intervention. In fact, all through November he kept assuring both his superiors and the general public that there was absolutely no danger of an uprising. He personally wrote to some citizens who were concerned about the situation. He also gave interviews to the newspapers, although he later claimed that the newspapers distorted the reports concerning his reservation. In all these letters and interviews he laid full blame for the restlessness on Sitting Bull. He continued to insist that, if Sitting Bull were arrested, no trouble would occur on Standing Rock. His major point, however, was that he could take care of the situation by himself, with the help of his Indian police force.[36]

Agent McLaughlin's correspondence during November and early December clearly shows that he approached the ghost dance purely through Sitting Bull's persona. He seemed obsessed with Sitting Bull and the idea of getting rid of him. He repeatedly stressed that the ghost dancing was confined to approximately 450 people, all connected to Sitting Bull's immediate following (for comparison, see the table in chapter 1). In this sense, as McLaughlin insisted, he seemed to have his reservation under relatively good control. He did not want or need any troops to aid him; he was convinced that he knew better than anyone how to deal with the Indians on his reservation. He assured the commissioner of Indian affairs in several communications that he would be able to arrest Sitting Bull when the time was right. Military intervention, he believed, would only lead to bloodshed.[37]

Despite his obvious personal dislike, McLaughlin tried to convince Sitting Bull that it would be best for him and his people to stop the ghost dances. On November 16 he visited Sitting Bull's camp and talked with him at length. He became convinced that Sitting Bull did not "fully believe in what he was professing and endeavoring so hard to make others believe." McLaughlin thought that Sitting Bull's proposition that they go together to the West to see the Messiah to learn whether or not his teachings were true was sufficient evidence of his disbelief. He had long discussions with many of the Indians and was convinced that his talk had a good effect on them. Even Sitting Bull said that his reasoning was good and that he believed McLaughlin "was a friend to the Indians as people," though McLaughlin did "not like him personally."[38]

This visit to Sitting Bull's camp further strengthened the agent's belief that he would be able to restrict the ghost dancers to a few of Sitting Bull's followers, and that he would eventually be able to arrest Sitting Bull. Following his talk with the chief, McLaughlin reported that many Indians had abandoned the ghost dance. On November 21, he again wrote that Sitting Bull and fifty other malcontents should be removed from the reservation before spring. At present, however, there was no need for arrests; everything was quiet. The agent also remarked that the press was exaggerating the situation and accusing him of losing control. He had not lost control, he assured his superiors.[39] Indeed, being in control seemed to be the agent's main concern.

That control was threatened when William F. Cody (Buffalo Bill) arrived at Standing Rock on November 28. Cody was sent by General Miles to discuss matters with his old friend Sitting Bull and to persuade him to abandon the ghost dance; failing this, he was authorized to arrest Sitting Bull. This infuriated McLaughlin, who immediately asked for permission to stop Buffalo Bill's mission. He did not share Miles's opinion that Buffalo Bill's friendship with Sitting Bull would have an effect on him. McLaughlin once again expressed his view that any interference in matters at Standing Rock would lead to trouble. He also stated that the time was not right for an arrest; he wanted to wait until the weather got colder, which would calm the ghost dancers. He wrote to the commissioner, "Few Indians still dancing, but [this] does not mean mischief at present. . . . I have matters well in hand, when [the] proper time arrives [I] can arrest Sitting Bull by Indian police without bloodshed." His requests were agreed to, and President Harrison ordered Buffalo Bill to turn back. With some nice maneuvering, McLaughlin managed to prevent Buffalo Bill from even meeting with Sitting Bull. Thus McLaughlin won the first round in the battle against the military and General Miles for control of Standing Rock Reservation.[40]

The matter of arresting Sitting Bull was not over, however. In early December Secretary of the Interior John W. Noble, under instructions from the president, informed the agents that arrests were to be made, but only after great consideration was taken, and bloodshed was to be avoided. Furthermore, the agents were not to act on their own; they were to follow the orders and instructions given by army officers, ultimately those of General Miles.[41]

The events following this message up to the tragic death of Sitting Bull have been well explored and will not be repeated here in detail. Some points, however, are worth mentioning. When he received orders to follow military instructions, Agent McLaughlin, instead of dropping the idea of using his own police force in Sitting Bull's upcoming arrest, managed to talk Lt. Col. William F. Drum, the commanding officer at Fort Yates, into following his suggestions. Thus a plan was made to use the Indian police as the arresting force and to have the army units only as a backup. The arrest was planned for December 20, but according to McLaughlin's reports, which were actually submitted after Sitting Bull's death, by December 14 he had already heard rumors that Sitting Bull planned to leave the reservation. The arrest was therefore moved to an earlier date, December 15. To conduct the arrest, McLaughlin put together a police force of more than forty men, some of them Sitting Bull's enemies and many of them Yanktonai Sioux.[42]

When the arrest failed and resulted in the killing of Sitting Bull on December 15, 1890, McLaughlin blamed the chief for his fate. According to the agent, all accusations made in the press against the agent's actions were false. There was no one to blame but Sitting Bull himself. When the police entered Sitting Bull's cabin, he initially agreed to go with them, but then changed his mind, and when outside the cabin, assisted by his followers, tried to escape. The agent wrote that the Indian policemen fired only when fired upon; they acted bravely under very trying circumstances and remained loyal to the government. McLaughlin further noted that there was no doubt that Sitting Bull had been planning to leave the reservation in order to join the Pine Ridge ghost dancers. This made the attempted arrest not only necessary but justifiable. It is noteworthy, however, that prior to Sitting Bull's death, McLaughlin made no mention to his superiors of Sitting Bull's plan to leave the reservation. In fact, on December 6, he assured Brig. Gen. Thomas Ruger that "Sitting Bull can be kept on reserve by Indian police without fear of escape." Only after Sitting Bull's death did the agent claim that he was planning to leave the reservation and that he was "in open rebellion against constituted authority and deluding the more ignorant Indians into the Messiah Craze and firing their minds against the government and all whites."[43]

Despite organizing the arrest practically on his own, McLaughlin claimed that Sitting Bull's arrest had been ordered by General Miles. That was indeed the case, but the orders were that the military, under Colonel Drum's command, was to conduct the arrest.[44] In fact, on December 1, Acting Commissioner of Indian Affairs R. V. Belt ordered McLaughlin to "co-operate and fully obey the orders of the military officers." In a second telegram on December 5 he ordered the agent to "make no arrests whatever except under orders of the military or upon order from the Secretary of the Interior." Thus McLaughlin disobeyed the direct order that came from his superiors and ultimately from the president.[45]

This, of course, was not McLaughlin's view of the matter. Immediately following Sitting Bull's death Secretary Noble demanded that the agent explain who authorized him to arrest Sitting Bull. In his reply, McLaughlin again explained that the orders came from General Miles, and that he had only cooperated with the army. The plan to arrest Sitting Bull was made jointly with Colonel Drum, so the agent claimed that he had only done what he was asked to do.[46]

Quite soon after Sitting Bull's death the press accused McLaughlin of planning his assassination. Even Congress reacted, ordering a thorough investigation into the matter.[47] Agent McLaughlin's decisions and actions have long puzzled historians. The circumstances certainly leave room for speculation. As early as 1891 the historian Willis Fletcher Johnson put these speculations into words: "There was a quiet understanding between the officers of the Indian and Military departments that it would be impossible to bring Sitting Bull to Standing Rock [agency] alive. . . . Under arrest he would still be a source of great annoyance, and his followers would continue their dances and threats. . . . There was, therefore, a complete understanding . . . that the slightest attempt to rescue the old medicine man should be a signal to send Sitting Bull to the happy hunting grounds."[48] Sitting Bull's followers, at least, concurred with this view. Some of them later told an army officer that "at Standing Rock all they [the whites] thought of was to . . . kill Sitting Bull."[49]

Be that as it may, it is certainly true that McLaughlin wanted to get rid of Sitting Bull, though we may never know whether he actually wanted him dead. No evidence of this exists. Some of his actions, however, such as the selection of the policemen, suggest that he hoped death would be the result. As an experienced agent, he surely knew that Sitting Bull, a Hunkpapa medicine man and leader, would find it difficult to surrender to policemen, especially to those who were Yanktonai Sioux. Furthermore, in a message to Bull Head, the leader of the police force, McLaughlin wrote only one day before the arrest, "You must not let him escape under any circumstances."[50] We can only guess how Bull Head, a known enemy of Sitting Bull, interpreted these orders.

Agent McLaughlin had all along assured his superiors that by using the Indian police, bloodshed would be avoided. He said that he had insisted on this because he wanted to show that he was being consistent in his policies for running the reservation, and that he wanted to put it on record that he never asked for the military. As late as February 1891, when Sitting Bull was already dead and the military had assumed control of the Lakota reservations, McLaughlin continued to declare that he could control his reservation. He did not want the military there. He wrote to the commissioner of Indian affairs on February 4, 1891, "In the future, as in the past, I feel fully competent to manage this reservation and agency without interference of any supervising power."[51]

Whether his policy was that of consistency or stubbornness taken to extremes is impossible to say. One person who still was not completely satisfied was Secretary Noble, who, after reading McLaughlin's report on Sitting Bull's death, wrote to the commissioner of Indian affairs, "Agent McLaughlin is so proud of his exploit that he rather suppresses the source of his action. But it is necessary that it be shown and understood that this was the act of *Military, without qualification*." Secretary Noble seems to have thought that Agent McLaughlin not only was acting on his own, but was tarnishing the reputation of both the Office of Indian Affairs and the Interior Department.[52]

It seems quite certain that for McLaughlin the ghost dance, although to be condemned and stopped, was not his major concern. The major concern, as it had been for almost a decade, was Sitting Bull. It is of interest that McLaughlin had complained already in an October 17 letter to the commissioner of Indian affairs that Sitting Bull was "such an abject coward that he will not commit any overt act at open offense himself" that would allow the agent to demand his arrest.[53] When Sitting Bull became the leader of the ghost dancing faction at Standing Rock, the agent got exactly what he wanted: an excuse to get him out of the way. Thus it can safely be said that Sitting Bull's death was more closely related to the power struggle on Standing Rock Reservation than to the ghost dance; it was all about control.

Cooperation and Complaints

Other Lakota agents welcomed the military's arrival. On Pine Ridge, however, Special Agent Cooper, assisted by Agent Royer, continued to send confusing messages to the Office of Indian Affairs. In the days following the military's arrival both men reported that the ghost dancers were assuming a hostile attitude and were preparing for a fight. "Serious trouble seems inevitable," Cooper wrote on November 22, but two days later he reported that the turmoil was subsiding and the military's presence was having a calming effect.

He blamed the newspapers for spreading exaggerated and false reports, but it seems likely that he himself was equally culpable of believing the same rumors on which the newspapers based many of their stories.[54]

On November 22, Cooper received a telegram from Special Agent Lea, who had witnessed a ghost dance ceremony a few days earlier on Pine Ridge. In his telegram Lea described the dancers as extremely hostile and ready to take to the warpath. They want to see the white men dead, Lea wrote: "They say they are going on a big hunt as soon as grass comes next spring, and that means warpath." This message obviously affected Cooper, who forwarded the information to the acting commissioner of Indian affairs and on November 28 reported that the hostile Indians were "riding their horses in a circle, a custom denoting war in past years." In his and Royer's opinion, some arrests should be made immediately. They listed sixty-six men who were to be imprisoned. There could be even more, Royer believed, but those sixty-six would do as a start.[55]

Both Cooper and Royer thought that the arrests should be made before December, since by November 24 most of the Indians would be at the agency for rations. They believed that it would be easy to arrest the main leaders and to disarm the rest. Military officers did not agree; they knew that disarming several hundred Lakota men would not be an easy task, especially since the officers believed that the Indians were very well armed.[56] Moreover, the agents reported that most of the Indians, even the ghost dancers, were camped close to the agency. The agents were also very concerned that a party of several hundred Brulés who arrived from Rosebud Reservation were committing depredations and were reportedly very hostile. They were dancing the ghost dances throughout the night only twenty miles from the agency. Despite this, the agents also reported that the presence of the military had "brought the ghost dances to a sudden stop" at Pine Ridge. The Brulés, or "lawless parties," as the agents called them, were also to be disarmed and arrested. The agents even wrote in a tone of complaint that General Brooke had been notified of the situation and that he should do something about it. The army's inaction obviously began to rankle the agents.[57]

The agents were not the only ones who complained about the army's decision to wait and see. The white population living close to the reservations and the newspaper correspondents shared the agents' eagerness to see some action. The Nebraska Militia, consisting of volunteers, was called on duty, and the settlers were organizing their own militia; both were prepared to attack the Indians.[58]

While listing the ghost dance leaders who should be arrested, Agent Royer exonerated Red Cloud from all accusations made against him. Royer commented on November 25 that although it was generally assumed that Red Cloud had sided with the ghost dancers, "I am not in possession of any evidence that goes to show that he is connected with the ghost dance, and since taking charge he has given me no trouble of any character."[59]

During the early part of December Royer and Cooper continued to be very dissatisfied with how things were shaping up. They repeatedly wrote about depredations and reported that after receiving reinforcements from Rosebud the ghost dancers' fighting force on Pine Ridge had grown to 1,000 warriors. These Indians, they believed, were very hostile; the only remedy they could think of was to round them up, arrest them, and send the Rosebud Indians back to their own reservation. To the agents' annoyance, General Brooke did not concur. The agents promised to leave the decision concerning the use of force to the military officers. They further complained that there was no order on the reservation: the day schools were all closed, the white employees and "friendly" Indians were forced to come to the agency for safety, and the "friendly" Indians had lost all their property in the depredations committed by the ghost dancers.[60]

Meanwhile, Agent Reynolds, in charge of Rosebud Reservation, reported that everything was quiet. Indeed, the majority of the Rosebud ghost dancers had gone to Pine Ridge. The agent reported that his Indian police force was watching Short Bull, who despite this managed to leave for Pine Ridge. Other than that, there was no cause for concern. The Indian scare, as the agent put it, would be settled soon: "It is my judgment, that within the next ten days the greater portion of the Indians now led astray by their leaders, will see the absolute folly of further resistance and return to their homes and to obedience to the powers that be." He was convinced that the schools would soon be reopened and the teachers would return to their jobs.[61]

In fact, Reynolds did not blame the Indians for the current trouble; he blamed the press and other irresponsible (white) people for exaggeration and falsification. Reynolds complained to the commissioner of Indian affairs, "About two thirds of all the reports in the daily papers about the state of affairs on the reservation, especially from Pine Ridge, is the most stupendous rot ever printed and if the Department had some way of suppressing it, it would be God's blessing." He continued, "It is well calculated to alarm the friends and relatives of those who are here in control and prejudice unjustly the public against the whole body of Indians and thus cripple future efforts for their civilization and development." The problem for Reynolds, however, was soon to be over; Agent J. George Wright, who, it will be recalled, was accused of pocketing money from extra rations, was reinstated on December 1, 1890, when the investigation failed to uncover any misconduct on his part.[62]

Wright concurred with Reynolds. Only a day after his arrival at Rosebud he informed the commissioner that everything was quiet; the Indians who remained on the reservation were "well disposed" and ready to go to work. He also commented on the people who left for Pine Ridge, saying that, since they were destroying property and disobeying orders, their leaders should be arrested. Otherwise, life on Rosebud would soon return to normal. This included an increase in rations, which would be carried out as soon as the ghost dance leaders were arrested.[63]

Three days later, on December 5, Wright further explained to the commissioner his views on the ghost dance excitement. The ghost dance had started on Rosebud in September, but the Indians did not plan to harm anybody. "No violence of any kind was contemplated nor arms carried," the agent wrote. He went on to say that nonprogressive leaders like Two Strike and Crow Dog took up the ghost dance mainly because they felt that their influence was diminishing, and they wanted to get some recognition from the government. Short Bull, he said, was neither a troublemaker nor aggressive; in fact, the agent believed that Short Bull was used by others for their own purposes. The ghost dance, however, had to be stopped since it was causing "excitement and physical prostration and attracting the Indians from other camps, abandoning their stock and homes, taking away the children from school and having a demoralizing effect generally." According to Wright there was no longer need for the military on Rosebud Reservation.[64]

In fact, Wright believed that it was the sudden appearance of the troops on November 20 that caused the exodus of approximately 1,100 Indians to Pine Ridge. They had previously asked for permission to go to Pine Ridge but were denied and told that those who did leave would be punished. Despite this, and purely out of fear of the army, they finally fled, the agent wrote. Furthermore, a few hundred Indians who lived in the borderlands between Pine Ridge and Rosebud joined the fleeing ghost dancers. Together these two groups numbered approximately 1,800 people. These people from the borderlands, the agent noted, where not ghost dancers at all, and by December many of them were willing to return, but Wright believed that because they had committed depredations en route to Pine Ridge they were afraid to return. "All Indians remaining at the agency [are] quiet and will remain so," he wrote. They were afraid of the army and asked for protection. Military presence, Wright believed, would become necessary only when those who went to Pine Ridge returned. He did not expect any trouble at Rosebud, but suggested that it would not be wise to disarm the Indians. The Indians at the agency did not buy their guns for any "evil purposes." This made disarmament completely unnecessary. The Indians, as well as the agent, wanted a return to normality; at first the increased rations would restore confidence, then eventually the Indians could leave the agency and go to their homes, where they could resume their work, care for their stock, and send their children to school.[65]

On Cheyenne River Reservation Agent Palmer was much more concerned than Agents Reynolds and Wright on Rosebud. On November 28, he briefly stated that he had visited several ghost dance camps. He wrote to the commissioner of Indian affairs that the ghost dancers refused to talk to him and their "temper was very bad." According to the agent, Big Foot was urging everyone to buy guns and to stay in one big camp for safety. The Indians were "very disobedient and do not respect any order or regulation."[66]

On December 1, Palmer described at length his visit to the ghost dance camps, which were located at Cherry Creek, approximately sixty miles from the agency, on the Cheyenne River. The agent took every precaution to arrive secretly at the Indian camps, but the Indians were prepared for his arrival and stopped dancing. Palmer concluded that many had gone home when they learned about his visit. However, he found 348 Indians who had been dancing day and night for six consecutive days. In addition, there were 200 onlookers. The information the agent gathered on this trip convinced him that the ghost dancers were well armed with "the best make of guns, revolvers and cartridges," sold to them by white traders. He also complained that none of the ghost dancers had worn citizen's clothes, that is, white man's clothes, in more than a month.[67] He believed that the ghost dancers were preparing for a fight and were planning for "an outbreak of some sort." Big Foot and Hump should be arrested.[68]

By December 9, however, Palmer had come to a different conclusion: "I apprehend no great trouble in stopping the dance at Cherry Creek," he wrote. Since Hump had abandoned the ghost dance, the only concern was Big Foot. But the agent believed that not even Big Foot would cause major trouble, since there were only about 200 people in his camp.[69] More and more were abandoning the ghost dance after becoming convinced that it was only a "delusion," as Palmer put it. Many had been dancing out of curiosity, but were now listening to the Christian Indians, who were doing good service for the government. Agent Palmer was so delighted over the developments in the past days that he was "hoping soon to be able to report the dancing at this agency entirely ended."[70] Ghost dancing on Cheyenne River was indeed coming to its end, but not in the manner the agent envisioned.

By December 15, things seemed to be quieting down on all four Lakota reservations. Agent McLaughlin continued to insist that everything was under control on Standing Rock Reservation. Agent Wright on Rosebud was reporting that everything was quiet there. On Pine Ridge, despite some ongoing depredations, things seemed to be relatively calm, and on Cheyenne River Agent Palmer hoped to settle the issue of ghost dancing in the near future. Then came the news of Sitting Bull's death.[71]

The refugees from Standing Rock arrived at Cheyenne River during the days following Sitting Bull's death. Agent Palmer's initial response was great concern; the refugees had gone to Big Foot's camp, among others, and the agent worried about the effect their arrival might have on the ghost dancers. Dancing was continuing in Big Foot's camp, and he even refused to come to the agency for rations. Palmer reported that the Standing Rock Indians were fleeing from the troops and were scared, but he would try to send them back to their own reservation. Despite his concerns, the agent did not expect any trouble. He was in daily communication with all the camps on the reservation and was concerned only about Big Foot. He even believed that many Christian Indians were happy about Sitting Bull's death.[72]

On December 22, Agent Palmer reported that 400 ghost dancers from the Cherry Creek camp were coming to the agency. Big Foot, however, was not among them, but fifty families of the Standing Rock people were willing to come in. After this, the agent believed, Big Foot would have only about fifty men with him. All the Indians who arrived at Cheyenne River Agency gave up their arms willingly. The agent informed the commissioner of Indian affairs that no Indians were absent from his reservation, rations were issued to those at the agency, and everything seemed to be peaceful. The agent's positive expectations were rewarded when he learned that Big Foot had surrendered to the military.[73]

That day, December 22, did not end as happily as Palmer anticipated. Big Foot surrendered, but then he escaped. The agent was as astonished as everybody else, but believed that Big Foot had planned his escape before he surrendered. However, in his annual report to the commissioner of Indian affairs on August 17, 1891, Palmer contradicted himself by writing that it was not probable that Big Foot had any hostile plans when he left for Pine Ridge. He also noted that the ghost dance was not alone to be blamed for the trouble; the circumstances on the reservations were equally responsible. "The Indians alone have been the sufferers so far as relates to this reserve," the agent wrote, and he further noted that all reports of Indians committing depredations on Cheyenne River Reservation were without foundation. In fact, he believed that white men had carried out these depredations. After Big Foot's disappearance the remaining Indians on the reservation gathered at the agency, and Palmer was able to report that they were willing to obey orders. The Indians planned to stay at the agency until Big Foot was "in some way taken care of." The majority actually stayed there until mid-January 1891, when all trouble was settled. In his annual report, Palmer wrote that the majority of Indians remained loyal to the government and that their assistance proved the key to a peaceful settlement on Cheyenne River Reservation.[74]

After Big Foot and his followers left, ghost dancing practically ended on Cheyenne River. Agent Palmer had survived the ghost dance trouble without bloodshed on his reservation. On Pine Ridge, however, things were still unsettled.

While the search for Big Foot continued, tensions seemed to be calming down on Pine Ridge. The ghost dancers camped in the Badlands started their slow trek toward Pine Ridge Agency.[75] A relative calm must indeed have existed, since Agents Royer and Cooper, who previously were so anxious to report to the commissioner, had practically no correspondence with him between the period of December 8 and the massacre at Wounded Knee on December 29. It seems that the agents were finally satisfied and allowed the military to take care of business. In fact, General Brooke quite efficiently took over control of Pine Ridge; the agents were more onlookers than participants in the events that took place there during December. Elaine Goodale Eastman, inspector of Indian schools, also noticed this state of affairs. She wrote in her memoirs that in December 1890 Pine Ridge Reservation was practically under martial law, the military having control of all daily business. By this time Brooke had issued orders restricting newspaper reporters' rights to use the telegraph; perhaps these restrictions were extended to the agents also.[76]

Still, it is quite puzzling that the agents reported practically nothing about the several councils and negotiations that took place on Pine Ridge, nor did they inform their superiors that in late December most of the ghost dancers were moving toward the agency, and that their surrender was imminent. They had been complaining about depredations and hostilities, but now, when peace efforts were in progress, Royer and Cooper remained silent.

Then, on December 29, Royer telegraphed the commissioner of Indian affairs that earlier that morning the military had been in a battle with Big Foot's Indians. Although he had not been present, he reported that while the Indians were being disarmed a fight took place. Several soldiers had been killed or wounded and 300 Indians had been killed. Still, he seemed to be more concerned about matters at the agency, where Two Strike and his men opened fire on the agency buildings. The skirmishing there caused

FIGURE 6. "Grand Council between Friendly and Hostile Indian Chiefs at Pine Ridge Agency S.D. Jan. 17th 1891." After the ghost dancers' surrender, the Lakotas held a council at Pine Ridge in January 1891. Kicking Bear is speaking. Denver Public Library, Western History Collection, North Western Photo Co., photographer unknown, call number x-31474.

casualties on both sides, Royer reported. He added, however, that it was the Indians from Rosebud and Cheyenne River who were causing trouble; the Pine Ridge Indians took no part in the war, as the agent called it.[77]

Cooper wrote in the same tenor on December 30. He also told about the incident at Pine Ridge Agency, but believed that the Indian casualties at Wounded Knee were not more than 150. He did not directly blame the Indians for the Wounded Knee fight, though he noted that "Big Foot's band attacked the military." Royer agreed, and further stated that the army's intention had been to feed and care for the Indians, but while they were being disarmed a medicine man yelled "Kill the soldiers," after which the Indians opened fire. Cooper also reported an incident in which the 9th Cavalry was attacked by the ghost dancers, and on January 2, 1891, Royer reported that the Indians attacked and burned two day schools and an Episcopal church. They also killed a rancher.[78] Royer said that more than 3,000 Indians were camped approximately fifteen miles from the agency; they were hostile, committing depredations, and refused to surrender to the military. Among them were Red Cloud, Little Wound, and Big Road, but the agent believed that they wanted to return to the agency. Short Bull, Kicking Bear, and Two Strike, however, threatened to kill them if they tried to leave, Royer reported.[79]

The early days of January 1891 were full of turmoil and minor skirmishes between the army and the Lakotas. The focus was on Pine Ridge Reservation; the other Lakota agents were able to report that everything was peaceful on Rosebud, Cheyenne River, and Standing Rock Reservations. The agents filed reports on the recent events, trying to identify the causes of the trouble. They were clearly expecting the trouble to be over soon and were in an explanatory mood. Agent McLaughlin's main theme in his communication with his superiors in January 1891, and indeed during the following months, seemed to be a defense of his actions relating to Sitting Bull's arrest. He insisted that he had all along been, and could still be, in full control of his reservation. The other agents seemed to be eager to return to normal life.[80]

The return to normal life came sooner than the agents expected. On January 12, General Miles was finally able to push through his plan to replace all civil agents in charge of the Lakota reservations with army officers. The agents were allowed to stay on location; Cooper was even assigned to investigate the depredations committed by the ghost dancers. But the military took control. The Lakota agents, who a couple of months earlier had reported that they had lost control of their respective reservations, finally lost actual control, not to the Indians, but to the U.S. Army. Even McLaughlin, who claimed that he had never lost control, finally had to yield to military authority.[81]

All in all, the Lakota agents' major contributions as a group during the "trouble" was condemning the ghost dance from its inception, demanding that it be stopped, arguing for the arrest of ringleaders, contributing to the general alarm, and finally calling for troops. All this consequently played a role in the events that led to the tragic affair at Wounded Knee.

THREE

"To Protect and Suppress Trouble"

The Army Responds

The relationship between the U.S. Army and the Lakotas culminated in the Wounded Knee massacre on December 29, 1890. That relationship was characterized not only by years of warfare and hatred, but also by mutual respect. The army had a long tradition of dealing with Indians. Before the Civil War, general knowledge of the western Indians among the white population and within the army had been quite poor, even though the army built a chain of forts in the western regions to protect settlers and to establish contacts with the Plains tribes. After the Civil War, the army turned its attention to the Plains Indians, due in part to the increasing number of settlers traveling across the plains and in part to the discovery of gold and silver in Montana and Colorado. During the era of the so-called Grant's Peace Policy the army faced the task of fighting what eventually became its most famous Indian wars. Despite the lack of decisive Indian policy over the years and many political problems within the army, it managed to end most Indian hostilities by the mid-1880s.[1]

Although the major Indian campaigns ceased after the surrenders of Sitting Bull in 1881 and the Apache leader Geronimo in 1886, the army maintained its readiness to wage war against the Indians. According to the historian Robert Wooster, the army did not realize at that time that the Indian wars were effectively over.[2] The army was still necessary, but its strategy was changing. With improving technical innovations, such as the telegram and the railroad, the army sought to quickly put down any Indian uprisings that might occur. The basic strategy was to use trains to move and concentrate "overwhelming" forces at the scene of trouble. This tactic proved effective, for example, in subduing the Cheyenne Indians in 1885.[3]

During the late 1880s the army was in total control of the vast area that used to be Sioux country. The Lakotas now lived on reservations, which were surrounded by army forts. Fort Niobrara and Fort Robinson in Nebraska controlled the Lakotas who lived on Pine Ridge and Rosebud Reservations. Fort Yates in North Dakota and Fort Bennett in South Dakota watched over the Hunkpapas on Standing Rock Reservation and the Minneconjous, who lived on Cheyenne River Reservation. These forts were well connected to other parts of the country by rail and telegraph. Rapid response to troubles caused by Indians was now possible.[4]

By 1890 the army was prepared to move forces quickly. Historically, the Division of the Missouri was more involved than other divisions in the Indian campaigns.[5] When the ghost dance seemed to be causing problems, the task of dealing with it once again fell to the Division of Missouri. In 1890 the commander of that division was Maj. Gen. Nelson A. Miles, one of the most successful Indian fighters of the 1870s and 1880s. It is worth noting that General Miles was one of the military leaders who hunted down the Lakotas during the winter of 1876–77, after the Little Big Horn battle.[6]

General Miles was appointed commander of the Division of the Missouri in September 1889, following Maj. Gen. George Crook's death and just prior to the spread of rumors concerning the ghost dance troubles.[7] Under General Miles's leadership, the Division of Missouri was granted wide authority during the ghost dance period. By the end of the disturbances, the largest U.S. Army force since the Civil War had been mobilized to subdue the anticipated Lakota outbreak. Brig. Gen. John R. Brooke was head of the Department of the Platte and was sent to the scene of the Lakota "outbreak," where he served as commanding officer on the field. General Miles remained overall commander of the troops. He kept the division headquarters in Chicago until the early days of December 1890, later moving to Rapid City, South Dakota, closer to the scene of the trouble. On December 30, General Miles took the field personally and established his headquarters at Pine Ridge Agency.[8]

Months before the army arrived on the scene of the alleged trouble there was general interest in the ghost dance religion as rumors of an Indian messiah spread across the United States. The first news that some kind of messiah or "delusion" had taken hold of several Indian tribes reached army officials in the East in the fall of 1889. Indian agents in Oklahoma reported that Indians in Wyoming were captivated by a new belief that promised the return of the old way of life. The Oklahoma rumors said that an Indian messiah was living in the mountains somewhere north of the Shoshone lands. These rumors, mainly stories about strange events that had taken place in the West, enticed the Indians in Oklahoma so much that they sent a delegation to meet with the Shoshones. Their return caused some excitement among the Oklahoma Indians. Even Commissioner of Indian Affairs Thomas J. Morgan, who toured the West in person, mentioned in his annual report the early excitement among several Indian tribes; he called it a "Messiah Craze."[9]

Rumors of the messiah continued to spread during the winter of 1889–90. This restless feeling in the West concerned some officials in Washington. The commissioner of Indian affairs, however, did not think that the spreading "superstition" would cause any considerable trouble among the Indians, although it obviously affected their progress toward civilization. Moreover, despite the rumors, no actual information about the doctrine or the teachings of the messiah, known also as the Great Medicine Man of the North, were received.[10]

Nobody knew the messiah's identity, or even whether he was Indian or white. Some suggested that he was a Mormon. The first news that seemed to give some substance to the rumors reached officials in Washington through the War Department during the summer of 1890. This was the story of Porcupine, a Cheyenne Indian, who traveled with the Lakota delegation to meet the messiah (see chapter 1). On June 15, Porcupine told his story to the commander of Camp Crook at the Tongue River Agency in Montana. The messiah's identity, however, remained a mystery. As late as October 1890 contradictory stories regarding the messiah's identity and whereabouts were reported. Stories suggested that he lived around the Snake River in Idaho or at Walker River in Nevada. His name was Johnson Sides, John Johnson, Bannock Jim, or Quitze Ow, depending on the report. One thing, however, became more and more evident as the year 1890 passed: this messiah was creating great excitement among the Indians. Delegations from many tribes headed west to meet with him, and officials were most concerned that the

Lakotas might also send people. They did not realize that a Lakota delegation had already met him.[11]

No real answers regarding the true origins of the "Messiah Craze" were received until the army took up the investigation. This task was given to the Indian scout Arthur I. Chapman. Under orders to find the "Indian Christ," he set out in late November 1890 from San Francisco for Nevada, where the messiah was rumored to live.[12]

Chapman eventually found his way to Mason Valley, Nevada, where he learned that the name of the messiah was Jack Wilson or Quitze Ow (Wovoka). On December 4, 1890, he finally contacted Wovoka at Walker River, Nevada, and recorded the first interview with the Indian Messiah. Wovoka explained his beliefs to Chapman and said that he hoped to protect Indians from white soldiers. He also urged all Indians to live in peace with the white men. Wovoka had discovered that the soldiers were looking for him, but he did not care. He wanted only to meet them and show them that no bad feelings existed. According to Chapman, the Messiah was well known throughout Nevada and had performed many miracles. The Indians followed his teachings, and Wovoka claimed that he was the chief of all the Indians who sent representatives to meet with him. Finally, Chapman mentioned in his report that the local whites considered the Paiutes very good and industrious people; only a few of the whites believed that the "Indian superstition" would cause any problems. He also said that the story he learned was similar to the one told earlier by Porcupine, the Cheyenne.[13]

Remarkably, Chapman's interview with Wovoka took place as late as December 1890, when the army had already been sent to the Lakota reservations. Thus it appears that the army arrived on the reservations before accurate information about the origins and nature of the Indian messiah's teachings were gathered. Information about the Lakotas, however, had been received from the Lakota agents, among others. To take proper action, the army started to carry out its own investigation of the situation on the Lakota reservations.

In 1890 the army took notice of troubles among various Indian tribes. Among the Lakotas, however, nothing serious was reported; only the partitioning of the Great Sioux Reservation and the resulting opening of the surplus Lakota lands to non-Indian settlement caused dissatisfaction among the Indians.[14]

The army learned about the ghost dance from Porcupine in June 1890 but did not act on the information. Only in the fall of 1890 did army officials turn their attention to the dance, focusing specifically on the Lakotas. According to General Brooke, the dissatisfaction and uneasiness among the Lakotas grew during the summer of 1890 but did not reach serious proportions until the fall. The commissioner of Indian affairs grew more alarmed as Indian agents started to report discontent among the Lakotas. Those reports and letters were the most important sources of information regarding conditions on the Lakota reservations during September and October 1890.[15]

In late October, however, one of the major sources of information was General Miles himself. During that month, he traveled to several western army forts and outposts. On October 28, he arrived at Pine Ridge. There he was able to make firsthand observations of the situation that had already caused problems between Agent Daniel F. Royer and the ghost dancers. He consulted with the agent and with the progressive leaders American Horse and Young Man Afraid of His Horse, urging them to use their influence to stop the ghost dances. More important, he tried to persuade the ghost dancers to stop dancing in their own best interest, although he did not think that anything serious would result from the dance. In fact, he told Agent Royer that, if left alone, ghost dancing would probably eventually stop by itself.[16] Despite this, General Miles apparently threatened the ghost dancers. If they would not stop he would bring such a large force of soldiers that he would be able to destroy everyone who caused trouble.[17]

Soon after he returned from his trip Miles received orders to conduct an investigation into conditions on the Lakota reservations. On October 31, Brig. Gen. Thomas H. Ruger, commander of the Department of Dakota, was sent to Standing Rock to investigate the situation there. Capt. C. A. Earnest of the 8th Cavalry, the inspector for Indian supplies at Rosebud Agency, was ordered to report on the condition of the Indians who lived on that reservation. Capt. J. H. Hurst, commanding officer of Fort Bennett, South Dakota, conducted the investigation on Cheyenne River Reservation. General Brooke eventually made the report regarding Pine Ridge.[18]

Before these investigations were completed, however, the letters from the Lakota agents to the commissioner of Indian affairs and to the army officers caused much concern in Washington. According to General Brooke, these letters were alarming and needed to be sent forward to the highest authorities in the country.[19] Secretary of the Interior John W. Noble, alerted by Royer's letters, counseled the president to consider sending troops to Pine Ridge. Secretary Noble wanted to send a force that would be "so great it will overwhelm the Indians from [the] beginning." President Harrison agreed; already on October 31 he had said that something had to be done to suppress possible outbreaks resulting from the Indians' belief in the "coming of the Indian messiah and the return of dead Indian warriors for crusade upon the whites."[20]

In the midst of these alarming letters came an army memorandum listing ten reasons for the trouble. It reported all the complaints made by the Lakotas, from the reduction of their reservation to the failure of crops and the reduction in their beef rations. It also stated that the beef was of poor quality and that there were serious delays in issuing it. The memorandum noted that the Lakotas were starving, which directly resulted in dissatisfaction; the "Messiah Craze" was a symptom of this ill feeling. According to the memorandum, however, the "Messiah Craze" was used by malcontents to agitate others and acted as a cover for a planned outbreak. Sitting Bull was believed to be urging people to join him the following spring, when he would distribute 1,500 stands of concealed arms to the Lakotas. It is interesting that the memorandum accuses the Lakotas of concealing weapons and planning an outbreak, but at the same time sympathizes with them.[21]

The results of the first actual army investigation of the Lakota reservations were received by mid-November. Captain Earnest reported from Pine Ridge and Rosebud on November 12 that there was disaffection among the Indians stemming from the total failure of crops, the cut in government rations, and the delay in ration issuance. He also mentioned the new census figures, which were one of the reasons for the cut in rations. The shortage of jobs for Indians on the reservations and the resulting lack of money caused problems in the Indians' daily lives. Furthermore, the Lakotas at Rosebud opposed Agent J. George Wright's suspension.[22]

Captain Earnest pointed out that the "Messiah Craze" was only a symptom of this bad feeling, a superstitious mania that would eventually die out by itself. For this to happen, however, it was necessary to fulfill all the Lakotas' expectations. They needed to receive their full rations and needed work to do on the reservations. Captain Earnest concluded that they also needed to get Agent Wright back. The best way to deal with the ghost dancers would have been to leave them alone, but the situation had deteriorated because, according to Earnest, "busybodies told them that if they didn't stop [the] soldiers would come and take away their ponies. As they originally meditated no violence, this gave the Indians war hearts."[23]

By mid-November, General Ruger reported from Cheyenne River Reservation that approximately 200 Minneconjous were dancing under the leadership of Hump and Big Foot. The Indians had started dancing around September 20 and were now out of the agent's control. Despite this, Ruger's report emphasized that there was no need for action; it was unlikely that an outbreak would occur. The ghost dancers made no threats against the agent or other employees at the agency. Ruger believed that there was more turmoil on Pine Ridge Reservation than on either Cheyenne River or Standing Rock.[24] Both of these reports echoed the sentiment in the undated memorandum mentioned earlier.

On November 13, however, the rumors about the restless Lakotas caused the president to act. In a letter to the secretary of war, President Harrison ordered the War Department to "assume the direction and responsibility for steps that may be necessary to prevent an outbreak." The president wanted to have troops in readiness in case of emergency. The troops should be "impressive and effective." Concurrently, the president wanted to avoid any issue that would cause an outbreak.[25]

As a direct result of this order, Maj. Gen. John M. Schofield ordered General Miles on November 14 to take whatever action "may be necessary in view of the existing situation, the object being first to prevent an outbreak . . . and second to bring to bear upon the disaffected Indians such military force as will compel prompt submission to the authority of the government; the arrest of such of the leaders as may be necessary to insure peaceful conduct of the tribes and such other measures as may hereafter be necessary to prevent the occurrence of like difficulties."[26]

In a telegram of November 17, General Schofield gave authority over the situation to General Miles: "You will please take such action as the circumstances require, if in your judgment immediate action is necessary." A telegram from Agent Royer had prompted Schofield's concern.[27]

Even though the army's own investigations reported no imminent danger, the army was ordered to move forces onto the Lakota reservations. The army wanted to rapidly deploy enough troops by railroad to suppress any outbreak attempts. The concentration of troops was to be carried out in secrecy. The army was under orders to capture and destroy any hostile Indians leaving their reservations, to separate the "friendly" Indians from the "hostile," and to arrest the leaders as necessary. According to Robert Wooster, punishing Indians who left their reservations without permission and separating the friendly Indians from the hostile Indians were common strategies throughout the Indian wars period.[28] In this case, however, the infantry was going to be used as protection for white settlements, while the task of fighting and destroying the "hostile" Indians fell to the cavalry. The cavalry gained additional firepower from Hotchkiss guns, although the difficult terrain was expected to prevent their efficient use. Despite this, one Hotchkiss gun was given to each cavalry squadron. Although the army received direct instructions on how to wage war against the Lakotas, the orders included a directive to avoid open confrontation and to give support and confidence to the "loyal" Indians.[29]

The army was expected to require very large numbers of men and equipment to carry out its duties promptly. Concentrating the troops, however, was not an easy task. The Division of the Missouri received the assignment for this operation, but it alone was not considered a sufficient force. In fact, General Miles complained that the troops in his division were ill equipped and, because there had been no war for a long time, their efficiency was severely impaired. Furthermore, he believed that the hostile Lakotas far outnumbered his troops. Miles complained that he had only twenty-eight troops of cavalry, 1,400 mounted men scattered across a vast area. He believed these troops faced 30,000 "disaffected" Indians, as many as 6,000 of them fighting warriors.[30]

To solve these problems, Miles was given wide authority to attach troops

CONCENTRATING TROOPS ON THE NORTHERN INDIAN AGENCIES.—DRAWN BY FREDERIC REMINGTON.—[SEE PAGE 947.]

FIGURE 7. The U.S. Army concentrating troops on the Lakota reservations, by Frederic Remington. *Harper's Weekly*, December 1890.

from other divisions under his command. Troops were eventually called to the Lakota reservations from as far as New Mexico and Arizona.[31] At first, however, the troops sent to Pine Ridge and Rosebud belonged to the Department of the Platte. These units were under the command of General Brooke, who was also very concerned about the troops' condition and the number of men he could use at this point.[32]

While the army prepared to move sufficient forces to overwhelm the Indians, the officers were clearly aware of the fact that the sudden appearance of troops might frighten the Lakotas and cause a general stampede of both "friendly" and "hostile" Indians. There was also a general understanding that the situation was serious, and that some of the seriousness was caused by Agent Royer, who was considered to be "much alarmed and at the same time inexperienced."[33] Still, the army could not take the situation lightly. The white citizens living close to the Lakota reservations were growing very alarmed. They wanted protection.[34]

Despite the many problems the army experienced in mobilizing the troops, it executed a simultaneous arrival at Pine Ridge and Rosebud Reservations during the night of November 19–20, 1890. The army even succeeded in arriving at both reservations in relative secrecy and took the Indians by surprise.[35]

Once he received his orders, General Brooke acted rapidly. He positioned his troops strategically around the reportedly most troublesome reservations, Pine Ridge and Rosebud. The general himself arrived at Pine Ridge from Rushville, Nebraska, early on the morning of November 20, 1890. After investigating circumstances on the reservation he carried out his first major task: the separation of the well-disposed from the disaffected, the "friendlies" from the "hostiles," that is, the nondancers from the ghost dancers. He asked Agent Royer to call on those who had not defied the agent's authority to come to the agency. As a result, a large number of Oglalas arrived at the agency during the following few days.[36]

The tension on the reservation was still high. At first, both General Brooke and General Miles expected that separating the well-disposed Indians from the ghost dancers would prove a simple task. Miles, however, pointed out that any "violent overt act of any small party of the desperate ones may cause a general uprising." He also believed that Sitting Bull was sending emissaries around the country in an attempt to persuade other tribes to join him in the spring of 1891 in the Black Hills, where a general uprising would occur.[37]

A few days after arriving at Pine Ridge, General Brooke realized that separating the "friendly" Indians from the "hostiles" was not going to be an easy task. Although many Indians gathered at the agency, even more fled to the ghost dancers' camps. Brooke reported that the disaffected were mostly those who had not signed the Agreement of 1889 and were led by Little Wound, Jack Red Cloud, and Big Road. Both Brooke and Miles believed that the chiefs were in full control of the ghost dancers and were gaining in prestige. The dancers were reported to be well armed and were assuming a hostile attitude, disobeying all directions and regulations. According to Brooke, the ghost dancers did not plan to attack the whites but were prepared to defend themselves if necessary.[38]

On Rosebud Reservation the arrival of troops had a similar impact. Some of the Brulés started to move toward Pine Ridge. Brooke noted that the immediate cause of the Indians' exodus was a rumor that soldiers were coming to take away their ponies. Similar rumors circulated among the Indians, causing a movement that, according to Brooke, was "like prairie fire, the people dropped everything when they heard the news. [They] started for the White River and then turned toward Pine Ridge."[39]

The Brulés' attempt to join the Oglalas on Pine Ridge Reservation was seen as a very dangerous development, especially since concurrent reports told of the Indians' intention to fight. Special Census Agent A. T. Lea at Pine Ridge filed reports claiming that half of the Indians of Pine Ridge and Rosebud were affected by the ghost dance, and that the Indians were planning to go on the warpath. Special Agent James Cooper at Pine Ridge backed Lea's reports.[40]

Partly owing to this information, General Miles was certain that the Indians planned an attack against Brooke at Pine Ridge. As a result, more troops were ordered to the scene. On November 23, Brooke assured Miles that there was no danger at the present time and that the troops on Pine Ridge were perfectly safe. In his telegram, Brooke emphasized that the Indians had just and fair grievances. "This should be corrected at once . . . their just claims to be granted without delay," he suggested. In this Miles agreed with him.[41]

General Miles also believed in the necessity of employing as many Indians as scouts as possible, more to give them something to do than to expect them to do any real fighting. As a result of his requests, he was allowed to enlist 500 Indians as scouts and as additional policemen on the Lakota reservations. At this point, Miles received orders from General Schofield not to disturb the ghost dancers or to do anything that might precipitate a conflict. Although the ghost dancers were greatly animated, there seemed to be no imminent threat of war. Miles, however, needed to continue to send more troops to the scene. Schofield urged him to use caution and take no action before enough troops were present. Miles wanted to act quickly, while many of the Indians were close to Pine Ridge Agency for the issuing of rations. Schofield thought that careful consideration was required before they undertook any action, and the army needed to prepare for a long winter campaign. He was not going to take the matter lightly. He pointed out that the decision to act against the Indians depended on the president, and much discretion was needed from the commanding officers.[42]

On December 3 General Schofield wrote that disarming the Indians would be an immensely difficult and dangerous task. He reasoned that the Indians could be disarmed, and kept disarmed, only if they were taken prisoners of war and kept under full military control for an indefinite period of time. This was not a practical solution and, in fact, would have violated the government's general Indian policy. Schofield also noted that the Indians had not so far shown any deliberate intention to commence hostilities against whites. Therefore, disarming them was irrelevant. In fact, Schofield thought that if the Indians did actually start a war, it might eventually be easier for the army to respond to that than to deal with the scattered defiant Indians in the current situation, where they had simply put themselves "in an attitude of defiance." However, it remained the War Department's duty to determine the initial action in any case. Secretary of War Redfield Proctor was of the opinion that the military should not make any move against the Indians unless it was absolutely necessary.[43] Thus it seems that after the arrival of the troops, while General Miles was seeking a quick military solution, his superiors and General Brooke tried to convince him to take a more measured approach.

During the last days of November and the early days of December the army continued to move additional troops onto the Lakota reservations. The army was not going to take any chances, and the plan of "showing overwhelming force" was put into effect.[44] Meanwhile, the general feeling on the Lakota reservations seemed peaceful. The Indians were said to be at the agencies for rations, with only a few of the disaffected staying away. According to Miles, the ghost dancing element was subsiding and all indications were peaceful.[45]

On November 27, General Brooke reported that everything was quiet at Pine Ridge, and "every hour lessens the strength of the ghost dancers." Little Wound and Big Road arrived at the agency, and even Short Bull had visited the agency the previous night. Brooke believed that Pine Ridge was now the place where all the restlessness would be settled. At that point the 7th Cavalry had arrived at Pine Ridge. Everything was also reported to be quiet on Rosebud, and General Ruger had already sent word from Cheyenne River that settlers who had fled to nearby cities were now quietly returning to their homes.[46]

Despite these favorable reports from his officers, Miles was worried. Some settlers living around the reservations still asked for protection. The rumor was that the Indians planned a full-scale outbreak and reportedly said that they would once again "beat out the brains of children and drink women's blood." The settlers said that Indians were damaging homes and stealing horses and other goods.[47] On November 26 Miles learned about a great Indian gathering at Pass Creek, where Short Bull reportedly preached about the new Indian paradise. Miles believed that Short Bull had gathered together 1,500 warriors under his direct leadership, and that these Indians were prepared to fight if the soldiers attempted to arrest them. Additionally, these Indians claimed that they had bulletproof shirts. Miles grew more and more concerned about the condition of the troops under his command. The Indians, he believed, could easily wipe out the poorly equipped soldiers.[48]

More and more information about the ghost dance and the living conditions of the Lakotas was gathered. Army officers from each Lakota reservation filed their reports by the end of November. The main points expressed in these reports were that the Indians had suffered for want of food, they had been unjustly and unfairly treated, their land was not suitable for farming, the time between beef issues was too long, and the beef that was issued shrank during the wintertime to almost half of its original size. The Lakotas had no means to support themselves and they suffered physically and mentally. In addition, the census conducted by Special Agent Lea gave a smaller figure than the actual number. According to the officers, the Indians saw the ghost dance as a feast where food was given to starving people. One officer thought that the dancing would stop if the Indians were given enough food. General Brooke was still convinced that all the Lakota grievances should be satisfied. He believed that the ghost dance was only a "means to an end." Yet although he clearly understood the suffering of the Lakota people, Brooke concluded his report saying that the suffering did not justify the ghost dancers' current behavior. Therefore, all the Indians living on Pine Ridge and Rosebud Reservations should be disarmed.[49]

On November 28, General Miles filed a report based on his own investigations and his officers' reports. He pointed out that although the army had subjugated the Indians, this did not mean an end to the Indian wars. In fact, he believed that Indians in general were better equipped for war than ever. While on the warpath, they could more successfully live on livestock than they did on buffalo during previous times. "There never has been a time when the Indians were as well armed and equipped for war as the present," the general wrote. It would not surprise him if the Indians made a final attempt in "the death struggle of their race." According to him, the Indians still remembered the old times of freedom and had enough intelligence to see that their race was doomed. This caused much hatred, and since they believed in supernatural powers they naturally grasped onto the hope the ghost dance offered. When they reached a frenzied religious state, they saw visions of a place from which their enemies were eliminated, and then the "ferocious nature of [the] savage takes over," Miles wrote. "The doctrine of destruction of [the] white race, restoration of their dead relatives and return of [the] buffalo is close to their heart."[50]

General Miles believed that the original ghost dance doctrine had been peaceful, but that false prophets, especially Sitting Bull, transformed it so that "deeds were necessary to show belief and hasten the coming of the

Messiah." This caused the turbulent warriors to believe that they were on a righteous crusade that could end in a "terrible pillage and massacre of innocent and unprotected settlers." Miles added that the "Messiah delusion" became even more dangerous because the Indians believed that they would be resurrected in the near future, so they might as well die. He stated that the "craze" had taken hold of Indians over an area larger than all the states east of the Mississippi, and that "most positive and vigorous measures should be taken."[51]

Despite the call for "vigorous measures," Miles, like General Brooke, listed several causes of the Lakotas' disaffection and their just grievances. Also like Brooke, he recommended that Congress immediately fulfill all its obligations to the Lakotas. "What the Indians need is sufficient food, occupation and just and positive government," Miles remarked. By "just and positive government" he meant that all civilian agents should be removed and the agencies put under military control. He strongly implied that poor and inexperienced agents were partly to blame for the current troubles. Only the military knew the Indians' needs, and only the military could control the turbulent element.

General Miles wrote these strong words criticizing the abilities of the civil agents after an occasion when he felt that Agent McLaughlin at Standing Rock had overstepped his authority. Both Miles and McLaughlin wanted Sitting Bull arrested, but they could not agree on how to accomplish it. To prevent the agent from conducting the arrest, Miles ordered Buffalo Bill Cody to arrest Sitting Bull. He gave Cody instructions to go to Sitting Bull's camp and eventually take him prisoner. Cody arrived at Standing Rock on November 27, but, as noted in chapter 2, McLaughlin prevented him from meeting with Sitting Bull. This angered Miles and strengthened his conviction that the agents could not control the reservations. He repeated those sentiments several times during the following days. On November 28, Miles left for Washington, where he hoped to convince federal officials to follow his recommendations.[52]

On his way to Washington Miles told newspaper reporters that the situation was very grave and required more vigorous measures. On this trip, Miles himself became one of the sources of alarmist reports. He told the press, and

later repeated it in his memoirs, that the ghost dance was a "threatened uprising of colossal proportions, extending over a far greater territory than did
the confederation inaugurated by the Prophet and led by Tecumseh, or the
conspiracy of Pontiac."[53] He continued in a similar vein in his official report
about the disturbances. He maintained that strong military measures were
necessary, as "the most serious Indian war of our history was imminent."
The states of Nebraska, South Dakota, North Dakota, Montana, Wyoming,
Colorado, Idaho, and Nevada and the territory of Utah, said Miles, "were
liable to be overrun by [a] hungry, wild, mad horde of savages."[54]

Miles's comments are somewhat surprising given that almost all the reports from his officers on the reservations denied any imminent threat of
an outbreak. As Robert M. Utley has noted, Miles was so concerned about
public opinion that he suddenly began to spew alarming declarations. It certainly seems that Miles deliberately exaggerated the danger to gain attention for himself. Perhaps he feared that this Indian war would not match the
glory of past Indian wars and that the political gains of a small Indian campaign would be marginal.[55]

Whatever his personal motivations or political goals might have been, the
fact is that his comments were widely reported by newspapers and caused
much discussion in Congress.[56] The direct result of his visit to Washington
was that the military was given full control over the Lakota reservations.
The agents were ordered to obey the military's orders and fully cooperate
with the commanding military officer on their respective reservations. The
president gave Miles extraordinary authority to use all possible means to deal
with the situation. Everything in "the way of men and material that can be
spared from other points will be supplied," the president promised.[57] This
was exactly what Miles had hoped for, and without a doubt the public sensation he had caused with his alarmist reports helped him achieve this goal.
At the same time, however, he pointed out publicly how important it was
for the government to fulfill all its treaty obligations with the Lakotas.[58]

Although the officers of the U.S. Army showed sympathy toward the
Lakotas, they also realized that trouble might lie ahead. Two courses of action were suggested. The first was to let the ghost dance subside by itself
during the coming winter. The second was to remove all the "troublemak-

ers" from the reservations and then eventually disarm the Indians. Both plans stemmed from the belief that ghost dancing was harmful and that it had to stop. There was no doubt among the army officers that the Lakotas could wreak considerable havoc if they actually took the warpath. For this reason the concentration of troops continued and firm handling of the situation was called for. Although they planned to avoid open hostilities, by December 1890 the army was ready to wage a full-scale war against the ghost dancing Lakotas if need be.

The Struggle to Avoid a Battle

The military buildup on the Lakota reservations continued during Miles's visit to Washington.[59] While Agent Royer on Pine Ridge filed reports about Indian depredations, the army officers reported that everything was relatively quiet on the Lakota reservations. Their biggest concern was the concentration of Indians at the Stronghold in the Badlands. According to army officers, the Indians stole some cattle on their way, but no serious acts of violence occurred. Some Lakotas were reported to be dancing in Sitting Bull's camp, but otherwise life on Standing Rock Reservation was peaceful; the Indian children were even attending school.[60]

To keep things quiet on the reservations, the secretary of war authorized General Brooke to increase beef rations. The politics of conciliation, said Brooke, soon bore good results. On Pine Ridge, the Indians started to feel confidence in the army and remained quietly in their camps. Brooke further noted that much of the restlessness on Pine Ridge and Rosebud was caused by a general belief that the army was sent to the reservations as an act of war. Thus the most important task for the army was to prove to the Indians that this was not the case. Issuing rations was the first step in assuring the Indians of the army's peaceful intentions. At the same time, however, Brooke reported that the cavalry was in good shape on Pine Ridge as well as on Rosebud and was ready to take the field at any moment.[61]

During the early days of December, the army sought to maintain peace. Several delegations of "friendly" Lakotas were sent to the ghost dancers' camp. Much information regarding the Lakotas' complaints came to the commanding officers, who promptly submitted reports to the officials in

Washington. All reports from Pine Ridge seemed to indicate that a peaceful end was in sight. Two Strike and Big Road were expected to arrive at Pine Ridge Agency and to camp close to the friendly Indians. Brooke was so delighted about these developments that he wrote, "Trouble with these Indians is in a fair way to speedy settlement." Miles, who believed that the presence of the troops had demoralized the Indians, echoed this sentiment. He reported that those who were warlike a week earlier were starting to show signs of submission. The anticipated arrival of Two Strike and Big Road would be a clear sign of the disintegration that supposedly was taking place among the ghost dancers. Miles also referred briefly to allegations made in the press that Two Strike planned to stab Brooke. According to Miles, there was no indication of such a plan.[62]

The main reason for these favorable predictions was the council held on Pine Ridge on December 6. Brooke sent Father John Jutz to the Stronghold to negotiate with the ghost dancers. Finally, after long talks in the ghost dance camp, Father Jutz managed to bring approximately thirty Indians to Pine Ridge. Despite their warlike appearance, a white flag waved in front of their column. Although the public press made big news out of the "warlike" arrival of the Indians, Brooke did not mention that aspect in his report or telegrams.[63]

The negotiations between Brooke and Two Strike and a few other prominent ghost dance leaders started immediately following the Indians' colorful arrival. According to Brooke, the Indians once again explained their grievances and complained that they had tried to get some understanding from the U.S. government but received none. They had nothing to eat and they had become frustrated. They asked Brooke for advice. He replied that he would give them food and try to find employment for as many of them as possible. But for all this to happen, he asked the Indians to return to the ghost dance camp and bring all of their followers, both Oglalas and Brulés, back to the agency. Brooke explained that there would be time for further negotiations after this first goal was achieved. According to Brooke, the Indians were happy to hear this and promised to return to the Badlands and bring back all the people to the agency as soon as possible. Brooke was very satisfied with the results of the council. Nonetheless, General Miles, in Chicago, was convinced that the Indians had taken over control of the council and blamed Brooke for mismanaging the situation.[64]

While these seemingly favorable events took place on Pine Ridge, Miles had to deal with the ghost dancers on Cheyenne River Reservation, where they had gathered around Big Foot and Hump. The first thing to do was to assure the Indians living there of the army's peaceful intentions. According to Miles, the best way to do this was to give them more clothes. They had not received their clothing annuity, and winter was fast approaching. On Cheyenne River as well as Pine Ridge Miles tried to appease the ghost dancers by sending negotiators to their camps. On Cheyenne River Capt. Ezra P. Ewers, who was called to duty from Texas, was very successful. He had served with Miles during the so-called Lame Deer and Nez Percé campaigns during which Hump had served as a scout under Ewers's command,[65] and later served seven years as agent for the people living on Cheyenne River Reservation. He had earned the Indians' respect and befriended Hump. General Miles hoped that this friendship would bear results. Indeed, Hump followed Ewers's advice and again enlisted as an army scout. This, according to Miles, was a most favorable development. It removed one of the most feared leaders from the ghost dance and caused disintegration among the remaining dancers on Cheyenne River Reservation. Miles believed that Big Foot would now start obeying orders. The presence of troops seemed to have had such favorable results that on December 11, Miles once again noted that the army's presence had averted a serious war. According to him, the agents had lost control of their agencies twenty-four days earlier, and only the army could take full control of the Indians. To take proper care of the agencies, all civil agents must be removed and replaced by military officers.[66]

Despite these favorable reports, Miles continued to ask for more troops and equipment "in view of the possible outbreak of the Indians, and it would be remarkable if it did not occur." In a telegram to General Schofield, he hinted at the fact that Agent McLaughlin at Standing Rock had interfered with Buffalo Bill's mission to arrest Sitting Bull, which might have serious consequences. According to Miles, Sitting Bull was now aware of the plan to arrest him, making him more dangerous than ever. He also pointed out that Buffalo Bill's failed mission might cause Sitting Bull to flee to Canada.

Miles predicted that all future attempts to arrest Sitting Bull would be much more difficult than before, especially if he fled to Canada.[67]

While Miles's attention again turned toward Sitting Bull, Brooke gained positive results from his efforts on Pine Ridge. More troops arrived almost daily, and Brooke was confident that they were ready for a long winter campaign, if necessary. Despite this, everything seemed calm on Pine Ridge. Brooke later recalled the situation on Pine Ridge and Rosebud Reservations on December 7: "All the Oglalas, except those with the Brulés on [the] edge of [the] Badlands and Young Man Afraid Of His Horse's band were in camp about the agency. All the Indians of Rosebud Agency not near the Badlands were at their homes on their reservation. There were seven (7) companies of infantry and two (2) troops of cavalry at Rosebud agency, nine (9) companies of infantry, twelve (12) troops of cavalry and Capron's battery [1st artillery under the command of Capt. Allyn Capron] at Pine Ridge Agency." More troops were still on their way. He wrote in his report that on December 7, "the temper of the Indians at Pine Ridge was apparently all that could be desired."[68]

Two Strike was on his way to Pine Ridge Agency with almost 1,500 Indians, just as he had promised. Before they reached the agency, however, a quarrel took place among the Indians and approximately 600 to 700 returned to the Badlands. Eventually, Two Strike led 850 Lakotas to a camp close to Pine Ridge Agency, where they received extra provisions. Brooke was extremely satisfied with the developments and noted that all efforts to avoid war and bloodshed had been made. The only issue that still concerned Brooke was the return of those Brulés and Oglalas to the Badlands.[69]

While Brooke filed favorable reports from Pine Ridge, the settlers around the Lakota reservations and even in Wyoming asked for protection, reporting that hostile Indians were seen all over the country. Officials in Washington— the secretary of the interior, the secretary of war, and the commissioner of Indian affairs—received letters from alarmed citizens and Indian agents who demanded that the army move against the hostile Indians. Generals Brooke and Ruger assured citizens that there was no cause for alarm. The Lakotas seen in Wyoming, led by Young Man Afraid of His Horse, were on a peaceful trip to visit the Crow Indians. Despite the army officials' opinions, the press made a great deal of the growing sense of alarm among the settlers. Soon rumors about battles between the Indians and the army began to spread.[70]

Meanwhile, General Miles grew more and more concerned about Sitting Bull, who, Miles believed, was behind all the trouble. Only by arresting Sitting Bull could the army reach a permanent peace. "No Indian has had the power of drawing to him so large a following of his race, and molding and wielding it against the authority of the United States, or of inspiring it with greater animosity against the white race and civilization," Miles wrote.[71]

After Buffalo Bill's unsuccessful mission, the president authorized Miles to use his own judgment regarding Sitting Bull's possible arrest. On December 10, Miles instructed General Ruger to send orders to Lt. Col. William F. Drum, the commanding officer at Fort Yates, North Dakota, "to secure the person of Sitting Bull, using any practical means." The arrest was planned for issue day, December 20, but as rumors spread that Sitting Bull planned to leave the reservation, the original plan was abandoned. The date was moved up to December 15. Colonel Drum's orders included instructions for Agent McLaughlin to render all necessary assistance and cooperation. In fact, McLaughlin did more than cooperate; he convinced Colonel Drum that the best way to arrest Sitting Bull was to leave it to the reservation Indian police. This was agreed upon, and the army detachment of the 8th Cavalry under Capt. E. G. Fechét was left behind as backup.[72]

Because the army was not actually present when the attempt to capture Sitting Bull was made, no army eyewitness accounts of Sitting Bull's death exist. The troops arrived on the scene after Sitting Bull and some of the Indian policemen were already dead and skirmishing was going on between the rest of the policemen and Sitting Bull's men. At first the army could not tell the difference between the policemen and the ghost dancers, but after a few cannon shells were fired toward Sitting Bull's cabin, the policemen waved a white flag to signal their location. After a short skirmish with Sitting Bull's men, the army quickly drove the Indians away. According to Captain Fechét, the Indians showed no desire to engage in hostile actions against the soldiers. Colonel Drum noted that Sitting Bull's people did not attempt to fight the troops, but scattered to the nearby woods and hills in great alarm. Eventually they either surrendered to the army or found their way to Cheyenne River Reservation. The army had no casualties.[73]

Immediately after Sitting Bull's death, the press, as well as Agent McLaughlin, praised the conduct of the army and the Indian police. Their opinions were echoed by General Ruger, who said that "the conduct of [the] Standing Rock police was remarkable for fidelity as well as courage." The blame for Sitting Bull's death was put entirely upon Sitting Bull himself. Later, after an investigation into the matter had been conducted, thirty-seven Medals of Honor were awarded to the Indian policemen involved.[74] The result pleased Miles, who wrote in his report that "the action of Captain Fechét was gallant, judicious and praiseworthy, and it had the effect of striking the first and most serious blow to the hostile element . . . and totally destroyed the hostile element in Standing Rock." Miles went on to say that Sitting Bull's "death, for which he alone was responsible, was a great relief to the country in which he had been the terror for many years."[75] In his memoirs, Miles continued to emphasize the importance of arresting Sitting Bull, portraying him as one of the greatest Indian war chiefs. In a nostalgic tone, he wrote that it was a tragedy that he had to die at the hands of his own people.[76]

After Sitting Bull's death the military faced three major problems: the first was trying to induce the Indians in the Badlands to surrender peacefully; the second was dealing with the refugees from Sitting Bull's camp; the third was stopping the ghost dancing on Cheyenne River Reservation. On Pine Ridge, the negotiation tactic of dividing the Indians proved successful. By mid-December, growing numbers of ghost dancers from the Badlands camp were on their way, and a peaceful settlement seemed certain.

On December 15, 1890, the army's "struggle to avoid a battle" was over. The ghost dance had its first casualties, all Lakotas. Interestingly, the fight took place on Standing Rock, where only a small percentage of the population were ghost dancers (see the table in chapter 1). Although the army was not directly involved in Sitting Bull's killing, during the aftermath the first actual battle between the U.S. Army and the ghost dancing Lakotas took place. The process of finding a peaceful end to the trouble had to begin all over again.

Negotiation by Force

The news of Sitting Bull's death spread rapidly across the Lakota reservations. Immediately after his death, the situation on Standing Rock became chaotic. The army tried to find a way to gain control of Sitting Bull's fleeing people. Most of them surrendered during the days that followed, but many found their way to Cheyenne River.[77]

On Pine Ridge, General Brooke had planned to surround and attack the group of ghost dancers who remained in the Stronghold in the Badlands. Brooke hoped to act quickly to prevent any attempts by the ghost dancers to leave the reservation. General Miles, however, did not support that plan and instructed Brooke to postpone the attack. He believed that the Lakotas could defeat the army in the difficult terrain so familiar to the Indians. Although Brooke did not agree with the orders he received from Miles, he was already obediently retreating from his plan when the news of Sitting Bull's death arrived at Pine Ridge. The Indians, led by Two Strike, left the agency and returned to the Badlands. The events following Sitting Bull's death called for a different kind of approach by the army; attacking the Stronghold was no longer an option, not even for Brooke. Now the plan was to position troops around the Stronghold and gradually force the Indians to abandon their refuge.[78]

Once the plan to attack the Stronghold was abandoned, General Brooke decided to continue efforts to create dissension among the ghost dancers, a tactic that had proved successful in the past. Brooke now sent forty Oglalas and Brulés to the ghost dance camp. This time their mission was unsuccessful. The ghost dancers met the delegates with great anxiety and contempt. After the delegation returned, a council was held at Pine Ridge Agency, where, according to Brooke, the Indians themselves decided to send another delegation, of 500 men, to the ghost dance camp to try to persuade the dancers to surrender. The plan was abandoned, however, and eventually a smaller delegation of 140 men led by Little Wound and Big Road, both former ghost dancers, tried to use their influence on the dancers. A few days later, Brooke was happy to learn that this mission was successful. He received a message that the delegation would bring in all the people from the ghost dance camp.[79]

During the negotiations on Pine Ridge, other events needing the army's attention took place on Cheyenne River Reservation. Big Foot welcomed the refugees from Sitting Bull's camp and provided them with as much shelter as he could. This did not please General Miles, who was growing more and more suspicious about Big Foot's intentions. He believed that Big Foot was planning to unite with the ghost dancers in the Badlands.[80]

On December 3, the army sent troops under Lt. Col. Edwin V. Sumner to watch over Big Foot and his ghost dancers. By now Big Foot had brought his people back from their ghost dance camp to their cabin village on Cherry Creek, near its juncture with the Cheyenne River. During the two weeks Colonel Sumner watched over Big Foot, the two men had developed a mutual understanding and respect. On December 8, after talking to Big Foot and other leaders, Sumner reported, "They are peacefully disposed and inclined to obey orders. I believe that they are really hungry, and suffering from want of clothing and covering." He later said that he understood why Big Foot gave shelter to Sitting Bull's people: the fleeing Indians were their relatives and were in a destitute condition.[81] In the following days Sumner maintained that the Indians on Cheyenne River Reservation were under control.[82]

Despite Sumner's reports, General Ruger thought it necessary to arrest Big Foot and his people. He was convinced that Big Foot was talking war while Hump tried to talk peace. He considered Big Foot a threat to the settlers living close to Cheyenne River Agency. To comply with the orders he received, Colonel Sumner promised to escort Big Foot and his people to Camp Cheyenne, a temporary military outpost.[83] However, Sumner was not satisfied with his orders. He complained that he did not have enough troops to properly execute all the required tasks: to watch Big Foot, to prevent him from leaving the reservation, to capture Sitting Bull's fugitives, and to protect settlers. He believed that his superiors had sent him orders that he could not follow properly.[84]

The officers in the field, Lt. Col. H. C. Merriam and Lieutenant Colonel Sumner, were not convinced that capturing Big Foot was necessary in the first place. Colonel Merriam noted several times that Big Foot's people planned to surrender peacefully; they were hungry and greatly frightened. He did not expect any problems with Big Foot. In addition, 175 of the fugitives from

Standing Rock had already surrendered peacefully.[85] Sumner informed Miles that no danger existed, since even Sitting Bull's people obeyed orders. "They were willing to do anything I wish," he informed Miles on December 21. The next day he wrote, "They seem a harmless lot, principally women and children. There is no danger of their going toward the Badlands."[86]

Colonel Sumner wanted to let the Indians stay the night in their own village, where he could give them additional provisions. He did not consider it necessary to start moving them immediately toward Cheyenne River Agency, as his orders demanded. Later he explained why he had not obeyed orders, saying that Big Foot asked him to let them stay in their homes rather than in a military camp. Sumner agreed, because the Indians had done nothing wrong, and he thought that they were "so pitiable, in sight that I at once dropped all thought of their being hostile or even worthy of capture." Moreover, the Indians were afraid of the army, which caused much restlessness, especially among the women and children. Had he taken the Indians to the military camp by force, it might have resulted in trouble. Sumner also fully trusted Big Foot and was sure that the chief had the power to control his people. When all this was settled, Sumner was again able to report that Big Foot and his people, altogether more than 330 Indians, were under military control.[87]

On December 22 General Miles informed his superiors that Big Foot and his Indians had been captured. This was most satisfying news since, according to Miles, Big Foot had been "most defiant and threatening." The next day Miles sent orders to Sumner authorizing him to put Big Foot and any of his people under arrest. Because Big Foot was still showing signs of hostility, Miles ordered Sumner to "secure Big Foot and the Standing Rock Indians there, round [them] up, if necessary and disarm them." General Ruger too felt that arresting Big Foot was necessary. He believed that it would be a positive step toward ending all the trouble.[88]

The next day, however, the news was no longer so positive. Miles received information that Big Foot had escaped. This confirmed his theory that Big Foot was indeed as hostile and treacherous as he had believed. Colonel Sumner had not acted according to orders, and the army suffered great humiliation. "Your orders were positive, and you have missed your opportunity," Miles wrote to him. Miles could not understand how a force of 200 men armed with two Hotchkiss guns could not control a group of Indians that included only some 100 men. "Big Foot has been defiant both to the troops and to the authorities, and is now harboring outlaws and renegades from other bands," Miles continued. After this, all possible measures were taken to capture the fleeing Indians. Big Foot was to be captured, disarmed, and arrested.[89]

Big Foot's escape came as a total surprise to Colonel Sumner. The Indians had been packing their belongings in preparation to move to Fort Bennett, near Cheyenne River Agency, as planned, on December 23. Then, according to Sumner, "a white man by the name of Dunn . . . got into their camp and told them I was on the road to attack and kill them all. . . . So they just stampeded and like rabbits they fled for shelter in the Badlands, carrying nothing and tracking so fast I could not overtake them." Sumner believed that the approaching column of Colonel Merriam's soldiers had also frightened the Indians, and that Big Foot had no other option than to lead his people away from the soldiers. Sumner did not want to pursue Big Foot too far because rumors reporting more hostile Indians approaching from other directions required his attention. Instead, he sent messages to other officers who could intercept the Indians on their way to the Badlands.[90]

General Miles acted quickly. Troops were ordered to the field from all directions. Some were sent from Fort Bennett to follow Big Foot; others were sent from Pine Ridge to intercept his escape. Miles wanted to stop him before he could join the ghost dancers at Pine Ridge. Meanwhile, although the developments on Pine Ridge continued to suggest a speedy settlement of the troubles there, Miles feared that Big Foot's arrival might cause problems. The troops pursued the Indians through a blizzard for several days without seeing a trace of them. Finally, they made contact.[91]

Maj. Samuel M. Whiteside captured Big Foot and his following of 120 men and approximately 250 women and children on December 28. Miles immediately ordered Brooke to send more troops to ensure that Big Foot could not escape. The task fell to Col. James W. Forsyth, commanding the 7th Cavalry. He had specific orders to hold troops at a safe distance; to be ready for treachery; to hold Big Foot, disarm him, and, if necessary,

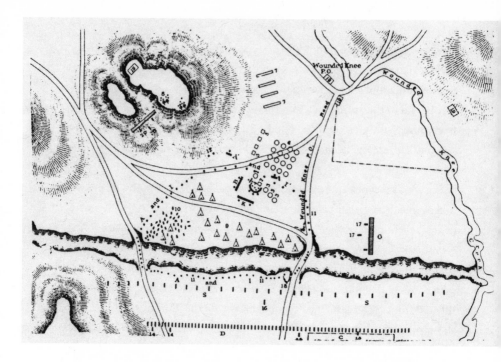

FIGURE 8. The Wounded Knee battlefield. Key: A–K: Army troops, S: Indian scouts, 1–3: Indian tents, 5–7: Army tents, 8: Hotchkiss cannons and troops, 9–10: Indian camps, 11–18: Army troops, 19: Indian houses, 20 Army troops, "Wounded Knee P.O." is the Wounded Knee Post Office. From *The Annual Report of the Secretary of War, 52nd Congress, 1st Session, House Executive Document*, Vol. 2, No. 1, Part 2, Vol. 1, Serial 2921 (Washington DC: Government Printing Office, 1892).

destroy him.[92] The next day, however, both Miles and Brooke seemed confused. Something had happened: a fight had taken place while Big Foot's men were being disarmed. There were casualties among the soldiers, and a few Indians had escaped. It was reported that the engagement took place at Wounded Knee Creek.[93]

During the following days more and more information about the Wounded Knee fight was received. According to army sources, Big Foot surrendered without resistance and was escorted to a camp at Wounded Knee Creek. During the night, Colonel Forsyth brought in the 7th Cavalry for reinforcement. The plan was to issue rations to the Indians in the morning, disarm them, and take them to Pine Ridge Agency.[94]

According to the army reports, on the morning of December 29, the

Indians refused to surrender all their guns, giving up only a few old carbines. Colonel Forsyth ordered the soldiers to conduct a search for arms among the women in the Indian camp. While the disarmament was carried out, the medicine man started to harangue the young men. He danced, shouted, and threw dust in the air. Finally, he signaled something to the men, and suddenly one of them opened fire on the soldiers. The Indians fired some fifty shots before the army returned fire. The Indians dispersed in all directions and were followed by troops, who kept calm and even helped wounded women and children. In the resulting fight most of Big Foot's men were killed, and some women and children had fallen. This, however, was mostly due to the confusion, as the soldiers could not differentiate between women and men. Army officers also claimed that the Indians themselves shot some of their own women and children during the confusion. The army lost one officer, six noncommissioned officers, and eighteen privates; four officers, eleven noncommissioned officers, and twenty-two privates were wounded. In addition, two civilians were wounded. Most of the earliest army accounts described the Indian resistance as vicious and the conduct of the troops as excellent and blamed the incident entirely on the Indians. Colonel Forsyth, for example, said that desperate Indians, crazed by religious fanaticism, started the fight and that only a few noncombatants were killed. Some reports even claimed that no women or children were killed.[95]

This view changed when more and more bodies of women and children were found on the battlefield, and even miles away from the actual scene of the battle. The behavior of the 7th Cavalry quickly became a subject of controversy. President Harrison directed that an inquiry be conducted into the killing of women and children on the Wounded Knee battlefield. Maj. J. Ford Kent and Capt. Frank D. Baldwin were ordered to investigate the matter. The inquiry was conducted during January 1891.[96]

General Miles relieved Colonel Forsyth from duty on January 4, 1891, because he believed that the disposition of troops had been such that it caused the soldiers to shoot one another in the crossfire. This, according to Miles, showed that Forsyth was incapable of commanding U.S. Army troops. Although Miles regretted the death of women and children, calling the army's actions unjustifiable and injudicious, he was more concerned about how his orders had been executed. The Kent-Baldwin investigation found no evidence of misconduct or disobedience. Eventually the 7th Cavalry was acquitted, and Colonel Forsyth resumed his command.[97]

Even though the bodies of a woman and three children who had been shot at close range were found three miles from the battlefield, arousing speculation that the soldiers had pursued and then shot them, the official opinion was that the army had performed well and the treachery of the Indians had caused all the trouble. General Schofield noted in February 1891 that "the conduct of the 7th Cavalry under very trying circumstances was characterized by excellent discipline and in many cases, by great forbearance." No further investigation would be necessary. In fact, eighteen Medals of Honor were later awarded to soldiers involved in the Wounded Knee affair.[98]

The news of the battle at Wounded Knee Creek caused intense fear and anger at Pine Ridge Agency. Miles reported that the news alarmed those who had already surrendered there; 3,000 Indians fled and joined Kicking Bear and Short Bull, who were still on their way to the agency. In addition, some 150 men led by Two Strike reportedly went to Wounded Knee, where they engaged in a battle with the 7th Cavalry. Afterward, the Indians returned to Pine Ridge Agency, where they fired toward the agency buildings, wounding two soldiers. General Brooke did not allow the soldiers to engage in a battle with the Indians, and the soldiers at the agency did not return fire. One officer, however, wanted to fire on the Indian camp behind Red Cloud's house, but fearing the results of such an act, Brooke gave strict orders not to respond to the Indians' fire. Only the Indian police fired back and drove away the attacking Indians. According to Brooke, the young Brulés and Oglalas now controlled the majority of the Indians who had fled the agency. Many Indians soon showed their desire to return to the agency, but they were held in the camp by the younger, "hostile" element.[99]

Immediately after the Wounded Knee affair, the army had to take action to prevent a major Indian war. According to Miles, the fight at Wounded Knee caused 3,000 Indians to be "thrown into a condition of hostility with a spirit of animosity, hatred and revenge." During the days following the Wounded Knee battle several skirmishes between the Indians and the army occurred, the most notable of them at the Holy Rosary Catholic Mission

FIGURE 9. "Gen. Miles and Staff during Late Indian War at Pine Ridge Agcy."
General Miles arrived at Pine Ridge on December 30, 1890, to take charge of
the field operations. From left to right: Capt. Ezra P. Ewers, Lt. John S. Mallory,
Capt. Francis E. Pierce, Lt. Col. Dallas Bache, Capt. Francis J. Ives, Maj. Jacob
Ford Kent, Lt. Col. Henry C. Corbin, Maj. Gen. Nelson A. Miles, Capt. Frank D.
Baldwin, Lt. Sydney A. Cloman, Capt. Charles F. Humphrey, and Capt. Marion
P. Maus. Denver Public Library, Western History Collection, photographer un-
known, call number x-31369.

(Drexel Mission) near Pine Ridge Agency. Troops of the 7th Cavalry, again
under the command of Colonel Forsyth, were nearly annihilated by a force
of Indian warriors. The arrival the 9th Cavalry troops saved the day for the
army. The small skirmishes following Wounded Knee resulted in few casualties on both sides but kept the tension high.[100]

Following the Wounded Knee battle, General Brooke prepared his troops
for Indian attacks. He ordered them to surround the hostile camp, now situated at White Clay Creek. At the end of December General Miles arrived at

Pine Ridge Agency and assumed command of the military operations. Miles continued to encircle the Indians and sent Brooke to the field to monitor operations. The military operations were conducted to cut off the Indians' escape routes, forcing them to move gradually toward Pine Ridge Agency.[101]

While the military tightened the cordon around the Indian camp, General Miles sent negotiators, both Indian and white, to the hostile camp to restore confidence. These negotiations bore favorable results, and on January 7, 1891, Miles reported that seventy Indians from the hostile camp came to the agency and surrendered. The rest, led by Red Cloud, Little Wound, Big Road, and Two Strike, were expected to arrive in the near future.[102]

Miles took utmost care to prevent further hostilities. Food was issued to the Indians, and Miles assured them that they would receive different treatment than Big Foot's people had at Wounded Knee. He noted that the Indians were very suspicious and afraid; restoring confidence after Wounded Knee would be extremely difficult. He believed that the Indians would surrender only if the army left the reservations, or if army officers replaced the civil agents. "An immediate and thorough change is needed," he wrote. He emphasized that the blame for the trouble lay partly on the agents and the general mismanagement of the government's Indian policy. Following Miles's repeated demands to replace the agents, orders for putting military officers in charge of the Lakota reservations came on January 6, 1891. Miles quickly replaced the agents with army officers.[103]

On January 10, the Indians, surrounded on three sides, started to move slowly toward Pine Ridge Agency. The military followed the Indians closely, preventing them from escaping in any direction; the only way open to them was toward the agency. The next day the whole group, 3,000 Indians, camped at White Clay Creek five miles away. Most of the Indians reportedly wanted to surrender. General Brooke kept the pressure on by following them closely.[104]

Two days later, on January 12, the Indians moved closer to Pine Ridge Agency, and Miles believed that the trouble was coming to an end. Nothing but an accident or a mistake could prevent a favorable result. He noted that the Indians were still very agitated, even wild. Many people in the camp were wounded, which kept tensions high and caused desperation and despair among the Indians. There was still a lot of work to be done before a permanent peace could be achieved, Miles reported. It was of utmost importance that the government show its good intentions to the Indians. A delegation of chiefs needed to go to Washington to meet with the commissioner of Indian affairs and the president. Miles believed that only in this way could a bridge to peace be established.[105]

During the following two days the Indians moved even closer. Finally, the long column arrived at Pine Ridge Agency under the watchful eyes of the U.S. Army. Miles gave orders to the chiefs to collect all arms from the Indians. He wrote that Kicking Bear was the first to give up his gun, and others soon followed. Altogether approximately 600 to 700 guns were gathered, 200 of which were rifles. This, Miles believed, was more than the Lakotas had ever surrendered before. The number of guns collected, however, was much less than anticipated.[106] The general impression throughout the trouble was that the Lakotas were well armed with very modern guns, some even with two Winchester rifles. These estimates are quite revealing, especially given that the Lakotas were poor and that new guns were expensive. The events at Wounded Knee and at the final surrender show that these estimates were highly exaggerated.

Throughout the trouble, Miles, along with his fellow officers, seemed to empathize with the Indians to a certain extent, but at the same time the officers, especially Miles, called for firm action. The officers clearly wanted justice to be done for the Indians. Their job, however, was to command the troops and to prevent an outbreak, which might have led to great loss of life. Miles's actions were particularly divided. At times he called for justice for the Indians; at least once, in his official report on September 24, 1891, he wrote that a careful investigation "seems to justify the opinion that no considerable number of them [the ghost dancers] had seriously intended to engage in hostilities against the United States, unless driven to such a course by unbearable hardship, or in self-defense." But at the same time he predicted the biggest Indian war ever and called for decisive military action. For example, he characterized Sitting Bull's death as a "first and serious blow to the hostile element," even though, according to the army's orders, the original goal was to avoid hostilities and to suppress a possible outbreak. This first blow, which pleased Miles, did not comply with those orders.[107]

Although Utley has noted that Miles had to combine force and diplomacy in the right proportions in order to prevent a major Indian war, it seems that in several cases he managed to ignore his officers' opinions, basing his actions instead on reports that amounted more to rumors than actual facts. In retrospect, Miles believed that his tactics would have been successful had not a few incompetent officers, including Sumner and Forsyth, spoiled his carefully drawn plans.[108]

Undoubtedly, the political play behind the scenes was also a factor during the ghost dance troubles. This occurred mainly on two levels: one involved Miles's own political goals; the other, the tension between the War and Interior Departments over the control of Indian affairs. To what extent Miles's personal ambitions affected his decisions and actions throughout his career is a question that has caused controversy among scholars. Wooster, for example, has noted that the sympathies Miles showed toward the Indians in his memoirs were not always evident in his official correspondence. According to Wooster, these late-born sympathies could well have been aimed at gaining the support of the influential eastern humanitarian groups for a projected presidential campaign. Whether true or not, the fact is that already during the campaign of 1890–91 accusations were made by some army officers and even by the public that Miles was using the Indian troubles to boost his own political career.[109]

Although the military campaign was over in January 1891, many questions went unanswered and many problems remained to be solved. During the following months, numerous investigations and inquiries were made into the ghost dance troubles, into the military's conduct, and into official Indian policy.[110] Even if no evidence to condemn the army's actions was found, and no hard historical evidence can be found today that goes to show there were any plans to kill so many Indians, it has to be noted that there was an undercurrent of sentiment around the reservations, among the reservations' white residents, ordinary soldiers, newspapermen, and Indians alike, that the army was there to teach the Lakotas a lesson. Showing the Lakotas that it was impossible to resist the power of the U.S. Army was not the military's official policy, but even General Miles stated as early as on December 30, 1890, that the Wounded Knee affair was a good lesson for the Lakotas.[111]

Be that as it may, the army ended the ghost dance troubles without loss of life or property among white settlers. The ghost dancing was stopped, the Indians were disarmed, and military officers controlled the Lakota reservations. The army had accomplished all that was expected: it had protected the settlers, it had divided the Indians, and it had conquered.

By January 15, 1891, the military campaign was over. Altogether almost 7,000 Lakotas were in camp around Pine Ridge Agency under the full control of the army. This also ended the largest military operation in the United States since the Civil War. During the whole campaign, including the fight on December 15, 1890, when Sitting Bull was killed, the Wounded Knee affair, and the skirmishes in January 1891, more than 200 Lakotas had been killed; around thirty soldiers and a few civilians who were with the army had also lost their lives. The military operation had cost 1.2 million dollars. Despite this, General Miles informed his superiors that the campaign had been most satisfactory: "A more complete submission to the military power has never been made by any Indians," he concluded.[112]

The campaign formally ended in a spectacular military parade that took place at Pine Ridge Agency during a snowstorm. Miles felt that it made a great impression on the Indians who witnessed it. He depicted the scene in his memoirs: "This review was one of the most interesting in my experience, as it occurred in midwinter and during a gentle snow storm. The vast prairie, with its rolling undulations, was covered with the mantle of winter. That cheerless, frigid atmosphere, with its sleet, ice, and snow, covered all the apparent life of nature. That scene was possibly the closing one that was to bury in oblivion, decay, and death that once powerful, strong, resolute race."[113]

FOUR

Missionary Views on the Lakota Ghost Dance

The earliest contacts between Euro-American explorers and the Sioux Indians took place in the seventeenth century, when men like Pierre Espirit Radisson and René-Robert Cavalier de la Salle encountered the people known today as the Sioux. Jesuit missionaries soon followed. Fathers Claude Jean Allouez and Louis Hennepin and others contacted the Sioux people in the second half of that century and the early eighteenth century. These missionaries were, to a certain extent, successful in introducing Christianity to the Sioux people, although these early contacts did not result in the establishment of permanent missions among the Sioux.[1]

By the mid-nineteenth century, Catholics and various Protestant groups competed vigorously over souls in the Eastern Sioux (Dakota) country, which roughly encompasses the present state of Minnesota. The missionaries quickly established missions and took up the task of translating biblical and other religious texts into the Dakota language. Many newly converted Sioux were trained as catechists, some of whom were elevated into the clergy. It soon became evident that the services of these Christian Sioux were vital in spreading the missionaries' message. Both the Protestants and the Catholics were convinced that Christianity and Indian education walked hand-in-hand.[2]

While the Dakotas were becoming familiar with Christian missionaries and their teachings, their western relatives, the Lakotas, remained outside the area of the missionaries' influence. The Jesuit missionary Father Pierre J. De Smet frequently visited the Sioux along the Missouri River during the mid-nineteenth century. But missionaries did not really affect the lives of the Lakotas until the 1860s, when increasing numbers of Dakotas moved westward or settled on reservations closer to the Lakota country. Christian missionaries followed the trails of this westward movement. By the early 1870s the Lakotas also were becoming used to these white men who ventured into their camps bringing stories of a new God. Some of these white men even spoke their language and were able to establish good relationships with them. Still, converting these nomadic people of the plains turned out to be a formidable task.[3]

In 1859 the Episcopal Church organized two mission areas west of the Mississippi River. In 1873 William Hobart Hare was appointed bishop of Niobrara, which encompassed the country of the Lakotas. During these early years of organized mission among the Lakotas, four Lakota agencies were assigned to the Episcopalians; the first Episcopal mission was established in 1879 at Pine Ridge Agency, and a church building was erected in 1881. Only Standing Rock Agency was assigned to the Catholics. In the 1880s, however, all Christian denominations were allowed to establish missions at all the Lakota agencies. Presbyterians established a mission, a school, and a church at Pine Ridge Agency in 1885–86. As noted above, missionary ideology dictated that Indians needed to be civilized before they could be good Christians. The first schools among the Lakotas were established in the late 1870s, and before the construction of churches, school buildings often served as places of worship. By 1885 the Episcopalians were operating two mission schools at Rosebud in addition to the seven government-operated schools at that agency. In 1886 the government established nine schools at Pine Ridge. The Jesuits also established schools on Pine Ridge and Rosebud in 1886 and 1887.

Many Lakotas, however, resisted both education and Christianity. In the late 1870s and early 1880s the vast Great Sioux Reservation still offered the possibility of avoiding contact with white men. Many Lakotas took advantage of this and lived far away from the agencies and the missions. Only after the Lakotas truly adapted to the reservation system in the late 1880s did Christian teachings begin to have a significant impact on these people.[4]

The beginning of Catholic mission work among the Lakotas can be traced to the early 1880s, when Catholic missionaries arrived at Pine Ridge

and Rosebud Agencies. Among these was Father Francis M. Craft, who established good contacts with the Oglalas and Brulés. He did not, however, establish any permanent missions on the Great Sioux Reservation. In
December 1885 Father John Jutz, together with Brother Ursus Nunlist, arrived at Rosebud. On January 1, 1886, they established the Catholic mission,
St. Francis, there. A year later Father Jutz established another mission, Holy
Rosary, at Pine Ridge. Catholic mission work at Standing Rock Agency had
begun in the late 1870s under the auspices of Bishop Martin Marty. Later, in
1884, Father Craft arrived at Standing Rock. Soon Protestant and Catholic
missions were working side by side, but not together, among the Standing
Rock Sioux. The first Catholic mission on Cheyenne River Reservation was
established as late as 1891.[5]

From the beginning, the missionaries looked to implement the government's assimilation policies and were quick to condemn Lakota traditional
beliefs and ceremonies. The activities of medicine men were of great concern to the missionaries, who believed that the medicine men were allies of
the devil. The missionaries also condemned polygamy as well as many traditional Indian dances and feasts, which they considered immoral.[6]

Missionary work among the Lakotas throughout the 1880s was extensive,
especially when success is measured in the growing numbers of missionaries, teachers, and other employees who participated in the attempt to civilize the Lakotas. By the end of the decade, the number of churches established for the Lakotas had grown from six to thirty-one, and the number
of missionaries rose from six to fifty-four. According to statistics provided
by the churches, the number of Christian Lakotas also rose, from a meager
few hundred in the early 1880s to 4,757 by the end of the decade. In 1889 on
Pine Ridge, for example, the number of Christian Lakotas who regularly attended church was reported to be 2,213 out of the total population of 5,611.
Similar growth was reported at other Lakota agencies.[7]

During the 1880s, growing numbers of Lakota children were sent to government boarding schools far away from their homes. Reservation boarding schools and day schools also were able to report success in educating and
Christianizing Lakota children.[8] Ironically, education and literacy became
means for Indians throughout the United States to communicate with each

other. This, of course, was essential for the rapid spread of the ghost dance religion in the late 1880s.

Although the numbers showed that mission work among the Lakotas was successful during the 1880s, only a fraction of Lakotas completely turned to Christianity. Many simply incorporated Christian concepts into their own traditional system of belief. But this did not mean that they did not consider themselves Christians at the same time. The Lakota way of thinking did not require that Christianity be excluded from traditional Lakota beliefs. The missionaries could not accept this; for them a Christian could not have any other gods or ways of worship. There are many accounts by missionaries, Catholic and Protestant alike, who encountered Lakotas whom they considered to be devoted Christians but who were secretly practicing their old "heathenish" religion. These encounters seem to have been devastating to the missionaries; time after time they were deeply disappointed and angered by such discoveries. To the missionaries, this was evidence that more hard, earnest work lay ahead.[9] It is therefore difficult to establish the actual number of Christian Lakotas by the time the news of the ghost dance started to spread among them.

When the ghost dance arrived at the newly reduced Lakota reservations in 1890, Father Emil Perrig was the superintendent of the Holy Rosary Mission School under the leadership of Father John Jutz. Father Florentine Digman, with two other priests, Fathers Aloysius Bosch and Joseph Lindebner, was in charge of the St. Francis Mission and School on Rosebud Reservation. These missions were located close to each other, and contacts between the priests were frequent; the priests also exchanged posts from time to time. Perrig and Digman, for example, worked at both the Holy Rosary and the St. Francis Missions. This was natural, since they were all members of the same religious order, the Jesuits, and from a single governance structure within the order, which at the time was located in Buffalo, New York. Fathers Jutz, Perrig, and Digman stayed at their posts throughout the ghost dance period. Other mission employees, including sixteen Jesuit brothers and several Franciscan nuns, who worked as schoolteachers, assisted them. In December 1890 Father Craft arrived at the Holy Rosary Mission and stayed there until January 1891. Secretary of War Redfield Proctor and Secretary of the Interior

John Noble sent him there to investigate the ghost dance and to try to prevent an uprising. He was to report his findings also to the director of the Bureau of Catholic Indian Missions, Father Joseph A. Stephan.[10]

By the time the ghost dance had arrived on the Lakota reservations the Protestants too were well established there. Episcopalian Bishop William Hobart Hare, who not only was in charge of the whole region but also visited Rosebud Reservation during the ghost dance period, was widely quoted by many newspapers. Another important missionary was the Congregationalist Mary C. Collins, who was stationed at Grand River on Standing Rock Reservation. She was watching the ghost dance closely and even visited Sitting Bull's camp on Grand River. Her opinions were published in many national newspapers. Phillip J. Deloria, a Yankton Sioux Episcopal priest, was a very important figure among the Christian Indians on that reservation.

The Protestant missionaries' point of view was expressed in the *Word Carrier* newspaper, published at Santee Agency in Nebraska. It reflects the missionaries' attitudes, but also the attitudes of literate Christian Indians. The paper was begun by the Reverend John P. Williamson in 1871 and was initially published in the Dakota language under the name *Iapi Oaye*, but from 1873 until 1884 it was published as one paper using both titles. In 1884 the paper was separated into two; from then on, the English version was published to serve Christian Indians and also white audiences in the East. The paper included descriptions of daily life on the reservations and tried to shed light on the situation among the Indians. The Dakota-language version of the paper, the *Iapi Oaye*, differed in content from the English version since it was intended for a different audience. It served as a platform for missionary work among the Dakotas and Lakotas alike. The articles in the *Iapi Oaye* were written by missionaries and Christian Indians; it included national and international news, prayers, hymns, inspirational readings, and Bible translations. The editorial staff of these newspapers consisted of Presbyterian and Congregationalist missionaries. The most important writers, in addition to John P. Williamson, were Stephen R. Riggs and his sons, Alfred, Thomas, and Frederick, all of whom had many years of experience of missionary work among the Sioux.[11]

Missionaries who were closely observing the effects of the ghost dance on the Lakotas were either situated on the Lakota reservations or they were individuals who had long experience with the Lakota people. To depict the situation among the missionaries, I consider in this chapter the perspectives of both Protestant and Catholic missionaries. I examine the missionaries' attitudes toward the ghost dance, but also explain the role the missionaries played in the actual chain of events that eventually led to the Wounded Knee massacre.

"The Appearance of Deviltry"

For the Jesuit missionaries the year 1890 began in the same fashion as the years before: they were engaged in organizing education for Lakota children as well as in converting as many people as possible. Since establishing their missions on the Lakota reservations, the Jesuit priests had baptized several hundred Lakota children. School attendance was reported to be growing. The missionaries' diaries and correspondence reveal that, until late August 1890, nothing out of the ordinary took place at the various missions on the Lakota reservations, and the missionaries were fully occupied with daily missionary work. The documents explain in great detail various church-related activities, as well as other social activities around the missions. The priests seem to have been especially proud of the schools and the success the Indian children were having in reading and other schoolwork.[12]

The ghost dance became an issue on August 24, 1890, when Father Perrig noted in his diary that the Indians were holding a large meeting only six miles north of Holy Rosary Mission. He wrote that the meeting was in response to "that silly talk about the apparitions of Jesus Christ." He described how the Indians defied authority by refusing to return to their homes. Agent Hugh D. Gallagher, who had been in Chadron, Nebraska, was called back to the agency. Immediately upon his arrival on August 24, he summoned his Indian police force and rode out to meet the Indians. Father Perrig described the meeting between the ghost-dancing Indians and the agent as one at which the Indians were prepared to fight. According to Perrig, a battle between the Indian policemen and the ghost dancers was imminent. He noted that at a critical point, the interpreter Phillip Wells intervened, explaining that they were there only to talk to the Indians and to ask them to go home because such gatherings were illegal. After some discussion the Indians agreed, and the agent with his policemen returned home.[13] The next day, however, Father Perrig noted that the Indians were meeting again, in other places, for the same purpose.[14]

On September 7, Perrig seemed discouraged. He noted briefly, "Our whole camp, six families[,] escaped, went to the Medicine dance in Medicine Root Creek. Only two Indians in Mass."[15] By September several ghost dance camps had been established throughout Pine Ridge Reservation; one of the major camps was on Medicine Root Creek. On September 20 Perrig wrote, "All our Indians . . . off to the ghost dance."[16] Father Perrig's comments substantiate that the ghost dance did not become a factor on that reservation before early September, and also that from the white point of view, order on the reservation started to collapse by late September.

On other Lakota reservations the ghost dance had not yet caused alarm among the missionaries. On September 26, however, Perrig reported that rumors were spreading among the white population that the Indians on Rosebud were planning an uprising and that they had arrived at St. Francis Mission wearing war paint and carrying arms. They also took their children out of school. Father Perrig noted that the new agent, Daniel F. Royer, had arrived at Pine Ridge.[17]

Despite the rumor about an impending uprising on Rosebud Reservation, Father Digman, at St. Francis, made no mention of anything to that effect in his papers. A few days later, on September 30, however, he wrote at length about the ghost dance. He traced its origins to the destitute situation among the Lakotas. He stated that the ghost dances had started on Pine Ridge in the spring of 1890 and then spread to Rosebud. He emphasized that the government's treatment of the Lakotas was one of the main reasons for disaffection; the cut in rations, disappointment in their farming efforts, loss of land, and hunger and diseases were to be blamed for the current dissatisfaction among the Lakotas. Because of that, the Indians "lent a willing ear to the gospel of chief Short Bull preaching the ghost dance and promising his followers old glorious times of the buffalo hunt and threatening those holding with the whites, they would be turned to dogs."[18] Whether this is actually what Short Bull said is not known.

Agent J. George Wright asked Father Digman and other missionaries to try to persuade the ghost dancers to give up their dances. Digman, accompanied by another priest, visited one of the ghost dance camps on White River. Digman describes the encounter:

> At our arrival the leaders just took a sweat bath, howling and singing and praying to the stones. Having finished they crawled out one by one with their long dripping hair. We invited them to their large dance hall nearby saying: "We have good news for you." But before they allowed me to speak their spokesman declaimed very bitterly against the agent, who had threatened not to issue any more rations or give them work and wages before they would give up dancing. "Obey [the] order then and quit dancing. Why after all are you bent on dancing?" "This is our way of worshipping the Great Spirit, who has taught us so." "I fear it is another spirit that leads you astray." Here he tapped me on the shoulder saying: "You are a Blackrobe. We know you speak the truth. For this reason chief Spotted Tail had asked the Great Father to send Blackrobes as teachers for his people. But instead he sent us White Robes, saying they are alike. Now you white folks have different prayers. The Blackrobe's prayers and that of the White Robes and you quarrel [with] each [other] saying the other is not right. We Indians do not want that strife. Let us along then, and let us worship the Great Spirit in our own way."[19]

Father Digman's description demonstrates the conflicting viewpoints between the Lakotas and the whites. The whites saw the ghost dance ritual as heathenish, while the Indians considered it a prayer or worship, similar to those prayers and rituals the whites were trying to impose on them. This exchange also illustrates the religious confusion among the Lakotas caused by the competition between Christian denominations.[20]

In his diary Digman noted that he was having difficulty keeping children in school, and that many Indians on Rosebud were afraid of Short Bull's threats. Therefore, he invited those who did not want to join the ghost dancers to come to the mission, which many of them did. In a letter to Father Stephan he wrote, "*Our* Indians keep pretty well aloof of them," evidently referring to those who stayed close to the mission.[21] Thus in late September and early October daily routines on Rosebud Reservation seem to have been more important to Digman than the ghost dance. He wrote about the visit of Bishop Martin Marty and the laying of the cornerstone for the new church. He also reported that thirty-one Lakotas had been confirmed.[22]

Father Perrig, on Pine Ridge, however, expressed concerns about the ghost dance. He believed that it would lead to disturbances and that it "gets more and more the appearance of deviltry." He said that the person the Indians claimed to be the Father, and who pretended "to be our Lord," expressed dislike toward baptized Indians. Perrig believed that the Indians pretended that they saw "the happy hunting grounds" in their visions, which caused dislike, distrust, contempt, and even hatred toward the whites.[23]

Father Digman wrote to Father Stephan on October 14, citing at length the problems that lay ahead if the Lakotas' living conditions were not improved. He mentioned the ghost dance, but emphasized that most of the Indians did not believe in it; however, because they were suffering from lack of food, they were ready to do whatever was needed to make their voices heard. Some were even prepared to take the warpath the following spring, Digman reported. "Hunger is an awful power, sharpening or conjuring up again the warlike spirit of the Sioux," he wrote. He had attended a council where the ghost dance was discussed both by those who believed in it and those who were not actively participating in the ceremonies. Hollow Horn Bear, one of the leading progressive chiefs, said, "Let them give us all the rations for twelve months, they will [last] about six months and then the ghosts will come and bring back many buffalos." Digman noted that although the chief's comments were made in jest, they reflected what many Lakotas believed: the whites were not going to help them, so why not look for help from supernatural powers? Interestingly, it seems that Hollow Horn Bear later joined the ghost dancers, at least for a while.[24]

Still, despite these rather gloomy descriptions, neither Perrig nor Digman reported any actual disturbances on the reservations. They were preparing for Bishop Marty's visit. Father Perrig, for example, dutifully reported that several Indian boys had been confirmed. Nothing indicated that trouble would occur at Holy Rosary or St. Francis Missions during early October

1890. The biggest problem on Rosebud seemed to be the possible removal of Agent Wright, who was accused of dishonesty. This was of special concern to Digman, who believed that Wright was the only white person whom the Indians trusted. Perrig also briefly noted that Father Jutz had gone "to see the Indian dance." It is not clear whether Perrig was referring to Jutz's visit to one of the ghost dance camps or to some other social event.[25]

On October 19, Perrig noted that not a single Indian attended mass. "They are dancing again," he wrote in his diary. It seems that October and November were not particularly joyful months for the people at Holy Rosary Mission. Perrig complained several times that they did not have any fresh vegetables, and his diary entries were very brief and rather gloomy. It appears that most of the Indians normally staying at or around the mission had gone, and only the white employees remained. However, Perrig describes the Indian boys enjoying the first snows and what they were given for dessert. So, despite comments to the contrary, some Indians obviously remained at the mission.[26]

It is worth noting that even if most of the Indians had left the mission, they had not necessarily joined the ghost dancers. In fact, Digman wrote that the missions were empty because the children were "taken home by the scared parents." Father Jutz also believed that the parents wanted to keep their children at home and did not want them to attend either school or mass.[27] This was especially true after November 20, when the military arrived on Pine Ridge and Rosebud Reservations.

The military's arrival was major news on both reservations and did not escape the missionaries' notice. Father Digman was asked by the military officers to talk to the Indians and to explain that the army was there only to protect the good Indians and would be hard only on the hostiles. "The excitement of the Indians was great. I called a meeting. . . . The pipe of peace went around and the situation was talked over. They asked for a white flag to distinguish them from the hostiles. This, however, was not granted for fear it might be abused to get the soldiers into a trap," Digman wrote. Fearing military action, the Indians were allowed to camp around the mission. Father Digman described the scene: "In one day a large village of tents arose around St. Francis, and the Indians bid us 'sleep quiet, we will watch that no harm is done.'"[28]

Father Perrig wrote on November 19 that 500 soldiers were on the march toward the reservation because a general Indian uprising was feared. He noted that all government employees on the reservation were ordered to the agency, and many left the reservation altogether. Even the new agent, Daniel F. Royer, had reportedly gone to Rushville. All the reservation schools were closed, and the white people at the agency were arming themselves. Despite this general sentiment, Perrig wrote, "Nothing, however, transpires of hostile Indian intentions."[29]

Mary C. Collins, on the other hand, presented a completely different view of the ghost dance. In early November she visited Sitting Bull's camp on Grand River, where she witnessed a ghost dance ceremony and talked with Sitting Bull. She said that Sitting Bull invited her to a tipi where he was sitting, his face painted red, green, and white. From this tipi he was directing the ghost dance ceremony, which was going on outside. Collins urged Sitting Bull to stop the dance to avoid trouble. She told him that he could fool the Indians and even some white men, but he could not fool God. By "mocking God" in this way, he would surely bring trouble upon himself and his people. Sitting Bull replied simply that he wanted only to let his people worship God in their own way. Despite her friendly conversation with Sitting Bull, Collins condemned the ghost dance fiercely. She also condemned Sitting Bull. According to her, he was using the ghost dance to start an uprising. If nothing were done, a general Indian war was imminent. She urged that Sitting Bull and a few others be arrested: "There is no time now for false sentiment. Better sacrifice a few than that the whole race be exterminated."[30]

Collins described the ongoing ghost dance ceremony quite accurately, even noticing that women wore feathers on their heads, which was not the usual custom among the Lakotas. Although she predicted that the ghost dance would lead to an outbreak, she was clearly more concerned about the possibility that it was leading the Indians away from civilization and back toward savagery. "It is nothing more than the old sun dance revived," she wrote, adding, "This is all done to keep the people savages."[31]

Collins also wrote that she believed that Sitting Bull and a few others were only pretending to believe in the coming of the messiah, using the ghost dance to further their plans for starting an uprising. At the same time, however, she wrote, "It is not true that the masses are deceived. A few simple ones are: the greater part are not." As she described the ghost dance ceremony, she also said that only some of those who opposed the previous year's land agreement participated in the dance. Most of the Indians had not joined "the enemy," as she called the ghost dancers.[32] There is some confusion and some contradiction in her statements. If only a few of Sitting Bull's followers were participating in the ghost dance, who would start the general uprising and war?

In fact, the situation was growing more confusing on Pine Ridge than it was on Standing Rock Reservation. In late November, Father Perrig wrote that there were contradictory rumors around, some arguing that the Indians were definitely going to fight and others saying that no such plan existed. Perrig wrote that most of the Indians and squaw men (the term for white men married to Indian women) on the reservation were summoned to Pine Ridge Agency and that only 100 were dancing the ghost dance a few miles from Holy Rosary Mission. He seemed to be most concerned about the fact that no Indians showed up for mass and that all the schoolboys had to be sent home. He was also concerned about the rumored plans to disarm the Indians. He believed that the Indians would not give up their arms unless forced to do so by a superior military force. To this effect, more and more soldiers were arriving on the reservation. On November 27, Father Perrig noted that there were already 1,200 soldiers at Rosebud Agency. This, of course, could easily lead to trouble.[33]

Both Perrig and Digman wrote that the threatened uprising was exaggerated by newspapers and circulating rumors. Digman wrote in a light-hearted fashion that, if the newspapers were to be believed, St. Francis Mission at Rosebud had already been burned down and all the personnel killed: "We were amused hearing this news and built our church, unmolested, protected by God and our faithful Indians." Perrig, on Pine Ridge, was not amused. "Who is responsible for this costly and unwarranted scare!" he wrote on November 23. He regretted that no one wanted to believe that there actually was no trouble on the part of the Indians.[34]

By the end of November things seemed to be calming down at both missions. Perrig noted that some Indians were returning to Holy Rosary and were again attending mass. Digman did not make any entries in his diary regarding the ghost dance in the final days of November.[35] By that time, most of the Rosebud ghost dancers had gone to Pine Ridge.[36]

Two significant articles were published in the November issue of the *Word Carrier*. One was written by Owen Lovejoy, a Santee Sioux, who worked as a teacher on Standing Rock. He had joined Mary Collins on her trip to Sitting Bull's village and had also visited Sitting Bull earlier, telling him that he wanted to teach in the chief's camp. He had talked to Sitting Bull about stopping the ghost dance, but Sitting Bull gave no reply. Lovejoy was certain that God would finally help him to persuade the ghost dancers to give up their ceremonies. He obviously still hoped to be able to return to Sitting Bull's camp. Another person who joined Mary Collins was Elian Gilbert, who described the meeting with Sitting Bull and the ghost dance ceremony in the January 1891 issue of the *Iapi Oaye*. He described how Sitting Bull, sitting in his tipi, painted all the dancers, who then joined together for the dance, during which they cried, prayed, and danced. Gilbert did meet with Sitting Bull, but he refused to talk much. The people were expecting to meet the spirits of the dead, and they believed that what they were doing was sacred. Gilbert, however, did not believe that anything good could come of the ghost dance.[37]

Another article in the November 1890 *Word Carrier* described the ghost dance as the devil's way to take hold of the ignorant Indians. "The only way of the devil to keep control of a people is to hold them in ignorance and barbarism," the anonymous writer claimed. However, the ghost dance seemed to be a novel idea created by the devil. Since the missionaries were doing such good work among the Sioux, the devil was forced to come up with a new plan because his old plans had failed:

> He [the devil] is experimentally wiser now and accordingly makes a combination of the old heathen dance and the idea of a Messiah brought in by a gleam of Christianity. Thus the strange phenomenon of a messianic delusion is a credit to these Indian people. It shows that even into the darkest minds of the most heathenish of them such a

Christian influence has begun to work that the Devil can not arouse savage frenzy on his old purely heathen plan. The imported idea must be recognized in present tactics. The New Testament in many instances shows that the devils are more apt than men to recognize God. In this instance the Devil has seen these Indians to be more largely influenced by Christian thought than even the missionaries had supposed. For, in this Indian craze, the messiah idea, when analytically unencumbered, is of Christian origin. Thus making a combination of some of the most heathenish dances with very perverted messianic notion, all the mental affinities of the less than semi-civilized Indians are employed in the Devil's sole purpose of leading to destruction.[38]

This lengthy quote is very revealing; it acknowledges the Christian origins of the ghost dance and underscores that the dance was a combination of old Lakota traditions and Christianity. The writer does not blame the Indians for believing in this delusion; on the contrary, he praises the Indians' progress in Christianity. At the same time, the writer emphasizes that the Indians were not yet fully civilized, and therefore were susceptible to the work of the devil, who perverted Christian teachings to suit his purposes.

In November the *Iapi Oaye* also commented on the ghost dance. An article written by Sam White Bird at the Lower Brulé Agency appeared on the front page under the title "Messiya Itonsni" (The Lie of the Messiah, or The False Prophet).[39] He warned Indians against believing in false prophets and expressed his sadness over the fact that so many believed in this lie. He also referred to the Bible verses warning about the last days and what would happen to those who believed in the false prophets who would appear before the end of time. The ghost dance messiah was clearly one of those false prophets who would lead the Indians to destruction instead of resurrection. He believed that the ghost dance was a trick of the devil, whom he called *wakhą́ šíca*. Traditionally *wakhą́ šíca* referred to any kind of bad or evil spirits, but in the Christian context it designated the devil.[40]

On the second page of the paper, the Reverend John P. Williamson launched an attack against the ghost dance. The headline of his lengthy article was "Wanagi Akdi Kda" (The Spirits Will Arrive). The article began with an introduction to the ideas of the ghost dance supported by letters from Christian Indians urging people to give up this new messiah. One of the Indians, Louis Mazawakiyanna, wrote from Pine Ridge, and the other, Samuel Spaniard, from Rosebud. They described how the ghost dance had arrived among the Lakotas, saying that at first no one really believed it, but soon more and more people started to dance. They described the ceremonies in which many people "died" and then suddenly came to life again. They did not think the ghost dance was good for the Indians.[41]

Williamson himself wrote that this new messiah could not really be the true Messiah, since no one knew when Jesus would again return to earth. Although all Christians knew that the second coming of Christ would soon occur, the time and place of his arrival was unknown to humans. The ghost dancers claimed that the messiah would arrive sometime in spring, maybe in the spring of 1891, and some believed that he had already arrived. Williamson quoted the biblical warning against believing in false prophets and taught that the true Messiah would come like the light, moving from the east to the west, showing himself to all mankind. He would not arrive secretly in a deserted place in the West, as the Indians believed. Williamson threatened the Indians, writing that only those who believed in the true Christ would one day be resurrected; those who believed in the ghost dance would surely not be among them. In the spring the Indians would see that no spirits would arrive to rescue them. In support of his argument, Williamson quoted several other passages from the Bible.[42]

Thus the first comment on the ghost dance in the *Iapi Oaye* was, to a certain extent, similar in nature to the articles published in the *Word Carrier* that condemned the dance. The historian Todd Kerstetter has noted that it was typical of *Iapi Oaye*'s responses to the ghost dance to emphasize Christianity and to argue that the dance was the work of the devil.[43] I fully agree with his view, but it is also important to realize that the *Word Carrier* also condemned the ghost dance, which on several occasions it claimed to be the work of the devil. In this sense these two papers did not differ from each other; the real difference was in the way the articles were composed. The *Iapi Oaye* wanted to warn, educate, and even threaten the Indians about the dangers of believing in such a delusion, while the *Word Carrier* clearly spoke more to the white audience.

In late November and early December ghost dances were performed regularly on all four Lakota reservations. In late November Episcopalian Bishop William H. Hare visited Rosebud Agency and planned to visit several ghost dance camps. His trip was described in November by many national newspapers. In the pages of the *New York Times,* for example, he described the doctrine of the ghost dance and claimed that the Indians had no need to attack the settlements because, according to ghost dance teachings, all the whites would be destroyed anyway. He understood that "it [the ghost dance] revives many dear memories and appeals to the race feeling even in the civilized Indians."[44]

On December 6, Bishop Hare reported to the commissioner of Indian affairs about his trip. His comments, privately and publicly, were relatively calm. He did not believe that the ghost dance would lead to any uprising or violence. He listed several causes of disaffection among the Indians, particularly their miserable living conditions. He also noted that many missionaries had been predicting that something like this might soon occur if the Indians were not treated better. He emphasized that the ghost dance had a profound impact on the Lakotas and that even some of the "civilized Indians" were affected by it.[45]

Edward Ashley, an Episcopal missionary, accompanied Bishop Hare on his trip. Ashley later told an interviewer that, because of a busy schedule and a snowstorm, Bishop Hare visited only Rosebud Agency. So instead of going to the ghost dance camps himself, he asked Ashley to go. Ashley later regretted that he never got to visit Sitting Bull; he believed that his visit might have had an impact and that the outcome might have been different. He noted that at the time he did not believe the Indians were planning to launch any attacks against white settlements. Another person who regretted that he never got to go to Sitting Bull's camp was Phillip J. Deloria, who was an Episcopal minister at the Wakpala Mission and a Yankton Sioux. Bishop Hare asked him if he would go to Sitting Bull's camp and try to talk him out of the ghost dance. Deloria was willing to go since he was concerned about the ghost dances himself. He had already asked Agent James McLaughlin to stop the ghost dances by force, if possible. But McLaughlin refused, telling him that the ghost dances would stop by themselves. As Deloria was preparing for the trip to Sitting Bull's camp, he received a message from McLaughlin, who had evidently changed his mind; Sitting Bull was to be arrested at once. There was no longer need for Deloria's services, so he never made the trip to Sitting Bull's camp.[46]

Even if Bishop Hare failed to make the trip to these remote ghost dance camps, he clearly tried to use his influence on the dancers and was very concerned about Sitting Bull. Whether Hare got his information through firsthand experience or through Ashley or other missionaries is not important. The important thing is that his views made headlines in national newspapers. These newspaper articles were significant because Bishop Hare, while condemning the ghost dance as immoral, also specified what he believed to be the causes of the trouble and emphasized that there was no immediate reason for alarm.[47] However, because Bishop Hare visited only Rosebud Agency, his views were somewhat limited.

Father Digman, at St. Francis Mission, also was not particularly concerned about the ghost dance on Rosebud. He did not even mention the dance in his diary entries in December. This confirms what has been noted in other chapters in this study: Rosebud ghost dancers had gone to Pine Ridge, and the majority of Indians on Rosebud Reservation were either camped at the agency or had returned to their homes.

The Lakotas from Rosebud, however, were causing concern on Pine Ridge Reservation. Even Father Perrig took notice of the roaming Rosebud Lakotas. Their intentions seemed unclear: first he heard that the Rosebud Indians had escaped out of fear of the soldiers, but later he heard that they had come to live permanently on Pine Ridge, or that they had come to fight the soldiers. Also, the number of Rosebud Lakotas now on Pine Ridge was unknown, although he believed that they numbered up to 500 lodges and were joined by 20 to 30 lodges of Oglalas.[48]

At this point Father Jutz became the source of information regarding the ghost-dancing Lakotas on Pine Ridge. In early December, as an emissary from Brig. Gen. John R. Brooke, he traveled to the Stronghold, the ghost dancers' camp located in the Badlands. Once in the ghost dance camp, Jutz entered Chief Two Strikes' tipi, where the chief met him in a polite and friendly atmosphere. Jutz tried to convince him that nothing good could result from the ghost dance. He also pointed out that the Indians could not live in the Badlands forever. Gradually, the tipi filled with Indians, who, according to Jutz, were willing to listen to his advice. They told him that they were afraid of the soldiers and regretted the dire circumstances in which they were living. Jutz tried to assure them that the army had come only to protect the peaceful people on the reservation, and that General Brooke was willing to negotiate and end the trouble without bloodshed. He also told the Indians that those who would give up the ghost dance would be provided with food and clothing. The Indians asked him to swear that all that he said was true. Father Jutz did so, after which the Indians decided to send a delegation to meet with General Brooke.[49]

The newspapers reported on Father Jutz's mission. According to the *New York Times,* Jutz remarked that the Stronghold was "remarkably well fortified" and "wholly inaccessible." He believed that there might be more than 2,000 armed men in the camp. During the conference the Indians tried to explain the reasons for their actions and told the priest that they did not want to go to the agency because they feared punishment.[50]

Father Perrig also wrote at length about Jutz's mission and about the ghost dancers' grievances and worries. He commented on the dancers' arrival at the mission and on the council they had with General Brooke at Pine Ridge Agency. He described the ghost dancers as a peaceful delegation and was more concerned about their safety than about their showing any signs of hostility. That was also Father Jutz's impression. He noted that the Indians' grievances were just and that they were afraid that, if they came to the agency, they would be arrested or attacked by the soldiers. The missionaries believed that the council with the Indians and General Brooke took place in a most positive and friendly manner.[51]

"The False Prophets": Destruction, Not Resurrection

In early December Perrig, Jutz, Digman, and Francis M. Craft, who had come to the Holy Rosary Mission to investigate the ghost dance, had a heated debate about the dance. Their main concern was the situation among the Christian Lakotas. They wanted to know how many Protestant and Catholic Indians embraced the ghost dance, but were not able to come to any conclusions. In fact, the missionaries became quite agitated toward one another. Father Craft threatened to leave the reservation, but finally decided to stay. Perrig and Digman seemed to be quite unhappy about Craft's presence; they probably did not know that he was sent there by Father Stephan and Secretaries Noble and Proctor.[52]

The trouble among the priests did not end there. On December 14, both Jutz and Digman wrote to Father Stephan asking about the purpose of Craft's mission. They complained that Father Craft had not told them the truth about his mission when he arrived at Holy Rosary. When asked about it, he had been evasive and did not want to cooperate with the Jesuit missionaries. Only when pressured did Craft show them a letter that explained that he was sent by Father Stephan to investigate the situation among the Lakotas. Digman noted that even Agent Wright was concerned about Craft's presence, since his previous stay on the reservation caused some controversy. Father Stephan replied on December 19, regretting that friction had developed among the missionaries. He explained that since Father Craft had been on his way to Pine Ridge and Rosebud anyway, he felt that he could act as an official emissary from the Bureau of Catholic Indian Missions. He did not explain why Craft had not told about his mission openly, nor did he say that he was sent by Secretaries Noble and Proctor. Perhaps he did not even know.[53]

Father Craft had long been considered a troublemaker among his fellow missionaries. Throughout his career he managed to stir up controversy wherever he was stationed. In the early 1880s his superiors banished him from Rosebud and Pine Ridge Agencies. While on Standing Rock, he also got into considerable trouble with his fellow missionaries, as well as with policy makers in the East. Thomas J. Morgan, the commissioner of Indian affairs, after being accused by Craft of mismanagement, suggested that Father Craft might be mentally unbalanced.[54] At times Craft's methods caused the controversies, but sometimes trouble arose simply because of a clash of personalities.

Father Craft had some very original ideas about how to bring Christianity to the Indians. He was very strict and did not allow himself or anybody else any exceptions in practicing the Catholic religion. Yet at the same time he was quite open-minded about some Indian customs; he even saw Christian parallels in some of their traditional ceremonies. When considered from this perspective it is perhaps not surprising that Craft was again in the middle of a controversy, nor that he described the ghost dance the way he did. Perrig provides one rather amusing example of Craft's behavior. Perrig wrote that after returning from a ghost dance camp late in the evening Craft could not get into Holy Rosary Mission because the doors were closed. He knew what to do, however: he broke a schoolhouse window and climbed inside. He was found there the following morning, sleeping peacefully on the floor. It seems that Father Craft was quite a colorful person among the missionaries.[55]

The matter of the number of Christian Lakotas among the ghost dancers caused anxiety among the missionaries on several occasions. Father Perrig pointed out that many families left the agency and the mission, and that some Christian Lakotas did become active ghost dancers. Father Digman noted similar movement on Rosebud Reservation, but he wrote that these people left because they were frightened; not all of them became ghost dancers. The *Word Carrier* printed conflicting articles regarding the numbers of ghost-dancing Christian Lakotas. In December 1890 it reported that Christian Indians were "unmoved" by the ghost dance, but admitted also that a few indeed did participate in ghost dance ceremonies.[56] Reverend Williamson wrote, "It has been a time to try the virtue of the Christian religion, and the trial has been a victory for Christ. The followers of Jesus have been true to the captain of their Salvation and loyal to the powers that be. . . . Of eleven hundred church-members not a dozen turned aside after the Indian Messiah or were led to hostilities. . . . Only [a] few hid their lights for a time but soon recovered. Others stood firm through the trouble." Still, he admitted that missionary work, especially on Pine Ridge, was disrupted by the ghost dance.[57]

This matter understandably was of great concern to the missionaries. For them, every Christian Indian who became a ghost dancer indicated that their efforts in pushing the Lakotas toward Christianity were insufficient. The missionaries' comments simply reveal how difficult it was, even then, to distinguish between those who were supporting the ghost dance and those who were not. Furthermore, as this study shows, the matter was much more complicated than even the missionaries realized; to divide the Lakotas into progressive Christians who rejected the ghost dance and nonprogressives who accepted it is far too simplistic and does not take into account other important aspects of the ghost dance among the Lakotas.[58]

On December 12, Father Perrig wrote that almost half the ghost dancers had decided to give up and had started toward Pine Ridge Agency. He reported that General Brooke had used Red Cloud, American Horse, and Big Road to induce the ghost dancers to come in.[59] The dancers finally arrived at Holy Rosary Mission on December 14, 1890. The moving camp consisted of 145 lodges of Oglalas and Brulés; approximately 107 lodges reportedly stayed in the Badlands. The Indians told Perrig that many more Indians were willing to come in, but they had not been allowed to. According to Perrig, even Short Bull wanted to come in, but the more fanatical Indians wanted him to stay in the Stronghold. The Indians put up their camp about two miles northwest of the mission. Father Craft spent the evening in the Indian camp and evidently witnessed a ghost dance ceremony. The following day Perrig quoted Craft's description of the ghost dance and wrote that Craft "found it to be all right, quite catholic and even edifying." During the day an angry Indian who wanted to find some white men he could kill brought in the first rumors of Sitting Bull's death. The rumors were confirmed later in the evening by Father Jutz, who had been at Pine Ridge Agency.[60]

On the following days more and more Indians arrived at Holy Rosary Mission and established their camps close by. It is unclear whether these people were the Oglalas sent by General Brooke to the Badlands to induce the rest of the people there to come to the agency, or whether these camps also included former ghost dancers. The majority probably consisted of Oglalas sent by Brooke, since on December 21 Father Perrig wrote that they had gone to the Badlands.[61]

The December issue of the *Word Carrier* presented two opposing views of the ghost dance. The first compared the ceremony to the old Dakota dance, *wakhą wachípi* (the sacred dance), which is not to be confused with the sun dance. The article said that the ghost dance was equally as humbug as the old traditional dances. The other article maintained that the ghost dance had nothing to do with traditional dances. Contradicting Mary Collins's earlier report, this article claimed that it was not the old sun dance revived but a totally new ceremony. While the sun dance affected people physically, the ghost dance caused mental exhaustion and fervor. Despite these contradictory assessments, the paper characterized the Indian dances as "utterly demoralizing. . . . They break down habits of industry that have been painfully gained: they impoverish the people and set [them] back from civilization to barbarism." What the Indians needed, argued the *Word Carrier*, was education, which would eventually lead to civilization. Then there would be "no more Indian troubles and no more Indians."[62]

The December issue also took notice of Sitting Bull's death. The Reverend G. W. Reed at Fort Yates, Standing Rock, gave his lengthy explanation of the events surrounding Sitting Bull's death. According to him, the reservation had been in utter confusion since the news of the chief's death became known. At first the missionaries could not believe the news, since there were at the time so many contradictory rumors circulating around the reservation. Reed's description of the events follow the explanations given by Agent James McLaughlin and are therefore not quoted here. The Reverend, however, believed that no more trouble was expected at Standing Rock; most Indians were living peacefully in their camps or close to the agency.[63] On another occasion Reed declared that he did not believe that Sitting Bull had ever planned to leave the reservation without permission. Bishop Martin Marty, as well as the Reverend Aaron Beede, an Episcopal missionary who was also stationed on Standing Rock Reservation, supported his views. Beede thought that the ghost dance was "nothing new, a form of worship to help the dead as well as the living and to get visions for the future." The missionaries maintained that Sitting Bull was actually quite positively disposed toward Christianity, especially the Episcopal denomination. Therefore, they did not think that Sitting Bull fully believed in the ghost dance doctrine. Both Beede and Reed, however, made these comments more than ten years after the ghost dance, so time may have changed their views to some extent. Mary Collins also reported later that Sitting Bull had always been very

polite toward the missionaries; he never, not even during the ghost dance period, prevented them from doing their work. According to Collins, he stated
his objections but never took matters further.[64]

On December 20, Father Craft also commented on Sitting Bull's death.
He directly accused Agent McLaughlin of responsibility for it. The only way
to avoid trouble now and in the future was to keep the army in control of
the reservations, Craft believed. He thus blamed the government for allowing civilian agents to take charge of the Lakota reservations. Then he listed
several causes of the trouble; "starvation, abject misery, and despair" were
among them. Father Craft did not blame the Indians at all; he clearly sympathized with them, and said that the current state of affairs was caused by
"the outrageous conduct of the Indian Department for many years."[65]

Father Perrig's notes of late December show that the situation on Pine
Ridge was still very confusing. At times he wrote that all the ghost dancers
were willing to come to the agency; at other times he noted that the soldiers had gone after them, or that there had already been a skirmish between
the Indians and the soldiers. Father Jutz explained in a letter on December
26 that things were looking good, but at the same time he complained that
they were having trouble with the Indians at the mission. He did not specify
the nature of the problem but noted that they were spending money meant
for the school to help the Indians in the current trouble. More confusion
was added by the news that the soldiers were following some Indians from
Cheyenne River Reservation who were rumored to be planning to move to
Pine Ridge. They were Big Foot's people, who had escaped from Lt. Col.
Edwin V. Sumner only a few days earlier.[66]

Father Perrig also reported several causes of the ghost dance trouble. He
believed that replacing Agent Gallagher with an inexperienced new agent,
Daniel F. Royer, was a crucial mistake. He noted that there had been no
problems when Agent Gallagher was in office, but Royer could not manage the situation. Father Jutz also complained about the new agent, who
was unable to deal with the situation and was unwilling to provide Indian
policemen to protect the mission, ignoring Father Jutz's repeated requests.
According to Perrig, Royer threatened the Indians but never made good on
his threats. He therefore lost all his influence among the Indians, ghost danc-

ers and nondancers alike. Other reasons for Indian restlessness were the loss of land and the cut in their rations, which Perrig believed caused a general feeling of dissatisfaction and distrust. "Into these already dissatisfied masses the Messiah revelations were thrown. Every day almost brought new revelations, which all aimed at filling the Indians with distrust or hatred of the whites and with the hope of soon getting free from the rule and control of the whites," Perrig wrote on December 27, 1890.[67]

The *Word Carrier* offered a completely different explanation of the causes of the ghost dance trouble. The paper argued that neither hunger, disease, the replacement of Agent Gallagher, nor the government's failure to live up to its promises had anything to do with the ghost dance. The reasons for the trouble were twofold: Sitting Bull and Red Cloud were instigating trouble and heathenism was rampant: "One of these mischief makers is Red Cloud. Only that he is too wily to go into open rebellion. Another was Sitting Bull who well deserved his death. But no more than Red Cloud." The paper went on to blame them for opposing every attempt to move the Lakotas toward civilization and progress. Finally, the article came to its main point: heathenism. All Indian dances and customs should be abolished. The ghost dance and other dances were a disguise under which savagery and hostility were born: "We need a firm hand here and the absolute stopping of savage customs. . . . The Government must educate by good Government as well as by schools. But even more than this is the urgent need of missions that go in the power of God's truth and his spirit for the regeneration of the hearts of the people." The article also noted that the ghost dance and the teachings of a new messiah were not contradictory to traditional Lakota beliefs. The Indian pantheon was large enough to take in Christian and other gods.[68]

The *Word Carrier* published three more articles dealing with the causes of the trouble, but these totally contradicted the one just quoted. Two of the articles were overall assessments of the situation, and one focused on the ghost dance on Rosebud Reservation. All three pointed out that the trouble lay in the government's mismanagement of the reservations, hunger, diseases, and, to some extent, in the old chiefs and medicine men, who wanted to retain their power. None of these articles blamed the Indians or accused them of hostile intentions. On the contrary, they maintained that, if the Indians had been treated better, there would never have been a ghost dance and the ensuing trouble.[69]

In December the *Iapi Oaye* continued its attack on the ghost dance. Another article entitled "Messiya Itonsni" (The False Prophet) was published. This time it was written by Fred B. Riggs. His main point was that one should not be deceived by false prophets. He quoted the Bible to support his claims:

> Jesus answered: "Watch out that no one deceives you. For many will come in my name, claiming, "I am the Christ," and will deceive many. You will hear of wars and rumors of wars, but see to it that you are not alarmed. Such things must happen, but the end is still to come. Nation will rise against nation, and kingdom against kingdom. There will be famines and earthquakes in various places. All these are the beginning of birth pains. Then you will be handed over to be persecuted and put to death, and you will be hated by all nations because of me. At that time many will turn away from the faith and will betray and hate each other, and many false prophets will appear and deceive many people. Because of the increase of wickedness, the love of most will grow cold, but he who stands firm to the end will be saved. And this gospel of the kingdom will be preached in the whole world as a testimony to all nations, and then the end will come. (Matt. 24:4–14)

Then Riggs decided to educate his readers. He said that some Indians and whites alike believed that Christ had come down from heaven to resurrect the dead, but this was not true. The ghost dance messiah was the last of a long list of false prophets, the first appearing in Palestine during the Roman Empire. According to Riggs, what these prophets had in common was that they always led to destruction and bloodshed. Then he urged people to read the November issue of the *Iapi Oaye,* in which John Williamson presented his arguments against the ghost dance. The message was clear: those who believed in such false prophets were not going to be saved or resurrected, despite the messiah's promises. Danger and destruction only was in store for those who were fooled by this current delusion.[70]

Clearly, the missionaries saw the ghost dance as also a political problem that threatened their missionary work. To them, Christianity was the only means of ridding the Lakotas of heathenism. Although the missionaries acknowledged the problems the Indians were facing, they still emphasized that the daily missionary work was suffering and that by dancing the ghost dance the Lakotas were resorting to heathenism. This sentiment was especially evident in the articles published in November and December in the *Iapi Oaye*. Based on these articles and the individual missionaries' comments, it seems safe to say that by late December 1890 the missionaries' views about the causes of the ghost dance were quite contradictory.[71]

The last days of December 1890 were filled with confusion at Holy Rosary Mission. On December 29, the first rumors about the fighting at Wounded Knee Creek reached the people at the mission. Soon groups of wandering Indians arrived; some were heading toward Wounded Knee, others were escaping from the battlefield. Soldiers too were passing by, adding to the confusion. Father Perrig reported that a skirmish between the Indians and the cavalry took place in the hills surrounding the mission. This skirmish between the 7th Cavalry and some Lakota ghost dancers became known as the (Drexel) Mission Fight, and the valley where the soldiers made their stand was called the "Bloody Pocket," even though not much blood was spilled that day. Perrig wrote that a lot of gunfire was heard around the mission and that some Indians even shot a few rounds toward the mission buildings. He believed that it was an unnecessary encounter, in which both sides made a lot of noise without actually accomplishing anything. The mission was in no danger, despite the rumors reporting that it had been burned down.[72]

Much confusion also resulted from the reports claiming that Red Cloud had joined the ghost dancers and that the dancers planned to fight until the end. Other rumors suggested that the Indians were fighting against each other, and that some were willing to return to the agency whereas others were looking for a fight. Every day the situation seemed to change; one day Father Perrig reported that the soldiers were at the mission to give them protection, and on other days he wrote that Indians were coming to the mission from the ghost dance camp either to seek help or to give assistance to the missionaries. Perrig did not report any hostilities shown toward the mission employees; on the contrary, he was very concerned about the Indians'

FIGURE 10. "'Bloody Pocket' in which 'The Mission Fight' occurred; Dec. 30th 1890, [Pine Ridge Reservation]." Following the Wounded Knee battle U.S. Army troops and a group of Lakotas had a skirmish near the Holy Rosary Catholic Mission at Pine Ridge. Denver Public Library, Western History Collection, photographer C. G. Morledge, call number X-31341.

well-being. The fate of the wounded children was of great concern to him. He complained that he had not been able to have mass in several days.[73] All in all, the days following the Wounded Knee massacre were very confusing on Pine Ridge Reservation, and Perrig's and Jutz's notes illustrate the situation very well.

Father Craft, who was critically wounded in the Wounded Knee affair, later gave a lengthy description of the event. He arrived at Wounded Knee on the evening of December 28 as an emissary from General Brooke. On the morning of December 29 he walked around the Indian camp assuring the Indians that no trouble would occur. Surprisingly, Craft described Big Foot's people as "the worst element of their Agency, whose camp had for years been the rendezvous of all the worst characters on the Sioux Reservation."

He also accused the Indians of starting the fight. He claims that they were deliberately planning an attack on the soldiers and that, during the disarmament, they carried out their plan. Craft maintained that the soldiers fired on the Indians only after they were first fired upon. In the ensuing melee Craft was stabbed in the back. He went on to defend the soldiers' behavior during the battle. He denied all allegations accusing the soldiers of killing innocent women and children.[74] Father Craft's comments are remarkable, since until the Wounded Knee affair he had defended the Indians and his comments regarding the ghost dance had been very mild in nature. It is difficult to judge his change of heart, but perhaps the fact that he was so severely injured affected his opinions of Big Foot, his people, and the events on December 29.

Beginning on January 10, 1891, Father Perrig's notes reveal that things were settling down around Holy Rosary Mission. Rumors were still circulating, but overall the situation seemed to be less intense. The major concern, according to Perrig, was that the Indians were afraid of being disarmed, which might lead to trouble. Day by day, however, more Indians were moving toward the agency, stopping at Holy Rosary Mission to rest and eat; Perrig reported that 734 armed men with more than 1,000 women and children passed by on January 12 alone. The Indians were not at all hostile, although some tension was still evident. One example is the killing of Lt. Edward Casey on January 7, 1891. This incident seemed to be of particular concern to Perrig because Casey was shot by an Indian who had attended a government boarding school. Perrig again speculated about the number of educated Lakotas who had joined the ghost dancers. Finally, on January 23, 1891, he reported that most of the soldiers were ordered to return to their forts and that many Indians were settled around the agency. Peace had returned to Pine Ridge.[75]

The January 1891 issue of the *Word Carrier* published several articles relating to the ghost dance. One was written by an Episcopal schoolteacher, Jennie B. Dickson, who was located on Pine Ridge Reservation. By January she was staying with other government employees at the agency, where she was able to observe the effects of the Wounded Knee affair. She wrote that they were trying to care for the wounded Indians and soldiers alike, but that the situation around the agency was chaotic and confusing. Nobody knew what the Indians were planning to do, but she believed that the majority of them were not going to give up without another fight. She also believed that the army was not ready to answer the threat the Indians posed to the people on the reservation. Therefore, they were living in constant fear. One brief article commented on the Lakotas' actions at Wounded Knee, saying that they once again showed their great bravery when attacking a force much larger than theirs. It is noteworthy that the article blamed the Indians for starting the battle, although it clearly sympathized with them in other respects. Another article offered a revealing comment about the Wounded Knee affair: "Taking it in its bearings on the whole condition of things among the rebellious Titon [Teton] Sioux it was a blessing. It was needful that these people should feel in some sharp terrible way the just consequences of their actions, and be held in wholesome fear from further folly. . . . It was better that two hundred should die than that a nation should perish."[76]

This comment seems to fit well with the *Word Carrier*'s old policy that advocated a similar ideology. Already in the 1870s, the paper wrote that the Sioux ought to be taught a lesson that they would remember forever.[77] Although some white people living around the Lakota reservations, as well as certain military officers and government officials, believed that the Lakotas needed to be subjugated by force, I have not been able to find these sentiments expressed so clearly in the context of the ghost dance in any other source that I have studied.

It is worth noting that neither Father Perrig nor Father Digman commented on the Wounded Knee massacre at any length. Both basically noted that the battle had occurred and that Father Craft was injured, but they offered no explanations for the incident or provided any further comments. Father Perrig briefly mentioned the wounded who were treated by the mission employees.[78]

The *Iapi Oaye* commented on the Wounded Knee affair only very briefly, in January 1891. The paper simply wrote that Big Foot's people opened fire on soldiers, and as a result 150 Indians died and 30 were wounded. Also 26 soldiers had reportedly died.[79]

The *Word Carrier*, however, wrote at length about the ghost dance and

Wounded Knee in February and March 1891. These articles, written by the
Congregationalist missionary Thomas L. Riggs, were quite insightful in explaining the Indian point of view. Although Riggs condemned the ghost
dance as immoral, he seemed to understand the Indians' motivations and
clearly sympathized with them. He questioned the reasons behind Sitting
Bull's arrest as well as the army's conduct at Wounded Knee. He knew
Big Foot personally and believed that he did not have any intention of
going on the warpath. He went on to say, "The fact is that not one Indian in
a hundred of our western Sioux had any thought of making war upon the
whites, of having an 'outbreak' and cutting up generally." Riggs noted that
the Indians were very excited about their new messiah, but the excitement
was only local. It was the arrival of the U.S. Army that forced the Indians
to become hostile.[80]

It must be said that both the Protestant and the Catholic missionaries were
convinced that the ghost dance had to be stopped, since it would lead only
to disaster and to the return of heathenism. At the same time, they did not
believe that it would lead to an uprising or revolt. However, the Protestant
missionaries used much harsher language than the Jesuits to condemn the
ghost dance and those who participated in it. The Protestant missionaries
attacked the ghost dance fiercely, using the newspapers, especially the *Iapi
Oaye*, as platforms. While the missionaries clearly recognized that starvation,
disease, and ill treatment by the government were the causes of the Lakotas'
dissatisfaction, it is evident that they ultimately blamed the ghost dance on
heathenism. And heathenism, of course, was caused by the devil.

FIVE

"In an Atmosphere Pregnant with Mysteries"
Press Coverage of the Ghost Dance

"From Our Special Correspondent"

The press played a very significant role during the ghost dance troubles. Several newspapers sent reporters to the scene of the "Sioux troubles." Many of them arrived at Pine Ridge Agency on November 20, 1890, together with the army. The reporters represented some of the largest newspapers in the country, including the *New York Herald*, the *New York World*, and the *Chicago Tribune*, as well as many smaller local newspapers.[1]

One of the most important newspapers reporting on the ghost dance troubles was the *Omaha Daily Bee* in Nebraska. The paper sent Charles "Will" Cressey to Pine Ridge, where he arrived with Brig. Gen. John R. Brooke on November 20, and stayed until the Indians' surrender. Another reporter from the same paper, possibly Charles H. Copenharve, subsequently joined him. Their role in the ghost dance reporting is important because their reports, especially Cressey's, ended up in the pages of many of those newspapers that did not send reporters to the scene. The *New York Times*, for example, never sent a reporter to the Lakota reservations but used the reports written by the *Omaha Daily Bee* correspondents extensively. The *Washington Post* did not send a correspondent either and probably used some of the *Bee*'s material, but it never specifically acknowledged the source, as the *New York Times* and the *Chicago Tribune* did. The *Chicago Tribune* sent at least one, possibly two reporters to Pine Ridge; despite this, the *Tribune* used the *Bee*'s material widely, especially after the Wounded Knee battle. Perhaps the *Tribune* correspondents, Edward B. Clark and Irving Hawkins, left Pine Ridge by the end of December 1890.[2]

All the reporters stayed at a small hotel on Pine Ridge run by a local entre-
preneur and postmaster, James A. Finley, and the hotel soon became known
as Hotel de Finley. There the reporters got together in the evenings to discuss
the day's events and to compare notes. In the Hotel de Finley this varied lot
of newspapermen wrote the stories that they then sent to their respective
papers via telegraph from Rushville, Nebraska. Thus many of the articles
appearing in the newspapers were "specials from Pine Ridge via Rushville."
The papers often designated these articles as "from our special correspondent." They were often presented as accounts from eyewitnesses or reliable
sources, even though, in fact, what they reported were merely rumors. When
the dispatches were taken to Rushville, newspapers were brought back to
Pine Ridge. This allowed the correspondents—and the Indians—to see the
results of their work within a few days. Even the eastern papers arrived at
Pine Ridge relatively quickly, often within a week. These newspaper reports
added to the already confusing situation on the Lakota reservations. They
angered and frustrated General Brooke, but also allowed the Indians to get
firsthand information about the sensation they were causing.[3]

By mid-December there were seventeen correspondents, including two
women, representing sixteen daily newspapers, two magazines, and the
Associated Press. *Harper's Weekly* sent its own reporter, the famous western
artist Frederic Remington. He first arrived at Pine Ridge with General Miles
in October but stayed only a short while. He returned to Pine Ridge in early
January 1891, and his articles were published in the magazine during January
and February 1891. Some of the reporters were quite inexperienced and were
hired only for this one occasion; others were long-time newspaper profes-
sionals. The "ghost dance war" became a media event widely documented
not only in printed articles but also in photographs.[4] Reporters came even
from Europe, one all the way from Finland, then an autonomous part of
Russia. This reporter, Konni Zilliacus, represented the *Svenska Dagbladet,* a
Swedish newspaper.[5]

The Press Discovers the Ghost Dance

Although Indians were not the most important issue in the newspapers
during the first months of 1890, some articles were printed that dealt with

Indians in general and a few that focused specifically on the Lakotas.[6] *Harper's Weekly* opened the year with a romantic article about life on an Indian reservation. The *Omaha Daily Bee* began the year by announcing that Sitting Bull was not as angry about the division of the Great Sioux Reservation as was generally believed. The paper quoted Agent James McLaughlin, who said that although Sitting Bull was a very conservative Indian and had little faith in civilized habits, the relations between himself and Sitting Bull were "most amicable."[7]

The opening of the Great Sioux Reservation to white settlers was major news in February 1890. Settlers were reportedly rushing in to claim homesteads, while Indian policemen, who were assigned to stop anyone attempting to move onto those lands before they were officially opened, watching helplessly. The *Omaha Daily Bee* was especially interested in the newly opened lands, calling the opening of the reservation a "transformation from darkness to light, from idleness to activity, from barbarism to civilization."[8]

After the initial excitement resulting from the opening of the reservation, no major articles about the Lakotas appeared until April 1890. The destitute situation among white farmers in the Dakotas received wide attention, while the suffering Lakotas received none.[9]

The next time attention turned to the Lakotas was on April 6 and 7, when the newspapers reported that the Lakotas were gathering to hold a great council and to dance. None of the papers, however, mentioned the ghost dance. In fact, the papers reported that the Lakotas were dancing their last war dance or holding their last powwow. The major issue discussed at this council was whether or not the Lakotas would take their lands in severalty. Sitting Bull and his followers were reported to be strongly opposed to any farming efforts, and the result of the council was that only some mixed bloods and squaw men agreed to take allotments.[10] It may be that this council was one of the earliest in which the Lakotas talked about the ghost dance after their delegation returned from Nevada (see chapter 1).

When the *Washington Post* next reported about the Lakotas, the tone was more alarming. The headline on April 16 was "Gone to Warpath." The article reported on Big Foot, who allegedly was on the warpath and was surrounded by soldiers. He refused to obey orders, and the army had cornered him and his band. Great trouble was expected. The paper, however, never followed up on these developments.[11]

A couple of days earlier the *Omaha Daily Bee* reported on "an Indian prophecy." This was the first article regarding the ghost dance, although the paper did not actually use the term "ghost dance." The article described a prophecy that was circulating among the tribes in the Northwest, causing great excitement. The Indians were expecting a great flood that would destroy all the whites, after which all the dead animals would be restored upon the earth. This was supposed to happen in three months.[12] The reporter wrote about the Indian messiah and questioned how the Indians, who lived thousands of miles apart, came to share the same belief. The Indians seemed to be mixing their old beliefs and Christianity into a new kind of religion.[13]

In May 1890, the *Bee* reported on the problems caused by the census conducted among the Indians at Rosebud Reservation. White speculators who were indifferent to the welfare of the Indians were causing problems among the Lakotas. The paper also noted that the Shoshones and Arapahos had been preparing for over a year for the coming of a new millennium with invocations and ceremonies. This had been going on in total secrecy; the whites had learned of their hopes only recently. The *Chicago Tribune* was also very much concerned about the Indians expecting their dead to be resurrected.[14]

During May and June the attention of the eastern papers, especially the *New York Times* and the *Washington Post*, was still turned away from the Lakotas. On June 6 the *Post* reported that the Cheyenne Indians had gone on the warpath, killing several settlers in Wyoming and Montana. Soldiers were sent after these Indians, who were stirred up over news of the coming of Christ, who would bring the Indians horses, cattle, and firewater. This was the first time the *Post* alluded to the ghost dance, although indirectly. The *New York Times* mentioned the incident also, but did not connect it with the ghost dance.[15]

The *Omaha Daily Bee* was also interested in the Cheyennes, but it did not connect the reported trouble with the new messiah beliefs. Rather, the paper blamed the lack of subsistence among the Cheyennes and referred to the incident as the annual Indian scare, started by rumors that were greatly exaggerated by settlers and newspapers.[16]

In late June, the *Omaha Daily Bee* commented that the Lakota Indians in the region were peaceable and had no desire to go on the warpath as long as the government lived up to its agreements with them. The article suggested that the Indian reunion in April was wrongfully believed to be an indication of an uprising, but added that trouble might lie ahead because the government had postponed the ration issue until July 1. This, the paper predicted on June 20, would cause hardship for the Lakotas.[17]

The first news regarding the Lakota ghost dance connected the ceremony to a "war dance" and to an eventual uprising. Indians dancing surely meant trouble. The *Omaha Daily Bee* was perhaps the most analytical and least alarmist of these newspapers. The general feeling, however, was that the "Messiah Craze" would eventually cause trouble.

"The Air Is Full of Rumors"

During the late summer of 1890 neither the ghost dance nor the Indians were considered important enough to be given space in the *Washington Post* or the *New York Times*. In fact, there were only a few articles commenting on the situation in the Dakotas and Nebraska, most of which reported on the difficulties faced by white farmers throughout the West. Although there was great concern for the white farmers, there seemed to be no concern for the welfare of the Indians, who were expected to support themselves by farming on their reservations.[18] In July, however, an article in the *Washington Post* was headlined "Caring for the Red Man." The Indians in the West were in great need of money and appropriations, but from the newspaper's point of view that need was not because the Indians were suffering or starving; the money was necessary for educating and civilizing them.[19]

Not until August 28 was there any report of trouble among the Lakotas. On that day the *Washington Post* quoted Special Agent A. T. Lea, who claimed that there were fewer Indians living on Rosebud Reservation than officially reported by the agent, and they were therefore receiving too many rations. The *Post* tried to be impartial, quoting J. George Wright, the agent on Rosebud Reservation, who claimed that diseases such as measles and smallpox took their toll on the population. There is no reason to go further into Lea's accusations here, but this shows that the eastern newspapers were not worried about the ghost dance or an Indian rebellion during the summer of 1890.[20] In fact, after early spring, no articles regarding the ghost dance appeared in the *Washington Post* or the *New York Times* until September 1890.

In contrast, during the summer the western papers were quite interested in the development of the "Messiah Craze." They reported that the Indians were becoming crazed by religion and were dancing and "having [a] good time." The papers also reported that Porcupine, the Cheyenne, had seen the Messiah (see chapter 1). They told Porcupine's story and expressed astonishment at its similarity to Christian teachings. What especially impressed the papers were the "commandments" the Messiah gave to the Indians. Despite the doctrine's reportedly peaceful nature, the Indians' excitement provoked fear among the settlers. The *Omaha Daily Bee*, however, reported that there was no need for panic, since the Indians were totally peaceable, did not want to go on the warpath, and, in fact, could not do so even if they wanted. "These annual Indian scares are getting very tiresome," the paper commented.[21] During the summer the western papers reported that drought was causing problems for farmers, but like the eastern papers they reported nothing really alarming regarding the Indians until September.[22]

Then, on September 26 and 27, the *Washington Post* and the *Chicago Tribune* published stories of disturbing behavior among 5,000 Indians, although neither paper specified who these Indians were. They obtained the information from an officer of the 7th Cavalry, who claimed that the biggest Indian uprising ever was ahead; the Indians were expecting a medicine man who would destroy the whites. This had already led to "incantations and religious orgies." As soon as the medicine man appeared the trouble would begin. The officer demanded that the number of soldiers be doubled in all garrisons in the West.[23] Thus the first news of the ghost dance to reach white audiences was quite alarming.

After this first alarm there were no more articles about the ghost dances in any of the newspapers until October 24, when the *Omaha Daily Bee* reported discontent among Indians living in Indian Territory. They were greatly excited over the expected coming of the new Christ.[24] In fact, on October 28, the *Bee*, the *Yankton Press and Dakotan*, the *Chicago Tribune,* and the *Washington Post* began to report more frequently on developments relating to the ghost dance. The *New York Times* followed, beginning on November 8, 1890.

On October 28, the major headline in the *Washington Post* was "Led by Sitting Bull. A General Uprising of the Sioux Indians Feared Next Spring." The article quoted Agent McLaughlin, who said that the ghost dance appealed to many Indians, even to those who were considered progressive and reasonable. According to McLaughlin, all the trouble was caused by Sitting Bull, who was "high priest and leading apostle of this latest Indian absurdity; in a word, he is the chief mischief-maker at this agency, and if he were not here this craze so general among the Sioux would never have gotten a foothold at this agency." McLaughlin also wanted to make clear that the ghost dance was very dangerous; even the Indian policemen feared to interfere with the dancing. Quoting McLaughlin, the *Post* noted that the ghost dance was very "demoralizing, indecent and disgusting."[25]

The *Chicago Tribune* and the *Yankton Press and Dakotan* published similar articles also quoting McLaughlin, but added that the soldiers were ready for Sitting Bull. The *Omaha Daily Bee* noted that Sitting Bull was in a very ugly mood and was stirring up the "young bucks." The paper called for a swift military response.[26] Thus the first substantial articles concerning the Lakota ghost dance blamed Sitting Bull for causing the trouble and painted a very alarming picture of the Indians' new religion.[27]

On October 29, the tone in the *Washington Post* was entirely different. The paper published an article written by Herbert Welsh, a representative of the Indian Rights Association.[28] Welsh claimed that Sitting Bull was being wronged; he was not trying to make war. In fact, Welsh had even received a letter from Sitting Bull giving assurance that he was not the cause of any trouble. Welsh also objected strongly to McLaughlin's comments on Sitting Bull's person.[29] The *Post* did not take any stand for or against these accusations. At this point it simply allowed both parties involved to make their views clear to the public. Even Sitting Bull was allowed to speak, although through the representative of the Indian Rights Association.

The *Omaha Daily Bee* also took notice of the ghost dance on October 29, calling it "The Indian Millennium." The paper published additional articles focusing on similar movements among American Indians. Such superstition was caused by the Indians' inability to cope with the whites without supernatural help. The paper did not believe that it would lead to any major uprising, since the Indians had practically no means to wage war against the whites; they were surrounded by towns and soldiers. Some local outbreaks and bloodshed, however, might occur. Sitting Bull's involvement was the only reason for concern, according to the *Bee*. The *Yankton Press and Dakotan* announced that several veterans of the 1876 Sioux war were volunteering for the army; they wanted to exact revenge on Sitting Bull and his warriors.[30]

The ghost dance next appeared on the pages of the *Washington Post* on November 7, when Maj. Gen. John M. Schofield tried to calm the public. He claimed that the Indian question was resolved and that the Indians were to receive humane treatment on their reservations. The army was needed only to control the young and restless elements so that they would not cause any trouble.[31]

The next day the eastern papers concentrated on the origins of the ghost dance. They accused the Mormons of instigating the whole madness and quoted General Miles, who claimed that the Mormons, who believed "in prophets and spiritual manifestations," were behind the trouble. The Mormons had had missions among some tribes for a long time; in fact, Miles suggested that the person or persons who claimed to be the Messiah were white. He believed this was almost certain, since no one had actually seen the Messiah's face, which he always kept disguised.[32]

Accusing the Mormons was not a new tactic for the newspapers. There were many articles, for example in the *New York Times*, about the Mormons' strange customs. The fact that Miles believed the Messiah to be a white man reflects the mystery surrounding the Messiah's identity and, indeed, the whole phenomenon of the ghost dance.[33]

When Miles was asked about a possible Lakota outbreak, he answered that the situation was not alarming in any way. About Sitting Bull he said, "No one is more ardent [about the ghost dance] than Sitting Bull, who is intensely Indian in all his ideas." Miles, however, stressed that because they were surrounded by white settlements and railroads, it would be very difficult for the Indians to escape from their reservations.[34]

The first articles show clearly that very little knowledge about the ghost dance was available. The two high-ranking army officers who were quoted tried to assure the public that there was nothing to fear; they expected no major outbreak.[35] Despite this, the ghost dance and an eventual outbreak were discussed in the papers as facts obvious to most observers. The newspapers studied here considered the ghost dance and the Lakota outbreak one inseparable and inevitable phenomenon. The situation was well described by the *Washington Post*: "The air is full of rumors . . . over an outbreak."[36] It is significant that only a few articles were written about the nature or origins of the ghost dance, and only a few were written about the more than thirty other tribes who were dancing. The Lakota ghost dance was the one that caused the headlines; especially Sitting Bull's involvement was of great concern.

The Army Steps In

"Gone to Fight the Indians" was a headline in the *Washington Post* on November 15, 1890. According to the paper, the situation was worse than anyone in the East had imagined. The Indians were so hostile that the settlers close to the Lakota reservations were terrified. The paper demanded that the army be sent to help the agents, who could not control the Indians. The *New York Times* too worried that the ghost dancers defied their agents, but wondered whether the Indians would really attempt an outbreak with winter coming on. Both papers were certain, however, that the military officers' idea was to show force and to avoid actual battle.[37] Although the *Washington Post* headline suggested that the army had already been sent to fight the Indians, the army did not arrive at Pine Ridge and Rosebud Reservations until November 20. The president's orders to the military had been given on November 13; perhaps the *Post* had some inside information relating to the upcoming military operation, or perhaps it was just relying on rumors. Whatever the case, the paper was five days ahead of actual events.[38]

The *Yankton Press and Dakotan* reported also on November 15 that "an Indian war" had begun and that the army was sent to the Lakota reservations to show the Indians that there was "a power which they must obey." The *Chicago Tribune* and the *Omaha Daily Bee* reported in a similar tone. The papers described Indians arming themselves and defying their agents. Settlers were reported to be fleeing, and the army was called in. The Lakotas were believed to be ready to go on the warpath. The turmoil was again attributed to Sitting Bull, who reportedly had influence even over the Cheyennes and the Kiowas in the Indian Territory.

Interestingly, in the midst of this reporting a short note appeared in the *Chicago Tribune* claiming that the turbulence was subsiding and the Indians were quietly hauling in their supplies for the winter. The *Yankton Press and Dakotan* also contradicted the news from November 15, reporting two days later that the Indians were not on the warpath, and the army officials expected no trouble with the Sioux.[39] This was the first time during the ghost dance reporting that any of these newspapers clearly contradicted itself.

On November 16, the *Washington Post* repeated the observation that the Indians were unable to make war in the winter because there was no food available for their ponies. Nonetheless, the Lakotas seemed to be continuing their war and sun dances, which were exciting the "young bucks," as the paper put it.[40] The same day, the *New York Times* published a lengthy report about the ghost dance religion written by a correspondent who toured various tribes and even participated in ghost dance ceremonies. The correspondent wrote about the ghost dance very objectively and described the experiences of the Cheyenne prophet Porcupine and the Arapaho prophet Sitting Bull. The story of the Lakota delegates was also included, and some of the Lakota ghost dance ceremonies were described. This article attempted to present both the doctrine and the ceremony of the ghost dance from the Indian point of view, depicting the dance as a religious movement rather than an expression of war or a revolt. The article also included a sensational report about a fight—not reported anywhere else—between the ghost dancers and the soldiers. The only surviving soldier in the clash was General Miles. This is an amazing report, considering that Miles at that time was not even close to the Lakota reservations.[41]

During the days prior to November 20, when the army finally entered the Lakota reservations, all the papers were filled with reports of Indians arming themselves and riding about with their weapons. Some, it was reported, were armed with two rifles apiece. The *New York Times* claimed that white settlers were being evacuated throughout the West because the army could not protect them. The Indians were supposed to be well armed, and some unscrupulous white traders had sold all their ammunition to them. The

Omaha Daily Bee also reported that settlers were fleeing, and estimated that there could be between 15,000 and 27,000 warriors ready for war. Similar articles appeared in the *Yankton Press and Dakotan*.

 The *New York Times* then published a report by General Miles, who emphasized that settlers were not being evacuated. Only a few fearful people had left their homes, and reports of danger were greatly exaggerated. Miles stressed, however, that if the Indians started trouble they could do much harm; they had at least 15,000 well-armed warriors available. If true, that would have been a tremendous fighting force. Miles reassured that there was no immediate danger; all necessary measures were being taken, but the spring might bring an uprising if the "madness" continued. The *Chicago Tribune* reported that the Indians were already committing depredations and that even some Indian policemen were turning their back on civilization and joining the ghost dancers. Still, the restlessness in the West, however great it was, was expected to be of short duration.[42] It is interesting that the estimate of the number of Lakota warriors ranged from 15,000 to 27,000, when the actual number of adult Lakota men, according to the census, was only approximately 5,000.

On November 19, both eastern papers printed very alarming headlines: "Sioux Outbreak. Varying Rumors of Trouble" and "The Avenging Messiah. Indians Say That Their Savior Will Do All of Their Fighting." Despite the headlines, both articles were, in fact, very reassuring. The *New York Times* reported troop movements and quoted Acting Commissioner of Indian Affairs R. V. Belt, who said that although the settlers' alarm was justified, no harm would come if the Indians were left alone. Therefore, Belt decided, there would be no arrests or attempts to stop the dances if no act of violence occurred. Otherwise, action might lead to violence. "Let [the] Indians dance themselves out. They will [lose] faith eventually and [the] whole delusion collapses," he said. Belt quoted a letter from Charles A. Eastman, one of the agency physicians and a Santee Sioux, who had talked with Red Cloud. The chief believed that "the enthusiasm of the men in it [the ghost dance] will melt away like a spring snow."[43]

The *Washington Post* quoted an officer who toured the reservations and claimed that the religion was not opposed to whites. "It is just [a] harmless religious affair equivalent to Christian communion that is a preparatory ceremony before the coming of the master," he said. He charged that some of the Indian agents, who were unused to the Indians' ways, were the actual cause of the trouble.[44] This was the first time in the ghost dance reporting that accompanying articles totally contradicted their headlines.

The *Washington Post* reported that settlers living close to the Lakota reservations were in full stampede, fleeing to Mandan, North Dakota. They were threatening to kill all Indians on sight if the government did not do something. The citizens were said to be arming themselves, and they believed the Indians on Pine Ridge Reservation were totally out of control. The *New York Times* reported just the opposite: the rumors of an uprising were unfounded, and the Indians were living peacefully on their reservations.[45]

The *Omaha Daily Bee* was of the same opinion: "All Sorts of Contradictory Rumors about the Indian Excitement" was the November 19 headline. The paper quoted Acting Commissioner Belt, but at the same time it described excited soldiers who were anxiously waiting to engage Sitting Bull, "the old foe." The paper blamed the new inexperienced agents for the trouble, and quoted General Miles, who now believed that the soldiers were going to face 27,000 fighting Indians. The *Yankton Press and Dakotan* also reported that the Indians were armed to the teeth, swarming around the white settlements, but at the same time it quoted Brig. Gen. Thomas H. Ruger, who maintained that there was no danger of war. The *Chicago Tribune* reported that troops had already been sent to the scene of the trouble, but that the danger had been averted and the settlers were returning to their homes.[46] So, on the eve of the military invasion of the Lakota reservations, the newspapers printed contradictory reports about tranquility and trouble, peace and war, at the same time.

Toward the end of November reports regarding the ghost dance took on even more alarming characteristics. Immediately after the military's arrival at Pine Ridge and Rosebud Reservations stories of battles began to spread. The *Chicago Tribune* and the *Omaha Daily Bee* reported on November 20 that a fight had taken place in which up to sixty people were killed. This, however, was not confirmed. Another rumor claimed that several hundred warriors belonging to Sitting Bull's band were missing from Standing Rock. Yet another rumor said that Sitting Bull was already in irons. Both papers reported extensively on the hostile Indians led by Little Wound, Red Cloud, and Sitting Bull, who were alleged to be planning an attack for the morning of November 21. The *Yankton Press and Dakotan* reported on the factionalism among the Lakotas, saying that American Horse and Young Man Afraid of His Horse were leading those who were for peace, whereas Red Cloud, Little Wound, Sitting Bull, Gall, and Hump were fomenting trouble. The paper called for utmost vigilance, but believed that things were gradually calming down.[47] It is interesting that Gall was portrayed as a troublemaker. As noted in chapter 1, he never took part in the ghost dance and kept most of his followers away from the ghost dance camps.

At the same time they were reporting about danger and fleeing settlers, the papers quoted General Miles, who stated that the army's appearance had a quieting effect. Agent McLaughlin was of the same opinion, adding that Sitting Bull had only approximately 100 followers dancing the ghost dance. Agent Royer at Pine Ridge, on the other hand, told reporters that his life was in grave danger and that he had taken his family to Rushville, Nebraska. The *Omaha Daily Bee* expressed a wish that Sitting Bull might accidentally run before federal rifles. The *Chicago Tribune*, however, claimed that there was no reason to expect an uprising; the paper pointed out that white men were sometimes equally animated by religion. The *Tribune* blamed the government for mistreating the Indians; it also blamed the local settlers, who out of pure greed sold weapons and liquor to the Indians. The *Bee* noted that the ghost-dancing Indians were wearing some kind of holy shirts.[48] This was the first time the newspapers mentioned the Lakota ghost dance shirts.

The *New York Times* was convinced that the Indians were very well armed and very well supplied with food. The paper also claimed on November 21 that Sitting Bull was already in irons, but Red Cloud and Little Wound declared that they were going to meet the troops in battle the next day, that being the day the Messiah would appear in the form of a buffalo. According to the paper, these two chiefs were causing trouble and belonged to the so-called "bad Indians."[49] The article was in fact almost identical to the articles published in the western papers one day earlier.

On November 21, the *Omaha Daily Bee*, the *Yankton Press and Dakotan*, and the *Chicago Tribune* reported extensively on the trouble among the Lakotas. The papers claimed that the Indians at Pine Ridge had the agency and the surrounding country in a state of terror. Sitting Bull was going to lead more than 200 warriors to meet other dancers, who were dancing with guns strapped to their backs and who were becoming more boisterous and threatening all the time. Officers on the ground feared that the hostile Indians, estimated to number as many as 8,000, were capable of annihilating the army detachments whenever they pleased. One officer described the danger in the following words: "I hope to God that reinforcements come before the red devils make their break." Sitting Bull, who was reported to have been in irons a day before, was now blamed for encouraging warriors to steal cattle and kill settlers. His influence was now said to be so great that even some of the Indian policemen threw off their uniforms and joined the dancers. They were threatening Agent McLaughlin, who was afraid to punish them. According to McLaughlin, however, the Indian police remained loyal to him throughout the ghost dance troubles (see chapters 1 and 2). The scene on Pine Ridge was portrayed as one in which fully armed Indians were swarming around the reservation looking for every opportunity to launch a major attack against the whites. The *Yankton Press and Dakotan* predicted that the largest Indian uprising since colonial times was ahead and that it would lead to a "complete extermination of the red man."[50]

The *New York Times* published the same story as the *Omaha Daily Bee* on November 22, noting that the Indian Office discredited the stories of an uprising, saying that they were greatly exaggerated. Acting Commissioner Belt did not believe that the Indians entertained hostile feelings against the whites. He said that inasmuch as the Indians expected their messiah to do it for them, there was no need for hostilities. Thus the doctrine itself prevented them from fighting, but Belt worried that trouble would come when the promises of the doctrine were not fulfilled.[51]

The *New York Times* published a series of articles expressing a variety of opinions about the ghost dance on November 22. The first article was written by a reporter who had visited a dance; the title was "How the Indians Work Themselves Up to a Fighting Pitch." The article portrayed the ceremony as very hostile; in fact, the dancers were for the first time called "hostiles."[52] The dancers were wearing white shirts, evidently ghost dance shirts, and the writer claimed that many of the Indians wore war paint. He believed that the ceremony showed the Indians to be insanely religious, banging their heads until blood began running. The ghost dance was "simply a dance of cruel endurance which is far more barbarous than the sun dance."[53]

Postmaster James Finley's wife at Pine Ridge Reservation painted an even more barbarous picture of the ceremony. She said that the Indians lost all their senses in the dance, believing that they were animals. She claimed that the Indians believed a man had turned into a buffalo even though he still looked like a man. "I suppose they have killed and eaten him by this time," she concluded. Nonetheless, she wanted to emphasize that, if the Indians were left alone, there would be no need for troops.[54] All in all, these articles in the *New York Times* gave some additional information to the eastern audience, albeit some of it false and misleading.

On November 22, *Harper's Weekly* was very critical of the government's Indian policy. The magazine believed that allotment and civilization were good for the Indians, but criticized the effect of the spoils system on the civilizing process: "So long as our practical relations with the Indians are in the hands of men appointed to promote the political fortunes of some man—or party, the Indian question continue[s] to be what it long has been—a disgrace."[55]

Meanwhile, the western papers reported further developments on the Lakota reservations. They once again blamed Sitting Bull and expressed the belief that there would be no uprising unless he ordered it. The *Yankton Press and Dakotan* briefly noted that the soldiers were doing good work on Pine Ridge in separating the "good and bad Indians." The paper contradicted itself by writing that no bloodshed was expected yet maintaining that the Indians were ready for a battle at any time. The *Chicago Tribune* listed all the leaders of the ghost dance; one of them was Red Cloud, even though he denied his involvement. The papers nonetheless portrayed Red Cloud as an intelligent man and a true politician. They published the speech in which he explained his views:

> I don't want to fight and I don't want my people to fight. We have lots of old women and we have lots of old men. We've got no guns and we can't fight, for we have nothing to eat, and are too poor to do anything.

. . . I haven't been to see the dancing. I will try to stop it. Those Indians are fools. The winter weather will stop it, I think. Anyway, it will be over by spring. I don't think there will be any trouble. They say that I have been in the dance. That is not right. I have never seen it.[56]

Yet the papers continued to present Red Cloud as one of the ghost dance leaders since his son Jack Red Cloud was considered one of the leading spirits of the dance. That same day the *Omaha Daily Bee* also described the Lakota ghost dance ceremony. Whereas other papers portrayed it as a horrible, even cannibalistic ritual, the *Bee* claimed that there was nothing warlike in the ceremony. It was nothing more or less than religious fanaticism.[57]

The next day several newspapers published a letter sent to Agent Royer by Little Wound:

I understand that the soldiers have come on the reservation. What have they come for? We have done nothing. Our dance is a religious dance and we are going to dance until spring. If we find then that the Christ does not appear we will stop dancing; but, in the meantime, troops or no troops, we shall start our dance on this creek in the morning. I have also understood that I was not to be recognized as a chief any longer. All that I have to say to that is neither you nor the white people made me a chief and you can throw me away as you please, but let me tell you, Dr. Royer, that the Indians made me a chief, and by them I shall be so recognized so long as I live. We have been told that you intended to stop our rations and annuities. Well, for my part, I don't care; the little rations we get do not amount to anything, but Dr. Royer, if such is the case, please send me a word so that me and my people will be saved the trouble of going to the agency. We do not intend to stop dancing.[58]

Remarkably, the papers interpreted this letter as open defiance of the troops. According to Royer, "The Sioux [Lakota] mean war. They have been ordered to stop dancing. They have refused to do so. It now remains for the soldiers to enforce their orders."[59] If the letter is read objectively, one can see that it is not written in a defiant tone; it is almost polite. Understandably for Royer the letter meant that he could not control the Indians, but it certainly was not an open declaration of war; rather, it was an explanation of the Indians' point of view, giving their reasons for their actions. This, however, was overlooked both by Royer and by the newspapers.

In the wake of this "letter of defiance," the newspapers went on to speculate on how the Lakotas would strike against the settlers and then go to the Big Horn Mountains or the Badlands to fight the soldiers. This rumor was strengthened by reports that some Lakotas were seen heading to the Big Horn Mountains. In fact, this was a group led by Young Man Afraid of His Horse, who had permission to leave Pine Ridge to visit the Crow Reservation.[60]

The *New York Times* reported that the Indians were massing, and that even Pawnees, Arapahos, Shoshones, and Kiowas were ready to join the Lakotas. The newspapers claimed that the Indians were dancing in a wilder manner than ever before and that they were threatening to shoot anyone who attempted to suppress the dance. The *Times* estimated that there could be up to 40,000 Indians dancing throughout the United States. Those people were led by some of the most "desperate and treacherous redskins in this part of the country." The paper was referring to, among others, Red Cloud. The *Omaha Daily Bee* even revealed "a devilish plot" to ambush the soldiers somewhere in the Badlands. Despite this, the papers also reported that thousands of peaceful Lakotas were coming to their agencies. According to the papers, everything was reported quiet at Standing Rock and Rosebud. Sitting Bull had lost almost all of his following, but still the settlers were fleeing and additional troops were called for. The newspapers' reporting was now completely contradictory. The *Yankton Press and Dakotan*, for example, wrote that Sitting Bull's messengers were urging Indians to slaughter the white men, yet it also reported that there were no new developments. The paper actually admitted that "the news from here [Pine Ridge] is meager and unsatisfactory, and consists mainly of rumors."[61]

Whereas the other newspapers were reporting frequently about the ghost dance, the *Washington Post* had kept silent since November 19, but on November 24 the paper took up the *Omaha Daily Bee*'s report from the previous day about the Indians' plan to ambush and kill the soldiers. "They Plot a Massacre" was the headline. Likewise, the *New York Times* noted the Indians' treacherous plan. Both papers believed that the Indians were better equipped than ever for war and suggested that the country was better suited for warfare than earlier, since now there were cattle for the Indians to steal.[62]

The western papers reported Two Strike's alleged plan to stab Brooke during negotiations. This was to be a sign to commence hostilities. The *Omaha Daily Bee* reported that hostile Indians, who were using Short Bull and his ghost dance as a pretence for starting a war, surrounded Pine Ridge Agency. Even the so-called friendlies could no longer be trusted, the *Bee* correspondent claimed. The *Washington Post* and the *New York Times* reported that Sitting Bull was planning a major assembly in the spring, which would mean war. At the same time these papers reported that no outbreak was expected; everything was peaceful in Sitting Bull's camp.[63]

The articles continued to be wildly contradictory. They told about whites killed by Indians and settlers fleeing from roving bands of Indians; at the same time they maintained that the situation was quiet and the friendly chiefs were fully supporting the agents. The *Omaha Daily Bee* provides a good example. One article reported that the Indians were generally not well armed, but a couple of paragraphs later the writer claimed that Pine Ridge Reservation was surrounded by heavily armed Indians. The papers also reported that more than 6,000 Lakota warriors had broken loose and that some Cheyennes had tried to join them; yet they also reported that everything was quiet among the Cheyennes in Montana and that Short Bull and Red Cloud were denying any hostile intentions. At this point the situation was very confusing for the settlers, agents, army officials, and reporters alike. There were simply too many rumors afloat. The army, however, moved more soldiers to the scene, and every soldier in the Division of the Missouri was reported to be in readiness to start for the Dakotas at a moment's notice. Agent Royer at Pine Ridge, who requested reinforcements for the Indian police, added to the confusion.[64]

On November 24, the *Washington Post* published an article with a totally different tone. This article quoted an army officer:

[The Indians] should be allowed to dance because they are naturally religious people. Dancing will give them something to do. The present system fails because the Indians have nothing to do. Farming is impossible in that country. Indians believe that Great Spirit doesn't want them to farm when always year after year crops fail. It is human nature to believe so and with Indians we are dealing with human nature.

The officer also criticized the reservation system, where the agents represented a kind of despot that did not exist anywhere else in the United States.[65]

Somewhat surprisingly, on the same day the *New York Times* published two articles about the effect the ghost dance had on the Indians. The first article was, in fact, a letter from an Indian agent who had worked among the Arapahos and Cheyennes for many years. In his letter, he assured readers that the doctrine was not meant to harm whites, even if it caused great excitement. He had heard only vague rumors about the origin of the doctrine, but he believed that it started somewhere near Pine Ridge. According to the agent, it was a doctrine that appealed mainly to the most nonprogressive Indians. It caused Indians to "neglect their work and to [lose] interest in their own progress and advancement and to spend a good part of their time in talking over the expected change which this Christ is about to make in their circumstances and surroundings."[66]

In another article on the same day the writer seriously doubted the need for military action:

> The present excitement may have been purposely exaggerated in the reports in order to get an increase of the army. No doubt some frontiersmen and traders find a profit in the presence of the soldiers and would be very glad to see a larger number of them, for purpose of trade. Still the alarm seems to be genuine enough now; and although it has been based in most cases on unsupported rumors . . . protection is due to them [the settlers].

He also noted that the important issue was not whether the army was able to put down a rebellion, but the cost of such action in human lives, time, and money. He referred to the costs of capturing the small bands of Geronimo and Chief Joseph some years earlier. Furthermore, he feared the possible effects of a joint uprising of ten to twenty tribes.[67]

The following day, November 25, the *Omaha Daily Bee* joined the eastern papers in changing its tone. "Hounded On by Hunger" and "Famine

Rather Than Religious Enthusiasm Has Excited the Indians" were two of the headlines. "The Indians are slowly starving to death. That is the real, the way down, deep cause of this war scare," the paper charged. The article further noted that it was no wonder that the Indians took up whatever hope they could get. General Brooke and Agent Royer were of the same opinion. Royer even commented that the only thing the Indians had enough of was soap. The *Bee* interviewed Two Strike and Little Wound, who said that they would stop dancing, but they did not like the way the newspapers portrayed them as bad people. The article went on to say that the Indians on Pine Ridge made no hostile demonstrations and the general feeling seemed to be that the immediate threat of war was subsiding, although the situation was still so delicate that one mistake could lead to a war. The paper reported that the actual ghost dance ceremony was not hostile at all; it was wild, but purely religious. The *Yankton Press and Dakotan* quoted an Indian who said that the dance was "perfectly natural and appropriate," since dancing was an Indian custom.[68]

These articles are particularly striking because they followed a series of articles reporting that the treacherous and barbarous Indians were preparing to go on the warpath. The change was very sudden, and was probably an effort to better inform readers about the ghost dance after the confusing and sensational picture of the dance that had in fact been created by the papers themselves. These articles were in a sense additional or supplementary to actual news reporting. Comments on newspaper sensationalism were even published by the papers themselves. It is worth noting that Indians like Little Wound and Two Strike willingly gave their opinions to the newspapers, and perhaps even tried to use the papers for their own purposes.[69]

Despite this change in attitude, the newspapers continued to print reports of threatened hostilities, descriptions of the fate of fleeing settlers, stories that the Indians had done no harm, and claims that the Indians still planned to massacre the troops. The eastern papers agreed that Sitting Bull's influence was growing and that it was dangerous even to try to negotiate with the rest of the dancers since the whites could not offer them what they wanted: their lands. The *Chicago Tribune* believed that Sitting Bull had invented the whole "Messiah Craze," but nonetheless argued that there was no need for alarm on Standing Rock Reservation. All three papers, however, agreed that the monthly ration day might cause trouble. The issue of rations was a cause of much apprehension, since thousands of Indians—including a few prominent ghost dancers—would come to their respective agencies. The situation was considered very delicate; at Pine Ridge it was believed to be even more alarming than on other reservations, as all kinds of rumors were afloat there. The *Washington Post* noted that it was very difficult to get reliable information because the correspondents were working "in an atmosphere pregnant with mysteries."[70]

The *New York Times*, the *Washington Post*, and the *Chicago Tribune* continued their reporting on November 25 with articles about the army. Even though it was the largest number of troops mustered since the campaign of 1876–77, the papers understood that the army was under orders not to attack the Indians. The army's task, according to the eastern papers, was to find out the truth about the quantity of rations the Indians were getting and whether or not the lack of rations was the reason for the trouble. According to the *Tribune*, the ghost dancers would not be pacified without strong measures. The paper added that General Miles was promising in earnest to suppress any attempted outbreak. The eastern papers also claimed that the Indian messiah had finally been located. He was allegedly living close to the city of Reno, Nevada, and he was known by the name Johnson Sides.[71]

The *New York Times* again published several different opinions about the ghost dance on November 26. According to the paper, the Indians were afraid that they would be corralled by the army and then annihilated. Their fear of the army was seen as a major problem that might eventually lead to a disaster. The paper claimed that the Indians agreed that there was no use to make war because they were surrounded by railroads and settlements, and even if they could destroy the soldiers at hand they would finally perish. Episcopal Bishop William H. Hare, who visited the Rosebud Agency, was also interviewed. His opinion was that no trouble would occur if the dancers were left alone, an opinion shared by Herbert Welsh of the Indian Rights Association, who blamed the government and the Interior Department for removing all able Indian agents and replacing them with men who were unfit for the job. An anonymous missionary woman (later revealed to be

the Congregationalist missionary Mary C. Collins), whose post was close
to Sitting Bull's camp, expressed a totally different opinion about the ghost
dance. She described it as the sun dance under a new name. According to
her, the Indians were wearing war dress and war paint. "Sitting Bull means
war. He is thoroughly and hopelessly bad," she claimed. The *Yankton Press
and Dakotan* used the same material but revealed that the missionary was
Mary C. Collins.[72]

The *Chicago Tribune* printed a completely contradictory description of the
situation on Pine Ridge Reservation. The people who were truly frightened
were the Indians, not the whites. The army's movements around the reservation almost caused a general stampede of the panic-stricken Indians. There
was a rumor that the soldiers had killed Indians at Wounded Knee Creek.
As a result, the Indians camped close to Pine Ridge Agency were preparing
to leave for the ghost dance camps, where they would be safe. The *Omaha
Daily Bee* told a similar story, but quoted Agent Royer, who believed that
even the friendlies were going to go on the warpath. The *Tribune* published
an interview with Big Road, who described the journey of the apostles and
the first dances. He strongly denied the rumors that the Indians were dancing with their guns on their backs. The *Bee* quoted another eyewitness who
said that no guns could be seen during the ceremony: "They have no idea
of being warlike and never had and are surprised that any objections should
be had to such a dance." He noted that the dancers wore simple shirts without ornaments. The paper included an interview with a squaw man, who
explained that the Indians were not preparing for war for three reasons: first,
they had no place to go; second, if they killed the soldiers on location they
knew that more soldiers would come; and, third, they would starve during
a winter campaign.[73]

These articles were followed by several other contradictory stories. Some
reported that a major battle had taken place between the Indians and the
army, while at the same time Miles continued to deny that any hostilities
had taken place and told instead about the peaceful and satisfactory developments as the ghost dancers moved closer to the agencies. Among them were
the people led by Short Bull and Little Wound. Even though the soldiers saw
this as a good sign, the settlers and local newspapers saw it as an attempt to

raid the settlements or as an attempt to join forces with Hump and Big Foot. The Indians were reported to have been destroying property en route. An example of these rumors and counterrumors, as the *Omaha Daily Bee* called them, was received on November 26, when it was reported that Indians led by Red Cloud had invaded a town. The truth turned out to be that Red Cloud visited the town as a witness in a legal case. The *Chicago Tribune* published an interview with Little Wound, who denied sending Agent Royer a letter a few days earlier and explained that the Indians needed this dance because it was a prayer. The chief claimed that they did not want to cause trouble and that the dance was a dance of peace for all nations. Despite Little Wound's promises to stop dancing, the *Tribune* estimated that 100,000 soldiers would be needed to suppress the trouble.[74] Little Wound's denial of sending the "letter of defiance" to Agent Royer is interesting. Did he lie about it, or was the letter actually written by someone else? Whatever the case, it was not included in Royer's official correspondence (see chapter 2).

On November 29, the *New York Times* reported that the Indians were dancing in circles and preparing to take the warpath. A scout verified this and claimed that Indians danced in that particular manner only when they were preparing for war. Furthermore, the ghost dancers' camps were made in the form of circles, which was considered further evidence of their preparation for war (about the actual significance of the camp circle, see the introduction). The paper reported that the army had been put on alert and that some of the soldiers had sworn eternal vengeance on the Lakotas. Miles considered the situation grave and believed that the army faced a winter campaign unless the Indians were dismounted and disarmed.[75]

The *Washington Post* predicted that "within thirty-six hours the troops will be ordered to disarm or shoot down the marauders and when the troops do start after them the end will be no Custer affair." The word "marauders" referred to the Rosebud Indians who were going to Pine Ridge, destroying property en route and threatening to kill every white man along the way. In the same article, however, the writer reported that citizens in North Dakota were no longer as afraid as they had been a week earlier. The paper also claimed that Sitting Bull was urging his men to dance more vigorously; he was more hostile and determined than ever. The *Yankton Press and Dakotan* agreed, but noted several times that the governor of South Dakota, Arthur C. Mellette, was certain that no cause for alarm existed. He said that every alarm had so far been groundless, and people should stay home and look after their regular business.[76]

The *New York Times* added to the confusion by reporting that the Rosebud Lakotas were spoiling for a fight. They were panic-stricken, believing that they would be disarmed and their ponies taken away. The dancers wore war paint, and the ghost dance had become a real war dance. They were even wearing what the paper called "new war shirts." The same article printed an interview with an Indian spy who had been among the ghost dancers and claimed that many educated Indians who could read the newspapers were among them. Because of this, the ghost dancers were able to laugh at the great alarm they were causing, but they could also read about troop movements and plans to disarm them. This had two consequences: the alarm seemed to them a sign of their power, a sign that the whites would eventually flee or disappear; and, since they knew the troop movements they could better plan their own strikes against the army. The *Chicago Tribune* reported similarly, but in a tone slightly more alarming, predicting a major battle between the Rosebud people led by Two Strike and the full army force led by General Brooke. The battle was expected to happen in the very near future. The Indians were swearing vengeance on the soldiers, but the article added that the trouble was largely caused by mismanagement of Indian affairs, inexperienced agents, lack of food, and the unnecessary concentration of troops.[77]

Harper's Weekly ran the most bellicose headline: "An Indian War." Yet the accompanying article only speculated about the possibility of an uprising and suggested that the onset of winter would prevent major hostilities. The situation was reported to be serious because the Indians were crazed over their new religion, which was considered a hostile movement. This was only natural, however, since the government treated the Indians so badly. The magazine criticized the U.S. government's method of treating its uncivilized wards as foes of the nation and rejoiced that General Miles, who knew and sympathized with the Indians, was in command of the troops sent to the Lakota reservations.[78]

"A Great Military Move," claimed a headline in the *Omaha Daily Bee* on

November 30, but the paper never explained what the actual move was. A *Chicago Tribune* headline that day was "To Arrest Sitting Bull," and the article briefly commented on the prospects of Sitting Bull's capture. Despite its headline, the article focused more on General Brooke's waiting tactic, which it believed to be very effective since more and more Indians were reported to be taking part in ordinary daily tasks on Pine Ridge Reservation. The greatest concern was the group of Rosebud Brulés who arrived at Pine Ridge under Two Strike's and Short Bull's leadership. The *Tribune* suggested that Brooke's plan was to wait for an opportunity, then arrest the leaders and eventually disarm the rest of the Indians.[79]

At the same time the newspapers reported that Indians on Pine Ridge were holding a council with Agent Royer, but Little Wound's clever answers to all questions left the whites in the dark. According to the *Washington Post*, Little Wound said that dancing was just their way of expressing their emotions and their needs. Royer's interpretation of this remark was "Sioux have grievances." Little Wound blamed the government for sending them a bad agent in a time of trouble. The final note about the council was that Little Wound was "the champion liar of the Sioux nation" and that, in fact, the Lakotas were planning to scalp General Miles, who for his part hoped for a bloodless suppression of the ghost dance.[80] At the time Miles was not even close to the Lakota reservations, and scalping him at his headquarters in Chicago or in Washington was most likely not planned by the ghost dancers.

November reporting ended with articles in the *New York Times* in which some of the well-known Friends of the Indian were allowed to present their opinions about the "craze." According to them, the Indians were not alone in their belief in a false Christ. More civilized and educated men, white and black, expected their messiah to arrive within a few years' time. They described the doctrines of several movements, and one article concluded that the Indian "is neither stronger nor weaker than his brother of other hues." The ghost dance was compared to movements that occurred among oppressed peoples all over the world, from Siberia to Arabia. It stressed that the ghost dance was not a "craze." The *Omaha Daily Bee*, on the other hand, reported on the "Messiah orgies" but believed that empty stomachs and white men's cruelty caused the Indians' behavior.[81]

Finally, on November 30, the papers reported the identity of the messiah of the ghost dance religion. They quoted a special census agent for Indians in Nevada who revealed that the Messiah was Jack Wilson, known also as We-Wo-Kar or Co-We-Jo, who lived in Mason Valley, Nevada—not Johnson Sides, as had been previously reported. The agent described the Messiah as an intelligent man with dramatic visions and noted that the religion was not dangerous. The Indians should be allowed to dance, the agent believed. He hoped that the Indians would be allowed to visit the Messiah, who expressed his wish to meet with Sitting Bull.[82]

From Confusion to Wounded Knee

"Pinned in by Troops. The Indian Problem to Be Solved by a Single Crushing Blow" was the headline in the *Washington Post* on December 1. The *New York Times* ran the same article under the headline "General Miles's Plan Revealed." The article itself told about a plan to surround the Indians. The *Times*, however, admitted that military officials were keeping quiet, so the article was purely speculative. An army of newspaper reporters was moving to the front, while the Indians were pillaging and burning the cabins of the settlers, who were fleeing for their lives. There was also a brief mention in both papers that an Indian was killed when a shirt that was "dipped in a fluid of wonderful charm" failed to protect him.[83]

Although the eastern papers claimed that Indians were destroying property, they also quoted General Brooke, who failed to confirm the reported depredations. On the contrary, he was very sympathetic toward the Indians. "The Indians here are suffering for food. I have nothing to give them. The proverbial improvidence of the Indian and the insufficiency of his food causes this," Brooke claimed.[84]

The *New York Times* published extracts from the annual report of the secretary of the interior urging Congress to keep its promises to the Indians. At the same time the secretary expressed the opinion that the 250,000 Indians in the United States possessed far more land than they needed. About the Lakotas the report said it "is believed that this tribe will presently be distinguished for its rapid progress toward civilization as it has heretofore been for bravery and intelligence in savage warfare."[85]

The *Chicago Tribune,* the *Yankton Press and Dakotan,* and the *Omaha Daily Bee* also printed reports about the fleeing settlers and the ghost dancers pillaging the settlers' abandoned property. The papers were much concerned about the Rosebud Brulés, who were moving toward Pine Ridge and the Badlands. These Indians were considered to be very hostile and uncontrollable. Their presence on Pine Ridge Reservation was expected to lead to trouble, because many of the friendlies there reportedly decided to join the Brulés. This, it vas believed, made the moving column a tremendous fighting force. The papers reported that the ghost dancers shot at some Indian policemen, but at the same time it was explained that there were so many rumors that there was no way of knowing the truth. "White liars, red liars, and all the intermediate tinges are busily at work. Stories of the most alarming character are told about once an hour and contradicted in less time," the *Tribune* correspondent complained. Despite their somewhat alarming reports, the western papers in fact understood the Indians' situation quite well. The *Omaha Daily Bee* believed that the Indians were suffering from lack of food and that it was understandable for superstitious people to believe in supernatural forces when there was no other hope left for them.[86] The reporting in the beginning of December contained as much confusion and as many contradictions as the reporting at the end of November.

During the following days all five newspapers reported that 1,000 to 2,000 of the friendlies were moving toward the Badlands to join the hostile camp there. On their way they were plundering other friendlies' homes and stealing thousands of cattle and wagonloads of flour. The army was sent after that "thieving band of rebels," as the *New York Times* put it, even though it admitted that army officials would not confirm that the alleged depredations had actually occurred. Even as the newspapers reported depredations and mounting danger, they still concluded that the danger was believed to be over. This was especially annoying to Royer, who considered the army's inaction inexcusable.[87]

On December 2, under the headline "Our Indian Policy," the *New York Times* questioned why no action had been taken earlier, especially when the lack of rations and Indian disaffection had been reported by Commissioner of Indian Affairs Thomas J. Morgan and Secretary of the Interior John M.

Noble as early as April 1890. According to the article, there might have been a miscalculation in rations sent to the Rosebud Lakotas, the Indians getting more than they were entitled to, but miscalculations in the opposite direction may have occurred as well. If a band received less food than it was entitled to, it was only natural to expect some raids on cattle. The article suggested that disaffection was to be expected given the fact that the Indians were losing their lands very quickly. The paper further noted that stealing Indian land was the main feature of the government's Indian policy in the year 1890. Such action was elevated into a moral and educational platform, while, in fact, economic and other reasons were behind the land theft.[88]

On the following day, December 3, the *New York Times*, the *Omaha Daily Bee*, and the *Washington Post* devoted considerable space to General Miles's thoughts. Like General Brooke, he did not blame the Indians for the situation, but white men who were holding back rations. "These hostiles have been started [it is "starved" in the *Bee*] into fighting and they will prefer to die fighting than starve peaceably." Miles commented, "We have overwhelming evidence from officers, inspectors, and testimony of agents as well, and also from Indians themselves, that they have been suffering for the want of food, more or less, for two years past, and one of the principal causes of disaffection is this very matter." Other causes included "the religious delusion and the innate disposition of the savage to go to war."[89]

Despite the sympathy Miles felt for the Indians, he noted that the "seriousness of the situation has not been exaggerated. The disaffection is more widespread than it has been at any time in years. . . . The conspiracy extends to more different tribes . . . over a larger area of country than in the whole history of Indian warfare." He continued, "It [the ghost dance] is a more comprehensive plot than anything ever inspired by the prophet Tecumseh or even Pontiac." Miles was convinced the 30,000 Indians in the Northwest could muster more than 6,000 fighting men. Of these, 4,000 would go on the warpath, and they could easily be joined by 4,000 from other parts of the country. This formidable force could cause much trouble. Thus Miles's objective was to avoid hostilities, even if he believed that such a happy ending to the trouble was improbable. He was certain that the Indians were able to go on the warpath in the winter because they had good horses, were well armed, and could live on cattle much as they had lived on buffalo before.[90] It is noteworthy that previously the newspapers estimated the Lakotas' fighting force at 15,000 to 27,000 men.

By early December some news of peace was also reported. Some of the ghost dancers were willing to come to the agency at Pine Ridge, raising hopes for a speedy settlement of the situation. Also, reports from officers who had visited the ghost dancers' camps claimed that everything was quiet. The only alarming element in the Indian situation, according to one officer, was the newspaper accounts.[91] In the following days, the papers published articles focusing on the discussion going on in Congress regarding the situation on the Lakota reservations. The papers called for an investigation of hunger among the Lakotas and blamed the spoils system for bringing about the change in agents at a critical time. This was considered especially significant for Pine Ridge and Cheyenne River Reservations.[92]

The newspapers also focused on Father John Jutz's mission to the Stronghold (see chapters 1 and 4) and reported on the conference between the ghost dancers and Father Jutz (the papers write "Jule"). The *Omaha Daily Bee* listed the Indians' grievances and described Father Jutz's mission in great detail. The *New York Times* followed the next day with exactly the same story under the headline "The Hostile Camp Visited." According to the *Times*, there seemed to be no doubt about the ghost dancers' ability to defend themselves. The *Times* also published General Schofield's letter to the secretary of the interior in which the general said that the Indians were well armed and supplied with ammunition. "Should they commence hostilities, there will be no room for doubt about the course to be pursued," he maintained, but added that disarming the Indians would cause immense problems, including the fact that holding Indians as prisoners of war would be against the policy of civilizing them. However, "it does not appear that the Indians have had any deliberate purpose to commence hostilities against the whites; they have so far as known simply put themselves in an attitude of defiance," the general concluded.[93]

The *Chicago Tribune* and the *Omaha Daily Bee* reported on December 7 that a meeting was held at Pine Ridge Agency between the ghost dance chiefs and General Brooke. In this council, the ghost dance leaders repeated to

Brooke all the reasons for their actions that they had given to Father Jutz a day earlier. These articles had a somewhat nostalgic tone, describing the Indians marching to the council as "noble savages," wearing their feathers and war paint. The *Bee* correspondent added that these Indians were "grim looking fellows," the most "brutal looking Indians" he had ever seen. Despite the tone, the papers reported the proceedings of the council in an unbiased manner. Both papers considered that the council was beneficial and reported that Brooke hoped to settle the whole matter in a couple of days. General Miles was also reported to be of the opinion that the disintegration among the ghost dancers would settle the trouble soon. Interestingly, the *Bee* correspondent, Charles Cressey, claimed that it was totally absurd for the newspapers to pay so much attention to what he called an "utterly groundless agitation about an Indian scare." The *Washington Post* ran a similar article on the following day, but added that some Indians were at the same time stealing horses and robbing houses. The article noted that such action by savages would not be tolerated in any other civilized country. The *Yankton Press and Dakotan* wrote that the council did not accomplish much; rather, it caused dissatisfaction among the peaceful Indians since Brooke promised food and provisions to those who had gone on the warpath. Why should they be rewarded for their bad behavior, was the question among the peaceful Indians. There was also much confusion during the council, and the paper claimed that the interpreters had mistranslated the Indians' words. This is not verified by any other source.[94]

The *Omaha Daily Bee* and the *Chicago Tribune* continued in a similar vein the following day, focusing on the poor living conditions on Pine Ridge Reservation. Under the headlines "Life among Red Men" and "The Monotony of Existence at the Pine Ridge Agency," the papers expressed deep sympathy for the Lakotas. They described Indian life as an "aimless existence," with sadness and misery a part of daily life. The *Bee* correspondent had invited Red Cloud and Little Wound to a dinner and characterized it as a great honor to have been allowed to host these men. In an attempt to understand the ghost dance, the *Bee* described other messianic religions, from ancient Egypt to the Mormons. The *Chicago Tribune* ran a similar article and added Porcupine's story. Both papers, however, noted that the situation on Pine

Ridge was still volatile since more and more Indians were heading toward the Badlands. They described the disposition of the troops in great detail and speculated on Miles's plans to surround and disarm the Indians. Miles was quoted as saying that he did not like the current reservation system, which allowed "savages to terrorize several states."[95]

While the newspapers were concerned with current events at Pine Ridge, *Harper's Weekly* published two articles by Frederic Remington. The first was titled "Chasing a Major-General" and was a romantic description of Remington's trip with Miles to Pine Ridge in October 1890. The general was portrayed as a true western hero, and the soldiers' life was described as hard but honest. The second article addressed the possibility of an Indian war. It was written earlier, perhaps in October or November, and Remington predicted that before his story was printed "the biggest Indian war since 1758 will be in progress, or that the display of military force will have accomplished its object, and the trouble gone." He added that the troop movements were to be carried out in secrecy because the Indians were able to read the newspapers and make their own moves accordingly. Remington blamed the Interior Department for mismanagement but believed that the blame for the trouble overall was to be divided among the Interior Department, some old medicine men, and the most desperate war chiefs.[96]

On December 6, *Harper's Weekly* published a third article relating to the Indians, written by Lt. Marion P. Maus and titled "The New Indian Messiah." The author claimed that he had visited a dance camp at Pine Ridge with Remington. The new religion was nothing more than a version of Christianity that suited the Indians' hopes and expectations. Most of the Indians were sincere in their beliefs, and even Red Cloud believed that the religion would spread over all the earth, Maus wrote. He described the doctrine and the visions seen in the ceremony. He listed Red Cloud, Sitting Bull, and Little Wound as the main apostles of the doctrine, and reported that Sitting Bull had visited the Messiah. Despite some obvious factual mistakes, the article clearly sympathized with the Lakota ghost dancers.[97]

On December 9, the *New York Times* reported that several skirmishes between the Indians and the settlers had occurred. It also reported that the Cheyennes, Arapahos, and Comanches were planning an uprising after a

Lakota runner had organized ghost dances among the Oklahoma Indians. Two days later the paper disputed the news of fighting. That day the headline reported "a false Indian alarm" caused by a white man's joke.[98] This was the first time that a correction of previously reported news was announced in a headline.

The *Omaha Daily Bee* continued in a tone similar to that of the day before, reporting on the poor living conditions among the Lakotas, who were always hungry, and predicted that it would take years before the Indians became civilized. The *Chicago Tribune* quoted the commissioner of Indian affairs, who claimed that the Indians had several just grievances, of which hunger was only one. The commissioner believed that the wrongs done to the Indians should be corrected. The paper offered another opinion on the matter, that of Special Agent Lea, who claimed that, in fact, the Lakotas had no lack of food.[99] General Miles was once again asked for his opinion; this time he suggested that nothing serious would result from the ghost dance. The *Tribune* also reported that cowboys and settlers were organizing a militia force to attack the ghost dancers.[100]

During the next few days, before the attempted arrest of Sitting Bull, the newspapers were filled with reports of Indians fighting each other, the soldiers, and the settlers. The fighting among Indians was reported to have caused up to forty casualties. Several casualties on both sides were reported in a fight that allegedly occurred between the soldiers and 500 ghost dancers lead by Kicking Bear. There were reports of cowboys ambushing Indians, as well as reports of Indians ambushing and killing cowboys. There were also reports of Indians surrendering, but these were outnumbered by reports of Indian hostilities. All in all, the situation was very unclear as the papers reported about fighting at the same time they quoted army officers who claimed that there was no need for alarm, no danger of an outbreak. These officers confirmed only the fighting among the Indians themselves. Despite such assurances, however, the reports published from December 10 to 15 would have convinced readers that a full-scale war had finally begun. The difficult task of reporting accurately was well described by Charles Cressey of the *Omaha Daily Bee*, who wrote that it was impossible to know what was going on since there were "lies all over."[101]

On December 13, *Harper's Weekly* printed an alarming story entitled "The Threatened War." The situation was deemed very serious; almost 4,000 Lakotas were preparing to take the warpath. They would be reinforced by 6,000 Indians from the Indian Territory. The article quoted General Miles, who believed that the largest Indian uprising ever was at hand. For this reason it was fortunate that Miles, who was considered a friend to the Indians, was in command of the troops. Despite the alarming tone, *Harper's Weekly* emphasized that the government and the spoils system were to be blamed for the current situation. "We teach the Indian to distrust us, and when they naturally turn against us, we destroy them," the article concluded.[102]

The *Washington Post* published an article criticizing the reservation system as inhumane, although reservations enabled the government to civilize the Indians. The *Omaha Daily Bee* believed that it was "bulls, not bullets, beef and not grief" that the starving Indians wanted and needed.[103] On December 15, both eastern newspapers published articles criticizing the government's Indian policy. The *New York Times* claimed that the causes for Indian wars lay in the agents' incompetence, business swindles, lack of supplies, and the friction between the War and Interior Departments.[104] The *Washington Post* quoted an army chaplain who listed the mistakes made in the management of Indian affairs. "Gross injustice [has been] done to the native inhabitants of the continent," the chaplain claimed. "We made some of them savages. In sheer desperation they commit those acts which are caused by constant invasion and aggression." The ghost dance was a result of the mismanagement of Indian affairs. "To expect a race to yield in any considerable degree in ten years is unreasonable," he claimed. The ghost dance was only a religious ceremony in which people danced naked, carrying absolutely nothing. "Does this look dangerous?" he asked. He believed that the danger rose from hunger and suffering. He added that the government should feed those it kept as prisoners and that the ghost dancers planned no outbreak. Even if the whites seemed to expect an outbreak, it was mostly because some Indian agents had become frightened and spread their fear across the country. According to the chaplain, things had gone so far that one drunken white man, or a drunken Indian, could start a bloody Indian war.[105]

These comments, very critical toward whites and the government and very sympathetic toward the Indians, were published in the midst of the many reports of fighting between Indians and whites. Clearly, the newspapers wanted to add some independent analysis to the alarming news reports. This additional information was sought from various sources: government officials, army personnel, special agents, and even an anonymous army chaplain. The *Omaha Daily Bee*, however, relied heavily on its correspondents on location. These additional or supplementary articles and editorials seemed to appear almost simultaneously in several newspapers, as though they unanimously decided that it was time to change the tone of the news reporting.

The Death of Sitting Bull

In early December, the newspapers took notice of Buffalo Bill's mission to capture Sitting Bull and the disagreements it caused between the Interior and War Departments. The *Washington Post* reported that Buffalo Bill believed Sitting Bull was behind the trouble but that he did not believe an uprising would occur before spring. Although Sitting Bull was not directly violating reservation rules, the *New York Times* accused him of violating the rules of the Indian Department by keeping children out of school. The *Chicago Tribune* reported that Sitting Bull was in Nevada, inciting the Indians there, clearly confusing the Lakota chief with the Arapaho ghost dance disciple of the same name. Sitting Bull's planned arrest became a controversial issue; most frontiersmen quoted by the papers believed that it would cause a general uprising.[106]

"The Last of Sitting Bull," "Sitting Bull Shot," "Sitting Bull's Last Fight," "Sitting Bull Shot Dead," and "Sitting Bull's Blood" were the major headlines on December 16. The newspapers published several articles regarding the chief's death, while admitting that the only thing known for certain was that a fight had occurred, and Sitting Bull, with several other Indians, was dead. No one seemed to know what really happened, whether Sitting Bull tried to escape or whether he tried to resist arrest. The general understanding was that Sitting Bull was going to leave the reservation, and that when the Indian policemen tried to arrest him he made a desperate attempt to escape and was then killed by the policemen. The *Chicago Tribune* claimed that

Sitting Bull's men attacked the Indian policemen before they were even able to demand Sitting Bull's surrender. General Miles defended the attempted arrest because he was convinced that Sitting Bull was going to lead more than 300 warriors to the Badlands. Miles did not believe that Sitting Bull's death would cause any general outbreak. On the contrary, he believed that it would crush the ghost dancers' spirit, but admitted that it might instead render them desperate and incite them to fight.[107]

None of the papers could give exact particulars of the events, but they tried to gather information through army officers and Agent McLaughlin. Four of the papers published McLaughlin's report to the secretary of the interior. In this report McLaughlin defended his actions and decisions. The *Yankton Press and Dakotan* quoted the agent only briefly but ran a story about Sitting Bull's death that was likely based on McLaughlin's report. The other papers published articles expressing the general feeling among the settlers living around the Lakota reservations: "The arch villain is dead," said one; another prophesied, "Before another sun has set Sitting Bull's celebrated chorus of dancers will be good Indians or prisoners," paraphrasing the old saying "The only good Indian is a dead Indian."[108]

Sitting Bull's death caused much speculation in the newspapers. There were reports of fleeing Indians and pursuing soldiers, reports of battles, and reports that denied any hostilities. The general sentiment, however, was that because Sitting Bull was killed by the Indian police his blood was not on the hands of the whites. In the midst of all these mixed news reports was an article in the *Washington Post* in which a merchant offered to pay 800 dollars for Sitting Bull's skin. At this point, official comments made by the president, several army officers, and Secretary Proctor all expressed regret at Sitting Bull's death. They hoped that it would eventually have favorable results.[109]

The *New York Times* published two articles describing Sitting Bull's life. They portrayed him as a cruel, sagacious, bloodthirsty enemy of the whites, who was to be blamed for the death of Colonel Custer as well as for the ghost dance. Because he was thought to be well aware of the political value of a messiah, there was no doubt that he was behind the whole ghost dance hysteria. Finally, the paper compared his death to "the slaying of a rogue elephant," adding, "No quadruped ever did so much widely-extended and long-continued mischief as Sitting Bull." The *Chicago Tribune* published articles in which Buffalo Bill, Agent McLaughlin, and General Miles expressed their views on Sitting Bull. Although the tone of these interviews was that Sitting Bull deserved his fate, a certain feeling of respect toward the dead leader can be detected. He was a man with more brains than courage, said the *Chicago Tribune*, more of a politician than a warrior.[110]

The *New York Times* continued in a similar vein, describing the events surrounding Sitting Bull's death quite accurately. One article ended with the comment that the Indian police made "a good Indian of him." The paper described the difficult situation on Standing Rock Reservation, including the power struggle among the different chiefs and between Sitting Bull and McLaughlin. It expressed the firm belief that Sitting Bull saw the ghost dance as his final chance to regain his prestige. The paper suggested that although the facts were not yet known, the Indians were to be blamed for Sitting Bull's fate. The army and the Indian police were praised for their actions. Somewhat surprisingly, despite all the negative reporting about Sitting Bull as a person, the paper also believed that his death aroused more apprehension than relief among local whites.[111]

An even more surprising article followed, as an army officer ridiculed the whole idea of an Indian uprising: "There is a great deal of humbug and political clap trap in the noise being made by the military officers on the frontier." The anonymous officer noted that the Indians, despite all reports to the contrary, were poorly armed. "The truth is that much more has been made of this threatened outbreak than the situation warranted," he believed.[112]

The western papers agreed that Sitting Bull's arrest was necessary, but noted that he alone could not be blamed for the trouble; there were whites who shared the blame as well, and the government should take better care of its wards. The *Yankton Press and Dakotan* wrote that Sitting Bull could never have become "a friendly Indian." He witnessed the destruction the whites brought upon his people but realized that he could not stop it, he could only fight it. The paper urged people to put themselves in Sitting Bull's place before they passed judgment on him. Although the *Omaha Daily Bee* portrayed Sitting Bull as a menace to peace, a bar to civilization, a savage, and an enemy of the whites, it also described him as a great warrior, a crafty leader, and a man who possessed "a devotion to his people, which among civilized mankind is called patriotism."[113]

While analyzing the events surrounding Sitting Bull's death, the western papers also reported rumors from the Lakota reservations. "Slain by the Indians" was one of the headlines. More than fifty soldiers were reported dead after a bloody encounter with the Indians. The soldiers were said to be on their way to apprehend the fleeing Indians loyal to Sitting Bull. At the same time the papers paid close attention to the effect Sitting Bull's death had on the Indians of Pine Ridge. To their surprise no general stampede or outbursts of anger occurred. On the contrary, hopes for a peaceful settlement of the trouble were reported. The situation was still considered very delicate, since the full effect of Sitting Bull's death could not yet be predicted. One correspondent apologized to his readers, saying that it was impossible to gain accurate information about the Indians or the troop movements.[114]

Several days following Sitting Bull's death the *New York Times* and the *Washington Post* were filled with news of severe fighting between the hostiles and the soldiers. The news of a battle in which more than fifty soldiers and countless Indians lost their lives was repeated in these newspapers. Settlers were reportedly killed and their ranches burned by the hostiles. These reports were partly denied by the military, but the general impression was of bloody encounters following Sitting Bull's death. Both papers reported that sounds of a battle and cannon firing were heard, but actual details of the fighting were lacking. An attack against the hostiles, which would probably result in their annihilation, was called for. According to both papers, the hostilities were believed to be so severe that an uprising would take place also among the Southern Utes, Kiowas, Comanches, and some tribes in Canada.[115]

The western papers also printed reports about skirmishes between the troops and the ghost dancers. Their reports, however, were not as sensationalist as those in the eastern papers. The *Omaha Daily Bee* especially seemed to be quite rational about the situation. One article listed all the problems the Lakotas had been facing for years and reported favorable developments as more and more ghost dancers were moving closer to Pine Ridge Agency. The western papers reported that a council had been held at Pine Ridge Agency during which Red Cloud tried to convince the rest of the several thousand Indians to remain calm and quiet. Red Cloud was reported to have expressed regret that there had been trouble, but said that it was understandable that the soldiers would eventually kill those who refused to surrender. The article includes a letter said to have been written by Red Cloud in which he explained his position on the ghost dance. The paper denied the earlier report of the battle in which fifty men were said to have been killed. Instead, there had been a skirmish on a ranch on Pine Ridge during which three Indians were killed. The *Omaha Daily Bee* in fact had already reported this incident on December 14, since the *Bee* correspondent, Charles Cressey, took part in the skirmish.[116]

Interestingly, the *Chicago Tribune* quoted General Miles, who believed that there was no hope for a peaceful settlement since there could be up to 750 hostile warriors determined to fight it out with the soldiers. The *Omaha Daily Bee* also quoted Miles, this time reporting the general's opinion that the situation was looking more favorable—this despite the fact that there were more than 1,000 warriors "on the warpath," as the paper put it. It is worth noting that now the estimates regarding the numbers of hostile warriors had dropped to a new low of around 1,000.

Both papers, however, were concerned about the possibility that all the hostile Indians would join forces in the Badlands. Sitting Bull's people were reportedly planning to join Big Foot, who would then lead a major fighting force toward the Badlands, where the Pine Ridge ghost dancers were still camped.[117]

On December 20, the *Chicago Tribune* reported that Sitting Bull's band planned to avenge their leader's death: "The dead chief's band decide to lift some scalps." This, according to a reliable messenger, was the plan of approximately 100 warriors. When the plan was revealed, the settlers in the vicinity fled to Fort Bennett. There was also a report of a lively skirmish between troops and several hundred Lakota warriors. The *Omaha Daily Bee* also reported this skirmish and the Indians' plan to avenge Sitting Bull's death. Big Foot supposedly led the party. But the paper contradicted itself by saying that approximately thirty of Sitting Bull's men had already surrendered, as had Hump and Big Foot. The *Bee* and the *Yankton Press and Dakotan* reported that Little Wound was extremely angry with the white officials for pitting Indian against Indian. In an almost romantic tone the article portrayed Little Wound as a chief magnificent in his anger.[118]

Little Wound was the focus of an article published in the *Chicago Tribune* on December 21. It was written by Emma C. Sickels, a schoolteacher on Pine Ridge Reservation, who visited Little Wound at his home on White Clay Creek. Little Wound explained to her all the reasons for the trouble, starting with broken promises and the starvation of his people. He wished everybody to know that he wanted peace, but his heart was sad, since there was nothing left for the Indians.[119]

Harper's Weekly focused on Sitting Bull and other noted chiefs on Standing Rock Reservation. The magazine described the factions on Standing Rock, where Sitting Bull was the leader of the hostile faction and Gall and John Grass were the friendly Hunkpapa leaders. Sitting Bull was portrayed as the major obstacle to civilization and the prominent ghost dance leader. John Grass and Gall were considered the most intelligent and progressive chiefs: "The strong faces of these two chiefs indicate their character, which unlike Sitting Bull, is fearless, upright, bright and progressive." Although the Sitting Bull faction was small, it was believed to be the most dangerous element, consisting of ambitious men who would be ready for war at any time. The paper suggested that the danger of war was imminent because never before had so many "diverse Indian tribes been so generally united upon one single idea." The Indian fanaticism over this idea was reportedly so overwhelming that one single spark could precipitate an Indian war far exceeding those led by Pontiac or Tecumseh, repeating General Miles's assessment of December 3. *Harper's Weekly* suggested that the Indians were not wholly to blame, however. The current excitement was caused to some extent by unscrupulous white people who hoped that a war would bring them profit and result in opening the reservation lands for settlement.[120] The article, clearly written before Sitting Bull's death, was alarmist in tone but followed the magazine's policy of placing a part of the blame on the white men.

The *Omaha Daily Bee* headline on December 21 read "Waiting for Developments," indicating that nothing important was going on. The whites on Pine Ridge Reservation were calling for action. The local cowboys especially were eager to face the Indian in battle. The army's tactic of waiting and negotiating did not please everybody. The *Bee* reflected this attitude by urging the army to go to the Badlands and end the trouble. If the army did nothing, the war was a farce. General Brooke was also quoted; he said that he did not understand the Indians, who promised one day this and another day that. One more peace effort, however, was going to be made.[121]

The following day the peace party was sent out, and General Miles believed that they would succeed in bringing the ghost dancers to the agency. Another favorable development was also reported: Hump was on his way to Cheyenne River Agency with forty of Sitting Bull's men. The paper noted that so far the Indians had not killed any white settlers or soldiers; twenty-three Indians, however, were believed to be dead. The main concern now was Big Foot. Col. Edwin V. Sumner, who was leading the force sent to capture Big Foot, was expected to have a lively struggle.[122]

On December 23, the western papers reported that Sitting Bull's band, now under Big Foot's leadership, had been captured without resistance. The two eastern papers reported the same on December 24. General Miles believed that had this force not been captured before reaching the Badlands, it "could have massacred as many settlers as the Sioux did in the Minnesota troubles of 1862." He also believed that Sitting Bull's death left the Indians without a real leader. Since Big Foot was now acting as a leader and was "most defiant and threatening," all the trouble on Cheyenne River and Standing Rock Reservations was expected to end with his capture. Big Foot's Indians were reported to be protesting any plan to disarm them, but they were not believed to be planning serious resistance. Big Foot's capture was expected to have a positive effect on those who were still in the Badlands since they no longer could hope to receive reinforcements from Cheyenne River Reservation.[123]

The newspapers also reported events among the hostiles in the Badlands, where the peace delegation sent by Brooke faced strong opposition and even threats against their lives. The general sentiment among the Indians in the Badlands was reported to be very hostile. Two Strike, leading the Brulés, announced that they would not surrender. The *Yankton Press and Dakotan*, however, believed that Short Bull was anxious to surrender and that he would soon lead a number of ghost dancers to the agency. Attention was again given to Sitting Bull's death. Agent McLaughlin's official report of his death was published, and Congress was demanding a full investigation into the matter.[124]

Thus, after Sitting Bull's death the actual news reporting continued in its usual contradictory fashion. The western papers, however, approached the situation somewhat more calmly than the eastern papers. In the wake of Sitting Bull's death they published additional information about the Lakotas, Sitting Bull, and the ghost dance. Even if Sitting Bull was to be blamed for his own death, the actual celebration of his death ended quite soon. In fact, Sitting Bull, the archvillain who was so critically portrayed while he was still alive, now began a slow transformation into a victim or even into a patriot, as the *Omaha Daily Bee* suggested. At the same time, Big Foot rose from relative anonymity to become the main enemy. Perhaps the papers were simply repeating General Miles's opinion of Big Foot.[125]

Big Foot's Surrender and the Wounded Knee Affair

"Tricked by the Sioux," claimed the *Washington Post* on December 25. "Making for the Badlands" was the headline in the *New York Times*. Both papers were certain that Big Foot had escaped in order to join the hostiles: "If these bucks unite with Kicking Bear's band in the latter's stronghold, there will be a bloody fight before the redskins are induced to surrender again." The *Chicago Tribune* only briefly commented that Big Foot had eluded the soldiers and was heading toward the Badlands. The *Yankton Press and Dakotan* seemed to miss Big Foot's escape and reported instead that his capitulation would end the trouble peacefully; Big Foot's men had already surrendered ninety-eight stands of arms. The *Omaha Daily Bee*, on the other hand, joined the eastern papers in making big news of Big Foot's escape: "Good bye to peace parleying. It is now plainer than ever that a slaughter of reds is at hand."[126]

The *Washington Post* explained that the whites were so afraid of the ghost dance because they believed the dance meant that the Indians were preparing to take scalps. The article tried to represent the Indian point of view, claiming that they were engaging in the ghost dance simply as a commemoration of the birth of Christ.[127]

During the next couple of days the newspapers reported bloody encounters between the Indians led by Kicking Bear and the soldiers. They also reported that the hostiles were surrendering in small groups on all Lakota reservations. The *Yankton Press and Dakotan* went so far as to announce in a headline "Peace." The paper also noted Big Foot's escape from the soldiers. Still, no more hostilities were expected, which was generally believed to be the result of the delegation that went to the Badlands to negotiate for peace. Those who surrendered gave up their arms, which were mostly of "very antiquated pattern." For the first time the papers reported that the Indians seemed not to be as well armed as had generally been thought. Disarming the Indians was seen as a dangerous job that could easily lead to a fight, but it was still considered necessary.[128]

At this point, the fate of Big Foot and his band was even more uncertain than the contradictory reports of fighting. There were reports that he had already joined the hostiles in the Badlands, but there were also reports that he had been recaptured. No one seemed to know where he really was; he had evaded all the troops that were sent after him. General Miles considered this most unfortunate and believed that Big Foot had deceived Colonel Sumner, who first captured him. The papers reported that the people in the Badlands were starting to move their camp toward Pine Ridge Agency. This was seen as a favorable development, although the Indians were still reported to be carrying on raids against ranches.[129]

Harper's Weekly published two lengthy pieces on December 27 relating to the Lakotas and the ghost dance. The first, an editorial, expressed the hope that Sitting Bull's death, though tragic, would result in a peaceful end to the trouble. The editorialist was of the opinion that there was not enough evidence to support Miles's claims that the ghost dance was a plot far exceeding that of Pontiac's. The writer emphasized that the spoils system was to be blamed for the trouble and demanded its dismantling. "Profound dissatisfaction there certainly is, and even suffering from hunger," the writer believed. The trouble was caused by "the bad faith of the white man. . . . When promises have been faithfully kept, there has been little serious trouble." Even education toward civilization would succeed better with a more humane and honest course.[130]

An article written by Frederic Remington speculated on the benefits of

HARPER'S WEEKLY

JOURNAL OF CIVILIZATION

Vol. XXXIV.—No. 1775.
Copyright, 1890, by Harper & Brothers.
All Rights Reserved.

NEW YORK, SATURDAY, DECEMBER 27, 1890.

TEN CENTS A COPY,
INCLUDING SUPPLEMENT.

ONE OF THE FORT KEOGH CHEYENNE SCOUT CORPS, COMMANDED BY LIEUTENANT CASEY.—Drawn by Frederic Remington.—[See Page 1004.]

FIGURE 11. An Indian scout. The army employed many Lakotas as scouts during the ghost dance troubles. *Harper's Weekly*, December 1891, cover by Frederic Remington.

234

employing Indians—Lakotas as well as other tribes—as regular cavalry. He believed that Indians made excellent soldiers, since it suited their lifestyle. They could be organized as troops based on their traditional tribes and bands. Every village would create a force, and the officer would be the head of the village. This would create a semicivilized military class that would eventually become self-supporting. Remington believed that trying to make the Indians farmers would fail, as would the entire government Indian policy, which he characterized as a gross case of mismanagement. He understood why Indians took up the ghost dance: "When he [the Indian] thinks of being a pure and simple farmer it chills his soul, and he welcomes the ghost dance, and would welcome anything else which would take him from his lazy starvation of the agency." Because of all the mismanagement of Indian affairs, thousands of soldiers were now forced to sleep in the snow during this military campaign and be called on to "shoot down a people who have the entire sympathy of every soldier in the ranks."[131]

On December 28, the *New York Times* published a correction to the previous day's news. Printed in very small type, the correction declared that there was no foundation for the news of skirmishes between the Indians and the soldiers, nor in the reports of murdered ranchmen. In fact, the paper claimed, not a shot had been exchanged between the Indians and the troops.[132]

That day both eastern papers tried to present the Indian point of view on the ghost dance. According to the *Washington Post*, dancing was a natural Indian ceremony; the ghost dance was only a way for Indians to express their feelings. The paper also commented on the character of Sitting Bull, who was not originally a chief but rose to power by his own merits, like Napoleon in Europe. The *New York Times* published an article about Indians' life in general and their "peculiar social system." It ended by saying that the Indian was much like the white man, with both good and bad characteristics.[133]

The western papers went even further in an attempt to understand the Lakotas. The *Omaha Daily Bee* reported extensively on the government's broken promises, the destruction of the buffalo, the failed attempts by the Lakotas to take up farming, and the reduction of the Lakota reservations, concluding that the Indians understandably felt cheated. "Under these circumstances it is not in human nature not to be discontented and restless, even turbulent or violent. They have been hungry, cold and sick. . . . To the great mass of them should be extended sympathy, help and last, but not least, justice." The *Chicago Tribune* approved of Miles's suggestion that the best way to treat the Lakotas was to put army officials in charge of the reservations. The paper specifically accused Agent McLaughlin of taking personal advantage of his post. He had allegedly amassed a huge fortune during his almost fifteen years as an Indian agent. Sitting Bull had officially complained about McLaughlin's methods, which caused the agent to cut off the Indians' rations. This led to ghost dancing and to Sitting Bull's death, which the paper blamed on McLaughlin.[134]

Despite these analyses, the western papers continued to warn of a possible war. "A Decisive Fight Imminent" and "News of Bloodshed May Be Expected within 48 hours" were among the headlines. Supposedly there were in the Badlands more than 800 heavily armed warriors, assisted by 500 able "squaws," spoiling for a fight. The papers also claimed that the ghost dancers, who were continuing their depredations, had killed the members of the so-called peace party. But the papers contradicted themselves by noting that the ghost dancers were peacefully moving toward Pine Ridge Agency and that Big Foot was the only cause for concern.[135]

Big Foot's capture was the major news on December 29. The papers were generally convinced that the war was now coming to an end, since Short Bull, with a band of 400 ghost dancers, was reported to be on his way to Pine Ridge Agency. The western papers reported that Big Foot came forward carrying a white flag to meet with Maj. Samuel Whiteside and after a short parley surrendered peacefully. General Miles was very pleased and expressed his gratitude to the friendly chiefs who persuaded the ghost dancers to move closer to the agency. It was now believed that no more lives would be lost. The *New York Times* quoted Miles, who expressed great disappointment in the government's manner of treating the Indians. He was certain that civilization was the only way for the Indians, but before that could happen the government needed to support its dependents. He said that he did not want to bring upon the people of the United States "the national disgrace of starving our dependents into rebellion and then killing them for rebelling." The *Omaha Daily Bee*, however, once again contradicted itself by saying that Big

Foot's surrender was not made in good faith and could still lead to a battle in which the soldiers would "have the drop on the prisoners."[136]

"Battle with Indians," "Desperate Act of Treachery," "Big Foot's Treachery Precipitates a Battle," "A Bloody Battle," and "Redskins All Wiped Out" were a few of the major headlines on December 30. All five newspapers and *Harper's Weekly* designated much space to accounts of the bloody encounter at Wounded Knee. *Harper's Weekly*, however, was not published until late January and early February. The tone of these articles varied only slightly from one paper to another. The *New York Times* described the battle at Wounded Knee objectively, saying that the Indians were in a very sullen and ugly mood because the women and children had no food and were harassed by the troops. The fight occurred when the army tried to disarm the Indians. Then "Big Foot's braves turned upon their captors" and the Indians were shot down ruthlessly.[137]

An article in the *Washington Post* declared that the 7th Cavalry once again displayed its bravery in action: "The troops were taken at a disadvantage by the treacherous foe." The paper suggested that the Indians probably wanted revenge for Sitting Bull's death, and predicted that the survivors of the 7th Cavalry would punish the hostiles severely. The *Chicago Tribune* took a similar tone, claiming that the Indians opened fire on the unsuspecting soldiers, who then fired back, killing most of them. The article noted that after the first volley the Indians were killed regardless of their age or sex. Still, the members of the 7th Cavalry "have once again shown themselves to be heroes in deeds of daring." Accounts of the battle in *Harper's Weekly* were similar in nature to those in the *Post* and the *Tribune*. Only the Indians were to be blamed; the soldiers performed excellently at a most critical time, and at Wounded Knee the largest Indian uprising was crushed. This, according to the magazine, was accomplished by wise and excellent use of U.S. troops.[138]

Most notable among the articles published on December 30 was the one written by Charles Cressey of the *Omaha Daily Bee*. Cressey took the field personally with Maj. Samuel Whiteside and was present when Big Foot surrendered. At the time of the attempted disarmament, Cressey was standing very close to the Indian men, who were sitting in front of Big Foot's tent. Thus Cressey evidently witnessed at least parts of the battle. His article in the *Bee* described the events leading to the actual disarmament of Big Foot's people quite objectively, but as in the other newspapers, Cressey reported that the Indians opened fire on the soldiers, who were taken totally by surprise. Cressey concluded that the army would no longer entertain sympathetic feelings toward the hostiles and expressed the opinion that it was time for the army to act and punish the Indians: "The country will not shed many tears, if the treacherous murderers of Captain Wallace and his men are sent to keep company with Sitting Bull." He also referred to the previous day's article that claimed that the Indians had not surrendered in good faith.[139]

At this point none of the newspapers knew what actually happened, but the events were described accurately up until the actual fight began. It was generally believed that the Indians fired the first shot that inaugurated the battle. The newspapers concluded that the Indians were fully responsible and that the military showed great heroism. At this point, on December 30–31, while the events of the battle were unclear, it seemed obvious to the newspapers that almost the entirety of Big Foot's band was annihilated. The army officers and officials in Washington believed that the Indians wanted revenge for Sitting Bull's death. All the papers reported extensively about the fighting that followed the battle at Wounded Knee, including the attack on Pine Ridge Agency and other skirmishes. Even the so-called friendly Indians were reported to be fleeing from the agency. A bloody war was expected.[140]

It is very likely that all the other newspapers studied here received the particulars of the fight at least partly from the *Omaha Daily Bee* and its correspondent Charles Cressey. After the battle, Cressey and a few other newspaper correspondents who were also present at Wounded Knee came together at a trading post close to the battlefield. There they compared notes and wrote the story of Wounded Knee. By 8 o'clock in the evening their story was delivered to the telegraph office at Rushville, Nebraska. The correspondents at Pine Ridge, however, had for weeks followed a system that allowed one correspondent's story each day to be sent first through the telegram. On December 29, the lucky person who got to wire first was William F. Kelley of the *Nebraska State Journal*. Cressey and his companions had to wait their turn. The first news of the battle of Wounded Knee reached the major newspapers through Kelley, a man who was not a professional correspondent and whom the other correspondents had ridiculed for being a "tenderfoot," thoroughly unfamiliar with Indians. Although Kelley's dispatch was the first to be sent, other newspapers used Cressey's story widely.[141]

"The Ghost Dance War"

The newspapers studied here took different approaches to the Wounded Knee affair and its aftermath on the last days of the year 1890. The *Washington Post* reported on the second fight between the soldiers and the Indians, in which Two Strike was defeated. "More than 30–40 Sioux warriors bite the dust," the paper reported, although it admitted that the information it received was contradictory. Articles in the *Omaha Daily Bee* and the *Chicago Tribune* mentioned several skirmishes between Indians and soldiers. Especially noteworthy was the battle at Drexel Mission, where the 7th Cavalry was reported to have been surrounded and almost wiped out by as many as 1,000 to 2,000 Lakota warriors. These papers painted a picture of full-scale warfare waged on the fields surrounding Pine Ridge Agency. Both papers published Cressey's latest account of the events at Wounded Knee in which he basically blamed the Indians for treachery and portrayed the 7th Cavalry as heroic victims. The women and children were not killed on purpose, but still the encounter was "the greatest slaughter of redskins of many a year," Cressey wrote. The *Bee* also quoted Miles, who believed that the Wounded Knee battle was a good lesson for the Lakotas. The general was not surprised that it happened to Big Foot, since, according to him, Big Foot's people were the most desperate.[142]

The *New York Times* too reported about the fight between Two Strike and the soldiers, but the different approach it took was published on page 4. "The Indian Massacre" was the headline, and the article claimed, "It would be an abuse of language to describe as a battle the encounter that took place on Monday." The event was called an act of desperation and insanity by the Indians, who were driven to fight because they knew that by giving up their arms "they were sealing their own doom." The paper noted that the Indians' last stand was a heroic attempt that would have been "besung and bepainted" had it been made, for example, by the French army. The *Times* wanted to find a scapegoat for the battle and accused the Interior Department,

and ultimately the president, for allowing the Indians to be starved into revolt. The article concluded by saying that the only way to keep peace was
to feed and disarm the Indians. *Harper's Weekly* expressed the same opinion
on January 24. The government Indian policy was a disgrace, which had
now led to bloodshed and great suffering. This article was very critical of
government Indian policy, which was set by politicians who had no knowledge of the Indian situation and no ear for the Indians. The Indian was not
a romantic figure but a crafty human who should be treated humanely.[143]
The *Washington Post* ended the year by reporting that President Harrison
and Secretary of War Proctor regretted the bloodshed, since the policy of
the government had been to avoid it.[144]

The *Omaha Daily Bee*, the *Washington Post,* and the *Chicago Tribune* started
the year 1891 with reports of a full-scale war: "All on the Warpath," "Redskins
Want Blood," "Reds in Their Warpaint," "Will Fight to Death," "The Roar of
the Cannon," "Miles's Flaming Sword," and "3,000 Braves on the Warpath"
were some of the headlines published in early January 1891. The *New York
Times* appeared to take a somewhat calmer approach. Its major headlines
were "Miles at Pine Ridge," "Hostiles Growing Bolder," and "Ready for the
Indians." The *Yankton Press and Dakotan* ran an even simpler headline: "From
Pine Ridge." The actual news reporting, however, was very similar in all
these newspapers. Mainly there were reports of sharp fighting between the
troops and the hostiles. The newspapers detailed the heroic mission of the
9th Cavalry to save the surrounded 7th Cavalry. There were reports of depredations, massacres, burial parties, and escaping settlers. According to the
newspapers there were thousands of hostile Indians who planned to kill all
the whites they could. Even Red Cloud was reported to be among the hostiles, as the Indians were now generally referred to. In contrast, the *Omaha
Daily Bee*, noted that Red Cloud was not hostile at all, but had been forced
to join the hostile party, and the *Chicago Tribune* claimed that Red Cloud
planned to escape from the hostiles' camp. Generally, however, it was believed that only a few friendly Indians remained at Pine Ridge Agency. The
only chief who remained loyal, according to the papers, was American Horse.
"There are no friendlies now," an article in the *Bee* commented on January
1. All the papers took notice of Miles's arrival at Pine Ridge. This was seen

HARPER'S WEEKLY

JOURNAL OF CIVILIZATION

Vol. XXXV.—No. 1779.
Copyright, 1891, by Harper & Brothers.
All Rights Reserved.

NEW YORK, SATURDAY, JANUARY 24, 1891.

TEN CENTS A COPY.
INCLUDING SUPPLEMENT.

IN THE TRENCHES AT PINE RIDGE.—From a Sketch taken on the Spot.

FIGURE 12. Soldiers digging trenches in preparation for a fight at Pine Ridge. *Harper's Weekly*, January 1891, cover by Frederic Remington.

as an indication of serious trouble ahead. The general sentiment is probably best described by this headline from the *Bee*: "The Bloodiest Battle of Indian History Is at Hand."[145]

Despite these stories, there were a few articles that tried to shed additional light on the matter. The *Chicago Tribune* commented on an article written by General Miles for the *North American Review* in which he tried to explain the reasons for the current trouble. Miles once again expressed his views on the mismanagement of government Indian policy; the Lakotas suffered for want of food, broken promises, and reduced rations. In this article, the general was again quoted as urging the government to replace the Indian agents with military officers. Despite his sympathy for the Indians, Miles believed that they were ready to wage a disastrous war against the U.S. Army, and, according to him, they were better armed than ever before. The *Tribune* article agreed with Miles on many points, but noted that the Indians never had any rights to the lands on which they lived since they were not using the land for farming. This, according to the paper, was justification enough for taking those lands. The *Yankton Press and Dakotan* suggested that the reservations should be abolished and the Lakotas sent to the East in small groups. There they would be surrounded by white civilization and would gradually be absorbed into mainstream society. That would solve the Indian question for good.[146]

The *Omaha Daily Bee* published an article by Herbert Welsh of the Indian Rights Association, who expressed his belief that the major reason for the trouble was the appointment of inexperienced agents who were unable to control the Lakota reservations. Another article, however, commented that the only way to civilize the Indians was to kill them; it was not a time to sentimentalize, but to punish. There were other arguments for and against the Indians, the ghost dance, and even the military campaign. The most notable of these, perhaps, was made by General Schofield: "The dances and the messiah craze in the first place were intended to be harmless, but during the past few days the Indians had come to the conclusion that they were to be disarmed for all time, and not having sufficient provisions, they feared suffering from the want of food and therefore preferred to fight their way out of the situation."[147]

The eastern newspapers supplemented their news reporting with additional articles and editorials. They focused more on the army and on the government and its Indian policy than on the Indians or the ghost dance. The papers blamed the Indian agents, Congress, and even the president for not being able to resolve the Indian question. The matter was of extreme importance because the citizens of the United States were the real sufferers of these recurring Indian wars. The *New York Times* predicted that the bloodiest Indian war in history was at hand and blamed the current administration for the inevitable bloodshed. Both eastern papers agreed that the best solution was to let the War Department take care of the Indians. To replace the civil agents with army officers, as Miles suggested, was the first step in a permanent solution to the Indian question.[148]

The actual news reporting continued in its usual bellicose fashion, but the focus shifted somewhat to the army's role in the Wounded Knee battle. The papers gave a lot of space to Col. James Forsyth, who was relieved from command. His actions during the battle were scrutinized, but it was generally agreed that he did all that he could to save his men and even the Indians. To relieve him of duty was considered unjust and unwise. The papers quoted many seasoned army officers and regular soldiers who testified that warfare against Indians was of a special nature. Neither Forsyth nor the 7th Cavalry were to be blamed for the events that took place at Wounded Knee; the Indians alone were responsible. The fact that women and children were killed was attributed to the special character of Indian warfare. In the heat of battle it was impossible to distinguish the men from the women; they all looked the same, and, in any case, the women participated in the fighting alongside the men. The paper suggested that Colonel Forsyth was relieved of duty not for the alleged massacre of women and children, but for incompetence in positioning his troops. This, according to General Miles, resulted in the soldiers shooting and killing one another. For the first time, however, the battle at Wounded Knee was called a slaughter and butchery. Some space was also given to a rumor claiming that Miles was killed by the hostile Indians. This, as well as other rumors of fighting between Indians and soldiers, was quickly refuted.[149]

On January 6 an article in the *Chicago Tribune* blamed the Democratic newspapers for exaggerating the situation in their eagerness to assail the Republican administration. The article suggested that those Democratic newspapers, together with the eastern sentimentalists—referring to the so-called Friends of the Indians—tried to blame the government and the army for Sitting Bull's death and the massacre at Wounded Knee. The article listed what it called facts regarding these incidents that purported to show that neither the army nor the Indian police could be blamed; Indian treachery alone was responsible for these tragic events. The *Omaha Daily Bee* too commented on inaccurate newspaper reporting, expressing a different view. The article referred to the wild reports that were circulating in the eastern cities that blamed newspaper reporters for the trouble, which started with "smart country correspondents, who can [only] partially read telegraphy." These men then sent their reports, which newspapers, "in their effort of notoriety," eagerly used.[150]

Also on January 6 the *Washington Post* published an article by Secretary of the Interior Noble, who strongly opposed the proposal to let the War Department take over control of Indian affairs. The secretary noted that the Interior Department was not responsible for the current trouble and that the stories of the Lakotas' starvation were much exaggerated. The paper followed this piece with a story on January 7 under the headline "Shall the Army Rule?" The article focused on Secretary Noble, who fiercely defended the Interior Department's way of managing Indian affairs. Secretary of War Proctor equally fiercely opposed him and urged the president to turn Indian affairs over to the War Department. While this battle of wills raged in the press, it seemed evident that the president was ready to approve Miles's idea of putting army officers in control of the Lakota reservations.[151]

By January 1891, as criticism of the newspapers grew, party politics was also becoming a major issue. According to the newspaper historian Elmo Scott Watson, each political party blamed the other for the mismanagement of Indian affairs. Watson observes that during the early part of January newspaper reporting became divided into two camps. Some papers attributed the Wounded Knee battle to Indian treachery and denied charges that the troops deliberately killed women and children; other papers called the Wounded Knee affair a slaughter and a massacre and blamed the army and Miles's personal aspirations for the disaster.[152] This division reflected the confusion that shadowed the Wounded Knee affair. To clarify the general confusion, the army and the government later conducted several investigations into the matter.[153]

The extent to which the development of these two opposed positions can be attributed to the general political play in the East, or to the influence of the eastern Friends of the Indian, is difficult to estimate. At some level Watson's analysis of the division within the newspapers does work. Yet his analysis presents some problems, since all the newspapers studied here published arguments for and against the army, for and against the government's Indian policy, and for and against the Indians. Typically, the newspapers were contradictory on these issues. For this reason it is very difficult to see any clear policy in the news reporting of any one of these newspapers. Thus Watson's division of the papers into two camps based on political allegiance does not hold. Nonetheless, his analysis does work on a general level; throughout the trouble, and especially after Wounded Knee, the eastern papers were more interested in the overall question of the management of Indian affairs than were the *Omaha Daily Bee,* the *Yankton Press and Dakotan,* or the *Chicago Tribune.* In fact, after Wounded Knee, the *Bee* and the *Press and Dakotan* did not concern themselves with the politics of Indian policy.[154]

This does not mean that the eastern newspapers were more accurate, or that they were more informative about the Lakotas or the ghost dance. It only means that they provided readers with commentary and additional information written by their own reporters or obtained from "experts." Such articles, not the news reporting, reflected the political play in the East. The eastern papers simply were more involved in policy making than their western counterparts. The western papers also provided additional information and commentary, but it often reflected the sentiments in the West or the actual—or rumored—events at the scene of the trouble. Neither of the eastern papers sent its own correspondents to the Lakota reservations. It is noteworthy that the eastern papers and the *Chicago Tribune* relied extensively on the expertise of General Miles and Agent McLaughlin. To a certain extent this is understandable, since both men were in positions such that their information and opinions were considered not only interesting, but reliable. Through the papers, their opinions became widely known; both men were even quoted in the U.S. Congress.[155] In fact, it is justifiable to say that these two men used the papers to further their own political agendas. Through Miles and McLaughlin, newspaper readers learned about thousands of fully armed Lakota warriors who were going to follow their leaders, especially Sitting Bull, on the warpath. The newspapers eagerly took up the allegations made against Sitting Bull and published estimates of the numbers of armed Lakotas that went as high as 27,000. Even in this sense the newspapers became involved in the political play surrounding the Lakota ghost dance.

The actual news reporting in early January, however, continued in the usual contradictory fashion. During the following days there were reports that several skirmishes had taken place, and it was even reported that the Indians had killed General Miles. Other reports claimed the Indians were planning a major attack against the soldiers and the settlements, that the Indians were surrounded by soldiers, or that the soldiers were surrounded by Indians. Once again, the best way to summarize the situation from January 5 to January 15 is a quote from the *Omaha Daily Bee*: "Terrible rumors get afloat, to be contradicted in a short time." Some details, however, are worth mentioning. The papers claimed that after Wounded Knee there were practically no friendlies left at Pine Ridge Agency. Thousands of Indians were reported to be on the warpath. Even Miles was still of the opinion that a great conspiracy of all the Indians was going to result in a major battle. On January 8, however, the surprising report was that many Indians were still at the agency. A census conducted among the Indians showed that there were more than 3,500 Indians camped peacefully at Pine Ridge Agency. Despite all the rumors to the contrary, more and more Indians were arriving daily. Even Red Cloud was on his way to rejoin the friendly camp. Miles expressed the opinion that there were no more than 300 to 400 Indian warriors ready to fight. Other reports had estimated up to 4,000 hostile Indians.[156]

Gradually the tone in the newspapers started to change. Even though there still were reports of fighting and depredations, the general feeling was that the trouble was coming to an end—one way or another. The *New York Times* and the *Washington Post* were of the opinion that the end would come only after a major battle, but the *Chicago Tribune* believed that the hostilities would end without further bloodshed. The influence of Young Man Afraid of His Horse over the hostile people was bearing favorable results, the *Tribune* reported. All three papers reported that several of the so-called hostile chiefs agreed to turn themselves in. The Indians were reported to be on verge of fighting each other; they were completely divided in the matter of whether to surrender or to continue their resistance.[157]

The *Omaha Daily Bee*, however, complained that the Indians only promised to come to the agency, but failed to live up to their promise. Red Cloud especially was to be watched. The *Chicago Tribune* believed that the hostiles were slowly making their way to the agency. Despite favorable developments there seemed to be a general apprehension that the eventual disarmament of the Indians could cause serious trouble. They were known to be afraid to give up their arms and were expected to fight rather than to surrender their weapons. For this reason Miles prepared the agency for the Indians' arrival. The *Bee* reported that the agency had been turned into a military garrison. The delicate situation, according to the newspapers, called for additional troops, and the papers followed the movements of the Nebraska Militia carefully. Indeed, the militiamen seemed to be eager to get their hands on the Indians.[158]

"The Militia men want to wipe out all Indians," declared the *Omaha Daily Bee* on January 12, but the major news in all newspapers was that the hostiles were not yet at the agency as they promised. Once again the *Bee* managed to contradict itself. First it claimed "They have started, that is all," implying that the ghost dancers did not even plan to come to the agency; then, on the following page, it noted, "Hostiles coming closer." Other papers simply reported that the Indians were moving, although slowly, closer to the agency. The *Chicago Tribune* and the *New York Times* also reported the slow progress the Indians were making on their way to the agency, but more important, they reported that a major skirmish had taken place between the army and the Indians.[159]

Undoubtedly, newspaper reporting played an important role during the entire duration of the trouble, and indeed played a role in creating the trouble. Immediately following the arrival of troops at Pine Ridge and Rosebud, after Sitting Bull's death, and especially after the Wounded Knee massacre, the newspapers created the impression that a full-scale war was raging, mainly on Pine Ridge Reservation. The papers were filled with descriptions of battle scenes, a heroic U.S. Army, and Indian treachery. This was especially true of the *Omaha Daily Bee*. Even before the Wounded Knee affair, the *Bee* created an impression of serious trouble brewing on Pine Ridge Reservation and even predicted that Big Foot's surrender would lead to a massacre of Indians—this only a few days before it actually happened.

Still, it has to be noted that the *Omaha Daily Bee* correspondent Charles Cressey, on location at Pine Ridge, was most likely reporting quite accurately about what he saw and heard around Pine Ridge Agency. He noted on several occasions that it was very difficult to tell what was really going on since so many contradictory rumors were circulating. Obviously, Cressey decided to report almost everything, regardless of the source or contradictory nature of the stories. This, according to the historian George R. Kolbenschlag, was true of many of the correspondents at Pine Ridge. He maintains that the correspondents there were in a difficult position since the officials did not give them enough information. To please their editors, they had to rely on what information—mainly rumors—they could gather. Kolbenschlag also believes that the newspaper editors were as responsible for the sensational nature of the news reporting as the correspondents themselves.[160]

Despite the exaggeration and resort to yellow journalism, Cressey was able to relate a vivid picture of life at the agency, and indeed of the Wounded Knee battle. At times the western papers seemed to echo the general frontier attitude of hatred toward Indians. This was mostly true, however, in their additional, or editorial, commentary. Despite his sensational style, Cressey was, in fact, quite sympathetic toward the Lakotas, especially before the Wounded Knee affair.

After Sitting Bull's death, the eastern newspapers clearly shifted from blaming the Indians to sympathizing with them. This was even truer after Wounded Knee. The papers did write about Indian treachery, skirmishes, and depredations, much like the *Omaha Daily Bee*, but these papers were the first to look critically at the army's conduct during the troubles. They, together with the *Chicago Tribune*, also characterized the Wounded Knee affair as a massacre and a slaughter. They called for investigations into the matter, and they started to discuss the party politics that allegedly controlled the government's Indian policy.

"Reds Finally Show Up" was the *Chicago Tribune* headline on January 13. "Sioux Bury Their Guns" was the *Washington Post* headline. The major news that day was that the hostile Indians were camped close to Pine Ridge Agency.

They arrived peacefully, but there was still much tension. The *Tribune* believed that Kicking Bear was trying to call for a great council, where he could talk in favor of continuing the war. The *Omaha Daily Bee* reported that the Indians were very restless over the rumors that they were going to be disarmed and that some of their leading men would be punished or sent away. All the newspapers described the great Indian gathering around Pine Ridge Agency. The *Tribune* described the women and children, who were greatly suffering from cold and lack of food. The army continued to watch the Indians closely, but Miles was reportedly convinced that all the trouble was over. The newspapers also noted the ongoing investigation into the Wounded Knee affair. The general opinion was that neither Colonel Forsyth, the 7th Cavalry, nor Agent Royer were to be blamed.[161]

On January 14 and 15 the newspapermen were busy describing the scene at Pine Ridge Agency. Indians and soldiers were coming and going, food was being issued, small groups were discussing matters, but no official negotiations were started. General Miles wanted to give the Indians a few days to "recover their nerves." Everything seemed to be peaceful, but the Indians were reported to be greatly scared, which kept tensions high. The *Washington Post* reporting was somewhat different; hundreds of hostiles escaped toward the Badlands, according to a headline, but the actual article was similar to those in the other three newspapers. Despite the headline, the *Post* agreed with the other papers in asserting that the major problem was to restore confidence. General Miles's promises to treat the Indians justly, to feed them, and to let them keep their weapons for a while quickly put an end to all hostile intentions. So, by mid-January, the newspapers were able to report that all hostilities were over. General Miles triumphed and the Indians surrendered. Finally, on January 15, 1891, the *Chicago Tribune* was able to declare in its headline "Peace at Pine Ridge."[162]

By mid-January 1891 the biggest "newspaper Indian war" was over. During the nearly four months of close coverage of the Lakota ghost dance, the five newspapers studied here went through many phases, from sympathizing with the Indians to extreme war sensationalism. Thus any attempt to generalize their reporting is very difficult and, for the most part, unfair. Many scholars who have used the newspapers as additional material for their studies have selected a few articles, for example, after such major incidents as the death of Sitting Bull and the Wounded Knee massacre, to substantiate their generalizations of yellow journalism.[163] After these major incidents the reporting tended to assume—naturally—more alarming and sensational characteristics. Yet day by day from January 1890 to January 1891, the fact is that there were many attempts to report objectively and from various viewpoints about the ghost dance and about the Lakotas and their living conditions. Many articles were very sympathetic toward the Lakotas, but they were overshadowed by more alarming headlines and reports. For this reason, scholars also have largely neglected these less obvious reports and given a generally negative interpretation of the newspaper reporting on the ghost dance.

Finally, even though there were many mistakes, exaggerations, and contradictions, it has to be said that to some extent the newspapers, the correspondents, and the editors all fell victim to the extremely difficult conditions on the Lakota reservations during the Lakota ghost dance "war."

SIX

The U.S. Congress and the Ghost Dance

The U.S. Congress took no notice of the ghost dance until December 3, 1890. Instead of focusing on the ritual itself, or on the ghost dancers, Congress was initially concerned with the white settlers living close to the Lakota reservations, who were thought to be in life-threatening danger. Thus Congress approached the problems resulting from the ghost dance solely from the perspective of the settlers.[1]

During 1889 and 1890, Congress discussed and decided to approve additional appropriations for several Indian tribes suffering from famine and disease. Funds were provided for the Arapaho, Yankton Sioux, Arikara, and Mandan Indians, among others, who were reported to be suffering because of the failure of their crops.[2] In discussions about the Lakotas, however, there was no mention of any major problems during that period. On the contrary, on January 15, 1889, O. S. Gifford, the representative from Dakota Territory, claimed that the Indians there had suffered no hardships since coming under territorial administration.[3]

During discussions on January 16, 1889, Congress painted a picture of the flourishing civilization in Dakota Territory. The country was at peace, the Indians were educated, and Sitting Bull and savagery had given way to civilization.[4] President Benjamin Harrison continued in a similar tone a year and a half later in his annual message to the Senate in December 1890. He noted that the allotment of Indian lands had been carried out successfully.[5]

This, however, was not the case among the Lakotas. Thomas J. Morgan, the commissioner of Indian affairs, wrote on May 8, 1890, and again in his

1891 annual report that although it was already completed among several other tribes, the allotment of lands on the Lakota reservations had only begun. Despite the problems among the Lakotas, Commissioner Morgan was extremely pleased with the way the Indians in general were progressing on the road to civilization. After visiting several reservations in the fall of 1890 he wrote that he was encouraged and strengthened in his conviction that the Indian Office was doing splendid work.[6] Two years after the passage of the General Allotment Act (the Dawes Act), however, no actual allotments had yet been made among the full-blood Lakotas on Pine Ridge, Rosebud, Cheyenne River, or Standing Rock Reservations.[7] The allotment of Lakota lands occurred mainly in the 1890s, following the ghost dance troubles.[8] In his message in December 1890, President Harrison noted that the Lakotas had not received all the appropriations due them. He expressed his strong belief that this mistake needed to be corrected. This was the first high-level comment heard in Congress during the year 1890 sympathizing with the Lakotas. The president, however, made no comment regarding the real problems: famine and disease. It has to be noted that the president was well informed about the problems among the Lakotas, since by December he had received several letters, telegraphs, and reports from the secretary of the interior as well as from army officers in the field that clearly portrayed the Lakotas' suffering.[9]

When viewed against this background, it is not surprising that Congress sided with the white settlers when discussing the ghost dance. In fact, it seems that even before the ghost dance appeared the Lakotas were portrayed in congressional debates somewhat more negatively than many other Indian tribes. The Lakotas' problems were not discussed at all, while other tribes throughout the United States were receiving some relief. The Lakotas were mentioned in debates mainly when the issue related to land. This was the case, for example, when President Harrison tried to explain the motivations and justifications for breaking up the Great Sioux Reservation in a message to Congress in February 1890.[10]

When Congress started to discuss the problems caused by the ghost dance, its focus remained on protecting the white population, not on solving the problems of the Indians. On December 3, 1890, a proposition was made in

Congress that 1,000 guns and sufficient ammunition be sent from federal warehouses to the states of Nebraska, South Dakota, and North Dakota so that the white population could protect itself from Indian attacks. A letter from Secretary of War Redfield Proctor that was introduced into the House of Representatives backed this proposal. The secretary pointed out that the proposed guns would help the people feel more secure.[11]

The congressmen believed that civilian fear of the ghost dancers escalated when nearly the entirety of the garrisons from Fort Robinson and Fort Niobrara were sent to the Lakota reservations. The surrounding country was thus left unprotected, and many settlers living close to the Lakota reservations left or planned to leave their homes. This exodus occurred despite the fact that the governors of the above-mentioned states had already distributed some weapons to the settlers.[12]

The federal weapons delivery proposal was approved by the Senate on December 6, 1890, but only after the House suggested that weapons should be provided for the states of Montana and Wyoming as well.[13] Congress took a firm hand on the situation by sending up to 5,000 weapons and sufficient ammunition to the settlers. This could be viewed as a continuation of the policy that had already caused the army to occupy the Lakota reservations. The idea of delivering weapons to civilians, however, caused some discussion in Congress before the decision was finally made. Senator Daniel W. Voorhees of Indiana attempted to turn Congress's attention to current Indian policy, focusing on the situation of the Lakota people.[14]

Senator Voorhees opened the debate with an appeal to the congressmen's Christianity. He claimed that the state of Indian affairs in general was so deplorable that it was a crime before the eyes of God and man. The senator expressed amazement that Congress would decide to deliver weapons to settlers instead of feeding the starving Indians. Referring to his discussion with Maj. Gen. Nelson A. Miles, he added that the Lakotas had been suffering for want of food for two years. This explained their desperation and determination to die with their guns in their hands rather than die from starvation. Voorhees declared that the Indians were dancing "the dance of death by starvation and the dance of desperation."[15]

The remarkable point in Voorhees's speech was his demand for Congress to focus on the Lakotas' standard of living. According to the senator, this was the real problem, not the actual dancing. He wanted to put things in correct perspective and blamed the government's official Indian policy for the Lakotas' famine. Thus the government was responsible for the unrest that threatened not only the lives of the Indians, but also the lives of soldiers and civilians. According to Voorhees, no one had done anything to solve the problem. He believed that giving food to the Indians might have solved the entire ghost dance problem, although things had developed so far that even this solution might come too late.[16] Voorhees was probably right about this. Issuing additional food to the Lakotas sooner, during the summer and early fall, might have solved many problems. The crop failures in the summer of 1890, along with the reduction in rations, gave the ghost dance the new impetus it needed. But it seems likely that not even food would have entirely solved the problem in December 1890.[17]

Senator Voorhees's allegations and accusations encountered strong opposition in Congress. Most ardent was Republican Senator Henry L. Dawes, chairman of the Senate Committee on Indian Affairs, who was considered the prominent expert on Indian affairs in the Congress. Dawes started by defending the basic approaches of the government's Indian policy and tried to explain the problems that were related to it. According to him, there was no single solution to the Indian problem; that was why there had been so many changes in official Indian policy during previous decades. The current strategy was to try to make the Indians work like white men. This policy of forcing the Indians to work or starve was, Dawes argued, justifiable because it had been explained to the Indians and was based on law. The amount of rations provided to the Indians would be gradually cut down each year in order to make them realize the necessity of working for their livelihood.[18]

Dawes argued that reducing the Lakotas' annual appropriations was justified because their numbers had dwindled since the 1868 Treaty. He did not take into account that this population loss was due to famine and epidemics. The senator added that nothing illegal was done toward the Lakotas during the previous year, when the Sioux Commission induced them to part with a great portion of their lands.[19] According to Dawes, this action was also properly explained to the Indians, and their leading men had approved it when they visited Washington.[20]

The question is whether these leading men were in a position in Lakota society to make such decisions for their people. The whites' conceptualization of leadership was totally different from the Lakotas'. In fact, the leaders' approval meant little because the Agreement of 1889 could become law only if the various tribes of the Sioux Nation approved it, according to the terms set forth in Article 12 of the 1868 treaty. That meant that three-fourths of the adult males had to sign it; it did not matter whether or not the chiefs signed it. At the time of the chiefs' visit to Washington, a sufficient number of signatures had already been gathered. Legally, the consent the chiefs gave in Washington meant nothing.[21]

Technically, Dawes was correct. The number of adult Lakotas who had signed was adequate, but whether the commission had behaved ethically is doubtful. The actions and promises of the Sioux Commission caused much discussion in Congress. A petition presented in December 1890 to the House of Representatives requested that the government fulfill the promises made by the commission, even though it had made those promises without full congressional authorization. Without those promises, the Lakotas might have refused to give up the land. The Lakotas expected to receive compensation for the lands they lost, but instead of getting an increase in their yearly annuities, as they anticipated, the annuities were reduced. Although the Sioux Commission did not recommend the cut in rations, the Indians were convinced that the reduction was a result of signing the agreement. This, according to Acting Commissioner of Indian Affairs R. V. Belt, was causing great discontent among the Lakotas.[22]

Even though the Sioux Commission recommended that the annual appropriations for the Lakotas be maintained at their current level, those appropriations were first reduced to 950,000 dollars and then to 850,000 dollars for the year 1890. This was 150,000 dollars less than the Lakotas had received for the years 1888 and 1889. Additionally, the decision to reduce the appropriation was made as late as August 19, 1890, when the situation among the Lakotas was critical: the supplies for that year were already exhausted. Congress also denied the additional 150,000 dollars promised to the Lakotas by the Sioux Commission for educational purposes, even though both the commissioner and the acting commissioner of Indian affairs asked Congress to appropriate the necessary funds. The commissioners also urged Congress to follow the suggestion made by the Sioux Commission to compensate the Lakotas for ponies they lost in 1876 and 1877.[23]

The discussion in Congress soon shifted back to the possible famine among the Lakotas. Dawes admitted that Voorhees was correct when he said that crop failures had caused hardships for the people, whites and Indians alike, in the midwestern states. He obviously could not deny that fact, since the *New York Times,* the *Washington Post,* and other newspapers had reported the failure of crops and other problems the farmers faced in those areas.[24] When talking about the Lakotas, however, Dawes emphasized that only those who were following their "fanatical chiefs" on the warpath were suffering for lack of food. He assured the congressmen that nearly 25 percent of all Sioux were self-sufficient, clear proof that the government's Indian policy was successful for the Lakotas as well.[25] But Dawes's comments prove to be incorrect when the Lakotas' farming activities and their degree of self-sufficiency are more closely examined.

In 1889, before the Great Sioux Reservation was divided, it comprised 12,845,521 acres. Of that, the Indians cultivated 17,681 acres, only 0.08 percent of the total area.[26] In addition, the size of individual farms was very small, averaging two to four acres, and the farms produced very little. The Lakotas who were engaged in farming were mostly mixed bloods, white men married to Indian women, or, in some cases, full bloods who belonged to the progressive faction. The full-blood Lakotas, however, were seldom involved in farming activities. In 1889, as many as 79 percent of all the people living on the Lakota reservations were fully dependent on food supplied to them by the U.S. government. In actuality, the number of Lakotas, especially full-blood Lakotas, dependent on government rations was probably much higher due to the 1889 and 1890 crop failures.[27]

A large portion of the land still in the Lakotas' possession was totally unfit for farming. Many whites understood this. Elaine Goodale Eastman, who worked in the Dakotas as the supervisor of education for the Office of Indian Affairs, described the situation in the summer of 1890 in these words: "In the persistent hot winds the pitiful little gardens of the Indians curled up and died."[28] As noted earlier in this study, the former agent at Pine Ridge Agency,

Valentine T. McGillicuddy, doubted whether even white men would be able to make their living by farming in the same area.[29] In 1886, Commissioner of Indian Affairs J. D. C. Atkins observed that on many reservations the soil was bad, the rains did not come regularly, the climate was harsh, and the growing season was so short that even a first-class white farmer would have problems making his living from the land. By the end of the 1880s all the Lakota agents in office concurred with that opinion.[30]

In his annual report for 1891 Commissioner of Indian Affairs Thomas J. Morgan, trying to find explanations for the troubles of 1890, suggested that the Lakotas had been forced to take up farming too quickly on land that was totally unsuitable. He added that the Lakotas' discontent was understandable when the land did not produce enough food and the government reduced their rations. Commissioner Morgan noted that it was natural for humans in such a situation to feel dissatisfied and even resort to violence.[31]

Bishop William H. Hare, who lived among the Dakotas and was well acquainted with the Lakotas as well, thought that the prolonged negotiations with the Sioux Commission in 1889 made the situation even worse. During the negotiations, while the Indians remained at the agencies to attend the councils, their crops dried up. He pointed out that the crop failures of 1890 were so complete that no matter how carefully the rations were used, they could not last more than two-thirds of the time for which they were planned. This, according to Bishop Hare, led in both years to terrible famines, followed by epidemics. His analysis is substantiated by American Horse, who claimed in a speech on April 15, 1890, before the Senate Committee on Indian Affairs and later at a meeting in November 1890 on Pine Ridge Reservation that the negotiations caused problems in farming and were the reason for much suffering among the Lakota people. Commissioner Morgan also mentioned that the negotiations were one of the major reasons for the Lakotas' destitution.[32] When reviewed in this light, Dawes's claims about Lakota self-sufficiency appear to be groundless. In fact, Dawes himself noted in 1890 that the negotiations of 1889 were the reason for the failure of crops among the Lakotas and that the reduction of rations had left the Lakotas in a state of "irritation and complaint."[33]

Senator Dawes was not the only congressman who held this opinion.

Senator Gilbert A. Pierce of North Dakota also took part in the discussion. He claimed that he had seen Indians in his hometown who were "sleeker and better fed" than even Senator Voorhees. According to Pierce, the statement that Indians were starving was not at all correct. Moreover, the idea that the Indians were taking the warpath because they were starving was totally incorrect. The senator thought that the problems arose from the Indians' nature: an Indian was always unsatisfied. Pierce was certain that the fact that the Indians were living altogether too well on their reservations was behind all the problems. "The devil always finds mischief for idle hands to do," he noted. Furthermore, he described how the poor settlers were fleeing the savage Indians, who "for pure mischief . . . are marching through the country and holding a war dance." The so-called friendly Indians, such as the Arikaras and Mandans, according to Pierce, were also taking part in these war dances, in which all the Indians were armed with modern Winchester rifles.[34]

Pierce's accusations seem incredible in comparison with other accounts of the behavior of the ghost dancers. Commissioner Morgan, for example, noted in his report that during the troubles the Indians did not try to get close to or destroy any white settlements. Not a single white person was killed outside the reservations, and even on the reservations only two white men were killed outside of actual battle. He also pointed out that only very little of the settlers' property inside the Lakota reservations was destroyed.[35] The historian George E. Hyde notes that it seems obvious that the ghost dancers were not trying to break out of their reservations at any stage of the trouble, even though they might have had the chance to do so.[36]

Although Pierce sided with Dawes, it can be assumed that his motives were rather different. As Voorhees pointed out directly, Pierce belonged to that portion of the white population living close to the Lakotas; he and his people, Voorhees declared, "long for the lands belonging to Indians and will get them as soon as possible." According to Voorhees, Pierce represented those people for whom "the only good Indian is a dead Indian" and who did not take into consideration that Indian wars always caused suffering and casualties among the whites as well.[37] Even Dawes pointed out that the white population in the Dakotas, who wanted to drive the Lakotas away from their lands, caused much of the trouble.[38]

As a senator from North Dakota, Pierce was very well aware of the sentiments of the people of the state he represented. In a telegram to Secretary
of War Proctor on November 18, 1890, Senator Pierce demanded protection
for the people of North Dakota. He demanded more troops, claiming that
a handful of troops is as good as nothing.[39] It has to be taken into account
that Pierce was at the time also preparing for the next election and was cam-
paigning to retain his seat in the Senate. Calling for strong action against the
Lakotas might have assured his popularity among the North Dakota voters.
His reelection campaign, however, was not successful.[40]

Although Dawes and Pierce expressed similar sentiments toward the ghost
dance, it strains credibility to believe that Dawes would have used the taking of Lakota lands to his personal advantage. This motivation may have
driven Pierce, however. Voorhees also believed in Dawes's sincerity, but
believed that Dawes did not possess sufficient power or ability to solve the
difficult Indian question.[41]

On December 4, 1890, Voorhees presented an article from the *Cincinnati
Enquirer* to support his own arguments. The paper published an interview
with Governor Charles Foster of Ohio, who had been the official chairman
of the Sioux Commission that negotiated the partitioning of the Great Sioux
Reservation in 1889. Thus he knew quite well the situation on the Lakota
reservations. In the article, Governor Foster criticized the government for
having a poorly administered Indian policy and for corruption. He was very
angry that the Lakotas' rations were reduced despite the commission's promises to keep them at the same level as the previous year. Voorhees ended his
commentary on the article with the words "The Sioux are starving."[42]

Voorhees did not receive much support from other senators. In the House of
Representatives, however, William S. Holman, a representative from Indiana,
supported Voorhees's position.[43] Holman said that he had spent some time
among the Sioux Indians and was fully convinced that they did not take the
warpath on "willful purpose." He believed that if these Indians had been
treated justly, they would have caused no trouble. Congressman Holman noted that the nature of the Indian in general was such that he felt very strongly whether the treatment he received was just or unjust. The Lakotas had
had enough of unjust treatment, Holman declared. He went on to criticize

official Indian policy and the ceding of Indian lands that was a direct consequence of that policy. He also emphasized that the widespread rumors of an uprising were "manifestly sensational" and were "calculated to create alarm among persons who know nothing of the condition of these tribes." He believed that there were individuals who sought personal gain from the situation in which unjust treatment and famine caused trouble among the Lakotas. He also urged Congress to determine what had happened to the money appropriated for the Lakotas and why they were starving. It is quite interesting that both Senator Voorhees and Representative Holman were so strongly in favor of the Lakotas. Holman had been appointed to investigate matters on the Lakota reservations, especially on Pine Ridge a few years earlier, but other than that, neither his nor Voorhees's correspondence or published speeches indicate that they had taken any previous special interest in Indian affairs during their long political careers.[44]

At this point, the discussion turned to the question of whether Congress had acted according to the law in matters relating to the Lakota people in general. Senator Henry M. Teller of Colorado believed that if nothing illegal had been done to the Lakotas they should not be given any more attention than other people, Indian or white, who suffered from the failure of crops.[45] In general, Congress was not interested in the way a law was put into effect, for example, if a law had to be enforced using military power. The important thing was that Congress acted according to the law.[46] Teller, however, as well as Pierce, belonged to the group of westerners who throughout the 1880s attempted to get as much Indian land as possible for themselves and their constituents.[47]

Several senators expressed their astonishment at Governor Foster's claim that the Lakotas had already begun suffering from lack of food in 1889 and nothing had been done to help them. They regretted that they had not been informed of the situation. One senator voiced amazement at the whole affair; he had believed that enough money was appropriated to feed the Lakotas as well as the other Indian tribes. He had assumed that the approximately 900,000 dollars that was provided for that purpose for the year 1889 would have been sufficient if it had been used as intended.[48]

Whether or not Congress was really so poorly informed about the situation is debatable. According to Maj. Gen. John M. Schofield, for example, all the members of Congress were fully aware of the situation on the Lakota reservations. In addition, during the year 1890 several councils were held with delegations of Lakota chiefs who appeared before the congressional committees on Indian affairs in Washington. The chiefs fully explained their situation and literally begged Congress to help them.[49] As noted earlier, Commissioners Morgan and Belt informed members of Congress about the situation among the Lakotas several times. Morgan wrote in April 1890 that a feeling of despair was growing among the Lakotas, which might eventually lead to trouble. "Men will take desperate remedies sooner than suffer from hunger," the commissioner wrote to the chairman of the House Committee on Indian Affairs on April 15, 1890.[50]

Dawes, however, continued his defense of the government's Indian policy by arguing that the Lakotas received all the rations called for in the 1889 agreement. He continued to express certainty that only those who tried to return to barbarism and turned their backs on civilization were starving. Dawes believed that, all in all, Indians had been treated well and justly for the past fifteen years. The state of affairs "is now such that cheating the Indian in the dark and by devices and by tricks has passed away," he said. Regarding Governor Foster's remarks, Dawes said that the last time the governor was on the Lakota reservations was in 1889, so his knowledge of the situation was not up to date. Dawes finally admitted that he was not completely sure that all the rations actually did reach the Lakotas, although he believed that they did.[51]

To support his claims, Dawes presented a letter written by Special Census Agent A. T. Lea, who was conducting the census among the Lakotas. In this letter, the agent maintained that not a single Indian on Pine Ridge Reservation complained to him about the lack of food. On the contrary, the Indians told him that they had more than enough. Agent Lea blamed the "Big Chiefs," who had lost their influence, for the trouble. He claimed that no one living on Pine Ridge Reservation really suffered. "Those who are most gluttonous in their natures, eat up their rations often a day or two before issue day, but they never go hungry," he concluded.[52]

Once again Dawes found a supporter in Pierce, who said that a Lakota man told him that the ghost dancers had stored up so much meat that they did not have enough wagons to move it all. But Voorhees pointed out that if this was true, it was probably not meat provided to the Lakotas by the government, but meat the ghost dancers obtained by stealing cattle during the past months. Thus Dawes's argument could not refute the assertion that the Lakotas had been starving for the past two years. Voorhees wanted to introduce the opinions of General Miles. He wondered how anyone could doubt the reports of such a high-ranking and well-respected officer, whose reports were based on information obtained from those who were on location: the soldiers, inspectors, Indian agents, and Indians themselves. Voorhees doubted Agent Lea's reports, since no one, not even Dawes, could tell him who Lea actually was and who had appointed him. Voorhees questioned his credibility and believed that since no one seemed to know anything about him he might have been appointed to "fix things."[53]

Without a doubt Agent Lea's information can be questioned, and on further scrutiny may be considered false. Substantiating this, however, is difficult. Perhaps the Lakotas whose homes Lea visited really gave the answers he described in his letter. Whether those answers assuring him that the Lakotas had sufficient food were his own interpretation or might be categorized as natural hospitality toward a visitor cannot be determined. In any case, with the help of this letter Dawes tried to demonstrate that the government had done no wrong to the Lakotas.[54]

The comments made by Dawes reflect his belief in the policy he had long pursued. He evidently felt that the ghost dance was only an attempt to resist the policy of Indian civilization. It was an obstacle to the policy he himself had created and in which he strongly believed. The ghost dance meant that the Lakotas were falling backward on the ladder of civilization, on which they had been moving upward since they were forced to abandon their nomadic lifestyle and take up farming.[55]

Remarkably, Dawes's comments, while clarifying his own views, disputed the arguments of Governor Foster and General Miles. It is especially noteworthy that he questioned the credibility of Miles, who, in the end, was the commander of the army sent to the Lakota reservations. In a way, Dawes was correct in his arguments about those he thought were taking part in the ghost dance, but he was wrong about those who were starving.

Congressional debate continued to criticize government Indian policy, the responsible officials, and also the Indians. In Congress, opinions about the Indians were diverse. Some senators and representatives showed clear hostility toward the Indians, claiming, for example, that they used every opportunity to take white men's scalps. Others emphasized the government's responsibility to support those whose means of living they had destroyed. All in all, Congress seemed to agree on only one thing: the ghost dance offered a serious threat of war and all necessary means were to be taken to avoid open conflict. They were clearly convinced that the Lakotas possessed the ability to go on the warpath and believed that the number of armed Lakotas was as high as 6,000 men. Moreover, Congress believed that these men were armed with modern Winchester rifles, a belief based on information they received from Indian agents, alarmed citizens, some army officers, and, undoubtedly, the press.[56]

The figure of 6,000 fighting men seems remarkable, especially since Dawes himself said on December 8 that the Lakotas had no more than 5,225 adult males. The latter figure was most likely based on information provided by the Office of Indian Affairs. The actual number as reported by Acting Commissioner Belt was 5,245 male Lakotas, including those living on Crow Creek and Lower Brulé Reservations.[57] Congress wanted to find out how this dangerous situation had developed. A commission was appointed to investigate the matter, as well as the possibility of corruption in the administration of Indian affairs. More important, as one senator suggested, was first to throw water on the flames rather than investigate the cause of the fire.[58]

Senator Dawes tried to lift the blame for the troubles off the shoulders of the government's Indian policy and thus off his own shoulders as well. He assured Congress that the Indians' best interest was his primary concern. Dawes eventually agreed to provide the Lakotas additional rations in order to quell the unrest, although he emphasized that it should be only a provisional arrangement; after the troubles were subdued, Congress should return to official Indian policy. He did not change his views on the guidelines of the Indian policy or on the Indians in general. These views were at least in part incorrect: he blamed Red Cloud and Sitting Bull for all the troubles among the Lakotas.[59]

Dawes also blamed the press: "The condition of things is being very much perverted and the public misled by an army of newspaper men." He went on to say that there seemed to be more newspapermen than military men on the Lakota reservations.[60] Privately, he implied in a letter to his wife that too much had been made of the current Indian problem and that there was no need to keep so large a number of troops on the Lakota reservations. Despite the reports and rumors, he did not believe that an outbreak was going to occur.[61]

Sitting Bull and Red Cloud as Scapegoats

During the December 1890 congressional debate Dawes pointed out on several occasions that only those Indians who followed the fanatical leaders, Red Cloud of the Oglalas and Sitting Bull of the Hunkpapas, on the warpath were suffering from lack of food. He considered Sitting Bull the driving force of the whole ghost dance hysteria. Dawes might have been correct when he claimed that Sitting Bull tried to take advantage of the situation by using the ghost dance to distance himself from the whites, but accusing him of trying to foment a war, to take revenge on the whites, and holding him responsible for the ghost dance troubles was unreasonable.[62]

At this point it is necessary to try to find out on what Dawes based his opinions. His speeches clearly show how he felt about Sitting Bull. For Dawes, Sitting Bull was the personification of Indian resistance to the civilization policy. He accused Sitting Bull of organizing Lakota resistance against the planned reduction of the Great Sioux Reservation as early as 1882, when Sitting Bull's presence during the negotiations helped the Lakotas to prevent the partitioning of their reservation.[63] Dawes also delighted in the fact that Sitting Bull fell ill and could not be present during the final moments of the 1889 negotiations, when the Sioux Commission was trying to induce the Lakotas to sign the Agreement of 1889. Whether Sitting Bull really was ill at that time or whether he was not informed of the signing date, as Sitting Bull himself claimed, is a totally different question and will not be pursued here.[64]

Dawes claimed that Sitting Bull controlled his people through fear and terror and lived on his reservation "in luxury and ease." According to the senator, it was the fear that the ordinary Indians felt toward Sitting Bull that might have prevented the Lakotas from signing the Agreement of 1889. Dawes's feelings toward the chief became public when he pronounced that Sitting Bull was the most "pious hypocrite in this country." He also called Sitting Bull a murderer, responsible for the deaths of Col. George A. Custer and his men at Little Big Horn in 1876.[65]

In the speech, Dawes referred to his correspondence with Agent James McLaughlin at Standing Rock Reservation. This explains in part the hostility he expressed toward Sitting Bull, as McLaughlin frequently expressed his own very negative feelings toward the chief.[66] Although McLaughlin's motives were personal and reflected his rivalry with Sitting Bull for control of Standing Rock Reservation, it is little wonder that Dawes's opinions became what they were. There is no reason to believe that the correspondence between McLaughlin and Dawes could have taken any other tone. It seems certain that Sitting Bull, as well as Red Cloud, became victims of their own reputations when their role in the ghost dance was discussed in Congress. Moreover, in regard to Sitting Bull, Dawes, as well as other whites, clearly confused the Lakota Sitting Bull with the person and actions of an Arapaho ghost dance apostle who had the same English name.[67]

Red Cloud's role in the troubles was even smaller than Sitting Bull's, as noted in chapter 1. Thus it seems amazing that he bore so much of the blame. Of course, he was one of the prominent leaders in the 1860s and 1870s, but by 1890 he was an old man, dedicated to establishing a balance between opposing groups rather than serving as an active leader.[68] During the final stages of the troubles, he even sought help from the U.S. Army when the ghost dancers threatened his life.[69]

Red Cloud responded strongly to the accusations made against him. A letter in which he defended himself was read in the House of Representatives on December 19, 1890. In this letter Red Cloud wondered how the whites could even think that the Lakotas would be able to make war, since they were practically surrounded by white settlements and railroads. Furthermore, he emphasized that famine had taken away the people's strength. According to

Red Cloud, on Pine Ridge Reservation alone 217 persons had died of starvation in the previous two years.[70]

Red Cloud claimed that some of the Brulés, who had been left without a leader after Spotted Tail's death in 1881, were causing the trouble. He believed that those Brulés were forced to wander to find food. This frightened the whites and caused a general feeling of unrest. Since they had no real leader they did what they pleased. Red Cloud, however, noted that although the Brulés destroyed some property belonging to Indians, they had not destroyed any property belonging to whites outside the reservation. Red Cloud claimed that he never urged anyone to participate in a ghost dance ceremony and had never even witnessed a ceremony himself. He asked the congressmen to take into account that he got along well with his previous agent, Hugh D. Gallagher, and with the white people who lived close to the reservation. According to Red Cloud, those white people helped his people during hard times. He blamed the famine and his people's destitute condition for causing the trouble. He regretted that their annual rations were reduced once again. Finally, he reminded the whites that he was their friend and for that reason he had agreed to convert to Catholicism a few years earlier.[71]

The letter caused a remarkable response from a congressman in the House of Representatives: "What is the name of this Indian? Is he dead or alive?" These questions shed light on the actual situation in the U.S. Congress. Knowledge of Indian affairs appeared to be minimal among the congressmen in general, given that the letter was written by one of the period's most famous Indians. Additional comments in the House mainly questioned the letter's authenticity and reliability. Doubts about Red Cloud's position as a leader were expressed. The House took note of the fact that not only Indians were suffering in the United States. According to some congressmen, there was no need to waste Congress's time in discussing Indians; it was more important to take care of the suffering white farmers. In the House of Representatives some attention was given to the fact that the Lakotas were starving. For example, Congressmen W. S. Holman and B. W. Perkins, the chairman of the House Committee on Indian Affairs, acknowledged that the Lakotas' living conditions were miserable and believed that Congress should offer some assistance.[72]

Congressional Inaction

The December 1890 congressional debate painted a picture of a Congress out of touch with the Indian situation. It had to rely for information on the expertise of a few congressmen. This expertise was often colored by personal motives and was based on sometimes questionable or even false information. There were strong differences of opinion regarding the ghost dance and the Lakotas in both the Senate and the House. However, congressmen seemed to agree on two issues. They were convinced that the danger of war was imminent; the decision to send arms and ammunition to protect the white population reflects this belief. They were also unanimous in considering the ghost dance a dangerous movement that had to be stopped.

For some congressmen the ghost dance signaled a return to barbarism and a breakdown in the Lakotas' progress toward assimilation and civilization. For these men, led by Dawes, the ghost dance was less a military threat than a failure, or at least a setback, of the Indian policy they espoused. For that reason, the ghost dance had to be suppressed. Some senators and representatives probably saw the ghost dance as a chance to get their hands, or those of their constituents, on the last Lakota lands. The fact was, however, that most Indian wars had ended in the opening of Indian lands for the whites; a war might have done the trick here, too. This, in fact, reflects the old political division between the westerners and the eastern humanitarians, who in their own way sought to help the Indians. This division was not new, and the Lakota ghost dance quickly became incorporated into this political play.

It is, however, too strong an argument to maintain that Congress deliberately sought a conflict with the Lakotas, although that might have been the intention of some congressmen. The use of military force was an option that could benefit both groups in Congress. According to army officials, a peaceful solution, if possible, was the army's primary objective. However, harsh measures would not be avoided if needed. That ideology becomes clear in letters from Secretary of War Proctor and General Schofield that were both read in the Senate on December 6, 1890.[73]

Whatever motivated individual congressmen, Congress's attitude toward the Lakota ghost dance in general was negative, suspicious, uncertain, and in some respects fearful. It appears that Congress did not really understand the movement it had to deal with. There seemed to be, as Voorhees pointed out, a certain "desire to hide and cover" things. At least there was a need to defend the government's Indian policy.[74] The ghost dance was seen as a threat, which in December 1890 it in some respects really was. Its development into a threat might have been avoided had it been accepted as a religious movement. This was emphasized by Elaine Goodale Eastman, who wrote in her memoirs, "No one with imagination could fail to see in the rite a genuine religious ceremony, a faith which, illusory as it was, deserved to be treated with respect."[75] Congress did not, however, discuss the ghost dance as a religious movement at any stage, nor did Congress discuss the essence or the true origin of the ghost dance. Although more than thirty Indian tribes were involved with the ghost dance in some way or other, Congress was interested only in the Lakota version and the potential trouble it might bring. This was the case even though trouble and unrest were characteristic of other tribes that had taken up the ghost dance as well.[76]

It is also worth noting that the two congressmen most sympathetic to the Lakotas were Senator Voorhees and Representative Holman, neither of whom had previously been specifically interested or involved in Indian affairs, although, as noted above, Holman had spent some time among the Lakotas in the mid-1880s. Perhaps, as outsiders to the administration of Indian affairs, they had nothing to lose or gain. That may in part explain why these two men from Indiana spoke their mind about the ghost dance, the Lakotas, and the general treatment of Indians. As noted earlier, Voorhees called it a crime before God and man not to help the suffering Indians. Yet it needs to be recognized that Voorhees and Holman represented the Democrats, who opposed the Republican administration, which had different views on the government's Indian policies in general.[77]

There was extensive debate in Congress about the famine among the Lakotas and its role in the troubles. However, Congress seemed to get sidetracked when the discussion turned to the issue of whether there was actual famine among the Lakotas and whether the U.S. government had in any way acted illegally toward them. Had something illegal occurred, the blame would fall, in part, on the congressmen themselves. Speakers in both the

Senate and the House failed to offer any suggestions that might have solved the Lakotas' problems. For Congress, the issue was largely a legal one, not one that involved real human lives. This attitude is characterized in a debate between two congressmen on December 19, 1890. Congressman B. McMillin asked, "Are they [the Lakotas] any worse off than they were yesterday?" To this question Congressman Perkins answered, "No worse off than on yesterday and as badly off as they will be to-morrow." "Well, then this can go over until to-morrow," replied Congressman McMillin, referring to the urgency, or the lack thereof, of discussing the problems of the Lakotas. This brief exchange is quite revealing since, as noted earlier, Congressman Perkins was the chairman of the House Committee on Indian Affairs.[78] It seems obvious that to many congressmen the ghost dance, as well as matters relating to Indians in general, were distant and immaterial.

When the fighting between the ghost dancers and the army began on December 15, 1890, Congress had no immediate comment. Even though the fighting took the lives of several Indians, including Sitting Bull and several of the Indian police, Congress remained silent. In the days following the incident on Standing Rock Reservation Congress focused on a street fight in which one man was killed. Congressmen also turned their attention to the issue of providing additional appropriations for several Indian tribes, although the Lakotas were not among them. On December 22, however, the House asked for information regarding the circumstances of Sitting Bull's arrest and the conduct of the Indian police force. When accusations started to circulate in the press that Sitting Bull had been unjustifiably murdered and his body barbarously mutilated, the House asked the secretary of the interior to submit all documents relating to the arrest. The affair had to be thoroughly investigated as a "matter of national honor." Interestingly, when the investigation was concluded Medals of Honor were awarded to thirty-seven of the Indian policemen at the suggestion of Agent McLaughlin and Brig. Gen. Thomas H. Ruger.[79]

Congress maintained a similar silence following the December 29 massacre at Wounded Knee. No comments were made regarding the incident until January 6, 1891, when a vague statement was made that the massacre and Sitting Bull's death both needed further investigation.[80] Army officers conducted the first investigation in January 1891, and during the following months and years the circumstances surrounding the Lakota ghost dance and the Wounded Knee affair were repeatedly investigated.[81]

During the ghost dance trouble Congress was not well informed about the situation on the Lakota reservations, nor was it well informed about the ghost dance itself. During the months that the Lakota ghost dance was becoming more and more troublesome, there were no congressional debates over the issue. The situation was not made any better by the fact that Congress was in recess from October until December. Not until December, when the situation was already complicated, were the congressmen able to discuss the matter. But instead of taking a leading role in the ghost dance trouble, Congress merely reacted, or tried to react, to events that were beyond its control. Congress was an onlooker rather than an active participant in matters relating to the Lakota ghost dance.

Conclusion:
Toward "a Great Story" of the Lakota Ghost Dance

Any investigation of the Lakota ghost dance necessarily begins with an understanding of the relationships between Lakotas and whites in the late 1880s. By then, most American Indians, including the Lakotas, were living on reservations, where the U.S. government expected them to abandon their traditional way of life, learn how to support themselves by farming, become educated, and adopt Christianity—in short, to become civilized. The Lakotas were divided, adopting opposing survival strategies to adapt to reservation life: some sought to cooperate with the whites and adapt to their culture, while others tried to hold on as much as possible to their traditional way of life.

It is apparent that Indians and white Americans viewed the ghost dance completely differently; their perspectives were shaped by their respective cultural and social values. For many Lakotas the ghost dance represented spiritual renewal and a chance for social and economic betterment; many white Americans saw it as an obstacle to the government's Indian policy and a setback for the Lakotas on the road to civilization. This basic conflict of interests is the starting point for any analysis of the ideologies and events surrounding the Lakota ghost dance.

When the Lakotas first learned about the ghost dance, their responses to it were shaped by their historical, political, religious, and cultural circumstances. By 1889 they had lost most of their lands, and the buffalo, on which their way of life had been based, were only a memory. When the U.S. government forbade their religious ceremonies they were forced to abandon another fundamental aspect of their culture and identity. Religion was as natural a part of Lakota life as hunting and fighting. With so much of their past way of life lost, the rumors of the ghost dance and its promise of a new life understandably affected these people deeply. The rumor was so compelling that the Lakotas sent representatives all the way to Nevada to learn about this new religion. When the delegation returned in the spring of 1890, the message they brought back was one of hope for a better future, when the Indians could live without white men, hunger, disease, and misery. The Lakota delegates brought a new kind of religion, a new way to practice religion in a form comfortably familiar to the Lakotas: a dance.

The Lakota delegates interpreted the ghost dance doctrine as preached by Wovoka the Messiah according to their own personal hopes and expectations, as well as their traditions and the history of the Lakota people. But they did not transform the ghost dance into a warlike demonstration against the white race, as so many scholars have suggested, nor did they deliberately pervert the doctrine in order to gain political prestige among their people.[1] There is no doubt about the Lakota delegates' sincere belief in the ghost dance. Wovoka's teachings fit easily into the traditional Lakota system of belief, which held to no single doctrine. It was a system constantly changing and developing, for example, through individuals' personal vision experiences. Whatever changes the Lakotas made in Wovoka's ghost dance teachings have to be understood from this perspective.

The Lakota version of the ghost dance doctrine did prophesy that the white men would be destroyed in a great earthquake, but so did Wovoka's original doctrine. There is no evidence whatsoever that the Lakota delegates called for taking up arms against the whites; on the contrary, they emphasized that the only thing required of the Indians was to dance, pray, and believe. The Messiah would take care of the rest. This is typical of revitalization movements throughout the world. When the ghost dance was inaugurated among the Lakotas in the spring of 1890 it was no more hostile toward the whites than the ghost dance among any other Indian tribe.

The ghost dance filled a religious void in Lakota culture that resulted from years of oppression by whites. The dance and its religious message appealed to many progressive Lakotas as well as to the nonprogressives. Even though the progressives, under such leaders as American Horse and Young Man Afraid of His Horse, did not turn to the ghost dance as a unified body, they did not deny its potential power. For years they had followed "the white man's road" as well as they could; their decision not to join the ghost dancers was based on their political convictions, not on a rejection of the ghost dance as a religious expression. The internal divisions within Lakota society, and the problems with the whites, determined the Lakotas' different approaches to the ghost dance, not the ghost dance itself.

The Lakota ghost dance quickly became a mixture of traditional Lakota beliefs, Christianity, and Wovoka's teachings as interpreted by, among others, Short Bull and Kicking Bear. Scholars have often overlooked the fact that Christian aspects of the doctrine remained throughout the ghost dance period. As demonstrated in chapter 1, some Christian Lakotas found in the ghost dance a powerful means to combine their traditional beliefs with Christianity.

Any attempt to quantify the number of Christian or progressive Lakotas who actually became active ghost dancers is problematic. If, for example, a person joined the ghost dance camp for a day or two and then returned to the progressive camp, should he be counted as a ghost dancer? Was he then no longer a progressive? Such back-and-forth movement was extensive, but there is no way of determining the exact numbers of progressive Indians who visited a ghost dance camp or occasionally participated in a ghost dance ceremony.

Indeed, exact figures are not even necessary. There is enough evidence to show that the ghost dance affected both progressive and nonprogressive Lakotas. The fact that, for example, the Protestant missionaries felt the need to attack the ghost dance on the pages of the *Iapi Oaye* clearly shows that they too were worried about the effect the ghost dance had on the progressive, Christian Lakotas. Contemporaries such as Commissioner of Indian Affairs Thomas J. Morgan as well as many scholars—following James Mooney— have claimed that the ghost dance was a movement that affected only the nonprogressive, that is, warlike, Lakotas. This, however, can be dismissed as political rhetoric used to justify the military action and to support the assumption that the ghost dancers had warlike intentions.

Still, it is important to realize that the ghost dance caused great tension among the Lakota people, although it was only the latest in a series of events that caused friction among them. The fact that it appeared at a time of extreme hardship caused tensions to mount, leading to several conflicts between the progressives and nonprogressives, or, more properly, the ghost dancing and nondancing Lakotas. In the spring of 1890 the ghost dance attracted enthusiastic crowds of Lakotas, but during the summer the enthusiasm faded. Had not the summer brought with it another failure of crops, another reduction in rations with resulting hunger and misery, the ghost dance might have died out altogether, as most of the Lakota agents anticipated.

During the Lakota ghost dance "trouble"—a period of less than a year, starting in the spring of 1890 and ending in January 1891—a total of seven different men were appointed Indian agents in charge of the four Lakota reservations where the dance took hold. In addition, Special Agent James A. Cooper was assigned the task of assisting Agent Daniel F. Royer at Pine Ridge Reservation. When the ghost dance began on the Lakota reservations, the more experienced agents were still in charge. When learning about the ghost dances, the agents first sought to investigate what the dance was all about. After that, they tried to convince the Indians, partly by reasoning and partly by threatening, to give it up. In this the agents had some limited success, since during the summer of 1890 there were no major ghost dance ceremonies among the Lakotas. At this point, the agents were fully convinced that the ghost dance had to be stopped, not because it presented a military threat but because it was demoralizing and, as they stated, sent the Indians back to savagery.

For the Lakota agents, therefore, the ghost dance was not a major problem during the spring and summer of 1890. They were more concerned about dissatisfaction resulting from the previous year's land commission. The reduction of the Great Sioux Reservation caused general anxiety among the Lakotas. This, the agents believed, was then used by the nonprogressive Indians to spark general restlessness. Adding to this, hunger and disease were the agents' major concerns. Despite these problems, none of the agents— Hugh D. Gallagher at Pine Ridge, J. George Wright at Rosebud, Charles E.

McChesney at Cheyenne River, or James McLaughlin at Standing Rock—
anticipated any immediate trouble. They believed that the arrest of some
of the most disaffected leaders, including Sitting Bull, would prevent any
future trouble.

In fact, the agents promptly arrested some of the ghost dance leaders,
which may in part have caused the ghost dance excitement to subside during the summer. The first standoff between the ghost dancers and the agents
occurred in August on Pine Ridge, where the ghost dancers were prepared
to defend themselves with arms, if necessary. That encounter ended without bloodshed, and in September Agent Gallagher and Special Agent Elisha
B. Reynolds were allowed to witness a ghost dance ceremony.

Both agents were alarmed by what they saw. For the first time, they suggested to the commissioner of Indian affairs that the ghost dance should be
stopped, not because they expected it to lead to an uprising or a revolt but
simply because it excited the Indians, had a "demoralizing" effect on them,
and interfered with the reservation's daily routines. The agents at Rosebud
and Cheyenne River Reservations concurred. The missionaries also began
to worry about the ghost dance in the early fall of 1890, since growing numbers of Lakotas left their schools and churches and only a few attended
mass regularly. Still, the missionaries expected no serious trouble from the
Indians' new dance.

The role of the U.S. Army, no longer actively needed for Indian campaigns,
was restricted to overseeing the Lakotas on their reservations. There was
some restlessness among various Indian tribes throughout 1889–90, but the
Lakotas caused no real concern for the military. Neither did the rumors of
the Indian messiah. Only on June 15, 1890, did the army learn in detail about
the ghost dance from Porcupine, the Cheyenne who traveled with the Lakota
delegation to meet the messiah. Although Porcupine's story did not worry
the military officers, the destitution among the Lakotas did concern some of
them in the late summer of 1890. In fact, it was the military that conducted
the first investigation into the origins of the ghost dance and the messiah's
identity, although this did not occur until November and December 1890.

Nor did the press consider the Lakotas, or Indians in general, an important problem during the early part of 1890. Their main interest regarding

the Lakotas was in the opening of the Great Sioux Reservation, which was portrayed as a milestone event in which barbarism gave way to civilization. Other than that, everything was reported to be peaceful among the Lakotas. Agent James McLaughlin was even quoted as saying that relations between himself and Sitting Bull were "most amicable."[2]

In April 1890, about the time the Lakota delegates returned from their journey to meet the messiah, the newspapers printed reports about the gatherings and councils the Lakotas were holding. In these initial reports the councils were called powwows or war dances. In April the first stories regarding the messiah and the ghost dance were also printed. During the summer, the *New York Times*, the *Washington Post,* and *Harper's Weekly* did not take any interest in the Lakota ghost dance, although the dance was reported to be the cause of excitement among other Indian tribes. The western papers followed the situation among the Lakotas more closely, but they did not expect any trouble from the ghost dance. On the contrary, the Lakotas were reported to be totally peaceful. The *Omaha Daily Bee* even reported that the Lakota ghost dance was only a form of religious excitement and was surprisingly close to Christianity in its teachings.

During the spring and summer of 1890 none of the papers studied here considered the Lakota ghost dance a threat, even though in the beginning it was referred to as a kind of war dance. The ghost dance in general was believed to excite the Indians and had the potential eventually to cause trouble, but the Lakotas were not in any way singled out as troublemakers.

Nor were the Lakotas a focal point of congressional debates during the first half of the year 1890. The matters discussed that related to Indian affairs mostly concerned issuing additional rations to several tribes suffering from lack of food. The situation among the Lakotas was portrayed as gradually progressing toward civilization, and no hardships were reported among the Lakotas during the 1889–90 congressional session. Congress was mainly interested in the successful partitioning of the Great Sioux Reservation and the subsequent plan to allot the remaining tribal lands to individual Lakotas.

The most remarkable congressional action affecting the Lakotas in the summer of 1890 was the decision to reduce their rations. This was due in part to the report made by Special Census Agent A. T. Lea and in part to the government's ongoing Indian policy, which sought to gradually reduce the Indians' rations so they would eventually be forced to take up farming and become self-supporting. By cutting the Lakotas' rations Congress continued this policy despite the reports submitted by Indian agents, the commissioner of Indian affairs, the military, the Sioux Commission, the press, and the Lakotas themselves, all of which indicated that the Lakotas could not support themselves by farming and were greatly suffering from lack of subsistence and from disease. By stubbornly clinging to established policy, Congress, probably unknowingly, played a critical role in creating future problems with the Lakotas and set in motion a chain of events that led first to the renewal of the ghost dances among the Lakotas in the fall of 1890 and eventually to the Wounded Knee massacre.

During the summer of 1890 none of the white voices studied here, despite some sensationalist newspaper articles, regarded the ghost dance among the Lakotas as a potentially dangerous movement. In fact, despite suggestions by Mooney and other scholars, during the summer of 1890 Lakota ghost dancing had come to an almost complete halt. There probably were councils and gatherings where the matter was discussed, but no major ceremonies were organized before August 1890.

By early fall, however, after a summer of misery, the ghost dance ceremonies were resumed, and the whites, especially in the press, took notice of it. In October 1890 the press characterized these dances as warlike manifestations, or even war dances. On several occasions, the press quoted "reliable sources" or "old frontiersmen" who maintained that the Indians danced in circles only when preparing to take the warpath. Although untrue, these accounts surely spread general alarm. Other newspaper accounts portrayed the Lakota ghost dance quite accurately, calling it a religious ceremony. But these articles were overshadowed by more alarming reports, some of which included accusations that the ghost dancers promised to beat out children's brains and drink the white man's blood; even worse, they claimed that during the ceremony the Lakota ghost dancers resorted to cannibalism.[3]

These news reports understandably alarmed eastern decision makers, including Senator Henry L. Dawes, who were concerned about the Lakotas' progress in civilization. Rituals like this surely meant that the Lakotas were slipping backward toward savagery; ghost dancing had to be stopped. The Indian agents agreed. Agents Gallagher and Reynolds deemed the ghost dance a heathenish practice, but considered it a religious ceremony nonetheless. The main issue for the agents was that the ghost-dancing Indians were beyond control and were returning to barbarism.

When ghost dancing intensified in the fall of 1890 the Lakota agents reacted by trying to stop the ceremonies. The ghost dancers responded by continuing the dances against the agents' orders. This in turn caused minor incidents between the ghost dancers and the agents, who often used the Indian police or progressive leaders as their spokesmen. By October 1890, these incidents, although related more to the internal division within the Lakota people than to the problems between whites and Indians, caused alarm and a public outcry in the press.[4] There is no doubt that the excitement among the Lakotas grew during October and November, but there is no indication that the Indians planned any violence against the whites.[5]

A major reason for the excitement stemmed from the Sioux Act of 1889 and the resulting partitioning of the Great Sioux Reservation, which left extremely deep wounds in Lakota society.

Those who did not sign the agreement blamed those who did sign it for the Lakotas' pitiful situation. In fact, many who finally signed did so because the Sioux Commission promised that rations would be maintained at the same level as previously. When the rations, especially the beef rations, were reduced in the summer of 1890, the Lakotas understandably interpreted this as a breach in the Agreement of 1889. Although this was not in fact the case, for many Lakotas the reduction clearly demonstrated the government's duplicity. Those who signed were then blamed for being fooled by the whites. This was only one factor that contributed to the division within the Lakota people, but it was the most recent and the most dramatic. During the fall of 1890 this division can be seen behind the restless feeling among the Lakotas; the trouble mainly occurred between the ghost dancers and the nondancers, and between the ghost dancers and the Indian police forces. Ultimately it was a conflict between those who did not sign the Agreement of 1889 and those who did.[6] Because the nondancers sided with the agents, the agents also became a part of this clash.

This conflict led to a situation in which, at least from the white point of view, order on the reservations collapsed. By mid-November the Lakota reservations were indeed in great turmoil, but the greatest misunderstanding by contemporaries and historians alike has been to interpret this as a sign of growing hostility toward the whites. It is important to recognize that the Act of 1889 resulted in much dissatisfaction among the Lakotas, and the ghost dance trouble was directly related to that act and to the events that preceded the actual partitioning of the Great Sioux Reservation.

Although the experienced Lakota agents did not deem the ghost dance warlike, the press certainly did. This occurred when the government appointed new agents to take charge of Pine Ridge, Cheyenne River, and Rosebud Reservations. The new agents had never seen a ghost dance, and they soon became as excited about it as were the local settlers and the press. Inexperienced as they were, the new agents failed to recognize the ghost dance as a religious movement; they understood it only in relation to the excitement it caused and believed that it was directed against the white population in general and the agents personally. Only Agent Reynolds, who took charge of Rosebud Reservation, seemed to maintain a degree of self-control and calm, although he too soon asked for military assistance. Agent Perain P. Palmer, in charge of Cheyenne River Reservation, also became very concerned and called for troops. Agent Royer, at Pine Ridge, was even more anxious; his appeals for help convinced the acting commissioner of Indian affairs to send Special Agent Cooper to Pine Ridge to assist Royer. Unfortunately, Cooper seems to have been equally concerned about the situation. Together they began sending excited, even frightened, messages to their superiors. Agents Royer, Reynolds, and Palmer maintained that they could not control their reservations without military assistance. This, along with reports by newspapers and alarmed citizens, finally prompted military intervention.

Royer's actions have been condemned by both his contemporaries and historians. This study also shows that there is no doubt that he was totally unfit to handle the situation. Perhaps in a less turbulent time he would have been able to perform adequately as an Indian agent, but on this occasion he was simply the wrong man for the purpose. The name the Lakotas gave him is quite illuminating of their view of him: Young Man Afraid of His Indians. Still, some sympathy has to be granted to Agent Royer. As the historian James C. Olson noted, Royer had not even wanted the job of Indian agent.[7] He had absolutely no experience with Indians, let alone the Lakotas. By the time he took over Pine Ridge Reservation the Lakotas were already dissatisfied and restless. They were distressed over the recent land agreement, lack of food, diseases, and, finally, the ghost dance. Things were in such turmoil on Pine Ridge that it is no wonder the inexperienced agent become frightened.

It is generally considered that the change of agents contributed significantly to the eventual bloodshed. I completely agree with that argument, but it has to be noted that Standing Rock, where the very experienced James McLaughlin was allowed to retain his position, was the first reservation where blood was spilled. On Standing Rock, only some 250 people were active ghost dancers, whereas on other reservations the number was much higher (see the table in chapter 1). This has been taken as evidence of McLaughlin's success in preventing the ghost dance from spreading among the rest of the people living on the reservation. However, it must be kept in mind that on Standing Rock Reservation the Indians were divided into rival factions; only those who followed Sitting Bull took an active part in the ghost dance. The rest either took no side or sided with the agent. Thus, in fact, the agent did not have much to do with preventing the spread of the ghost dance. Sitting Bull was his problem, not the ghost dance. McLaughlin's actions contributed to the death of several people and to the flight of approximately 150 of Sitting Bull's followers, some of whom were later killed at Wounded Knee. Therefore it has to be concluded that McLaughlin played a role at least as critical—although in a different way—as Royer's in contributing to the general confusion on the Lakota reservations, and even among the white population.

The events at Standing Rock, however, do not contradict the fact that the change in agents certainly escalated the problem, but whether more experienced agents could have prevented bloodshed altogether is an unanswerable question. Perhaps they would not have called in troops so quickly. But, as we have seen, there were other forces in play also. When the army was finally sent to the Lakota reservations, the agents, except for McLaughlin, became more or less observers. They welcomed the army and, despite some complaints, cooperated with the military on all major issues. The new agents certainly were inexperienced and brought about the military intervention, but McLaughlin did no better.

Even before ordered to take the field, the U.S. military conducted an investigation into the situation on the Lakota reservations. They found that there was growing dissatisfaction among the Lakotas caused by the failure of crops, reduction of rations, delay in ration issuance, loss of land, hunger, and disease. The report concluded that the ghost dance was only a symptom of this ill feeling, and that it would not lead to trouble. The army understood the situation clearly, or at least better than the new agents did. Despite this, the president ordered the military to assume control of the Lakota reservations.

The army's task was to overwhelm the Indians by a show of force, to separate the "hostiles" from the "friendlies," that is, the ghost dancers from the nondancers, in order to protect the settlers and to suppress any attempted outbreak. Still, Maj. Gen. John M. Schofield, the commander of the U.S. Army, emphasized that all measures should be taken to avoid trouble. He further ordered that no attempts to disarm the Indians were to be made, not only because it was dangerous and could lead to hostilities, but it was also contrary to the government's Indian policy. While the army officers in the field expected a relatively easy task in dealing with the Lakotas, they also understood that the military's appearance on the reservations could frighten the Indians and cause a general panic. This was exactly what happened on November 20. The panic-stricken Indians fled. Brig. Gen. John R. Brooke, commanding the troops in the field, decided to wait and see what the Indians would do. He set out to use negotiation instead of force in dealing with the Lakota ghost dancers.

In fact, General Brooke, like other officers in the field, was of the opinion that the ghost dancers did not present any real threat to the army or the settlers. Maj. Gen. Nelson A. Miles, in command of the entire military operation, was of a different opinion. He estimated that the Lakota ghost dancers could number as many as 27,000, of whom 6,000 would be fully armed warriors. On at least one occasion he even estimated that the Indians, including the Lakotas and other tribes, might have up to 15,000 warriors in arms. He also complained that he did not have enough troops under his command and that the troops he had were poorly equipped. Despite this, he favored rapid military action. General Schofield, however, sided with General Brooke and other officers who favored a more patient approach; the army was not going to take the first military step. Still, the army did prepare for a long and difficult winter campaign. It is worth noting that from the beginning Miles did not concur with his fellow officers about the manner in which the campaign was to be carried out, but he agreed with them that the Lakotas were facing serious problems and that the government needed to take necessary measures to help them. In this matter the military officers clearly sympathized with the Lakotas.

It was no secret that Miles was of the opinion that the military did not have enough control over Indian affairs. He believed that only the army was capable of dealing with Indians, and he therefore repeatedly called for more funds and power for the military. This, of course, was only one symptom of the old rivalry between the War and Interior Departments over control of Indian affairs. The ghost dance gave Miles an excuse to call for more control for the army and to request the removal of the civilian agents in charge of the Lakota reservations.

On several occasions in November and December 1890 Miles predicted that the ghost dance was going to lead to the greatest Indian war ever. In this, he completely contradicted the opinions of his fellow officers. He even contradicted himself; only a month earlier he had said that the Indians were powerless to leave their reservations since they were surrounded by railroads and white settlements. Yet during his trip to Washington in late November he gave interviews to the press in which he predicted that the country was going to be "overrun by [a] hungry, wild, mad horde of savages."[8] His opinions were widely quoted. Miles's trip to Washington helped him gain support for his requests; the army was put in full control of the Lakota reservations and the civilian agents were ordered to obey military authorities. Thus, by predicting that a major Indian uprising was ahead, Miles won a temporary victory for the military in their old feud with the Interior Department.

In late November and early December the press, reflecting the settlers' views, accused the army of not doing enough to settle the turmoil caused by the ghost dance. Even Agents Royer and Cooper on Pine Ridge were disappointed in the army's decision to wait and see. This kind of negative public opinion was not what Miles wanted. To gain more control for the military, and to carry out a successful military campaign, an adversary worth fighting was required. Several thousand Lakota warriors on the warpath was exactly what Miles needed to accomplish his political goals. Perhaps Miles feared that the gains of a minor campaign would have been marginal and an unsuccessful campaign disastrous for his political career.[9] By releasing several alarmist reports, the press played nicely into Miles's hands.

While calling for military action, Miles accused certain "false prophets" of distorting the originally peaceful ghost dance doctrine by transforming it into a doctrine of war. He quickly singled out Sitting Bull as the main leader of the ghost dance trouble among the Lakotas. The press adopted this view, and, as we have seen, Sitting Bull was considered the major foe by some congressmen as well. The only solution they could think of in dealing with Sitting Bull was to arrest him. The questions were, how should he be arrested and who should do it?

In fact, troubles on Standing Rock Reservation were even more directly related to the factional division within the Lakota people than on other reservations. This power struggle had initially three dimensions: Agent McLaughlin versus Sitting Bull, Sitting Bull versus progressive leaders such as Gall and John Grass, and Sitting Bull versus the Indian police force. These power struggles and the clash of personalities were the main factors that led to Sitting Bull's death. When the military took control in late November, it added a fourth dimension to the power struggle: McLaughlin versus the military, represented by General Miles. The situation on Standing Rock Reservation became the focal point because of the interest in Sitting Bull shown by the press, Congress, Agent McLaughlin, and General Miles.

It is extremely difficult to explain why Miles believed that Sitting Bull was behind the whole ghost dance phenomenon. McLaughlin certainly promoted this belief, but his motives differed from those of Miles. Perhaps Miles really believed that his old foe was still the principal enemy.[10] To him, Sitting Bull was the personification of Lakota resistance. He believed that by removing Sitting Bull the whole problem of Lakota resistance might be settled. On December 19, he wrote to his wife, "I was intensely anxious to know whether I would have to encounter my old antagonist, Sitting Bull."[11] He clearly did not want to enter once again into a long campaign against Sitting Bull.

For both McLaughlin and Miles, Sitting Bull represented the spirit of Lakota resistance, and for that reason they wanted him to be removed from the reservation. For McLaughlin, however, arresting Sitting Bull was a personal matter. He wanted to be in complete control on Standing Rock Reservation, and Sitting Bull stood in his way.

Agent McLaughlin considered it an embarrassment to have the military take charge of his reservation. In fact, he had for some time urged Sitting Bull's arrest. He even regretted that Sitting Bull never committed any "overt act" that would be an excuse to arrest him.[12] The ghost dance finally gave him that excuse. As a leader of this "heathenish" ceremony, Sitting Bull was disobeying the agent's orders, thereby providing the justification for his arrest. It would be far too strong an argument to maintain that McLaughlin wanted Sitting Bull dead, but it is fair to say that he cleverly used the reservation's internal divisions to arrange for his arrest, which culminated in Sitting Bull's death. McLaughlin also manipulated both the army and the press to further the general impression that Sitting Bull was behind all the trouble. By this maneuvering he not only got control of the Indians on his reservation but also won a temporary victory over General Miles.

McLaughlin defended the decision to arrest Sitting Bull by claiming that the Hunkpapa leader was going to leave Standing Rock for Pine Ridge, where he could join the other ghost dancers. All Indian accounts, supported by a few accounts from white observers, claim that at the time of the attempted arrest Sitting Bull did not have any specific plans to leave. He was invited by the ghost dancers to visit Pine Ridge, and he even asked McLaughlin for permission to do so. Inasmuch as Sitting Bull's camp was almost sixty miles from Standing Rock Agency, he could have left whenever he pleased. Many of the ghost dancers, in fact, traveled between the reservations freely. Sitting Bull, however, did not leave; perhaps he did not want to give the agent a

reason for making an arrest by leaving the reservation without permission. But McLaughlin believed that Sitting Bull planned to leave on December 15. This may be no coincidence, especially taking into account that the army was preparing to arrest him in the near future, something that McLaughlin did not want to see happen. Sitting Bull's alleged intention to leave at that particular time seems to have suited McLaughlin's plans almost too well to be only a coincidence.

Discussion of Agent McLaughlin's motives will not stop here. While debating his motives, scholars do mainly credit him for his ability to prevent the ghost dancing from spreading beyond Sitting Bull's immediate following. As noted earlier, the Indians on Standing Rock Reservation were so sharply divided into rival factions that there was little the agent could do to accomplish this task. The Indians generally followed their leaders, and this was the case with the ghost dance as well. Those Lakotas who followed Sitting Bull's adversaries were not going to abandon their leaders in any great number in order to join Sitting Bull's ghost dancers. With all this in mind, I have to agree with the anthropologist Raymond J. DeMallie, who noted, "For all intents and purposes, Sitting Bull's death was unrelated to the ghost dance."[13] Sitting Bull's death, however, initiated a chain of events that directly led to Wounded Knee.

The Christian missionaries among the Lakotas were also concerned about the ghost dance, although the Protestant and Catholic missionaries viewed it somewhat differently. The ghost dance was not a major issue for the Catholic missionaries. They condemned it as a heathenish ritual, but they were not particularly concerned about it. Father Francis Craft even said that it was "all right." On Rosebud, Father Florentine Digman did not devote much of his writing to the ghost dance, which implies that it really did not have a great impact on that reservation. That the situation was tenser on Pine Ridge is reflected in Father Emil Perrig's writings. He carefully commented on what he saw and heard around Holy Rosary Mission and did not believe that the Indians had any hostile intentions toward the whites. Even after the Wounded Knee massacre, Perrig reported that, despite various rumors and regardless of some skirmishes, most of the Indians were peaceably disposed.

Neither the mission nor the missionaries were in danger at any point, but the ghost dance did affect daily life. For most of November and December the schools were closed and few Indians attended mass, when mass was held at all. The disruption of the normal routine was also one of the major concerns for the Protestant clergy. One can easily understand that this worried the missionaries, who had labored to educate, Christianize, and civilize the Lakotas. In this sense the ghost dance surely was a setback in the missionaries' efforts.

Although the Jesuit missionaries did not anticipate any trouble resulting from the ghost dance, their Protestant colleagues did not always share that opinion. The Congregationalist missionary Mary C. Collins was one of those who spread rumors of Sitting Bull's alleged war plans, and the *Word Carrier* proclaimed that the Lakotas must be taught a lesson before they could be properly civilized. In *Iapi Oaye* the Protestant missionaries condemned the ghost dance and essentially threatened the Indians who believed in what the missionaries called "false prophets." The ghost dance was considered a dangerous plan, devised by the devil, that would lead to the return of heathenism and the destruction of the Indians. In fact, it can be argued that the Protestant missionaries were more concerned about the ghost dance than were the Jesuits. They were also more influential in shaping public opinion than were the Jesuits. Although both Bishop William H. Hare and Mary Collins, for example, were widely quoted in the national newspapers, Bishop Hare's opinions were relatively calm and analytical, whereas Collins presented a very negative picture of the ghost dance.

In the end, the missionaries did not play a significant role during the ghost dance period. Those who were on location on Pine Ridge, Rosebud, and Standing Rock Reservations were in a perfect position to make observations about the effect of the ghost dance on the Lakotas, and their observations are therefore of utmost value. The extent to which the missionaries, Jesuits and Protestants alike, were able to persuade the Lakotas not to join the ghost dance is difficult to determine. Perhaps the missionaries were personally able to convince some Lakotas that the ghost dance would not help them, or perhaps the articles in, for example, the *Iapi Oaye* that warned the Indians about the consequences of believing in false prophets did accomplish what they were intended to do. There are, however, no records to show what the results of these efforts were, and as noted in this study, despite the missionaries' efforts, some educated, Christian Lakotas did turn to the ghost dance, while others visited the ghost dance camps as spectators. The majority of those considered to be devoted Christians probably did not join the ghost dancers at all. Chief Gall is a good example of the latter. This leads us to the question of the numbers of Lakotas who actually did participate in the ghost dance ceremonies.

Contemporary estimates of the numbers of ghost dancers varied greatly. This examination has to start with the agents. On November 12 Agent Royer claimed that more than 50 percent, approximately 2,500, of the Pine Ridge Lakotas were ghost dancers. A few days later he gave a more detailed account and estimated the ghost dancers at 1,300 people. On Cheyenne River, the agent listed the followers of Big Foot and Hump as ghost dancers, numbering approximately 400 to 500 people. On Rosebud, the agent listed Two Strike and Crow Dog as the main leaders but never gave any estimate of the ghost dancers' numbers. Agent Wright, however, said in December that 1,800 Indians from Rosebud left for Pine Ridge in order to join the ghost dancers there. However, some 700 nondancers had joined them en route, which would leave us with the approximate number of 1,100 actual ghost dancers from Rosebud Reservation. On Standing Rock, Agent McLaughlin said that only 10 percent of the Indians were ghost dancers. These numbers are strikingly close to the estimates presented in this study (see the table in chapter 1), which suggests that only 28 percent, that is, 4,200 of the 15,329 Lakotas, were ghost dancers. When all other circumstances are taken into account, even that number is most likely an exaggeration.

It is therefore important to note that the white voices selected for this study estimated the Lakota ghost dancers as numbering from 6,000 to almost 30,000. The highest estimates were presented in the press, but it is noteworthy that some newspapers, when presenting those figures, quoted General Miles! As noted above, General Miles did in fact present quite extraordinary numbers relating to the Lakota ghost dancers. Furthermore, according to Miles, the Lakotas would get reinforcements of 4,000 men from other Indian tribes. The press, understandably, took up Miles's estimates. He was considered to be a reliable source and his views were presented during the congressional debate in December 1890. Senator Dawes, for example, concurred with Miles and stated that almost 6,000 Lakota men were on the warpath. This is remarkable, since only a few days earlier Dawes himself noted that there were only 5,225 Lakota males altogether, including young boys and old men.

Before going further, it is necessary to ask an important question: Because the actual number of ghost dancers was much smaller than the whites generally believed, was military intervention justified? From the white point of view, the answer has to be yes. The way the ghost dance was presented in November by the press, the agents, and General Miles left the white public with only one impression: the ghost dance meant impending war. Scholars such as Mooney, who follow the official records that report the ghost dancers' numbers as very high, generally agree. However, given that the number of ghost dancers was only 28 percent or less of the Lakota population, sending in the military seems an overreaction. This is especially true when there was no evidence that the ghost dancers ever planned an outbreak.

As we have seen, many misunderstandings regarding the Lakota ghost dance have prevailed. A good example, used particularly by scholars to substantiate the claim that the ghost dancers intended war, is the misinterpretation of the ghost dance shirts and dresses. They were introduced among the Lakotas around August or September 1890, after Kicking Bear returned from a visit to the Arapaho Indians, who already wore them in the ghost dance. Only then did they become popular among the Lakotas. It therefore seems that these ritual garments were adopted by the Lakotas from the Arapahos, but it is possible that their origin may be traced back to Wovoka, whom the Lakota delegates saw wearing some kind of special clothing. Then, as Black Elk explained, some of the dancers saw these shirts and dresses in visions, which instructed the Lakotas to start making and wearing them. The ghost dance shirts and dresses became an integral part of the ceremony for many Indian tribes. The Lakota ghost dance shirts, however, were thought to be bulletproof, a characteristic not reported by any other tribe.

The idea that the ghost dance shirts and dresses were bulletproof was strongly based in Lakota tradition. Sacred shields, as well as special shirts, were believed to be bulletproof; indeed, a human being could be bulletproof. The important thing here is that it was the power manifested in the item—the shield or the shirt—that made it bulletproof, not the material of which it was made. A shirt could be as bulletproof as a shield. The ghost dance shirts, which the Lakotas called *oglé wakhą́*, that is, sacred or holy shirts, were thus not an innovation for the Lakotas. The shirts are simply further evidence of the ever-developing Lakota ghost dance ceremony.

Scholars have interpreted the fact that the Lakotas did not decorate their ghost shirts with objects that derived from the white man's culture as an expression of their hostility toward the whites. This assertion can be dismissed as far-fetched. The shirts were, in fact, made of cloth obtained from the whites. That the Lakota ghost dancers did not decorate themselves with the white man's items probably reflects their dislike of the whites and their expectation of living in a world where no whites would exist, but it does not give the ghost shirt, or the ghost dance, a warlike meaning. Moreover, if the doctrine prevented the Lakotas from using objects originating in white culture, how could they carry guns during the ceremony, as some scholars have suggested? These two ideas clearly contradict each other, and the latter idea is, in fact, discredited by this study.

Furthermore, if there was nothing warlike going on among the Lakotas during the summer of 1890, why would they have started to make these bulletproof shirts at that time, as suggested by some scholars? The dancers were not anticipating facing bullets until after the military intervened. Therefore, the shirts assumed their bulletproof nature late in the fall, not, as claimed by Mooney and others, during the summer.

White contemporaries did not express much interest in these shirts, or in their bulletproof nature. The Lakota agents mentioned them only a few times, referring to them as some kind of sacred shirts. The military officers and the press mentioned them only randomly. General Brooke's joking comment when learning about an unlucky incident in which a ghost dancer was wounded in the thigh while trying to demonstrate the shirt's power is revealing. He quipped, "Probably the shirt was not long enough."[14] The bulletproof nature of these shirts is apparently more significant to scholars than it was to contemporary white observers.

In fact, it is quite certain that the ghost shirts did not assume their bullet-proof nature until late November 1890, after the military had arrived on the Lakota reservations. On October 9, Kicking Bear mentioned in a speech that the white man's powder would not harm the Indians, and on October 31, Short Bull said that he would make his men wear sacred shirts and sing, after which the soldiers would fall to the ground. Neither of the speeches directly mentions the shirts as bulletproof, although the idea may already have been present. However, when the Lakotas were forced to face the military might of the United States, they needed something to keep them united; there was a social call for these shirts. With the bulletproof shirt there was no longer any reason to be afraid of the army. These shirts, together with the promise that all the dead Indians would come alive again in the near future, helped the ghost dancers deal with the situation. In that sense the bulletproof ghost shirts surely made the ghost dancers believe more firmly in their strength, and also made them more boisterous and defiant toward the authorities. But, again, that happened only after the military invasion of the Lakota reservations.

Contemporary public opinion, especially as represented in the press, placed a strong emphasis on the act of dancing. Since October the press had condemned the ghost dance as a war dance and predicted that it would lead to a major Indian uprising. In the early phase of ghost dance reporting, such eastern newspapers as the *Washington Post* and the *New York Times* expressed much more alarm than papers closer to the Lakota reservations. Their headlines were more alarmist and the tone of their articles was more negative toward the ghost dancers than those articles published in the western papers. Even when the articles in the eastern press were taken directly from, for example, the *Omaha Daily Bee*, the headlines were altered to give them a more sensationalist effect. As noted above, Sitting Bull's death and the Wounded Knee massacre somewhat changed this pattern in the sense that the eastern papers turned the "ghost dance war" into an issue of politics. In contrast, the *Omaha Daily Bee* assumed a more hostile tone toward the Lakotas after Wounded Knee, but this may in part be explained by the fact that Charles Cressey, the paper's reporter, had witnessed the Wounded Knee affair, and his bias is apparent in his reports.[15]

The newspapers studied here covered the Lakota ghost dance troubles extensively. *Harper's Weekly*, given its weekly format, was not able to publish as many articles, but used its own correspondent, Frederic Remington, whenever possible. Even if the eastern newspapers were somewhat more alarmist in the beginning, it was obvious that by the spring of 1890 all newspapers considered the ghost dance a dangerous and barbaric movement that needed to be suppressed. Despite this, however, before the fall of 1890 the newspapers were relatively moderate in their comments regarding the ghost dance; they were concerned, rather than alarmed. Newspaper editors sought additional information from many sources: Indian agents, the commissioner of Indian affairs, army officers, missionaries, and sometimes even the Indians.

When the army was finally sent to the scene, the news reporting assumed a stance toward the Indians that can best be described using the word the newspapers themselves so frequently used to describe the Indians: hostile. In part, the local settlers and traders who saw their opportunity to profit from the army's presence and from an eventual war brought about this hostility. The historians Elmo Watson and George R. Kolbenschlag both believe that many inexperienced correspondents were told fabricated stories that they, without hesitation, believed and filed with their editors as quickly as they could. During the ghost dance troubles, especially before professional correspondents arrived on the scene, there were many "space writers," who wrote whatever they thought would sell. This was the real beginning of ghost dance newspaper sensationalism. Kolbenschlag claims that the sensationalist tone was partly due to the writing style of the day and partly to the popular perceptions of the "Wild West."[16]

Articles appearing in *Harper's Weekly* adopted a romantic tone in portraying life in the West. In this it remained true to the style it had used to report the Indian wars of the 1860s and 1870s. After the Wounded Knee affair, *Harper's Weekly* joined the other newspapers studied here in blaming the Indians for the trouble. Before Wounded Knee, however, it was very sympathetic toward the Lakotas; the wrongs done to them and their suffering were mentioned in almost every article. Despite the overall romantic style, both the articles written by Remington and the editorials offered severe criticism of

Indian policy. *Harper's Weekly* unquestionably saw the ghost dance trouble as a political issue resulting from bad Indian policy.

Historians generally agree that newspaper reporting of the Lakota ghost dance trouble was alarmist and sensational.[17] This study fully concurs with that view; the reporting was for the most part contradictory, confusing, and even false. The papers copied one another, published stories lacking in foundation, and resorted to unprofessional journalism. But this study has brought to light additional information concerning the nature of the newspaper reporting, namely, that there were a surprisingly large number of articles in all five newspapers and *Harper's Weekly* that fully sympathized with the Lakotas. This fact has escaped most historians, who, by randomly selecting a few newspaper articles, have created their generalizations about the news reporting. Such generalizations are insufficient, since all the papers selected for this study included articles both positive and negative toward the Lakotas. To generalize, for example, that the eastern papers were more negative toward the Indians than the western papers, or vice versa, is inaccurate. On some occasions, the eastern papers were more alarmist and sensational, while at other times the western papers took a more alarmist tone. This is partly due to the fact that the same material was used in slightly different forms by all of the newspapers studied here. Any generalizations are therefore difficult and probably misleading, as Kolbenschlag has also suggested. The Lakota ghost dance became a closely watched affair, a "war" of confusion, contradictions, exaggeration, and distortion, indeed a showcase of sensational journalism. The reporters were a mixed lot, and they reported for many purposes and from varied premises. Furthermore, there is no way to determine the extent to which the editors pressured correspondents to write sensational stories, and there is no way of knowing how extensively the editors rewrote their correspondents' reports.

The role of the press during the ghost dance trouble was extremely important, since it affected the general public, increased the settlers' feeling of alarm, and influenced the opinions of the decision makers in Washington. The newspapers were used by certain people on the frontier who, by feeding sensational reports to the inexperienced correspondents, hoped to profit from a war with the Lakotas. The papers were also used by men like General Miles and Agent McLaughlin to further their personal agendas, and the papers directly affected developments on the Lakota reservations. Since some of the Lakota mixed bloods could read English, the ghost dancers were able to follow the sensation they caused through the newspapers. This had three consequences: (1) the Indians were able to read about troop movements; (2) this led to a deterioration of relationships between General Brooke and the newspapermen, resulting in complaints about the army's inaction; and (3) some of the Indians objected to the way they were portrayed in the press, which led to a growing sense of injustice and discontent. Indians such as Little Wound and Red Cloud, complained that they were not able to present their views at all. Thus the newspaper reporting during November and December 1890 contributed significantly to the growing alarm and confusion on the Lakota reservations as well as among the white population.

The general confusion and misunderstandings surrounding the Lakota ghost dance were clearly reflected in the December 1890 congressional debate. Instead of trying to solve the Lakotas' problems, Congress approached the Lakota ghost dance as a threat—not necessarily a threat in a military sense, but a threat to the government's Indian policy. Congress was unanimous in insisting that the ghost dance had to be suppressed, but the congressmen came to this conclusion for various reasons. They were not unanimous about what the Lakota ghost dance really represented. In fact, the congressmen can be divided into four groups, each of which represents different approaches to the Lakota ghost dance. The first group consisted of congressmen who believed that ghost dancing had to be stopped because it meant a setback in the Lakotas' progress toward civilization. For this group, represented by Senator Henry L. Dawes, the ghost dance was evidence of the failure of government Indian policy. The second group comprised the humanitarian congressmen, represented by Senator Daniel W. Voorhees and Representative William S. Holman, who believed that the Lakotas' problems stemmed from mismanagement of the government's Indian policy. The third group of congressmen argued that ghost dancing must be stopped because it meant an impending war. This perspective was articulated by Senator Gilbert A. Pierce, who represented some western interest groups that advocated the use of military force to stop the dance and hoped that this might eventually result in opening more Lakota lands to white settlement. Furthermore, the military presence would be a boost to the local economy. The fourth group consisted of the majority of congressmen, who had no real interest in the Lakotas or the ghost dance and were content to leave the matter to the army.

Given these differing approaches to the ghost dance, congressional debate focused more on the legal aspects of the government's Indian policy than on solving problems among the Lakotas. When talking about the Lakotas and the ghost dance, Congress relied on rumors, on information received through newspapers, and on the expertise of a few biased fellow congressmen. This was especially true during the discussion regarding the numbers of Lakota ghost dancers and their alleged intentions to take the warpath under the leadership of Sitting Bull and Red Cloud.

As to the question of whether the Lakotas were suffering from lack of food, Congress also relied on biased information. Only after several days' discussion did Congress order an increase in rations for the Lakotas. This matter was extremely important in the wider context of the ghost dance trouble. Had the rations been increased earlier, much of the trouble might have been averted. There is no doubt that the congressmen knew that the Lakotas were starving; there certainly was enough information on this. Yet Congress made this too a political issue instead of a humanitarian one. Congress's approach to the Lakota ghost dance was in this sense blatantly hypocritical.

Ultimately, Congress played a surprisingly minor role during the ghost dance period. In fact, it may be said that the Congress did not act in matters relating to the Lakota ghost dance; it merely reacted.

Toward the end of December 1890 the ghost dance trouble seemed to be coming to a peaceful close as the ghost dancers on Pine Ridge gradually yielded to the peace efforts launched by General Brooke. In growing numbers they were returning to the agency. Even the newspapers, despite some alarming reports to the contrary, were predicting a peaceful resolution. The army officers, especially Brooke, were very optimistic. Then, following Sitting Bull's death, Big Foot and his followers left Cheyenne River Reservation to go to Pine Ridge. Big Foot's action led to increasing confusion on Pine Ridge and Cheyenne River.

When Big Foot eluded the soldiers, General Miles was furious. He accused the Indians of treachery and demanded that Big Foot be captured at all costs. He immediately deemed Big Foot's action a hostile demonstration. According to him, Big Foot was now the main troublemaker. Miles's opinions are noteworthy, since he again totally contradicted his fellow officers, particularly Lt. Col. Edwin V. Sumner, who was personally in contact with Big Foot and was convinced that Big Foot had no hostile intentions. Sumner claimed that the day Miles ordered the arrest of the hostile and defiant Big Foot, the chief was, in fact, "quietly occupying his village with his people, amenable to orders, having given no provocation whatever to my knowledge for attack, and no more deserving punishment than peaceable Indians at any time on their reservation." Sumner later observed, "I was not aware that Big Foot or his people were considered hostile, and am now at a loss to understand why they were so considered, every act of theirs being within my experience directly to the contrary, and reports made by me were to the effect that the Indians were friendly and quiet."[18]

Indian accounts also maintain that Big Foot fled simply out of fear of the troops; he sought protection from Red Cloud and other powerful leaders at Pine Ridge. Whatever his reasons were, he was blamed both by Miles and the public press. Miles ordered troops to go after him, to capture and disarm him, and, if necessary, to destroy his followers. The press went so far as to predict a "slaughter of reds."[19]

When Big Foot was eventually captured, every measure was to be taken to keep him under control. He was to be disarmed and imprisoned. For Miles, Big Foot's escape was a major embarrassment, and the army could not afford to let that happen again.[20] Clearly, Miles believed that Sumner's opinion of Big Foot was incorrect. As the overall commander, Miles viewed the military situation in the field differently than Sumner did. Miles was in constant communication with his superiors, who informed him about the letters from frightened agents and citizens living near the Lakota reservations. He was therefore under pressure to keep those citizens safe. However, it is difficult to understand why the opinions of these officers differed so radically. Big Foot's escape assured Miles that he had been correct all along.

This leads us to the massacre at Wounded Knee Creek on December 29,

1890. It is not necessary to go into the details of the battle here, but some particulars are worth noting. The beginning of the fight has been closely scrutinized by contemporaries and scholars alike. Contemporaries—the army, the press, Agent Royer, and even Father Craft—claimed that the Indians opened fire on the soldiers in a deliberate act of resistance. Indian accounts, however, unanimously deny this. In fact, the accounts given by mixed-blood army scouts, who understood both English and Lakota, are most valuable in answering the questions relating to the beginning of the fight. There is no doubt that an Indian fired the first shot during, or immediately following, a medicine man's dance around the circle in which Big Foot's men were sitting. Many contemporary white accounts state that the medicine man harangued the Indians and finally threw dirt in the air as a signal to open fire on the soldiers. Many historians have taken this as the standard interpretation of the battle's beginning.[21]

However, when the medicine man's performance is put into the context of Lakota religious practices, it becomes evident that he was performing a ritual, a prayer, of which the throwing of dust was a part. Phillip Wells, a mixed-blood army scout, verifies this. He said that the medicine man was only praying, but while he was performing other events took place leading to a gunshot and the subsequent fight. Undoubtedly the situation was tense, and the fact that the Indians could not understand the commanding officers' intentions, and vice versa, contributed significantly to the dramatic beginning of the battle. But it is quite obvious that the Indians did not plan any resistance, although they did not expect to be disarmed either. In fact, the families were preparing for a peaceful march to Pine Ridge Agency.

It is worth noting that by ordering the Indians' disarmament, General Miles contravened the orders given by his superiors; General Schofield, commanding the U.S. Army, repeatedly said that disarmament could lead to trouble and was to be avoided. Had the Indians been allowed to keep their arms, there most likely would not have been a Wounded Knee massacre.

Still, accusations that the army planned revenge for the 1876 Little Big Horn battle, where the Lakotas annihilated the 7th Cavalry, are without any historical foundation. Perhaps such sentiments were expressed in the heat of the moment, but historical facts do not credit any premeditated plans to kill the Indians in revenge. There are, however, newspaper accounts as well as some individual statements that describe the general atmosphere on Pine Ridge prior to the Wounded Knee affair as such that a decisive battle was expected. Reading between the lines, one might speculate on the possibility that some individual soldiers, perhaps some congressmen, and certainly some among the white residents living close to the Lakota reservations were hoping to inflict such a blow on the Lakotas that it would end their resistance for good. The Wounded Knee massacre did actually accomplish that task. Furthermore, some eyewitnesses, scouts, mixed-blood interpreters, and a few white men who were with the army claim that alcohol was provided to both the soldiers and the officers. Some claim that Col. James W. Forsyth was in an especially bad mood during the early morning disarmament because of the heavy drinking he had done the previous night.[22] There are, however, only random references to the matter, none of which can be accepted as historical evidence. In the end, it must be concluded that the Wounded Knee affair was the result of many tragic misunderstandings, and that neither the Indians nor the army planned a wholesale act of war. The interpretations regarding the causes of the Wounded Knee fight are only further examples of the many misunderstandings that have prevailed concerning the Lakota ghost dance.

Immediately following Wounded Knee all peaceful developments on Pine Ridge ceased. The Indians were frightened, angry, and desperate. The army had to prepare for a possible war, but also to start negotiations all over again. The press described the situation as a full-scale war. The situation was extremely chaotic for a few days, but gradually, after some skirmishing between the Indians and the soldiers, life on the reservation began to calm down, leading to an end of the trouble by mid-January 1891.

After the Wounded Knee fight Congress and the U.S. Army were forced to face accusations relating to the killing of women and children at the battle. The press quickly turned its praise of the army into charges of brutal massacre. To reply to the growing criticism, the army ordered a thorough investigation into the Wounded Knee matter. Thus the Lakota "ghost dance war" became a political issue. This was reflected in newspaper reporting, which began to assume some partisan characteristics in January 1891. The investigations, however, did not lead to any serious condemnation of the army's conduct during the Wounded Knee affair.

The Great Story of the Lakota ghost dance revolves around fundamental misunderstanding on a collective level; the whites and the Lakotas were simply unable to understand each other. Since Lakotas and whites viewed the ghost dance from their own cultural perspectives, conflict between them seems inevitable. From the basic misunderstanding of the ghost dance itself stemmed additional misunderstandings and conflicts on both the collective and individual levels. Further complications stemmed from various individual interests among whites and Indians alike. Contemporary whites failed to understand the Lakota ghost dance as a religious phenomenon. From the very beginning many whites associated it with war dances and assumed that the dancing implied an impending uprising. This study, however, clearly demonstrates that the Lakota ghost dance was no more hostile toward whites than was the ghost dance among other American Indian tribes. The Lakotas did indeed introduce changes in both the doctrine and the ceremony of Wovoka's ghost dance, but these changes were based on Lakota traditions and reflected their own religious beliefs.

This study shows that the Lakota ghost dance cannot be understood as a phenomenon in isolation from the rest of Lakota culture. When the Lakota ghost dance is studied outside the context of Lakota culture, the result is inevitably biased and insufficient. This is the second basic misunderstanding regarding the Lakota ghost dance: the failure of scholars to understand the nature of the Lakota ghost dance. Most of the material historians have used consists of documents that convey the white man's viewpoint. Despite this, the same material has also been used to explain the little that scholars have considered necessary to represent the Indians' point of view. For this reason, historical accounts of the Lakota ghost dance, with few exceptions, are biased and fail to understand the Lakota ghost dance as what it really was: a religious ceremony.[23] Mooney tried to approach the Lakota ghost dance as a religious ceremony, but since the Lakotas were reluctant to give him any information he had to rely on other sources. He also did not have the benefit of historical hindsight. However, later scholars, following Mooney, have generally failed to conceptualize the ghost dance in the context of Lakota culture and have promoted the belief that the dance was a political or military movement that sought to further the Indians' cause by resorting to violence. To understand the Lakota ghost dance it is vital to understand the Lakotas' point of view. Historians' unwillingness, or inability, to place the ghost dance in the context of Lakota culture has so far left us with inadequate interpretations of the Lakota ghost dance.[24]

As DeMallie noted, "To dismiss the ghost dance as only a reaction to land loss and hunger does not do it justice, to dismiss it as merely a desperate attempt to revitalize a dead or dying culture is equally unsatisfactory. . . . The ghost dance has to be seen as part of the integral, ongoing whole of Lakota culture and its suppression as part of the historical process of religious persecution led by Indian agents and missionaries against the Lakotas."[25] This is what this study has sought to accomplish: an understanding of the Lakota ghost dance in the context of the history and culture of Lakotas and white Americans alike. The method chosen for this study shows how differently these peoples actually viewed the Lakota ghost dance and helps us to understand the differing viewpoints within each group.

The fact that contemporary whites condemned the ghost dance ceremony among the Lakotas as warlike is in part explained by circumstances surrounding the ghost dance. Natural suspicions toward Indians, historical circumstances, and personal ambitions all clearly contributed to the general alarm the Lakotas' ceremony caused. This is to some extent also understandable; only sixteen years had passed since the Lakotas had wiped out Colonel Custer's entire column at the Little Big Horn River. The Lakotas were still feared and considered dangerous and wild Indians. There is no doubt that the Lakota ghost dance ceremony, with its trances and excitement, was "wild," and for those who only heard rumors or read newspaper descriptions of it, it must have seemed even wilder than it actually was.

For some white contemporaries, the Lakota ghost dance meant a collision with their own religious interests; for some it was an issue of political and economic interests; and for yet others the ghost dance was simply in conflict with their personal moral beliefs. Despite such differences, all the white voices studied here concurred on one thing: if the ghost dance would not stop by itself, it had to be stopped. The Lakota ghost dance affected a variety of white people representing different interests and interest groups in American society. For this reason, the dance, although an Indian creation, has to be seen as an integral part of the cultural, political, economic, religious, racial, and ideological fabric of white America as well.

The multidimensional historical method advocated by Berkhofer provides us with an exciting, yet challenging, way of writing history. Creating "a Great Story" based on various "voices" and "viewpoints" can at its best be very rewarding. However, the larger the selection of voices, or the longer the period of time under investigation, the more difficult it is for the historian to keep the structure of the work together and repetition to a minimum. This, I believe, is the real challenge of writing "a Great Story" of any historical event. Despite this, I am convinced that Berkhofer's method helps us to achieve more comprehensive interpretations of the past. In this study, the Lakota ghost dance serves as an example, but the method could as readily be applied in many other studies of the history of the American West, where it would prove especially valuable in examining cultural, religious, ethnic, and racial conflicts.

In fact, many of the problems among the Lakotas today are direct results of those controversies that trace back to the nineteenth century. The questions relating to Indian lands, education, and poverty, for example, are still part of daily life on the Lakota reservations. In this sense, I hope this study may prove useful in trying to understand some of the reasons behind the present problems between the Lakota Indians and the United States.

A Chronology of Events During the Lakota Ghost Dance Period

Summer 1889	The first news of the ghost dance and the messiah reaches the Lakota reservations. The Sioux Land Commission negotiates for the reduction of the Great Sioux Reservation. Hunger and other hardships afflict the Lakotas
Fall–Winter 1889–90	The Lakota delegation is sent to meet with the messiah. The Great Sioux Reservation is opened to white settlers and the Sioux Act of 1889 is passed.
April–May 1890	The delegation returns, inaugurating the ghost dance among the Lakotas. Newspapers take notice of the Lakota ghost dance. A settler in South Dakota warns the commissioner of Indian affairs about the potential problems caused by the ghost dance. The agents arrest some ghost dance leaders.
June–July 1890	The ghost dance is discontinued on the Lakota reservations. Hardships continue to plague the Lakotas. Congress decides to cut the Lakotas' rations. The Lakota agents suggest that nonprogressive leaders such as Sitting Bull should be arrested.

The ghost dance is not a major concern to the agents.

The army learns about the ghost dance through Porcupine, a Cheyenne Indian.

August–September 1890   Hardships among the Lakotas continue.

The ghost dance causes concern among white settlers.

The first incidents occur between the ghost dancers and their agents.

Ghost dances are performed on Pine Ridge, Rosebud, and Cheyenne River Reservations.

October 1890   Kicking Bear introduces the ghost dance on Standing Rock Reservation.

Agent James McLaughlin urges Sitting Bull's arrest and tries to stop a ghost dance in his camp.

Several ghost dance camps are established on various Lakota reservations.

Newspapers publish sensational articles on the ghost dance.

The new agents take charge of Pine Ridge, Rosebud, and Cheyenne River Reservations.

The agents become alarmed and call for assistance. Agent James McLaughlin believes he can control the Indians on Standing Rock without assistance.

Minor incidents occur between the ghost dancers and the agents.

Short Bull preaches to the ghost dancers on October 31.

November 1890   More alarmed newspaper articles are published.

On November 13, President Benjamin Harrison orders the military to assume control of the Lakota reservations.

The agents, especially Daniel F. Royer, send telegrams to their superiors reporting their alarm and fear.

The military arrives at Pine Ridge and Rosebud on November 20.

Newspaper reporters arrive on the Lakota reservations in late November and "war correspondence" begins.

Panic among the Indians follows the military's arrival. Ghost dancers on Pine Ridge move to the Stronghold in the Badlands.

The army tries to separate the progressive from the nonprogressive Indians, that is, ghost dancers from nondancers.

Lakotas from Rosebud travel to Pine Ridge to join the ghost dancers there.

The bulletproof ghost shirts are introduced.

Sitting Bull's arrest is planned by Gen. Nelson A. Miles and William F. (Buffalo Bill) Cody.

Gen. Nelson A. Miles travels to Washington, gaining support for his military campaign.

The ghost dance causes a sensation in the press.

Negotiations begin between the ghost dancers and the army officers on the Lakota reservations.

December 1890

Newspaper sensationalism grows to even larger proportions.

Father John Jutz visits a ghost dancers' camp. Negotiations to end the dancing continue.

William F. Cody's mission to arrest Sitting Bull is stopped by Agent James McLaughlin.

Agent James McLaughlin launches his own plan for Sitting Bull's arrest.

There are peaceful developments on Pine Ridge and Cheyenne River. Little Wound, Big Road, and Hump give up the ghost dance.

Disagreements occur among the ghost dancers in the Stronghold.

Congressional debate on the Lakota ghost dance begins.

Sitting Bull is killed.

Big Foot escapes the soldiers and starts a journey toward Pine Ridge; the army pursues him.

Peaceful developments on Pine Ridge cease when the Indians learn about Sitting Bull's fate.

Newspapers continue to spread alarm.

Big Foot is captured on December 28 and escorted to Wounded Knee Creek.

Lakotas are massacred at Wounded Knee on December 29.

Gen. Nelson A. Miles personally takes command of the troops in the field.

January 1891   Fighting between Lakotas and the U.S. Army follows the Wounded Knee massacre.

Debate about Wounded Knee begins in the press.

Congress orders investigation into the Wounded Knee affair. The U.S. Army begins its own investigation into the Wounded Knee affair.

Negotiations take place between the ghost dancers and the army.

On January 15 the ghost dancers surrender. The ghost dance among the Lakotas is over.

APPENDIX 2

Phonetic Key to the Lakota Language

There are several systems of writing Lakota. In this study the orthography developed by the University of Colorado Lakhota Project is used. This method of writing Lakota is also used by the American Indian Studies Research Institute at Indiana University when teaching the Lakota language. This orthography has proven to be especially useful in expressing the pronunciation of the Lakota language. The following brief phonetic key is based on Allan R. Taylor and David S. Rood, *Elementary and Intermediate Lakota* (Boulder: Colorado Lakhota Project, 1976) and James R. Walker, *Lakota Society,* ed. Raymond J. DeMallie (Lincoln: University of Nebraska Press, 1992), appendix 2.

The phonetic symbols with special significance used in this study are the following:

č   is pronounced *ch*
ǧ   is pronounced as in the Spanish *pagar*
ȟ   is pronounced as in the German *ach*
ž   is pronounced *zh*
š   is pronounced *sh*

Glottal stops are indicated by a backward superscript hook, as in čik̇ála.

Nasalization is indicated by a "hook" under the letter, as in wakḣá.

Accent marks indicate stress, as in náǧi.

The Messiah Letters

Arapaho Version

What you get home you make dance, and will give (you) the same. When you dance four days and (in night) one day, dance daytime, five days and then fifth, will wash five for every body. He likes you (flok) you give him good many things, he heart been satting feel good. After you get home, will give good cloud, and give you chance to feel good. And he give you good spirit. And he give you (al) good paint.

You folks want you to come in three [months] here, any tribs from there. There will (be) good bit snow this year. Sometimes rain's, in fall, this year some rain, never give you any thing like that. Grandfather said when he die never (no) cry. No hurt anybody. No fight, good behave always, it will give you satisfaction, this young man, he is a good Father and mother, don't tell no white man. Jueses was on ground, he just like cloud. Every body is alive again, I don't know when they will (be) here, may be this fall or spring.

Everybody never get sick, be young again,—(if young fellow no sick any more) work for white men never trouble with him until you leave, when it shake the earth don't be afraid no harm any body.

You make dance for six (weeks) night, and put your foot [food?] in dance to eat for every body and wash in the water. That is all to tell, I am in to you. And you will received a good words from him some time, Don't tell lie.

Cheyenne Version

When you get home you have to make dance. You must dance four nights and one day time. You will take bath in the morning, before you go to yours homes, for every body, and give you all the same as this. Jackson Wilson likes you all, he is glad to get good many things. His heart satting fully of gladness, after you get home, I will give you a good cloud and give you chance to make you feel good. I give you a good spirit, and give you all good paint, I want you people to come here again, want them in three months any tribs of you from there. There will be a good deal snow this year. Some time rains, in fall this year some rain, never give you any thing like that, grandfather, said, when they were die never cry, no hurt any body, do any harm for it, not to fight. Be a good behave always. It will give a satisfaction in your life. This young man is good father and mother. Do not tell the white people about this, Juses is on the ground, he just like cloud. Every body is alive again. I don't know when he will be here, maybe be in this fall or spring. When it happen it may be this. There will be no sickness and return to young again. Do not refuse to work for white man or do not make any trouble with them until you leave them. When the earth shakes do not be afraid it will not hurt you. I want you to make dance for six weeks. Eat and wash good clean yourselves. [The rest of the letter has been erased.]

Free Rendering

When you get home you must make a dance to continue five days. Dance four successive nights, and the last night keep up the dance until the morning of the fifth day, when all must bathe in the river and then disperse to their homes. You must all do in the same way.

I, Jack Wilson, love you all, and my heart is full of gladness for the gifts you have brought me. When you get home I shall give you a good cloud [rain?] which will make you feel good. I give you a good spirit and give you all good paint. I want you to again in three months, some form each tribe there [the Indian Territory].

There will be a good deal of snow this year and some rain. In the fall there will be such a rain as I have never given you before.

Grandfather [a universal title of reverence among Indians, and here meaning the messiah] says, when your friends die you must not cry. You must not hurt anybody or harm to anyone. You must not fight. Do right always. It will give you satisfaction in life. This young man has a good mother and father.

[Possibly this refers to Casper Edson, the young Arapaho who wrote down this message of Wovoka for the delegation.]

Do not tell the white people about this. Jesus is now upon the earth. He appears like a cloud. The dead are all alive again. I do not know when they will be here; maybe this fall or in the spring. When the time comes there will be no more sickness and everyone will be young again.

Do not refuse to work for the whites and do not make any trouble with them until you leave them. When the earth shakes [at the coming of the new world] do not be afraid. It will not hurt you.

I want you to dance every six weeks. Make a feast at the dance and have food that everybody may eat. Then bathe in the water. That is all. You will receive good words again from me some time. Do not tell lies.

Source: James Mooney, *The Ghost Dance Religion and the Sioux Outbreak of 1890*, 14th Annual Report of the Bureau of Ethnology to the Secretary of the Smithsonian Institution 1892–1893, Washington DC 1893 (Lincoln: University of Nebraska Press, 1991).

Kicking Bear's Speech, October 9, 1890

My brother, I bring you the promise of a day in which there will be no white man to lay his hand on the bridle of the Indian's horse; when the red men of the prairie will rule the world and not be turned from the hunting grounds by any man. I bring you word from your fathers the ghosts, that they are now marching to join you, led by the Messiah who came once to live on earth with white men, but was cast and out and killed by them. I have seen the wonders of the spirit-land, and have talked with the ghosts [*wanáǧi*]. I traveled far and am sent back with a message to tell you to make ready for the coming of the Messiah and return of the ghosts in the spring.

In my tepee on the Cheyenne reservation I rose after the corn-planting sixteen moons ago, and prepared for my journey [description of the journey omitted]. On the evening of the fourth day, when we were weak and faint from our journey, we looked for a camping-place, and were met by a man dressed like an Indian, but whose hair was long and glistening like the yellow money of the white man. His face was very beautiful to see, and where he spoke my heart was glad and I forgot hunger and the toil I had gone through. And he said: "How, my children. You have done well to make this long journey to come to me. Leave your horses and follow me." And our hearts sang in our breasts and we were glad. He led the way up a great ladder of small clouds, and we followed him up through an opening in the sky. . . . He whom we followed took us to the Great Spirit and his wife, and we lay prostrate on the ground, but I saw that they were dressed as Indians. Then from an opening in the sky we were shown all the countries of the earth and the camping-grounds of our fathers since the beginning; all were there, the tepees, and the ghosts of our fathers, and great herds of buffalo, and a country that smiled because it was rich and the white man was not there. Then he whom we had followed showed us his hands and feet, and there were wounds in them, which had been made by the whites when he went to them and they crucified him. And he told us that he was going to come again on earth, and this time he would remain and live with the Indians, who were his chosen people. . . . And the Great Spirit spoke to us saying:

"Take this message to my red children and tell it to them as I say it. I have neglected the Indians for many moons, but I will make them my people now if they obey me in this message. The earth is getting old, and I will make it new for my chosen people, the Indians, who are to inhabit it, and among them will be all those of their ancestors who have died, their fathers, mothers, brothers, cousins and wives— all those who hear my voice and my words through the tongue of my children. I will cover the earth with new soil to a depth of five times the height of a man, and under this new soil will be buried the whites, and all the holes and the rotten places will be filled up. The new lands will be covered with sweet-grass and running water and trees, and herds of buffalo and ponies will stray over it, that my red children may eat and drink, hunt and rejoice. And the sea to the west I will fill up so that no ships may pass over it, and the other seas I will make impassable. And while I am making the new earth the Indians who have heard this message and who dance and pray and believe will be taken up in the air and suspended there, while the wave of the new earth is passing; then set down among the ghosts of their ancestors, relatives and friends. Those of my children who doubt will be left in undesirable places, where they will be lost and wander around until they believe and learn the songs and the dance of the ghosts. And while my children are dancing and making ready to join the ghosts, they shall have no fear of the white man, for I will take from the whites the secret of making gunpowder, and the powder they now have on hand will not burn when it is directed against the red people, my children, who know the songs and the dances of the ghosts; but that powder which my children, the red men, have, will burn and kill when directed against the whites and used by those who believe. And if a red man die at the hands of the whites while he is dancing, his spirit will only go to the end of the earth and there join the ghosts of his fathers and return to his friends next spring. Go then, my children, and tell these things to all the people and make all ready for the coming of the ghosts."

. . . Then we were shown the dances and taught the songs that I am bringing to you my brothers, and we were led down the ladder of clouds by him who had taken us up.

Source: James McLaughlin, *My Friend the Indian* Lincoln: University of Nebraska Press, 1989), 185–89 (orig. pub. 1910).

Short Bull's Speech, October 31, 1890

My friends and relations: I will soon start this thing in running order. I have told you that this would come to pass in two seasons, but since the whites are interfering so much, I will advance the time from what my father above told me to do, so the time will be shorter. Therefore you must not be afraid of everything. Some of my relations have no ears, so I will have them blown away.

Now there will be a tree sprout up, and there all the members of our religion and the tribe must gather together. That will be the place where we will see our dead relations. But before this time we must dance the balance of this moon, at the end of which time the earth will shiver very hard. Whenever this thing occurs, I will start the wind to blow. We are the ones who will then see our fathers, mothers, and everybody. We, the tribe of Indians, are the ones who are living a sacred life. God, our father himself, has told and commanded and shown me to do these things.

Our father in heaven has placed a mark at each point of the four winds. First, a clay pipe, which is at the setting of the sun and represents the Sioux tribe. Second, there is a holy arrow lying in the north, which represents the Cheyenne tribe. Third, at the raising of the sun there lies hail, representing the Arapaho tribe. Fourth, there lies a pipe and a nice feather at the south, which represents the Crow tribe. My father has shown me these things, therefore we must continue this dance. If the soldiers surround you four deep, three of you, on whom I have put holy shirts, will sing a song, which I have taught, around them, when some of them will drop dead. Then the rest will start to run, but their horses will sink into the earth. The riders will jump from their horses, but they will sink into the earth also. Then you can do as you desire with them. Now, you must know this, that all the soldiers and that race will be dead. There will be only five thousand of them left living on the earth. My friends and relations, this is straight and true.

Now, we must gather at Pass creek where the tree is sprouting. There we will go among our dead relations. You must not take any earthly things with you. Then the men must take off all their clothing and the women must do the same. No one shall be ashamed of exposing their persons. My father above has told us to do this, and we must do as he says. You must not be afraid of anything. The guns are the only things we are afraid of, but they belong to our father in heaven. He will see that they do no harm. Whatever white men may tell you, do not listen to them, my relations. That is all. I will now raise my hand up to my father and close what he has said to you through me.

Sources: *Annual Report of the Secretary of War*, 52nd Congress, 1st Session, House Executive Document, Vol. 2, No. 1, Part 2, Vol. 1, Serial 2921 (Washington DC: Government Printing Office, 1892), 142–43; James Mooney, *The Ghost Dance Religion and the Sioux Outbreak of 1890*, 14th Annual Report of the Bureau of Ethnology to the Secretary of the Smithsonian Institution 1892–1893, Washington DC, 1893 (Lincoln: University of Nebraska Press, 1991), 788–89.

NOTES

Abbreviations

AAG   Assistant Adjutant General

ABD   Aaron Beede Diary

ACIA   Acting Commissioner of Indian Affairs

AG   Adjutant General

AISRI   American Indian Studies Research Institute, Indiana University

AIUSD   Wilcomb E. Washburn, ed., *American Indian and the United States: A Documentary History*, vols. 1–4

AIWKSC   Reports and Correspondence Relating to the Army Investigations of the Battle at Wounded Knee and to the Sioux Campaign of 1890–1891

ARCIA   *Annual Report of the Commissioner of Indian Affairs*

ARSW   *Annual Report of The Secretary of War*

ATMIU   Archives of Traditional Music, Indiana University

BBMG   Buffalo Bill Museum and Grave, Golden, Colorado

BCIM   Bureau of Catholic Indian Missions

BHP   Benjamin Harrison Papers, Library of Congress

CIA   Commissioner of Indian Affairs

DAID   Vine Deloria Jr. and Raymond J. DeMallie, eds., *Documents of American Indian Diplomacy. Treaties, Agreements and Conventions 1775–1979*, vols. 1–2

DUSIP   Francis Paul Prucha, ed., *Documents of the United States Indian Policy*

EBMC   Eugene Buechel Manuscript Collection, Marquette University Libraries

HCIAP   House Committee on Indian Affairs Papers

HLDP   Henry L. Dawes Papers

HRMSCA   Holy Rosary Mission Special Collections and Archives, Marquette University Libraries

IUL   Indiana University Library

IULAL	Indiana University Law Library
IULL	Indiana University Lilly Library
JMLP	James McLaughlin Papers
LC	Library of Congress
LSASPR	Letters Sent to the Office of Indian Affairs by the Agents or Superintendents at the Pine Ridge Agency 1875–1914
MHS	Minnesota Historical Society, St. Paul
MUA	Marquette University Archives
NAMFP	Nelson A. Miles Family Papers
NARS	National Archives Records and Administration Services
NDHS	North-Dakota Historical Society, Bismarck
RG	Record group
SBD	Short Bull Document
SBM	Short Bull Manuscript
SC 188	Special Case No. 188—The Ghost Dance, 1890–1898
SCIAP	Senate Committee on Indian Affairs Papers
TJMLB	Thomas Jefferson Morgan Private Letter Press Books
UOLA	University of Oklahoma Libraries and Archives
WMCC	Walter Mason Camp Manuscript Collection
WSCMC	Walter S. Campbell Manuscript Collection

Preface

1. U.S. Special Indian Agent Elisha B. Reynolds to the CIA Thomas J. Morgan, September 25, 1890, NARS, RG 75; SC 188), M 4728, Roll 1, 1/22–26. For the area covered by the ghost dance, see figure 1.

2. Mooney, *The Ghost-Dance Religion*, 780–81. For more about Wovoka and his message, see the introduction.

3. For more about U.S. Indian policy and the Lakotas, see the introduction.

4. See Mooney, *The Ghost-Dance Religion*, 1016, and foreword by Raymond J. DeMallie, xv–xxv. For further commentary, see Maddra, *Hostiles?*, 27–44.

5. For a useful survey of the literature relating to the Lakota ghost dance, see Sievers, "The Historiography of 'The Bloody Field.'"

6. Robert E. Bieder, "Multiculturalism: The Term, the Debate," paper presented at the Nordic Conference, August 9–13, 1995, Oslo, Norway (in the author's possession); discussions with Professor Robert E. Bieder in Tampere, Finland, during the winter of 1997–98, and in Bloomington IN during 1999–2001. For more about multiculturalism, see C. Taylor et al., *Multiculturalism*.

7. See Limerick, *The Legacy of Conquest*, 20–40. The historians Patricia N. Limerick and Richard White represent a new tradition known as "the new western histo-

ry." This approach challenges the traditional frontier ideology set forth by Frederick Jackson Turner in the late nineteenth century. Recently, the new western history has stimulated extensive debate among scholars in the United States. See Limerick, *The Legacy of Conquest*, 18–55; White, *It's Your Misfortune;* Limerick, Millner, and Rankin, *Trails;* Nash, "Point of View," 4; Faragher, "The Frontier Trail," 107–8; Hurtado, "Whose Misfortune?," 286–91; Allen, "The New Western History Stillborn," 203; Francis E. Flavin, "What Is The New Western History?," unpublished manuscript in the author's possession, 1997. See also Berkhofer, *Beyond the Great Story,* 161–90. For more about Turner's theories on the West and the frontier, see F. J. Turner, *The Frontier in American History;* F. J. Turner, "The Significance of the Frontier in American History."

8. See Berkhofer, *Beyond the Great Story,* 139–201.

9. See Berkhofer, *Beyond the Great Story,* 157–201.

10. DeMallie, "'These Have No Ears,'" 526, 532. See also Limerick, *The Legacy of Conquest,* 26, 291–92.

11. DeMallie, "'These Have no Ears,'" 532.

12. For a discussion of the ethnohistorical method and the role of ethnohistory as an intermediary between anthropology and history, see Dark, "Methods of Synthesis," 249–54; Hudson, "Folk History and Ethnohistory," 52–67; Sturtevant, "Anthropology, History, and Ethnohistory"; Euler, "Ethnohistory in the United States"; Martin, "Ethnohistory"; Limerick, *The Legacy of Conquest,* 222. For more about the use of oral tradition in writing history, see Sturtevant, "Anthropology, History, and Ethnohistory," 455–67; Euler, "Ethnohistory in the United States," 204; Vansina, *Oral Tradition as History.*

13. Discussion with Professor Douglas R. Parks, December 25, 2000, Bloomington IN. This orthography is used in A. R. Taylor and Rood, *Elementary and Intermediate Lakhota.* These textbooks are used at Indiana University for teaching the Lakota language. Another valuable guide to the Lakota language is Eugene Buechel, *Lakota English Dictionary* (Pine Ridge SD: Red Cloud Indian School, Holy Rosary Mission, 1983).

Introduction

1. See Dippie, *The Vanishing American,* 3–11. For accounts of the early days of the U.S. Indian policy see Prucha, *American Indian Policy in the Formative Years* and *The Great Father,* 1:35–314; Viola, *Thomas L. McKenney;* See also DAID 1:6–8.

2. Prucha, *American Indian Policy in the Formative Years,* 224–25; Prucha, *Americanizing the American Indian,* 2–3; Hoxie, *A Final Promise,* 2.

3. Viola, *Thomas L. McKenney,* 200–201; Washburn, *Indian in America,* 209–13; Berkhofer, *The White Man's Indian,* 157; Bieder, *Science Encounters the Indian,* 94–99.

4. For more about Indian removal, see Prucha, *American Indian Policy in the Formative Years*, 224–49; Viola, *Thomas L. McKenney*, 200–222; Dippie, *The Vanishing American*, 56–78. See also Bieder, *Science Encounters the Indian*, 94–99.

5. Prucha, *Americanizing the American Indian*, 3; Berkhofer, *The White Man's Indian*, 33–69; Dippie, *The Vanishing American*, 81–94; Hoxie, *A Final Promise*, xiv.

6. For more about the Peace Policy, see Mardock, "The Plains Frontier"; Prucha, *American Indian Policy In Crisis*, 33–71; Prucha, *The Great Father*, 1:479–533; Grobsmith, "The Plains Culture Area," 197. In 1872, seventy-three agencies were assigned to thirteen different religious groups. The division, however, was not equal. The Methodists were the largest group, with fourteen agencies; the Catholics were in charge of seven agencies; and the smallest group was the Lutherans, with only one agency (Prucha, *American Indian Policy in Crisis*, 53; Prucha, *The Great Father*, 1:516–19; Grobsmith, "The Plains Culture Area," 197). For more about the controversy between the Protestants and the Catholics regarding Indian education, see Prucha, *The Churches and the Indian Schools*, 1–44. For contemporary accounts, see Barrows, *Proceedings of the 9th Annual Meeting of the Lake Mohonk Conference of the Friends of the Indian 1891*, 54–58. For a good account of the development of the Indian Office, see Stuart, *The Indian Office*.

7. Mardock, "The Plains Frontier," 187–201; E. Hoxie, "The End of the Savage," 150; Stuart, *The Indian Office*, 32–35; Prucha, *The Great Father*, 1:516–19. For problems with the Peace Policy, see Prucha, *Americanizing the American Indian*, 4; Prucha, *American Indian Policy in Crisis*, 72–102; Hoxie, "The End of the Savage," 158; Robert M. Utley, *The Indian Frontier*, 129–201. As examples of the problems between the Department of the Interior and the Department of War, see Transfer of Indian Affairs to the Department of the Interior, March 3, 1849, DUSIP, 80; House Debate on Civil versus Military Control of Indian Affairs 1866, AIUSD, 3:1444–55; Senate Debate on the Administration of Indian Affairs 1867, AIUSD, 3:1456–87.

8. Hoxie, "The End of the Savage," 160. For more about these disturbances, see Andrist, *The Long Death*.

9. Senator Henry L. Dawes as quoted in Hoxie, "The End of the Savage," 160.

10. Prucha, *American Indian Policy in Crisis*, 132–68; Henriksson, *The Indian on Capitol Hill*, 109–10. For more about Indian education and Christianity, see Prucha, *American Indian Policy in Crisis*, 265–327; Bowden, *American Indians and Christian Missions*, 164–97; M. C. Coleman, *Presbyterian Missionary Attitudes;* Prucha, *The Great Father*, 2:688–715. For information regarding the development of Indian education and Christianity in the late nineteenth and early twentieth centuries, see Prucha, *The Churches and the Indian Schools*. For more about contemporary attitudes toward Indian civilization, education, and Christianity, see Prucha, *Americanizing the American Indian;* Bieder, *Science Encounters the Indian*, 191–95, 234–39.

11. See, for example, Bannan, *Reformers and the "Indian Problem,"* 87–89; Prucha, *The Great Father,* 1:500–501. Several organizations were established by "the Friends of the Indians." Most notable perhaps were the National Indian Defense Association, headed by Thomas A. Bland, and the Indian Rights Association, led by Episcopalian Herbert Welsh (Bannan, *Reformers and the "Indian Problem,"* 87–102; Prucha, *The Great Father,* 2:612–29). For more about The Indian Rights Association, see Hagan, *The Indian Rights Association,* 11–37; Prucha, *Americanizing the American Indian.*

12. Prucha, *Americanizing the American Indian,* 31–37; Hoxie, "The End of the Savage," 160; Hoxie, *A Final Promise,* 12; Hagan, *The Indian Rights Association,* 65–76; Prucha, *The Great Father,* 2:655–58. Some nineteenth-century ideas were based on the belief that, if the Indian could no longer hunt he would not only need less land, but eventually would die out as a race (Bieder, *Science Encounters the Indian,* 96–99).

13. Eggan, *American Indian,* 142–70; Berkhofer, *The White Man's Indian,* 33–69; Dippie, *The Vanishing American,* 95–111; Bieder, *Science Encounters the Indian,* 55–105, 191–95, 234–39. For more about theories regarding human development, see La Barre, *The Ghost Dance,* 33–40.

14. Berkhofer, *The White Man's Indian,* 117–18; Hoxie, *A Final Promise,* 14–19, 38–39; Bieder, *Science Encounters the Indian,* 94–99.

15. Hoxie, "The End of the Savage," 165; Bieder, *Science Encounters the Indian,* 191–95, 216, 234–39; Prucha, *American Indian Policy in Crisis,* 292–352. For interesting Lakota thoughts about education, see 50th Cong., 2nd Sess., *Senate Executive Document,* No. 17; 51st Cong., 1st Sess., *Senate Executive Document,* No. 51.

16. See *The Statutes at Large,* 24 Stat., 388–91. See Dippie, *The Vanishing American,* 171–76; Hoxie, *A Final Promise,* 72–73; Prucha, *The Great Father,* 2:659–71; Henriksson, *The Indian on Capitol Hill,* 165–72. The idea of the allotment of Indian lands was not totally new. It had already been explored and, to some extent, tried as early as the 1830s (Bieder, *Science Encounters the Indian,* 241–43).

17. Hoxie, "The End of the Savage," 166–67; Dippie, *The Vanishing American,* 172–77; Hagan, *The Indian Rights Association,* 65–66; Henriksson, *The Indian on Capitol Hill,* 177, 247, 270–86. For more about acculturation and assimilation, see Taske and Nelson, "Acculturation and Assimilation," 351–67.

18. *Statutes at Large,* 24 Stat., Section 10, 390. See Hoxie, "The End of the Savage," 167.

19. Senator Henry L. Dawes as quoted in Hoxie, "The End of the Savage," 169. In this case the word "work" refers to farming. See also Prucha, *Americanizing the American Indian,* 7; Bieder, *Science Encounters the Indian,* 7–8, 36–37; Henriksson, *The Indian on Capitol Hill,* 108.

20. *Statutes at Large,* 24 Stat., Section 6, 390; Report of Commissioner of Indian Affairs J. D. C. Atkins, October 5, 1885, AIUSD, 1:358–60. For more about Indian citi-

zenship, see Prucha, *Americanizing the American Indian*, 57–65; Hoxie, *A Final Promise*, 52–53, 77–80; Bieder, *Science Encounters the Indian*, 36–53, 73–80, 241–43; Henriksson, *The Indian on Capitol Hill*, 92–95, 165–77.

21. Hoxie, "The End of the Savage," 172–75. For information about Indian education in the late nineteenth century, see Prucha, *The Churches and the Indian Schools*.

22. Hoxie, "The End of the Savage," 178–79.

23. Senator Henry L. Dawes at a meeting of the Board of Indian Commissioners in Washington, *Fifteenth Annual Report of the Board of Indian Commissioners 1883*, 69–70, as quoted in Prucha, *Americanizing the American Indian*, 29. See also Hagan, *The Indian Rights Association*.

24. Hyde, *Spotted Tail's Folk*, 4–5; Hassrick, *The Sioux*, 3–6, 61–75; White, "The Winning of the West," 321–24; DeMallie, "Sioux Until 1850," 718–20; DeMallie, "Teton," 794; personal correspondence with Professor Raymond J. DeMallie, February–March 2003.

25. For a discussion of the usage of the terms "Dakota" and "Sioux," see DeMallie, "Sioux Until 1850," 719, 749.

26. It is worth noting that during the nineteenth century, the Santees spoke of the Seven Councilfires as an ancestral league from which all Sioux people descended. However, no eighteenth-century writer mentions the Seven Councilfires, which suggests that it is a nineteenth-century origin myth, probably of Santee origin. The Lakotas seem not to have spoken of the Seven Councilfires until the twentieth century, and when they did, they associated it with the stars of the Big Dipper, and they usually thought of the seven as being all the Lakota groups excluding the other Sioux (DeMallie, "Sioux Until 1850," 735, 748; personal correspondence with Professor Raymond J. DeMallie, February–March 2003).

27. Discussion with Professor Douglas R. Parks and Professor Raymond J. DeMallie, December 25, 2000, Bloomington IN. See also DeMallie, "Sioux Until 1850," 718–19.

28. John Blunt Horn, Antoine Herman, and James R. Walker in Walker, *Lakota Society*, 13–21. See Hyde, *Red Cloud's Folk*, 3; Hassrick, *The Sioux*, 3–6; DeMallie, "Sioux Until 1850," 725.

29. Hyde, *Spotted Tail's Folk*, 5; Hassrick, *The Sioux*, 3–6, 61–75; White, "The Winning of the West," 321–33; DeMallie, "Sioux Until 1850," 731–732; DeMallie, "Teton," 794.

30. Lowie, *Indians of the Plains*, 4; Hyde, *Spotted Tail's Folk*, 3–4; White, "The Winning of the West," 328–30; DeMallie, "Sioux Until 1850," 719–21, 731–34. For more about the Lakotas' daily life, see Hassrick, *The Sioux*, 107–242; DeMallie, "Teton," 791–812. For estimations of the Lakota population, see DeMallie, "Sioux Until 1850," Table 6, 748.

31. Hyde, *Red Cloud's Folk*, 126; Hassrick, *The Sioux*, 76–100; Standing Bear, *My People the Sioux*, 57; DeMallie, "Teton," 805–6. The historian Richard White, for example, believes that Lakota warfare was not only periodic skirmishing, but at times

also aimed at economic advantage or at conquering lands from other tribes (White, "The Winning of the West," 320). For more about Lakota warfare, see DeMallie and Parks, "Plains Indian Warfare" 66–75.

32. See Thomas Tyon, Little Wound, American Horse, Lone Star, George Sword, Bad Heart Bull, and Short Bull in Walker, *Lakota Belief and Ritual* 176–91; Spotted Elk and James R. Walker in Walker, *Lakota Society*, 21–23. See also W. K. Powers, *Oglala Religion*, 40–41; W. K. Powers, *Sacred Language*, 35. An interesting eyewitness account of these periodic group movements is provided by Francis Parkman, who lived among the Lakotas in the 1840s. See Parkman, *The Oregon Trail*, 110–253. For more about the significance of the buffalo, see J. E. Brown, *Animals of the Soul*, 5–17.

33. For accounts of the structure of the Lakota society, see Antoine Herman, James R. Walker, Charles Garnett, Bad Bear, Thomas Tyon, John Blunt Horn, and Iron Tail in Walker, *Lakota Society*, 3–7, 14–19, 20–36. See also Hassrick, *The Sioux*, 3–31; Price, *The Oglala People*, 2–17; DeMallie, "Teton," 800–803. The fullest account of the Lakota bands and sub-bands during the nineteenth century can be found in DeMallie, "Sioux Until 1850," 742–48.

34. In this study the Lakota band and tribe names are usually written as they are generally written in the English literature.

35. DeMallie, "Teton," 799; DeMallie and Parks, "Plains Indian Warfare," 70–73.

36. For accounts of the camp circle and the divisions of the Lakota, see John Blunt Horn, Antoine Herman, James R. Walker, and Spotted Elk in Walker, *Lakota Society*, 13–23. See also Hassrick, *The Sioux*, 12–16; Price, *The Oglala People*, 2–8; DeMallie, "Teton," 800–803. The largest Lakota camp was probably the one that faced the forces of Col. George A. Custer in 1876. There too the camp circles were organized according to tradition. See, for example, Statement of Flying By in IULL, Walter Mason Camp Manuscript Collection (hereafter WMCC), Box 5, Folder 1, Envelope 41.

37. For further information of the distribution of power among the Lakotas, see James R. Walker, Charles Garnett, Bad Bear, Thomas Tyon, John Blunt Horn, Iron Tail, Woman Dress, and Red Feather in Walker, *Lakota Society*, 23–36. See also Pennington, "An Analysis," 146–53; Hassrick, *The Sioux*, 24–31; Densmore, *Teton Sioux Music and Culture*, 284–332; Price, *The Oglala People*, 8–18; DeMallie, "Teton," 801–3. About the importance of kinship, see James R. Walker and Thomas Tyon in Walker, *Lakota Society*, 44–50; E. C. Deloria, *Speaking of Indians*, 24–38. See also DeMallie, "Change in American Indian Kinship Systems," 222–38; DeMallie, "Kinship and Biology in Sioux Culture," 130–43; DeMallie, "Kinship: The Foundation," 306–50.

38. Hyde, *Red Cloud's Folk*, 67–68; Pennington, "An Analysis," 153; Hyde, *A Sioux Chronicle*, 164. For more about Red Cloud, see Olson, *Red Cloud and the Sioux Problem;* Larson, *Red Cloud.* About Crazy Horse, see Sandoz, *Crazy Horse;* Sajna, *Crazy Horse;* Bray, *Crazy Horse.*

39. See Hyde, *Red Cloud's Folk*, 53–54; Olson, *Red Cloud and the Sioux Problem*, 19–22; White, "The Winning of the West," 338; Larson, *Red Cloud*, 58–61; C. A. Eastman, *The Soul of the Indian*, 108–10; Parkman, *The Conspiracy of Pontiac*, 138–39.

40. See Treaty of 1851, September 17, 1851, DUSIP, 84–85. See also Hyde, *Spotted Tail's Folk*, 45–46; Utley, *The Indian Frontier*, 61; Lazarus, *Black Hills/White Justice*, 16–18; DeMallie, "Teton," 794–95.

41. Treaty of 1851, Article 5, DUSIP, 84–85. See, for example, Hyde, *Spotted Tail's Folk*, 46; Lazarus, *Black Hills/White Justice*, 18.

42. See, for example, Hyde, *Spotted Tail's Folk*, 55, 61; Lazarus, *Black Hills/White Justice*, 23–24; Larson, *Red Cloud*, 66–75; DeMallie, "Teton," 795.

43. See Indian Peace Commission Report to President Andrew Johnson, January 7, 1868, AIUSD, vol. 1, 153; White, "The Winning of the West," 341–42. For fuller accounts of the events of 1850–1860, see Hyde, *Red Cloud's Folk*, 69–98; Olson, *Red Cloud and the Sioux Problem*, 15–26; Larson, *Red Cloud*, 50–73.

44. Utley, *The Indian Frontier*, 78–79. For more about the so-called Minnesota uprising, see Oehler, *The Great Sioux Uprising*.

45. Lazarus, *Black Hills/White Justice*, 27–28. In this study these terms are used when the white attitudes are described.

46. Hyde, *Red Cloud's Folk*, 101–13; Hyde, *Spotted Tail's Folk*, 90–92; Andrist, *The Long Death*, 88–92; Utley, *The Indian Frontier*, 93. For more about Spotted Tail, see Hyde, *Spotted Tail's Folk*. As noted above, the Cheyennes and Arapahos were thus included in the Lakota alliance, *lakhólkičhiyapi*.

47. Hyde, *Spotted Tail's Folk*, 102–3; D. Brown, *Bury My Heart at Wounded Knee*, 102–42.

48. See Hyde, *Red Cloud's Folk*, 114–33; Mardock, "The Plains Frontier," 187–90; Utley, *The Indian Frontier*, 95–100; Ostler, *The Plains Sioux*, 44–46.

49. Hyde, *Red Cloud's Folk*, 115–16; Hyde, *Spotted Tail's Folk*, 107–13; Olson, *Red Cloud and the Sioux Problem*, 27–40; Larson, *Red Cloud*, 88–92. For more about Sitting Bull's role during the war of 1865–66, see Vestal, *Sitting Bull*, 70–82; Hoover, "Sitting Bull," 155–57; Utley, *The Lance and the Shield*, 65–75.

50. Red Cloud's position among the Lakotas has raised questions also among scholars. Some argue that he was already a chief in 1866; others believe that he was only a shirt wearer or a war leader. In any case, he was not the kind of head chief the whites thought he was. For this discussion, see Hyde, *Red Cloud's Folk*, 142–43; Olson, *Red Cloud and the Sioux Problem*, 22–26; Andrist, *The Long Death*, 103; Utley, *The Indian Frontier*, 99; Lazarus, *Black Hills/White Justice*, 35–36; Price, *The Oglala People*, 66–67; Larson, *Red Cloud*, 88–90.

51. See Hyde, *Red Cloud's Folk*, 138–43; Olson, *Red Cloud and the Sioux Problem*, 34–37; Andrist, *The Long Death*, 101–3; Mattingly, "The Great Plains Peace Commission," 23–24; Price, *The Oglala People*, 57–58; Larson, *Red Cloud*, 91–93.

52. See Treaty with the Oglala and Brulé Sioux, June 27, 1866, DAID, vol. 2, 1368–70. See also Hyde, *Spotted Tail's Folk*, 114–16; Olson, *Red Cloud and the Sioux Problem*, 37; Lazarus, *Black Hills/White Justice*, 36–37.

53. For more about Red Cloud's war, see Hyde, *Red Cloud's Folk*, 134–61; Olson, *Red Cloud and the Sioux Problem*, 41–57; Andrist, *The Long Death*, 97–134; Larson, *Red Cloud*, 74–104; Ostler, *The Plains Sioux*, 44–50.

54. See Indian Peace Commission Report to President Andrew Johnson, January 7, 1868, AIUSD, vol. 1, 144–45. See also Mardock, "The Plains Frontier," 187–201; Mattingly, "The Great Plains Peace Commission," 23–37; Ostler, *The Plains Sioux*, 45–49.

55. Treaty of 1868, Articles 2, 11, and 16, AIUSD, vol. 4, 2517–25. See also Olson, *Red Cloud and the Sioux Problem*, 58–95.

56. Treaty of 1868, Article 4, AIUSD, vol. 4, 2517–25. See, Hyde, *Red Cloud's Folk*, 177; Olson, *Red Cloud and the Sioux Problem*, 96–117; Lazarus, *Black Hills/White Justice*, 61. For accounts of Indian delegations to Washington, see C. C. Turner, *Red Men Calling;* Viola, *Diplomats in Buckskins*.

57. Hyde, *Red Cloud's Folk*, 253; Olson, *Red Cloud and the Sioux Problem*, 83–84, map between pages 270–71; Schusky, "The Lower Brulé Sioux Reservation," 423–24.

58. Hyde, *Spotted Tail's Folk*, 182.

59. 44th Cong., 2nd Sess., *House Executive Document*, No. 1, Serial 1749, DUSIP, 147–51. See Hyde, *Spotted Tail's Folk*, 182, 187. For more about life and struggles on the Great Sioux Reservation between 1868 and 1874, see Olson, *Red Cloud and the Sioux Problem*, 114–213; Larson, *Red Cloud*, 137–69. For a comprehensive account of the Oglalas' progress in farming, see Smedman, *Sotureista ja Metsästäjistä maanviljelijöitä*.

60. Hyde, *Spotted Tail's Folk*, 188, 194–96; Olson, *Red Cloud and the Sioux Problem*. See also 42nd Cong., 3rd Sess., *House Executive Document*, No. 1, Serial 1560, DUSIP, 137–41.

61. Report of the Commissioner of Indian Affairs Edward P. Smith, November 1, 1874, AIUSD, vol. 1, 200–201. See Hyde, *Spotted Tail's Folk*, 202, 206, 215; Olson, *Red Cloud and the Sioux Problem*, 199–216; Lazarus, *Black Hills/White Justice*, 80–83; Larson, *Red Cloud*, 185–98; Ostler, *The Plains Sioux*, 58–62.

62. See Hyde, *Spotted Tail's Folk*, 219–21; Olson, *Red Cloud and the Sioux Problem*, 215–17; Larson, *Red Cloud*, 197–99.

63. The literature relating to the summer 1876 fighting and Little Big Horn is extensive. Accounts of these events are included in, for example, Vestal, *Sitting Bull*, 1957, 138–180; Hyde, *Spotted Tail's Folk*, 224–25; Andrist, *The Long Death*, 248–52, 261–92; Hoover, "Sitting Bull," 157–62; DeMallie, "'These Have No Ears,'" 515–34; Sandoz, *Crazy Horse*, 302–59; Utley, *The Lance and the Shield*, 122–64; Sajna, *Crazy Horse*, 271–99.

64. See, for example, Hyde, *Red Cloud's Folk*, 277–93; Vestal, *Sitting Bull*, 1957, 181–213; Olson, *Red Cloud and the Sioux Problem*, 199–235; Andrist, *The Long Death*, 297; Schusky,

"The Lower Brulé Sioux Reservation," 433; Hoover, "Sitting Bull," 157–61; Lazarus, *Black Hills/White Justice*, 91–92; Sandoz, *Crazy Horse*, 335–59; Utley, *The Lance and the Shield*, 174–82; Sajna, *Crazy Horse*, 300–320.

65. Indian Department Appropriations Act (Termination of Treaty Making Process), March 3, 1871, AIUSD, vol. 3, 2181–85. See DAID, vol. 1, 233–48. See also Henriksson, *The Indian on Capitol Hill*, 70–74. The Indian tribes were no longer considered independent nations, but domestic dependent nations. Treaties were no longer needed; agreements, ratified by both the Senate and the House of Representatives, were considered sufficient. This gave more power to the House, since earlier treaties were ratified by the Senate alone. Thus in 1871 the treaties made with the Indians suffered a kind of fall in status. Indians, however, did not understand this technical difference. In practice, treaty making continued after 1871, but the legal status was no longer the same (Henriksson, *The Indian on Capitol Hill*, 70–74; Hyde, *Red Cloud's Folk*, 277–93).

66. *Statutes at Large*, 19 Stat., Act of February 28, 1877, Article 1-11, 254–57. See Hyde, *Red Cloud's Folk*, 277–93; Olson, *Red Cloud and the Sioux Problem*, 223–30; Lazarus, *Black Hills/White Justice*, 92–93.

67. See, for example, Vestal, *Sitting Bull*, 181–230; Hyde, *Spotted Tail's Folk*, 248; Andrist, *The Long Death*, 298; Hoover, "Sitting Bull," 160–62; Sandoz, *Crazy Horse*, 259–62, 406–13; Utley, *The Lance and the Shield*, 165–210; Sajna, *Crazy Horse*, 320–24. For an account of the events leading to Crazy Horse's surrender from the Indian viewpoint, see DeMallie, "'These Have No Ears,'" 526–32. Several Indian accounts relating to Crazy Horse's death can be found in the Eli S. Ricker Manuscript Collection. The Ricker interviews are published in Jensen, *Voices of the American West*, vols. 1-2.

68. Hyde, *Red Cloud's Folk*, 302–3; Hyde, *Spotted Tail's Folk*, 254–63; Olson, *Red Cloud and the Sioux Problem*, 247–63.

69. 44th Cong., 2nd Sess., *House Executive Document*, No. 1, Annual Report of the Commissioner of Indian Affairs, October 30, 1876, Serial 1749, DUSIP, 145–51. See Hyde, *A Sioux Chronicle*, 29–30; Hyde, *Spotted Tail's Folk*, 266–67; Utley, *The Indian Frontier*, 235–41; McLaughlin, *My Friend the Indian*, 90. For more about the Lakota delegations to Washington, see Viola, *Diplomats in Buckskins*.

70. See Hyde, *A Sioux Chronicle*, 76–77; Vestal, *Sitting Bull*, 231–34; Utley, *The Lance and the Shield*, 234–59.

71. The Lakotas based their demands on the treaties of 1851 and 1868. In these treaties the government promised to pay annual appropriations for them. See Treaty of 1851, AIUSD, vol. 4, 2479–80; Treaty of 1868, AIUSD, vol. 4, 2517–25.

72. Hyde, *A Sioux Chronicle*, 69; Youngkin, "Prelude to Wounded Knee," 335.

73. Report of Acting Commissioner of Indian Affairs E. M. Marble, November 1, 1880, AIUSD, vol. 1, 288–89; 45th Cong., 2nd Sess., *House Executive Document*, No. 1,

Serial 1800, 398–99, DUSIP, 151; Valentine T. McGillicuddy in IULL, WMCC, Box 4, Folder 3, Envelope 4. See also Twiss, "A Short History of Pine Ridge," 36–37. For more about traditional men's societies, see Thomas Tyon and John Blunt Horn in Walker, *Lakota Belief and Ritual*, 260–70; Hassrick, *The Sioux*, 14–25.

74. Report of the Commissioner of Indian Affairs Hiram Price, October 24, 1881, AIUSD, vol. I, 308–9. See DeMallie, "Teton," 814. For accounts of the role of the *akičhita*, see Thomas Tyon, John Blunt Horn, and Iron Tail in Walker. *Lakota Society*, 28–34; Hassrick, *The Sioux*, 16–24.

75. 47th Cong., 1st Sess., *House Executive Document*, No. 1, Serial 2018, 1–3, DUSIP, 155–57. See Twiss, "A Short History of Pine Ridge," 38; Dippie, *The Vanishing American*, 263; DeMallie, "Teton," 814–15.

76. Hyde, *A Sioux Chronicle*, 164. For more about Agent Valentine T. McGillicuddy and Red Cloud, see Olson, *Red Cloud and the Sioux Problem*, 264–85; Julia B. McGillicuddy, *Blood on the Moon;* Larson, *Red Cloud*, 217–48.

77. Hyde, *A Sioux Chronicle*, 164; Utley, *The Indian Frontier*, 236; Lazarus, *Black Hills/White Justice*, 98–99.

78. See Hassrick, *The Sioux*, 31; Price, *The Oglala People*, 172–73; DeMallie, "Teton," 812. For a sense of the negotiations of 1888 and 1889, see 50th Cong., 2nd Sess., *Senate Executive Document*, No. 17, vol. I, Serial, 2610, 1–283; 51st Cong., 1st Sess., *Senate Executive Document*, No. 51, Vol. 5, Serial 2682, 1–215. For more about the communities living on the new districts at Pine Ridge, see ARCIA, 1884, Report of Agent Valentine T. McGillicuddy, September 1, 1884, 82. See also Vassenden, *Lakota Trail*, 56–69; DeMallie, "Teton," 812.

79. Report of the Commissioner of Indian Affairs J. D. C. Atkins, September 28, 1886, AIUSD, vol. I, 405; *Statutes at Large*, 24 Stat, 388–91. See also Hyde, *A Sioux Chronicle*, 107–4; Prucha, *American Indian Policy in Crisis*, 169–92; Hoxie, "The End of the Savage," 167–72; Hagan, *The Indian Rights Association*, 38–41; Prucha, *The Great Father*, 2:659–71; Henriksson, *The Indian on Capitol Hill*, 165–72.

80. See 50th Cong., 2nd Sess., *Senate Executive Document*, No. 17, Vol. I, Serial, 2610, 1–283; 51st Cong., 1st Sess., *Senate Executive Document*, No. 51, Vol. 5, Serial 2682, 1–215. See also *Statutes at Large*, 25 Stat., Act of 1889, Section 1–7, 888–90; Statement of American Horse in 51st Cong., 1st Sess., House of Representatives Committee on Indian Affairs, Unpublished Hearing, April 15, 1890, IUL, Microfiche, Card 1, 1–3. Fuller analysis of the negotiations can be found in, for example, Greene, "The Sioux Land Commission"; Youngkin, "Prelude to Wounded Knee," 337–40; Prucha, *American Indian Policy in Crisis*, 177–92; Hagan, *The Indian Rights Association*, 47–64; Hoover, "The Sioux Agreement," 57–75; Utley, *The Lance and the Shield*, 268–80.

81. *Statutes at Large*, 25 Stat., Act of 1889, Section 1–7, 888–90. See also Greene, "The Sioux Land Commission," 50–66; Hoxie, "From Prison to Homeland," 2; Ut-

ley, *The Indian Frontier*, 232; Prucha, *The Great Father*, 2:631–40; Hoover, "The Sioux Agreement," 67–70.

82. Youngkin, "Prelude to Wounded Knee," 340–41, 343; McLaughlin, *My Friend the Indian*, 90.

83. For more about these divisions, see Agent Perain Palmer to CIA, October 29, 1890, NARS, RG 94, AIWKSC, M 983, Roll 1, Vol. 1, 29; ARCIA 1891, Report of James McLaughlin, October 17, 1890, 126–27; Little Soldier, UOLA, WSCMC, Box 104, Folder 6; One Bull, UOLA, WSCMC, Box 104, Folder 21; Shoots Walking, UOLA, WSCMC, Box 104, Folder 5. See also Zahn, *The Crimson Carnage*, 3; Hyde, *A Sioux Chronicle*, 152–53; Hagan, *Indian Police and Judges*, 96–97; Utley, *The Indian Frontier*, 234–36.

84. C. A. Eastman, *The Soul of the Indian*, 4–5, 18–21; Lazarus, *Black Hills/White Justice*, 100–101; E. C. Deloria, *Speaking of Indians*, 98–109. For more about the official ideas concerning "barbarous" rituals, the power of the chiefs, and the nonprogressives, see 48th Cong., 1st Sess., *House Executive Document*, No. 1, Serial 2190, x–xii, DUSIP, 160–62. For more about Christianity among the Lakotas, see chapter 4.

85. Letters by Little Wound, Young Man Afraid of His Horse, and Fast Thunder in Gallagher to CIA, July 23, 1890, NARS, RG 75, LSASPR, M 1282, Roll 10, 335–38; ARCIA 1891, Report of the Commissioner of Indian Affairs T. J. Morgan, October 1, 1891, 132–33; Senator Henry L. Dawes in Cong. Rec., 51st Cong., 2nd Sess., Vol. 22, Part 1, December 3, 1890, 46–47. See also Treaty of 1868, Article 8–10, AIUSD, Vol. 1, 2517–25; *Statutes at Large*, 19 Stat., Act of 1877, Article 3–8, 255–56. For more about the discussion of the Lakota rations, see Gallagher to CIA, August 28, 1890, NARS, RG 75, LSASPR, M 1282, Roll 10, 385; 51st Cong., 2nd Sess., *Senate Executive Document*, No. 2, Vol. 1, Serial 2818, 15–21; Agent Valentine T. McGillicuddy to General Colby, January 15, 1891, as quoted in Mooney, *The Ghost-Dance Religion*, 831–33; Cong. Rec., 51st Cong., 2nd Sess., Vol. 22, Part 1, December 3, 1890, 46–47. For more about the promises and suggestions made by Gen. George Crook and other commissioners, see 51st Cong., 1st Sess., *Senate Executive Document*, No. 51, Vol. 5, Serial 2682, 23–32.

86. Youngkin, "Prelude to Wounded Knee," 340–43; Lazarus, *Black Hills/White Justice*, 112–13. For more about the reduction of rations, see chapter 6.

87. Lesser, "Cultural Significance of the Ghost Dance," 115; Clemhout, "Typology of Nativistic Movements," 14; Siikala, *Cult and Conflict*, 15.

88. La Barre, *The Ghost Dance*, 277–96; Siikala, *Cult and Conflict*, 15. Cultural assimilation is considered one aspect of cultural change and acculturation processes, which stem from cultural contact and conflict. Cultural assimilation eventually leads to a total submission of the weaker culture. See, for example, Taske and Nelson, "Acculturation and Assimilation," 351–67.

89. Linton, "Nativistiset liikkeet," 191–92; Siikala, *Cult and Conflict*, 52. See also Overholt, "The Ghost Dance of 1890," 38–58.

90. See Wallace, "Revitalization Movements," 264; Clemhout, "Typology of Nativistic Movements," 14; La Barre, *The Ghost Dance*, 197–223, 225–48, 253–73, 299–321; Siikala, *Cult and Conflict*, 15–19, 32, 52; Mooney, *The Ghost-Dance Religion*, 657–763.

91. Clemhout, "Typology of Nativistic Movements," 14; Overholt, "The Ghost Dance of 1890," 37–38; Taske and Nelson, "Acculturation and Assimilation," 357–67; Siikala, *Cult and Conflict*, 18–19.

92. Wallace, "Revitalization Movements," 265–67. For more about the types of revitalization movements, see Clemhout, "Typology of Nativistic Movements," 14.

93. Moses, "'The Father Tells Me So!,'" 1985, 36; Mooney, *The Ghost-Dance Religion*, 764–65; Hittman, *Wovoka*, 29.

94. Boring, *Wovoka*, 17–20; Fowler and Liljeblad, "Northern Paiute," 455–58. For accounts of Wovoka's life among the whites and his early years, see Bailey, *Ghost Dance Messiah*, 11–37; Hittman, *Wovoka*, 27–62, 107–24. See also Phister, "The Indian Messiah," 105; Boring, *Wovoka*, 20–23; Moses, "'The Father Tells Me So!,'" 337–38; Mooney, *The Ghost-Dance Religion*, 764–65, 771–72.

95. Boring, *Wovoka*, 27; Moses, "'The Father Tells Me So!,'" 339; Mooney, *The Ghost-Dance Religion*, 771–72. For information on the Paiute circle, or round dance, see Hittman, *Wovoka*, 63–65.

96. Mooney, *The Ghost-Dance Religion*, 771–74; Fowler and Liljeblad, "Northern Paiute," 451–52. For an analysis of the eclipse of the sun in 1889 and its effect on Indians, see Hittman, *Wovoka*, 63–68. About Wovoka's trances, miracles, and tricks see, for example, Danberg, "Wovoka," 12–15; Hittman, *Wovoka*, 66–84.

97. For accounts of Wovoka as a person and a shaman, see Danberg, "Wovoka"; Boring, *Wovoka*; Hittman, *Wovoka*. About his later years, see Danberg, "Wovoka," 40–52; Stewart, "Contemporary Document on Wovoka"; Moses, "'The Father Tells Me So!,'" 343–46; Hittman, *Wovoka*, 167–76.

98. See McCann, "The Ghost Dance," 28–30; La Barre, *The Ghost Dance*, 205–23; Mooney, *The Ghost-Dance Religion*, 662–763, 928–47.

99. Thornton, *American Indian Holocaust*, 138–40.

100. Jorgensen, "Ghost Dance," 660–61; Thornton, *American Indian Holocaust*, 138–40. For more about the 1870 ghost dance, see Hittman, "The 1870 Ghost Dance," 247–71.

101. McCann, "The Ghost Dance," 28–30; Bailey, *Ghost Dance Messiah*, 11–18; Thornton, *American Indian Holocaust*, 136; Mooney, *The Ghost-Dance Religion*, 764–66; Utter, *Wounded Knee*, 3. Mooney wrote that Wodziwob and Tavivo (known also as Tavibo, Waughzeewaughber, and Numitaivo) were the same person. If so, Wovoka's father was the founder of the 1870 ghost dance. Mooney was not absolutely sure that this was the case, however. Today's scholars believe that Tavivo was a follower of Wodziwob, not the founder of the religion (Hittman, "The 1870 Ghost Dance,"

250–51; Hittman, *Wovoka*, 29–34; Thornton, *American Indian Holocaust*, 136; Mooney, *The Ghost-Dance Religion*, 765; Utter, *Wounded Knee*, 3).

102. Mooney claims that Mormon influence on these religions cannot be disputed, but later scholars are somewhat doubtful, although they do not totally rule out the idea. More about this discussion can be found in Utley, *Last Days*, 65; Smoak, "The Mormons and the Ghost Dance"; Bailey, *Ghost Dance Messiah*, 143–49; Jorgensen, "Ghost Dance," 661–62; Thornton, *American Indian Holocaust*, 13; Mooney, *The Ghost-Dance Religion*, 766, 792–93; Hittman, *Wovoka*, 84–86.

103. For more about the Dreamers, see McCann, "The Ghost Dance," 28–30; Trafzer and Beach, "Smohalla," 313–22.

104. Moses, "'The Father Tells Me So!,'" 337–38; Trafzer and Beach, "Smohalla," 311–13; Mooney, *The Ghost-Dance Religion*, 771; Hittman, *Wovoka*, 79–80. It has remained somewhat unclear whether Wovoka personally saw or met any of the Shakers or the Dreamers. Mooney claims that Wovoka never left Mason Valley, but Moses and Bailey, for example, believe that he had traveled in California, Oregon, Washington, and Nevada. Moses bases his opinion on the memoirs of E. A. Dyer, a long-time friend of Wovoka. Whatever the truth, Wovoka seems to have been well aware of the teachings of Smohalla and John Slocum, as well as of the teachings of the Mormons and other Christians (Moses, "'The Father Tells Me So!,'" 337–38; Bailey, *Ghost Dance Messiah*, 34–51; Mooney, *The Ghost-Dance Religion*, 763–71; Utter, *Wounded Knee*, 4; Hittman, *Wovoka*, 19–22, 55–61, 79–80).

105. Mooney, *The Ghost-Dance Religion*, 771–73, 777. See also Phister, "The Indian Messiah," 117.

106. Mooney, *The Ghost-Dance Religion*, 771–72, 780–86. When doing his research among the Cheyennes, Mooney was shown a letter by an educated Arapaho Indian reporting directly on a speech by Wovoka that outlines his doctrine. Mooney saw two versions of the letter, one that Wovoka gave to the Cheyennes, the other to the Arapahos. These letters, which Mooney refers to as "the Messiah Letters," are reproduced in Appendix 3. See also Hittman, *Wovoka*, 297–98.

107. Boring, *Wovoka*, 34; Mooney, *The Ghost-Dance Religion*, 777–86. For more about the symbolism of colors in Wovoka's doctrine, see Hittman, *Wovoka*, 179–94.

108. Mooney, *The Ghost-Dance Religion*, 777–86. See Phister, "The Indian Messiah," 107; Hittman, *Wovoka*, 90. See also Appendix 3.

109. Mooney, *The Ghost-Dance Religion*, 802–19, 926–27. See Boring, *Wovoka*, 36; Thornton, *American Indian Holocaust*, 144. In addition to the Paiute, the ghost dance had followers in at least the following tribes: Arapaho, Arikara, Assiniboine, Bannock, Cheyenne, Gosi-Ute, Gros Ventre, Hidatsa, Mandan, Nez Percé, Shoshone, Sioux, Ute, Canadian Sioux, Southern Arapaho, Caddo, Comanche, Delaware, Iowa, Kansa, Kickapoo, Kiowa, Kiowa-Apache, Oto-Missouri, Pawnee, Wichita, Cheme-

huevi, Walapai, Havasupai, Taos Pueblo, and Kichai. Mel Boring claims that there might have been more than 60,000 active dancers, but he does not say how he has got this number. Perhaps he has misinterpreted Mooney, who maintains that there were more than 60,000 people in these thirty tribes. It is very difficult to estimate the number of active dancers, since not all of the people in those tribes can be considered active dancers, although they might have known of Wovoka's doctrine. Thus the number 60,000 has to be considered a rough and somewhat exaggerated estimate. Mooney does not give an exact account of the number of dancers, but we can safely speak of tens of thousands of Indians who were affected by the ghost dance in one way or another. See Boring, *Wovoka*, 36; Mooney, *The Ghost-Dance Religion*, 802–19. See also Hittman, *Wovoka*, 89–90.

110. Utley, *The Last Days*, 67; Thornton, *American Indian Holocaust*, 145.

111. For more about the miracles Wovoka made, see Hittman, *Wovoka*, 66–70, 75–77, 82–88. See also Danberg, "Wovoka," 13–15; Mooney, *The Ghost-Dance Religion*, 775–76; Utter, *Wounded Knee*, 4–5.

112. Mooney, *The Ghost-Dance Religion*, 785–86, 791. See Curtis, *The Indians' Book*, 45–47. For accounts of Lakota concepts of spirits, see Good Seat and Thomas Tyon in Walker, *Lakota Belief and Ritual*, 71–72, 123; Malan and Jesser, *The Dakota Indian Religion*, 10.

1. Wanáǧi Wachípi kį

1. William T. Selwyn to E. W. Foster (Agent at the Yankton Agency), November 25, 1890, NARS, RG 75, SC 188, M 4728, Roll 1, 2/97–3/2. See also E. G. Eastman, "The Ghost Dance War," 1; Hyde, *A Sioux Chronicle*, 239; Smith, *Moon of the Popping Trees*, 70; Ostler, *The Plains Sioux*, 243–56.

2. Selwyn to Foster, November 25, 1890, NARS, RG 75, SC 188, M 4728, Roll 1, 2/97–3/2. See also Mooney, *The Ghost-Dance Religion*, 819–20; Larson, *Red Cloud*, 265–66; W. S. E. Coleman, *Voices of Wounded Knee*, 5–7.

3. Short Bull Manuscript, SBM, EBMC, HRMSCA, 1–2. This text has been translated into English by Professor Raymond J. DeMallie, Dennis M. Christafferson, and Rani-Henrik Andersson, American Indian Studies Research Institute, Indiana University, Bloomington, 2005, from Father Buechel's original Lakota manuscript. This translation of the text is published also in Maddra, *Hostiles?*, appendix 5, 211–18. Another English version of the text has been published in Buechel, *Lakota Tales*, but unfortunately the text differs somewhat from the original manuscript and also contains some errors. A retranslation was therefore essential. Short Bull Document, 1–2; Short Bull in Haberland, *Die Oglala Sammlung Weygold*, 37–38; Selwyn to Foster, November 25, 1890, NARS, RG 75, SC 188, M 4728, Roll 1, 2/97–3/2. See also Hyde, *A Sioux Chronicle*, 240; W. S. E. Coleman, *Voices of Wounded Knee*, 9–10; Ostler, *The Plains Sioux*, 243–56.

4. SBM, EBMC, HRMSCA, 1–2; SBD, BBMG, 1–2; Selwyn to Foster, November 25, 1890, NARS, RG 75, SC 188, M 4728, Roll 1, 2/97–3/2. Shorter versions of the delegates' journey were told by Short Bull in Curtis, *The Indian's Book*, 45–47; Short Bull in Haberland, *Die Oglala Sammlung Weygold*, 37–38; Kicking Bear in McLaughlin, *My Friend the Indian*, 185–89. See Utley, *The Last Days*, 61; Mooney, *The Ghost-Dance Religion*, 820. See also Hyde, *A Sioux Chronicle*, 240; Smith, *Moon of the Popping Trees*, 71; Miller, *Ghost Dance*, 40–41; W. S. E. Coleman, *Voices of Wounded Knee*, 8–10, 25, 32; Ostler, *The Plains Sioux*, 243–56; Maddra, *Hostiles?*, 35–44.

5. SBM, EBMC, HRMSCA, 1–2; SBD, BBMG, 1–2. See also Hyde, *A Sioux Chronicle*, 240; Smith, *Moon of the Popping Trees*, 80–81; Miller, *Ghost Dance*, 45–47; W. S. E. Coleman, *Voices of Wounded Knee*, 10. For more about Kicking Bear, see Miller, *Ghost Dance*, 288–89. About Short Bull, see Wilhelm Wildhage, "Material on Short Bull," 35–41. When the word "apostle" is used hereafter, it refers to Kicking Bear, Short Bull, and other delegates, as is generally done in the literature.

6. SBM, EBMC, HRMSCA, 1–2; SBD, BBMG, 1–2; Short Bull in Curtis, *The Indian's Book*, 45–47; Short Bull in Haberland, *Die Oglala Sammlung Weygold*, 37–38. Short Bull's accounts of the journey are somewhat obscure, especially with times and places. See also Kicking Bear in McLaughlin, *My Friend the Indian*, 185–86; Hyde, *A Sioux Chronicle*, 240–41; Thornton, *American Indian Holocaust*, 145; Mooney, *The Ghost-Dance Religion*, 820–22.

7. SBM, EBMC, HRMSCA, 1–2.

8. See George Sword in Sickels, "The Story of the Ghost Dance," 28–36; Mooney, *The Ghost-Dance Religion*, 820–22. Mooney got the story from Emma C. Sickels, who at the time was the superintendent of the Indian school at Pine Ridge (see Raymond J. DeMallie, introduction to Mooney, *The Ghost Dance Religion*, xxiii). George Sword was the first captain of the Pine Ridge Indian police force. See, for example, Valentine T. McGillicuddy, IULL, WMCC, Box 5, Folder 4, Envelope 41.

9. Sword in Sickels, "The Story of the Ghost Dance," 28–36; Mooney, *The Ghost-Dance Religion*, 797–98, 820–22; Short Bull in Curtis, *The Indian's Book*, 45–46; Kicking Bear in McLaughlin, *My Friend the Indian*, 185–89. See also W. S. E. Coleman, *Voices of Wounded Knee*, 29–31.

10. Sword in Sickels, "The Story of the Ghost Dance," 28–36; Mooney, *The Ghost-Dance Religion*, 797–98, 820–22; Short Bull in Curtis, *The Indian's Book*, 45–47. See also Miller, *Ghost Dance*, 51–53.

11. In translating this text we tried to maintain as much of the Lakota style of speech as possible. The English version is, therefore, somewhat repetitive, but at the same time it gives a wonderful insight into Short Bull's experiences.

12. SBM, EBMC, HRMSCA, 1–6. For slightly different accounts, see SBD, BBMG, 1–3; Short Bull in Curtis, *The Indian's Book*, 45–46; Short Bull in Haberland, *Die Oglala Sammlung Weygold*, 37–38.

13. SBM, EBMC, HRMSCA, 5.

14. See, for example, Utley, *The Last Days*, 72–73; Mooney, *The Ghost-Dance Religion*, 822. The historian Sam A. Maddra has noted that both Kicking Bear and Short Bull continued to believe in the ghost dance well after Wounded Knee. They were known to have instructed other believers as late as 1902 (Maddra, *Hostiles?*, 186–88).

15. DeMallie, "The Lakota Ghost Dance," 390–91; Bad Wound and Short Bull in Walker, *Lakota Belief and Ritual*, 124, 144. See also Miller, *Ghost Dance*, 53, 106. For comparison, see Utley, *The Last Days*, 71–75.

16. SBM, EBMC, HRMSCA, 3; Porcupine's account of the journey, June 28, 1890, NARS, RG 75, SC 188, M 4728, Roll 1, 1/16–20, published also in Mooney, *The Ghost-Dance Religion*, 793–96. See also Moses, "'The Father Tells Me So!,'" 340. For the Messiah letters, see Mooney, *The Ghost-Dance Religion*, 780–81. See also Appendix 3.

17. Selwyn to Foster, November 22, 1890, NARS, RG 75, SC 188, M 4728, Roll 1, 2/97–3/2; Selwyn to Foster, November 25, 1890, NARS, RG 75, SC 188, M 4728, Roll 1, 2/85–96. See the report of William T. Selwyn in Mooney, *The Ghost-Dance Religion*, 820–21. See also Miller, *Ghost Dance*, 45, 51–53.

18. See DeMallie, "The Lakota Ghost Dance," 394–98.

19. The Lakota concept of religion is different from the Euro-American concept. The Lakota language, for example, has no specific word for "religion." For this reason, to avoid confusion, such words as "religion" and "doctrine" are used in this study as they are understood in Euro-American culture.

20. Porcupine, June 28, 1890, NARS, RG 75, SC 188, M 4728, Roll 1, 1/16–20; SBM, EBMC, HRMSCA, 1–6; SBD BBMG, 1–3. See also Short Bull in Curtis, *The Indian's Book*, 46; Mooney, *The Ghost-Dance Religion*, 793–96, 817–18. For comparison, see Sword in Sickels, "The Story of the Ghost Dance," 28–36 and in Mooney, *The Ghost-Dance Religion*, 797–98, 821–22; Utley, *The Last Days*, 87; DeMallie, "The Lakota Ghost Dance," 385–405; W. S. E. Coleman, *Voices of Wounded Knee*, 31; Ostler, *The Plains Sioux*, 260–64; Maddra, *Hostiles?*, 27–44. Mooney believed that these white men whom Porcupine mentioned might have been Mormons (Mooney, *The Ghost-Dance Religion*, 792, 812–13).

21. See, for example, Phister, "The Indian Messiah," 107; Hittman, *Wovoka*, 90.

22. See Utley, *The Last Days*, 87; Larson, *Red Cloud*, 266. Similar ideas have been expressed in Boyd, *Recent Indian Wars;*; W. F. Johnson, *The Red Record of the Sioux*, 171; Lowie, *Indians of the Plains*, 181; D. M. Johnson, "Ghost Dance," 45–46; Utley and Washburn, *Indian Wars*, 294–95; Smith, *Moon of the Popping Trees*, 75; Utter, *Wounded Knee*, 12–17. A good analysis regarding the nature of the Lakota ghost dance doctrine can be found in Maddra, *Hostiles?*, 7–8, 27–44.

23. DeMallie, "Lakota Belief and Ritual," 34.

24. See DeMallie, "The Lakota Ghost Dance," 387–88.

25. About the first meetings and ghost dance ceremonies, see Short Bull, EBMC,

HRMSCA, 1–3; Young Skunk, EBMC, HRMSCA, 1–6; Pretty Eagle, EBMC, HRMSCA, 1–6. (These accounts by Young Skunk and Pretty Eagle have also been translated by Raymond J. DeMallie, Dennis M. Christafferson, and Rani-Henrik Andersson from Father Buechel's original manuscript.) SBD, BBMG, 3; Agent Hugh D. Gallagher to CIA, June 10, 1890, NARS, RG 75, LSASPR, M 1282, Roll 10, 307; Gallagher to CIA, June 14, 1890, NARS, RG 75, LSASPR, M 1282, Roll 10, 315. See also Utley, *The Last Days*, 74–75; Standing Bear, *My People the Sioux*, 218; Smith, *Moon of the Popping Trees*, 71–73; Miller, *Ghost Dance*, 56–57, 63–64. For more about the allotment of the Lakota lands and the Lakotas' development in farming during the 1880s and 1890s, see Textor, *Official Records*, 154; Paulson, "The Allotment of Land"; Henriksson, *The Indian on Capitol Hill*, 183; Smedman, *Sotureista ja metsästäjistä maanviljelijöitä*.

26. Utley, *The Last Days*, 75.

27. ARCIA 1891, Report of the Commissioner of Indian Affairs T. J. Morgan, October 1, 1891, 126–27. See also Utley, *The Last Days*, 75; Schusky, "The Roots of Factionalism," 269.

28. ARCIA 1891, Report of the Commissioner of Indian Affairs T. J. Morgan, October 1, 1891, 126–27; Gallagher to CIA, June 10, 1891, NARS, RG 75, LSASPR, M 1282, Roll 10, 305–7; Gallagher to CIA, June 14, 1890, NARS, RG 75, LSASPR, M 1282, Roll 10, 314. See also Hyde, *A Sioux Chronicle*, 243–44; Smith, *Moon of the Popping Trees*, 81–82; Miller, *Ghost Dance*, 71–72. For more about the agents, see chapter 2.

29. ARCIA 1891, Report of Superintendent of Indian Schools Daniel Dorchester, September 30, 1890, 529–31. See Mooney, *The Ghost-Dance Religion*, 916–17; Utley, *The Last Days*, 76; Ostler, *The Plains Sioux*, 274–76. See also Gallagher to CIA, June 10, 1890, NARS, RG 75, LSASPR, M 1282, Roll 10, 305–7; Gallagher to CIA, June 14, 1890, NARS, RG 75, LSASPR, M 1282, Roll 10, 315; Gallagher to CIA, August 28, 1890, NARS, RG 75, LSASPR, M 1282, Roll 10, 385.

30. Letters by Little Wound, Young Man Afraid of His Horse, and Fast Thunder in Gallagher to CIA, July 23, 1890, NARS, RG 75, LSASPR, M 1282, Roll 10, 335–38; Statement of American Horse in 51st Cong., 1st Sess., House of Representatives Committee on Indian Affairs, Council Held with a Delegation of Sioux Indians, Unpublished Hearing, April 15, 1890, IUL, Microfiche, Card 1, 1–9. See also introduction.

31. Gallagher to CIA, August 28, 1890, NARS, RG 75, LSASPR, M 1282, Roll 10, 385–87. See C. A. Eastman, *From Deep Woods to Civilization*, 99–101. See also Miller, *Ghost Dance*, 127–30. About the role of American Horse and other chiefs during the negotiations of 1888 and 1889, see 50th Cong., 2nd Sess., *Senate Executive Document*, No. 17, Vol. 1, Serial 2610; 51st Cong., 1st, Sess., *Senate Executive Document*, No. 51, Vol. 5, Serial 2682; Gallagher to CIA, NARS, RG 75, LSASPR, M 1282, Roll 10, 385–87. See also Utley, *The Lance and the Shield*, 268–80; Larson, *Red Cloud*, 257–64.

32. Complaints made by American Horse in Royer to CIA, October 17, 1891, as a

part of ARSW, 1891, Report of Maj. Gen. Nelson A. Miles, September 24, 1891, 136. See also Statement of American Horse in 51st Cong., 1st Sess., House of Representatives Committee on Indian Affairs, Unpublished Hearing, April 15, 1890, IUL, Microfiche, Card 1, 1–3.

33. SBD, BBMG, 3. See Prucha, The Great Father, 2:727; Miller, *Ghost Dance*, 120–23; Mooney, *The Ghost-Dance Religion*, 843, 848–49; W. S. E. Coleman, *Voices of Wounded Knee*, 54; Ostler, *The Plains Sioux*, 274–76.

34. Mooney, *The Ghost-Dance Religion*, 977.

35. Red Cloud to T. A. Bland, December 10, 1890 in Cong. Rec., 51st Cong., 2nd Sess., December 19, 1890, 702–3; Red Cloud as quoted in Charles A. Eastman to Frank Wood (forwarded to ACIA), November 11, 1890, NARS, RG 75, SC 188, M 4728, Roll 1, 1/98–100. See also C. A. Eastman, *From Deep Woods to Civilization*, 100; Miller, *Ghost Dance*, 40–41, 56; Larson, *Red Cloud*, 268–69. Red Cloud was also quoted by the newspapers. See chapter 5.

36. Little Wound as quoted in *New York Times*, November 23, 1890, 5; *Chicago Tribune*, November 23, 1890, 1; *Omaha Daily Bee*, November 23, 1890, 1; Little Wound as quoted in Hyde, *A Sioux Chronicle*, 250; Little Wound as quoted in E. G. Eastman, "The Ghost Dance War," 30. See Phillip Wells in Jensen, *Voices of the American West*, 1:139–41. See also Miller, *Ghost Dance*, 56; W. S. E. Coleman, *Voices of Wounded Knee*, 48–49.

37. Royer to CIA, November 8, 1890, NARS, RG 94, AIWKSC, M 983, Roll 1, Vol. 1, 62–65. See Young Skunk, EBMC, HRMSCA, 1–2. See also Boyd, *Recent Indian Wars*, 183. For an estimation of the number of Lakota ghost dancers, see the table in chapter 1.

38. Utley, *The Last Days*, 84–85; Olson, *Red Cloud and the Sioux Problem*, 323.

39. See Phillip Wells in Jensen, *Voices of the American West*, 1:146–48; Gallagher to CIA, August 28, 1890, NARS, RG 75, LSASPR, M 1282, Roll 10, 387–88; ARCIA 1891, Report of the Commissioner of Indian Affairs T. J. Morgan, October 1, 1891, 274–75. See also Boyd, *Recent Indian Wars*, 179; Olson, *Red Cloud and the Sioux Problem*, 325; Miller, *Ghost Dance*, 82–85.

40. Cong., Rec., 51st Cong., 2nd Sess., Vol. 22, Part 1, December 12, 1890, 47–48. See "Ghost-Dances in the West: Origin and Development of the Messiah Craze and the Ghost-Dance," *Illustrated American*, January 17, 1891, 327; Boyd, *Recent Indian Wars*, 179.

41. Hyde, *A Sioux Chronicle*, 251; Miller, *Ghost Dance*, 82.

42. According to the 1868 treaty, the government was supposed to build a school for every thirty Lakota children. However, in 1880 there was only fifteen schools on the Great Sioux Reservation and the average attendance was 319 pupils. In the Act of 1889 it was agreed that thirty more schools would be established. By 1890 there were forty-four schools on the Lakota reservations, with the capacity of approxi-

mately 2,700 pupils, but the average attendance as late as 1891 was only 1,300 pupils (Treaty of 1868, AIUSD, Vol. 4, 2517–25; *Statutes at Large,* The Sioux Act of 1889, sec. 20, 896; ARCIA 1891, Report of the Commissioner of Indian Affairs T. J. Morgan, October 1, 1891. See also Smedman, *Sotureista ja metsästäjistä maanviljelijöitä*). During the ghost dance troubles some of the schools were closed for as long as three or four months (ARCIA 1891, Report of Superintendent of Indian Schools Daniel Dorchester, September 30, 1890, 533).

43. Standing Bear, *My People the Sioux,* 221; Mooney, *The Ghost-Dance Religion,* 92; Miller, *Ghost Dance,* 91–93. Luther Standing Bear was a prominent progressive on the Rosebud Reservation. He was educated at the Carlisle Training School in Pennsylvania and was a schoolteacher at Rosebud. See Standing Bear, *My People the Sioux.*

44. ARCIA 1891, Report of the Commissioner of Indian Affairs T. J. Morgan, October 1, 1891, 127–28. See also Mooney, *The Ghost-Dance Religion,* 848; Hyde, *A Sioux Chronicle,* 254; Prucha 1984, 2:727–28. For more about the agents, see chapter 2.

45. Standing Bear, *My People the Sioux,* 219–20; SBD, BBMG, 1–4. See Hyde, *A Sioux Chronicle,* 254, 260–61; Utley, *The Last Days,* 95; W. S. E. Coleman, *Voices of Wounded Knee,* 54. See also chapter 2.

46. Joseph Horn Cloud in Jensen, *Voices of the American West,* 1:191–208; Dewey Beard in Jensen, *Voices of the American West,* 1:208–26. The Eli S. Ricker Interviews with Joseph Horn Cloud and Dewey Beard are also published in Danker, "The Wounded Knee Interviews," 164–200. See also Hyde, *A Sioux Chronicle,* 258; Smith, *Moon of the Popping Trees,* 88–94; Seymour, *Sitanka,* 53; Miller, *Ghost Dance,* 95; Mooney, *The Ghost-Dance Religion,* 848.

47. See, for example, Joseph Horn Cloud in Jensen, *Voices of the American West,* 1:191–208; Dewey Beard in Jensen, *Voices of the American West,* 1:208–26.

48. Hagan, *Indian Police and Judges,* 82–96. For more about the success of the Lakota Indian police force before the ghost dance troubles, see ARCIA 1889, Report of Agent Charles E. McChesney, August 26, 1889, Report of Agent Hugh D. Gallagher, August 25, 1889, Report of Agent L. F. Spencer, August 23, 1889, Report of Agent James McLaughlin 1989, August 26, 1889, 134, 153, 159, 169; ARCIA 1890, Annual Report of the Commissioner of Indian Affairs T. J. Morgan, September 5, 1890; Valentine T. McGillicuddy, IULL, WMCC, Box 4, Folder 3, Envelope 4.

49. See Standing Bear, *My People the Sioux,* 219. See also Hyde, *A Sioux Chronicle,* 269–70. For more about the significance of the camp circle, see Spotted Elk and James R. Walker in Walker, *Lakota Society,* 21–23. See also introduction.

50. For more about U.S. Indian policy during the 1880s, see introduction and Hoxie, "The End of the Savage," 157–79.

51. Utley, *The Last Days,* 74; Larson, *Red Cloud,* 266–68.

52. DeMallie, "The Lakota Ghost Dance," 56; discussion with Professor Raymond

J. DeMallie, April 30, 2000, Bloomington IN. This was also the opinion of Agent James McLaughlin. See chapters 2 and 5.

53. ARCIA 1891, Report of the Commissioner of Indian Affairs T. J. Morgan, October 1, 1891, 131. This claim made by Commissioner Morgan either reflects his lack of knowledge of the situation or was an attempt to convince the authorities that the situation was better managed than it actually was. There are many examples of this kind of falsification of facts and corruption within the Bureau of Indian Affairs. See, for example, *The Annual Report of the Board of Indian Commissioners,* 1869, DUSIP, 127–29; House Miscellaneous Report No. 167, 44th Cong., 1st Sess., Vol. 5, Serial 1702, 1–18, 180–87. See also Hyde, *Spotted Tail's Folk,* 188; Henriksson, *The Indian on Capitol Hill,* 43–44.

54. Neihardt and Black Elk, *Black Elk Speaks,* 241–42; DeMallie, *The Sixth Grandfather,* 258–60; Miller, *Ghost Dance,* 76. See also Palmer to CIA, November 10, 1890, NARS, RG 94, AIWKSC, M 983, Roll 1, Vol. 1, 30–32.

55. Hultkrantz, "Naturfolkets religion," 6; DeMallie and Lavenda, "Wakan"; C. A. Eastman, *The Soul of the Indian,* 27–28.

56. Little Wound, Good Seat, and James R. Walker in Walker, *Lakota Belief and Ritual,* 68–74. See Hultkrantz, *De Amerikanska indianernas religion,* 5; DeMallie and Lavenda, "Wakan," 153–59, 163–64; W. K. Powers, *Sacred Language,* 111–13, 118. According to Hultkrantz, most "primitive peoples" perceive God as a kind of higher being, *Deus otosius,* that observes the world from high above (Hultkrantz, *De Amerikanska indianernas religion,* 107).

57. Little Wound, Good Seat, and James R. Walker in Walker, *Lakota Belief and Ritual,* 68–74; Little Wound, Good Seat, James R. Walker, George Sword, Bad Wound, No Flesh, Short Feather, Ringing Shield, Finger, John Blunt Horn, William Garnett, Thomas Tyon, and Thunder Bear in Walker, *Lakota Society,* 68–124. See also DeMallie and Lavenda, "Wakan," 154–59; W. K. Powers, *Oglala Religion,* 170–71; DeMallie, "Lakota Belief and Ritual," 27–32.

58. Malan and Jesser, *The Dakota Indian Religion,* 8; W. K. Powers, *Oglala Religion,* 170–71; DeMallie, "Lakota Belief and Ritual," 29.

59. Little Wound, Good Seat, James R. Walker, George Sword, Bad Wound, No Flesh, Short Feather, Ringing Shield, Finger, John Blunt Horn, William Garnett, Thomas Tyon, and Thunder Bear in Walker, *Lakota Belief and Ritual,* 68–124. See Malan and Jesser, *The Dakota Indian Religion,* 10; DeMallie and Lavenda, "Wakan," 153–59, 163–64; DeMallie, "Lakota Belief and Ritual," 29–31; Amiotte, "The Lakota Sun Dance," 86–89; Grobsmith, "The Plains Culture Area," 190.

60. See SBM, EBMC, HRMSCA, 1.

61. James R. Walker in Walker, *Lakota Belief and Ritual,* 73–74. See Malan and Jesser, *The Dakota Indian Religion,* 12–13; J. E. Brown, *The Sacred Pipe,* 45; W. K. Powers,

Oglala Religion, 56–63. See also DeMallie, "Lakota Belief and Ritual," 29; Grobsmith, "The Plains Culture Area," 191.

62. More about the division of the *wichášha wakhá* can be found in J. E. Brown, *The Sacred Pipe*, 45; W. K. Powers, *Sacred Language*, 164–65, 180–83, 194. For convenience the term "medicine man" is used also in this study to describe all *wichášha wakhá* unless otherwise translated.

63. See, for example, Neihardt and Black Elk, *Black Elk Speaks*, 28–47; DeMallie, "Lakota Belief and Ritual," 33–42; Walker, *Lakota Belief and Ritual*, 68, 73–74, 91–96.

64. Little Wound, American Horse, Lone Star, James R. Walker, George Sword, Bad Wound, No Flesh, and Thomas Tyon in Walker, *Lakota Belief and Ritual*, 68, 73–74, 91–96. See Malan and Jesser, *The Dakota Indian Religion*, 12–13; J. E. Brown, *The Sacred Pipe* (ed.), 45; W. K. Powers, *Sacred Language*, 164–65; Grobsmith, "The Plains Culture Area," 191.

65. W. K. Powers, *Sacred Language*, 111–13. William Powers makes the comparison to Christian ritual of baptism, where the water becomes sacred. A similar comparison is presented by V. Deloria Sr., "The Establishment of Christianity," 109.

66. J. E. Brown, *The Sacred Pipe*, 3–9; W. K. Powers, *Oglala Religion*, 86–88. For more about the significance of the pipe, see George Sword in Walker, *Lakota Belief and Ritual*, 82–83, 87–90; Neihardt and Black Elk, *Black Elk Speaks*, 1–6, 291–96; Hassrick, *The Sioux*, 257–65; Looking Horse, "The Sacred Pipe," 67–73.

67. Hassrick, *The Sioux*, 260; Mooney, *The Ghost-Dance Religion*, 1062–63.

68. J. E. Brown, *The Sacred Pipe*, 31–43; W. K. Powers, *Oglala Religion*, 135–36. For further information on the Lakota sweat lodge ceremony, see Bucko, *The Lakota Ritual*.

69. See J. E. Brown, *The Sacred Pipe*, 10–30; W. K. Powers, *Oglala Religion*, 93–95; C. A. Eastman, *The Soul of the Indian*, 18–24; DeMallie, "Lakota Belief and Ritual," 34–42; Densmore, *Teton Sioux Music and Culture*, 77–84.

70. Malan and Jesser, *The Dakota Indian Religion*, 12–1; Hultkrantz, *De Amerikanska indianernas religion*, 63–64; J. E. Brown, *The Sacred Pipe*, 44–46; Grobsmith, "The Plains Culture Area," 190–91; Densmore, *Teton Sioux Music and Culture*, 172–203. For more about the importance of the vision and of Black Elk's development into a medicine man, see Neihardt and Black Elk, *Black Elk Speaks*, 160–216; for further understanding of his experience, see DeMallie, *The Sixth Grandfather*, 111–41.

71. Thomas Tyon, Little Wound, American Horse, Lone Star, Bad Heart Bull, Short Bull, and James R. Walker in Walker, *Lakota Belief and Ritual*, 176–91. See J. E. Brown, *The Sacred Pipe*, 67–100; Grobsmith, "The Plains Culture Area," 192–94. A good description of the communal buffalo hunt is given by James R. Walker in Walker, *Lakota Society*, 74–94, and of the sun dance by High Bear, 96–99. See also Hassrick, *The Sioux*, 188–200; Densmore, *Teton Sioux Music and Culture*, 84–151.

72. J. E. Brown, *The Sacred Pipe,* 101–38. For more about Lakota kinship, see Thomas Tyon and James R. Walker in Walker, *Lakota Society,* 44–67; E. C. Deloria, *Speaking of Indians,* 24–38. See also DeMallie, "Change in American Indian Kinship Systems," 221–37; DeMallie, "Kinship and Biology," 130–43; DeMallie, "Kinship: The Foundation," 330–34, 339–50; DeMallie, "Teton," 808.

73. W. K. Powers, *Oglala Religion,* 47–54; W. K. Powers, *Sacred Language,* 127–44; Amiotte, "The Lakota Sun Dance," 75–88; DeMallie, "Lakota Belief and Ritual," 29. About the seven councilfires, *ochéthi šakówj,* see introduction.

74. For more about the importance of the circle, see Wissler, *Some Protective Designs,* 40–43; Neihardt and Black Elk, *Black Elk Speaks,* 198–200; J. E. Brown, *The Sacred Pipe,* 7. For more about the camp circle, see introduction.

75. Utley, *The Indian Frontier,* 243–45; M. Powers, *Oglala Woman,* 92; Lazarus, *Black Hills / White Justice,* 100–101. For more about Christianity and traditional Lakota religion, see C. A. Eastman, *The Soul of the Indian,* 18–24; E. C. Deloria, *Speaking of Indians,* 98–108. See also Markowitz, "The Catholic Mission and the Sioux."

76. ARCIA 1889, Report of Agent Hugh D. Gallagher, August 27, 1889, 150–57; ARCIA 1878, Report of the Commissioner of Indian Affairs Ezra A. Hayt, November 1, 1878, 779–81. See Olmstead, *History of Religion,* 415; M. Powers, *Oglala Woman,* 192–93.

77. The vision of Fast Thunder as told in *Illustrated American* 17, January 1891, 332, published also in Boyd, *Recent Indian Wars,* 193–94.

78. See Neihardt and Black Elk, *Black Elk Speaks,* 241–42; DeMallie, *The Sixth Grandfather,* 82–88 (introduction), 260–66. Black Elk had a vision, which became real in the form of the ghost dance ceremony. He saw the sacred tree and people dancing in a circle. In the vision he saw the return of the Lakota way of life and the restoration of the sacred hoop. To him, this was exactly what the ghost dance represented.

79. DeMallie, "The Lakota Ghost Dance," 404.

80. Mooney, *The Ghost-Dance Religion,* 918–19. See Miller, *Ghost Dance,* 59.

81. Bucko, *The Lakota Ritual,* 40–41, 255. See also *Illustrated American* 17, January 1891, 323; Boyd, *Recent Indian Wars,* 183–84; E. C. Deloria, *Speaking of Indians,* 81.

82. Mooney, *The Ghost-Dance Religion,* 822–23; Bucko, *The Lakota Ritual,* 40.

83. Mooney, *The Ghost-Dance Religion,* 823–24, 1062–63; *Illustrated American* 17, January 1891, 331; Boyd, *Recent Indian Wars,* 184. For more about the sacred pipe and the legend of the White Buffalo Calf Woman, see J. E. Brown, *The Sacred Pipe,* 3–9, 74–76; Neihardt and Black Elk, *Black Elk Speaks,* 1–6, 291–96; Hassrick, *The Sioux,* 257–65; Looking Horse, "The Sacred Pipe," 67–73.

84. Mooney, *The Ghost-Dance Religion,* 823, 915–16, 1063–64; J. E. Brown, *The Sacred Pipe,* 69; Miller, *Ghost Dance,* 60–61. A good description of a Lakota ghost dance ceremony was written by Special Agent Elisha B. Reynolds, who witnessed a ghost dance on Pine Ridge in September 1890. For his account, see Reynolds to CIA, Sep-

tember 25, 1890, NARS, RG 75, SC 188, M 4728, Roll 1, 1/22–26 (see also preface to this study). Another description can be found in E. G. Eastman, "The Ghost Dance War," 32–33. Short Bull later described the ceremonies: see Short Bull, Young Skunk, Pretty Eagle, EBMC, HRMSCA.

85. Discussion with Professor Raymond J. DeMallie, Bloomington IN, April 30, 2001. See Wissler, *Some Protective Designs*, 40–41.

86. W. K. Powers, *Voices from the Sprit World*, 28; Mooney, *The Ghost-Dance Religion*, 1061. Another opening song can be found in Mooney, *The Ghost-Dance Religion*, 1070. See also Reynolds to CIA, September 25, 1890, NARS, RG 75, SC 188, M 4728, Roll 1, 1/24–25.

87. Reynolds to CIA, September 25, 1890, NARS, RG 75, SC 188, M 4728, Roll 1, 24–26. See also Mooney, *The Ghost-Dance Religion*, 823, 920–21, 1061. For comparison to the Paiute ghost dance ceremony, see Hittman, *Wovoka*, 90–96. For more about traditional Lakota dances, see Densmore, *Teton Sioux Music and Culture*, 84–151, 468–84. See also Ostler, *The Plains Sioux*, 64–65.

88. Reynolds to CIA, September 25, 1890, NARS, RG 75, SC 188, M 4728, Roll 1, 24–26. See Mooney, *The Ghost-Dance Religion*, 920–21; *Illustrated American* 17, January 1891, 329.

89. Reynolds to CIA, September 25, 1890, NARS, RG 75, SC 188, M 4728, Roll 1, 24–25. See Mooney, *The Ghost-Dance Religion*, 920–22.

90. Mooney, *The Ghost-Dance Religion*, 915–21.

91. See *Illustrated American* 17, January 1891, 329; Thomas Tyon, William Garnett, George Sword, and John Blunt Horn in Walker, *Lakota Belief and Ritual*, 108; Neihardt and Black Elk, *Black Elk Speaks*, 241; J. E. Brown, *The Sacred Pipe*, 78–79; DeMallie, *The Sixth Grandfather*, 258–60; Mooney, *The Ghost-Dance Religion*, 823–24, 788. The newspapers are studied more carefully in chapter 5.

92. Pretty Eagle, EBMC, HRMSCA, 4–6; Young Skunk, EBMC, HRMSCA, 1–6; Reynolds to CIA, September 25, 1890, NARS, RG 75, SC 188, M 4728, Roll 1, 1/25–26. See Mooney, *The Ghost-Dance Religion*, 920–21. See also Wissler, *Some Protective Designs*, 40–45; Lesser, "Cultural Significance of the Ghost Dance," 110; Feher-Elston, *Raven Song*, 79. For more about traditional games, see Densmore, *Teton Sioux Music and Culture*, 485–91.

93. Mooney, *The Ghost-Dance Religion*, 916–17, 921; Feher-Elston, *Raven Song*, 79.

94. Young Skunk, EBMC, HRMSCA, 1–6; Pretty Eagle, EBMC, HRMSCA, 1–6; Mooney, *The Ghost-Dance Religion*, 915–16. See *Illustrated American* 17, January 1891, 332. See also chapter 2.

95. Sickels, "The Story of the Ghost Dance," 32–36; Mooney, *The Ghost-Dance Religion*, 1061–75. These songs are also published in L. W. Colby, "Wanagi Olovan Kin," Nebraska State Historical Society Proceedings and Collections, 1(3), 1895, 131–50. Songs by Young Skunk and Pretty Eagle can be found in EBMC, HRMSCA. Three songs were

published in Curtis, *The Indian's Book*, 47–48, 63–67. See also W. K. Powers, *Voices from the Spirit World*, 8–76; Wildhage, *Geistertanz-Lieder der Lakota*, 9–40. Performances of some of these Lakota ghost dance songs are recorded on *The Willard Rhodes Collection of North American Indian Music*, Catalogue 54–022–F, ATMIU.

96. Sickels, "The Story of the Ghost Dance," 32–36; Mooney, *The Ghost-Dance Religion*, 1061, 1065–70; W. K. Powers, *Voices from the Spirit World*, 27–45; Wildhage, *Geistertanz-Lieder Der Dakota*, 9–40.

97. Mooney, *The Ghost-Dance Religion*, 1064, 1069.

98. Mooney, *The Ghost-Dance Religion*, 1070. This song was sung by Short Bull to Natalie Curtis and is also published in Curtis, *The Indian's Book*, 48, 66; Wildhage, *Geistertanz-Lieder Der Dakota*, 9, 15, 18, 26. The song is also found on *The Willard Rhodes Collection of North American Indian Music*, Catalogue 54–022–F, ATL 58.6, ATMIU.

99. See, for example, Feher-Elston, *Raven Song*, 79. For more about the Lakota concepts of birds, see J. E. Brown, *Animals of the Soul*, 32–37.

100. Mooney, *The Ghost-Dance Religion*, 1068, 1072. See also Feher-Elston, *Raven Song*, 80.

101. Mooney, *The Ghost-Dance Religion*, 1072; also published in Wildhage, *Geistertanz-Lieder Der Dakota*, 27.

102. For comparison with the ghost dance songs of other nations, see Mooney, *The Ghost-Dance Religion*, 958–1055, 1081–102. For additional information on traditional Lakota songs, see Curtis, *The Indian's Book*, 49–90; Densmore, *Teton Sioux Music and Culture*, 12–62, 332–427. For comparison of the Lakota ghost dance songs and war songs, listen to the Lakota ghost dance songs on *The Willard Rhodes Collection of North American Indian Music*, Catalogue 54–022–F, ATMIU, and war songs on *The Joseph K. Dixon Collection*, Catalogue 54–109–F, ATMIU.

103. *Illustrated American* 17, January 1891, 330; Boyd, *Recent Indian Wars*, 189; Mooney, *The Ghost-Dance Religion*, 922–26.

104. An account given by Mrs. Z. A. Parker in ARCIA 1891, Report of Superintendent of Indian Schools Daniel Dorchester, September 30, 1890, 529–31; Z. A. Parker as quoted in Mooney, *The Ghost-Dance Religion*, 917.

105. Young Skunk, EBMC, HRMSCA, 1–6.

106. Young Skunk, EBMC, HRMSCA, 1–6.

107. Pretty Eagle, EBMC, HRMSCA, 4–6.

108. DeMallie, *The Sixth Grandfather*, 263–64. See also Neihardt and Black Elk, *Black Elk Speaks*, 245.

109. *Illustrated American* 17, January 1891, 330–31. Little Wound told about his vision through an interpreter. According to the writer of the article, the English text is an exact translation of Little Wound's speech. Little Wound's vision is also published in Boyd, *Recent Indian Wars*, 189–91. Other descriptions of visions were told by Short Bull, Young Skunk, and Pretty Eagle in EBMC, HRMSCA.

110. See E. C. Deloria, *Speaking of Indians*, 83.

111. See Colby, "The Sioux Indian War," 147; Mooney, *The Ghost-Dance Religion*, 788–89. See Zahn, *The Crimson Carnage*, 2; Hyde, *A Sioux Chronicle*, 261, 269. Except for Mooney, scholars generally believe that arms were carried during the ceremonies, but they are unsure about how frequently this really happened. The number of guns in the possession of the ghost dancers is also unclear. See Mooney, *The Ghost-Dance Religion*, 788; Zahn, *The Crimson Carnage*, 2; Hyde, *A Sioux Chronicle*, 261, 269. See also chapters 4–6.

112. Short Bull in Curtis, *The Indian's Book*, 45; Big Road as quoted in *Chicago Tribune*, November 26, 1890, 1, 5; anonymous eyewitness as quoted in *Omaha Daily Bee*, November 26, 1890, 1.

113. E. G. Eastman, "The Ghost Dance War," 33. There were incidents when the ghost dancers met the authorities with arms in their hands. Such an incident took place on Pine Ridge on August 24, but the dancing had already stopped, so no one can say whether guns were carried during the dance. See Gallagher to CIA, August 28, 1890, NARS, RG 75, LSASPR, M 1282, Roll 10, 387–88.

114. The policemen's story as told in McLaughlin to CIA, October 17, 1890, NARS, RG 75, SC 188, M 4728, Roll 1, 1/31–43, published also in ARCIA 1891, Report of the Commissioner of Indian Affairs T. J. Morgan, October 1, 1891, 125–26. See One Bull, UOLA, WSCMC, Box 104, Folders 10–11. See also McLaughlin, *My Friend the Indian*, 191; Hagan, *Indian Police and Judges*, 98–100; DeMallie, "The Lakota Ghost Dance," 394.

115. One Bull, UOLA, WSCMC, Box 104, Folders 10–11; John Carignan as quoted in NDHS, ABD, Vol. 2, 242. See Utley, *The Last Days*, 98; Miller, *Ghost Dance*, 107; Vestal, *Sitting Bull*, 272–73; W. S. E. Coleman, *Voices of Wounded Knee*, 74–75. Sitting Bull was reported to be interested in Christianity; he was especially fond of the Episcopalian denomination. Even James McLaughlin noted that Sitting Bull was sympathetic toward Christianity. See Mary C. Collins, IULL, WMCC, Box 6, Folder 3, Envelope, 78; Berghold, *The Indians' Revenge*, 193–96; Statement of Bishop Martin Marty in Berghold, *The Indians' Revenge*, 225–27; Father Aaron Beede as quoted in Hoover, "Sitting Bull," 166–67; discussion with Professor Raymond J. DeMallie, April 30, 2001, Bloomington IN. For more about James McLaughlin's comments, see chapter 2. Furthermore, the old Lakota religion, as noted above, did not rule out Christianity as such.

116. See, for example, D. M. Johnson, "Ghost Dance," 46; Malm, *Dödsdans i Dakota*, 92; Smith, *Moon of the Popping Trees*, 106; McLaughlin, *My Friend the Indian*, 192; Mooney, *The Ghost-Dance Religion*, 854–55; W. S. E. Coleman, *Voices of Wounded Knee*, 74–75.

117. *Illustrated American* 17, January 1891, 328; Boyd, *Recent Indian Wars*, 182. For newspaper accounts see chapter 5.

118. See One Bull, Mrs. One Bull, and Four Blanket Woman, IULL, WMCC, Box 5,

Folder 1, Envelope 41; Robert P. Higheagle, UOLA, WSCMC, Box 104, Folder 22; Old Bull, UOLA, WSCMC, Box 105, Notebook 11; Mary C. Collins, IULL, WMCC, Box 6, Folder 3, Envelope, 78. See also Smith, *Moon of the Popping Trees*, 103–5; Miller, *Ghost Dance*, 100–105; Vestal, *Sitting Bull*, 278; W. S. E. Coleman, *Voices of Wounded Knee*, 76–77. Miller's informants were, among others, One Bull (Sitting Bull's nephew), Henry Kills Alive, Louis Looking Horse, and White Bird. See Miller, *Ghost Dance*, 300.

119. John Carignan as quoted in NDHS, ABD, Vol. 2, 242; One Bull, UOLA, WSCMC, Box 104, Folders 10–11. See Utley, *The Last Days*, 100–102; Miller, *Ghost Dance*, 112–16; Mooney, *The Ghost-Dance Religion*, 848. About Mrs. Catherine Weldon and Sitting Bull, see W. F. Johnson, *The Red Record*, 187, 318–31; Smith, *Moon of the Popping Trees*, 101–3, 108–10; Miller, *Ghost Dance*, 66–69. Some of Weldon's letters can be found in Vestal, *New Sources*, 98–114.

120. The ghost dance was introduced to Lower Brulé and Crow Creek Reservations in November 1890. The agent promptly subdued it and the ghost dance never got a foothold on these reservations. See A. Dixon to ACIA (telegram), November 21, 1890, NARS, RG 75, SC 188, M 4728, Roll 1, 2/8–9; Dixon to CIA (telegram), November 28, 1890, NARS, RG 75, SC 188, M 4728, Roll 1, 2/52; Dixon to CIA (telegram), December 3, 1890, NARS, RG 75, SC 188, M 4728, Roll 1, 3/50; ARCIA, 1891, Report of Agent A. Dixon, August 28, 1891, 403; ARCIA 1891, Report of the Commissioner of Indian Affairs T. J. Morgan, October 1, 1891, 126. See also Schusky, "The Roots of Factionalism," 269. For this reason, these two reservations are left out of this study.

121. Torn Belly in Reynolds to CIA, NARS, RG 75, SC 188, M 4728, Roll 1, 1/23. See also Berghold, *The Indians' Revenge*, 212; Utley, *The Last Days*, 9, 96–98; Standing Bear, *My People the Sioux*, 219.

122. Neihardt and Black Elk, *Black Elk Speaks*, 246–48; Malm, *Dödsdans i Dakota*, 60; Mooney, *The Ghost-Dance Religion*, 788–91.

123. Indians were allowed to raise cattle on the Lakota reservations in the 1880s. At first the authorities were afraid to let them do so, because it was too close to the traditional nomadic Lakota life and so might have been a hindrance to their progress in civilization. However, the Act of 1889 encouraged cattle raising by promising more land to those who took up ranching. The harsh climate caused problems for cattle as well as for farming, but in some areas it was rather successful. Thus in 1890 the Lakotas had some cattle of their own in addition to the government's annual appropriations. See *Statutes at Large*, 25 Stat., Act of 1889, Sec. 8, 890. See also Textor, *Official Records*, 150; Hoxie, "From Prison to Homeland," 4.

124. Mooney, *The Ghost-Dance Religion*, 788–90. See also Wissler, *Some Protective Designs*, 31. In this study these sacred shirts are called "ghost shirts" or "ghost dance shirts" to avoid confusion.

125. For additional descriptions of the ghost dance shirts, see Pretty Eagle, EBMC,

HRMSCA, 4–6; George Sword in Sickels, "The Story of the Ghost Dance," 3; Mooney, *The Ghost-Dance Religion*, 789–90, 798, 919–20; Thomas Tyon, William Garnett, Thunder Bear, George Sword, and John Blunt Horn in Walker, *Lakota Belief and Ritual*, 108. See also Wissler, *Some Protective Designs*, 31–40; Feher-Elston, *Raven Song*, 92. A thorough study of the symbolism of colors, numbers, decorations, and designs used in the ghost dance clothing is presented in Thomas, *Crisis and Creativity*, 55–202.

126. See Thomas, *Crisis and Creativity*, 190–202.

127. See, for example, J. E. Brown, *The Sacred Pipe*, 6; J. E. Brown, *Animals of the Soul*, 32–37. For a comparison of the significance of birds in the traditional Lakota thought, and in the ghost dance, see Thomas, *Crisis and Creativity*, 72–78.

128. Sword in Sickels, "The Story of the Ghost Dance," 3; Mooney, *The Ghost-Dance Religion*, 797–798. See also Feher-Elston, *Raven Song*, 92; Miller, *Ghost Dance*, 81.

129. Mrs. Z. A. Parker as quoted in ARCIA 1891, Report of Superintendent of Indian Schools Daniel Dorchester, September 30, 1890, 529–31; Mrs. Z. A. Parker as quoted in Mooney, *The Ghost-Dance Religion*, 916–17. Mrs. Parker says that she asked why there were no metal objects or other commonly used decorations in the ghost shirts. The reply was that they were forbidden, since they were things brought by the white man. See also E. G. Eastman, "The Ghost Dance War," 32–33. A comprehensive analysis of the designs and decorations used in the ghost dance shirts is presented in Thomas, *Crisis and Creativity*.

130. Miller, *Ghost Dance*, 60.

131. Thomas, *Crisis and Creativity*, 53, 122.

132. Mooney, *The Ghost-Dance Religion*, 789–90.

133. See Boring, *Wovoka*, 50; Feher-Elston, *Raven Song*, 93; Hittman, *Wovoka*, 82–86.

134. Mooney, *The Ghost-Dance Religion*, 789–91; Hittman, *Wovoka*, 82–86. More about the Mormon influence can be found in Smoak, "The Mormons and the Ghost Dance of 1890"; Maddra, *Hostiles?*, 50–52.

135. Mrs. Z. A. Parker as quoted in ARCIA 1891, Report of Superintendent of Indian Schools Daniel Dorchester, September 30, 1890, 529; Reynolds to CIA, September 25, 1890, NARS, RG 75, SC 188, M 4728, Roll 1, 1/24. See Mrs. Z. A. Parker as quoted in Mooney, *The Ghost-Dance Religion*, 916, 917. See also Hyde, *A Sioux Chronicle*, 250; Utley, *The Last Days*, 76; Mooney, *The Ghost-Dance Religion*, 789–91; W. S. E. Coleman, *Voices of Wounded Knee*, 40–41. It is noteworthy that neither the army officers nor the press mentioned the ghost shirts before late November 1890. See chapters 3 and 5.

136. Neihardt and Black Elk, *Black Elk Speaks*, 245–48; DeMallie, *The Sixth Grandfather*, 259–62; Pretty Eagle, EBMC, HRMSCA, 4–6.

137. McLaughlin to CIA, October 17, 1890, NARS, RG 75, SC 188, M 4728, Roll 1, 1/31–33. Part of the letter is published in ARCIA 1891, Report of James McLaughlin October 17, 1890, 126–27. See Miller, *Ghost Dance*, 100. Kicking Bear's speech is in appendix 4.

138. McLaughlin to CIA, October 17, 1890, NARS, RG 75, SC 188, M 4728, Roll 1, 1/31–33. See Hyde, *A Sioux Chronicle*, 248. Hyde does not indicate where he got this information. Larson implies that the bulletproof shirts would have been used already in May 1890, but that is highly unlikely (Larson, *Red Cloud*, 269). Kicking Bear's speech is also published in the memoirs of Agent James McLaughlin. The speech was repeated to McLaughlin by One Bull, who was Sitting Bull's nephew but at that time was also a member of the Indian police force at Standing Rock (McLaughlin, *My Friend the Indian*, 185–89).

139. Short Bull in ARSW 1891, Report of the Major-General Commanding the Army, September 24, 1891, 142–43. The speech is also published in Mooney, *The Ghost-Dance Religion*, 788–89. See Appendix 5. See also SBD, BBMG, 4.

140. Phister, "The Indian Messiah," 107; Danberg, "Wovoka," 13–15; Thornton, *American Indian Holocaust*, 149; Hittman, *Wovoka*, 82–86.

141. Discussion with Professor Raymond J. DeMallie, December 25, 2000, Bloomington IN.

142. Pretty Eagle, EBMC, HRMSCA, 4–6; *Illustrated American* 17, January 1891, 330–31.

143. Mooney, *The Ghost-Dance Religion*, 1072–73. Another song that refers to the ghost shirt is in Mooney, *The Ghost-Dance Religion*, 1072. See also W. K. Powers, *Voices from the Spirit World*, 21; Wildhage, *Geistertanz-Lieder Der Dakota*, 27.

144. Short Bull in Walker, *Lakota Belief and Ritual*, 143.

145. *Illustrated American* 17, January 1891, 333; Wissler, *Some Protective Designs*, 33–39; Utley, *The Last Days*, 165.

146. Mooney, *The Ghost-Dance Religion*, 789–90. See also Thunder Bear in Walker, *Lakota Belief and Ritual*, 270–81; James R. Walker in Walker, *Lakota Society*, 99–107. For an analysis of traditional protective designs and paintings used in shields and in the ghost shirts, see Thomas, *Crisis and Creativity*, 121–55. A good analysis of the significance of the shield in Plains Indian cultures can be found in Hämäläinen, "The Study of the Plains Indian Shields." Vivid Lakota descriptions of Crazy Horse's "warmedicine" can be found in Jensen, *Voices of the American West*, vol. 1. See also Sandoz, *Crazy Horse*, 103–6; Sajna, *Crazy Horse*, 139–46.

147. Sword in Sickels, "The Story of the Ghost Dance," 31; Sword as quoted in Mooney, *The Ghost-Dance Religion*, 798. See Maddra, *Hostiles?*, 32. The new translation of George Swords's text was made by Raymond J. DeMallie, May 2007.

148. *Illustrated American* 17, January 1891, 330–31.

149. DeMallie, "The Lakota Ghost Dance," 392–93. See *Illustrated American* 17, January 1891, 327–28. The general feeling among the whites is well illustrated in the newspapers, which are studied in chapter 5.

150. Maj. Gen. Nelson A. Miles was the commander of the Division of Missouri and one of the military leaders who had subdued the tribes, including the Lakotas,

during the 1870s. See, for example, Mattes, "The Enigma of Wounded Knee," 3; Andrist, *The Long Death*, 286–300; Wooster, *The Military*, 65–66. More about General Miles's visit can be found in chapter 3.

151. Little Wound as quoted in Royer to ACIA, October 30, 1890, NARS, RG 75, SC 188, M 4728, Roll 1, 1/48–49. See Hyde, *A Sioux Chronicle*, 260; Utley, *The Last Days*, 104–5; Mooney, *The Ghost-Dance Religion*, 849.

152. See, for example, Red Cloud to T. A. Bland, December 10, 1890, in Cong. Rec., 51st Cong., 2nd Sess., December 19, 1890, 702–3; Red Cloud as quoted in Charles A. Eastman to Frank Wood (forwarded to ACIA), November 11, 1890, NARS, RG 75, SC 188, M 4728, Roll 1, 1/98–100. See also Olson, *Red Cloud and the Sioux Problem*, 327–28; Utley, *The Last Days*, 104; Larson, *Red Cloud*, 267–69, 275. When Red Cloud's actions during the ghost dance troubles are studied, it has to be taken into account that he was already an old man, approximately sixty-six, and he was going blind. See Royer to ACIA, October 30, 1890, NARS, RG 75, SC 188, M 4728, Roll 1, 1/48–49. See also chapter 2.

153. Short Bull as quoted in ARSW 1891, Report of the Major-General Commanding the Army, September 24, 1891, 142–43. See also Mooney, *The Ghost-Dance Religion*, 788–89, 849. The historian Jeffrey Ostler suggests that the speech might be a fabrication altogether (Ostler, *The Plains Sioux*, 295–96). For an interpretation of Short Bull's speech, see DeMallie, "The Lakota Ghost Dance," 394–95. The speech is in appendix 5.

154. Utley, *The Last Days*, 106; Miller, *Ghost Dance*, 119–20; Mooney, *The Ghost-Dance Religion*, 788–90. Approximately 1,800 Indians from Rosebud moved toward Pine Ridge. See SBD, BBMG, 4.

155. Utley, *The Last Days*, 106–7. See also *Illustrated American* 17, January 1891, 328.

156. See SBD, BBMG, 4–5. See also Maddra, *Hostiles?*, appendix 5, 199–200.

157. See Reynolds to CIA, September 25, 1890, NARS, RG 75, SC 188, M 4728, Roll 1, 1/22–23; Robert O. Pugh in Jensen, *Voices of the American West*, 2:67–71. See also C. A. Eastman, *The Soul of the Indian*, 94–95; Miller, *Ghost Dance*, 127–30. For more about the old rivalry among the Oglala People, see Hyde, *Red Cloud's Folk*, 55–57; Olson, *Red Cloud and the Sioux Problem*, 19–21.

158. Although the division followed the progressive–nonprogressive line to some extent, these groups are from now on referred to as the ghost dancers and the non-dancers when their attitudes directly toward the ghost dance are described. These terms illustrate the situation better and do not reflect the contemporary white attitudes. When the words "nonprogressive" and "progressive" or "hostiles" and "friendlies" are used, they describe these groups as understood by the contemporary whites and do not necessarily relate to the ghost dance.

159. C. A. Eastman, *From Deep Woods to Civilization*, 95; Mooney, *The Ghost-Dance Religion*, 848.

160. Neihardt and Black Elk, *Black Elk Speaks*, 242; Utley, *The Last Days*, 106. See also Little Wound, Kicking Bear, Two Strike, and American Horse as quoted in Colby, "The Sioux Indian War," 186–90. For more about the symbolic meaning of the good red road and the black road of error and destruction, see J. E. Brown, *The Sacred Pipe*, 7.

161. Little Wound, Kicking Bear, Two Strike, and American Horse as quoted in Colby, "The Sioux Indian War," 186–90. See also DeMallie, "The Lakota Ghost Dance," 393–94.

162. The table was constructed using ARCIA 1890, Report of Agent James McLaughlin, August 26, 1890, Report of Agent Charles E. McChesney, August 25, 1890, Report of Agent J. George Wright, August 26, 1890, and Report of Agent Hugh D. Gallagher, August 28, 1890, 37, 42, 50, 57, 450. The percentages are taken from Utley, *The Last Days*, 112. There were 1,791 Yanktonai Sioux living on Standing Rock Reservation and 167 Northern Cheyenne on Rosebud and 517 on Pine Ridge. Because these people were not Lakotas, they are excluded from the table. Since the ghost dance never became a major issue on the Lower Brulé and Crow Creek Reservations the 2,084 Indians living there are also excluded.

163. Utley, *The Last Days*, 112. Agent James McLaughlin also stated that the percentage on Standing Rock Reservation was approximately 10 (McLaughlin, *My Friend the Indian*, 192). See also Royer to ACIA, October 30, 1890, NARS, RG 75, SC 188, M 4728, Roll 1, 1/48. The Lakota agents' estimations are more carefully studied in chapter 2.

164. Mooney, *The Ghost-Dance Religion*, 926–27; Andersson, "Henkitanssi," 92–94; Andersson, "Wanáǧi Wachípi kį," 149–52. The 2,084 people living on the Lower Brulé and Crow Creek Reservations are not included in the 15,000 mentioned here. The total number of all the Sioux people was approximately 26,000, and Mooney mistakenly based his estimate on this number. The white estimates of the Lakota ghost dancers' strength ranged from 6,000 to 27,000. For contemporary white estimates, see chapters 2–3, 5–6.

165. Mooney, *The Ghost-Dance Religion*, 847–48; Andersson, *Henkitanssi*, 92–94; Andersson, "Wanáǧi Wachípi kį," 148–52.

166. See Josephine Waggoner Papers, "Notes on Gall," Museum of the Fur Trade, Chadron NE. See also E. C. Deloria, *Speaking of Indians*, 100–101.

167. See chapters 2–3, 5–6.

168. See, for example, Royer to ACIA, October 30, 1890, NARS, RG 75, SC 188, M 4728, Roll 1, 1/47–50, published also in ARSW 1891, 144; Royer to CIA (telegram), November 15, 1890, NARS, RG 75, SC 188, M 4728, Roll 1, pp, 1/91–92, published also in ARCIA 1891, Report of the Commissioner of Indian Affairs T. J. Morgan, October 1, 1891, 128. See also Hyde, *A Sioux Chronicle*, 263; Utley, *The Last Days*, 109; Mooney, *The Ghost-Dance Religion*, 849. For more about the developments leading to the troops' arrival, see chapters 2 and 3.

169. Most notable, as mentioned in the introduction, was the seven-year-long struggle between Red Cloud and Agent Valentine T. McGillicuddy at Pine Ridge. This power struggle came to an end when the agent was relieved of duty in 1887. It is also worth mentioning that despite extreme tensions on Pine Ridge, the agent never called for the army. The agent himself said that both he and Red Cloud understood the situation perfectly, and from the first moments they realized that they were rivals. From that point on it was a battle of wills. See, for example, Valentine T. McGillicuddy, IULL, WMCC, Box 4, Folder 3, Envelope 4; ARCIA 1883, Report of Agent Valentine T. McGillicuddy, August 10, 1883, 35; ARCIA 1884, Report of Agent Valentine T. McGillicuddy, September 1, 1884, 81. See also Olson, *Red Cloud and the Sioux Problem*, 282–86; Larson, *Red Cloud*, 217–48.

170. C. A. Eastman, *From Deep Woods to Civilization*, 100–101; Mattes, "The Enigma of Wounded Knee," 3; Standing Bear, *My People the Sioux*, 223.

171. Utley, *The Last Days*, 117; Miller, *Ghost Dance*, 137–38.

172. Weasel as quoted in Boyd, *Recent Indian Wars*, 194–95.

173. Two Strike and Crow Dog as quoted in Colby, "The Sioux Indian War," 187–89; George Little Wound in Jensen, *Voices of the American West*, 1:232–33. See also Utley, *The Last Days*, 118; Mooney, *The Ghost-Dance Religion*, 850–52. These 700 Oglalas were dissatisfied because they had been forced to move from their homes due to the new line of the reservation border, established by the Act of 1889. Their location had caused problems during the census and they were not allowed to move from Rosebud to Pine Ridge, even if they wanted to (Gallagher to CIA, July 18, 1890, NARS, RG 75, LSASPR, M 1282, Roll 10, 327–28). About the borders, see *Statutes at Large*, 25 Stat., Act of 1889, Sec. 1–2, 888–90. In general, the problem of reservation borders had been festering for several years. An old Indian commentary was "Why does not the white man take boundaries made by God, like the rivers and mountain ranges or buttes?" ("An Indian Joke," IULL, WMCC Box 4, Folder 3, Envelope 4). The issue of the borderlines became a major problem during the negotiations of 1888 and 1889. By this time the Indians clearly understood the importance of borderlines and they were strongly opposed to any new arrangements. Although they still had difficulty understanding the maps the commissioners showed them, they realized the main point: that the borderlines were not as they had been promised in their negotiations with government officials. For more information, see 50th Cong., 2nd Sess., *Senate Executive Document*, No. 17, Vol. 1, Serial, 2610; 51st Cong., 1st Sess., *Senate Executive Document*, No. 51, Vol. 5, Serial 2682. See also chapter 2.

174. ARSW 1891, Report of Maj. Gen. Nelson A. Miles, September 24, 1891, 147. See also Mooney, *The Ghost-Dance Religion*, 861–62. More about Agent Palmer appears in chapter 2.

175. See, for example, One Bull, UOLA, WSCMC, Box 104, Folder 11. See also Zahn,

The Crimson Carnage, 3; Malm, *Dödsdans i Dakota,* 164–66; Hagan, *Indian Police and Judges,* 100.

176. Wooster, *The Military,* 193–94. For more about the army's strategy, see chapter 3.

177. C. A. Eastman, *From Deep Woods to Civilization,* 101; Utley, *The Last Days,* 118; Miller, *Ghost Dance,* 139–40.

178. Hyde, *A Sioux Chronicle,* 271; Utley, *The Last Days,* 120–21; Smith, *Moon of the Popping Trees,* 134.

179. SBD, BBMG, 4–5. See Maddra, *Hostiles?,* appendix 5, 199–200. See also Two Strike and Short Bull as quoted in W. S. E. Coleman, *Voices of Wounded Knee,* 112–14. Descriptions of the Stronghold can be found in Malm, *Dödsdans i Dakota,* 159; Utley, *The Last Days,* 121–22; Smith, *Moon of the Popping Trees,* 134–35; Standing Bear, *My People the Sioux,* 226–27; Miller, *Ghost Dance,* 152–58; DeMallie, *The Sixth Grandfather,* 269; Mooney, *The Ghost-Dance Religion,* 852–53. After the trouble, several hundred Lakotas filed claims for the depredations of the ghost dancers. Special Agent James A. Cooper conducted an investigation, in which he determined that 744 of these claims were acceptable, and altogether $98,383.46 was finally appropriated for these claimants. Interestingly, among the 744 Lakotas who received money were Short Bull, No Water, Jack Red Cloud, Red Cloud, and Big Road, all more or less accused of being ghost dance leaders (52nd Cong., 2nd Sess., *Senate Executive Document,* No. 93, Vol. 8, Serial 3062, 1–13). See also Eli R. Paul, "Dakota Resources: The Investigation of Special Agent Cooper and Property Damage Claims in the Winter of 1890–1891," *South Dakota History* 24(3–4), 1994.

180. Hyde, *A Sioux Chronicle,* 270, 272. Hyde does not give any source for this information.

181. About Plenty Horses and the killing of Lieutenant Casey, see ARCIA 1891, Report of the Commissioner of Indian Affairs T. J. Morgan, October 1, 1891, 132. See also Utley, *The Indian Frontier,* 245.

182. Standing Bear, *My People the Sioux,* 221–22; Miller, *Ghost Dance,* 91–93, 139–40.

183. Utley, *The Last Days,* 121; Smith, *Moon of the Popping Trees,* 133–35; Miller, *Ghost Dance,* 152–58; Mooney, *The Ghost-Dance Religion,* 851.

184. SBD, BBMG, 4–5. See also Maddra, *Hostiles?,* appendix 5, 199–200. See Man Above in Jensen, *Voices of the American West,* 1:240–41; ARCIA 1891, Report of the Commissioner of Indian Affairs T. J. Morgan, October 1, 1891, 131. See Short Bull and Two Strike as quoted in W. S. E. Coleman, *Voices of Wounded Knee,* 112–14. See also Miller, *Ghost Dance,* 301.

185. Miles to the AG (telegram), November 24, 1890, NARS, RG 94, AIWKSC, M 983, Roll 1, Vol. 1, 209, 219. See also Colby, "The Sioux Indian War," 152; Utley, *The Last Days,* 135; Standing Bear, *My People the Sioux,* 219–21.

186. Man Above in Jensen, *Voices of the American West*, 1:240–41. See W. F. Johnson, *The Red Record*, 304–10; Miller, *Ghost Dance*, 152–58; Kreis, *Rothäute, Schwarzröcke und Heilige Frauen*, 83–84.

187. Man Above in Jensen, *Voices of the American West*, 1:240–41. See also Hyde, *A Sioux Chronicle*, 274; Standing Bear, *My People the Sioux*, 227; Smith, *Moon of the Popping Trees*, 143–45; Kreis, *Rothäute, Schwarzröcke, und Heilige Frauen*, 84.

188. Utley, *The Last Days*, 120; McGillicuddy, *Blood on the Moon*, 259–63; Miller, *Ghost Dance*, 142–52.

189. W. F. Johnson, *The Red Record*, 304–10, 414–19; Neihardt and Black Elk, *Black Elk Speaks*, 252; Miller, *Ghost Dance*, 169–71; Kreis, *Rothäute, Schwarzröcke, und Heilige Frauen*, 102–3. The footnote in *Black Elk Speaks* says that the Black Robe was Father J. M. Craft, but according to other sources, it was Father John Jutz (Neihardt and Black Elk, *Black Elk Speaks*, 252). The work by Karl Markus Kreis is valuable because it contains discussions between the ghost dance leaders and Father Jutz taken from the priest's personal accounts, written in German. They are preserved in the Marquette University Archives (Milwaukee WI) and published by Kreis with very little editing (Kreis, *Rothäute, Schwarzröcke, und Heilige Frauen*, preface). See chapter 4. See also Short Bull, as quoted in W. S. E. Coleman, *Voices of Wounded Knee*, 115.

190. Hyde, *A Sioux Chronicle*, 274–75; Miller, *Ghost Dance*, 171. According to Hyde, the apostles had promised, among other things, that there would be no winter at all, but in December 1890 the cold weather arrived as always (Hyde, *A Sioux Chronicle*, 274–75).

191. For more about the death of Crazy Horse, see Sandoz, *Crazy Horse*, 259–62; Sajna, *Crazy Horse*, 320–24; Bray, *Crazy Horse*, 360–91.

192. Neihardt and Black Elk, *Black Elk Speaks*, 252–53; Smith, *Moon of the Popping Trees*, 143–45; Miller, *Ghost Dance*, 172–74. Short Bull himself later noted that he urged the ghost dancers to go back to the agency, sell their ponies, and, with the money, pay for the cattle they had killed. He did not want any trouble and did not like the idea of killing other people's cattle. See SBD, BBMG, 1–4. See also W. S. E. Coleman, *Voices of Wounded Knee*, 165–66.

193. Utley, *The Last Days*, 143–44; Miller, *Ghost Dance*, 173–74.

194. Indian policeman Lone Man, IULL, WMCC, Box 5, Folder 1, Envelope 41; One Bull, UOLA, WSCMC, Box 104, Folders 10–11. See Miller, *Ghost Dance*, 49, 116; W. S. E. Coleman, *Voices of Wounded Knee*, 76. Agent McLaughlin's version of the events can be found in chapter 2.

195. Miller, *Ghost Dance*, 116; McLaughlin, *My Friend the Indian*, 206–7; Vestal, *Sitting Bull*, 277.

196. Sitting Bull to James McLaughlin, as quoted in Vestal, *Sitting Bull*, 283–84. See One Bull, UOLA, WSCMC, Box 104, Folder 11; John Carignan, NDHS, ABD, Vol. 2, 242. See

also Utley, *The Last Days*, 152–53; Smith, *Moon of the Popping Trees*, 150; Miller, *Ghost Dance*, 117; Vestal, *Sitting Bull*, 279, 282–85.

197. Mary C. Collins, IULL, WMCC, Box 6, Folder 3, Envelope 78; Sitting Bull to McLaughlin, as quoted in Vestal, *Sitting Bull*, 283–84. See also Smith, *Moon of the Popping Trees*, 150; Miller, *Ghost Dance*, 116.

198. Indian policeman Grey Eagle, IULL, WMCC, Box 5, Folder 1, Envelope 41. About Sitting Bull and Grey Eagle, see Mary C. Collins, IULL, WMCC, Box 6, Folder 3, Envelope 78; G. W. Reed, IULL, WMCC, Box 5, Folder 1, Envelope 41. Both Mary C. Collins and the Reverend G. W. Reed were convinced that Sitting Bull had no intentions of leaving. Reed furthermore said that the only indication that Sitting Bull had been planning to leave was that he was feeding his horses (G. W. Reed, IULL, WMCC, Box 5, Folder 1, Envelope 41). Indian accounts concur that Sitting Bull did not intend to leave the reservation. See Four Blanket Woman, One Bull, Mrs. One Bull, IULL, WMCC, Box 5, Folder 1, Envelope 41. See also W. F. Johnson, *The Red Record*, 187, 318–31; Smith, *Moon of the Popping Trees*, 152; Miller, *Ghost Dance*, 66–69, 134–36.

199. One Bull, "Prophecy of Sitting Bull Would be Killed by His Own People" UOLA, WSCMC, Box 104, Folder 21. See Vestal, *Sitting Bull*, 278; Utley, *The Lance and the Shield*, 290. See also Miller, *Ghost Dance*, 116; Mooney, *The Ghost-Dance Religion*, 855. Miller's informant was Sitting Bull's nephew One Bull.

200. Four Blanket Woman, One Bull, Mrs. One Bull, Indian policemen Lone Man and Grey Eagle, IULL, WMCC, Box 5, Folder 1, Envelope 41. The events surrounding the arrest and death of Sitting Bull are documented in ARSW 1891, 146–47. For Indian accounts of the arrest, see Walter Mason Camp Collection (several informants), IULL, WMCC, Box 5, Folder 1, Envelope 41; Shoots Walking, UOLA, WSCMC, Box 104, Folder 5; Little Soldier, UOLA, WSCMC, Box 104, Folder 6; One Bull, UOLA, WSCMC, Box 104, Folders 10–11; Robert P. Higheagle, UOLA, WSCMC, Box 104, Folder 22; Old Bull, UOLA, WSCMC, Box 105, Notebook 11. Lone Man and Robert P. Higheagle as quoted in Vestal, *New Sources*, 45–55; Miller, *Ghost Dance*, 182–90; Vestal, *Sitting Bull*, 286–302. Miller's informants were policemen White Bull and Little Soldier, One Bull's wife, John Sitting Bull, and Henry Sitting Bull. See Miller, *Ghost Dance*, 303.

201. Indian policeman Lone Man, IULL, WMCC, Box 5, Folder 1, Envelope 41. See also Zahn, *The Crimson Carnage*, 4; Malm, *Dödsdans i Dakota*, 164; Hagan, *Indian Police and Judges*, 100–102; Miller, *Ghost Dance*, 76. One Bull, Sitting Bull's nephew, told about a policeman who asked One Bull to kill him because "we're all drunk. We ruined each other here" (Miller, *Ghost Dance*, 190). The policemen "smelled of Whiskey," claimed Four Blanket Woman (IULL, WMCC, Box 5, Folder 1, Envelope 41). However, Robert M. Utley has noted that the stories of the policemen being drunk were not substantiated by any other source nor by the actions of the policemen during the arrest (Utley, *The Lance and the Shield*, 310). For more about the dispute between Sitting Bull and Bull Head, see Utley, *The Last Days*, 150.

202. Indian policemen Grey Eagle and Lone Man, IULL, WMCC, Box 5, Folder 1, Envelope 41. Among the casualties was Crow Foot, Sitting Bull's son. Policeman Lone Man said they killed him because he was the cause of the trouble. However, some eyewitnesses say that Crow Foot never said a word and was viciously killed by the policemen (Four Blanket Woman and Mrs. One Bull, IULL, WMCC, Box 5, Folder, 1, Envelope 41). For more about the army's conceptions of these events, see chapter 3. Excellent studies of these events can be found in Miller, *Ghost Dance*, 182–90; Mooney, *The Ghost-Dance Religion*, 857–58; Utley, *The Lance and the Shield*, 291–305. Sitting Bull's death immediately raised questions about the circumstances under which he died, and many stories were published in newspapers and books soon after his death. Some newspaper accounts are discussed in chapter 5. For early accounts of Sitting Bull's life and death, see W. F. Johnson, *The Red Record*; Boyd, *Recent Indian Wars*.

203. W. F. Johnson, *The Red Record*, 426–27; Utley, *The Last Days*, 165; Miller, *Ghost Dance*, 186–88; Utley, *The Lance and the Shield*, 396. Sitting Bull joined Buffalo Bill's *Wild West Show* in 1885, and his favorite horse learned to react to shooting. During the fighting on December 15, Sitting Bull's horse became excited because of the gunfire and started to perform the tricks it had been taught during its years in Buffalo Bill's show. This made many Indians wonder whether the spirit of Sitting Bull had entered the horse. However, Utley has noted that this story, although very often told, is probably apocryphal since it is not substantiated by Indian accounts. Whatever the truth, the story is a good one, and as Utley noted, it has lived through many accounts of Sitting Bull's death. See W. F. Johnson, *The Red Record*, 426–27; Utley, *The Last Days*, 165; Utley, *The Lance and the Shield*, 396. For more about Sitting Bull's life in Buffalo Bill's *Wild West Show*, see Utley, *The Lance and the Shield*, 260–69.

204. See also DeMallie, "The Lakota Ghost Dance," 394.

205. For more about the tensions during the negotiations with the Sioux commission, see the introduction.

206. Joseph Horn Cloud in Jensen, *Voices of the American West*, 1:191–208; Dewey Beard in Jensen, *Voices of the American West*, 1:208–26. See Mattes, "The Enigma of Wounded Knee," 3; Utley, *The Last Days*, 173–86; Danker, "The Wounded Knee Interviews," 164–200; Miller, *Ghost Dance*, 198–200.

207. Miller, *Ghost Dance*, 196–97. For more about these events, see chapters 3 and 5.

208. Joseph Horn Cloud in Jensen, *Voices of the American West*, 1:191–208; Dewey Beard in Jensen, *Voices of the American West*, 1:208–26; Andrew Good Thunder, IULL, WMCC, Box 6, Folder 14, Envelope 90. See ARSW 1891, Report of Maj. Gen. Nelson A. Miles, September 24, 1891, 147. See also Utley, *The Last Days*, 132; Mooney, *The Ghost-Dance Religion*, 862. For more about General Miles's tactics and Captain Ewers's efforts, see chapter 3.

209. Andrew Good Thunder, IULL, WMCC, Box 6, Folder 14, Envelope 90; Joseph

Horn Cloud in Jensen, *Voices of the American West*, 1:191–208; Dewey Beard in Jensen, *Voices of the American West*, 1:208–26; Beard in Walker, *Lakota Society*, 158; Dewey Beard, Louise Weasel Bear, Bertha Kills Close to Lodge, Rough Feather, and Nellie Knife in McGregor, *The Wounded Knee Massacre*, 95, 101, 106, 119, 130.

210. Joseph Horn Cloud in Jensen, *Voices of the American West*, 1:191–208; Dewey Beard in Jensen, *Voices of the American West*, 1:208–26. See also Utley, *The Last Days*, 178; Smith, *Moon of the Popping Trees*, 166–68; Miller, *Ghost Dance*, 200.

211. Big Foot as quoted in ARSW 1891, Statement of Interpreter Felix Benoit, January 18, 1891, 237–38; Joseph Horn Cloud in Jensen, *Voices of the American West*, 1:191–208; Dewey Beard in Jensen, *Voices of the American West*, 1:208–26. See also Bull Eagle, IULL, WMCC, Box 4, Folder 4, Envelope 5; Andrew Good Thunder, IULL, WMCC, Box 6, Folder 14, Envelope 90. Lt. Col. E. V. Sumner was totally convinced that Big Foot's intentions were peaceful. See Sumner to Miles, December 21 and December 22, 1890, in ARSW 1891, Report of Major-General Commanding the Army, September 24, 1891, 232–33; Miles to AG (telegram), December 24, 1890, NARS, RG 94, AIWKSC, M 983, Roll 1, Vol. 1, 608. See also chapter 3.

212. Andrew Good Thunder, IULL, WMCC, Box 6, Folder 14, Envelope 90; Joseph Horn Cloud in Jensen, *Voices of the American West*, 1:191–208; Dewey Beard in Jensen, *Voices of the American West*, 1:208–26. See also Beard in Walker, *Lakota Society*, 158–59.

213. Andrew Good Thunder, IULL, WMCC, Box 6, Folder 14, Envelope 90; Joseph Horn Cloud in Jensen, *Voices of the American West*, 1:191–208; Dewey Beard in Jensen, *Voices of the American West*, 1:208–26; ARSW 1891, Statement of Interpreter Felix Benoit, January 18, 1891, 237–38; ARSW 1891, Statement of John Dunn, no date, 235–37. See also Beard in Walker, *Lakota Society*, 158–59. Despite their popular style of writing, these events are well portrayed in Smith, *Moon of the Popping Trees*, 172–74; Seymour, *Sitanka*, 127–31; Miller, *Ghost Dance*, 200–201.

214. The best accounts of the escape are given by Joseph Horn Cloud in Jensen, *Voices of the American West*, 1:191–208; Dewey Beard in Jensen, *Voices of the American West*, 1:208–26; Andrew Good Thunder, IULL, WMCC, Box 6, Folder 14, Envelope 90; Beard in Walker, *Lakota Society*, 160. See also W. F. Johnson, *The Red Record*, 426–27; McGregor, *The Wounded Knee Massacre*, 95–98; Seymour, *Sitanka*, 136–47; Miller, *Ghost Dance*, 205, 208–11. Miller's informants were Pipe On Head and Iron Hail. Walker's and McGregor's informant, Beard, is also known as Dewey Beard, Dewey Horn Cloud, and Iron Hail (Walker, *Lakota Society*, 122).

215. Andrew Good Thunder, IULL, WMCC, Box 6, Folder 14, Envelope 90; James Grass, 75th Cong., 1st Sess, House Committee on Indian Affairs, Published Hearing, March 7 and May 12, 1938, IULAL, Microfiche, Group 3, Card 5, 48. James Grass was one of the scouts for the troops.

216. Andrew Good Thunder, IULL, WMCC, Box 6, Folder 14, Envelope 90; Joseph

Horn Cloud in Jensen, *Voices of the American West*, 1:191–208; Dewey Beard in Jensen, *Voices of the American West*, 1:208–26; John Shangrau in Jensen, *Voices of the American West*, 1:256–64; James Pipe On Head, 75th Cong., 1st Sess, House Committee on Indian Affairs, Published Hearing, March 7 and May 12, 1938, IULAL, Microfiche, Group 3, Card 4, 17. See also James Pipe On Head, Louise Weasel Bear, White Lance, and Dog Chief in McGregor, *The Wounded Knee Massacre*, 98, 101, 109, 124–25.

217. Andrew Good Thunder, IULL, WMCC, Box 6, Folder 14, Envelope 90; Dewey Beard in Jensen, *Voices of the American West*, 1:208–26; Beard in Walker, *Lakota Society*, 161–63; Dewey Beard, Bertha Kills Close to Lodge, Edward Owl King, Kills Plenty, Peter Stand, and Dog Chief in McGregor, *The Wounded Knee Massacre*, 95–96, 106, 107–8, 116, 124–25. See also Zahn, *The Crimson Carnage*, 5; Mattes, "The Enigma of Wounded Knee," 3; Miller, *Ghost Dance*, 218–23; Jensen, "Big Foot's Followers," 194–99.

218. Andrew Good Thunder, IULL, WMCC, Box 6, Folder 14, Envelope 90; John Shangrau in Jensen, *Voices of the American West*, 1:256–64; Joseph Horn Cloud in Jensen, *Voices of the American West*, 1:191–208; Dewey Beard in Jensen, *Voices of the American West*, 1:208–26; James Pipe On Head, 75th Cong., 1st Sess, House Committee on Indian Affairs, Published Hearing, March 7 and May 12, 1938, IULAL, Microfiche, Group 3, Card 4, 17; Beard in Walker, *Lakota Society*, 163–64; Louise Weasel Bear, George Running Hawk, Mrs. Mousseau, Bertha Kills Close to Lodge, and Mrs. Rough Feather in McGregor, *The Wounded Knee Massacre*, 101, 102, 105, 106–7, 119–20. Dewey Beard later claimed that the men carried no guns under their blankets when they were in the circle. He said that the soldiers who were killed there were shot by other soldiers, not by Indians. See Dewey Beard, 75th Cong., 1st Sess, House Committee on Indian Affairs, Published Hearing, March 7 and May 12, 1938, IULAL; Microfiche, Group 3, Card 4, 22.

219. Joseph Horn Cloud in Jensen, *Voices of the American West*, 1:191–208; Dewey Beard in Jensen, *Voices of the American West*, 1:208–26; Phillip Wells in Jensen, *Voices of the American West*, 1:126–63; Statement of the Survivors, IULL, WMCC, Box 4; Folder 4, Envelope 5 (the statement is written in Lakota and translated by Rani-Henrik Andersson); Beard in Walker, *Lakota Society*, 163–65; Dewey Beard, Rough Feather, Bertha Kills Close to Lodge, White Lance, John Little Finger, and Richard Afraid of Hawk in McGregor, *The Wounded Knee Massacre*, 95–96, 99–100, 106, 109, 111, 121; Testimony of Interpreter Phillip F. Wells, NARS, RG 94, AIWKSC, M 983, Roll 1, Vol. 1, 711–16. See also Neihardt and Black Elk, *Black Elk Speaks*, 266–67; Smith, *Moon of the Popping Trees*, 184–88; Miller, *Ghost Dance*, 224, 227–28.

220. See Mooney, *The Ghost-Dance Religion*, 917.

221. Andrew Good Thunder, IULL, WMCC, Box 6, Folder 14, Envelope 90; Dewey Beard in Jensen, *Voices of the American West*, 1:208–26; Louie Mousseau in Jensen, *Voices of the American West*, 1:226–32; James Pipe On Head, 75th Cong., 1st Sess,

House Committee on Indian Affairs, Published Hearing, March 7and May 12, 1938, IULAL, Microfiche, Group 3, Card 4, 18–19; Dewey Beard, 75th Cong., 1st Sess, House Committee on Indian Affairs, Published Hearing, March 7 and May 12, 1938, IULAL, Microfiche, Group 3, Card 4, 22–24; Beard in Walker, *Lakota Society*, 164–65; Statements of the survivors in McGregor, *The Wounded Knee Massacre*, 95–130; Danker, "The Wounded Knee Interviews," 226–33. Phillip Wells, who was an army scout, maintains that if the Indians had planned any resistance, they would have resisted before coming to Wounded Knee Creek, where they were actually prisoners of war. According to Wells, the Indians could have taken advantage of the terrain and their greater numbers at the time they first met the soldiers. This, he argued, shows that no plan for resistance existed (Phillip Wells in Jensen, *Voices of the American West*, 1:126–63). For different interpretations and for a discussion of the beginning of the fight, see Zahn, *The Crimson Carnage*, 5–6; McGregor, *The Wounded Knee Massacre*, 95–130; Mattes, "The Enigma of Wounded Knee," 4, 6; Utley, *The Last Days*, 212–13; Sievers, "The Historiography of 'The Bloody Field,'" 37–39; Seymour, *Sitanka*, 156–70; Miller, *Ghost Dance*, 229–30; Mooney, *The Ghost-Dance Religion*, 884–86. For more about the significance of showing grief among the Lakotas, see Thomas Tyon in Walker, *Lakota Belief and Ritual*, 163–64.

222. Dewey Beard in Jensen, *Voices of the American West*, 1:208–26; Beard in Walker, *Lakota Society*, 165; Statement of the Survivors, IULL, WMCC, Box 4; Folder 4, Envelope 5; James Pipe On Head, 75th Cong., 1st Sess, House Committee on Indian Affairs, Published Hearing, March 7 and May 12, 1938, IULAL, Microfiche, Group 3, Card 4, 18–19; Joseph Horn Cloud in Jensen, *Voices of the American West*, 1:191–208. See Sievers, "The Historiography of 'The Bloody Field,'" 50; Miller, *Ghost Dance*, 229–30.

223. Mooney, *The Ghost-Dance Religion*, 868–69, 884–86; Andrew Good Thunder, IULL, WMCC, Box 6, Folder 14, Envelope 90; Statements of the survivors in McGregor, *The Wounded Knee Massacre*, 95–130; Statements of Frog and Help Them, January 7, 1891, NARS, RG 94, AIWKSC M 983, Roll 1, Vol. 1, 717–20. For comparison, see Utley, *The Last Days*, 205–13; Smith, *Moon of the Popping Trees*, 187–98; Seymour, *Sitanka*, 171–82; Utter, *Wounded Knee*, 22. See also chapter 3.

224. Andrew Good Thunder, IULL, WMCC, Box 6, Folder 14, Envelope 90; Dewey Beard in Jensen, *Voices of the American West*, 1:208–26; Joseph Horn Cloud in Jensen, *Voices of the American West*, 1:191–208; William Garnett in Jensen, *Voices of the American West*, 1:99–100; Statement of the Survivors, IULL, WMCC, Box 4; Folder 4, Envelope 5; James Pipe On Head, 75th Cong., 1st Sess, House Committee on Indian Affairs, Published Hearing, March 7 and May 12, 1938, IULAL, Microfiche, Group 3, Card 4, 18–19; Beard in Walker, *Lakota Society*, 165; Dewey Beard, James Pipe On Head, Rough Feather, White Lance, John Little Finger, Donald Blue Hair, Afraid of the Enemy, Richard Afraid of Hawk, Dog Chief, and Charlie Blue Arm in McGregor,

The Wounded Knee Massacre, 97–100, 109, 111, 117–18, 121–22, 125, 128. See also Smith, *Moon of the Popping Trees*, 188–91; Miller, *Ghost Dance*, 229–31; Mooney, *The Ghost-Dance Religion*, 884–86.

225. Dewey Beard in Jensen, *Voices of the American West*, 1:208–26; Joseph Horn Cloud in Jensen, *Voices of the American West*, 1:191–208; Man Above in Jensen, *Voices of the American West*, 1:240–41; John Shangrau in Jensen, *Voices of the American West*, 1:256–64; William Garnett in Jensen, *Voices of the American West*, 1:99–100; Peter Mc-Farland in Jensen, *Voices of the American West*, 2:1–10; William Peano in Jensen, *Voices of the American West*, 1:233–37; Dewey Beard, 75th Cong., 1st Sess, House Committee on Indian Affairs, Published Hearing, March 7 and May 12, 1938, IULAL, Microfiche, Group 3, Card 4, 22–24; James Pipe On Head, 75th Cong., 1st Sess, House Committee on Indian Affairs, Published Hearing, March 7 and May 12, 1938, IULAL, Microfiche, Group 3, Card 4, 18–19. For more about the events during the fight from the Indians' point of view, see Beard in Walker, *Lakota Society*, 165–68; Statements of the survivors in McGregor, *The Wounded Knee Massacre*, 95–130. See also Miller, *Ghost Dance*, 233–44. See also the Indians' descriptions of the events given on February 11, 1891, in ARCIA 1891, Report of the Commissioner of Indian Affairs T. J. Morgan, October 1, 1891, 179–81, published also in Mooney, *The Ghost-Dance Religion*, 884–86.

226. A vivid description of these events is provided by Black Elk, who was among the 150 warriors and who was wounded during the fight. See Neihardt and Black Elk, *Black Elk Speaks*, 259–68; DeMallie, *The Sixth Grandfather*, 272–75. See John Little Finger in McGregor, *The Wounded Knee Massacre*, 112; Mooney, *The Ghost-Dance Religion*, 873. For a comprehensive account of the Indians with Big Foot at Wounded Knee, see Jensen, "Big Foot's Followers," 194–212. A good analysis of the casualties can also be found in Utley, *The Last Days*, 227–28.

227. William Peano in Jensen, *Voices of the American West*, 1:233–37; W. A. Birdsall in Jensen, *Voices of the American West*, 2:45–48. See ARCIA 1891, Report of the Commissioner of Indian Affairs T. J. Morgan, October 1, 1891, 130–31. See also Mattes, "The Enigma of Wounded Knee," 4; Olson, *Red Cloud and the Sioux Problem*, 330; Miller, *Ghost Dance*, 245.

228. Standing Bear, *My People the Sioux*, 224. See also Mooney, *The Ghost-Dance Religion*, 873–74.

229. Andrew Good Thunder, IULL, WMCC, Box 6, Folder 14, Envelope 90; Dewey Beard in Jensen, *Voices of the American West*, 1:208–26; Joseph Horn Cloud in Jensen, *Voices of the American West*, 1:191–208; William Garnett in Jensen, *Voices of the American West*, 1:99–100; Statement of the Survivors, IULL, WMCC, Box 4; Folder 4, Envelope 5; James Pipe On Head, 75th Cong., 1st Sess, House Committee on Indian Affairs, Published Hearing, March 7 and May 12, 1938, IULAL, Microfiche, Group 3, Card 4, 18–19. See statements of the survivors in McGregor, *The Wounded Knee Massacre*,

95–130. See also Olson, *Red Cloud and the Sioux Problem*, 330; Twiss, "A Short History of Pine Ridge," 37; Miller, *Ghost Dance*, 253; Larson, *Red Cloud*, 280.

230. For the battles of January 1891, see John Shangrau in Jensen, *Voices of the American West*, 1:256–64; Neihardt and Black Elk, *Black Elk Speaks*, 263–70. See also Utley, *The Last Days*, 236–41; Miller, *Ghost Dance*, 250–53, 256–57; Kreis, *Rothäute, Schwarzröcke, und Heilige Frauen*, 106–8; DeMallie, *The Sixth Grandfather*, 276–82. For different estimations of the Lakotas' numbers at the Drexel Mission fight, see chapters 3–5.

231. Utley, *The Last Days*, 251–52. For more about the army's strategy, see chapter 3.

232. Neihardt and Black Elk, *Black Elk Speaks*, 268–71; Utley, *The Last Days*, 255; Miller, *Ghost Dance*, 257; DeMallie, *The Sixth Grandfather*, 280–81.

233. Hyde, *A Sioux Chronicle*, 308; Neihardt and Black Elk, *Black Elk Speaks*, 270–71; Miller, *Ghost Dance*, 260–62; Utley, *The Last Days*, 257–58.

234. Utley, *The Last Days*, 258–59; Mooney, *The Ghost-Dance Religion*, 887.

235. Neihardt and Black Elk, *Black Elk Speaks*, 269; Standing Bear, *My People the Sioux*, 228–29; Miller, *Ghost Dance*, 264–65. For an account of George Sword's mission to Crazy Horse's camp, see DeMallie, "'These Have No Ears,'" 528–32.

236. See, for example, Curtis, *The Indian's Book*, 45–47. Kicking Bear and Short Bull together with twenty-five other ghost dance leaders were imprisoned after their surrender. Kicking Bear and Short Bull were even sent to Europe with Buffalo Bill's *Wild West Show* (see Utley, *The Last Days*, 271–72; Maddra, *Hostiles?*, 86–190). An interesting comment on Kicking Bear's and Short Bull's experience with Buffalo Bill was written by William F. Cody himself. He stated that both men were doing perfectly well on the tour and caused no problems whatsoever. See William F. Cody (Buffalo Bill) to Gen. Nelson A. Miles, April 14, 1891, NAMFP, Box 1, Cody File. For an excellent study regarding the ghost dancers' experiences with Buffalo Bill, see Maddra, *Hostiles?*, 57–109.

237. See, for example, Mattes, "The Enigma of Wounded Knee," 4–5; Utley, *The Last Days*, 261; Miller, *Ghost Dance*, 266–68.

238. See Walker, *Lakota Society*, 151; Cheney, *The Big Missouri Wintercount*, 41–42.

2. The Indian Agents and the Lakota Ghost Dance

1. See Utley, *The Last Days*, 18–59; Olson, *Red Cloud and the Sioux Problem*, 114–319; McGillicuddy, *Blood on the Moon*; McLaughlin, *My Friend the Indian*.

2. See, for example, McLaughlin to CIA, May 5, 1890, MHS, JMLP, M 230, Roll 21, 10–224; ARCIA 1889, Report of Agent Charles E. McChesney, August 26, 1889, Report of Agent Hugh D. Gallagher, August 27, 1889, Report of Agent L. F. Spencer, August 23, 1889, Report of Agent James McLaughlin August 26, 1889, 129–35, 151–61, 165–70; ARCIA 1890, Report of Agent Charles E. McChesney, August 25, 1890, Report

of Agent Hugh D. Gallagher, August 28, 1890, Report of Agent J. George Wright, August 26, 1890, Report of Agent James McLaughlin August 26, 1890, 37–62. See also Olson, *Red Cloud and the Sioux Problem*; McGillicuddy, *Blood on the Moon*; McLaughlin, *My Friend the Indian*.

3. ARCIA 1890, Report of Agent Charles E. McChesney, August 25, 1890, Report of Agent Hugh D. Gallagher, August 28, 1890, Report of Agent J. George Wright, August 26, 1890, Report of Agent James McLaughlin, August 26, 1890, 37–62. See also chapters 1 and 6.

4. Gallagher to CIA, January 21, 1890, NARS, RG 75, LSASPR, M 1282, Roll 10, 65; Gallagher to CIA, January 31, 1890, NARS, RG 75, LSASPR, M 1282, Roll 10, 108; Gallagher to CIA, February 17, 1890, NARS, RG 75, LSASPR, M 1282, Roll 10, 116; Gallagher to CIA, June 10, 1890, NARS, LSASPR, M 1282, Roll 10, 305; Gallagher to CIA, October 4, 1890, NARS, RG 75, LSASPR, M 1282, Roll 10, 436; McLaughlin to CIA, August 9, 1890, MHS, JMLP, M 230, Roll 21, 154–56. See also ARCIA 1890, Report of Agent Charles E. McChesney, August 25, 1890, Report of Agent Hugh D. Gallagher, August 28, 1890, Report of Agent J. George Wright, August 26, 1890, Report of Agent James McLaughlin August 26, 1890, 37–62.

5. See Charles L. Hyde to the Secretary of the Interior John W. Noble, May 29, 1890, NARS, RG 75, SC 188, M 4728, Roll 1, 1/1. See also Mooney, *The Ghost-Dance Religion*, 843. For the newspaper accounts, see chapter 5.

6. Gallagher to CIA, June 10, 1890, NARS, RG 75, LSASPR, M 1282, Roll 10, 305–7; Gallagher to CIA, June 14, 1890, NARS, RG 75, SC 188, M 4728, Roll 1, 1/2. See also Hyde, *A Sioux Chronicle*, 247–48.

7. McChesney to CIA, June 16, 1890, NARS, RG 75, SC 188, M 4728, Roll 1, 1/3–4; Wright to CIA, June 16, 1890, NARS, RG 75, SC 188, M 4728, Roll 1, 1/5–7. See also ARCIA 1890, Report of Agent Charles E. McChesney, August 25, 1890, Report of Agent Hugh D. Gallagher, August 28, 1890, Report of Agent J. George Wright, August 26, 1890, Report of Agent James McLaughlin, August 26, 1890, 37–62.

8. McLaughlin to CIA, June 18, 1890, NARS, RG 75, SC 188, M 4728, Roll 1, 1/8–10. The emphasis is McLaughlin's.

9. Gallagher to CIA, August 28, 1890, NARS, RG 75, LSASPR, M 1282, Roll 10, 385–87; McLaughlin to CIA, August 9, 1890, MHS, JMLP, M 230, Roll 21, 154–56; ARCIA 1891, Report of Agent James McLaughlin August 26, 1891, Report of Agent Perain Palmer, August 17, 1891, Report of Acting Agent Charles G. Penney, September 1, 1891, Report of Agent J. George Wright, August 27, 1891, 324–94, 408–12. See Olson, *Red Cloud and the Sioux Problem*, 323–24; Mooney, *The Ghost-Dance Religion*, 843–55.

10. Gallagher to CIA, August 28, 1890, NARS, RG 75, LSASPR, Roll 10, 387–88; Reynolds to CIA, September 25, 1890, NARS, RG 75, SC 188, M 4728, Roll 1, 1/22–26 (see also preface in this study). For comparison, see Utley, *The Last Days*, 92; Mooney, *The Ghost-Dance Religion*, 846–47; Ostler, *The Plains Sioux*, 274–76.

11. Gallagher to CIA (emphasis in original), August 28, 1890, NARS, RG 75, LSASPR, Roll 10, 387–88; Reynolds to CIA, September 25, 1890, NARS, RG 75, SC 188, M 4728, Roll 1, 1/22–26; Phillip Wells in Jensen, *Voices of the American West*, 1:146–48. An excellent account of the incident can be found in Utley, *The Last Days*, 91–94. For a different interpretation, see chapter 1.

12. ARCIA 1891, Report of Agent J. George Wright, August 27, 1891, 411–12. For more about the excitement caused by the rumor, see chapter 1. Withholding rations was efficiently used on several occasions during the 1870s and 1880s to subdue restlessness on the reservations. See, for example, Olson, *Red Cloud and the Sioux Problem*.

13. ARCIA 1891, Report of Agent J. George Wright, August 27, 1891, 411–12. See Utley, *The Last Days*, 95; Mooney, *The Ghost-Dance Religion*, 847. Agent Lea's role is studied in chapters 1, 3, and 6.

14. See, for example, Hyde, *A Sioux Chronicle*, 249–50; Olson, *Red Cloud and the Sioux Problem*, 307; W. S. E. Coleman, *Voices of Wounded Knee*, 59–61. See CIA to Herbert Welsh, December 13, 1889, TJMLB, AISRI, 122–23; CIA to Herbert Welsh, December 12, 1890, TJMLB, AISRI, 308–9; CIA to L. E. Quick, December 12, 1890, TJMLB, AISRI, 310–11.

15. Olson, *Red Cloud and the Sioux Problem*, 325. Daniel F. Royer wanted to be named receiver of the Land Office at Huron, but was sent to Pine Ridge.

16. Much has been written about the change of agents and especially about Agent Royer's character and his abilities as agent. Historians and even contemporaries generally agree that he was totally unfit for the position of Indian agent. See, for example, Phillip Wells in Jensen, *Voices of the American West*, 1:148–51; Colby, "The Sioux Indian War," 184; C. A. Eastman, *From Deep Woods to Civilization*, 84; E. G. Eastman, "The Ghost Dance War," 32; D. M. Johnson, "Ghost Dance," 47; Hyde, *A Sioux Chronicle*, 254; Utley, *The Last Days*, 96, 103; Olson, *Red Cloud and the Sioux Problem*, 325; Smith, *Moon of the Popping Trees*, 120–21; Graber, *Sister to the Sioux:*, 145; Mooney, *The Ghost Dance Religion*, 848; W. S. E. Coleman, *Voices of Wounded Knee*, 60; Ostler, *The Plains Sioux*, 291.

17. Agent Perain Palmer to CIA, October 11, 1890, NARS, RG 75, SC 188, M 4728, Roll 1, 1/29–30. See also Utley, *The Last Days*, 96–97; Mooney, *The Ghost Dance Religion*, 848.

18. For General Miles's thoughts on Big Foot, see chapter 3. A different view of Big Foot's alleged hostile intentions is presented in chapter 1.

19. Palmer to CIA, October 29, 1890, NARS, RG 75, SC 188, M 4728, Roll 1, 1/51–53.

20. Agent James McLaughlin to CIA, October 17, 1890, NARS, RG 75, SC 188, M 4728, Roll 1, 1/31–43; ARCIA 1891, Report of Agent James McLaughlin August 26, 1891, 327–39. See McLaughlin, *My Friend the Indian*, 184–91. See also Utley, *The Last Days*, 97–98.

21. McLaughlin to CIA, October 17, 1890, NARS, RG 75, SC 188, M 4728, Roll 1, 1/31–43, published also in ARCIA 1891, Report of the Commissioner of Indian Affairs T. J. Morgan, October 1, 1891, 125–26. See McLaughlin to Herbert Welsh, January 12, 1891,

MHS, JMLP, M230, Roll 22, 47–64; McLaughlin to Mary Collins, December 26, 1890, MHS, JMLP, M 230, Roll 22, 27–30; McLaughlin to Mrs. Winfield Jennings, January 4, 1891, MHS, JMLP, M 230, Roll 22, 33; ARCIA 1891, Report of Agent James McLaughlin August 26, 1891, 327–39. See also McLaughlin, *My Friend the Indian*, 180–83; Hoover, "Sitting Bull," 163–70; McLaughlin, *Account of the Death of Sitting Bull*; Ostler, *The Plains Sioux*, 292.

22. McLaughlin to CIA, October 17, 1890, NARS, RG 75, SC 188, M 4728, Roll 1, 1/31–43; ARCIA 1891, Report of Agent James McLaughlin August 26, 1891, 327–39. See McLaughlin, *My Friend the Indian*, 192–93. See also D. M. Johnson, "Ghost Dance," 46–47; Utley, *The Last Days*, 97–100; Hoover, "Sitting Bull," 167–70; Mooney, *The Ghost-Dance Religion*, 847–48. For a discussion of Sitting Bull and the episode with the peace pipe, see chapter 1.

23. Royer to ACIA, October 30, 1890, NARS, RG 75, SC 188, M 4728, Roll 1, 1/47–50.

24. Royer to ACIA, October 30, 1890, NARS, RG 75, SC 188, M 4728, Roll 1, 1/47–50. For more about General Miles's visit, see chapters 1 and 3.

25. Royer to ACIA, October 30, 1890, NARS, RG 75, SC 188, M 4728, Roll 1, 1/47–50. See also C. A. Eastman, *From Deep Woods to Civilization*, 88–100.

26. Reynolds to CIA, November 2, 1890, NARS, RG 75, SC 188, M 4728, Roll 1, 1/56–59.

27. Royer to CIA, November 8, 1890, NARS, RG 75, SC 188, M 4728, Roll 1, 1/65–68. See also Royer to CIA (telegram), November 11, 1890, NARS, RG 75, SC 188, M 4728, Roll 1, 1/64–68; Royer to CIA (telegram), November 12, 1890, 1890, NARS, RG 75, SC 188, M 4728, Roll 1, 1/75–79.

28. Royer to CIA, November 8, 1890, NARS, RG 75, SC 188, M 4728, Roll 1, 1/65–68; Royer to CIA (telegram), November 11, 1890, NARS, RG 75, SC 188, M 4728, Roll 1, 1/64–68; Royer to CIA (telegram), November 12, 1890, 1890, NARS, RG 75, SC 188, M 4728, Roll 1, 1/75–79; Royer to ACIA, November 12, 1890, NARS, RG 75, SC 188, M 4728, Roll 1, 1/93.

29. See Royer to CIA, November 11, 1890, NARS, RG 75, SC 188, M 4728, Roll 1, 1/91–92. See also C. A. Eastman, *From Deep Woods to Civilization*, 93–99; Utley, *The Last Days*, 107–9.

30. Royer to CIA (telegram), November 12, 1890, 1890, NARS, RG 75, SC 188, M 4728, Roll 1, 1/75–79; Royer to ACIA, November 12, 1890, NARS, RG 75, SC 188, M 4728, Roll 1, 1/93. See Utley, *The Last Days*, 107–9.

31. Royer to ACIA (telegram), November 15, 1890, NARS, RG 75, SC 188, M 4728, Roll 1, 1/89–90. See Utley, *The Last Days*, 111; Olson, *Red Cloud and the Sioux Problem*, 325–27; Smith, *Moon of the Popping Trees*, 123–25. Commissioner of Indian Affairs Thomas J. Morgan was in Oklahoma inspecting Indian schools. See Thomas J. Morgan Correspondence, December 1890–January 1891, TJMLB, AISRI. See also Utley, *The Last Days*, 100.

32. See chapter 3.

33. See Palmer to CIA, November 4, 1890, NARS, RG 75, SC 188, M 4728, Roll 1, 1/60–61; Palmer to CIA, November 5, 1890, NARS, RG 75, SC 188, M 4728, Roll 1, 1/55; Palmer to CIA, November 6, 1890, NARS, RG 75, SC 188, M 4728, Roll 1, 1/64–72; Palmer to CIA, November 10, 1890, NARS, RG 75, SC 188, M 4728, Roll 1, 1/82–84; Palmer to CIA (telegram), November 20, 1890, NARS, RG 75, SC 188, M 4728, Roll 1, 2/5; Reynolds to CIA, November 2, 1890, NARS, RG 75, SC 188, M 4728, Roll 1, 1/56–59; Reynolds to CIA (telegram), November 21, 1890, NARS, RG 75, SC 188, M 4728, Roll 1, 2/6. For further commentary on the movement of the Rosebud ghost dancers to Pine Ridge, see chapters 1 and 3.

34. President Harrison's correspondence leading to the decision to send troops can be found in BHP, October–November 1890, Microfilm, Series 1, Roll 29.

35. See Special Agent James A. Cooper to CIA (telegram), November 21, 1890, NARS, RG 75, SC 188, M 4728, Roll 1, 2/7; Cooper to ACIA, November 21, 1890, NARS, RG 75, SC 188, M 4728, Roll 1, 2/16–17; Royer to ACIA (telegram), November 21, 1890, NARS, RG 75, SC 188, M 4728, Roll 1, 2/17; Royer to ACIA, November 21, 1890, NARS, RG 75, SC 188, M 4728, Roll 1, 2/66; Cooper to ACIA, November 21, 1890, NARS, RG 75, SC 188, M 4728, Roll 1, 2/68–69. See also Utley, *The Last Days*, 116; Smith, *Moon of the Popping Trees*, 126. For newspaper accounts of Royer's trip to Rushville, see chapter 5.

36. See McLaughlin to Martin Marty, October 18, 1890, MHS, JMLP, M 230, Roll 20, 450–51; McLaughlin to Emma Harnet, November 13, 1890, MHS, JMLP, M 230, Roll 21, 421; McLaughlin to John Haget, November 17, 1890, MHS, JMLP, M 230, Roll 21, 427; McLaughlin to George Bingenheimer, November 18, 1890, MHS, JMLP, M 230, Roll 21, 428; McLaughlin to David Carey, November 19, 1890, MHS, JMLP, M 230, Roll 21, 429; McLaughlin to CIA, November 19, 1890, MHS, JMLP, M 230, Roll 21, 430–37; McLaughlin to Reverend Martin Marty, November 20, 1890, MHS, JMLP, M 230, Roll 21, 467; McLaughlin to Miss Francis, November 24, 1890, MHS, JMLP, M 230, Roll 21, 450–51; McLaughlin to A. C. Hewdekoper, November 25, 1890, MHS, JMLP, M 230, Roll 21, 454–55; McLaughlin to John Dady, November 28, 1890, MHS, JMLP, M 230, Roll 21, 463; McLaughlin to Mrs. A. Langenworthy, November 28, 1890, MHS, JMLP, M 230, Roll 20, 464; McLaughlin to Herbert Welsh, November 25, 1890, MHS, JMLP, M 230, Roll 20, 469–72. For Agent McLaughlin's comments published in the press, see chapter 5.

37. McLaughlin to CIA, November 19, 1890, NARS, RG 75, SC 188, M 4728, Roll 1, 2/18–25; McLaughlin to CIA, November 29, 1890, NARS, RG 75, SC 188, M 4728, Roll 1, 2/75–81. See also McLaughlin, *My Friend the Indian*, 193–200; W. S. E. Coleman, *Voices of Wounded Knee*, 69–71.

38. McLaughlin to CIA, November 19, 1890, NARS, RG 75, SC 188, M 4728, Roll 1, 2/18–25. See McLaughlin, *My Friend the Indian*, 201–8; W. S. E. Coleman, *Voices of Wounded Knee*, 68–70, 79–82.

39. McLaughlin to CIA, November 19, 1890, NARS, RG 75, SC 188, M 4728, Roll 1, 2/18–25;

McLaughlin to CIA (telegram), November 21, 1890, NARS, RG 75, SC 188, M 4728, Roll 1, 2/10–11; McLaughlin to CIA, November 29, 1890, NARS, RG 75, SC 188, M 4728, Roll 1, 2/75–81. See also W. F. Johnson, *The Red Record*, 170–77; Utley, *The Last Days*, 100–102; McLaughlin, *My Friend the Indian*, 201–8; Vestal, *Sitting Bull*, 277–78; Mooney, *The Ghost-Dance Religion*, 854–55; Utley, *The Lance and the Shield*, 287–89.

40. McLaughlin to CIA (telegram), November 28, 1890, NARS, RG 75, SC 188, M 4728, Roll 1, 2/8–9; McLaughlin to CIA, November 29, 1890, NARS, RG 75, SC 188, M 4728, Roll 1, 2/75–81; McLaughlin to CIA, December 1, 1890, NARS, RG 75, SC 188, M 4728, Roll 1, 2/93–94; McLaughlin to CIA, December 4, 1890, MHS, JMLP, M 230, Roll 21, 483–486; McLaughlin, *My Friend the Indian*, 209–11. For more about William F. Cody's mission, see Utley, *The Last Days*, 122–26; Vestal, *Sitting Bull*, 280–85. See also chapters 1 and 3.

41. President Benjamin Harrison to Noble, December 4, 1890, NARS, RG 75, SC 188, M 4728, Roll 1, 2/96–97; Noble to CIA, December 1, 1890, NARS, RG 75, SC 188, M 4728, Roll 1, 2/25; Noble to CIA, December 6, 1890, NARS, RG 75, SC 188, M 4728, Roll 1, 2/83. See chapter 3.

42. For accounts of Sitting Bull's death and of the events leading to it, see W. F. Johnson, *The Red Record*, 183–88; Utley, *The Last Days*, 146–66; Hoover, "Sitting Bull," 168–70; Vestal, *Sitting Bull*, 280–307; Mooney, *The Ghost-Dance Religion*, 854–60; Utley, *The Lance and the Shield*, 291–305. See also chapter 1. Agent McLaughlin's own accounts can be found in McLaughlin to CIA, December 16, 1890, NARS, RG 75, SC 188, M 4728, Roll 1, 4/96–5/1; McLaughlin to CIA, December 24, 1890, NARS, RG 75, SC 188, M 4728, Roll 1, 5/55–77; ARCIA 1891, Report of Agent James McLaughlin August 26, 1891, 327–38. Agent McLaughlin further explained the events surrounding Sitting Bull's death in McLaughlin, *My Friend the Indian*, 211–22, 406–17; McLaughlin, *Account of the Death of Sitting Bull*.

43. McLaughlin to CIA (telegram), December 15, 1890, NARS, RG 75, SC 188, M 4728, Roll 1, no page number; McLaughlin to CIA, December 16, 1890, NARS, RG 75, SC 188, M 4728, Roll 1, 4/96–5/1; McLaughlin to CIA, December 24, 1890, NARS, RG 75, SC 188, M 4728, Roll 1, 5/55–77; ARCIA 1891, Report of Agent James McLaughlin August 26, 1891, 327–38; John M. Carignan to McLaughlin (telegram), December 14, 1890, NARS, RG 75, SC 188, M 4728, Roll 1, 5/5–6. It was this message by the Grand River Day School teacher John M. Carignan that prompted McLaughlin's actions. Carignan reported that Sitting Bull was asking for permission to leave for Pine Ridge but would leave even if he did not get permission. See Carignan to McLaughlin (telegram), December 14, 1890, NARS, RG 75, SC 188, M 4728, Roll 1, 5/5–6; McLaughlin, *Account of the Death of Sitting Bull*. See also Vestal, *New Sources*, 7–14; Utley, *The Last Days*, 147–48; McLaughlin, *My Friend the Indian*, 211–22; Mooney, *The Ghost-Dance Religion*, 855; Utley, *The Lance and the Shield*, 296–97; W. S. E. Coleman, *Voices of Wounded Knee*, 176–93.

44. See chapter 3.

45. See, for example, McLaughlin to CIA, December 16, 1890, NARS, RG 75, SC 188, M 4728, Roll 1, 4/96–5/1; McLaughlin to CIA, December 24, 1890, NARS, RG 75, SC 188, M 4728, Roll 1, 5/55–77; ACIA to McLaughlin (telegram), December 1, 1890, NARS, RG 75, SC 188, M 4728, Roll 1, 5/3; ACIA to McLaughlin (telegram), December 5, 1890, NARS, RG 75, SC 188, M 4728, Roll 1, 5/4; ARCIA 1891, Report of Agent James McLaughlin August 26, 1891, 327–38; McLaughlin, *My Friend the Indian*, 211–22; McLaughlin to Miss Winfield Jennings, January 4, 1891, MHS, JMLP, M 230, Roll 22, 33. See also Utley, *The Last Days*, 146–66; Smith, *Moon of the Popping Trees*, 147–52; Hoover, "Sitting Bull," 168–71; Vestal, *Sitting Bull*, 286–87; Mooney, *The Ghost-Dance Religion*, 854–60.

46. Noble to McLaughlin (telegram), December 20, 1890, NARS, RG 75, SC 188, M 4728, Roll 1, 7/56; McLaughlin to Noble (telegram, never sent), December 30, 1890, NARS, RG 75, SC 188, M 4728, Roll 1, 7/56–58, McLaughlin to CIA, January 23, 1891, NARS, RG 75, SC 188, M 4728, Roll 1, 7/60–64.

47. See chapters 5 and 6.

48. W. F. Johnson, *The Red Record*, 178–79. For a discussion of McLaughlin's motives, see Utley, *The Last Days*, 147–48, 167–69; Hoover, "Sitting Bull," 168–69; Vestal, *Sitting Bull*, 287, Mooney, *The Ghost-Dance Religion*, 854–60. McLaughlin later explained his actions and motives in several occasions. See, for example, McLaughlin to CIA, December 16, 1890, NARS, RG 75, SC 188, M 4728, Roll 1, 4/96–5/1; McLaughlin to CIA, December 24, 1890, NARS, RG 75, SC 188, M 4728, Roll 1, 5/55–77; McLaughlin, *My Friend the Indian*, 215–22, 406–17; McLaughlin, *Account of the Death of Sitting Bull*.

49. Statement of Hunkpapa and Blackfoot prisoners of war in Guy H. Preston to the Commanding Officer, February 17, 1891, NARS, RG 75, SC 188, M 4729, Roll 2, 9/91–92.

50. McLaughlin to Bull Head, December 14, 1890, MHS, JMLP, M 230, Roll 20, 502–3. See also Vestal, *New Sources*, 15.

51. McLaughlin to CIA, November 29, 1890, NARS, RG 75, SC 188, M 4728, Roll 1, 1/75–81; McLaughlin to CIA, February 4, 1891, NARS, RG 75, SC 188, Roll 2, 8/63–69.

52. Noble to CIA (emphasis in original), December 31, 1890, NARS, RG 75, SC 188, M 4728, Roll 1, 5/81.

53. McLaughlin to CIA, October 17, 1890, NARS, RG 75, SC 188, M 4728, Roll 1, 1/36. See also McLaughlin, *My Friend the Indian*, 197; Vestal, *Sitting Bull*, 287.

54. See Cooper to CIA, November 20, 1890, NARS, RG 75, SC 188, M 4728, Roll 1, 2/2–4; Cooper to CIA (telegram), November 21, 1890, NARS, RG 75, SC 188, M 4728, Roll 1, 2/7; Cooper to CIA (telegram), November 22, 1890, NARS, RG 75, SC 188, M 4728, Roll 1, 2/12; Cooper to ACIA, November 22, 1890, NARS, RG 75, SC 188, M 4728, Roll 1, 2/31; Cooper to CIA (telegram), November 24, 1890, NARS, RG 75, SC 188, M 4728, Roll 1, 2/13–14; Royer to CIA, November 25, 1890, NARS, RG 75, SC 188, M 4728, Roll 1, 3/31–33; Royer to

CIA (telegram), November 26, 1890, NARS, RG 75, SC 188, M 4728, Roll 1, 2/43–44. For newspaper accounts, see chapter 5.

55. Cooper to CIA, November 20, 1890, NARS, RG 75, SC 188, M 4728, Roll 1, 2/2–4; Cooper to CIA (telegram), November 21, 1890, NARS, RG 75, SC 188, M 4728, Roll 1, 2/7; Cooper to CIA (telegram), November 22, 1890, NARS, RG 75, SC 188, M 4728, Roll 1, 2/12; Cooper to ACIA, November 22, 1890, NARS, RG 75, SC 188, M 4728, Roll 1, 2/31; Cooper to CIA (telegram), November 24, 1890, NARS, RG 75, SC 188, M 4728, Roll 1, 2/13–14; Special Agent A. T. Lea to Cooper (telegram), November 22, 1890, NARS, RG 75, SC 188, M 4728, Roll 1, 2/38–40; Cooper to CIA (telegram), November 25, 1890, NARS, RG 75, SC 188, M 4728, Roll 1, 2/41–42; Royer to CIA, November 25, 1890, NARS, RG 75, SC 188, M 4728, Roll 1, 3/31–33; Royer to CIA (telegram), November 26, 1890, NARS, RG 75, SC 188, M 4728, Roll 1, 2/43–44; Cooper to CIA (telegram), November 27, 1890, NARS, RG 75, SC 188, M 4728, Roll 1, 2/45–46. The historian Robert Utley maintains that Agent Royer listed sixty-five men to be arrested, but the correct number is sixty-six. See Royer to CIA, November 25, 1890, NARS, RG 75, SC 188, M 4728, Roll 1, 3/31–33; Utley, *The Last Days*, 123.

56. See chapter 3.

57. Cooper to ACIA, November 24, 1890, NARS, RG 75, SC 188, M 4728, Roll 1, 2/52; Cooper to ACIA, November 25, 1890, NARS, RG 75, SC 188, M 4728, Roll 1, 3/18; Royer to ACIA, November 25, 1890, NARS, RG 75, SC 188, M 4728, Roll 1, 3/36; Cooper to CIA, (telegram), November 25, 1890, NARS, RG 75, SC 188, M 4728, Roll 1, 2/41–42; Cooper to CIA (telegram), November 26, 1890, NARS, RG 75, SC 188, M 4728, Roll 1, 2/43–44; Cooper to CIA (telegram), November 27, 1890, NARS, RG 75, SC 188, M 4728, Roll 1, 2/45–46; Royer to CIA (telegram), November 27, 1890, NARS, RG 75, SC 188, M 4728, Roll 1, 2/47–50; Royer to ACIA, November 27, 1890, NARS, RG 75, SC 188, M 4728, Roll 1, 3/34–35; Cooper to ACIA, November 27, 1890, NARS, RG 75, SC 188, M 4728, Roll 1, 3/38–39; Royer and Cooper to CIA (telegram), November 28, 1890, NARS, RG 75, SC 188, M 4728, Roll 1, 2/59–60.

58. As examples of the settlers' feelings, see R. M. Tuttle to President Harrison, November 18, 1890, NARS, RG 75, SC 188, M 4728, Roll 1, 2/55–56; J. Fitzgerald to CIA, November 25, 1890, NARS, RG 75, SC 188, M 4728, Roll 1, 2/65–66. For accounts of the militia, see Colby, "The Sioux Indian War," 144–77; Utley, *The Last Days*, 143–44; W. S. E. Coleman, *Voices of Wounded Knee*, 167–72. For more about the newspaper correspondents, see chapter 5.

59. Royer to CIA, November 25, 1890, NARS, RG 75, SC 188, M 4728, Roll 1, 3/31–33. See also Utley, *The Last Days*, 135–36. For further discussion about Red Cloud's role in the ghost dance, see chapters 1 and 6.

60. Royer to ACIA, December 1, 1890, NARS, RG 75, SC 188, M 4728, Roll 1, 3/86–87; Royer and Cooper to ACIA, December 1, 1890, NARS, RG 75, SC 188, M 4728, Roll 1, 3/88–90;

Royer to ACIA, December 4, 1890, NARS, RG 75, SC 188, M 4728, Roll 1, 3/98–99; Royer to ACIA, December 5, 1890, NARS, RG 75, SC 188, M 4728, Roll 1, 4/18; Royer to CIA, December 8, 1890, NARS, RG 75, SC 188, M 4728, Roll 1, 4/6.

61. Reynolds to CIA, November 26, 1890, NARS, RG 75, SC 188, M 4728, Roll 1, 3/15–17.

62. Reynolds to CIA, November 26, 1890, NARS, RG 75, SC 188, M 4728, Roll 1, 3/15–17. See also Utley, *The Last Days*, 95.

63. Wright to CIA (telegram), December 2, 1890, NARS, RG 75, SC 188, M 4728, Roll 1, 3/47–49.

64. Wright to CIA, December 5, 1890, NARS, RG 75, SC 188, M 4728, Roll 1, 4/50–56; ARCIA 1891, Report of Agent J. George Wright, August 27, 1891, 411–13.

65. Wright to CIA, December 5, 1890, NARS, RG 75, SC 188, M 4728, Roll 1, 4/50–56; Wright to CIA (telegram), December 14, 1890, NARS, RG 75, SC 188, M 4728, Roll 1, 4/58. See also ARCIA 1891, Report of the Superintendent of Indian Schools, Daniel Dorchester, September 30, 1890, 532–33.

66. Palmer to CIA, November 28, 1890, NARS, RG 75, SC 188, M 4728, Roll 1, 3/62–63. See chapter 1.

67. By late 1880s Indians predominantly wore white man's clothing. In fact, wearing "citizen's" clothing was considered an important part of the civilization process. Reports of the number of Indians wearing citizen's clothes were regularly included in the agents' annual reports. See, for example, ARCIA 1889, Report of Agent Charles E. McChesney, August 26, 1889, Report of Agent Hugh D. Gallagher, August 27, 1889, Report of Agent L. F. Spencer, August 23, 1889, Report of Agent James McLaughlin, August 26, 1889, 498–501; ARCIA 1890, Report of Agent Charles E. McChesney, August 25, 1890, Report of Agent Hugh D. Gallagher, August 28, 1890, Report of Agent J. George Wright, August 26, 1890, Report of Agent James McLaughlin August 26, 1890, 450–51; ARCIA 1891, Report of Agent James McLaughlin August 26, 1891, Report of Agent Perain Palmer, August 17, 1891, Report of Acting Agent Charles G. Penney, September 1, 1891, Report of Agent J. George Wright, August 27, 1891, 764–76, 768–69.

68. Palmer to CIA, November 28, 1890, NARS, RG 75, SC 188, M 4728, Roll 1, 3/62–63; Palmer to CIA, December 1, 1890, NARS, RG 75, SC 188, M 4728, Roll 1, 3/64–67; ARCIA 1891, Report of Agent Perain Palmer, August 17, 1891, 390.

69. For comparison, see Jensen, "Big Foot's Followers," 194–98.

70. Palmer to CIA, December 9, 1890, NARS, RG 75, SC 188, M 4728, Roll 1, 3/61–63; ARCIA 1891, Report of Agent Perain Palmer, August 17, 1891, 390. For more about Chief Hump, see chapters 1 and 3.

71. For the effect of Sitting Bull's death on the Indians, see chapter 1.

72. Palmer to CIA, December 17, 1890, NARS, RG 75, SC 188, M 4728, Roll 1, 4/92–94;

Palmer to CIA, December 22, 1890, NARS, RG 75, SC 188, M 4728, Roll 1, 5/15; ARCIA 1891, Report of Agent Perain Palmer, August 17, 1891, 390.

73. Palmer to CIA, December 22, 1890, NARS, RG 75, SC 188, M 4728, Roll 1, 5/15; Palmer to CIA, December 22, 1890, NARS, RG 75, SC 188, M 4728, Roll 1, 5/37–38; Palmer to CIA, December 22, 1890, NARS, RG 75, SC 188, M 4728, Roll 1, 5/39.

74. Palmer to CIA, December 27, 1890, NARS, RG 75, SC 188, M 4728, Roll 1, 5/89–90; ARCIA 1891, Report of Agent Perain Palmer, August 17, 1891, 390.

75. See chapters 1 and 3.

76. See E. G. Eastman, "The Ghost Dance War," 33–34. See also chapters 1, 3, and 5.

77. Royer to CIA (telegram), December 29, 1890, NARS, RG 75, SC 188, M 4728, Roll 1, 5/46–48.

78. For an account of the killing of the rancher, see Utley, *The Last Days*, 254, 265. In fact, the Indians did not actually burn or destroy any churches during the trouble (see chapter 1).

79. Cooper to CIA (telegram), December 30, 1890, NARS, RG 75, SC 188, M 4728, Roll 1, 5/49–50; Royer to CIA, December 31, 1890, NARS, RG 75, SC 188, M 4728, Roll 1, 6/6–8; Royer to CIA (telegram), January 2, 1891, NARS, RG 75, SC 188, M 4728, Roll 1, 5/91–93.

80. See, for example, Wright to CIA (telegram), January 6, 1891, NARS, RG 75, SC 188, M 4728, Roll 1, 6/9; McLaughlin to CIA, January 7, 1891, NARS, RG 75, SC 188, M 4728, Roll 1, 6/36; McLaughlin to CIA, January 9, 1891, NARS, RG 75, SC 188, M 4728, Roll 1, 6/68–69; McLaughlin to CIA (telegram), January 10, 1891, NARS, RG 75, SC 188, M 4728, Roll 1, 6/28–29; Cooper to CIA, January 10, 1890, NARS, RG 75, SC 188, M 4728, Roll 1, 7/23–28; Palmer to CIA, January 19, 1891, NARS, RG 75, SC 188, M 4728, Roll 1, 7/22; Wright to CIA, January 23, 1891, NARS, RG 75, SC 188, M 4728, Roll 1, 7/86–95. Agent James McLaughlin's attempts to defend his actions can be found throughout the Special Case 188 collection and will not be singled out in detail here.

81. See chapter 3. See also Utley, *The Last Days*, 279–81. For the results of Agent Cooper's investigations, see Paul, "The Investigation of Special Agent Cooper," 212–35.

3. "To Protect and Suppress Trouble"

1. McDermott, "The Primary Role of the Military," 1–2, 22; Mattingly, "The Great Plains Peace Commission," 22; Socolofsky, "Great Plains Studies," 2; Wooster, *The Military*, 2–16, 30. For an account of the structure of the U.S. military before 1890, see Wade, "The Military Command Structure," 5–20. For more about the power struggle within the army and the problems with the army and other government institutions, see McDermott, "The Primary Role of the Military," 1; Youngkin, "Prelude to Wounded Knee," 334–35; Wooster, *The Military*, 19–21, 77–89.

2. McDermott, "The Primary Role of the Military," 1; Wooster, *The Military*, 29; Paul, "Your Country Is Surrounded," 25.

3. Socolofsky, "Great Plains Studies," 2–3; Wade, "The Military Command Structure," 16; Wooster, *The Military*, 40, 192–93; Ostler, "Conquest and the State," 227–31.

4. Boyd, *Recent Indian Wars*, 200–201; Colby, "The Sioux Indian War," 146; Mattingly, "The Great Plains Peace Commission," 22; Paul, "Your Country Is Surrounded," 25–26. For a general account of the military and its efforts to control the Great Plains area, see Wade, "The Military Command Structure," 5–21.

5. Wade, "The Military Command Structure," 15. The Military Division of the Missouri was composed of subordinate departments, which varied from time to time. By 1890 the Department of the Platte and the Department of the Dakota belonged to the Division of the Missouri. For more about the structure of the U.S. Army, see Wade, "The Military Command Structure," 5–20; Wooster, *The Military*, 17–26. For a historical account of the role of the Division of Missouri from the 1860s to 1891, see Wade, "The Military Command Structure," 9–20.

6. Wade, "The Military Command Structure," 14–15; Utley, *The Indian Frontier*, 255. For accounts of General Miles's life and career before the ghost dance troubles, see Miles, *Personal Recollections*; Miles, *Serving the Republic*; V. W. Johnson, *The Unregimented General*; Wooster, *Nelson A. Miles*. According to Wooster, Miles was a successful officer, but his success was somewhat shadowed by accusations of taking credit for the work of other officers. Also, his political ambitions caused some discussion. Virginia W. Johnson, however, argues that Miles did not use the military to boost his political career. Wooster maintains that Miles was more concerned with his own success than the welfare of the Indians (V. W. Johnson, *The Unregimented General*, 274–75; Wooster, *The Military*, 66; Wooster, *Nelson A. Miles*, 163–75). See also Seymour, *Sitanka*, 143–47.

7. See Miles, *Serving the Republic*, 233–34; V. W. Johnson, *The Unregimented General*, 261–63; Utley, *The Indian Frontier*, 255; Wooster, *Nelson A. Miles*, 163–75.

8. Usually major generals headed the divisions and brigadier generals headed the departments. At the time of the ghost dance troubles the chain of command was the following: Brig. Gens. John R. Brooke and Thomas H. Ruger reported to Maj. Gen. Nelson A. Miles, whose superior was Maj. Gen. John M. Schofield, the general of the army, in Washington. Schofield's superior was Secretary of War Redfield Proctor, who was appointed by the president, at this time Benjamin Harrison (Wooster, *The Military*, 17; Paul, "Your Country Is Surrounded," 26). See also Miles, *Serving the Republic*, 233–34; Socolofsky, "Great Plains Studies," 2–3; Wooster, *Nelson A. Miles*, 175; Green, *After Wounded Knee*, 27.

9. ARCIA 1891, Report of the Commissioner of Indian Affairs T. J. Morgan, October 1, 1891, 123–24. See also Kelley, "The Indian Troubles," 31.

10. ARCIA 1891, Report of the Commissioner of Indian Affairs T. J. Morgan, October 1, 1891, 123–24. See also Thomas J. Morgan, personal correspondence, November

1890–January 1891, TJMLB, AISRI. For rumors and newspaper accounts regarding the ghost dance among the Shoshones, Arapahos, and Cheyennes, see chapter 5.

11. See Maj. Guy W. Henry to AAG, October 14, 1890, NARS, RG 94, AIWKSC, M 983, Roll 1, Vol. 1, 1–2; Maj. E. R. Kellog to AAG, October 27, 1890, NARS, RG 94, AIWKSC, M 983, Roll 1, Vol. 1, 4–5; ARSW 1891, Report of A. I. Chapman in Report of Operations Relative to the Sioux Indians in 1890 and 1891, October 19, 1891, 190–94. For Porcupine's account of the journey, see June 28, 1890, NARS, RG 75, SC 188, M 4728, Roll 1, 1/16–20. See Mooney, 812–13. For newspaper accounts of the messiah's identity, see chapter 5. See also chapters 1 and 2.

12. ARCIA 1891, Report of the Commissioner of Indian Affairs T. J. Morgan, October 1, 1891, 123–24; ARSW 1891, Report of A. I. Chapman, December 6, 1890 in Report of Operations Relative to the Sioux Indians in 1890 and 1891, October 19, 1891, 190–94. See Hittman, *Wovoka*, 7–12, 231–336; Ostler, *The Plains Sioux*, 248–49. For early newspaper accounts of the Paiute ghost dance, see Hittman, *Wovoka*, 259.

13. ARSW 1891, Report of A. I. Chapman, December 6, 1890 in Report of Operations Relative to the Sioux Indians in 1890 and 1891, October 19, 1891, 190–94. See also Hittman, *Wovoka*, 7–12, 231–36.

14. Report of Brig. Gen. John R. Brooke in Brooke to AAG March 2, 1891, NARS, RG 94, AIWKSC, M 983, Roll 2, Vol. 2, 1670; ARSW 1891, Report of Maj. Gen. Nelson A. Miles, September 24, 1891, 55.

15. Report of Brig. Gen. John R. Brooke in Brooke to AAG, March 2, 1891, NARS, RG 94, AIWKSC, M 983, Roll 2, Vol. 2, 1670. For the agents' reports and letters, see chapter 2.

16. Maj. Gen. Nelson A. Miles to Maj. Gen. John M. Schofield, November 14, 1890, NARS, RG 94, AIWKSC, M 983, Roll 1, Vol. 1, 34; ARSW 1891, Report of Maj. Gen. Nelson A. Miles, September 24, 1891, 143; Royer to ACIA, October 30, 1890, NARS, RG 75, SC 188, M 4728, Roll 1, 47–50. See Hyde, *A Sioux Chronicle*, 260; Utley, *The Last Days*, 104–5; Paul, "Your Country Is Surrounded," 26; Wooster, *Nelson A. Miles*, 177–78; Ostler, "Conquest and the State," 232–33. See also chapters 1 and 2.

17. See, for example, W. S. E. Coleman, *Voices of Wounded Knee*, 65–66. See also chapter 5.

18. AAG to Miles, October 31, 1890, NARS, RG 94, AIWKSC, M 983, Roll 1, Vol. 1, 6; Miles to Schofield, November 14, 1890, NARS, RG 94, AIWKSC, M 983, Roll 1, Vol. 1, 34; Brig. Gen. John R. Brooke to the Commanding Officer at Fort Niobrara (telegram), November 17, 1890, NARS, RG 94, AIWKSC, M 983, Roll 2, Vol. 1, 1704; Report of Brig. Gen. John R. Brooke, in Brooke to AAG March 2, 1891, NARS, RG 94, AIWKSC, M 983, Roll 2, Vol. 2, 1671; ARSW 1891, Report of Maj. Gen. Nelson A. Miles, September 24, 1891, 134–39. See also Youngkin, "Prelude to Wounded Knee," 334–37.

19. Report of Brig. Gen. John R. Brooke in Brooke to AAG, March 2, 1891, NARS, RG 94, AIWKSC, M 983, Roll 2, Vol. 2, 1671. See also Paul, "Your Country Is Surrounded," 27. For more about the agents' letters, see chapter 2.

20. Secretary of the Interior John W. Noble to President Benjamin Harrison, November 7, 1890, NARS, RG 94, AIWKSC, M 983, Roll 1, Vol. 1, 33; President Harrison to Secretary of War Redfield Proctor, October 31, 1890 LC, BHP, Roll 29, Series 1.

21. Memoranda, undated (between letters dated November 6 and November 10, 1890), unsigned, NARS, RG 94, AIWKSC, M 983, Roll 1, Vol. 1, 47. The belief that the Lakotas had concealed weapons for future purposes was quite common among the army officers as well as officials in Washington. As examples of this discussion, see 51st Cong., 2nd Sess., *Senate Executive Document*, No. 2, Vol. 1, Serial 2818, 1–14; 51st Cong., 2nd Sess., *Senate Executive Document*, No. 9, Vol. 1, Serial 2818, 2–51.

22. Report of Capt. C. A. Earnest, November 12, 1890, NARS, RG 94, AIWKSC, M 983, Roll 1, Vol. 1, 78–82. See chapters 1 and 2.

23. Report of Capt. C. A. Earnest, November 12, 1890, NARS, RG 94, AIWKSC, M 983, Roll 1, Vol. 1, 78–82.

24. Report of Brig. Gen. Thomas H. Ruger in AAG to Miles (telegram), November 16, 1890, NARS, RG 94, AIWKSC, M 983, Roll 1, Vol. 1, 85–86; ARSW 1891, Report of Brig. Gen. Thomas H. Ruger, November 26, 1890, 189–91.

25. President Harrison to Secretary of War Redfield Proctor (telegram), November 13, 1890, NARS, RG 94, AIWKSC, M 983, Roll 1, Vol. 1, 19–20; Harrison to Secretary of the Interior John W. Noble, November 13, 1890, LC, BHP, Roll 29, Series 1. See also Noble to Harrison, November 7, 1890, NARS, RG 94, AIWKSC, M 983, Roll 1, Vol. 1, 33.

26. Schofield to Miles, November 14, 1890, NARS, RG 94, AIWKSC, M 983, Roll 1, Vol. 1, 71.

27. Schofield to Miles (telegram), November 17, 1890, NARS, RG 94, AIWKSC, M 983, Roll 1, Vol. 1, 36.

28. Wooster, *The Military*, 31–34.

29. AAG to Brooke (telegram), November 17, 1890, NARS, RG 94, AIWKSC, M 983, Roll 1, Vol. 1, 94; AAG to Brooke (telegram), November, 17, 1890, NARS, RG 94, AIWKSC, M 983, Roll 1, Vol. 1, 97; AAG to Brooke (telegram), November 17, 1890, NARS, RG 94, AIWKSC, M 983, Roll 1, Vol. 1, 98; AAG to Brooke (telegram), November 17, 1890, NARS, RG 94, AIWKSC, M 983, Roll 1, Vol. 1, 99; AAG to Brooke (telegram), November 18, 1890, NARS, RG 94, AIWKSC, M 983, Roll 1, Vol. 1, 100.

30. Miles to AG (telegram), November 17, 1890, NARS, RG 94, AIWKSC, M 983, Roll 1, Vol. 1, 104–5; ARSW 1891, Report of Maj. Gen. Nelson A. Miles, September 24, 1891, 145. See also Utley, *The Last Days*, 114–15. General Miles had for a few years past been concerned about the condition of the army and had been asking for additional appropriations for his division. On this issue he was on a constant collision course with several other army officers, and with Congress. See Wooster, *Nelson A. Miles*, 163–75; Ostler, "Conquest and the State," 228–32. For different estimates of the number of Lakota warriors, see chapters 1, 2, 5, 6.

31. See Orders of Maj. Gen. John M. Schofield, November 21, 1890, NARS, RG 94, AIWKSC, M 983, Roll 1, Vol. 1, 145–47; Schofield to Miles (telegram), November 22, 1890, NARS, RG 94, AIWKSC, M 983, Roll 1, Vol. 1, 176; Memorandum, Troops Ordered to the Division of the Missouri, December 4, 1890, NARS, RG 94, AIWKSC, M 983, Roll 1, Vol. 1, 422. Altogether General Miles had approximately 3,500 troops under his direct command; this was almost half of the infantry and cavalry of the regular army. Additionally 2,000 troops were in readiness (Utley, *The Last Days*, 251).

32. Brooke to AAG (telegram), November 16, 1890, NARS, RG 94, AIWKSC, M 983, Roll 1, Vol. 1, 75. See Utley, *The Last Days*, 115–16.

33. AAG to Brooke (telegram), November 18, 1890, NARS, RG 94, AIWKSC, M 983, Roll 1, Vol. 1, 100; AAG to Brooke (telegram), November 18, 1890, NARS, RG 94, AIWKSC, M 983, Roll 1, Vol. 1, 101.

34. See, for example, Governor of North Dakota John Miller to Noble (telegram), November 17, 1890, NARS, RG 94, AIWKSC, M 983, Roll 1, Vol. 1, 106; Settlers of New England ND to Proctor, November 26, 1890, NARS, RG 94, AIWKSC, M 983, Roll 1, Vol. 1, 246–47; Senator Gilbert A. Pierce ND to Proctor (telegram), November 18, 1890, NARS, RG 94, AIWKSC, M 983, Roll 1, Vol. 1, 109; R. M. Tuttle to President Harrison, November 18, 1890, NARS, RG 75, SC 188, M 4728, Roll 1, 2/55–56; J. Fitzgerald to CIA, November 25, 1890, NARS, RG 75, SC 188, M 4728, Roll 1, 2/65–66.

35. Utley, *The Last Days*, 114–16; Paul, "Your Country Is Surrounded," 27–28.

36. Report of Brig. Gen. John R. Brooke in Brooke to AAG, March 2, 1891, NARS, RG 94, AIWKSC, M 983, Roll 2, Vol. 2, 1671. See also chapters 1 and 2.

37. Miles to AAG (telegram), November 20, 1890, NARS, RG 94, AIWKSC, M 983, Roll 1, Vol. 1, 142; Miles to AAG (telegram), November 21, 1890, NARS, RG 94, AIWKSC, M 983, Roll 1, Vol. 1, 144. This rumor was often repeated in newspapers. See chapter 5.

38. Miles to AG (telegram), November 22, 1890, NARS, RG 94, AIWKSC, M 983, Roll 1, Vol. 1, 180–81; Report of Brig. Gen. John R. Brooke in Brooke to AAG, March 2, 1891, NARS, RG 94, AIWKSC, M 983, Roll 2, Vol. 2, 1673–74.

39. Miles to AG (telegram), November 22, 1890, NARS, RG 94, AIWKSC, M 983, Roll 1, Vol. 1, 180–81; Report of Brig. Gen. John R. Brooke in Brooke to AAG, March 2, 1891, NARS, RG 94, AIWKSC, M 983, Roll 2, Vol. 2, 1673–74.

40. Agent Cooper in ACIA to Secretary Noble, November 22, 1890, NARS, RG 94, AIWKSC, M 983, Roll 1, Vol. 1, 177; Agent Lea in Miles to AG (telegram), November 22, 1890, NARS, RG 94, AIWKSC, M 983, Roll 1, Vol. 1, 180–81. For more about Agent Cooper, see chapter 2, and about Agent Lea, see chapters 1, 2, 5, and 6.

41. Miles to AG (telegram), November 22, 1890, NARS, RG 94, AIWKSC, M 983, Roll 1, Vol. 1, 184; Miles to AG (telegram), November 23, 1890, NARS, RG 94, AIWKSC, M 983, Roll 1, Vol. 1, 192.

42. Miles to AG (telegram), November 22, 1890, NARS, RG 94, AIWKSC, M 983, Roll

1, Vol. 1, 184; Miles to AG (telegram), November 23, 1890, NARS, RG 94, AIWKSC, M 983, Roll 1, Vol. 1, 192; Miles to AG (telegram), November 24, 1890, NARS, RG 94, AIWKSC, M 983, Roll 1, Vol. 1, 201; Schofield to Miles (telegram), November 24, 1890, NARS, RG 94, AIWKSC, M 983, Roll 1, Vol. 1, 202; Schofield to Miles (telegram), November 24, 1890, NARS, RG 94, AIWKSC, M 983, Roll 1, Vol. 1, 206–7; Miles to AG (telegram), November 24, 1890, NARS, RG 94, AIWKSC, M 983, Roll 1, Vol. 1, 209; Schofield (copy of 1st endorsement), November 26, 1890, NARS, RG 94, AIWKSC, M 983, Roll 1, Vol. 1, 210.

43. Schofield to Proctor, December 3, 1890, 51st Cong., 2nd Sess., *Senate Executive Document*, No. 2, Vol. 1, Serial 2818, 2–3; Proctor to the President of the United States Senate, December 6, 1890, 51st Cong., 2nd Sess., *Senate Executive Document*, No. 2, Vol. 1, Serial 2818, 1. Agents Royer and Cooper kept on insisting that the Indians should be disarmed and imprisoned. See chapter 2.

44. For troop movements see, for example, Schofield to Miles (telegram), November 24, 1890, NARS, RG 94, AIWKSC, M 983, Roll 1, Vol. 1, 226; Miles to Schofield (telegram), November 24, 1890, NARS, RG 94, AIWKSC, M 983, Roll 1, Vol. 1, 228; Brig. Gen. Wesley Merritt to Schofield (telegram), November 25, 1890, NARS, RG 94, AIWKSC, M 983, Roll 1, Vol. 1, 236; Schofield to Merritt (telegram), November 25, 1890, NARS, RG 94, AIWKSC, M 983, Roll 1, Vol. 1, 238; Miles to AG (telegram), November 25, 1890, NARS, RG 94, AIWKSC, M 983, Roll 1, Vol. 1, 243; Memorandum, Troops Ordered to the Division of the Missouri, December 4, 1890, NARS, RG 94, AIWKSC, M 983, Roll 1, Vol. 1, 422. See also Utley, *The Last Days*, 118–19.

45. Miles to AG (telegram), November 24, 1890, NARS, RG 94, AIWKSC, M 983, Roll 1, Vol. 1, 219; Miles to AG (telegram), November 25, 1890, NARS, RG 94, AIWKSC, M 983, Roll 1, Vol. 1, 235.

46. Ruger to AG (telegram), November 23, 1890, NARS, RG 94, AIWKSC, M 983, Roll 1, Vol. 1, 195; Miles to AG (telegram), November 26, 1890, NARS, RG 94, AIWKSC, M 983, Roll 1, Vol. 1, 263; Miles to AG (telegram), November 27, 1890, NARS, RG 94, AIWKSC, M 983, Roll 1, Vol. 1, 268. See Boyd, *Recent Indian Wars*, 217–18.

47. See, for example, *Yankton Press and Dakotan*, November 28, 1890, 1; *Washington Post*, November 27, 1890, 1. See also chapter 5.

48. Miles to AG (telegram), November 26, 1890, NARS, RG 94, AIWKSC, M 983, Roll 1, Vol. 1, 244–45; Miles to AG (telegram), November 26, 1890, NARS, RG 94, AIWKSC, M 983, Roll 1, Vol. 1, 264. For the feelings of the settlers, see Letter by Settlers of New England City ND to Proctor, November 26, 1890, NARS, RG 94, AIWKSC, M 983, Roll 1, Vol. 1, 246–47; Letter by settlers of Chadron NE (no recipient), November 26, 1890, NARS, RG 94, AIWKSC, M 983, Roll 1, Vol. 1, 252–54. See Boyd, *Recent Indian Wars*, 227. For Short Bull's speech, see chapter 1. These rumors were spread by the newspapers also. See chapter 5.

49. Report of Lt. Col. J. S. Poland to AAG (telegram), November 29, 1890, NARS,

RG 94, AIWKSC, M 983, Roll 1, Vol. 1, 288–92; Brooke to AAG (telegram), November 30, 1890, NARS, RG 94, AIWKSC, M 983, Roll 1, Vol. 1, 296–301; Report of Capt. F. A. Whitney, November 27, 1890, NARS, RG 94, AIWKSC, M 983, Roll 1, Vol. 1, 307–11; ARSW 1891, List of Causes of Disaffection on Different Reservations, November 27, November 30, December 7, 1890, 134–39.

50. Miles to AG, November 28, 1890, NARS, RG 94, AIWKSC, M 983, Roll 1, Vol. 1, 279–85; ARSW 1891, Report of Maj. Gen. Nelson A. Miles, September 24, 1891, 132–44.

51. Sources of quotations in this and the following paragraph are Miles to AG, November 28, 1890, NARS, RG 94, AIWKSC, M 983, Roll 1, Vol. 1, 279–85; ARSW 1891, Report of Maj. Gen. Nelson A. Miles, September 24, 1891, 132–44. For more on Miles's ideas about resolving the "Indian question," see *North American Review*, January 1891, 1–11. See also Youngkin, "Prelude to Wounded Knee," 341–43.

52. Proctor to Miles (telegram), November 28, 1890, NARS, RG 94, AIWKSC, M 983, Roll 1, Vol. 1, 348; Schofield to Miles (telegram), November 29, 1890, NARS, RG 94, AIWKSC, M 983, Roll 1, Vol. 1, 347; ARSW 1891, Report of the Major General Commanding the Army, September 24, 1891, 145–46. See also Miles, *Serving the Republic*, 238–39; Zahn, *The Crimson Carnage*, 3; V. W. Johnson, *The Unregimented General*, 278–79; Utley, *The Last Days*, 122–27; Youngkin, "Prelude to Wounded Knee," 342–43; Paul, "Your Country Is Surrounded," 31–32; Wooster, *Nelson A. Miles*, 181–82. For Agent McLaughlin's opinions about Buffalo Bill's mission, see chapter 2.

53. Miles, *Serving the Republic*, 238; Seymour, *Sitanka*, 143–47. General Miles's comments were directly quoted in the newspapers. See chapter 5. Tecumseh was a Shawnee chief who led a war against the whites in the early nineteenth century. Pontiac was an Ottawa chief who led a long campaign against the whites in the 1760s. For more about Tecumseh, see Sugden, *Tecumseh*. For more about Pontiac, see Parkman, *The Conspiracy of Pontiac*, 621–846.

54. ARSW 1891, Report of the Major General Commanding the Army, September 24, 1891, 144. See Seymour, *Sitanka*, 145–47.

55. Utley, *The Last Days*, 127. See also Seymour, *Sitanka*, 143–47; W. S. E. Coleman, *Voices of Wounded Knee*, 97–98, 145–46; Ostler, "Conquest and the State," 236–39.

56. See Cong. Rec., 51st Cong., 2nd Sess., Vol. 12, Part 1, December 3–8, 1890, 44–48, 68–74. For the effects Miles's comments caused in the press and in Congress, see chapters 5 and 6.

57. Noble to CIA, December 1, 1890, NARS, RG 94, AIWKSC, M 983, Roll 1, Vol. 1, 392; Proctor to Miles, December 1, 1890, NARS, RG 94, AIWKSC, M 983, Roll 1, Vol. 1, 401.

58. See Hyde, *A Sioux Chronicle*, 279–80; V. W. Johnson, *The Unregimented General*, 275; Utley, *The Last Days*, 127–30; Youngkin, "Prelude to Wounded Knee," 334–35, 347–49; Wooster, *Nelson A. Miles*, 182.

59. See Schofield to the Commanding Generals of the Division of the Missouri,

Division of the Pacific, Department of Dakota, Department of the Platte, Department of Texas (telegrams), December 1, 1890, NARS, RG 94, AIWKSC, M 983, Roll 1, Vol. 1, 363–66; Miles to AAG (telegram), December 1, 1890, NARS, RG 94, AIWKSC, M 983, Roll 1, Vol. 1, 389.

60. ACIA to Proctor, December 1, 1890, NARS, RG 94, AIWKSC, M 983, Roll 1, Vol. 1, 356; AAG to AG (telegram), December 1, 1890, NARS, RG 94, AIWKSC, M 983, Roll 1, Vol. 1, 360; AAG to AG (telegram), December 1, 1890, NARS, RG 94, AIWKSC, M 983, Roll 1, Vol. 1, 371; AAG to AG (telegram), December 1, 1890, NARS, RG 94, AIWKSC, M 983, Roll 1, Vol. 1, 397; Report of Brig. Gen. John R. Brooke in Brooke to AAG, March 2, 1891, NARS, RG 94, AIWKSC, M 983, Roll 2, Vol. 2, 1675–76.

61. Noble to CIA (telegram), December 1, 1890, NARS, RG 94, AIWKSC, M 983, Roll 1, Vol. 1, 395; Brooke to Schofield (telegram), December 1, 1890, NARS, RG 94, AIWKSC, M 983, Roll 1, Vol. 1, 393; Brooke to AAG (telegram), December 5, 1890, NARS, RG 94, AIWKSC, M 983, Roll 1, Vol. 1, 428; Report of Brig. Gen. John R. Brooke in Brooke to AAG, March 2, 1891, NARS, RG 94, AIWKSC, M 983, Roll 2, Vol. 2, 1675–76.

62. Miles to AG, (telegram), December 5, 1890, NARS, RG 94, AIWKSC, M 983, Roll 1, Vol. 1, 430; Miles to AG (telegram), December 7, 1890, NARS, RG 94, AIWKSC, M 983, Roll 1, Vol. 1, 451–52; Miles to AG (telegram), December 10, 1890, NARS, RG 94, AIWKSC, M 983, Roll 1, Vol. 1, 485. For the allegations made in the press against Two Strike, see chapter 5.

63. Report of Brig. Gen. John R. Brooke in Brooke to AAG, March 2, 1891, NARS, RG 94, AIWKSC, M 983, Roll 2, Vol. 2, 1676–78. See Boyd, *Recent Indian Wars*, 235–38; Utley, *The Last Days*, 137–39. See also chapter 2.

64. Report of Brig. Gen. John R. Brooke in Brooke to AAG, March 2, 1891, NARS, RG 94, AIWKSC, M 983, Roll 2, Vol. 2, 1676–78. For the mission of Father Jutz, see chapter 3. About newspaper accounts of his efforts and the negotiations of December 6, see chapter 5. See also Hyde, *A Sioux Chronicle*, 273–76; Utley, *The Last Days*, 137–40.

65. For accounts of the Lame Deer and Nez Percé campaigns, see Miles, *Personal Recollections*, 248–56, 259–80; Miles, *Serving the Republic*, 169–81; V. W. Johnson, *The Unregimented General*, 173–209; Beal, *"I Will Fight No More Forever,"* 233–311; Wooster, *Nelson A. Miles*, 92–93, 96–110.

66. Miles to AAG (telegram), December 10, 1890, NARS, RG 94, AIWKSC, M 983, Roll 1, Vol. 1, 485; Miles to AG, December 10, 1890, NARS, RG 94, AIWKSC, M 983, Roll 1, Vol. 1, 504–5; ARSW 1891, 147. See also V. W. Johnson, *The Unregimented General*, 277–78; Utley, *The Last Days*, 131–33; Mooney, *The Ghost-Dance Religion*, 862.

67. Miles to Schofield (telegram), December 6, 1890, NARS, RG 94, AIWKSC, M 983, Roll 1, Vol. 1, 448; Miles to AG (telegram), December 8, 1890, NARS, RG 94, AIWKSC, M 983, Roll 1, Vol. 1, 458. For accounts of General Miles's previous campaigns against Sitting Bull, see Miles, *Serving the Republic*, 137–68; V. W. Johnson, *The Unregimented General*, 75–170; Utley, *The Indian Frontier*, 186–89; Wooster, *Nelson A. Miles*, 76–94.

68. Report of Brig. Gen. John R. Brooke in Brooke to AAG, March 2, 1891, NARS, RG 94, AIWKSC, M 983, Roll 2, Vol. 2, 1679–82.

69. Report of Brig. Gen. John R. Brooke in Brooke to AAG, March 2, 1891, NARS, RG 94, AIWKSC, M 983, Roll 2, Vol. 2, 1679–82; Miles to AAG (telegram), December 11, 1890, 1890, NARS, RG 94, AIWKSC, M 983, Roll 1, Vol. 1, 510; Miles to AG (telegram), December 13, 1890, NARS, RG 94, AIWKSC, M 983, Roll 1, Vol. 1, 516; AAG to AG (telegram), December 15, 1890, NARS, RG 94, AIWKSC, M 983, Roll 1, Vol. 1, p 556.

70. See, for example, Petition by Citizens of Keya Paha Country NE in Congressman W. E. Dorsey to Proctor, December 9, 1890, NARS, RG 94, AIWKSC, M 983, Roll 1, Vol. 1, 177–79; Governor F. E. Warren WY to Proctor, December 13, 1890, NARS, RG 94, AIWKSC, M 983, Roll 1, Vol. 1, 518–19; Mayor M. S. Elliot WY, to Proctor (telegram), November 22, 1890, NARS, RG 94, AIWKSC, M 983, Roll 1, Vol. 1, 521; Statement of Brig. Gen. Thomas H. Ruger, December 19, 1890, in Proctor to Dorsey, January 5, 1891, NARS, RG 94, AIWKSC, M 983, Roll 1, Vol. 1, 484; Brooke to Warren, November 21, 1890, NARS, RG 94, AIWKSC, M 983, Roll 1, Vol. 1, 525–26; Ruger to AG (telegram), December 14, 1890, NARS, RG 94, AIWKSC, M 983, Roll 1, Vol. 1, 534; Miles to AG (telegram), December 14, 1890, NARS, RG 94, AIWKSC, M 983, Roll 1, Vol. 1, 543. For accounts in the press, see chapter 5.

71. ARSW 1891, Report of the Major General Commanding the Army, September 24, 1891, 143, 146–47. See also V. W. Johnson, *The Unregimented General*, 281.

72. ARSW 1891, Report of Operations Relative to the Sioux Indians in 1890–1891, by Brig. Gen. Thomas H. Ruger, October 19, 1891, 181–82. See V. W. Johnson, *The Unregimented General*, 278–80; Utley, *The Last Days*, 146–48; Hagan, *Indian Police and Judges*, 100; Utley, *The Lance and the Shield*, 294–95; Wooster, *Nelson A. Miles*, 183–84; W. S. E. Coleman, *Voices of Wounded Knee*, 183–89. See also chapter 2.

73. ARSW 1891, Report of Capt. E. G. Fechet, December 17, 1890, 197–98; ARSW 1891, Report of Lt. Col. W. F. Drum, February 27, 1891, 194–97; Report of Brig. Gen. Thomas H. Ruger in Ruger to AAG, March 26, 1891, NARS, RG 94, AIWKSC, M 983, Roll 2, Vol. 2, 1275–76. For a list of casualties, see 52nd Cong., 1st Sess., *Senate Executive Document*, No. 84, Vol. 6, Serial 2901, 1–11. See also Utley, *The Last Days*, 161–64; Wooster, *Nelson A. Miles*, 183–84.

74. See Report of Brig. Gen. Thomas H. Ruger in Ruger to AAG, March 26, 1891, NARS, RG 94, AIWKSC, M 983, Roll 2, Vol. 2, 1275–76; 52nd Cong., 1st Sess., *Senate Executive Document*, No. 84, Vol. 6, Serial 2901, 1–11. For the newspaper accounts, see chapter 5. For more about Agent James McLaughlin, see chapter 2.

75. ARSW 1891, Report of Major General Commanding the Army, September 24, 1891, 146–147. See Utley, *The Last Days*, 169.

76. Miles, *Serving the Republic*, 239–40.

77. Miles to AG (telegram), December 22, 1890, NARS, RG 94, AIWKSC, M 983, Roll 1,

Vol. 1, 604. See Hyde, *A Sioux Chronicle*, 291–92; Mattes, "The Enigma of Wounded Knee," 3; Utley, *The Last Days*, 168–72.

78. Report of Brig. Gen. John R. Brooke in Brooke to AAG, March 2, 1891, NARS, RG 94, AIWKSC, M 983, Roll 2, Vol. 2, 1682–83. See also Miles, *Serving the Republic*, 240–41; V. W. Johnson, *The Unregimented General*, 276–77; Wooster, *Nelson A. Miles*, 182–83.

79. Report of Brig. Gen. John R. Brooke in Brooke to AAG, March 2, 1891, NARS, RG 94, AIWKSC, M 983, Roll 2, Vol. 2, 1863–64.

80. Miles to AG (telegram), December 22, 1890, NARS, RG 94, AIWKSC, M 983, Roll 1, Vol. 1, 604; Miles to Col. H. C. Merriam (telegram), ARSW 1891, Report of Col. H. C. Merriam, January 30, 1891, 205. See Miles, *Serving the Republic*, 241; Utley, *The Last Days*, 173; Paul, "Your Country Is Surrounded," 32.

81. For commentary on the Lakota concepts of kinship and family relationships, see the introduction.

82. Sumner to Miles (telegram), December 8, 1891, ARSW 1891, Report of Lt. Col. E. V. Sumner, February 3, 1891, 228; Sumner to AAG (telegram), December 16, 1891, ARSW 1891, Report of Lt. Col. E. V. Sumner, February 3, 1891, 229; Sumner to Miles (telegram), December 19, 1891, ARSW 1891, Report of Lt. Col. E. V. Sumner, February 3, 1891, 230. See also Utley, *The Last Days*, 173–74; Seymour, *Sitanka*, 115–43; Wooster, *Nelson A. Miles*, 184–85. See chapter 1.

83. Ruger to Merriam (telegram), December 18, 1890, ARSW 1891, Report of Col. H. C. Merriam, January 30, 1891, 204–5; Sumner to Miles, February 21, 1891, LC, NAMFP, Box 4; ARSW 1891, Report of Lt. Col. E. V. Sumner, February 3, 1891, 223–24; ARSW 1891, Statement of Second Lt. H. E. Hale, December 26, 1890, 200–210; ARSW 1891, Statement of Capt. J. H. Hurst, January 9, 1891, 201–2. See also Utley, *The Last Days*, 173–74; Jensen, "Another Look at Wounded Knee," 17; Wooster, *Nelson A. Miles*, 184–85.

84. Sumner to Brooke (telegram), December 12, ARSW 1891, Report of Lt. Col. E. V. Sumner, February 3, 1891, 228–29; Sumner to Miles (telegram), December 18, ARSW 1891, Report of Lt. Col. E. V. Sumner, February 3, 1891, 229; Sumner to Col. E. A. Carr (telegram), December 19, ARSW 1891, Report of Lt. Col. E. V. Sumner, February 3, 1891, 230–31; Sumner to Miles, February 21, 1891, LC, NAMFP, Box 4.

85. Merriam to Miles (telegram), December 20, 1891, ARSW 1891, 206; Merriam to AG (telegram), December 20, 1891, ARSW 1891, 206; Merriam to AAG (telegram), December 20, 1891, ARSW 1891, 206; Merriam to Miles (telegram), December 22, 1891, ARSW 1891, 209.

86. Sumner to Miles (telegram), December 21, 1891, ARSW 1891, Report of Lt. Col. E. V. Sumner, February 3, 1891, 232; Sumner to Miles (telegram), December 21, 1891, ARSW 1891, Report of Lt. Col. E. V. Sumner, February 3, 1891, 232; Sumner to Miles (2 telegrams), December 22, 1891, ARSW 1891, Report of Lt. Col. E. V. Sumner, February 3, 1891, 233; ARSW 1891, Report of Lt. Col. E. V. Sumner, February 3, 1891, 224–25. For an account of Big Foot's followers, see Jensen, "Big Foot's Followers," 194–212.

87. ARSW 1891, Report of Lt. Col. E. V. Sumner, February 3, 1891, 224–28; Sumner to Miles, February 21, 1891, LC, NAMFP, Box 4. See also Jensen, "Another Look at Wounded Knee," 17.

88. Miles to AG (telegram), December 22, 1890, NARS, RG 94, AIWKSC, M 983, Roll 1, Vol. 1, 604; Miles to Sumner (telegram), December 23, 1890, ARSW 1891, Report of Lt. Col. E. V. Sumner, February 3, 1891, 231; Ruger to AG (telegram), December 22, 1890, NARS, RG 94, AIWKSC, M 983, Roll 1, Vol. 1, 615.

89. Miles to Sumner (2 telegrams), December 24, 1890, ARSW 1891, Report of Lt. Col. E. V. Sumner, February 3, 1891, 235. Sumner later replied to General Miles's accusations, saying that he had obeyed his orders and had only tried to avoid bloodshed. See Sumner to Miles, February 21, 1891, LC, NAMFP, BOX 4.

90. Sumner to Carr (telegram), December 23, 1890, ARSW 1891, Report of Lt. Col. E. V. Sumner, February 3, 1891, 234; Sumner to Miles (telegram), December 23, 1890, ARSW 1891, Report of Lt. Col. E. V. Sumner, February 3, 1891, 234; ARSW 1891, Report of Lt. Col. E. V. Sumner, February 3, 1891, 225–26; Sumner to Merriam (message by courier), December 26, 1890, ARSW 1891, Report of Lt. Col. H. C. Merriam, January 30, 1891, 210; Sumner to Merriam (message by courier), December 27, 1890, ARSW 1891, Report of Lt. Col. H. C. Merriam, January 30, 1891, 210–11. For more about John Dunn, see Jensen, "Another Look at Wounded Knee," 17–18. See also chapter 1.

91. For a sense of the search for Big Foot, see Miles to AG (telegram), December 24, 1890, NARS, RG 94, AIWKSC, M 983, Roll 1, Vol. 1, 608; Miles to AG (telegram), December 25, 1890, NARS, RG 94, AIWKSC, M 983, Roll 1, Vol. 1, 609; AAG to Merriam (telegram), December 26, 1890, ARSW 1891, Report of Lt. Col. H. C. Merriam, January 30, 1891, 211–12; Miles to Merriam (telegram), December 27, 1890, ARSW 1891, Report of Lt. Col. H. C. Merriam, January 30, 1891, 212; Merriam to Sumner, December 28, 1890, ARSW 1891, Report of Lt. Col. H. C. Merriam, January 30, 1891, 212–13; Sumner to Merriam, December 28, 1890, ARSW 1891, Report of Lt. Col. H. C. Merriam, January 30, 1891, 212–13; Sumner to Carr, December 26, 1890, ARSW 1891, Report of Lt. Col. H. C. Merriam, January 30, 1891, 215; Report of Brig. Gen. John R. Brooke in Brooke to AAG, March 2, 1891, NARS, RG 94, AIWKSC, M 983, Roll 2, Vol. 2, 1684–86. The movements of troops during the search for Big Foot are well described in Utley, *The Last Days*, 187–99. See also Report of Maj. Samuel M. Whiteside, January 1, 1891, NARS, RG 94, AIWKSC, M 983, Roll 1, Vol. 2, 822–23.

92. Miles to AG (telegram), December 28, 1890, NARS, RG 94, AIWKSC, M 983, Roll 1, Vol. 1, 626; Lt. Fayette W. Roe (for Brooke) to Col. James W. Forsyth, December 26, 1890, NARS, RG 94, AIWKSC, M 983, Roll 1, Vol. 2, 751; Brooke to Maj. Samuel M. Whiteside, December 27, 1890, NARS, RG 94, AIWKSC, M 983, Roll 1, Vol. 2, 752; Roe (for Brooke) to Whiteside, December 27, 1890, NARS, RG 94, AIWKSC, M 983, Roll 1, Vol. 2, 753; Testimony of Brig. Gen. J. R. Brooke, January 18, 1890, NARS, RG 94, AIWKSC, M 983,

Roll 1, Vol. 2, 740–47. See also Zahn, *The Crimson Carnage*, 5; Mattes, "The Enigma of Wounded Knee," 4; Smith, *Moon of the Popping Trees*, 179; Seymour, *Sitanka*, 74–75.

93. See Forsyth to Brooke, December 29, 1890, NARS, RG 94, AIWKSC, M 983, Roll 1, Vol. 2, 758; Miles to AG (2 telegrams), December 29, 1890, NARS, RG 94, AIWKSC, M 983, Roll 1, Vol. 1, 633–34. See also Jensen, "Big Foot's Followers," 194–99.

94. ARSW 1891, Report of Major General Commanding the Army, September 24, 1891, 150.

95. For actual army accounts of the battle, see Forsyth to Brooke, December 29, 1890, NARS, RG 94, AIWKSC, M 983, Roll 1, Vol. 2, 758; Forsyth to AAG, December 31, 1890, NARS, RG 94, AIWKSC, M 983, Roll 1, Vol. 2, 760–61; Testimonies of Maj. S. M. Whiteside, Capt. M. Moylan, Capt. C. A. Varnum, Lt. W. J. Nicholson, Assistant Surgeon J. V. B. Hoff, Capt. E. S. Godfrey, Lt. S. Rice, Lt. C. W. Taylor, Capt. G. S. Ilsley, Capt. H. Jackson, Capt. W. S. Edgerly, Lt. W. W. Robinson Jr., Lt. T. Q. Donaldson Jr., Lt. S. R. H. Tompkins, Capt. A. Capron, Capt. H. J. Nowlan, Assistant Surgeon C. B. Ewing, Col. J. W. Forsyth, NARS, RG 94, AIWKSC, M 983, Roll 1, Vol. 2, 656–710. An excellent account of the Wounded Knee affair from the military point of view can be found in Utley, *The Last Days*, 200–230. See also Colby, "The Sioux Indian War," 155–57; Kelley, "The Indian Troubles," 40–44; Zahn, *The Crimson Carnage*, 5–6; Mattes, "The Enigma of Wounded Knee," 3–8; Smith, *Moon of the Popping Trees*, 184–96. An interesting account of the battle can be found in Lathrop, "Another View of Wounded Knee," 248–68. Lathrop used a soldier's diary to construct a story of Wounded Knee and the days following it from a regular soldier's point of view. Since the diary's authenticity cannot be fully established, the article is not used further in this study. Still, it is worth mentioning.

96. Special Orders, No. 8, January 4, 1890, NARS, RG 94, AIWKSC, M 983, Roll 1, Vol. 2, 653–54; Special Orders, No 10, January 6, 1890, NARS, RG 94, AIWKSC, M 983, Roll 1, Vol. 2, 655. For a full account of the Kent-Baldwin investigations, see Report of Investigations into the Battle at Wounded Knee Creek, South Dakota, Fought December 29, 1890, NARS, RG 94, AIWKSC, M 983, Roll 1, Vol. 2, 651–1134. See also Kelley, "The Indian Troubles," 41–44; Godfrey, "Tragedy at White Horse Creek," 1–11; Wooster, *Nelson A. Miles*, 189–92. For a discussion of the 7th Cavalry's role in the Wounded Knee affair, see Sievers, "The Historiography of 'The Bloody Field,'" 39–40.

97. Colonel Forsyth later submitted two reports in which he defended his conduct and expressed his opinions about the circumstances surrounding the Wounded Knee affair. See Reports of Brig. Gen. James W. Forsyth to Secretary of War Daniel S. Lamont, September 1, 1895, December 21, 1896, NARS, RG 94, AIWKSC, M 983, Roll 2, Vol. 4, 1–41. See ARSW 1891, Report of Major General Commanding the Army, September 24, 1891, 149–50. See also Miles, *Serving the Republic*, 243; Wooster, *Nelson A. Miles*, 189–92.

98. See Capt. Frank D. Baldwin to AAG, January 21, 1891, NARS, RG 94, AIWKSC, M 983, Roll 1, Vol. 2, 732–33; Report of Brig. Gen. John M. Schofield, February 4, 1891, NARS, RG 94, AIWKSC, M 983, Roll 1, Vol. 1, 268; Lt. Col. R. H. Brennan, 75th Cong. 1st Sess., House Committee on Indian Affairs, Published Hearing, March 7 and May 12, 1938, IULAL, Microfiche, Group 3, Card 5, 33–40. See also *Illustrated American* 7, February 1891, 334; Miles, *Serving the Republic*, 242–43; Mattes, "The Enigma of Wounded Knee," 8–9; Green, "The Medals of Wounded Knee."

99. Miles to AG (telegram), January 1, 1891, NARS, RG 94, AIWKSC, M 983, Roll 1, Vol. 2, 771; Forsyth to Brooke, December 31, 1890, NARS, RG 94, AIWKSC, M 983, Roll 1, Vol. 2, 760–61; Report of Brig. Gen. John R. Brooke in Brooke to AAG, March 2, 1891, NARS, RG 94, AIWKSC, M 983, Roll 2, Vol. 2, 1686–87; William Peano in Jensen, *Voices of the American West*, 1:233–37; George E. Bartlett, in Jensen, *Voices of the American West*, 2:27–37; General Augustus W. Corliss, in Jensen, *Voices of the American West*, 2:324–25. See also Twiss, "A Short History of Pine Ridge," 37; Utley, *The Last Days*, 231–34; Mooney, *The Ghost-Dance Religion*, 874–76; Paul, "Your Country Is Surrounded," 35–26. Interesting accounts of military life on Pine Ridge during the early days of January 1891 can be found in Erisman and Erisman, "Letters from the Field," 28–45; Green, *After Wounded Knee*, 48–74; Buecker, "'The Men Behaved Splendidly.'" For contemporary accounts, see W. A. Birdsall, in Jensen, *Voices of the American West*, 2:45–48; E. M. Keith, in Jensen, *Voices of the American West*, 2:63–67; Peter McFarland, in Jensen, *Voices of the American West*, 2:1–10.

100. For contemporary accounts of the Mission fight and other skirmishes, see ARSW 1891, Report of Brigadier General Commanding the Army, September 24, 1891, 150–52; Report of Lt. Col. James W. Forsyth, December 31, 1890, NARS, RG 94, AIWKSC, M 983, Roll 2, Vol. 2, 1092–94; Reports of Brig. Gen. James W. Forsyth to Secretary of War Daniel S. Lamont, September 1, 1895, December 21, 1896, NARS, RG 94, AIWKSC, M 983, Roll 2, Vol. 4, 1–41; Report of Capt. J. B. Kerr, January 2, 1891, NARS, RG 94, AIWKSC, M 983, Roll 2, Vol. 2, 1710–12; Report of Maj. G. V. Henry, January 17, 1891, NARS, RG 94, AIWKSC, M 983, Roll 2, Vol. 2, 1792–93; John Shangrau, in Jensen, *Voices of the American West*, 1:256–64; Phillip Wells, in Jensen, *Voices of the American West*, 1:126–63; Peter McFarland, in Jensen, *Voices of the American West*, 2:1–10. For more about these events, see Utley, *The Last Days*, 231–41; John V. Lauderdale to Josephine (Joe) Lauderdale, January 5–16, 1891, in Green, *After Wounded Knee*, 53–70; Erisman and Erisman, "Letters from the Field," 28–45.

101. See Report of Brig. Gen. John R. Brooke in Brooke to AAG, March 2, 1891, NARS, RG 94, AIWKSC, M 983, Roll 2, Vol. 2, 1689–94; ARSW 1891, Report of Brigadier General Commanding the Army, September 24, 1891, 150–52; Miles to AG, January 5, 1891, NARS, RG 94, AIWKSC, M 983, Roll 2, Vol. 2, 812–15; Peter McFarland, in Jensen, *Voices of the American West*, 2:1–10. See also Miles, *Serving the Republic*, 242–43.

102. Miles to AG (telegram), January 5, 1891, NARS, RG 94, AIWKSC, M 983, Roll 1, Vol. 2, 810; Miles to AG (telegram), January 7, 1891, NARS, RG 94, AIWKSC, M 983, Roll 1, Vol. 2, 881. See also Utley, *The Last Days*, 254–57; Mooney, *The Ghost-Dance Religion*, 887; John V. Lauderdale to Josephine (Joe) Lauderdale January 7–11, 1891, in Green, *After Wounded Knee*, 58–60.

103. Miles to Schofield (telegram), January 3, 1891, NARS, RG 94, AIWKSC, M 983, Roll 1, Vol. 2, 795; Miles to AG (telegram), January 6, 1891, NARS, RG 94, AIWKSC, M 983, Roll 1, Vol. 2, 825; Schofield to Miles (telegram), January 6, 1891, NARS, RG 94, AIWKSC, M 983, Roll 1, Vol. 2, 827; Miles to Schofield (telegram), January 7, 1891, NARS, RG 94, AIWKSC, M 983, Roll 1, Vol. 2, 917; Report of Major General Commanding the Army, September 24, 1891, ARSW 1891, 151–52. See *North American Review*, January 1891, 1–11; Miles, *Serving the Republic*, 243–44; Wooster, *Nelson A. Miles*, 186–87, 191–92.

104. For troop movements during January 1891, see Miles to Schofield (telegram), January 3, 1891, NARS, RG 94, AIWKSC, M 983, Roll 1, Vol. 2, 795; Miles to AG (telegram), January 11, 1891, NARS, RG 94, AIWKSC, M 983, Roll 1, Vol. 2, 941; Miles to AG (telegram), January 12, 1891, NARS, RG 94, AIWKSC, M 983, Roll 1, Vol. 2, 942; ARSW 1891, Report of Major General Commanding the Army, September 24, 1891, 151–52; Report of Brig. Gen. John R. Brooke in Brooke to AAG, March 2, 1891, NARS, RG 94, AIWKSC, M 983, Roll 2, Vol. 2, 1693–96. See also V. W. Johnson, *The Unregimented General*, 290–99; Utley, *The Last Days*, 251–61.

105. Miles to AG (2 telegrams), January 12, 1891, NARS, RG 94, AIWKSC, M 983, Roll 1, Vol. 2, 942, 946; Miles to AG (telegram), January 14, 1891, NARS, RG 94, AIWKSC, M 983, Roll 1, Vol. 2, 954; ARSW 1891, Report of Major General Commanding the Army, September 24, 1891, 152–55.

106. ARSW 1891, Report of Major General Commanding the Army, September 24, 1891, 154–55. See also Utley, *The Last Days*, 260–61. For further discussion of the guns in the Lakotas' possession, see 51st Cong., 2nd Sess., *Senate Executive Document*, No. 2, Vol. 1, Serial, 2818, 1–14; 51st Cong., 2nd Sess., *Senate Executive Document*, No. 2, Vol. 1, Serial, 2818, 2–51. See also chapters 1, 5, and 6.

107. Miles to Schofield (telegram), December 19, 1890, 1890, NARS, RG 94, AIWKSC, M 983, Roll 1, Vol. 1, 585; Frank Wood to ACIA, November 24, 1890, NARS, RG 75, SC 188, M 4728, Roll 1, 3/28–29; ARSW 1891, Report of Major General Commanding the Army, September 24, 1891, 56; Miles to Mary Miles, as quoted in V. W. Johnson, *The Unregimented General*, 288–89. See Miles, *Serving the Republic*, 238–43.

108. Youngkin, "Prelude to Wounded Knee," 333–37, 340–51; Utley, *The Indian Frontier*, 257.

109. See, for example, Youngkin, "Prelude to Wounded Knee," 332–35, 345–51; Seymour, *Sitanka*, 143–47; Utley, *The Indian Frontier*, 257; Wooster, *The Military*, 65–66; Wooster, *Nelson A. Miles*, 181–92; W. S. E. Coleman, *Voices of Wounded Knee*, 96–97. See also chapter 5.

110. For additional information about the army's actions and the investigations relating to the ghost dance troubles during the year 1891, see 52nd Cong., 1st Sess., *Senate Executive Document*, No. 58, Vol. 5, Serial 2900, 1–185; NARS, RG 94, AIWKSC, M 983, Roll 1–2, Vol. 2–4, 651–2006. See also Wooster, *Nelson A. Miles*, 188–92.

111. *Omaha Daily Bee*, December 30, 1890, 1. Elaine Goodale Eastman, for example, noted that many officers thought that the army's presence was not necessary, while at the same time ordinary soldiers were bored with the inaction and were "spoiling for a fight" (E. G. Eastman, "The Ghost Dance War," 30). For further commentary, see Ostler, *The Plains Sioux*, 350–52. See also chapters 5, 6.

112. Miles to Schofield (telegram), January 15, 1891, NARS, RG 94, AIWKSC, M 983, Roll 1, Vol. 2, 964; Miles to AG (telegram), January 15, 1891, NARS, RG 94, AIWKSC, M 983, Roll 1, Vol. 2, 967; ARSW 1891, Report of Major General Commanding the Army, September 24, 1891, 154–55. See also Miles, *Serving the Republic*, 243–44; Mattes, "The Enigma of Wounded Knee," 4–5; Utley, *The Last Days*, 259–67.

113. Boyd, *Recent Indian Wars*, 281–86; Miles, *Serving the Republic*, 245–46. The belief that Indians were a dying race was nothing new, and was entertained by many scientists and politicians as well. See introduction.

4. Missionary Views on the Lakota Ghost Dance

1. Woodruff, "The Episcopal Mission," 553–56; Markowitz, "The Catholic Mission and the Sioux," 119–23, Enochs, *The Jesuit Mission*, 1–14.

2. Woodruff, "The Episcopal Mission," 553–59; Hein, "Episcopalianism," 14–16.

3. See Enochs, *The Jesuit Mission*, 12–35.

4. See Barton, *John Williamson*, 176; Olmstead, *History of Religion*, 412–17; Anderson, *400 Years*, 81–106; Enochs, *The Jesuit Mission*, 20–26, 39; Hein, "Episcopalianism," 14–16; Foley, *Father Francis M. Craft*, 11–30.

5. Markowitz, "The Catholic Mission," 113–25; Enochs, *The Jesuit Mission*, 29, 3–41; Foley, *Father Francis M. Craft*, 11–49. See Father Emil Perrig Diary (hereafter Perrig Diary), MUA, BCIM, Holy Rosary Mission Collection; Florentine Digman Papers (hereafter Digman Papers), MUA, BCIM, History of St. Francis Mission 1886–1922, St. Francis Mission Collection.

6. Markowitz, "The Catholic Mission," 113–25; Enochs, *The Jesuit Mission*, 29, 3–41; Foley, *Father Francis M. Craft*, 85.

7. See Enochs, *The Jesuit Mission*, 35; Anderson, *400 Years*, 87–115.

8. See introduction.

9. See Hein, "Episcopalianism," 14–16; Markowitz, "The Catholic Mission," 128–29; Anderson, *400 Years*, 87–115; Foley, *Father Francis M. Craft*.

10. Markowitz, "The Catholic Mission," 113–25; Enochs, *The Jesuit Mission*, 29, 3–41; Foley, *Father Francis M. Craft*, 85. See Father Perrig to Father Stephan, March

26, 1890, MUA, BCIM, Series 1–1, Roll 20; Father Digman to Father Stephan May 12, 1890, MUA, BCIM, Series 1-1, Roll 20. For more about daily life at the missions, see Perrig Diary; Digman Papers.

11. Barton, *John Williamson*, 130–38, 145–255; Littfield and Parins, *American Indian and Alaska Native Newspapers and Periodicals*, 151–57, 403–7; Kerstetter, "Spin Doctors at Santee," 46–49.

12. See Perrig Diary, January–August 1890; Digman Papers, January–August 1890. Much information relating to the activities at the missions in early 1890 can be found in the correspondence between Fathers Jutz, Perrig, Digman, and Stephan. See Holy Rosary Mission and St. Francis Mission, Correspondence, January–April 1890, MUA, BCIM, Series 1-1, Roll 20. See also Enochs, *The Jesuit Mission*, 35–52.

13. Perrig Diary, August 24, 1890. For more about this incident, see chapters 2 and 3.

14. Perrig Diary, August 25, 1890.

15. Perrig Diary, September 7, 1890.

16. Perrig Diary, September 20, 1890.

17. Perrig Diary, September 26, 1890.

18. Digman Papers, September 30, 1890.

19. Digman Papers, September 30, 1890. Father Digman repeated his experience in a letter to Father Stephan in October 1890. See Digman to Stephan, October 2, 1890, MUA, BCIM, Series 1-1, Roll 20.

20. A good description of this competition is presented in Foley, *Father Francis M. Craft*, 16–77.

21. Digman Papers, September 30, 1890; Digman to Stephan, October 2, 1890, MUA, BCIM, Series 1-1, Roll 20, The emphasis is Father Digman's.

22. Digman Papers, October 16, October 19, 1890.

23. Perrig Diary, September 26, 1890.

24. Digman to Stephan, October 14, 1890, MUA, BCIM, Series 1-1, Roll 20. For more about Hollow Horn Bear, see chapter 1.

25. See Perrig Diary, September 27–October 17, 1890; Digman to Stephan, October 14, 1890, MUA, BCIM, Series 1-1, Roll 20. For more about Agent Wright, see chapter 2.

26. Perrig Diary, October 18–November 19, 1890.

27. Digman Papers, November 28, 1890; Jutz to Stephan, MUA, BCIM, Series 1-1, Roll 20.

28. Digman Papers, exact date not given, November 20–28, 1890.

29. Perrig Diary, November 19–20, 1890.

30. Mary C. Collins in *Word Carrier*, November 1890, 30; Mary C. Collins, IULL, WMCC Box 6, Folder 3, Envelope 78. See also Kerstetter, "Spin Doctors at Santee," 51–53. Mary Collins was also quoted by many national newspapers. See chapter 5.

31. Mary C. Collins in *Word Carrier*, November 1890, 30; Mary C. Collins, IULL, WMCC, Box 6, Folder 3, Envelope 78.

32. Mary C. Collins in *Word Carrier*, November 1890, 30, 31; Mary C. Collins, IULL, WMCC, Box 6, Folder 3, Envelope 78.

33. Perrig Diary, November 20–28, 1890.

34. Perrig Diary, November 20–27, 1890; Digman Papers, between November 20–28, 1890.

35. Perrig Diary, November 25–31, 1890; Digman Papers, November 28, 1890.

36. See chapters 1, 2.

37. Owen Lovejoy in *Word Carrier*, November 1890, 31; Elian Gilbert in *Iapi Oaye*, January 1891, 1.

38. *Word Carrier*, November 1890, 29.

39. "Messiya Itonsni" may be translated as "The lie of the Messiah", but in this context I believe that a better translation would be "False Prophet" since it refers to the false prophets mentioned in the quotations from the Bible that are used in the *Iapi Oyaye*.

40. Sam White Bird in *Iapi Oaye*, November 1890, 38, quotation from Matt. 24:3–24. See Kerstetter, "Spin Doctors at Santee," 54–55. For more about spirits, see chapter 1.

41. Louis Mazawakiyanna and Samuel Spaniard in *Iapi Oaye*, November 1890, 39

42. John Williamson *Iapi Oaye*, November 1890, 39, quotations from Isa. 49:6, 1 Thess. 1:10, 1 Thess. 4:15–17, Matt. 24:27, Luke 21:27, Jer. 5:28–29, Matt. 24:23–26.

43. Kerstetter, "Spin Doctors at Santee," 55. (Kerstetter's translation is also somewhat different.) See also Littfield and Parins, *American Indian and Alaska Native Newspapers and Periodicals*, 151–57, 403–05.

44. See *New York Times*, November 26, 1890, 1–2.

45. Bishop William B. Hare to CIA December 6, 1890, NARS, RG 75 SC 188, M 4728, Roll 1, 4/34; Bishop Hare as quoted in *New York Times*, November 26, 1890, 1–2.

46. Edward Ashley Papers 1883–1931,File A 5/2; Phillip J. Deloria, IULL, WMCC, Box 55, Folder 12, Envelope 65; Bishop William B. Hare to CIA, December 6, 1890, NARS, RG 75, SC 188, M 4728 Roll 1, 4/34. According to Deloria family tradition, Phillip J. Deloria would have actually met Sitting Bull the night before his death. There is, however, strong evidence that the meeting never took place. Phillip Deloria himself later said at least once that he did not meet Sitting Bull at that time. Discussion with Professor Phillip Deloria, October 4, 2007, Oklahoma City; discussion with Professor Raymond J. DeMallie, October 4, 2007, Oklahoma City. Phillip J. Deloria's own account can be found in IULL, WMCC, Box 55, Folder 12, Envelope 65.

47. See Bishop William B. Hare to CIA, December 6, 1890, NARS, RG 75, SC 188, M 4728 Roll 1, 4/34; Bishop Hare as quoted in *New York Times*, November 26, 1890, 1–2.

48. Perrig Diary, November 29–December 6, 1890.

49. Father Jutz to Stephan, December 14, 1890, MUA, BCIM, Series 1-1, Roll 20. See Kreis, *Rothäute, Schwarzröcke, und Heilige Frauen*, 102–3; Enochs, *The Jesuit Mission*, 57–58. For Father Jutz's visit, see also chapters 1 and 5.

50. *New York Times*, December 7, 1890, 14; *Omaha Daily Bee*, December 6, 1890, 1. See also chapter 5.

51. Perrig Diary, December 5–8, 1890; Father Jutz to Stephan, December 14, 1890, MUA, BCIM, Series 1-1, Roll 20.

52. Perrig Diary, December 12–13, 1890.

53. Digman to Stephan, December 14, 1890, MUA, BCIM, Series 1-1, Roll 20; Jutz to Stephan, December 14, 1890, MUA, BCIM, Series 1-1, Roll 20; Stephan to Jutz, December 19, 1890, MUA, BCIM, Series 1-1, Roll 20.

54. See CIA to L. E. Quigg, January 10, 1891, TJMLB, AISRI, 389–90; Statement of Commissioner Morgan, December 20, 1892, TJMLB, AISRI, 26. For more about Father Craft, see Foley, *Father Francis M. Craft*.

55. See Foley, *Father Francis M. Craft*; Perrig Diary, December 12–13, 1890.

56. Perrig Diary, November 1890–January 1890; Digman Papers, November–December 1890. See Mary Collins in *Word Carrier*, November 1890, 31; *Word Carrier*, December 1890, 35; *Word Carrier*, January 1891, 1–4. See also T. L. Riggs in *Word Carrier*, February 1891, 5; T. L. Riggs in *Word Carrier*, March 1891, 10.

57. John Williamson as quoted in Barton, *John Williamson*, 176–77.

58. For more about this division, see chapter 1.

59. Perrig Diary, December 12, 1890. See chapter 1.

60. Perrig Diary, December 14–15, 1890.

61. Perrig Diary, December 16–21, 1890.

62. *Word Carrier*, December 1890, 33.

63. G. W. Reed in *Word Carrier*, December 1890, 34. See Kerstetter, "Spin Doctors at Santee," 56.

64. G. W. Reed, IULL, WMCC, Box 5, Folder 1, Envelope 41; Mary C. Collins, IULL, WMCC, Box 6, Folder 3, Envelope 78; Aaron Beede, NDHS, ABD, Vol. 5, 50–53; Bishop Martin Marty as quoted in Berghold, *The Indians' Revenge*, 225–27; Aaron Beede as quoted in Hoover, "Sitting Bull," 166–67.

65. Father F. M. Craft as quoted in Foley, *Father Francis M. Craft*, 86. Father Craft's comment was initially published in *New York Freeman's Journal*.

66. Perrig Diary, December 22–27, 1890; Jutz to Stephan, December 26, 1890, MUA, BCIM, Series 1-1, Roll 20. For more about Big Foot, see chapter 1.

67. Perrig Diary, December 27, 1890; Jutz to Stephan, December 26, 1890, MUA, BCIM, Series 1-1, Roll 20.

68. *Word Carrier*, December 1890, 34.

69. *Word Carrier*, December 1890, 34.

70. Fred B. Riggs in the *Iapi Oaye*, December 1890, 42; footnotes deleted.

71. *Word Carrier*, December 1890, 34–35; *Iapi Oaye*, November 1890, 38–39; *Iapi Oaye*, December 1890, 41–42. See also Kerstetter, "Spin Doctors at Santee," 57.

72. Perrig Diary, December 28, 1890–January 10, 1891; Jutz to Stephan December 31, 1890, MUA, BCIM, Series 1-1, Roll 20. For more about the fight at the mission, see chapters 1 and 3.

73. Perrig Diary, December 28, 1890–January 10, 1891; Jutz to Stephan December 31, 1890, MUA, BCIM, Series 1-1, Roll 20.

74. Father F. M. Craft as quoted in Foley, *Father Francis M. Craft*, 87–93. Foley has used a journal written by Father Craft. The journal is in Foley's possession.

75. Perrig Diary, January 11–25, 1891.

76. *Word Carrier*, January 1891, 1–4.

77. Kerstetter, "Spin Doctors at Santee," 50.

78. See Perrig Diary, December 29, 1890–January 20, 1891; Digman Papers, December 29, 1890–January 20, 1891.

79. *Iapi Oaye*, January 1891, 1.

80. T. L. Riggs in *Word Carrier*, February 1891, 5; T. L. Riggs in *Word Carrier*, March 1891, 10.

5. "In an Atmosphere Pregnant with Mysteries"

1. For more about the correspondents, see Watson, "The Last Indian War," 208–10; Kolbenschlag, *Whirlwind Passes*, xi, 15–26.

2. Watson, "The Last Indian War," 208–10; Kolbenschlag, *Whirlwind Passes*, xi, 15–26.

3. Watson, "The Last Indian War," 205–6, 214; Jones, "Teresa Dean," 659; Kolbenschlag, *Whirlwind Passes*, 15–16, 40. See also chapters 1 and 3.

4. Watson, "The Last Indian War," 209; Kolbenschlag, *Whirlwind Passes*, 15–26; Carter, "Making Pictures," 39, 44–45. A comprehensive selection of pictures taken during the ghost dance troubles is presented in Jensen, Paul, and Carter, *Eyewitness at Wounded Knee*, 62–192. For an analysis of earlier Indian wars and the press, see Coward, *The Newspaper Indian*, 23–154.

5. Watson, "The Last Indian War," 210; Jones, "Teresa Dean," 656–62; Kolbenschlag, *Whirlwind Passes*, 82; Lindberg, "Foreigners in Action"; W. S. E. Coleman, *Voices of Wounded Knee*, 388. Coleman erroneously writes Zillucus instead of Zilliacus. He also maintains that he represented the *Chicago Swedish Tribune*. He attributes this information to Watson, but Watson does not mention this at all. Kolbenschlag believes that he was not a working journalist, but was named honorary correspondent by the other correspondents (Watson, "The Last Indian War," 210; Kolbenschlag, *Whirlwind Passes*, 82; Lindberg, "Foreigners in Action," 170–71; W. S. E. Coleman, *Voices of Wounded Knee*, 388).

6. The newspapers used the name "Sioux" instead of "Lakota."

7. *Harper's Weekly*, January 4, 1890, 10–11; *Omaha Daily Bee*, January 1, 1890, 1; *Omaha Daily Bee*, January 3, 1890, 1.

8. *Omaha Daily Bee*, February 11, 1890, 1, 4; *Omaha Daily Bee*, February 13, 1890, 1; *Omaha Daily Bee*, February 17, 1890, 2; *Washington Post*, February 11, 1890, 1; *New York Times*, February 11, 1890, 1; *Harper's Weekly*, March 8, 1890, 534; *Chicago Tribune*, February 11, 1890, 2.

9. See, for example, *Chicago Tribune*, January 28, 1890, 2; *Chicago Tribune*, January, 30, 2; *Omaha Daily Bee*, January 17, 1890, 8; *Omaha Daily Bee*, February 1, 1890, 1; *Washington Post*, January 28, 1890, 1; *Washington Post*, February 13, 1890, 5; *Washington Post*, March 8, 1890, 6; *Washington Post*, March 9, 1890, 1; *Washington Post*, March 18, 1890, 4; *New York Times*, January 28, 1890, 3; *New York Times*, February 13, 1890, 4; *New York Times*, March 17, 1890, 4.

10. *Omaha Daily Bee*, April 6, 1890, 1; *Washington Post*, April 6, 1890, 1; *Chicago Tribune*, April 7, 1890, 9; *New York Times*, April 6, 1890, 1. For more about the allotment of Lakota lands, see introduction and chapter 6.

11. *Washington Post*, April 6, 1890, 1; *Washington Post*, April 16, 1890, 2.

12. *Omaha Daily Bee*, April 12, 1890, 1.

13. *Omaha Daily Bee*, April 27, 1890, 1.

14. *Omaha Daily Bee*, May 2, 1890, 2; *Omaha Daily Bee*, May 14, 1890, 4; *Omaha Daily Bee*, May 29, 1890, 4; *Chicago Tribune*, May 28, 1890, 1.

15. See *Washington Post*, May 4, 1890, 9; *Washington Post*, May 16, 1890, 2; *Washington Post*, June 6, 1890, 1; *Washington Post*, June 8, 1890, 2; *Washington Post*, June 9, 1890, 1; *New York Times*, May 1, 1890, 10; *New York Times*, May 5, 1890, 5; *New York Times*, June 6, 1890, 1; *New York Times*, June 9, 1890, 2. See also *Chicago Tribune*, June 7, 1890, 2.

16. *Omaha Daily Bee*, June 12, 1890, 1; *Omaha Daily Bee*, June 13, 1890, 1, 4; *Omaha Daily Bee*, June 14, 1890, 2. See chapters 1, 3, and 6.

17. *Omaha Daily Bee*, June 19, 1890, 1; *Omaha Daily Bee*, June 20, 1890, 1. See also *Chicago Tribune*, June 12, 1890, 1.

18. *Washington Post*, July 21, 1890, 6; *Washington Post*, August 24, 1890, 1. See also *Washington Post*, August 4, 1890, 7; *Washington Post*, August 18, 1890, 5; *New York Times*, July 16, 1890, 1; *New York Times*, July 29, 1890, 2; *New York Times*, August 5, 1890, 1.

19. *Washington Post*, July 23, 1890, 7; *Washington Post*, July 24, 1890, 7.

20. *Washington Post*, August 28, 1890, 6; *New York Times*, August 14, 1890, 1. For more about Agent Lea, see chapters 1, 2, and 6.

21. *Chicago Tribune*, July 12, 1890, 1; *Omaha Daily Bee*, June 19, 1890, 1; *Omaha Daily Bee*, June 20, 1890, 1; *Omaha Daily Bee*, July 7, 1890, 6.

22. See, for example, *Chicago Tribune*, July 22, 1890, 6; *Chicago Tribune*, July 25, 1890, 9; *Chicago Tribune*, August 8, 1890, 9; *Omaha Daily Bee*, August 9, 1890, 2: *Omaha Daily Bee*, August 12, 1890, 4.

23. *Chicago Tribune*, September 26, 1890, 1; *Washington Post*, September 27, 1890, 1.

24. *Omaha Daily Bee*, October 26, 1890, 6; *Washington Post*, October 28, 1890, 4.

25. *Washington Post*, October 28, 1890, 1.

26. *Yankton Press and Dakotan*, October 28, 1890, 1; *Chicago Tribune*, October 28, 1890, 1; *Omaha Daily Bee*, October 28, 1890, 1. See also Smith, *Moon of the Popping Trees*, 110–12.

27. *New York Times*, October 28, 1890, 3. For an account of Sitting Bull's image in the press before the ghost dance, see Coward, *The Newspaper Indian*, 158–91.

28. The paper wrote that Herbert Welsh represented the Indian Defense Association, but he actually represented the Indian Rights Association. See introduction.

29. *Washington Post*, October 29, 1890, 7. For more about Herbert Welsh and The Indian Rights Association, see Hagan, *The Indian Rights Association*. For more about The Indian Rights Association and the ghost dance, see Hagan, *The Indian Rights Association*, 115–26.

30. *Omaha Daily Bee*, October 29, 1890, 1; *Yankton Press and Dakotan*, November 3, 1890, 1.

31. *Washington Post*, November 7, 1890, 7. See also *Chicago Tribune*, November 7, 1890, 6. For more about General Schofield's views, see chapter 3.

32. *Washington Post*, November 8, 1890, 1; *New York Times*, November 8, 1890, 5. For more about the Mormons and the ghost dance, see introduction.

33. See, for example, *New York Times*, October 12, 1890, 9; *New York Times*, October 15, 1890, 3; *New York Times*, November 17, 1890, 2. See also Smoak, "The Mormons and the Ghost Dance," 269–94.

34. *Washington Post*, November 8, 1890, 1; *New York Times*, October 22, 1890, 2.

35. See also chapter 3.

36. *Washington Post*, November 18, 1890, 1.

37. *Washington Post*, November 15, 1890, 6; *New York Times*, November 15, 1890, 1. For information about other newspaper reports during November and December 1890 and January 1891, see Kolbenschlag, *Whirlwind Passes*, 26–86; Smith, *Moon of the Popping Trees*, 126–41. See also Jensen, Paul and Carter, *Eyewitness at Wounded Knee*, 39–183.

38. For the military operation, see chapter 3.

39. *Yankton Press and Dakotan*, November 15, 1890, 1; *Yankton Press and Dakotan*, November 17, 1890, 1; *Chicago Tribune*, November 16, 1890, 1; *Chicago Tribune*, November 17, 1890, 1; *Omaha Daily Bee*, November 16, 1890, 1; *Omaha Daily Bee*, November 17, 1890, 1.

40. *Washington Post*, November 16, 1890, 1.

41. *New York Times*, November 16, 1890, 11. General Miles came to Pine Ridge in late December 1890. See chapter 3.

42. *New York Times*, November 17, 1890, 1; *New York Times*, November 18, 1890, 1; *Omaha Daily Bee*, November 17, 1890, 1; *Omaha Daily Bee*, November 18, 1890, 1; *Chicago Tribune*, November 18, 1890, 1; *Yankton Press and Dakotan*, November 17, 1890, 1–2; *Yankton Press and Dakotan*, November 18, 1890, 1.

43. *New York Times*, November 19, 1890, 2. See Charles A. Eastman to Frank Wood (forwarded to ACIA), November 11, 1890, NARS, RG 75, SC 188, M 4728, Reel 1, 1/98–100. Charles A. Eastman was an educated Santee Sioux serving as a physician among the Lakotas at Pine Ridge. For his life, see C. A. Eastman, *From Deep Woods to Civilization* and *The Soul of the Indian*.

44. *Washington Post*, November 19, 1890, 1.

45. *Washington Post*, November 19, 1890, 1; *New York Times*, November 19, 1890, 2. See Boyd, *Recent Indian Wars*, 216–17; Smith, *Moon of the Popping Trees*, 114–16. For more about the organization of local militia goups against the Lakotas, see Colby, "The Sioux Indian War."

46. *Omaha Daily Bee*, November 19, 1890, 2; *Chicago Tribune*, November 19, 1890, 1; *Yankton Press and Dakotan*, November 19, 1890, 1–2.

47. *Omaha Daily Bee*, November 20, 1890, 1, 4; *Chicago Tribune*, November 20, 1890, 1, 4; *Yankton Press and Dakotan*, November 20, 1, 4.

48. *Omaha Daily Bee*, November 20, 1890, 1, 4; *Chicago Tribune*, November 20, 1890, 1, 4. For more about newspaper reporting after the military's arrival, see Boyd, *Recent Indian Wars*, 220–21; Smith, *Moon of the Popping Trees*, 126–28; Kolbenschlag, *Whirlwind Passes*, 35–42.

49. *New York Times*, November 21, 1890, 1.

50. *Chicago Tribune*, November 21, 1890, 1–2, 9; *Omaha Daily Bee*, November 21, 1890, 1; *New York Times*, November 22, 1890, 1; *Yankton Press and Dakotan*, November 21, 1890, 1–2. Interestingly, the actual army reports were totally different in nature. See chapter 3.

51. *New York Times*, November 22, 1890, 2.

52. As mentioned in the introduction, during Indian wars whites traditionally divided the Indians into friendlies and hostiles. During the ghost dance troubles the newspapers, as well as the whites in general, quickly adopted these terms to differentiate between the ghost dancers and those who did not openly join them. To retain some of the style of the newspaper reporting, the words "hostiles" and "friendlies" are used in this chapter as the newspapers used them. See also Kolbenschlag, *Whirlwind Passes*, 34.

53. *New York Times*, November 22, 1890, 1–2.

54. *New York Times*, November 22, 1890, 2. Mrs. Finley's account was also published in *Chicago Tribune*, November 22, 1890, 2.

55. *Harper's Weekly*, November 22, 1890, 902.

56. *Chicago Tribune*, November 22, 1890, 1; *Omaha Daily Bee*, November 22, 1890, 1; *Yankton Press and Dakotan*, November 22, 1890, 1–2.

57. *Chicago Tribune*, November 22, 1890, 1; *Omaha Daily Bee*, November 22, 1890, 1.

58. *New York Times*, November 23, 1890, 5; *Chicago Tribune*, November 23, 1890, 1; *Omaha Daily Bee*, November 23, 1890, 1.

59. *New York Times*, November 23, 1890, 5; *Chicago Tribune*, November 23, 1890, 1; *Omaha Daily Bee*, November 23, 1890, 1.

60. For more about Man Afraid of His Horse's trip, see *New York Times*, November 21, 1890, 5.

61. *Omaha Daily Bee*, November 23, 1890, 1–2; *Yankton Press and Dakotan*, November 23, 1890, 1; *Chicago Tribune*, November 23, 1890, 1–3; *New York Times*, November 23, 1890, 5.

62. *Washington Post*, November 24, 1890, 1; *New York Times*, November 24, 1890, 1.

63. *Yankton Press and Dakotan*, November 23, 1890, 1; *Washington Post*, November 24, 1890, 1; *New York Times*, November 24, 1890, 1; *Chicago Tribune*, November 24, 1890, 1–2; *Omaha Daily Bee*, November 24, 1890, 1.

64. *Washington Post*, November 24, 1890, 1; *New York Times*, November 24, 1890, 1; *Chicago Tribune*, November 24, 1890, 1–2; *Omaha Daily Bee*, November 24, 1890, 1; *Yankton Press and Dakotan*, November 25, 1890, 1.

65. *Washington Post*, November 24, 1890, 1. For more about the Lakotas' success in farming, see the introduction and chapter 6.

66. *New York Times*, November 24, 1890, 2.

67. *New York Times*, November 24, 1890, 2.

68. *Omaha Daily Bee*, November 25, 1890, 1, 4; *Yankton Press and Dakotan*, November 25, 1890, 1.

69. See, for example, *Omaha Daily Bee*, November 25, 1890, 4. For additional commentary on the ghost dance reporting in November 1890, see Boyd, *Recent Indian Wars*, 217; Smith, *Moon of the Popping Trees*, 131–32, 137–41; Kolbenschlag, *Whirlwind Passes*, 35–42.

70. *Washington Post*, November 25, 1890, 1; *New York Times*, November 25, 1890, 5; *Chicago Tribune*, November 25, 1890, 1, 5.

71. *New York Times*, November 25, 1890, 5; *Washington Post*, November 25, 1890, 1; *Chicago Tribune*, November 25, 1890, 1, 5. For more about various names attributed to Wovoka, see the introduction and chapter 3.

72. *New York Times*, November 26, 1890, 1–2; *Yankton Press and Dakotan*, November 26, 1890, 1. See *Yankton Press and Dakotan*, November 28, 1890, 1; *Washington Post*, November 27, 1890, 1. See also chapter 4.

73. *Chicago Tribune*, November 26, 1890, 1, 5; *Omaha Daily Bee*, November 26, 1890, 1. See also *Yankton Press and Dakotan*, November 25, 1890, 2.

74. *New York Times*, November 27, 1890, 1; *New York Times*, November 28, 1890, 5; *Washington Post*, November 27, 1890, 1; *Washington Post*, November 28, 1890, 1; *Omaha Daily Bee*, November 26, 1890, 1; *Omaha Daily Bee*, November 27, 1890, 1; *Chicago Tribune*, November 27, 1890, 1; *Chicago Tribune*, November 28, 1890, 2.

75. *New York Times*, November 29, 1890, 5.

76. *Washington Post*, November 29, 1890, 1; *Yankton Press and Dakotan*, November 29, 1890, 1. See *Omaha Daily Bee*, November 28, 1890, 1.

77. *New York Times*, November 30, 1890, 2; *Chicago Tribune*, November 29, 1890, 1–2. See also *Omaha Daily Bee*, November 29, 1890, 1, *Yankton Press and Dakotan*, December 2, 1890, 3.

78. *Harper's Weekly*, November 29, 1890, 922–33.

79. *Omaha Daily Bee*, November 30, 1890, 1; *Chicago Tribune*, November 30, 1890, 4.

80. *New York Times*, November 30, 1890, 2; *Washington Post*, November 30, 1890, 1; *Omaha Daily Bee*, November 30, 1890, 1; *Chicago Tribune*, November 30, 1890, 4.

81. *New York Times*, November 29, 1890, 8; *New York Times*, November 30, 1890, 11; *Omaha Daily Bee*, November 30, 1890, 1, 4, 9–11; *Chicago Tribune*, November 30, 1890, 4. The *New York Times* did not specify who these whites were who were expecting their Messiah. The paper most likely meant the Mormons (*New York Times*, November 29, 1890, 8. See also Smoak, "The Mormons and the Ghost Dance of 1890").

82. *New York Times*, November 30, 1890, 2; *Washington Post*, November 30, 1890, 1; *Omaha Daily Bee*, November 30, 1890, 1; *Chicago Tribune*, November 30, 1890, 4. For a contemporary account of the messiah's identity, see John C. Mayhugh to CIA, November 24, 1890, NARS, RG 75, SC 188, M 4728, Roll 1, 2/74–79. See also introduction and chapter 3.

83. *New York Times*, December 1, 1890, 5; *Washington Post*, December 1, 1890, 1.

84. *Omaha Daily Bee*, December 1, 1890, 1; *New York Times*, December 1, 1890, 5; *Washington Post*, December 1, 1890, 1; *Yankton Press and Dakotan*, December 1, 1890, 1.

85. The Annual Report of the Secretary of the Interior as quoted in *New York Times*, December 1, 1890, 10.

86. *Chicago Tribune*, December 1, 1890, 1–2; *Omaha Daily Bee*, December 1, 1890, 1; *Yankton Press and Dakotan*, December 1, 1890, 1; *Yankton Press and Dakotan*, December 2, 1890, 1.

87. *New York Times*, December 2, 1890, 2; *Washington Post*, December 2, 1890, 1; *Omaha Daily Bee*, December 2, 1890, 1; *Yankton Press and Dakotan*, December 2, 1890, 1–2; *Chicago Tribune*, December 2, 1890, 1.

88. *New York Times*, December 2, 1890, 4.

89. *New York Times*, December 3, 1890, 2; *Washington Post*, December 5, 1890, 1; *Omaha Daily Bee*, December 3, 1890, 1; *Omaha Daily Bee*, December 5, 1890, 1.

90. *New York Times*, December 3, 1890, 2; *Omaha Daily Bee*, December 3, 1890, 1; *Yankton Press and Dakotan*, December 4, 1890, 1. For comparison, see chapters 3 and 6.

91. *New York Times*, December 3, 1890, 2; *Washington Post* December 5, 1890, 1.

92. *New York Times*, December 4, 1890, 4; *Washington Post*, December 4, 1890, 2; *Omaha Daily Bee*, December 4, 1890, 1; *Omaha Daily Bee*, December 5, 1890, 1; *Chicago Tribune*, December 5, 1890, 5.

93. *Omaha Daily Bee*, December 6, 1890, 1; *New York Times*, December 7, 1890, 14. See also chapter 3.

94. *Omaha Daily Bee*, December 7, 1890, 1; *Chicago Tribune*, December 7, 1890, 3, 25; *Washington Post*, December 8, 1890, 1; *Yankton Press and Dakotan*, December 11, 1890, 1.

95. *Omaha Daily Bee*, December 8, 1890, 2, 4, 6; *Chicago Tribune*, December 8, 1890, 5, 9. See *Yankton Press and Dakotan*, December 3, 1890, 1.

96. *Harper's Weekly*, December 6, 1890, 946–47.

97. *Harper's Weekly*, December 6, 1890, 946–47.

98. *New York Times*, December 9, 1890, 6; *New York Times*, December 11, 1890, 2. The excitement in Oklahoma was also reported in *Omaha Daily Bee*, December 9, 1890, 2; *Chicago Tribune*, December 9, 1890, 2.

99. For more about Agent Lea, see chapters 1, 2, and 6. See also W. S. E. Coleman, *Voices of Wounded Knee*, 147–48.

100. *Washington Post*, December 9, 1890, 4; *Omaha Daily Bee*, December 9, 1890, 1–2, 4; *Chicago Tribune*, December 9, 1890, 2. See also chapters 3 and 6.

101. See *Omaha Daily Bee*, December 10, 1890, 1; *Omaha Daily Bee*, December 11, 1890, 1; *Omaha Daily Bee*, December 12, 1890, 1; *Omaha Daily Bee*, December 13, 1890, 1; *Omaha Daily Bee*, December 14, 1890, 1; *Omaha Daily Bee*, December 15, 1890, 1; *Yankton Press and Dakotan*, December 9, 1890, 1–2; *Yankton Press and Dakotan*, December 13, 1890, 1; *Yankton Press and Dakotan*, December 14, 1890, 1; *Chicago Tribune*, December 11, 1890, 2; *Chicago Tribune*, December 12, 1890, 1; *Chicago Tribune*, December 13, 1890, 1; *Chicago Tribune*, December 14, 1890, 2, 31; *Chicago Tribune*, December 15, 1890, 1; *New York Times*, December 12, 1890, 2; *New York Times*, December 14, 1890, 5; *Washington Post*, December 14, 1890, 1.

102. *Harper's Weekly*, December 13, 1890, 967.

103. *Washington Post*, December 14, 1890, 2; *Omaha Daily Bee*, December 14, 1890, 4.

104. *New York Times*, December 15, 1890, 6.

105. *Washington Post*, December 15, 1890, 1. For more about news reporting from December 1 to 15, see Kolbenschlag, *Whirlwind Passes*, 43–53.

106. *New York Times*, December 2, 1890, 2; *New York Times*, December 3, 1890, 2; *Washington Post*, December 2, 1890, 1; *Washington Post*, December 3, 1890, 1; *Omaha Daily Bee*, December 2, 1890, 1; *Chicago Tribune*, December 2, 1890, 1.

107. *Chicago Tribune*, December 16, 1890, 1, 6; *Omaha Daily Bee*, December 16, 1890,

1; *Yankton Press and Dakotan*, December 16, 1890, 1; *New York Times*, December 16, 1890, 1; *Washington Post*, December 16, 1890, 1.

108. *Chicago Tribune*, December 16, 1890, 1, 6; *Omaha Daily Bee*, December 16, 1890, 1; *Washington Post*, December 16, 1890, 1; *New York Times*, December 16, 1890, 1; *Yankton Press and Dakotan*, December 17, 1890, 1. Agent McLaughlin's report and his account of the events are discussed in chapter 2.

109. *Chicago Tribune*, December 16, 1890, 1, 6; *Omaha Daily Bee*, December 16, 1890, 1; *Yankton Press and Dakotan*, December 17, 1890, 1; *New York Times*, December 16, 1890, 1; *Washington Post* , December 16, 1890, 1; *Washington Post*, December 17, 1890, 1. For further commentary on newspapers and Sitting Bull's death, see Coward, *The Newspaper Indian*, 184–91.

110. *New York Times*, December 16, 1890, 1, 4; *Chicago Tribune*, December 16, 1890, 1, 6. See also Coward, *The Newspaper Indian*, 158–91.

111. *New York Times*, December 17, 1890, 2; *New York Times*, December 18, 1890, 2.

112. *New York Times*, December 17, 1890, 2.

113. *Chicago Tribune*, December 17, 1890, 4; *Omaha Daily Bee*, December 17, 1890, 2, 4; *Yankton Press and Dakotan*, December 19, 1890, 1–2.

114. *Chicago Tribune*, December 17, 1890, 1; *Omaha Daily Bee*, December 17, 1890, 1; *Yankton Press and Dakotan*, December 18, 1890, 1.

115. *New York Times*, December 18, 1890, 1; *New York Times*, December 19, 1890, 2; *New York Times*, December 20, 1890, 3; *Washington Post*, December 17, 1890, 1; *Washington Post*, December 18, 1890, 1; *Washington Post*, December 19, 1890, 1; *Washington Post*, December 20, 1890, 1; *Washington Post*, December 23, 1890, 1. For comparison, see chapters 1–3.

116. *Omaha Daily Bee*, December 14, 1890, 1; *Chicago Tribune*, December 18, 1890, 1–2; *Chicago Tribune*, December 19, 1890, 5; *Yankton Press and Dakotan*, December 19, 1890, 1–2; *Yankton Press and Dakotan*, December 20, 1890, 1. For more about this incident, see Utley, *The Last Days*, 143–44; Kolbenschlag, *Whirlwind Passes*, 54; W. S. E. . Coleman, *Voices of Wounded Knee*, 167–72.

117. *Chicago Tribune*, December 18, 1890, 1–2; *Chicago Tribune*, December 19, 1890, 5; *Omaha Daily Bee*, December 18, 1890, 1; *Omaha Daily Bee*, December 19, 1890, 1.

118. *Chicago Tribune*, December 20, 1890, 2; *Omaha Daily Bee*, December 20, 1890, 1; *Yankton Press and Dakotan*, December 23, 1890, 2.

119. *Chicago Tribune*, December 21, 1890, 25.

120. *Harper's Weekly*, December 20, 1890, 995. See also chapter 6.

121. *Omaha Daily Bee*, December 21, 1890, 1, 4; *Yankton Press and Dakotan*, December 20, 1890, 1; *Yankton Press and Dakotan*, December 22, 1890, 1.

122. *Omaha Daily Bee*, December 22, 1890, 1. For comparison, see chapters 1 and 3.

123. *Omaha Daily Bee*, December 23, 1890, 1; *Omaha Daily Bee*, December 24, 1890,

1; *Yankton Press and Dakotan*, December 23, 1890, 1; *Chicago Tribune*, December 23, 1890, 1; *Washington Post*, December 24, 1890, 1; *New York Times*, December 23, 1890, 1. During the Minnesota war several hundred whites were killed and approximately 30,000 settlers fled their homes. The Indian casualties were also extensive. For more about that war, see Oehler, *The Great Sioux Uprising*.

124. *Omaha Daily Bee*, December 23, 1890, 1; *Omaha Daily Bee*, December 24, 1890, 1; *Yankton Press and Dakotan*, December 23, 1890, 1; *Chicago Tribune*, December 23, 1890, 1; *New York Times*, December 24, 1890, 6; *Washington Post*, December 25, 1890, 1.

125. See chapter 3.

126. *Yankton Press and Dakotan*, December 24, 1890, 1; *Yankton Press and Dakotan*, December 26, 1890, 1; *New York Times*, December 25, 1890, 1; *Washington Post*, December 25, 1890, 1; *Chicago Tribune*, December 25, 1890, 1; *Omaha Daily Bee*, December 25, 1890, 1.

127. *Washington Post*, December 25, 1890, 1.

128. *Washington Post*, December 27, 1890, 1; *New York Times*, December 26, 1890, 2; *New York Times*, December 27, 1890, 1; *Omaha Daily Bee*, December 27, 1890, 1; *Chicago Tribune*, December 26, 1890, 1, 6; *Yankton Press and Dakotan*, December 27, 1890, 1.

129. *Chicago Tribune*, December 28, 1890, 4; *Omaha Daily Bee*, December 27, 1890, 1; *Washington Post*, December 27, 1890, 1; *New York Times*, December 26, 1890, 2; *New York Times*, December 27, 1890, 1. See also Kolbenschlag, *Whirlwind Passes*, 61–62. For comparison, see chapters 1–3.

130. *Harper's Weekly*, December 27, 1890, 1002.

131. *Harper's Weekly*, December 27, 1890, 1002, 1004–6.

132. *New York Times*, December 28, 1890, 2. The newspapers wrote quite often about the ghost dancers' Stronghold, even though none of the newspapermen ever saw the place. They relied purely on secondhand information. See Kolbenschlag, *Whirlwind Passes*, 45–46.

133. *Washington Post*, December 28, 1890, 16; *New York Times*, December 28, 1890, 17.

134. *Omaha Daily Bee*, December 28, 1890, 3, 14; *Chicago Tribune*, December 28, 1890, 4. For comparison, see chapters 1–3.

135. *Omaha Daily Bee*, December 28, 1890, 1; *Chicago Tribune*, December 28, 1890, 4.

136. *Washington Post*, December 29, 1890, 1; *New York Times*, December 29, 1890, 1; *Yankton Press and Dakotan*, December 29, 1890, 1; *Omaha Daily Bee*, December 29, 1890, 1.

137. *New York Times*, December 30, 1890, 1; *Washington Post*, December 30, 1890, 1; *Omaha Daily Bee*, December 30, 1890, 1; *Chicago Tribune*, December 30, 1890, 1; *Yankton Press and Dakotan*, December 31, 1890, 1; *Harper's Weekly*, January 24, 1891, front cover and 59–61; *Harper's Weekly*, February 7, 1891, 106–7. For further commentary on

newspaper accounts relating to the massacre of Wounded Knee and its aftermath, see Watson, "The Last Indian War," 213–14; Kolbenschlag, *Whirlwind Passes*, 63–74. A good selection of photographs relating to the Wounded Knee massacre can be found in Jensen, Paul, and Carter, *Eyewitness at Wounded Knee*, 102–17, 130–32.

138. *Washington Post*, December 30, 1890, 1; *Chicago Tribune*, December 30, 1890, 1–2; *Harper's Weekly*, January 24, 1891, front cover and 61; *Harper's Weekly*, February 7, 1891, 106–7.

139. *Omaha Daily Bee*, December 30, 1890, 1. See also Watson, "The Last Indian War," 212–15; Kolbenschlag, *Whirlwind Passes*, 63–65.

140. *New York Times*, December 30, 1890, 1; *Washington Post*, December 30, 1890, 1; *Omaha Daily Bee*, December 30, 1890, 1, 4; *Chicago Tribune*, December 30, 1890, 1–2; *Yankton Press and Dakotan*, December 31, 1890, 1. See also Kolbenschlag, *Whirlwind Passes*, 63–74.

141. See Watson, "The Last Indian War," 212–14; Kolbenschlag, *Whirlwind Passes*, 62–72. William Kelley actually took part in the fight and reportedly killed at least one Indian. Among the newspaper correspondents he was known as a man who believed and reported everything that he heard. When told that an Indian chief had visited the agency, he reported in an article that Chief Wounded Knee had secretly come to Pine Ridge Agency, not then realizing that Wounded Knee was the name of a creek, not a person (Kolbenschlag, *Whirlwind Passes*, 23). Kelley's account of the battle was later published by the Nebraska Historical Society. See Kelley, "The Indian Troubles."

142. *Washington Post*, December 31, 1890, 1; *Chicago Tribune*, December 31, 1890, 1–2; *Omaha Daily Bee*, December 30, 1890, 1. See also *Yankton Press and Dakotan*, January, 2, 1891, 1.

143. *New York Times*, December 31, 1890, 1, 4; *Harper's Weekly*, January 24, 1891, 59.

144. *Washington Post*, December 31, 1890, 1.

145. See *Omaha Daily Bee*, January 1, 1891, 1; *Omaha Daily Bee*, January 2, 1891, 1, 4; *Omaha Daily Bee*, January 3, 1891, 1, 4; *Omaha Daily Bee*, January 4, 1891, 1, 4; *Omaha Daily Bee*, January 5, 1891, 1; *Yankton Press and Dakotan*, January, 2, 1891, 1; *Chicago Tribune*, January 1, 1891, 1–2; *Chicago Tribune*, January 2, 1891, 5; *Chicago Tribune*, January 3, 1891, 1; *Chicago Tribune*, January 4, 1891, 1; *Chicago Tribune*, January 5, 1891, 1; *Washington Post*, January 1, 1891, 1; *Washington Post*, January 2, 1891, 4, 6; *Washington Post*, January 3, 1891, 1, 4; *Washington Post*, January 4, 1891, 1, 4; *Washington Post*, January 5, 1891, 1; *New York Times*, January 1, 1891, 1; *New York Times*, January 2, 1891, 5; *New York Times*, January 3, 1891, 4–5; *New York Times*, January 4, 1891, 5; *New York Times*, January 5, 1891, 5. For more about the January 1891 skirmishes, see chapters 1–4. For an account of the 9th Cavalry and its role during the ghost dance troubles, see Buecker, "'The Men Behaved Splendidly.'"

146. *Chicago Tribune,* January 3, 1891, 4; *Chicago Tribune,* January 5, 1891, 5; *Yankton Press and Dakotan,* January, 2, 1891, 1; *Yankton Press and Dakotan,* January, 3, 1891, 2. See also *North American Review,* January 1891, 1–10.

147. *Omaha Daily Bee,* January 3, 1891, 1; *Omaha Daily Bee,* January 4, 1891, 3–4.

148. *New York Times,* January 3, 1891, 4; *New York Times,* January 6, 1891, 4; *Washington Post,* January 2, 1891, 4; *Washington Post,* January 3, 1891, 4.

149. *Chicago Tribune,* January 6, 1891, 1, 4; *Chicago Tribune,* January 7, 1891, 1; *Omaha Daily Bee,* January 6, 1891, 1; *Omaha Daily Bee,* January 7, 1891, 1, 4; *New York Times,* January 6, 1891, 5; *Washington Post,* January 6, 1891, 1, 4; *Washington Post,* January 7, 1891, 1.

150. *Chicago Tribune,* January 6, 1891, 4; *Omaha Daily Bee,* January 6, 1891, 1. From the beginning of the ghost dance trouble, government officials and other newspapers severely criticized the newspapermen at Pine Ridge. See Kolbenschlag, *Whirlwind Passes,* 26–28, 89–90. See also chapter 2.

151. *Washington Post,* January 6, 1891, 2; *Washington Post,* January 7, 1891, 1; *Washington Post,* January 8, 1891, 2.

152. See Watson, "The Last Indian War," 206–7, 216–17; Kolbenschlag, *Whirlwind Passes,* 72–74.

153. See chapter 3.

154. See Watson, "The Last Indian War," 212–17.

155. See chapter 6.

156. See *Washington Post,* January 7, 1891, 1; *Washington Post,* January 8, 1891, 1; *Washington Post,* January 9, 1891, 1; *Chicago Tribune,* January 7, 1891, 1; *Chicago Tribune,* January 8, 1891, 1, 4, 6, 9; *Chicago Tribune,* January 9, 1891, 5; *Omaha Daily Bee,* January 6, 1891, 1; *Omaha Daily Bee,* January 7, 1891, 1; *Omaha Daily Bee,* January 8, 1891, 1–2; *Omaha Daily Bee,* January 9, 1891, 2; *Yankton Press and Dakotan,* January 3, 1891, 1–2; *Yankton Press and Dakotan,* January 5, 1891, 1; *Yankton Press and Dakotan,* January 8, 1891, 1; *Yankton Press and Dakotan,* January 10, 1891, 1; *New York Times,* January 8, 1891, 2.

157. *New York Times,* January 10, 1891, 1; *New York Times,* January 11, 1891, 1; *Washington Post,* January 10, 1891, 1; *Washington Post,* January 11, 1891, 1; *Yankton Press and Dakotan,* January 12, 1891, 1–2; *Yankton Press and Dakotan,* January 3, 1891, 1; *Omaha Daily Bee,* January 10, 1891, 1, 3–4; *Omaha Daily Bee,* January 11, 1891, 1; *Chicago Tribune,* January 10, 1891, 1, 6; *Chicago Tribune,* January 11, 1891, 1–2. See also chapter 1.

158. *Omaha Daily Bee,* January 10, 1891, 1, 3–4; *Omaha Daily Bee,* January 11, 1891, 1; *Yankton Press and Dakotan,* January 10, 1891, 2; *Chicago Tribune,* January 10, 1891, 1, 6; *Chicago Tribune,* January 11, 1891, 1–2. For more about the Nebraska Militia, see Colby, "The Sioux Indian War." See also chapter 3.

159. *Omaha Daily Bee,* January 12, 1891, 1–2; *Yankton Press and Dakotan,* January 13, 1891, 1; *Chicago Tribune,* January 12, 1891, 1–2, 9; *New York Times,* January 12, 1891, 5; *Washington Post,* January 12, 1891, 1.

160. Kolbenschlag, *Whirlwind Passes*, 16–18, 72–73, 87–94. See also Watson, "The Last Indian War," 212–15, 218–19.

161. *Chicago Tribune*, January 13, 1891, 1; *Omaha Daily Bee*, January 13, 1891, 1, 4; *New York Times*, January 13, 1891, 1; *Washington Post*, January 13, 1891, 1.

162. *Chicago Tribune*, January 14, 1891, 1; *Chicago Tribune*, January 15, 1891, 2; *Omaha Daily Bee*, January 14, 1891, 1, 3; *Omaha Daily Bee*, January 15, 1891, 1, 4; *Yankton Press and Dakotan*, January 15, 1891, 1; *New York Times*, January 14, 1891, 1; *New York Times*, January 15, 1891, 1; *Washington Post*, January 14, 1891, 1; *Washington Post*, January 15, 1891, 1. For more about news reporting between January 1 and 15, 1891, see Kolbenschlag, *Whirlwind Passes*, 77–86.

163. See Kolbenschlag, *Whirlwind Passes*, 16, 47–48, 87–90. As examples of studies of the Lakota ghost dance that have randomly used newspapers, see Boyd, *Recent Indian Wars*; W. F. Johnson, *The Red Record*; Utley, *The Last Days*; Smith, *Moon of the Popping Trees*; Utter, *Wounded Knee*; Utley, *The Lance and the Shield*; W. S. E. Coleman, *Voices of Wounded Knee*.

6. The U.S. Congress and the Ghost Dance

1. Cong. Rec., 51st Cong., 1st Sess., Vol. 21, Part 14, December 3, 1890, 45. See Colby, "The Sioux Indian War," 144–46. Congress was on recess from October to December 1890.

2. For more about the issuing of rations, see Cong. Rec., 51st Cong., 1st Sess., Vol. 21, Part 3, January 21, 1890, 658; Cong. Rec., 51st Cong., 1st Sess., Vol. 21, Part 12, June 4, 1890, 5961; Cong. Rec., 51st Cong., 1st Sess., Vol. 21, Part 21, September 3, 1890, 11633–34; Cong. Rec., 51st Cong., 1st Sess., Vol. 21, Part 13, June 2, 1890, 6739; Cong. Rec., 51st Cong. 1st Sess., Vol. 21, Part 21, September 30, 1890, 11633–34; 51st Cong., 2nd Sess, *House Executive Document*, No. 139, Vol. 33, Serial 2863, 1–3. See also *Washington Post*, July 23, 1890, 7; *New York Times*, December 26, 1890, 3.

3. Cong. Rec., 50th Cong., 2nd Sess., Vol. 20, Part 2, January 15, 1889, 909. North and South Dakota became states in the fall of 1889. See Richardson, *Messages and Papers of the Presidents*, 20–21. For additional information about the early stages of South Dakota's statehood, see Lamar, "Perspectives on Statehood," 10–13.

4. Cong. Rec., 50th Cong., 2nd Sess., Vol. 20, Part 2, January 16, 1889, 849.

5. Cong. Rec., 51st Cong., 2nd Sess., Vol. 22, Part 1, December 1, 1890, 5. See also Second Annual Message to the Senate, December 1, 1890, in Richardson, *Messages and Papers of the Presidents*, 107–29.

6. CIA to Senator Henry L. Dawes, May 8, 1890, NARS, RG 46, SCIAP, BOX 57; ARCIA 1891, Report of the Commissioner of Indian Affairs T. J. Morgan, October 1, 1891. See also CIA to Gen. S. C. Armstrong, December 19, 1890, TJMLB, AISRI, 315–16; CIA to J. S. Lockwood, December 19, 1890, TJMLB, AISRI, 319; CIA to John Jay, December 29, 1890, TJMLB, AISRI, 321–22.

7. CIA to Dawes, May 8, 1890, NARS, RG 46, SCIAP, Box 57; ARCIA 1889, Report of Agent Charles E. McChesney, August 26, 1889, Report of Agent Hugh D. Gallagher, August 27, 1889, Report of Agent L. F. Spencer, August 23, 1889, Report of Agent James McLaughlin, August 26, 1889, 130, 134, 151–52, 155, 157, 166; ARCIA 1890, Report of Agent James McLaughlin, August 26, 1890, Report of Agent Charles E. McChesney, August 25, 1890, Report of Agent Hugh D. Gallagher, August, 28, 1890, Report of Agent J. George Wright, August 26, 1890, 36–37, 42, 46, 48–49, 50, 58. See also Textor, *Official Records,* 154; Paulson, "The Allotment of Land in Severalty," 132–53.

8. Henriksson, *The Indian on Capitol Hill,* 183–84. See also Paulson, "The Allotment of Land in Severalty," 132–53. The allotment of Indian lands continued into the twentieth century; in fact, during the years 1900–1921, eight times more Indian land was allotted than during the years 1887–1900 (Henriksson, *The Indian on Capitol Hill,* 178).

9. Cong. Rec., 51st Cong., 2nd Sess., Vol. 22, Part 1, December 1, 1890, 5. See Second Annual Message to the Senate, December 1, 1890 in Richardson, *Messages and Papers of the Presidents,* 117. See also the correspondence between the secretary of the interior, the secretary of war, and President Harrison, November–December 1890, LC, BHP, Series 1, Rolls 29–30.

10. Cong. Rec., 51st Cong., 1st Sess., Vol. 21, Part 4, February 11, 1890, 1149–50, 1164. See also Special Message to the Senate and the House of Representatives, February 10, 1890, in Richardson, *Messages and Papers of the Presidents,* 61–62. For more about the partitioning of the Great Sioux Reservation, see the introduction.

11. Cong. Rec., 51st Cong., 1st Sess., Vol. 21, Part 14, December 3, 1890, 45; Cong. Rec., 51st Cong., 1st Sess., Vol. 21, Part 14, December 5, 1890, 128–29, Letter of Secretary of War Redfield Proctor, December 2, 1890, read in the House of Representatives on December 5, 1890.

12. Cong. Rec., 51st Cong., 1st Sess., Vol. 21, Part 14, December 3, 1890, 45; Cong. Rec., 51st Cong., 1st Sess., Vol. 21, Part 14, December 5, 1890, 129, Letter of Secretary of War Redfield Proctor, December 2, 1890, read in the House of Representatives on December 5, 1890. As an example of the settlers' sentiments, see Petition of Citizens of Chadron NE, November 26, 1890, NARS, SCIAP, RG 46, Box 117, and NARS, HCIAP, RG 233, Box 106; Joint Resolution by the House of Representatives of the State of South Dakota (S 4894), NARS, SCIAP, RG 46, Box 117. See chapters 1, 2. See also Colby, "The Sioux Indian War," 146–48; Kelley, "The Indian Troubles," 31–32.

13. Cong. Rec., 51st Cong., 2nd Sess., Vol. 22, Part 1, December 4, 1890, 88; Cong. Rec., 51st Cong., 2nd Sess., Vol. 22, Part 1, December 5, 1890, 129; Cong. Rec., 51st Cong., 2nd Sess., Vol. 22, Part 1 December 6, 1890, 166. See Henriksson, *The Indian on Capitol Hill,* 60.

14. Daniel W. Voorhees was a long-term senator and a Democrat. He was born in

1827 in Ohio but was elected to the Senate as a representative for Indiana, where his family lived most of his life. More about Senator Voorhees is available in Charles C. Voorhees, *Speeches of Daniel W. Voorhees,* vii–xii; Cecilia Voorhees et al., *Forty Years of Oratory,* 1–7.

15. Cong. Rec., 51st Cong., 1st Sess., Vol. 21, Part 14, December 3, 1890, 45–46. Parts of the Congressional debate are reproduced in W. F. Johnson, *The Red Record,* 519–36; W. S. E. Coleman, *Voices of Wounded Knee,* 130–45, 150–53.

16. Cong. Rec., 51st Cong., 1st Sess., Vol. 21, Part 14, December 3, 1890, 46.

17. See chapter 1.

18. Cong. Rec., 51st Cong., 1st Sess., Vol. 21, Part 14, December 3, 1890, 46; 51st Cong., 2nd Sess., *House Executive Document,* No. 36, Vol. 25, Serial 2855, 1–6; 51st Cong., 2nd Sess., *House Executive Document,* No 37, Vol. 25, Serial 2855, 1–4. See also Henry L. Dawes, "Past and Present Indian Policy," address delivered to the annual meeting of the American Missionary Association, Hartford CT, 1892, LC, HLDP, Box 43, Speeches 1890–1900. For more about the annuities and the treaties they were based on, see the introduction.

19. For more about the proceedings of the negotiations with the Sioux Commission of 1889 and the Lakotas, see 51st Cong., 1st Sess., *Senate Executive Document,* No 17, Vol. 1, Serial 2610. For additional commentary about the commission, see Greene, "The Sioux Land Commission," 41–72; Prucha, *The Great Father,* 2:638–40; Hoover, "The Sioux Agreement," 57–94. See also introduction.

20. Cong. Rec., 51st Cong., 1st Sess., Vol. 21, Part 14, December 3, 1890, 46–47.

21. See *Statutes at Large,* 25 Stat., Act of March 2, 1889, Sec. 28, 899; Treaty of 1868, Article 12, AIUSD, Vol. 4, 2517–25. See also Colby, "The Sioux Indian War," 176–77.

22. Cong. Rec., 51st Cong., 1st Sess., Vol. 21, Part 14, December 8, 1890, 192; 51st Cong., 2nd Sess., *House Executive Document,* No. 36, Vol. 25, Serial 2855, 1–6; ACIA to Noble, December 4, 1890, in 52nd Cong., 2nd Sess., *Senate Executive Document,* No. 2, Vol. 1, Serial 2818, 17–20; *The Memorial of the Religious Society of Friends, In Pennsylvania, New Jersey and Delaware,* NARS, RG 46, SCIAP, Box 117, and NARS RG 233, HCIAP, Box 106. For commentary on the tactics used by the commission, see The National Indian Defense Association, *The Sioux Nation,* 21–27; Colby, "The Sioux Indian War," 176–77; Greene, "The Sioux Land Commission," 45–63; Graber, *Sister to the Sioux,* 136–37; Utley, *The Lance and the Shield,* 268–80. For more about the Lakota conceptions of the promises made by the Sioux Commission, see Statement of Chief American Horse at a meeting on Pine Ridge on November 27, 1890, in ARSW 1891, Report of Maj. Gen. Nelson A. Miles, September 24, 1891, 136, also published in 51st Cong., 2nd Sess., *House Executive Document,* No. 36, Vol. 25, Serial 2855, 6. See also 51st Cong., 1st Sess., United States Congress House of Representatives, House Committee on Indian Affairs, Council Held with a Delegation of Sioux Indians, April 15, 1890, Un-

published Hearing, IUL, Microfiche, Card 1, 1–9; 51st Cong., 1st Sess, House Committee on Indian Affairs, Minutes of Proceedings, January 7, 1890, 1.

23. See CIA to B. V. Perkins, April 15, 1890, NARS, RG 233, HCIAP, Box 67, Papers Relating to the Sioux Indians; CIA to Noble, April 23, 1890, NARS, RG 233, HCIAP, Box 67, Papers Relating to Sioux Indians; CIA to Dawes, December 9, 1890, NARS, RG 46, SCIAP, Box 55, Folder 5; ACIA to Noble, December 1, 1890, NARS, RG 46, SCIAP, Box 55, Folder 5; 51st Cong., 2nd Sess., *House Executive Document*, No. 36, Vol. 25, Serial 2855, 1–6; 51st Cong., 2nd Sess., *House Executive Document*, No 37, Vol. 25, Serial 2855, 1–4; ARCIA 1891, Report of the Commissioner of Indian Affairs T. J. Morgan, October 1, 1891, 133–34; ACIA to Noble, December 4, 1890, in 52nd Cong., 2nd Sess., *Senate Executive Document*, No. 2, Vol. 1, Serial 2818, 17–20. The cut in the money appropriated for Lakota annual rations was dramatic. For the year 1884 the annual appropriation was 1,325,000 dollars and by 1888 it had already been cut down to 1,000,000 dollars. See 52nd Cong., 2nd Sess., *Senate Executive Document*, No. 2, Vol. 1, Serial 2818, 21. For the recommendations made by the Sioux Commission, see 51st Cong., 1st Sess., *Senate Executive Document*, No 51, Vol. 4, Serial 2682, 23–31.

24. See, for example, *Washington Post*, July 21, 1890, 6; *Washington Post*, August 18, 1890, 5; *Washington Post*, August 24, 1890, 1; *New York Times*, July 16, 1890, 1; *New York Times*, July 29, 1890, 2; *New York Times*, August 5, 1890, 1. See Lamar, "Perspectives on Statehood," 10–11. See also chapter 5.

25. Cong. Rec., 51st Cong., 1st Sess., Vol. 21, Part 14, December 3, 1890, 46–47.

26. Report of the Commissioner of Indian Affairs J. D. C. Atkins, September 28, 1886, AIUSD, Vol. 1, 405; ARCIA 1890, Report of the Commissioner of Indian Affairs T. J. Morgan, Report of Agent James McLaughlin, August 26, 1890, Report of Agent Charles E. McChesney, August 25, 1890, Report of Agent Hugh D. Gallagher, August, 28, 1890, Report of Agent J. George Wright, August 26, 1890, 36–46, 48–64. In a recent study the historian Rainer Smedman estimates that the total area cultivated by the Lakotas was only 13,304 acres, which was only 0.06 percent of the total area of the Great Sioux Reservation. See Smedman, *Sotureista ja metsästäjistä maanviljelijöitä*, 219.

27. Report of the Commissioner of Indian Affairs J. D. C. Atkins, September 28, 1886, AIUSD, Vol. 1, 393; ARCIA 1889, Report of Agent Charles E. McChesney, August 26, 1889, Report of Agent Hugh D. Gallagher, August 27, 1889, Report of Agent L. F. Spencer, August 23, 1889, Report of Agent James McLaughlin, August 26, 1889, 130, 134, 151–52, 155, 157, 166; ARCIA 1890, Report of Agent James McLaughlin August 26, 1890, Report of Agent Charles E. McChesney, August 25, 1890, Report of Agent Hugh D. Gallagher, August, 28, 1890, Report of Agent, J. George Wright, August 26, 1890, 37–61; CIA to Dawes, May 8, 1890, NARS, SCIAP, RG 46, Box 57. See Hyde, *A Sioux Chronicle*, 169, 171.

28. E. G. Eastman, "The Ghost Dance War," 29; Graber, *Sister to the Sioux,* 137.

29. Hyde, *A Sioux Chronicle,* 71.

30. Report of the Commissioner of Indian Affairs J. D. C. Atkins, September 28, 1886, AIUSD, Vol. I, 393; ARCIA 1889, Report of Agent Charles E. McChesney, August 26, 1889, Report of Agent Hugh D. Gallagher, August 27, 1889, Report of Agent L. F. Spencer, August 23, 1889, Report of Agent James McLaughlin, August 26, 1889, 130, 134, 151–52, 155, 157, 166; ARCIA 1890, Report of Agent James McLaughlin August 26, 1890, Report of Agent Charles E. McChesney, August 25, 1890, Report of Agent Hugh D. Gallagher, August, 28, 1890, Report of Agent J. George Wright, August 26, 1890, 36–46, 48–64; 51st Cong., 2nd Sess., *House Executive Document,* No. 1, Part 5, Vol. 2, Serial 2841, 37, 42–46, 48–53, 58–61.

31. ARCIA 1891, Report of the Commissioner of Indian Affairs T. J. Morgan, October 1, 1891, 132–35. See also *The Memorial of the Representatives of the Religious Society of Friends, In Pennsylvania, New Jersey, and Delaware,* NARS, SCIAP, RG 46, 117, and NARS, HCIAP, RG 233, Box 106.

32. Bishop W. H. Hare to Noble, January 7, 1891, G. D. [Ghost Dance] Doc. 2440-1891, as quoted in Mooney, *The Ghost Dance Religion,* 85; Chief American Horse at a meeting on Pine Ridge on November 27, 1890, in ARSW 1891, Report of Maj. Gen. Nelson A. Miles, September 24, 1891, 136, also published in 51st Cong., 2nd Sess., *House Executive Document,* No. 36, Vol. 25, Serial 2855, 1–6; Morgan to Perkins, April 15, 1890, NARS, HCIAP, RG 233, Box 67, Papers Relating to the Sioux Indians; Commissioner of Indian Affairs Thomas J. Morgan, Memorandum (undated, between letters dated January 3 and 5, 1891), TJMLB, AISRI, 371–376. See also 51st Cong., 1st Sess., United States Congress House of Representatives, House Committee on Indian Affairs, Council Held with a Delegation of Sioux Indians, April 15, 1890, IUL, Unpublished Hearing, Microfiche, Card 1, 1–9. For Bishop Hare's views on the ghost dance, see Hare to Noble, January 1, 1891, NARS, RG 75, SC 188, M 4728, Roll 1, 7/10–11. See also chapter 4.

33. 51st Cong., 2nd Sess., *House Executive Document,* No. 36, Vol. 25, Serial 2855, 5. See also CIA to Dawes, May 8, 1890, NARS, SCIAP, RG 46, Box 57.

34. Cong. Rec., 51st Cong., 1st Sess., Vol. 21, Part 14, December 3, 1890, 48. For comparison, see chapters 1–3 and 5.

35. ARCIA 1891, Report of Commissioner of Indian Affairs T. J. Morgan, October 1, 1891. The ghost dancers destroyed altogether $98,383.46 worth of property during the troubles. This property, however, belonged to the so-called friendly Indians, not to white settlers (52nd Cong., 2nd Sess., *Senate Executive Document,* No 93, Vol. 8, Serial 3062, 1–3). See also Paul, "The Investigation," 212–23.

36. Hyde, *A Sioux Chronicle,* 308–9. See also Colby, "The Sioux Indian War"; Kelley, "The Indian Troubles."

37. Cong. Rec., 51st Cong., 1st Sess., Vol. 21, Part 14, December 3, 1890, 48.

38. Henry L. Dawes to Electa Dawes, December 2, 1890, LC, HLDP, Box 15, Folder August–December 1890. Many contemporaries, including some of the Lakota agents, echoed the idea that certain elements of the white population wanted to profit from the situation. See, for example, W. F. Johnson, *The Red Record*, 468–71; C. A. Eastman, *From Deep Woods to Civilization*, 103. See also chapter 2.

39. Senator Gilbert A. Pierce to Proctor (telegram), November 18, 1890, NARS, RG 94, AIWKSC, M 983, Roll 1, Vol. 1, 109.

40. See, for example, *Chicago Tribune*, October 28, 1890, 2; *Chicago Tribune*, October 30, 1890, 2; *Chicago Tribune*, November 10, 1890, 2; *New York Times*, January 12, 1891, 1; *New York Times*, January 18, 1891, 1. See also 52nd Cong., 1st Sess., *Senate Executive Document*, No. 84, Vol. 6, Serial 2901, 6.

41. Cong. Rec., 51st Cong., 1st Sess., Vol. 21, Part 14, December 4, 1890, 68. About Senator Henry L. Dawes's ideas relating to the Indian question, see Fifteenth Annual Meeting of the Board of Indian Commissioners 1883 in Prucha, *Americanizing the American Indian*, 27–30, and a speech by Henry L. Dawes at the Lake Mohonk Conference in 1887 in Prucha, *Americanizing the American Indian*, 101–10; Henry L. Dawes, "Past and Present Indian Policy," address delivered to the annual meeting of the American Missionary Association, Hartford CT 1892, LC, HLDP, Box 43, Speeches 1890–1900; Barrows, *Proceedings of the 8th Annual Meeting of the Lake Mohonk Conference;* Barrows, *Proceedings of the 9th Annual Meeting of the Lake Mohonk Conference,* 8–12, 78–85.

42. Cong. Rec., 51st Cong., 1st Sess., Vol. 21, Part 14, December 4, 1890, 68, an interview with Governor Charles Foster in *Cincinnati Enquirer*, read in the Senate on December 4, 1890. Governor Foster was quoted by other newspapers also. See chapter 5.

43. William S. Holman was a long-term politician and a Democrat from Indiana. He served in the U.S. Congress from 1859 to 1897. More about William S. Holman is available in Introduction to William S. Holman Papers, IULL, Bibliographical Folder.

44. Cong. Rec., 51st Cong., 1st Sess., Vol. 21, Part 14, December 5, 1890, 129. See, for example, Charles S. Voorhees, *Speeches of Daniel W. Voorhees*; Cecilia Voorhees et al., *Forty Years of Oratory*; Personal correspondence of William S. Holman in William S. Holman Papers, IULL, Folders 1885–1891. More about the Holman Committee is available in Olson, *Red Cloud and the Sioux Problem*, 300–308; Hyde, *A Sioux Chronicle*, 103.

45. Cong. Rec., 51st Cong., 1st Sess., Vol. 21, Part 14, December 4, 1890, 68–69.

46. Henriksson, *The Indian on Capitol Hill*, 267.

47. Senator Henry M. Teller had demanded earlier that all Indian lands be opened to white settlers so that the Indians could be civilized by living in the midst of white

settlements. He had also been involved in western cattle companies and acted as an attorney for a western railway company. This background can be seen in his activities as secretary of the interior from 1882 to 1885. Teller saw Indian education as the means to resolve the entire Indian problem (Henriksson, *The Indian on Capitol Hill*, 114, 121, 170). About the actions of Henry M. Teller and other westerners in the 1880s, see Phillips, "The Indian Ring," 345–76; Hoxie, "The End of the Savage," 162; Hoxie, *A Final Promise*, 36–37.

48. Cong. Rec., 51st Cong., 1st Sess., Vol. 21, Part 14, December 4, 1890, 70. See also Henry L. Dawes, Draft of a Paper for *Boston Journal*, January 1891, LC, HLDP, Box 29, Folder January 1891.

49. Schofield to Proctor, December 20, 1890, NARS, RG 94, AIWKSC, M 983, Roll 1, Vol. 1, 585–86; House Committee on Indian Affairs, Minutes of Proceedings, January 7, 1890, 1; 51st Cong., 1st Sess., United States Congress House of Representatives, House Committee on Indian Affairs. Council Held with a Delegation of Sioux Indians, April 15, 1890, IUL, Unpublished Hearing, Microfiche, Card 1, 1–9.

50. CIA to Perkins, April 15, 1890, NARS, HCIAP, RG 233, Box 67, Papers Relating to Sioux Indians.

51. Cong. Rec., 51st Cong., 1st Sess., Vol. 21, Part 14, December 3, 1890, 47; Cong. Rec., 51st Cong., 1st Sess., Vol. 21, Part 14, December 4, 1890, 69.

52. A. T. Lea to CIA, November 28, 1890, NARS, RG 75, SC 188, M 4728, Roll 1, 3/38–39; Cong. Rec., 51st Cong., 1st Sess., Vol. 21, Part 14, December 8, 1890, 197, Report by Special Census Agent A. T. Lea, November 28, 1890, read in the Senate on December 8, 1890. See also ACIA to Noble, December 4, 1890, in 51st Cong., 2nd Sess., *Senate Executive Document*, No 2, Vol. 1, Serial 2818, 15–16. Later in January 1891 Senator Dawes still emphasized that the cut in rations was justifiable since it was based on the census count taken by Agent Lea (Henry L. Dawes, Draft of a Paper for *Boston Journal*, January 1891, LC, HLDP, Box 29, Folder January 1891). For more about Special Agent Lea, see chapter 2.

53. Cong. Rec., 51st Cong., 1st Sess., Vol. 21, Part 14, December 8, 1890, 197–201. See also Henry L. Dawes, Draft of a Paper for *Boston Journal*, January 1891, LC, HLDP, Box 29, Folder January 1891. For more about General Miles's comments, see chapters 3 and 5. Despite Senator Voorhees's doubts, A. T. Lea was, in fact, a special agent of the Office of Indian Affairs.

54. For a critical comment about Agent Lea's reports, see W. F. Johnson, *The Red Record*, 468.

55. More about Dawes's ideas on the ghost dance and Indian policy is available in Henry L. Dawes, Draft of a Paper for *Boston Journal*, January 1891, LC, HLDP, Box 29, Folder January 1891; Henry L. Dawes, "Past and Present Indian Policy," address delivered to the annual meeting of the American Missionary Association, Hartford CT

1892, LC, HLDP, Box 43, Speeches 1890–1900. See also Barrows, *Proceedings of the 9th Annual Meeting of the Lake Mohonk Conference,* 80–85. For more about ideas regarding Indian civilization, see the introduction.

56. Cong. Rec., 51st Cong., 1st Sess., Vol. 21, Part 14, December 3, 1890, 47; Cong. Rec., 51st Sess., Vol. 21, Part 14, December 8, 1890, 198. For the discussion about weapons in Lakota possession, see 51st Cong., 2nd Sess., *Senate Miscellaneous Document,* No 28, Vol. 3, Serial 2821, 1; 51st Cong., 2nd Sess., *Senate Executive Document,* No 2, Vol. 1, Serial 2818, 3–14; 51st Cong., 2nd Sess., *Senate Executive Document,* No. 9, Vol. 1, Serial 2818, 2–51. For comparison, see chapters 1, 3, and 5.

57. Cong. Rec., 51st Cong., 1st Sess., Vol. 21, Part 14, December 3, 1890, 47; Cong. Rec., 51st Sess., Vol. 21, Part 14, December 8, 1890, 198; ACIA to Noble, December 5, 1890 in 51st Cong., 2nd Sess., *Senate Executive Document,* No. 2, Vol. 1, Serial 2818, 22–23; Noble to Dawes, December 5, 1890 in 51st Cong., 2nd Sess., *Senate Executive Document,* No. 2, Vol. 1, Serial 2818, 20–21. For additional information about the actual number of Lakotas in 1890, see ARCIA 1890, Report of Agent James McLaughlin, August 26, 1890, Report of Agent Charles E. McChesney, August 25, 1890, Report of Agent Hugh D. Gallagher, August 28, 1890, Report of Agent J. George Wright, August 26, 1890, 37–61, 450–51. See also the table in chapter 1.

58. Cong. Rec., 51st Cong., 1st Sess., Vol. 21, Part 14, December 4, 1890, 70–74.

59. Cong. Rec., 51st Cong., 1st Sess., Vol. 21, Part 14, December 3, 1890, 46–47; Henry L. Dawes, Draft of a Paper for *Boston Journal,* January 1891, LC, HLDP, Box 29, Folder January 1891.

60. Cong. Rec., 51st Cong., 1st Sess., Vol. 21, Part 14, December 4, 1890, 69. Henry L. Dawes to Electa Dawes, December 2, 1890, LC, HLDP, Box 15, Folder August–December 1890. The role of the press is discussed in chapter 5.

61. Henry L. Dawes to Electa Dawes, December 3, 1890, LC, HLDP, Box 15, Folder August–December 1890.

62. Cong. Rec., 51st Cong., 1st Sess., Vol. 21, Part 14, December 4, 1890, 69–70. See also Henry L. Dawes, Draft of a Paper to *Boston Journal,* January 1891, LC, HLDP, Box 29, Folder January 1891.

63. For more about the negotiations of 1882, see Greene, "The Sioux Land Commission," 42–43; Hoover, "The Sioux Agreement," 60–65.

64. For further information about this particular event during the negotiations of 1889 and about Sitting Bull's role in it, see 51st Cong., 1st Sess., *Senate Executive Document,* No 17, Vol. 1, Serial 2610, 194–213.

65. Cong. Rec., 51st Cong., 1st Sess., Vol. 21, Part 14, December 4, 1890, 69–70; Henry L. Dawes, Draft of a Paper to *Boston Journal,* January 1891, LC, HLDP, Box 29, Folder January 1891.

66. See McLaughlin, *My Friend the Indian,* 180, 182. See also chapter 2.

67. For more about the Arapaho ghost dance and Sitting Bull (Hänä'chä-thi'ak) the Arapaho, see Mooney, *The Ghost-Dance Religion*, 894–902. The name Sitting Bull also appeared several times in the newspapers that are studied in chapter 5. However, it is clear that the newspapers confused these two men who had the same name. For example, the papers even reported that Sitting Bull (the Lakota) was seen in Oklahoma and Nevada, exciting the Indians there—an obvious reference to the Arapaho Sitting Bull. See chapter 5.

68. See W. F. Johnson, *The Red Record*, 461–68; C. A. Eastman, *From Deep Woods to Civilization*, 100–101; Hyde, *A Sioux Chronicle*, 254; Utley, *The Last Days*, 104; Olson, *Red Cloud and the Sioux Problem*, 324–28. See also chapter 1.

69. Olson, *Red Cloud and the Sioux Problem*, 330; Hyde, *A Sioux Chronicle*, 308; Twiss, "A Short History," 37. See chapter 1.

70. Red Cloud to T. A. Bland, December 10, 1890, read in the House of Representatives on December 19, 1890, in Cong. Rec., 51st Cong. 1st Sess., Vol. 21, Part 14, December 19, 1890, 702–3. See also chapters 1, 2..

71. Red Cloud to Bland, December 10, 1890, read in the House of Representatives on December 19, 1890, in Cong. Rec., 51st Cong., 1st Sess., Vol. 21, Part 14, December 19, 1890, 702–3.

72. Cong. Rec., 51st Cong., 1st Sess., Vol. 21, Part 14, December 19, 1890, 703–4.

73. Secretary of War Redfield Proctor to the Senate, December 6, 1890, and Maj. Gen. J. M. Schofield to the Senate, December 3, 1890, read in the Senate on December 6, 1890, in Cong. Rec., 51st Cong., 1st Sess., Vol. 21, Part 14, December 6, 1890, 167. See also 51st Cong., 2nd Sess., *Senate Executive Document*, No. 2, Vol. 1, Serial 2818, 2–3.

74. Cong. Rec., 51st Cong., 1st Sess., Vol. 21, Part 14, December 8, 1890, 200.

75. Graber, *Sister to the Sioux*, 148. See also *The Memorial of the Representatives of the Religious Society of Friends, In Pennsylvania, New Jersey, and Delaware*, NARS, SCIAP, RG 46, Box 117, and NARS, HCIAP, RG 233, Box 106.

76. See, for example, *Washington Post*, June 6, 1890, 1; *Washington Post*, June 8, 1890, 2; *Washington Post*, June 9, 1890, 1; *New York Times*, June 6, 1890, 1; *New York Times*, June 9, 1890, 2; *Chicago Tribune*, June 7, 1890, 2; *New York Times*, August 14, 1890, 1. See also chapter 5.

77. See Cong. Rec., 51st Cong., 1st Sess., Vol. 21, Part 14, December 3, 1890, 45–46. For more about different approaches to U.S. Indian policies, see Hoxie, *A Final Promise*.

78. Cong. Rec., 51st Cong., 1st Sess., Vol. 21, Part 14, December 19, 1890, 701.

79. Cong. Rec., 51st Cong., 1st Sess., Vol. 21, Part 14, December 17, 1890, 558–89; Cong. Rec., 51st Cong., 1st Sess., Vol. 21, Part 14, December 17, 1890, 600, 611; 51st Cong., 2nd Sess., *House Miscellaneous Document*, No. 80, Vol. 1, Serial 2869, 1; 51st Cong., 2nd Sess., House Report No. 3375, Vol. 1, Serial 2885, 1; 52nd Cong., 1st Sess., *Senate Executive Document* (correspondence attached), No. 84, Vol. 6, Serial 2901, 1–12. See also

Ruger to McLaughlin, December 17, 1890, MHS, JMLP, M230, Roll 20, 501; McLaughlin to Senator Gilbert Pierce, MHS, JMLP, M 230, Roll 20, 496–500; McLaughlin to Pierce, March 3, 1891, NARS, RG 75, SC 188, M 4728, Roll 2, 9/66–69.

80. Cong. Rec., 51st Cong., 1st Sess., Vol. 21, Part 14, January 6, 1890, 964; 51st Cong., 2nd Sess., House Report No. 3375, Vol. 1, Serial 2885, 1.

81. For more about the army investigation relating to the Wounded Knee Massacre, see chapter 3. As examples of the investigations conducted among the Lakotas, see 52nd Cong., 1st Sess., *Senate Executive Document*, No., 58, Vol. 5, Serial 2900, 1–1251; 75th Cong., 3rd Sess., House Committee on Indian Affairs, Sioux Indians, Wounded Knee Massacre, Published Hearing, March 7 and May 12, 1938, IULAL, Microfiche Group 3, Card 4–5.

Conclusion

1. See chapter 1.

2. See *Omaha Daily Bee*, January 1, 1890, 1. See also chapter 5.

3. See *New York Times*, November 22, 1890, 2; *Chicago Tribune*, November 22, 1890, 2. See also chapter 5.

4. The historian Jeffrey Ostler argues that the press did not publish alarming reports until the military was sent to the Lakota reservations in mid-November 1890, and therefore played no major role in creating the trouble. This study, however, shows that the press did indeed play an important role, even before the military intervention. For comparison, see Ostler, "Conquest and the State," 217–48.

5. This was also the opinion of many of the army officers. See chapter 3.

6. This division is, however, only a rough approximation. It would be a worthwhile subject for further scholarly research to delve further into the relationship between the 1889 act and the ghost dance in the sense of a division between ghost dancers–nonsigners and nondancers–signers.

7. Olson, *Red Cloud and the Sioux Problem*, 325.

8. ARSW 1891, Report of Major General Commanding the Army, September 24, 1891, 144. See also chapter 3.

9. See, for example, Utley, *The Last Days*, 126–30.

10. For accounts of previous encounters between Sitting Bull and General Miles, see Miles, *Personal Recollections*, 212–56, 306–18; Miles, *Serving the Republic*, 137–68; V. W. Johnson, *The Unregimented General*, 117–70; Hoover, "Sitting Bull," 158–63; Vestal, *Sitting Bull*, 190–205; Wooster, *Nelson A. Miles*, 76–95.

11. Nelson A. Miles to Mary Miles, December 19, 1890, as quoted in V. W. Johnson, *The Unregimented General*, 281.

12. McLaughlin to CIA, October 17, 1890, NARS, RG 75, SC 188, M 4728, Reel 1, 1/36. See also chapter 2.

13. DeMallie, "The Lakota Ghost Dance," 57.

14. See *Omaha Daily Bee*, November 30, 1890, 1. See also chapters 3 and 5.

15. See Smith, *Moon of the Popping Trees*, 131–32; Kolbenschlag, *Whirlwind Passes*, 72.

16. Watson, "The Last Indian War," 206–12; Kolbenschlag, *Whirlwind Passes*, 16, 58, 87–90. See also Jones, "Teresa Dean," 659.

17. See, for example, Watson, "The Last Indian War"; Kolbenschlag, *Whirlwind Passes*; Utley, *The Last Days*; Smith, *Moon of the Popping Trees*.

18. ARSW 1891, Report of Lt. Col. E. V. Sumner, February 3, 1891, 227–28; Sumner to Miles, February 21, 1891, LC, NAMFP, Box 4.

19. See *Omaha Daily Bee*, December 25, 1890, 1. See also chapter 5.

20. Report of Brig. Gen. Nelson A. Miles, January 5, 1891, NARS, RG 94, AIWKSC, M 983, Roll 1, Vol. 2, 812–13.

21. See, for example, Mooney, *The Ghost-Dance Religion*, 868–69; W. F. Johnson, *The Red Record*, 435–57; D. M. Johnson, "Ghost Dance," 48–49; Utley, *The Last Days*, 208–13; Utley and Washburn, *Indian Wars*, 299.

22. For discussion of the possible use of alcohol before the Wounded Knee battle, see Richard C. Stirk, in Jensen, *Voices of the American West*, 2:285–89; William Garnett, in Jensen, *Voices of the American West*, 1:99–100; Zahn, *The Crimson Carnage*, 6–7; Mattes, "The Enigma of Wounded Knee," 9; V. W. Johnson, *The Unregimented General*, 286; Utley, *The Last Days*, 199; Smith, *Moon of the Popping Trees*, 179; Sievers, "The Historiography of 'The Bloody Field,'" 39–40; Twiss, "A Short History," 37; Seymour, *Sitanka*, 156; Miller, *Ghost Dance*, 233–39; W. S. E. Coleman, *Voices of Wounded Knee*, 293–94.

23. One of the best attempts to understand the Lakota ghost dance as a religious movement is Raymond J. DeMallie's brief article "The Lakota Ghost Dance: An Ethnohistorical Account." For comparison, see Ostler, *The Plains Sioux*, 260–64.

24. This category includes such works as Hyde, *A Sioux Chronicle*, Utley, *The Last Days of the Sioux Nation*, D. M. Johnson, "Ghost Dance," Smith, *Moon of the Popping Trees*, Utley and Washburn, *Indian Wars*, to name a few. In fact, most of the scholarly works used in this study fail to see the ghost dance in the context of the Lakota culture.

25. DeMallie, "The Lakota Ghost Dance," 54.

BIBLIOGRAPHY

Archival Sources

Aaron Beede Diary, North-Dakota Historical Society, Bismarck ND.

Bureau of Catholic Indian Missions Records, Series 1-1, Correspondence, Pine Ridge Agency Holy Rosary Mission, Rosebud Agency St. Francis Mission, Standing Rock Agency, Fort Yates, Microfilm, Reels 19–20, Special Collections and Archives, Marquette University Libraries, Milwaukee WI.

Benjamin Harrison Papers, Microfilm, Series 1, Rolls 29–30, Library of Congress, Washington DC.

Edward Ashley Papers 1883–1931, Archives of the Episcopal Church, Episcopal Diocese of South Dakota, Center for Western Studies, Sioux Falls SD.

Eli S. Ricker Manuscript Collection, M 3541–44, Reels 1–4, Nebraska State Historical Society, Lincoln NE 1957.

Emil Perrig Diary, Holy Rosary Mission, Special Collections and Archives, Marquette University Libraries, Milwaukee WI.

Eugene Buechel Manuscript Collection, Short Bull, Young Skunk, Pretty Eagle manuscripts, Holy Rosary Mission, Special Collections and Archives, Marquette University Libraries, Milwaukee WI.

Florentine Digman Papers, St. Francis Mission, Marquette University Libraries, Milwaukee WI.

Henry L. Dawes Papers, Library of Congress, Washington DC.

House Committee on Indian Affairs Papers, Records of the United States Congress, House of Representatives, Record Group 233, National Archives and Records Service, General Services Administration, Washington DC.

House Committee on Indian Affairs, Minutes of Proceedings, National Archives and Records Service, General Services Administration, Washington DC.

Josephine Waggoner Papers, Museum of the Fur Trade, Chadron NE.

James McLaughlin Papers, Minnesota Historical Society, St. Paul MN.

Letters Sent to the Office of Indian Affairs by the Agents or Superintendents at the Pine Ridge Agency 1875–1914, M 1282, Vol. 9, Roll 10, Record Group 75, Records of the Bureau of Indian Affairs, National Archives and Records Service, General Services Administration, Washington DC 1985.

Nelson A. Miles Family Papers, Library of Congress, Washington DC.

Reports and Correspondence Relating to the Army Investigations of the Battle at Wounded Knee and to the Sioux Campaign of 1890–1891, M 983, Vol. 1, Rolls 1–2, Record Group 94, Records of the Adjutant General's Office 1780–1917, National Archives and Records Service, General Services Administration, Washington DC 1974.

Senate Committee on Indian Affairs Papers, Records of the United States Congress, Senate, Record Group 46, National Archives and Records Service, General Services Administration, Washington DC.

Short Bull Document, handwritten document recorded by George C. Crager, "As Narrated by Short Bull," Buffalo Bill Museum and Grave, Golden CO.

Special Case No. 188—The Ghost Dance, 1890–1898, M 4728–29, Reels 1–2, Record Group 75, Records of the Bureau of Indian Affairs, National Archives and Records Service, General Services Administration, Washington DC, microfilm publication 1973.

Thomas Jefferson Morgan Private Letter Press Books, American Indian Studies Research Institute, Indiana University, Bloomington IN.

U.S. Congress, House of Representatives, 51st Congress, 1st Session, House Committee on Indian Affairs, Council Held with a Delegation of Sioux Indians, April 15, 1890, Unpublished Hearing, Microfiche, Card 1, Indiana University, Main Library, Bloomington IN.

U.S. Congress, House of Representatives, 75th Congress, 3rd Session, House Committee on Indian Affairs, Sioux Indians, Wounded Knee Massacre, March 7 and May 12, 1938, Published Hearing, Microfiche, Group 3, Indiana University, Law Library, Bloomington IN.

Walter Mason Camp Manuscript Collection, Indiana University, Lilly Library, Bloomington IN.

Walter S. Campbell Manuscript Collection, University of Oklahoma Libraries and Archives, Norman OK.

William Steele Holman Papers, 1836–1998, Indiana University, Lilly Library, Bloomington IN.

Published Sources

50th Congress, 2nd Session, *Senate Executive Document*, No. 17, Vol. 1, Serial 2610. Washington DC: Government Printing Office, 1889.

51st Congress, 1st Session, *Senate Executive Document*, No. 51, Vol. 5, Serial 2682. Washington DC: Government Printing Office, 1890.

51st Congress, 2nd Session, *Senate Executive Document*, No. 2, Vol. 1, Serial 2818. Washington DC: Government Printing Office, 1891.

51st Congress, 2nd Session, *Senate Executive Document*, No. 9, Armament of Certain Indians, Vol. 1, Serial 2818. Washington DC: Government Printing Office, 1891.

51st Congress, 2nd Session, *Senate Miscellaneous Document*, No 28, Vol. 3, Serial 2821. Washington DC: Government Printing Office, 1891.

51st Congress, 2nd Session, *House Executive Document*, No. 36, Sioux Indian Appropriation, Vol. 25, Serial 2855. Washington DC: Government Printing Office, 1891.

51st Congress, 2nd Session, *House Executive Document*, No. 37, Additional Provisions for Sioux, Vol. 25, Serial 2855. Washington DC: Government Printing Office, 1891.

51st Congress, 2nd Session, *House Executive Document*, No. 139, Vol. 33, Serial 2863. Washington DC: Government Printing Office, 1891.

51st Congress, 2nd Session, *House Miscellaneous Document*, No. 80, Vol. 1, Serial 2869. Washington DC: Government Printing Office, 1891.

51st Congress, 2nd Session, *House Report*, No. 3375, Vol. 1, Serial 2885. Washington DC: Government Printing Office, 1891.

52nd Congress, 1st Session, *Senate Executive Document*, No 58, Vol. 5, Serial 2900. Washington DC: Government Printing Office, 1892.

52nd Congress, 1st Session, *Senate Executive Document*, No. 84, Vol. 6, Serial 2901. Washington DC: Government Printing Office, 1892.

52nd Congress, 2nd Session, *Senate Executive Document*, No. 93, Vol. 8, Serial 3062. Washington DC: Government Printing Office, 1893.

Allen, Michael. "The New Western History Stillborn." *The Historian*, 57, 1994: 201–8.

Amiotte, Arthur. "The Lakota Sun Dance: Historical and Contemporary Perspectives." In *Sioux Indian Religion: Tradition and Innovation*, ed. Raymond J. DeMallie and Douglas R. Parks. Norman: University of Oklahoma Press, 1987: 75–89.

Anderson, Owanah. *400 Years: Anglican/Episcopal Mission among American Indians*. Cincinnati OH: Forward Movement Publications, 1997.

Andersson, Rani-Henrik. "Henkitanssi—Lupaus paremmasta tulevaisuudesta" [The Ghost Dance: A Promise for a Better Future]. Master's thesis, University of Tampere, Finland, 1996.

——. *"Wanáǧi Wachípi kị: The Ghost Dance among the Lakota Indians in 1890"—A Multidimensional Interpretation*. Tampere, Finland: Tampere University Press, 2003.

Andrist, Ralph. *The Long Death: Last Days of the Plains Indian*. New York: Macmillan, 1969.

Annual Report of the Commissioner of Indian Affairs 1878, House Executive Document,

No 1, 45th Cong., 2nd Sess., Vol. 9, Serial 1850. Washington DC: Government Printing Office, 1879.

Annual Report of the Commissioner of Indian Affairs 1883, 48th Congress, 1st Session, House Executive Document, No. 1, Vol. 2, Serial 2191. Washington DC: Government Printing Office, 1884.

Annual Report of the Commissioner of Indian Affairs 1884, 48th Congress, 2nd Session, House Executive Document, No. 1, Vol. 12, Serial 2287. Washington DC: Government Printing Office, 1885.

Annual Report of the Commissioner of Indian Affairs 1889, 51st Cong. 1st Sess. House Executive Document 1, Part 5, Vol. 2, Serial 2725. Washington DC: Government Printing Office, 1890.

Annual Report of the Commissioner of Indian Affairs 1890, 51st Congress, 2nd Session, House Executive Document, No. 1, Part 5, Vol. 2, Serial 2841. Washington DC: Government Printing Office, 1891.

Annual Report of the Commissioner of Indian Affairs 1891, 52nd Congress, 1st Session, House Executive Document, No. 1, Part 5, Vol. 2, Serial 2934. Washington DC: Government Printing Office, 1892.

Annual Report of the Secretary of War, 52nd Congress, 1st Session, House Executive Document, Vol. 2, No. 1, Part 2, Vol. 1, Serial 2921. Washington DC: Government Printing Office, 1892.

Bailey, Paul. *Ghost Dance Messiah*. Tucson AZ: Westernlore Press, 1986.

Bannan, Helen Marie. *Reformers and the "Indian Problem" 1878–1887 and 1922–1934*. Syracuse NY: Syracuse University Press, 1976.

Barrows, Isabel, ed. *Proceedings of the 8th Annual Meeting of the Lake Mohonk Conference of the Friends of the Indian*. Lake Mohonk NY: Lake Mohonk Conference, 1890.

———, ed. *Proceedings of the 9th Annual Meeting of the Lake Mohonk Conference of the Friends of the Indian*. Lake Mohonk NY: Lake Mohonk Conference, 1891.

Barton, Winifred W. *John Williamson: A Brother to the Sioux*. New York: Fleming H. Rewell, 1919.

Beal, Merrill D. *"I Will Fight No More Forever": Chief Joseph and the Nez Percé War*. New York: Ballantine Books, 1989.

Berghold, Alexander. *The Indians' Revenge, or Days of Horror: Some Appalling Events in the History of the Sioux*. San Francisco: P. J. Thomas Printer, 1891.

Berkhofer, Robert F., Jr. *Beyond the Great Story: History as Text and Discourse*. Cambridge MA: Harvard University Press, 1995.

———. *The White Man's Indian: Images of the American Indian from Columbus to the Present*. New York: Vintage Books, 1979.

Bieder, Robert E. *Science Encounters the Indian 1820–1880: The Early Years of American Ethnology*. Norman: University of Oklahoma Press, 1986.

Boring, Mel. *Wovoka, the Story of an American Indian*. Minneapolis MN: Dillon Press, 1981.

Bowden, Henry Warner. *American Indians and Christian Missions: Studies in Cultural Conflict*. Chicago: University of Chicago Press, 1981.

Boyd, James P. *Recent Indian Wars: Under the Lead of Sitting Bull and Other Chiefs; With Full Account of the Messiah Craze and Ghost Dances*. Philadelphia: Publishers Union, 1891.

Bray, Kingsley M. *Crazy Horse: A Lakota Life*. Norman: University of Oklahoma Press, 2006.

Brown, Dee. *Bury My Heart at Wounded Knee: An Indian History of the American West*. New York: Bantam Books, 1979.

Brown, Joseph Epes. *Animals of the Soul: Sacred Animals of the Oglala Sioux*. Rockport MA: Element Books, 1997.

———, ed. *The Sacred Pipe: Black Elk's Account of the Seven Rites of the Oglala Sioux*. Forge Village MA: Murray Printing Co., 1973.

Bucko, Raymond A. *The Lakota Ritual of the Sweat Lodge: History and Contemporary Practice*. Studies in the Anthropology of North American Indians. Lincoln: University of Nebraska Press, 1998.

Buechel, Eugene. *Lakota Tales and Texts: Wisdom Stories, Customs, Lives and Instruction of the Dakota People*. Ed. Paul Manhardt. Pine Ridge SD: Red Cloud Indian School, Holy Rosary Mission, 1978.

Buecker, Thomas R. "'The Men Behaved Splendidly': Guy V. Henry's Famous Cavalry Rides." *Nebraska History* 78(2), 1997: 54–63.

Carter, John E. "Making Pictures for a News-Hungry Nation." In *Eyewitness at Wounded Knee*, ed. Richard E. Jensen, Eli R. Paul, and John E. Carter. Lincoln: 1991: University of Nebraska Press, 37–60.

Cheney, Roberta C. *The Big Missouri Wintercount*. Happy Camp CA: Naturegraph, 1979.

Clemhout, Simone. "Typology of Nativistic Movements." *Man* 7, 1964: 14–15.

Colby, L. W. "The Sioux Indian War of 1890–1891." In *Transactions and Proceedings of the Nebraska Historical Society*. Vol. 3. Fremont NE: Hammond Bros., 1892: 144–90.

———. "Wanagi Olowan Kin." *Nebraska State Historical Society Proceedings and Collections*, 1(1), 1895: 131–50.

Coleman, Michael C. *Presbyterian Missionary Attitudes toward American Indians 1837–1893*. Jackson: University Press of Mississippi, 1985.

Coleman, William S. E. *Voices of Wounded Knee*. Lincoln: University of Nebraska Press, 2000.

Congressional Record: Containing the Proceedings and Debates of the Fiftieth Congress, Second Session, Vol. 20, Parts 1–3. Washington DC: Government Printing Office, 1889.

Congressional Record: Containing the Proceedings and Debates of the Fifty-First Congress, First Session also Special Session of the Senate, Vol. 21, Parts 1–11. Washington DC: Government Printing Office, 1889.

Congressional Record: Containing the Proceedings and Debates of the Fifty-First Congress, Second Session, Vol. 22, Parts 1–2. Washington DC: Government Printing Office, 1891.

Coward, John M. *The Newspaper Indian: Native American Identity in the Press.* Urbana: University of Illinois Press, 1999.

Curtis, Natalie. *The Indian's Book: Songs and Legends of the American Indians.* New York: Dover, 1950. (Orig. pub. 1907.)

Danberg, Grace. "Wovoka." *Nevada Historical Quarterly* 11(2), 1968: 5–53.

Danker, Donald F. "The Wounded Knee Interviews of Eli S. Ricker." *Nebraska History* 62(2), 1981: 151–243.

Dark, Philip. "Methods of Synthesis in Ethnohistory." *Ethnohistory* 4(3), 1957: 231–78.

Deloria, Ella C. *Speaking of Indians.* Lincoln: University of Nebraska Press, 1998. (Orig. pub. 1944.)

Deloria, Vine, Sr. "The Establishment of Christianity among the Sioux." In *Sioux Indian Religion: Tradition and Innovation,* ed. Raymond J. DeMallie and Douglas R. Parks. Norman: University of Oklahoma Press, 1987: 91–111.

Deloria, Vine, Jr., and Raymond J. DeMallie, eds. *Documents of American Indian Diplomacy: Treaties, Agreements and Conventions 1775–1979.* Vols. 1–2. Norman: University of Oklahoma Press, 1999.

DeMallie, Raymond J. "Change in American Indian Kinship Systems: The Dakota." In *Currents in Anthropology: Essays in Honor of Sol Tax,* ed. Robert Hinshaw. The Hague: Mouton, 1979: 221–41.

———, vol. ed. *Handbook of North American Indians.* Vol. 13, part 2, *Plains Indian.* Washington DC: Smithsonian Institution, 2001.

———. "Kinship and Biology in Sioux Culture." In *North American Indian Anthropology: Essays on Society and Culture,* ed. Raymond J. DeMallie and Alfonso Ortiz. Norman: 1994: University of Oklahoma Press, 125–46.

———. "Kinship: The Foundation for Native American Society." In *Studying Native Americans: Problems and Prospects,* ed. Russell Thornton. Madison: University of Wisconsin Press, 1998: 306–54.

———. "Lakota Belief and Ritual in the Nineteenth Century." In *Sioux Indian Religion: Tradition and Innovation,* ed. Raymond J. DeMallie and Douglas R. Parks. Norman: University of Oklahoma Press, 1987: 25–43.

———. "The Lakota Ghost Dance: An Ethnohistorical Account." *Pacific Historical Review* (51)4, 1982: 385–405.

————. "Sioux Until 1850." In *Handbook of North American Indians*. Vol. 13, part 2, *Plains Indian*, ed. William C. Sturtevant. Washington DC: Smithsonian Institution, 2001: 718–60.

————, ed. *The Sixth Grandfather: Black Elk's Teachings Given to John G. Neihardt*. Lincoln: University of Nebraska Press, 1985.

————. "Teton." In *Handbook of North American Indians*. Vol. 13, part 2, *Plains Indian*, ed. William C. Sturtevant. Washington DC: Smithsonian Institution, 2001: 794–820.

————. "'These Have No Ears': Narrative and the Ethnohistorical Method." *Ethnohistory* (40)4, 1993: 515–38.

DeMallie, Raymond J., and Robert H. Lavenda. "Wakan: Plains Siouan Concepts of Power." In *The Anthropology of Power: Ethnographic Studies from Asia, Oceania, and the New World,* ed. Richard Adams and Raymond D. Fogelson. New York: Academic Press, 1977: 153–65.

DeMallie, Raymond J., and Alfonso Ortiz, eds. *North American Indian Anthropology: Essays on Society and Culture*. Norman: University of Oklahoma Press, 1994.

DeMallie, Raymond J., and Douglas R. Parks. "Plains Indian Warfare." In *The People of the Buffalo*, vol. 1, ed. Colin F. Taylor and Hugh A. Dempsey. Wyk auf Foehr, Denmark: Tatanka Press, 2003: 66–76.

DeMallie, Raymond J., and Douglas R. Parks, eds. *Sioux Indian Religion: Tradition and Innovation*. Norman: University of Oklahoma Press, 1987.

Densmore, Frances. *Teton Sioux Music and Culture*. Lincoln: University of Nebraska Press, 1992.

Dippie, Brian W. *The Vanishing American: White Attitudes and U.S. Indian Policy*. Lawrence: University Press of Kansas, 1982.

Eastman, Charles Alexander (Ohiyesa). *From Deep Woods to Civilization: Chapters in the Autobiography of an Indian*. Boston: Little, Brown, 1916.

————. *The Soul of the Indian: An Interpretation*. Lincoln: University of Nebraska Press, 1980. (Orig. pub. 1911.)

Eastman, Elaine Goodale. "The Ghost Dance War and Wounded Knee Massacre of 1890–1891." *Nebraska History* 26(1), 1945: 26–42.

Edmunds, R. David, ed. *American Indian Leaders: Studies in Diversity*. Lincoln: University of Nebraska Press, 1980.

Eggan, Fred. *American Indian Perspectives for the Study of Social Change*. Chicago: Aldine, 1966.

Enochs, Ross. *The Jesuit Mission to the Lakota Sioux: A Study of Pastoral Ministry, 1886–1975*. Kansas City MO: Sheed and Ward, 1996.

Erisman, Fred, and Patricia L. Erisman. "Letters from the Field: John Sylvanus Loud and the Pine Ridge Campaign of 1890–1891." *South Dakota History* 26(1), 1996: 24–45.

Euler, Robert C. "Ethnohistory in the United States." *Ethnohistory* 19, 1972: 201–5.

Faragher, John Mack. "The Frontier Trail: Rethinking Turner and Reimaging the American West." *American Historical Review* 98(1), 1993: 106–17.

Feher-Elston, Catherine. *Raven Song: The Natural and Fabulous History of Ravens and Crows*. Flagstaff AZ: Northland, 1991.

Foley, Thomas W. *Father Francis M. Craft: Missionary to the Sioux*. Lincoln: University of Nebraska Press, 2002.

Fowler, Catherine S., and Sven Liljeblad. "Northern Paiute." In *Handbook of North American Indians*, vol. 1, *Great Basin*, ed. William C. Sturtevant. Washington DC: Smithsonian Institution, 1986: 435–65.

Godfrey, Edward S. "Tragedy at White Horse Creek: Edward S. Godfrey's Unpublished Account of an Incident Near Wounded Knee." *The Westerner's Brand Book*, 19(3–4), 1977.

Graber, Kay, ed. *Sister to the Sioux: The Memoirs of Elaine Goodale Eastman, 1885–1891*. Lincoln: University of Nebraska Press, 1985.

Green, Jerry, ed. *After Wounded Knee: Correspondence of Major and Surgeon John Vance Lauderdale While Serving with the Army Occupying the Pine Ridge Indian Reservation, 1890–1891*. East Lancing: Michigan State University Press, 1996.

———. "The Medals of Wounded Knee." *Nebraska History* 75(2), 1994: 200–208.

Greene, Jerome. "The Sioux Land Commission of 1889: Prelude to Wounded Knee." *South Dakota History* 1(1), 1970: 41–72.

Grobsmith, Elizabeth S. "The Plains Culture Area." In *Native North Americans: An Ethnohistorical Approach*, ed. Daniel L. Boxberger. Dubuque IA: Kendall/Hunt, 1990: 167–213.

Haberland, Wolfgang, ed. "Die Oglala Sammlung Weygold im Hamburgischen Museum fur Völkerkunde" [Weygold's Oglala Collections in the Hamburg Museum of Ethnology]. In *Museum fur Völkerkunde Hamburg*. Hamburg, Germany: Mitteilungen aus dem Museum fur Völkerkunde, 1977.

Hagan, William T. *Indian Police and Judges: Experiments in Acculturation and Control*. Lincoln: University of Nebraska Press, 1966.

———. *The Indian Rights Association: The Herbert Welsh Years 1882–1904*. Tucson: University of Arizona Press, 1985.

Hämäläinen, Riku. "The Study of Plains Indian Shields: Some Observations Concerning Previous Studies and Future Tasks." In *Styles and Positions: Ethnographic Perspectives in Comparative Religion*, ed. Tuula Sakaranaho, Tom Sjöblom, Terhi Utriainen, and Heikki Pesonen. Comparative Religion 8. Helsinki, Finland: University of Helsinki Press, 2002: 250–70.

Hassrick, Royal B. *The Sioux: Life and Customs of a Warrior Society*. Norman: University of Oklahoma Press, 1964.

Hein, David. "Episcopalianism among Lakota/Dakota Indians." *The Historiographer* 40, 2002: 14–16.

Henriksson, Markku. *The Indian on Capitol Hill: Indian Legislation and the United States Congress, 1862–1907*. Jyväskylä, Finland: Gummerrus, 1988.

Hittman, Michael. "The 1870 Ghost Dance at the Walker River Reservation: A Reconstruction." *Ethnohistory* 20(3), 1973: 247–78.

———. *Wovoka and the Ghost Dance*. Lincoln: University of Nebraska Press, 1997.

Hoover, Herbert T. "The Sioux Agreement of 1889 and Its Aftermath." *South Dakota History* 19(1), 1989: 56–94.

———. "Sitting Bull." In *American Indian Leaders: Studies in Diversity*, ed. R. David Edmunds. Lincoln: University of Nebraska Press, 1980: 152–74.

Hoxie, Frederick E. "The End of the Savage: Indian Policy in the United States Senate, 1880–1900." *Chronicles of Oklahoma* 55, 1977: 157–79.

———. *A Final Promise: The Final Campaign to Assimilate the Indian 1880–1920*. Lincoln: University of Nebraska Press, 1984.

———. "From Prison to Homeland: The Cheyenne River Reservation before wwi." *South Dakota History* 10(1) 1979: 1–24.

———, ed. *Indian in America. History: An Introduction*. Arlington Heights IL: David Harlan, 1988.

Hudson, Charles. "Folk History and Ethnohistory." *Ethnohistory* 13(1–2), 1966: 52–70.

Hultkranz, Åke. *De Amerikanska indianernas religion* [The Religions of the American Indians]. Svenska Bokförlaget. Stockholm, Sweden: Scandinavian University Books, 1967.

———. "Naturfolkets religion" [Religion of Primitive People]. In *Primitiv religion och magi* [Primitive Religion and Magic], ed. Åke Hultkrantz. Stockholm, Sweden: Bonniers, 1955: 1–18.

———, ed. *Primitiv religion och magi*. Stockholm, Sweden: Bonniers, 1955.

Hurtado, Albert L. "Whose Misfortune? Richard White's Ambivalent Region." *Reviews in American History* 22(2), 1994: 286–91.

Hyde, George E. *Red Cloud's Folk: History of the Oglala Sioux Indians*. Norman: University of Oklahoma Press, 1937.

———. *A Sioux Chronicle*. Norman: University of Oklahoma Press, 1956.

———. *Spotted Tail's Folk: A History of the Brulé Sioux*. Norman: University of Oklahoma Press, 1961.

Jensen, Richard E. "Another Look at Wounded Knee." In *Eyewitness at Wounded Knee*, ed. Richard E. Jensen, Eli R. Paul, and John E. Carter. Lincoln: University of Nebraska Press, 1991: 1–21.

———. "Big Foot's Followers at Wounded Knee." *Nebraska History* 71(4), 1990: 194–212.

————, ed. *Voices of the American West*, Vol. 1, *The Indian Interviews of Eli S. Ricker 1903–1919*. Lincoln: University of Nebraska Press, 2006.

————, ed. *Voices of the American West*, Vol. 2, *The Settler and Soldier Interviews of Eli S. Ricker, 1903–1919*. Lincoln: University of Nebraska Press, 2006.

Jensen, Richard E., Eli R. Paul, and John E. Carter, eds. *Eyewitness at Wounded Knee*. Lincoln: University of Nebraska Press, 1991.

Johnson, Dorothy M. "Ghost Dance, Last Hope of the Sioux." *Montana: The Magazine of Western History* 6(3), July 1956: 42–50.

Johnson, Virginia Weisel. *The Unregimented General: A Biography of Nelson A. Miles*. Boston: Riverside Press, 1962.

Johnson, Willis Fletcher. *The Red Record of the Sioux: Life of Sitting Bull and History of the Indian War of 1890–1891 . . . story of the Sioux nation; their manners and customs, ghost dances and Messiah craze. . . .* Philadelphia: Edgewood, 1891.

Jones, Douglas C. "Teresa Dean: Lady Correspondent among the Sioux Indians." *Journalism Quarterly* 49, 1972: 656–62.

Jorgensen, Joseph G. "Ghost Dance, Bear Dance and Sun Dance." In *Handbook of North American Indians*, Vol. 40, *Great Basin*, ed. William C. Sturtevant. Washington DC: Smithsonian Institution, 1986: 660–72.

Kelley, William F. "The Indian Troubles and the Battle of Wounded Knee." In *Transactions and Reports of the Nebraska State Historical Society*, Vol. 4. Lincoln NE: State Journal Company, 1892: 30–42.

Kerstetter, Todd. "Spin Doctors at Santee: Missionaries and the Dakota-Language Reporting of the Ghost Dance and Wounded Knee." *Western Historical Quarterly* 28, Spring 1997: 45–67.

Kolbenschlag, George R. *Whirlwind Passes: News Correspondents and the Sioux Indian Disturbances of 1890–1891*. Vermillion: University of South Dakota Press, 1990.

Kreis, Karl Markus. *Rothäute, Schwarzröcke und Heilige Frauen: Berichte aus den Lakhota-Missionen in den Reservationen Rosebud und Pine Ridge (sud-Dakota) 1886–1891* [Redskins, Blackrobes, and Holy Women: Stories from the Lakota Missions on Rosebud and Pine Ridge Reservations (South Dakota)]. Dortmundt, Germany: Fachhochschule, 1999.

La Barre, Weston. *The Ghost Dance: Origins of Religion*. Prospect Heights IL: Waveland Press, 1990.

Lakota–English Dictionary. Pine Ridge SD: Red Cloud Indian School, Inc., Holy Rosary Mission, 1983.

Lamar, Howard R. "Perspectives on Statehood: South Dakota's First Quarter Century, 1889–1914." *South Dakota History* 19(1), 1989: 2–25.

Larson, Robert W. *Red Cloud: Warrior-Statesman of the Oglala Lakota*. Norman: University of Oklahoma Press, 1997.

Lathrop, Alan K. "Another View of Wounded Knee." *South Dakota History* 16(3), 1986: 249–68.

Lazarus, Edward. *Black Hills, White Justice: The Sioux Nation versus the United States, from 1775 to the Present.* New York: Harper Collins, 1991.

Lesser, Alexander. "Cultural Significance of the Ghost Dance." *American Anthropologist* 35, 1933: 108–15.

Limerick, Patricia N. *The Legacy of Conquest: The Unbroken Past of the American West.* New York: Norton, 1987.

Limerick, Patricia N., Clyde A. Millner II, and Charles E. Rankin, eds. *Trails: Toward a New Western History.* Lawrence: University Press of Kansas, 1991.

Lindberg, Christer. "Foreigners in Action at Wounded Knee." *Nebraska History* 71(4), 1990: 170–81.

Linton, Ralph. "Nativistiset liikkket" [Nativistic Movements]. In *Uskonto ja Yhteisö: Tutkimuksia uskontosiologian alalta* [Religion and Society: Studies in Sociology of Religion], ed. Pentikäinen Juha. Helsinki, Finland: Gaudeamus, 1974: 189–204.

Littfield, Daniel F., Jr., and James W. Parins. *American Indian and Alaska Native Newspapers and Periodicals 1826–1924.* Westport CT: Greenwood Press, 1984.

Looking Horse, Arval. "The Sacred Pipe in Modern Life." In *Sioux Indian Religion: Tradition and Innovation,* ed. Raymond J. DeMallie and Douglas R. Parks. Norman: University of Oklahoma Press, 1987: 67–73.

Lowie, Robert H. *Indians of the Plains.* Anthropological Handbook 1. New York: McGraw-Hill, 1954.

Maddra, Sam A. *Hostiles? The Lakota Ghost Dance and Buffalo Bill's Wild West.* Norman: University of Oklahoma Press, 2006.

Malan, Vernon D., and Clinton J. Jesser. *The Dakota Indian Religion: A Study of Conflict in Values.* Rural Sociology Department, Bulletin 473. Brookings: Agricultural Experiment Station, South Dakota State College, 1959.

Malm, Einar. *Dödsdans i Dakota* [Death Dance in Dakota]. Stockholm, Sweden: Rabén and Sjögren, 1961.

Mardock, Robert W. "The Plains Frontier and the Indian Peace Policy 1865–1880." *Nebraska History* 49(2), 1968: 187–201.

Markowitz, Harvey. "The Catholic Mission and the Sioux: A Crisis in the Early Paradigm." In *Sioux Indian Religion: Tradition and Innovation,* ed. Raymond J. DeMallie and Douglas R. Parks. Norman: University of Oklahoma Press, 1987: 113–37.

Martin, Calvin. "Ethnohistory: A Better Way to Write Indian History." *Western Historical Quarterly,* 9, January 1978: 42–56.

Mattes, Merril J. "The Enigma of Wounded Knee." *Plains Anthropologist* 5(9), 1960: 1–11.

Mattingly, Arthur H. "The Great Plains Peace Commission of 1867." *Journal of the West* 15(3), 1976: 23–37.

McCann, Frank, Jr. "The Ghost Dance: Last Hope of the Western Tribes, Unleashed the Final Tragedy." *Montana: The Magazine of Western History* 16(1), 1966: 25–34.

McDermott, Louis M. "The Primary Role of the Military on the Dakota Frontier." *South Dakota History* 2(1), 1971: 1–22.

McGillicuddy, Julia B. *Blood on the Moon: Valentine McGillicuddy and the Sioux.* Lincoln: University of Nebraska Press, 1969.

McGregor, James H. *The Wounded Knee Massacre: From the Viewpoint of the Sioux.* Rapid City SD: Fenske Printing, 1997.

McLaughlin, James. *Account of the Death of Sitting Bull and of the Circumstances Attending It.* Philadelphia 1891. Available at http://www.pbs.org/weta/the west/wpa ges/wpgs680/sbarrest.html (accessed November 25, 1997).

———. *My Friend the Indian.* Lincoln: University of Nebraska Press, 1989. (Orig. pub. 1910.)

Miles, Nelson A. *Personal Recollections and Observations of General Nelson A. Miles: Embracing a Brief View of the Civil War or From New England to the Golden Gate and the Story of His Indian Campaigns with Comments on the Exploration, Development and Progress of Our Great Western Empire.* Chicago: Werner Company, 1896.

———. *Serving the Republic: Memoirs of the Civil and Military Life of Nelson A. Miles.* New York: Harper and Brothers Publishers, 1911.

Miller, David Humphreys. *Ghost Dance.* Lincoln: University of Nebraska Press, 1985.

Mooney, James. *The Ghost-Dance Religion and the Sioux Outbreak of 1890.* Lincoln: University of Nebraska Press, 1991. (Orig. pub. as part of the 14th Annual Report of the Bureau of Ethnology to the Secretary of the Smithsonian Institution 1892–1893, Washington DC, 1893).

Moses, L. G. "'The Father Tells Me So!' Wovoka the Ghost Dance Prophet." *American Indian Quarterly* 40(3), 1985: 335–51.

Nash, Gerald D. "Point of View: One Hundred Years of Western History." *Journal of the West* 32(1), 1993: 3–4.

The National Indian Defense Association. *The Sioux Nation and the United States: A Brief History of the Treaties of 1868, 1876, and 1889, Between that Nation and the United States.* Washington DC: National Indian Defense Association, 1891.

Neihardt, John G. *A Cycle of the West.* New York: Macmillan, 1949.

Neihardt, John G., and Black Elk. *Black Elk Speaks: Being the Life Story of a Holy Man of the Oglala Sioux.* Lincoln: University of Nebraska Press, 1961. (Orig. pub. 1932.)

Oehler, C. M. *The Great Sioux Uprising.* New York: Oxford University Press, 1997.

Olmstead, Clifton E. *History of Religion in the United States.* Englewood Cliffs NJ: Prentice-Hall, 1961.

Olson, James C. *Red Cloud and the Sioux Problem.* Lincoln: University of Nebraska Press, 1965.

Ostler, Jeffrey. "Conquest and the State: Why the United States Employed Massive Military Force to Suppress the Lakota Ghost Dance." *Pacific Historical Review* 65(2), 1996: 217–48.

———. *The Plains Sioux and U.S. Colonialism from Lewis and Clark to Wounded Knee.* Cambridge, England: Cambridge University Press, 2004.

Overholt, Thomas W. "The Ghost Dance of 1890 and the Nature of the Prophetic Process." *Ethnohistory* 21(1), 1974: 37–63.

Parkman, Francis. *The Conspiracy of Pontiac.* New York: Literary Classics of the United States of America, 1991.

———. *The Oregon Trail.* New York: Literary Classics of the United States of America, 1991. (Orig. pub. 1844.)

Paul, Eli R. "The Investigation of Special Agent Cooper and Property Damage Claims in the Winter of 1890–1891." *South Dakota History* 24(3–4), 1994: 212–35.

———. "Your Country Is Surrounded." In *Eyewitness at Wounded Knee,* ed. Richard E. Jensen, Eli R. Paul, and John E. Carter. Lincoln: University of Nebraska Press, 1991: 23–36.

Paulson, Howard W. "The Allotment of Land in Severalty to the Dakota Indians before the Dawes Act." *South Dakota History* 1(2), 1971: 132–53.

Pennington, Robert. "An Analysis of the Political Structure of the Teton-Dakota Indian Tribe of North America." *North Dakota History* 20, July 1953: 141–56.

Phillips, George H. "The Indian Ring in Dakota Territory, 1870–1890." *South Dakota History* 2(4), 1972: 344–76.

Phister, Nat P. "The Indian Messiah." *American Anthropologist* 4(2), 1891: 105–8.

Powers, Marla. *Oglala Woman, Myth, Ritual and Reality.* Chicago: University of Chicago Press, 1988.

Powers, William K. *Oglala Religion.* Lincoln: University of Nebraska Press, 1977.

———. *Sacred Language: The Nature of Supernatural Discourse in Lakota.* Norman: University of Oklahoma Press, 1986.

———. *Voices from the Spirit World: Lakota Ghost Dance Songs.* Kendall Park NJ: Lakota Books, 1990.

Price, Catherine. *The Oglala People, 1841–1879: A Political History.* Lincoln: University of Nebraska Press, 1996.

Prucha, Francis Paul. *American Indian Policy in Crisis: Christian Reformers and the Indian, 1865–1900.* Norman: University of Oklahoma Press, 1976.

———. *American Indian Policy in the Formative Years: The Trade and Intercourse Acts, 1790–1834.* Lincoln: University of Nebraska Press, 1970.

———, ed. *Americanizing the American Indian: Writings by the "Friends of the Indian" 1880–1900.* Lincoln: University of Nebraska Press, 1973.

———. *The Churches and the Indian Schools 1888–1912.* Lincoln: University of Nebraska Press, 1979.

———, ed. *Documents of the United States Indian Policy*. Lincoln: University of Nebraska Press, 1975.

———. *The Great Father: The United States Government and the American Indian*. Vols. 1–2. Lincoln: University of Nebraska Press, 1986.

Richardson, James D., ed. *Messages and Papers of the Presidents 1789–1897: A Compilation*. Vol. 9. Washington DC: Government Printing Office, 1898.

Sajna, Mike. *Crazy Horse: The Life behind the Legend*. New York: Wiley, 2000.

Sandoz, Mari. *Crazy Horse: The Strange Man of the Oglalas*. Lincoln: University of Nebraska Press, 1992.

Schusky, Ernest L. "The Lower Brulé Sioux Reservation: A Century of Misunderstanding." *South Dakota History* 7(4), 1977: 422–37.

———. "The Roots of Factionalism among the Lower Brulé Sioux." In *North American Indian Anthropology: Essays in Society and Culture*, ed. Raymond J. DeMallie and Alfonso Ortiz. Norman: University of Oklahoma Press, 1994: 250–77.

Seymour, Forrest W. *Sitanka: The Full Story of Wounded Knee*. West Hanover MA: Christopher Publishing House, 1981.

Sickels, Emma C. "The Story of the Ghost Dance, as Told in the Indian Tongue by Major George Sword." *Folk-Lorist* 1(1), 1892: 28–36.

Sievers, Michael A. "The Historiography of 'The Bloody Field . . . That Kept the Secret of the Everlasting Word': Wounded Knee." *South Dakota History* 6(1), 1975–76: 33–54.

Siikala, Jukka. *Cult and Conflict in Tropical Polynesia: A Study of Traditional Religion, Christianity and Nativistic Movements*. Helsinki, Finland: Helsingin Liikekirjapaino, 1982.

Smedman, Rainer. *Sotureista ja metsästäjistä maanviljelijöitä: Oglalat valkoisen miehen tiellä 1868–1887* (From Warriors and Hunters to Farmers: Oglalas on the White Man's Road 1868–1887, with and English summary). Tampere, Finland: Tampere University Press, 2001.

Smith, Rex Allan. *Moon of the Popping Trees: The Tragedy at Wounded Knee and the End of the Indian Wars*. Lincoln: University of Nebraska Press, 1975.

Smoak, Gregory E. "The Mormons and the Ghost Dance of 1890." *South Dakota History* 16(3), 1986: 269–94.

Socolofsky, Homer E. "Great Plains Studies—Part I. Military Organization, Functions, and Personal Activities." *Journal of the West* 15(3), 1976: 1–3.

Standing Bear, Luther. *My People the Sioux*. Lincoln: University of Nebraska Press, 1975. (Orig. pub. 1928.)

The Statutes at Large, Laws, Treaties and Proclamation of the United States of America 1859–1975. Boston: Little, Brown, 1863–66; Washington DC: Government Printing Office, 1877–1976.

Stewart, Omer C. "Contemporary Document on Wovoka (Jack Wilson) Prophet of the Ghost Dance in 1890." *Ethnohistory* 24(3), 1977: 219–22.

Stuart, Paul. *The Indian Office: Growth and Development of an American Institution, 1865–1900.* Studies in American History and Culture, No. 12. Ann Arbor MI: University Microfilms International, 1979.

Sturtevant, William C. "Anthropology, History, and Ethnohistory." In *Introduction to Cultural Anthropology: Essays in the Scope and Methods of the Science of Man,* ed. James A. Clifton. Boston: Houghton Mifflin, 1968: 451–75.

———, general ed. *Handbook of North American Indians.* Washington DC: Smithsonian Institution, 1986–2001.

Sugden, John. *Tecumseh: A Life.* New York: Henry Holt, 1998.

Taske, Raymond H. C., Jr., and Bardin H. Nelson. "Acculturation and Assimilation: A Classification." *American Ethnologist* 1(2), 1974: 351–68.

Taylor, Allen R., and David S. Rood. *Elementary and Intermediate Lakhota.* Boulder: University of Colorado Lakhota Project, 1976.

Taylor, Charles, K. Anthony Appiah, Jürgen Habermas, Steven C. Rockefeller, Michael Walzer, and Susan Wolf. *Multiculturalism: Examining the Politics of Recognition.* Princeton NJ: Princeton University Press, 1994.

Textor, Lucy. *Official Records between the United States and the Sioux Indians.* Palo Alto CA: Leland Stanford University Press, 1896.

Thomas, Trudy Carter. *Crisis and Creativity: Visual Symbolism of the Ghost Dance Tradition.* Ann Arbor MI: University Microfilms, 1990.

Thornton, Russel. *American Indian Holocaust and Survival: A Population History Since 1492.* Norman: University of Oklahoma Press, 1987.

———, ed. *Studying Native Americans: Problems and Prospects.* Madison: University of Wisconsin Press, 1998.

Trafzer, Clifford E., and Margery Ann Beach. "Smohalla, the Washani and Religion as a Factor in Northwestern History." *American Indian Quarterly* 9(3), 1985: 309–24.

Turner, Catherine C. *Red Man Calling on the Great White Father.* Norman: University of Oklahoma Press, 1951.

Turner, Frederick Jackson. *The Frontier in American History.* Huntington NY: R. E. Krieger, 1976. (Orig. pub. 1920.)

———. "The Significance of the Frontier in American History." In *History, Frontier, and Section: Three Essays.* Albuquerque: University of New Mexico Press, 1993, 1–38. (Orig. pub. 1893.)

Twiss, Gayla. "A Short History of Pine Ridge." *Indian Historian* 11(1), 1978: 36–39.

Utley, Robert M. *The Indian Frontier of the American West 1846–1890.* Albuquerque: University of New Mexico Press, 1984.

———. *The Lance and the Shield: The Life and Times of Sitting Bull.,* New York: Ballantine Books, 1993.

————. *The Last Days of the Sioux Nation*. New Haven CT: Yale University Press, 1963.

Utley, Robert M., and Wilcomb E. Washburn. *Indian Wars*. Boston: Houghton Mifflin, 1977.

Utter, Jack. *Wounded Knee and the Ghost Dance Tragedy: A Chronicle of Events Leading to and Including the Massacre at Wounded Knee, South Dakota, on December 29, 1890*. Lake Ann MI: National Woodlands, 1991.

Vansina, Jan. *Oral Tradition as History*. Madison: University of Wisconsin Press, 1985.

Vassenden, Kaare. *Lakota Trail on Man Afraid of His Horses*. Bergen, Norway: John Grieg, 2000.

Vestal, Stanley. *New Sources of Indian History 1850–1891*. Norman: University of Oklahoma Press, 1934.

————. *Sitting Bull: The Champion of the Sioux*. Norman: University of Oklahoma Press, 1989. (Orig. pub. 1932.)

Viola, Herman J. *Diplomats in Buckskins: A History of Indian Delegations in Washington City*. Bluffton SC: Rivilo Books, 1995.

————. *Thomas L. McKenney: Architect of America's Early Indian Policy: 1816–1830*. Chicago: Sage Books, 1974.

Voorhees, Cecilia, His three sons and his daughter, eds. *Forty Years of Oratory: Daniel Voorhees Lectures, Addresses and Speeches*. Vols. 1-2. Indianapolis IN: Bowen-Merril, 1897.

Voorhees, Charles C., ed. *Speeches of Daniel W. Voorhees of Indiana: Embracing His Most Prominent Forensic, Political, Occasional and Literary Addresses*. Cincinnati OH: Robert Clarke and Co. Printers, 1875.

Wade, Arthur P. "The Military Command Structure: The Great Plains, 1853–1891." *Journal of the West* 15(3), 1976: 5–22.

Walker, James R. *Lakota Belief and Ritual*. Ed. Raymond J. DeMallie Elaine A. Jahner. Lincoln: University of Nebraska Press, 1991.

————. *Lakota Society*. Ed. Raymond J. DeMallie. Lincoln: University of Nebraska Press, 1992.

Wallace, Anthony. "Revitalization Movements." *American Anthropologist* 58, 1956: 264–81.

Washburn, Wilcomb E., ed. *American Indian and the United States: A Documentary History*. Vols. 1-4. Westport CT: Greenwood, 1973.

————. *Indian in America*. New York: Harper & Row, 1975.

Watson, Elmo Scott. "The Last Indian War, 1890–1891—A Study of Newspaper Jingoism." *Journalism Quarterly* 20(1), 1943: 205–19.

White, Richard. *It's Your Misfortune and None of My Own: A New History of the American West*. Norman: University of Oklahoma Press, 1991.

————. "The Winning of the West: The Expansion of the Western Sioux in the Eighteenth and Nineteenth Centuries." *Journal of American History* 65(2), 1978: 319–43.

Wildhage, Wilhelm. *Geistertanz-Lieder Der Lakota: Eine Quellensamlung* [Lakota Ghost Dance Songs: A Collection of Sources]. Wyk Auf Foehr, Denmark: Verlag fur Amerikanistik, 1991.

————. "Material on Short Bull." *European Review of Native American Studies* 4(1), 1990: 35–42.

Wissler, Clark. *Some Protective Designs of the Dakota*. Vol. 1, Part 2. New York: Anthropological Papers of the American Museum of Natural History, 1907.

Woodruff, K. Brent. "The Episcopal Mission to the Dakotas 1860–1898." *South Dakota Historical Collections* 17, 1934: 553–603.

Wooster, Robert. *The Military and United States Indian Policy 1865–1903*. Lincoln: University of Nebraska Press, 1988.

————. *Nelson A. Miles and the Twilight of the Frontier Army*. Lincoln: University of Nebraska Press, 1993.

Youngkin, Stephen D. "Prelude to Wounded Knee: The Military Point of View." *South Dakota History* 4(3), 1974: 333–51.

Zahn, Frank B. *The Crimson Carnage of Wounded Knee: An Astounding Story of Human Slaughter*. Bottineau ND: Bottineau Courant Print, 1967.

INDEX

ghost keeping ceremony, 51

ghost shirts: avoidance of Euro-American artifacts on, 36, 68, 289, 342n129; bulletproofness of, 70–72, 140, 217, 288–90; development of idea of, 64, 67–73; effect on ghost dancers, 72, 75; misinterpretation of, 288–89; in news reports, 204, 206, 215; worn at arrest of Sitting Bull, 86; worn at Wounded Knee, 92

Gifford, O. S. (Representative from Dakota Territory), 251

Gilbert, Elian (missionary), 174

gold, effect of discovery of (1874), 14

Good Thunder (ghost dancer), 31, 44

Good Thunder, Andrew (member of Big Foot's band), 89, 90–91, 93

Grant, Ulysses S., Peace Policy of, 2–3, 128

Grass, John (progressive Hunkpapa leader), 21, 77, 230

Grattan, John, L. (Lt.), 10

Great Sioux Reservation: and Congress, 252; establishment of (1868), 13; newspaper coverage of, 194; organization of tribes on, 18–19; partition of, 22, 132, 274, 275–76. *See also* Sioux Act of 1889

Great Spirit (Wakȟáŋ Tȟáŋka), 48–49, 52–54, 335n56

"Great Story" method of history, 300

Grey Eagle (policeman), 84–85

guns and ammunition: absent on sacred shirts, 68; in agents' reports, 104; and army, 220; in army reports, 133, 138, 367n21; and Congress, 263; at ghost dances, 64–65, 340n111, 340n113; at ghost dances, denials of, 213; in news reports, 201, 209, 233; for white settlers, 253, 267. *See also* disarmament of Indians

Hare, William Hobart (Bishop), 163, 166, 177–78, 212, 257, 286

Harper's Weekly: after Wounded Knee, 240–42; on ghost dance, 222, 291; on Indian policy, 206, 215; on Miles as true western hero, 222; on possibility of uprising, 215, 224; reports on Lakota life, 194; on Sitting Bull, 230; on Sitting Bull's death, 233–34; tone of

articles in, 193, 291–92; on Wounded Knee affair, 237. *See also* Remington, Frederic

Harrison, Benjamin (President): blamed by press, 242; gives Miles extraordinary authority, 143; on Indians in message to Senate, 251, 252; orders arrest of Sitting Bull, 115, 148; orders troops to reservations, 111–12, 133, 134; and plan to give army control of Indian affairs, 244; regrets bloodshed, 240

Hawkins, Irving (correspondent), 192

Hennepin, Louis (early missionary), 162

Hollow Horn Bear (ghost dancer), 81, 170

Holman, William S. (Congressman), 259–60, 266, 268, 293

holy men, 50. *See also* chiefs and medicine men

Holy Rosary Catholic Mission (Drexel Mission): background of, 164, 165–66; Indians staying at, 171, 182; skirmish at, 96, 156–57, 187–91, 229, 239

Horn Cloud, Joseph (member of Big Foot's band), 89, 92, 93

Horse Creek Treaty (1851), 10, 11, 324n71

"hostile" *vs.* "friendly" Indians: and army, 135, 138; and hostiles equated with ghost dancers, 205–6, 281, 385n52; separation of, at Pine Ridge and Rosebud, 137–38. *See also* Lakotas, divisions within

Hump (Minneconjou leader): after Sitting Bull's death, 87–88, 229, 231; and agent, 106, 123; and army, 134, 146; as ghost dance leader, 46, 79; gives up ghost dance, 88; in news reports, divisions within Indians, 204; as nonprogressive, 21

hunger. *See* food shortages and famine

Hunkpapas (Lakota tribe), 6, 77, 87. *See also* Standing Rock Reservation

Hurst, J. H. (Captain), 132

Iapi Oaye (missionary newspaper): background of, 166; and effect of ghost dance on Christians, 273; on ghost dance as false prophecy, 175–77, 186–87, 286–87; on Sitting Bull, 174; on Wounded Knee affair, 190–91

Indian agents. *See* agents